Facilitating Infant and
Early Childhood Development

Primary Prevention of Psychopathology
George W. Albee and Justin M. Joffe, *General Editors*

Facilitating Infant and Early Childhood Development

Lynne A. Bond and
Justin M. Joffe, editors

Published for the Vermont Conference on
the Primary Prevention of Psychopathology
by University Press of New England
Hanover and London, 1982

University Press of New England

Brandeis University

Brown University

Clark University

Dartmouth College

University of New Hampshire

University of Rhode Island

Tufts University

University of Vermont

Library of Congress Catalog Card Number 81-69944
International Standard Book Number 0-87451-205-0

Printed in the United States of America

Library of Congress Cataloging in Publication data will be
found on the last printed page of this book.

Contents

vi   Contents

Preface

The Vermont conferences on the primary prevention of psychopathology started, in 1975, as a result of conversations between George Albee and Faith and James Waters of the Waters Foundation. The Foundation was seeking ways to stimulate efforts to enhance the cognitive, social, and emotional development of children; George Albee was studying ways to ameliorate suffering by preventing emotional distress rather than by ministering to the victims. The topic of preventing psychopathology was a meeting point for these related interests and one with prophetic aspects. As a result of the enthusiasm of James and Faith Waters and the generous financial support of the Waters Foundation, the 1975 Conference became the first in a series of annual conferences.

This volume contains a record of the papers presented at the sixth conference, the topic of which is an outgrowth of conceptual developments attributable in large degree to the intellectual stimulus of earlier conferences. The first five conferences, and the volumes that resulted from them, can be said to have done two things other than focusing the attention of people from a wide range of relevant professional disciplines—psychology, education, social work, medicine, amongst others—on the concept of prevention.

In the first place they provided an outline of most of the major topics and issues relevant to the field. Indeed this was the explicit intention of the first conference, devoted to an overview of the issues in the field. Some of these issues were fleshed out and additional areas of concern identified in subsequent conferences. The second conference focused on environmental factors and psychopathology; the third on ways of building competence and coping skills in children; the fourth on building these skills in adults; and the fifth with issues of political action and social change, a theme that arises so often in the course of attempting to deal with other questions that it needed explicit attention.

Aside from thus drawing the first crude map of a hitherto largely uncharted domain the first five conferences also contained, as a recurrent pattern, a growing emphasis on the promotion of competence as a more significant conceptual shift from treatment-oriented approaches to psychopathology than the concept of primary prevention alone. What will probably characterize future conferences, beginning with the one reported here, is more detailed examination of topics identified in the first 5 years and an increasing emphasis on the promotion of competence. Competence promotion appears to be a concept that represents not only a strategically more promising approach to preventing psychopathology than the idea of obviating or removing psychopathogenic influences, but one that entirely redefines the arena of the debate between treatment and prevention and between "medical models" and psychobiosocial models of disturbed functioning. The concept is part of a process of shifting emphasis from individual aberration as a cause of disturbance to institutional determinants such as socioeconomic conditions.

This volume is a good place to start a more systematic examination of the fruitfulness of the concept. Since it deals with very early development there is in any case less focus on "undoing" earlier deleterious influences—that is, less emphasis on treatment—and even more important, many of the authors are committed to a philosophy of development wherein health or optimal development is much more than simply the absence of adverse conditions or experiences. Within this broadened view of optimizing general development, an emphasis on the complex and dynamic nature of development emerges. Although it is stated in varied ways, the message is consistent: development must be viewed within the context of a multilevel system of reciprocal influences. Everything interacts with everything. The organism must be recognized as an organized system nested within other such organized systems.

The implications of this perspective are profound. Insofar as research is concerned, it suggests that we must move away from the search for simple causal links in development and, instead, study the properties and principles of organization of systems. Insofar as intervention is concerned it highlights the futility of dealing with any one level of the system in isolation. Since we need to focus on enduring influences in order to promote enduring change, we must simultaneously work with many levels of nested systems.

The following chapters provide a representative although not exhaustive overview of theory, research, social policy, and programming issues relevant to facilitating infant and early childhood development. The ideas presented are in various stages of formulation. Some, although soundly based on research and theory, are in early stages of construction. Others reflect the outcome of years of testing. All were selected for inclusion in this volume because they represented a dimension of the most current thinking and activity in this field.

The concept of facilitating optimal development or promoting competence is not a simple one. Nevertheless our hope is that clarification of the concept will be advanced by the papers in this book.

Burlington, Vermont   L.A.B.
August 1981   J.M.J.

PART I

Perspectives on Development: Prevention and Promotion

Introductory Notes

Inherent in any effort to facilitate infant and early childhood development is an explicit or implicit assumption about the nature of development. In order to consider the primary prevention of pathology and the promotion of development, one must work within a set of premises concerning the bases and dynamics of healthy development. Therefore, this book begins with five papers that examine perspectives on the nature of development and the implications of these views for facilitating early development.

Lynne Bond's paper begins by calling for a new focus for primary prevention efforts. She points out the limitations of the historically accepted goal of preventing the development of negative outcomes and urges a focus on the more general aim of promoting positive development. This shift from the prevention of disorder to the facilitation of development is apparent in many of the chapters in this book. Programmatic constraints have typically led us to focus on predominantly preventive measures and hence to implement isolated, short-lived, expensive programs when disaster seemed impending. Bond argues that the shift toward promotion is best approached by incorporating promotive features into the typical daily functioning of our society. Programs such as those of Minde, Shosenberg, and Marton, and Belsky and Benn, which are described in Part III, are excellent illustrations of this possibility.

Bond proceeds to delineate her perspective on the nature and bases of development as a framework for approaching efforts at promotion. Highlighting current research and theory on the character of human development, she concludes that development is a product of the organism's own active interaction with the environment and, consequently, it is the individual's propensity toward such interaction which must be promoted. Her review of the empirical and theoretical literature elaborates on Robert White's notion of an intrinsic motive to achieve effective interaction. She uses current research to document her argument that this motivation is both modified by experience and related to subsequent developmental competence. Moreover, in accord with her constructivist, transactional perspective on development, and her goal of integrating promotion into the structure of society, Bond recognizes the individual infant as simply one dynamic component of a multilevel system. She contends that the perceived efficacy of the infant is inherently tied to that of the caregiver–infant dyad, family triad, community, and society as a whole. Thus, reviewing prevention programs and elaborating upon the implications of her model for promotion, Bond suggests the need to address the self-sustaining motivational processes that simultaneously underlie a sense of efficacy at many levels of the system. With this goal in mind, she outlines concrete suggestions for the design and implementation of programs and for bringing about societal change that will emphasize promotion.

Dale Goldhaber, like Bond, looks beyond prevention to promotion, basing his approach on a life-span and constructivist view of development. Influenced by the work of Robert White and Jean Piaget, Goldhaber defines "competent" individuals as those "who can deal with a variety of situations, who are aware of themselves as agents of change, and who can take strategies developed in one setting and use them in another." Therefore, according to Goldhaber, attempts to promote individual competence must shift away from efforts to accelerate the emergence of specific skills. He proposes that encouraging greater breadth of experience is necessary in order to facilitate early development.

Goldhaber's paper contrasts traditional early intervention programs with his vision of a cognitive–developmental alternative and concludes that the generally disappointing outcomes of the former may be a result of their narrow view of human development. He argues that intervention and prevention programs must be consistent with the premise that development is a lifelong process, which cannot simply be equated with learning. He reviews several areas of research that support the emphasis on breadth of development and structural organization of interrelationships of diverse behaviors. Goldhaber suggests that both the general research on environmental correlates of cognitive growth and the specific evaluations of constructivist early childhood education programs support a focus on the breadth of development as basic to the facilitation of competence. He concludes his chapter by outlining general implications of this perspective for the design, administration, and evaluation of children's intervention and prevention programs.

The final three papers in this section offer perspectives on developmental continuities and discontinuities. Ann Clarke's paper gives specific emphasis to discontinuities of development and the various forms they may assume. She notes that measurement and evaluation problems may lead us to deemphasize this characteristic of development. Hence, Clarke reviews six areas of research to illustrate the nature of developmental discontinuities: these areas include early and late adoption, children rescued from severe deprivation, studies of cumulative deficit, social influences upon achievement, and outcomes of early intervention programs. From her review of the literature she finds support for her long-held position that discontinuities exist under normal and deviant conditions of development. In addition, Clarke considers the possibility of both biological and social trajectories from which individuals might deviate but to which they will return when they are in an "adequate" environment. This notion of a "self-righting tendency" is certainly not new, but it is increasingly gaining adherents, particularly with the growth of a transactional view of development. Perhaps most noteworthy among Clarke's conclusions is her conviction that only broadly based, enduring support can effect enduring change in the course of both child and adult development. This theme is reiterated in many of the chapters of this book.

Victor Denenburg is an outspoken critic of much of the traditional study of behavioral development. He argues that our rigid adherence to simple causal models of development has led us to engage in fruitless pursuits such as the question of causal links between early experiences and later development. Claiming that the continuity vs. discontinuity issue is, in fact, a pseudo-argument, Denenberg maintains that we must abandon our causal model if we hope to advance our knowledge of development. Reviewing the work of animal researchers published in the early 1960s, Denenberg shows that an interactional perspective on development was strongly supported two decades ago and wonders at human researchers' perseveration in efforts to disprove the traditional critical period hypothesis. His chapter illustrates and emphasizes the need for collaboration between animal and human researchers.

Denenberg offers general systems theory as a more viable framework for considering the organizational complexity of development—an approach implied in Bond's chapter and detailed in that of Ramey, MacPhee, and Yeates' (Part III). He reviews earlier animal research supporting the position that there is a need for such an interactional perspective. He then discusses his own recent research on the interaction of early experience and brain laterality in rodents as an illustration of the complex interactional nature of developmental processes. The implications of his research for examining human development include replacing a learning model with a psychobiological model and replacing linear cause–effect terms with systems terminology.

Marian Sigman integrates data from animals and humans as she examines the issue of plasticity in development and its implications for intervention. While recognizing the methodological problems in the literature concerning recovery from central nervous system lesions, she cites evidence for substantial recovery of brain function among lesioned children and lower-order animals; she also notes limitations to this plasticity as in the case of central nervous system damage related to congenital malformations. Turning to studies of environmental remediation of brain damage and the effects of early enrichment and deprivation upon adult characteristics, Sigman once again documents the plasticity of development and notes, as Denenberg emphasized, that these effects are not necessarily linear.

Sigman and her colleagues working on the UCLA Longitudinal Study of Preterm Infants have examined the complex interplay of pediatric, behavioral, and cognitive factors relating to later development. For example, she explains that their path analyses of the relationships between postnatal medical complications, pediatric complications, caregiver–infant interaction, and subsequent development reveal a fascinating situation, "two different and opposing links between early illness and later performance." Although Sigman's methodology is short of a system's approach, her results appear to reflect the complex interactional nature of development espoused by Denenberg. With this understanding, Sigman, like others in this book, points to the role played by the family and by the social milieu in effective intervention.

From Prevention to Promotion:
Optimizing Infant Development

Lynne A. Bond

A primary prevention approach to psychopathology has been deemed
the latest revolution in mental health (Albee, 1980). We are called to focus upon preventing the development of disorders rather than to await
their emergence and dwell upon identification and treatment. Thus, two
tactics are commonly suggested: (1) attempts to modify the environment
in order to reduce or eliminate stressful agents, and (2) efforts to enhance
the coping skills of individuals so that they can deal more effectively with
stressful events.

This orientation toward preventing the development of negative outcomes is easily adopted in work with infants. Infancy has long been characterized as a period of great importance for the individual and, more
recently, as a time during which the infant significantly affects its environment (e.g., Bell, R. Q., 1968, 1971; Lewis and Rosenblum, 1974).
Existing disorders are infrequently identified among infant as compared
with adult populations. Infants are more commonly perceived as "at
risk" for the development of pathology rather than as "diseased" and in
need of treatment. The recent efforts to delineate contributors to vulnerability or risk have provided a foundation on which to build prevention programs. Thus, infants and, specifically, infants "at risk" have
become a priority target for primary prevention efforts (Task Force on
Prevention, 1978), including attempts both to modify infant environments (e.g., through parent training) and to strengthen infant coping
skills (e.g., through programmed infant stimulation).

Meanwhile, the focus of primary prevention has remained, as the label
suggests, on the *prevention* of the development of negative outcomes (cf.
Caplan, 1964; Roberts, 1970; Wagenfeld, 1972). We presume that disaster is impending in our lives and that our efforts should be focused
upon its diversion. Before we accept this common working mode of primary prevention, we should reconsider prevention within the broader
context of promotion. Protecting ourselves from negative influences is,
at most, a narrow perspective on the course of growth and well-being.

This chapter discusses an orientation for reconceptualizing primary prevention in terms of the promotion of development. Emerging from a transactional, constructivist perspective of the nature of development, this paper suggests that promoting optimal development might best be approached by promoting the motivational system underlying infants' own active, adaptive interaction with the environment. Following a review of the research on infants' intrinsic motivation toward effective interaction, this chapter examines empirical literature that supports the notion that this motivational system is modified by contingency-related experiences and, in turn, has impact upon developmental competence. At the same time, it is stressed that a similar framework underlies the larger, multilevel transactional network (involving caregivers, family, community, etc.) of which infant development is only a part. This chapter concludes by discussing the implications of this model for structuring programs designed to optimize infant development.

Let us distinguish between the notion of prevention and the more general notion of enhancement or promotion. While prevention typically focuses upon avoiding negative outcomes, defects, or disease, promotion aims toward facilitating growth and adaptation. In discussing the philosophy of medicine, for example, Hoke (1968) points out that "*curing* disease and *preventing* disease . . . are but two aspects of a single orientation—the disease orientation. The focus is on disease and its causes. The object is, through therapeutics, to cure the disease or, through hygiene, to keep it away" (p.269). He suggests that while "health and disease have been regarded as polar opposites with health being the absence of disease" (p.269), to the contrary, "they are not mutually exclusive, dualistic, entities. . . . Promotive medicine seeks to promote healthy, positive adaptive responses. . . . Health is not a static end-point but a way of pursuing one's goals" (p.270).

In theory, promotion is not a new idea. For example, Goldston (1977) advocated "that *prevention* be used . . . to refer to actions which aim either to (1) anticipate a disorder or (2) foster optimal health" (p.20). According to Goldston, "the goals of primary prevention are two-fold: first, to prevent needless psychopathology and symptoms, maladjustment, maladaptation, and misery regardless of whether an end-point might be mental illness; and second, to promote mental health by increasing levels of 'wellness' among various defined populations" (p.21).

Meanwhile, the need for a distinction between prevention and promotion has been maintained. According to Klein and Goldston (1977), "Prevention is directed toward reducing the incidence of a highly predictable undesirable consequence. The term should not be used interchangeably with 'promotion of mental health' or 'improving the quality of life.'"

(p.vii). Danish and his colleagues (e.g., Danish and D'Augelli, 1980; Danish, Smyer, and Nowak, 1980), strong advocates of an enhancement approach, also suggest the need for a distinction between "enriching interventions" and primary prevention. They refer to the contrasting implications of these two perspectives for expected outcomes, implementation, evaluation of interventions, and acceptance of interventions by policy makers and the public. Of course, the basis for their arguments was the restricted focus of existing efforts in primary prevention. Whether we need to provide or maintain distinct labels is perhaps a secondary issue. Of primary concern is the fact that mental health programs are not fulfilling their potential. When we move beyond theory to practice, "promotion" rarely seems to be the goal.

The focus on prevention not only assumes a limited perspective of optimal development but also generates serious constraints in the programs it inspires. With its orientation toward avoiding the development of disorders, prevention typically is translated into a framework in which stress is seen as a negative factor and stressful events are to be avoided. This denies the constructive, growth-enhancing potential of crises and stress situations (e.g., Danish, 1977; Danish and D'Augelli, 1980; Danish et al., 1980; Lazarus, 1980; Riegel, 1975). It further presupposes a static model of human nature in which the goal is simply "problem reduction," that is, returning to conditions that existed prior to the problem (Danish and D'Augelli, 1980).

Perhaps in part because of limited resources, prevention efforts have tended to rely upon supplemental programs, specifically designed and designated for select samples of the population. The economics of these ventures have inevitably led to short-lived projects that are difficult to implement on a significant scale. If more than a token effort, they have tended to involve expensive and intensive additions to ongoing practices rather than fundamental reorganizations with long-term and wide-scale potential. Instead of incorporating the programs into the overall structure of societal institutions, thus spreading their responsibility, involvement, impact, and drain of resources, administration and implementation have typically been channeled to a limited group of human service agencies. Thus, competitive resources and priorities remain an unstable factor and the breadth and availability of services remain limited. Furthermore, the designation of any specific program for a defined subpopulation is accompanied by a more general danger—the value of the targeted experiences for the remainder of the population is deemphasized. Consider, for example, the flexible alternative education practices designed for "gifted" children that have deemphasized the fact that all school children might benefit from such alternatives in the system. Similarly, the supplemental, experiential learning situations provided for slow learners are often overlooked as valuable components of all children's education.

All of this is not to say that we should diminish our concern for high-risk populations or that we should abandon specific efforts directed toward these groups. But I would argue that the needs of these groups and the population at large might be better met if considered within the broader context of promotion, enhancement, and optimization of positive growth. It is only in this manner that we will move beyond the short-term interventions that are implemented intermittently when disaster seems impending to focus on broad-scale, long-term restructuring toward self-sustaining supportive systems as integral parts of our lives.

How shall we proceed? How can society go about the task of promoting optimal growth? The goal of prevention in its narrowest sense, averting the development of negative outcomes, appears ominous in magnitude. Working within the broader context of promoting positive growth may present more overwhelming difficulties given the absence of a consensus on definition. What is it that we want to or need to promote? Notions such as competence, life satisfaction, and positive quality of life come to mind. What do these entail? How do we promote them? As Ansbacher (1978) and others have suggested, it may be precisely this lack of a definition of positive mental health that has led us to focus our energies on dealing with negative environmental influences and negative outcomes. In attempting to specify our goals, Hoke's (1968) description of promotive medicine seems pertinent.

Promotive medicine . . . will require understanding health in *process* terms rather than in static or ontologic terms . . . . [It] views health, not as an entity that is lost or gained, nor a quantity, but as a developmental process involving multilevel responses to a total environment. (p.270)

This focus on process terms rather than static terms also appears in descriptions of "competence." Connolly and Bruner (1974) explain that "when we talk about competence we are talking about intelligence in the broadest sense, operative intelligence *knowing how* rather than simply *knowing that.* For competence involves action, changing the environment as well as adapting to the environment" (p.3). Mason (1970) describes intelligence as the process by which the organism adjusts as a whole; intelligent behavior involves the process of bringing a fit between the needs of the organism and the restrictions of the environment. Murphy and Frank (1979) report: "The outcomes of interactions between vulnerabilities and the environment . . . will not depend solely on how benign the efforts of others in behalf of the beleaguered child or adult may be, but on how the vulnerable person uses the environment along with his or her own resources" (p.198). They see the "process of restoring and maintenance of equilibrium as a basic aspect of coping which goes beyond culturally recognized and demanded cognitive and social skills" (p.203). Thus, although a shift from prevention to promotion might lead us to the problem of "how to structure a child's world so that experience has the maximum positive effect on growth and development" (White, 1967, p.204), it appears that promotive efforts require we proceed from our understanding not only of the pattern of human development but of the very processes underlying this development. We will see that a promotive rather than preventive approach fits well with our current conceptualization of the nature of development, and it is from this conceptualization that we can attempt to redefine our task of promotion.

Infant Competence

The amazing competencies of the newborn are now well documented (e.g., Ainsworth, 1973; Appleton, Clifton, and Goldberg, 1975; Osofsky, 1979; Stone, Smith, and Murphy, 1973). Infants' abilities to perceive, process, and respond to the environment far exceed our earlier expectations. For example, although Piaget's (1952) conceptualization of sensorimotor intelligence was once suspected of overestimating the infant's skills, it is now clear that it falls somewhat short of acknowledging the extensive cognitive and social competencies of the first 2 years of life. Not only have we been impressed by the infant's competence in responding to the environment but we are more than ever struck by the infant's ability to affect the environment. The image of the infant as a passive blob at the mercy of impinging stimuli is grossly outdated. Extensive literature has revealed the remarkably active role that infants play in shaping their own environments and, hence, their own development (e.g., Ainsworth and Bell, 1974; Bell, 1968, 1971; Bell and Ainsworth, 1972; Goldberg, 1977; Lewis and Rosenblum, 1974; Schaffer, 1977a; Stern, 1971).

Infant Preadaptation

A special facet of our understanding of infant competence is the growing appreciation of newborns' preadaptation to attend to stimuli in a manner that facilitates the infants' own social, cognitive, perceptual, and motor development. Consider, for example, infants' tendencies to orient toward stimuli that are moderately discrepant from those which they have previously experienced (e.g., Charlesworth, 1969; Hunt, 1965; Kagan, 1970) and infants' propensity to repeat, with slight modifications, those acts which they have most recently mastered (e.g., Piaget, 1952). Newborns appear "pretuned" to focus on stimuli that are characteristic of human responsiveness and interaction (e.g., Appleton et al., 1975; Papoušek and Papoušek, 1978; Richards, 1974; Stern, 1974; Trevarthen, 1977). For example, they demonstrate unusual attentiveness to visual stimuli characteristic of the human face (e.g., Bond, 1972; Cohen, De-Loache, and Strauss, 1979; Haaf and Bell, 1967; Packer and Rosenblatt, 1979); adults spontaneously exaggerate facial expressions when interacting with infants (Stern, 1974). There is also a match between infant auditory sensitivity and the range of frequencies of adult-to-infant speech (e.g., Eisenberg, 1965; Stern, 1974) and auditory discriminations which are unique to human speech (e.g., Eimas, Siqueland, Jusczk, and Vigorito, 1971).

Constructivist Perspective

There has been a move from empiricist and nativist arguments toward a constructivist notion of development "which holds that human organisms actively build their constructs, knowledge base, and views of reality through engagement with the environment" (Sigel and Cocking, 1977, p.225). Inspired by Piagetian theory and subsequent work by Kelly (1955), this perspective is best articulated by Sigel and Cocking (1977). Individuals are seen neither as passive shapes waiting to be molded nor as preprogrammed machines with a fixed developmental plan. Rather, humans are recognized as active processors of information who construct their own realities. The individual does not learn through the passive absorption of information; one's perception or understanding is not a carbon copy of some external reality. Instead, an individual's reality is constructed through active physical and mental manipulation of the environment. Organisms assimilate new experiences to their existing conceptual frameworks as a function of the interaction which, in turn, leads to restructuring these frameworks and hence new levels of environmental manipulation. Thus development is a product of the interactional process itself, not only in social and cognitive domains but in motor and perceptual activities as well (e.g., Held and Hein, 1963; Kohler, 1962; White, 1969). If we construe the term "understanding" in the broadest sense of perceiving, feeling, acting, and knowing, it appears to be the case that "to understand is to invent" (Piaget, 1976, p.1).

Life-Span Orientation

A life-span developmental orientation has emerged in many of the social and natural sciences, with its major propositions delineated, to a large extent, by Baltes and his colleagues (e.g., Baltes, 1978; Baltes and Brim, 1979; Baltes, Reese, and Lipsitt, 1980). Development is recognized as a lifelong process with no single period claiming primacy for the origin and occurrence of development; rather, many phases are seen as involving maximum change. Development is recognized as entailing a system of pluralistic change. It is not unilinear, irreversible, or endstate oriented. Instead, it is multilinear, multidirectional, heterogeneous, and plastic. The multiple origins of influences upon development are emphasized. Age-graded variables have long been considered (biological maturation and socialization). However, normative history-graded influences (e.g., war, economic depressions, technological advances), and nonnormative life events (e.g., accidents, career shifts) are now receiving serious attention.

Moreover, the dialectic nature of development is increasingly appreciated (e.g., Baltes et al., 1980; Riegel, 1975). The multiple forces reflected in development are not always synchronous nor synergistic; a balance or equilibrium may be the exception rather than the rule. In fact, the asynchronies or "crises" that continually emerge through interaction appear to be the basis for developmental restructuring. Thus crises are not to be avoided but, on the contrary, are an integral part of development (e.g., Danish and D'Augelli, 1980; Danish et al., 1980; Lazarus, 1980; Riegel, 1975).

Transactional Perspective

The roots of the transactional approach go at least as far back as the turn of the century (e.g., Baldwin, 1902) with the recognition that "persons become both factors and products in the social organizations of which they are a part" (Cairns, Green, and MacCombie, 1980, p.80). Certainly, much of the work of Piaget and Bowlby also portrays infants as active organisms "born with behavioral propensities and tendencies that shaped their experiences and contributed to their own development" (Lamb, 1979, p. 68). And Cairns et al. point to the transactional perspective, long espoused in research on nonhuman development (e.g., Kuo, 1967; Schneirla, 1966).

There is now widespread acknowledgment of the transactional nature of human development with much recent attention to the work of Sameroff and his colleagues (e.g., Sameroff, 1975a, 1975b, 1977; Sameroff and Chandler, 1975). It is recognized that individuals play an active role in shaping their environment and are simultaneously affected by the environment they are altering. Thus the infant–caregiver interaction is not simply a matter of each individual impacting on the other but rather, this interaction involves "*the changing pattern of the mutual perceptions and behaviors of both infant and caretaker vis-à-vis each other as a result of their respective previous mutual perceptions and behaviors vis-à-vis each other*" (Rosenthal,

1973, p.302), and, of course, vis-à-vis other animate and inanimate aspects of their environments. Parent and child characteristics change over time. Each changes the environment and is changed by the changes each has created. As Beckwith (1979) has summarized, development may well proceed "through a sequence of regular restructurings within and between the infant and his/her environment" (p.700). Thus the child's individuality and his/her environment are placed in a common reciprocal system. Individual functioning is "the outcome of an interactive process in which the infant's characteristics are only one of the multiplicity of factors in the social context of development" (Beckwith, 1979, p. 700).

Perhaps as a function of the methodological and statistical difficulties involved in reliable observation and assessment of behavioral transactions (e.g., see discussion by Packer and Rosenblatt, 1979), research and interventions have lagged behind theory in adopting a transactional perspective. Nevertheless, research and intervention techniques are slowly reorienting in this direction. Consider, for example, the focus on family systems theory and family-oriented education or intervention programs (Schaefer, 1970). Or consider the focus on reciprocity, synchrony, and dialogue in the context of the infant–caregiver relationship. For example, Kaye (1977) studied the emergence of "turn-taking" by mother and infant during feeding situations where the bursts and pauses of the infant's sucking and the jiggling by the mother show the controlled and controlling characteristics, that is, the mutual regulation of adult dialogue. Green, Gustafson, and West (1980) have demonstrated the increasing emergence of give-and-take games through infancy, with infants initiating more interactions from 6 to 12 months and mothers increasingly presenting games in which the infant is required to be an active participant. Thus, as Cairns et al. (1980) suggest, "developmental changes in young pace changes in their environments, which, in turn, feedback to produce subsequent alterations in their behaviors" (p.92).

To summarize, human infants are highly competent organisms who are capable of interacting with, processing information from, and responding to the environment as well as affecting it. Their development is transactional in nature with the infant and environment constantly in the process of mutual influence and regulation. The infant's development is best conceptualized in the context of a whole, organized, interrelated system of influence.

The transactional developmental process continues throughout life in a multilinear, multidirectional fashion with the specific characteristics of life task demands continually changing. As these demands change "so must the actions that are deemed adaptive or optimal" (Cairns et al., 1980, p. 102). Furthermore, as Bruner and Connolly have explained, "it is characteristic of [humans] that [they] must create the patterns of behavior that suit the very environmental conditions which [they have] also created" (1974, p. 309). Meanwhile, the infant seems pretuned to interact in such a way as to promote its own development, actively creating those conditions which precipitate its own development.

Thus, we come to recognize human infants and their environments in the context of a larger system of biological and behavioral adaptation. It is from this conceptualization, the adaptive behavioral system, that we can orient toward promoting positive growth within the structure of the lives of the population at large. Although we could identify and support specific skills associated with competency, this approach is not easily adapted to broad-scale implementation and the continually changing nature of individuals' needs. We must abandon our search for "experts" who will enhance the lives of the "masses". We cannot hope to provide each infant with some optimal pattern of stimulation even if such an unlikely formula were to exist. Instead, we must emphasize self-sustaining supportive systems within the population at large. That is, we need to focus on promoting the individual's own adaptive response system to allow for the unique and changing demands of the individual's development. The active, selective behavior of each individual leads to transactions which are the bases of the individual's growth and construction of reality, the process by which development occurs. Thus, to promote the optimal development of each individual, we can encourage the individual's own propensity toward creating those conditions conducive to its own development. These conditions involve the individual's active, adaptive interaction with the environment.

Toward Infant-Environment Interaction

What is it that affects the infant's tendency to interact with the environment? Noting the persistent, selective, directive nature of the infant's behavior, R. W. White (1959) proposed the existence of an intrinsic motivation to attain "competence", that is, "to interact effectively with [the] environment" (p. 297). Citing rich illustrations from the work of Piaget (1952), White suggested that the child seems to select "for continuous treatment those aspects of his environment which he finds it possible to affect in some way" (p. 320). That is, there appears to be an intrinsic motive to explore the consequences of one's behavior upon the environment and the effects which the environment has upon oneself. This was alternatively described as a motive to develop an "effective familiarity" with the environment (White, 1959, p. 321) and labeled more precisely, "effectance motivation."

Effectance motivation must be conceived to involve satisfaction—a feeling of efficacy—in transactions in which behavior has an exploratory, varying, experimental character and produces changes in the stimulus field. Having this character, the behavior leads the organism to find out how the environment can be changed and what consequences flow from these changes. (White, 1959, p. 329)

Effectance motivation, manifested in characteristics such as curiosity and exploration, was presumed to propel much of the infant's interaction with the environment. Effectance motivation would lead to exploration of one's effects upon the environment (i.e., mastery attempts). The perception of effects that are contingent upon one's behavior would result in feelings of efficacy. Feelings of efficacy appeared to be intrinsically reinforcing and therefore would serve to increase or sustain the effectance motivation. Thus competent (i.e., effective) behavior was seen as self-rewarding and leading to an adaptive, self-sustaining cycle which perpetuated infant–environment transactions.

Although White's model has been refined and elaborated (e.g., Harter, 1978; Harter and Zigler, 1974), there remains widespread agreement that infants enter the world with the tendency to explore their control of and control by the environment (e.g., Watson, 1979). From the first days of life, infants not only detect but also learn to control contingent stimulation (Papoušek, 1961). Watson (1966) suggested that infants are engaged in a continual process of contingency analysis, and interesting effects in the environment may lead the infant to "scan or read back its memory record . . . to select that behavior emitted just prior to the reception of the rewarding stimulus" (p. 124). Watson's (1979) recent model of contingency perception suggests the astounding complexity of the analyses in which infants are engaged and expounds on the various structural forms of contingencies (e.g., R→S, S→R, and S↔R or stimulus-response synchrony) which infants may perceive through multiple analytic indices. This elaborate, comprehensive perspective on contingency analysis fits well with White's (1959) notion of developing "effective familiarity" with the environment. Thus the focus is toward both the control of and control by the environment. Competence involves affecting the environment as well as adapting to it (see also Connolly and Bruner, 1974). The infant's orientation to explore contingencies in the environment is a central feature of its overall adaptive behavioral system; it propels the infant to interact with the environment, thereby providing the basis for the infant's own development.

There is much evidence that the infant's effective interaction with the environment is reinforcing in its own right rather than propelled by extrinsic rewards (e.g., Papoušek and Papoušek, 1978). As Appleton et al.

(1975) suggest, if mastery were not self-rewarding, the many failures and falls involved in mastering a task such as walking would quickly condition the infant to cease its efforts. Sroufe and his colleagues have demonstrated that laughter accompanies mastery in cognitive tasks and is positively related to the degree to which the infant is involved as an active participant in the experience (e.g., Sroufe and Waters, 1976; Sroufe and Wunsch, 1972). Watson (1972) and Watson and Ramey (1972), among others, have shown the smiling and cooing which accompany infants' experience with mobiles which turn contingently upon their behavior. In fact, Watson (1972) concluded that infants may find social stimuli rewarding precisely because these stimuli (i.e., adults) engage in "the game" of contingent responding. "Contingency may be a source of potency in its own right for eliciting social responsiveness" (Watson, 1979, p. 34).

Bower (1974) argues that the schedule of reinforcement rather than the reinforcement itself often seems to be a motivating factor since "the schedule can pose problems to the infant, and problem solving is the true motivation for human infants in a learning situation" (Bower, 1974, p. 8). Papoušek and Bernstein (1969) found infants highly motivated to solve difficult problems although they appeared inattentive to, and disinterested in, the visual display which the experimenters employed as the "reward". When Papoušek (1969) "reinforced" specific patterns of head turns by the illumination of light, infants' response rates rapidly increased whenever the experimenter changed the problem's solution (i.e., the pattern leading to the "reward"). However, once the infants learned the new pattern, there was a marked decrease in their responding until the solution was changed once again. Thus it appeared to be the opportunity to solve problems, that is, to explore new effective relationships, which was the motivational factor for interaction within this setting. In fact, the motivation toward effective, adaptive responding not only appears independent of physiological drives such as hunger or thirst, but may sometimes function as a more powerful motivator than such drives (Bower, 1974; Papoušek, 1967).

Infants will also express displeasure when unsuccessful in organizing effective responses. Trevarthen (1977) discussed research in which 2-month-old babies were presented with an image of their mother's face while she was either monitoring and responding to her infant's ongoing behavior or was interacting with another person who was off-screen. Although all the babies initially moved their arms and legs and vocalized to their mother's face, those in the noncontingent condition became withdrawn, agitated, and cried. Brazelton, Tronick, Adamson, Als, and Weise (1975) have also reported infant distress and helplessness emerging in experimental situations in which mothers intentionally refrain from synchronous, contingent responding. Indeed, it appears that objects that provide response-contingent feedback elicit approach and exploration (e.g., McCall, 1974); even unfamiliar objects (Gunnar, 1980; Gunnar-vonGnechten, 1978), people (Levitt, 1980), and events (Seligman, 1975) elicit less fear and distress, and more exploration when their activity is contingent rather than noncontingent upon the infant's behavior.

Thus the infant's interaction with the environment is propelled, in part, by a tendency to explore its effective relationships and is perpetuated by the intrinsically reinforcing properties associated with perception of efficacy. The consequent interaction provides the nutriment for growth and adaptation; it is the process whereby the infant constructs its reality. Therefore as one's tendency to explore and develop effective familiarity with the environment increases or decreases, so may one's developmental progress.

The Effective Infant

Over a decade ago, Lewis and Goldberg (1969) suggested that mothers who respond promptly and contingently to their infants do more than merely reinforce the specific preceding infant behavior. The mother also fosters the development of a generalized expectancy of effectiveness on the part of the child, that is, the infant learns the rule that its behavior has environmental consequences. The generally reinforcing effects of this sense of self-efficacy promote novel responding and exploration in new situations as well. This ensuing interaction leads to the discovery of new environmental consequences, promoting the sense of self-efficacy and motivation toward further interaction.

Indeed, observational studies reveal positive correlations between maternal responsiveness and both infant exploratory behavior (e.g., Riksen-Walraven, 1978) and children's initiative and responsiveness to strangers (Beckwith, 1972). Furthermore, Yarrow, Pedersen, and Rubenstein (1977) observed that the degree to which infants manipulated novel objects, emitted reaching and grasping behaviors, and engaged in goal-directed behaviors corresponded to the responsiveness of the objects in the infant's environment (i.e., the degree of visual, tactual, or auditory feedback elicited from the object by an infant's action on it). Provence and Lipton (1962) reported that orphanage-reared infants showed a decrease in their tendencies to approach and explore objects and initiate social contacts over the first year of life. Within this non-responsive institutional environment, the infants appeared to have learned that their behaviors (e.g., fussing for food or a diaper change) were, in fact, of little consequence. The phenomenon "learned helplessness," widely documented among humans and nonhumans alike (Seligman, 1975), emerges in situations in which subjects perceive a lack of control of their circumstances. Watson (1966) suggested that the majority of infants may spend their first few months in a state of "natural deprivation" of learning experiences, related to the noncontingent quality of the early care-giving environment. He argued that a change in these conditions may have positive, long-term developmental consequences.

The results of experimentally manipulated contingency experiences confirm interpretations of naturalistic observations. Early associations with response-contingent stimulation influence the infant's subsequent tendency to explore and discover contingent relationships (e.g., Finkelstein and Ramey, 1977; Papoušek, 1967; Ramey and Finkelstein, 1978; Watson and Ramey, 1972). For example, experience with response-noncontingent mobile turning led to significant difficulty in learning to affect a response-contingent mobile even 6 weeks later while response-contingent mobile turning enhanced infants' subsequent ability to effect such consequences (Watson and Ramey, 1972). Furthermore, the facilitory effects of early contingency experiences not only transfer from one task to another (Finkelstein and Ramey, 1977), but from one behavioral setting to another as well (Ramey and Finkelstein, 1978).

The enhanced contingency analysis or "effectance" which follows from early contingency experiences may be mediated, specifically, by a shift in attentional strategy (Finkelstein and Ramey, 1977; Ramey and Finkelstein, 1978). Infants who had been exposed to supplemental response-contingent stimulation attended more equally to both stimulus presentations and response manipulandum than infants with supplemental noncontingent experience, who paid more attention to the stimulus presentation alone. The strategy of equally divided attention seems more likely to reveal effective relationships between two events. As Appleton et al. (1975) suggest, "the infant learns to learn by finding that attention and activity result in new and interesting experiences" (p. 158).

Thus, we have found that experiences with response-contingent and noncontingent stimulation modify the infant's pursuit of an effective familiarity with the environment. Meanwhile, it is this pursuit which propels transactions with the environment, the substance from which development emerges. Therefore, the responsiveness of the infant's early environment should have a significant impact upon the infant's developmental progression.

Research supports this prediction of a positive relationship between environmental contingencies and developmental competence. For example, observational studies have revealed significant correlations between the responsiveness of infants' inanimate environments and their intellectual and motor development. Yarrow et al. (1975) found the responsiveness of objects within reach of the infant to correlate positively with scores of both mental and psychomotor development on the Bayley; cognitive-motivational variables (goal-directedness, reaching and grasping, secondary circular reactions) have shown particularly strong associations suggesting a powerful relationship between environmental responsiveness and the infant's exploratory behavior. Wachs (1978) reported a positive relationship between the number of audio-visually responsive toys in the infant's environment from 12 to 24 months and the Stanford-Binet score at 31 months. Jennings, Harmon, Morgan, Gaiter, and Yarrow (1979) found responsiveness of toys in the infant's 6-month environment was related to the continuity of play and the infant's production of effects from the environment (i.e., production of auditory and/or visual feedback) at 1 year. Meanwhile, Wachs, Uzgiris, and Hunt (1971) summarized their work as suggesting that "high intensity stimulation from which the infant cannot escape and involuntary exposure to an excessive variety of circumstances are negatively correlated with several aspects of psychological development" (p. 309) during the first 2 years of life.

The responsiveness of the infant's social environment (maternal responsiveness in particular) has been associated with enhanced development of infants' social and cognitive skills (e.g., Clarke-Stewart, VanderStoep, and Killian, 1979; Cohen and Beckwith, 1979). Latency of maternal response to infant crying or vocalization is inversely related to the infant's habituation rate to repeated stimulation, a measure of early concept development and predictive among 1-year-olds of Stanford Binet IQ score and concept formation performance at 3½ years (Lewis and Goldberg, 1969). Maternal responsiveness to infant behaviors, vocalization, and distress is also associated with the following:

• superior psychomotor (Yarrow et al., 1975) and mental development scores on the Bayley (Clarke-Stewart, 1973; Yarrow et al., 1975)

• gross and fine motor skills and cognitive-motivational measures (Yarrow et al., 1975)

• indices of object and person permanence (Bell, 1970)

• initiation, number, variety, and clarity of infant communication signals (Ainsworth and Bell, 1974; Bell and Ainsworth, 1972; Yarrow et al., 1975).

In summarizing her own extensive observational research, Clarke-Stewart (1973) stated:

Maternal responsiveness was, in fact, more highly related to measures of the child's general competence and motivation than it was to the frequency of the specific infant behaviors responded to (looking at mother, vocalizing to her, approaching her, giving or showing her objects). Responsiveness was related to the child's Bayley mental score, to his speed of processing information, and to his schema development, as well as to language, social, and emotional indices of competence. This finding is one step toward confirming the suggestion that contingent responsiveness to an infant's behavior does more than reinforce specific behaviors, that it created in the infant an expectancy of control which generalizes to new situations and unfamiliar people. (p.71)

Although much of the support for the promotive impact of contingency relationships has come from research examining maternal responsiveness to infant distress in particular, Clarke-Stewart (1973) suggested that maternal responsiveness to the infant's social signals (other than distress) may reveal an even stronger relationship to the enhancement of social and intellectual competencies and motivation. In a report on a longitudinal study of premature babies, Beckwith, Cohen, Kopp, Parmelee, and Marcy (1976) state:

Infants who were assessed at 9 months as more skillful in sensorimotor performance had at 1 month more mutual caregiver–infant gazing, at 3 months more interchanges of smiling during mutual gazing and more contingent response to their fuss cries, and at 8 months experienced greater levels of social interaction including more contingent responsiveness to their nondistress vocalizations. The significant dimension appears to be reciprocal social transactions, that is, transactions that occur contingently to the infant's signals, either simultaneously as in mutual gazing or successively as in contingency to distress or contingency to nondistress vocalizations. (pp. 585–86)

They propose that their study revealed "an effective similarity of contingent behaviors, although each contingent behavior acquired salience at different ages" (p. 586).

The infant's exploration of its control of and control by the environment is fundamental to the emergence of reciprocal turn taking within the caregiver–infant dyad. The development of these caregiver–infant "dialogues" or reciprocal exchanges is receiving growing attention as the basis of early communication (e.g., Brazelton, Koslowski, and Main, 1974; Newson, 1977, 1979; Richards, 1974; Trevarthen, 1977) and as the precursor to mature language and general social dialogue (e.g., Bruner, 1977; Cairns et al., 1980; Jones, 1979; Kaye, 1977; Schaffer, 1977a, 1977b). As Lamb (1979) remarked:

It is evident . . . that infants must develop concepts of themselves as effective social beings (i.e., individuals whose behaviors affect those with whom they are interacting) as well as expectations regarding the behavior of others before they can be viewed as intentionally social beings rather than persons whose behavior has unanticipated social significance . . . . [Some] have argued that, by assuring responses to the infant's actions, parental sensitivity permits babies to develop notions of their own effectance as well as expectations regarding the mode and predictability of others' behavior. (p.70)

This preverbal dialogue may serve as the mechanism whereby the infant's actions acquire meaning and intentionality for the infant as well as for others (Jones, 1979; Newson, 1979; Richards, 1974). Caregivers tend to interpret the infant's behavior in the same way that they interpret the behaviors of others engaged in a social dialogue and respond discriminately to those infant behaviors that have meaning in a typical social exchange. Thus a nonresponsive parent not only decreases an infant's tendency to explore its surroundings but also interferes with the cultural mediation of socially significant gestures and the phasing and reciprocity critical to the development of mature social exchange. That is, both the structure and the content of social dialogue may be influenced.

The Effective Dyad

Armed with this knowledge, how do we proceed toward the goal of optimizing infant development? Surely we could design individualized infant stimulation programs that would include extensive contingency experience. But such an approach is inadequate for broad-scale promotion. It returns us to the gross inefficiencies of one-to-one interventions and, in fact, becomes an absurd impossibility when targeting the general population. Furthermore, infant development occurs via transactions that are nested within larger systems. Thus we need to focus on restructuring the system rather than the individual, with the further goal of promoting a self-sustaining system. Expanding simply to the point of the caregiver–infant dyad or family triad lends a new perspective to the task of promotion.

Analyses of the synchrony in early mother–infant interaction suggest that mothers normally assume the responsibility for establishing the earliest interactional "synchronies" (e.g., Cairns et al., 1980; Trevarthen, 1977). They may begin by sequencing their behaviors around those of their infants, producing "pseudo-dialogues" (Jones, 1979; Newson, 1977, 1979; Schaffer, 1977a, 1977b, 1979), while they carefully monitor infant behavior, responding repetitively and with slight variation given indications of waning infant interest (e.g., Stern, 1974; Stern, Beebe, Jaffe, and Bennett, 1977). Over the first few days and weeks of life, however, infants spend more time in alert states and become more responsive to maternal solicitations (e.g., Packer and Rosenblatt, 1979). These developmental changes are accompanied by increasing mutual exchange and infant-initiated interactions (Green et al., 1980; Gustafson, Green, and West, 1979). Thus, the infant and caregiver rapidly become increasingly equal partners in regulating reciprocal interchanges (e.g., Kaye, 1977). As Korner (1979) suggests, the early "synchrony (or asynchrony) of interaction will, of course, in turn affect in a self-perpetuating way subsequent attempts at mutual regulation" (p. 777).

Goldberg (1977) has emphasized that caregivers' experiences affect their feelings of efficacy, as well. Adults embark upon parenthood with both general feelings of self-efficacy relevant to their pursuit of life goals, career, relationships, and so forth and certain specific expectations of their abilities to interact effectively with their baby. As with infants, caregivers' feelings of efficacy affect their tendencies to initiate responses; the expectation of being effective encourages the exploration of responses which may produce desired consequences. Feelings of self-efficacy also promote the caregiver's tendency to attend to and analyze the infant's behavior in terms of its contingent relationship to the caregiver's, allowing subtle changes in the infant's behavior to be used as cues for subsequent contingent responding by the caregiver.

As Goldberg (1977) explains (see Figure 1), caregivers' feelings of efficacy are influenced by their experiences in much the same manner as infants' feelings of efficacy. Interactions with a responsive, predictable, readable infant enhance the caregiver's feelings of efficacy, competence, and control. The likelihood increases that this caregiver will respond in a quick, contingent manner and will attend to the subtle changes in the infant's behavior which, in turn, both sustain the caregiver's feelings of efficacy and serve as cues for subsequent contingent responding to the infant. On the other hand, experiences with an infant who is unresponsive, unpredictable, and difficult to "read" will engender feelings of failure or helplessness on the part of the caregiver, decreasing the adult's tendency to respond quickly or contingently and, in turn, decreasing the response-contingent stimulation for the infant.

As we speak in terms of the "responsive caregiver" and the "responsive, predictable, readable infant," it becomes clear that we are not referring to independent characteristics of parent or child but rather to mutually dependent and evolving characteristics of an infant–caregiver transactional system (nested within still broader systems). The notion of a competent or effective dyad emerges (Ainsworth and Bell, 1974; Goldberg, 1977). Perceptions of efficacy not only influence the individual's tendency to explore and initiate responses but they simultaneously lead to behaviors that are effective in eliciting responsive behaviors from others. The

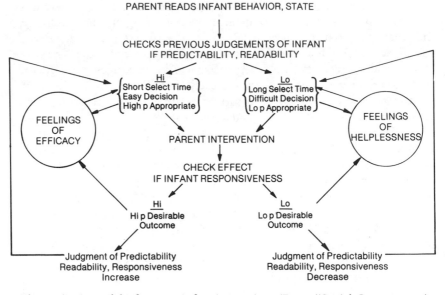

PARENT READS INFANT BEHAVIOR, STATE

CHECKS PREVIOUS JUDGEMENTS OF INFANT
IF PREDICTABILITY, READABILITY

Hi
{ Short Select Time
Easy Decision
High p Appropriate }

Lo
{ Long Select Time
Difficult Decision
Lo p Appropriate }

FEELINGS
OF
EFFICACY

FEELINGS
OF
HELPLESSNESS

PARENT INTERVENTION

CHECK EFFECT
IF INFANT RESPONSIVENESS

Hi
Hi p Desirable
Outcome

Lo
Lo p Desirable
Outcome

Judgment of Predictability
Readability, Responsiveness
Increase

Judgment of Predictability
Readability, Responsiveness
Decrease

Figure 1. A model of parent–infant interaction. (From "Social Competence in Infancy: A Model of Parent–Infant Interaction" by S. Goldberg, *Merrill-Palmer Quarterly*, 1977, *23*, 163–177. Copyright 1977 by the Wayne State University Press. Reprinted by permission.)

effective, responsive individual (caregiver or infant) behaves in a manner that is more likely to elicit effective responsive interaction with others, which, in turn, increases both the individual's and the others' perceptions of efficacy and subsequent tendency for future exploration and effective interaction. Meanwhile, the least effective infants and caregivers, those in most need of feedback regarding their own effects, behave in a manner least likely to elicit such experiences from others. Thus, the competent dyad fosters increasing growth and efficacy on the part of both members, while the incompetent dyad experiences spiralling decreases in feelings of effectiveness, which presumably decrease dyadic interaction and transactions in general.

This model has recently been implied in discussions of several patterns of developmental delay or difficulty. For example, Rossetti Ferreira (1978) argues that diminished synchronous, reciprocal, contingent interaction may mediate the relationship between malnutrition, environment, and retarded intellectual development. Citing evidence of the poor behavioral organization, muscle tone, visual orientation, and the diminished responsiveness of prenatally malnourished infants, she contends that these children will be less capable of eliciting responsive behavior on the part of their caregivers. Thus the behavioral state of the malnourished infant interacts with characteristics of the caregiver in such a way as to decrease the likelihood of either member of the dyad behaving in a manner which would promote responsiveness from the other. Thus the interactive initiative of each is decreased, thereby leading to a developmental retardation. Describing a longitudinal study by Chavez, Martinez, and Yaschine (1974) of mother–child dyads in a poor, rural Mexican community, Rossetti Ferreira (1978) notes that children from a nutritionally supplemented group were more active, independent, and demanding. Not only did their nutritionally supplemented mothers subsequently respond to them more often, but their nonsupplemented fathers also became more active participants in their caretaking and had higher expectations of their childrens' future. Thus the nutritionally supplemented infants gained more opportunity to learn of their behavioral impact upon the environment, and their increased engagement may have enhanced the responsiveness of their environment.

Similarly, Goldberg (1979) suggests that certain of the developmental difficulties of the premature infant may be related to factors that may have interfered with the early establishment of effective, mutually responsive transactions. The relative immaturity and disorganized behavioral state of premature infants hinders the clarity and predictability of their signals and responses. Thus premature infants are less effective in eliciting and supporting responsive caregiving. Furthermore, the premature infant's early separation from caregiver and placement into an intensive-care nursery diminishes the opportunity for caregiver and infant to develop an effective familiarity with one another. Both parent and infant are, in fact, relatively ineffective within such a context.

Jones (1979) compared the development of preverbal mother–infant "dialogue" or turn-taking between Down's syndrome and normal infants (8–18 months), and he described this communication process as one in which the "child learns to recognize what his own actions mean to others" (p. 179). Although Down's infants were involved in more interactional exchanges than typical infants, and their mothers more actively offered communicative support (i.e., treated any infant response as fitting appropriately into the dyadic exchange), Down's infants demonstrated less social initiative (e.g., reduced referential eye contact), and their mothers were more directive. Moreover, the Down's infants displayed timing in their interactional exchanges which was inappropriate for allowing turn-taking to occur (e.g., inappropriate time lags and phasing of utterances and lack of sensitivity to the caregiver's role). Jones concludes that Down's syndrome infants provide themselves with a less responsive, less stimulating environment. By making it more difficult for the caregiver to be responsive, these infants decrease their own opportunities for acquiring an understanding of their own social effects.

In summary, the caregiver's sensitivity and responsiveness to the child will vary with the caregiver's psychological and physiological state, expectations of the child's performance, and perceptions of, or affective feelings toward, the child. An infant's sensitivity and responsiveness to the caregiver will depend upon the infant's perceptual abilities, autonomic maturity, motor ability, and abilities to sustain an alert responsive state (Packer and Rosenblatt, 1979). But while the characteristics of infant and caregiver affect those of the other, they are simultaneously altered by their consequences in a manner which continually shapes the ability of each to interact effectively.

Promoting Optimal Development

How do we go about the task of promoting optimal development? We are coming to recognize the inherent dangers of attempting to prescribe the enhancement of specific skills or characteristics (e.g., Bruner and Connolly, 1974). For example, in appraising past efforts to promote social competence, White concludes that "mental health workers have rushed in where shrewder observers feared to tread" (1979, p. 5). He explains that the term "social competence" has assumed different meanings through history as a function of the changing values of society. What we choose to enhance in one decade may be considered far less significant in another. Thus, it appears wiser to focus on more basic, nonspecific emotional and intellectual characteristics, which, being neither situation- nor task-specific, allow the individual to monitor circumstances relevant to his or her own particular environment (see Laosa, 1979).

Interventionists have begun to consider Hunt's (1961, 1965) concept of the "problem of match" in their intervention designs; they have pointed to the importance of diagnosing the individual's level of functioning before determining the environmental circumstances optimal for promoting the individual's growth. From this perspective, it is claimed that a particular intervention cannot be expected to affect all people uniformly given the variations in "match" (e.g., Ulvund, 1980). Although this argument is certainly valid, it may be interpreted as calling for the development of unique formulas of optimal stimulation for each individual. Such a scheme is simply not feasible on a broad-scale basis. Moreover, the dialectics of development are such that the child's orientation toward producing effects upon the environment continually generates contradictions or asynchronies that move the individual toward greater articulation and integration (Laosa, 1979). Therefore, the optimal match for each individual continues to change, requiring constant reformulation. Thus, while the match between environment and child or parent and child may contribute significantly to development, it appears more fruitful to enhance the underlying tendency of the individual to seek circumstances that continually allow for growth. At the same time, while we can try to educate parents about their children's needs and the manner in which to meet them, it seems more productive to maximize parents' own tendencies to seek out and continually analyze the effectiveness of their varied behavioral transactions with their children.

I think we have reached a consensus that it is *enduring influences* which have enduring effects (e.g., Clarke and Clarke, 1976). Therefore, we need to focus upon promoting the self-sustaining and hence enduring characteristics of the individual and environment which underlie growth and development. Given the multidirectional, transactional nature of development, the variations within and between individuals, and the changing life task demands across the life span and across cultures, we cannot provide each individual with an "optimal" environment. Thus, we need to promote individuals who are more likely to promote optimal conditions for their own development, whatever their environment may be. Enhancing feelings of effectiveness and contingency seeking and analyses on the part of both members of the parent–infant dyad may be one important step toward optimizing development within the general population since these factors appear to underlie the individual's interaction with the environment which is, in turn, the basis of development.

In retrospect, the success of several major early intervention projects may be attributable, in part, to the large extent to which the programs promoted children's exploration of effective relationships with the environment. In both Beller's (1979) discussion of the consistent positive, long-term effects emerging from the varied preschool intervention programs of the Consortium of Longitudinal Studies (Lazar and Darlington, 1978), and Bruner's (1970) reflections on the similar impact of seemingly diverse preschool curricula (Weikart and Lambie, 1970), it was suggested that each of the effective programs shared an environment responsive to the children, one in which their behaviors had consequences. Thus the children learned that they could have some control of and impact on their environment.

A number of interventions have specifically integrated contingent, responsive stimulation into their infant programs. For example, Mahrer, Levinson, and Fine (1976) propose a model of "infant psychotherapy" based upon effectance facilitation. Although the label "infant psychotherapy" seems an unfortunate choice given its narrow treatment connotation, the approach is toward enhancing the infant's self-initiated and effective interaction, and it encourages recognition of the infant as an effective behavior initiator by both infant and parent ("therapist"). Ramey, Starr, Pallas, Whitten, and Reed (1975) provided supplemental contingent stimulation to failure-to-thrive infants based on the argument that nonorganic physical, intellectual, and social retardation may be related to a history of an inadequate frequency and/or variety of response—contingent experiences (Ramey, Hieger, and Klisz, 1972).

There also have been efforts to promote mutually contingent, responsive stimulation for both infant and caregiver. Badger's (1971, 1972) training program for lower-class mothers emphasized maternal responsivity to infant signals, stressing to mothers that their behaviors would have significant consequences on their babies' development. Fraiberg's (1971) work with parents of blind infants enhanced contingent responding to infant signals by facilitating parents' abilities to read infant cues and by demonstrating that their blind infants were responding selectively to parental stimulation.

Meanwhile, Riksen-Walraven (1978) reported one of the few direct attempts to modify infant–environment interaction and exploration by enhancing infants' feelings of self-efficacy. Moreover, she accomplished this task through parent education, a model with far-reaching potential for broad-scale implementation. Parents of 9-month-olds were given 1 of 4 50-page workbooks that stressed one of the following: that the infant needs large quantities of stimulation (stimulation group); that the infant learns best from the effects of its own behavior (responsiveness group); that both stimulation and responsiveness are important; or that neither stimulation nor responsiveness is important (control group). When observed just 3 months after the workbooks were distributed, caregivers with the responsiveness program showed significant increases in responsiveness. Moreover the infants of parents in the responsiveness group showed increased mastery of contingency tasks and increased exploratory behavior in general. Such data may provide the foundation for a longitudinal examination of the self-sustaining character of exploratory behaviors and their developmental impact. Of particular interest was Riksen-Walraven's report that

in informal talks at the end of the study, many parents, especially those who received a *Responsiveness*-program, remarked spontaneously that they had learned much during the experiment: they paid more attention to their infant's behavior and they noticed that they could have much more *influence* on the development of their child. . . . In the present study [the] expectation of non-efficacy seems to have disappeared, at least in some parents who received a Responsiveness-program. It is assumed here that parents' expectations of self-efficacy are changed by the same process by which the infants' expectancy of self-efficacy remains stable, because it gives rise to behavior which, by its consequences, confirms that expectation. (p.128)

Thus the infant clearly must be viewed within the context of a caregiver–infant system, and this system must be considered the target of our efforts to enhance feelings of efficacy; the effective dyad must be the goal.

Promoting self-sustaining feelings of efficacy within the dyad is not a simple task in our society. For example, in other cultures and other times, individuals developed confidence as effective, competent caregivers in their youth through observing practices of the extended family and by caring for younger siblings. Today parents are choosing to have fewer children. Furthermore, the population is typically segregated by age in education, social gatherings, and employment; the old and the young are rarely incorporated into the mainstream of economic, political, and social spheres. With the industrialization of our economy and the increased mobility of the population, we find increasing isolation of the nuclear family. Connolly and Bruner (1974) reported that 50 years ago more than half the families in Massachusetts had an older relative living with them, or within one mile of the home whereas fewer than 1 in 20 families were so situated in 1974. There has been a dramatic increase in single parenting, particularly as a result of divorce. Political, cultural, and economic changes have led to increased pressure for women and men alike to be employed in full-time jobs. Our society gives little prestige to those fully occupied with caregiving activities, whether professionally or otherwise. In sum, the situation is not conducive for either parents or children to observe and engage in childrearing activities and to develop expectations of competence in this role. There has been a change in the role of the family as a principal support system both of the young and the adult.

Compounding these problems is the increasing technology of the childrearing business. Childbirth has grown into a massive medical industry which has taken much control and responsibility for the young out of parents' hands. The message is that parents are not capable of providing adequate care for the newborn. Even parents of healthy, full-term babies are often deprived of opportunities for early continuous interaction with their neonates. The opportunity to become acquainted with the infant and develop early parenting skills is often delayed until the parents are home and without the support of professionals. The proliferation of childrearing theories, guides, educational toys and paraphernalia contrasts the "guesswork" of parenting with the "facts" and "knowledge" of the "experts." It is no wonder that adults lack confidence about their abilities as effective caregivers.

Therefore, just as the infant must be considered as a part of a larger caregiver–infant system, the dyad must be recognized within the context of a larger family system that is part of a community which, in turn, is enmeshed within a larger social structure. If we intend to promote optimal development on a broad-scale, long-term basis, it will mean restructuring the many levels of the social system so that people have more control of and impact on their own lives; they must recognize themselves as competent problem seekers and problem solvers.

The task of promotion may be approached simultaneously through many levels of systems, and it is this multilevel approach which seems to be most promising. Beyond certain obvious implications of our discussion for promotion efforts, broad guidelines for the content and structure of these activities emerge as well.

Emphasis upon the caregiver as effective.
The emphasis shifts from training a series of "do's and don'ts" of child rearing to encouraging caregivers' tendencies to monitor and analyze their own impact. A sensitivity toward the continual mutual regulation within the dyad, with simultaneous recognition of the uniqueness of each individual, places the parent–infant relationship in a meaningful perspective. As we have seen, increased parental sensitivity tends to be self-sustaining; it increases attention to the infant's signals, enhancing the likelihood of contingent responding by the parent which, in turn, will lead to a more responsive, predictable and readable infant, thus building the parent's efficacy and attention to effective interaction. The competent dyad behaves in a manner that is likely to sustain itself.

Therefore, our social institutions must focus on parents as effective caregivers and problem solvers rather than usurp their role. Practices need be adopted which increase the parent's sense of control and responsibility for the child; birthing options and educational alternatives are two examples. In a discussion of birthing practices, Richards (1979) notes that, "perhaps the crucial thing is a recognition that 'contact' is not enough: parents must feel a continued responsibility for their babies and a real sense of involvement in their care" (p.51).

When evaluating the impact of societal practices we must assess their effects upon parents' self-concepts and attitudes toward their infants. Even when arguing against an early "critical period", we must recognize that early perceptions assume great significance since they appear to lead to behaviors that are likely to confirm original expectations. That is, these attitudes are critical in the early establishment of self-supporting transactional patterns which consequently may have long-term impact upon developmental outcome (see Broussard, 1976; Broussard and Hartner, 1971).

Parent-centered and family-centered problem-solving orientation.

An emphasis upon parents as effective caregivers and problem solvers suggests a move from child-centered programs to parent- or family-centered programs. Since enduring influences have enduring effects, not surprisingly we find that family-centered intervention programs will have the most positive and long-lasting effects (e.g., Bronfenbrenner, 1974; Lazar and Darlington, 1978; Ramey, Sparling, and Wasik, 1979; Schaefer, 1970; Weikart and Lambie, 1970). This conclusion has led to programs in which parents rather than professionals are trained to implement curricula that have been carefully designed by specialists. But this move alone is not a solution since parents continue to be treated as actors reading someone else's script; they are encouraged to depend upon the recipes of experts with little thought toward the process of creating their own. Given the multilinear, multidimensional character of development, it is important not to promote one "optimal" course of behavior. Furthermore, deviation from that path then denotes parental "failure". Parents themselves must develop confidence and skills as "curriculum designers" with the recognition that the curriculum will be continually under reconstruction by both parent and infant. Just as there is no single formula for optimizing the development of all individuals, no single plan remains optimal for an individual across time and circumstances. Caregivers themselves need to be effective detectors, analyzers, and synthesizers of information (see Ramey, Sparling, and Wasik, 1979, and Shure and Spivack, 1978 for two successful applications of this notion).

In sum, positive, enduring impact is most likely to come about through programs and institutional restructuring directed not only toward the parent or family but also toward the processing and problem-solving skills of the caregiver. Of course, this orientation is an integral part of any attempt to enhance caregiver responsiveness and sensitivity to infant responsiveness. Again, the discovery of the self as a competent problem solver leads to behaviors that are more likely to confirm and sustain this self-image.

Educational orientation.

Proactive, promotive, educationally oriented systems focusing upon strengths as well as weaknesses will emerge as nonthreatening opportunities for continued growth and change. Crises will be treated neither as pathological nor as problematic but as an inherent part of the developmental process (Danish, 1977; Danish and D'Augelli, 1980; Danish et al., 1980; Huntington, 1979). With greater emphasis upon giving Psychology away to the public (Miller, 1969), we must reconceptualize and restructure "interventions" to make information more accessible to large portions of the population (e.g., Danish, 1977; Danish and D'Augelli, 1980; Danish et al., 1980; Gordon, 1977). "Education" needs to be redefined independently of formal institutions and incorporated into the daily experiences of life.

Development of self-help groups, natural caregivers, and support systems.

An inherent part of self-help groups is the implication that individuals are competent in diagnosing and affecting their own circumstances. Self- and peer-reliance are emphasized rather than dependence upon professionals; individuals are recognized as capable of contributing to both their own and others' development. Thus, the very structure of the self-help group enhances the individual's sense of efficacy and skills as a problem solver (e.g., see Silverman, 1978).

Huntington (1979) points out that parents learn best from each other. Increasing numbers of programs have capitalized upon this notion by employing former program participants as "trainers" for new members. These trainers occupy their roles for only a limited period at which time a new group of recent participants assume their jobs. This procedure prevents the emergence of a cadre of indoctrinated "experts" and emphasizes the expertise of each participant.

At the same time, mental health professionals are beginning to take advantage of the great potential of natural caregivers and support systems by promoting their development. Neighbors and friends remain the most common and accessible resource for help with problems of living. Farsighted programs are already supporting the skills of these native helpers (e.g., Collins and Pancoast, 1976; Danish and D'Augelli, 1980).

New emphases in training mental health professionals.

As the National Director of the Home Start Training Centers and the Child and Family Resource Program, O'Keefe stated "if we were planning Home Start all over again, we would have helped home visitors obtain adult education skills very early in the program because the focus of Home Start is an adult—a parent" (1977, p. 9, cited by Ramey et al., 1979). Mental health professionals need to be trained as educators who are skilled in encouraging the development of learning and problem-solving skills of others (Danish and D'Augelli, 1980). With a shift toward an educational approach and the development of self-help groups and natural support systems, the mental health professional needs to be well acquainted with teaching skills and variations in learning styles and social structures within subcultures of the population.

More than ever, there is a need for interdisciplinary exchange and a firm background in and exposure to normal developmental patterns. Training has typically centered on supervised office visits with troubled individuals; there must be greater exposure to the varied developmental characteristics of untroubled individuals within naturalistic settings.

Promotion of behaviors relevant for changing the social system.
Hess (1974) noted that studies of social development often dwell upon "person-relevant" behaviors, that is, those which relate persons to one another or to small groups. In contrast "system relevant" behaviors which "relate individuals to institutions and to political and social systems" (1974, p. 283) are rarely considered. We have seen that competence involves both adaptation to, as well as modification of, the environment. Individuals need to be effective both in coping with institutions and in altering those structures to meet their needs. Hess's (1974) analysis of elementary school social studies texts revealed that major sources of national tensions were infrequently mentioned and were portrayed as capable of resolution by the current social system, thus encouraging the status quo and the maintenance of ongoing tensions and stress rather than promoting skills in effecting productive societal changes.

Just as increased feelings of efficacy regarding person-relevant behaviors lead to actions that are likely to confirm effectiveness with others, increased feelings of efficacy regarding system-relevant behaviors may promote skills that support institutional and societal effectiveness. In an analysis of nursery settings, Tizard (1974) found that both staff behavior and child development were significantly related to social organization. Institutional structures that fostered staff feelings of autonomy and control appeared to lead to more effective staff behavior. With regard to families, Kagan (1970) argued that "a sense of control over one's future and a stake in the next day are likely to develop if the parent *believes* that a specific set of changes in daily practices is reasonable and the parent knows that he or she has the option to choose the procedures" (p. 24).

In summary, promoting competent individuals involves supporting individual's feelings of efficacy with regard to both person- and system-relevant behaviors. The self-supporting characteristics of efficacy are most likely to encourage the wide-scale, enduring promotion of development which we seek. Central to our concern is a recognition that we must view this process within the context of a multilevel response system. This takes us beyond the individual infant or infant–caregiver dyads (or triads) to consider the structures of the family, community, and society. If we hope that primary prevention in the broadest sense of promotion will become a way of life, we have to integrate responsive, supportive systems into our social structure; that is, we must work toward a society which itself is growth-promoting, one in which individual and group efficacy is real.

References

Ainsworth, M. D. The development of infant–mother attachment. In B. M. Caldwell and H. N. Ricciuti (Eds.), *Review of child development research* (Vol. 3). Chicago: University of Chicago, 1973.

Ainsworth, M. D., and Bell, S. M. Mother–infant interaction and the development of competence. In K. J. Connolly and J. S. Bruner (Eds.), *The growth of competence*. New York: Academic Press, 1974.

Albee, G. W. The fourth mental health revolution. *Journal of Prevention*, 1980, *1*(2), 67–70.

Ansbacher, H. L. What is positive mental health? In D. G. Forgays (Ed.), *Primary prevention of psychopathology*, Vol. 2: *Environmental influences*. Hanover, N.H.: University Press of New England, 1978.

Appleton, T., Clifton, R., and Goldberg, S. The development of behavioral competence in infancy. In F. D. Horowitz (Ed.), *Review of child development research* (Vol. 4). Chicago: University of Chicago Press, 1975.

Badger, E. A mother's training program—The road to a purposeful existence. *Children*, 1971 *18*(5), 168–173.

Badger, E. A mother's training program—A sequel article. *Children Today*, 1972, *1*(3), 7–12.

Baldwin, J. M. *Social and ethical interpretations in mental development: A study in social psychology* (3rd ed.). New York: Macmillan, 1902.

Baltes, P. B. (Ed.). *Life-span development and behavior* (Vol.1). New York: Academic Press, 1978.

Baltes, P. B., and Brim, O. G., Jr. (Eds.). *Life-span development and behavior* (Vol.2). New York: Academic Press, 1979.

Baltes, P. B., Reese, H. W., and Lipsitt, L. P. Life-span developmental psychology. *Annual Review of Psychology*, 1980, *31*, 65–110.

Beckwith, L. Relationships between infants' social behavior and their mothers' behavior. *Child Development*, 1972, *43*, 397–411.

Beckwith, L. Prediction of emotional and social behavior. In J. D. Osofsky (Ed.), *Handbook of infant development*. New York: John Wiley, 1979.

Beckwith, L., Cohen, S. E., Kopp, C. B., Parmelee, A. H., and Marcy, T. G. Caregiver-infant interaction and early cognitive development in preterm infants. *Child Development*, 1976, *47*, 579–587.

Bell, R. Q. A reinterpretation of the direction of effects in studies of socialization. *Psychological Review*, 1968, *75*, 81–95.

Bell, R. Q. Stimulus control of parent or caretaker behavior by offspring. *Developmental Psychology*, 1971, *4*, 63–72.

Bell, S. M. The development of the concept of object as related to infant-mother attachment. *Child Development*, 1970, *41*, 291–311.

Bell, S. M., and Ainsworth, M. D. Infant crying and maternal responsiveness. *Child Development*, 1972, *43*, 1171–1190.

Beller, K. Discussant. In F. Palmer (Chair), *Persistence of preschool effects: Evidence of impact*. Symposium presented at the meeting of the Society for Research in Child Development, San Francisco, March 1979.

Bond, E. K. Perception of form by the human infant. *Psychological Bulletin,* 1972, *77,* 225–245.

Bower, T. G. *Development in infancy.* San Francisco: W. H. Freeman, 1974.

Brazelton, T. B., Koslowski, B., and Main, M. The origins of reciprocity: The early mother-infant interaction. In M. Lewis and L. A. Rosenblum (Eds.), *The effect of the infant on its caregiver.* New York: Wiley, 1974.

Brazelton, T. B., Tronick, E., Adamson, L., Als, H., and Weise, S. Early mother-infant reciprocity. In Ciba Foundation Symposium 33, *Parent-infant interaction.* Holland: Elsevier, 1975.

Bronfenbrenner, U. Is intervention effective? *Teachers College Record,* 1974, *76,* 279–304.

Broussard, E. Neonatal prediction and outcome at 10/11 years. *Child Psychiatry and Human Development,* 1976, *7,* 85–93.

Broussard, E. R., and Hartner, M. S. Further considerations regarding maternal perception of the newborn. In J. Hellmuth (Ed.), *Exceptional infant,* Vol. 2: *Studies in abnormalities.* New York: Brunner/Mazel, 1971.

Bruner, J. S. Discussion: Infant education as viewed by a psychologist. In V. H. Denenberg (Ed.), *Education of the infant and young child.* New York: Academic Press, 1970.

Bruner, J. S. Early social interaction and language acquisition. In H. R. Schaffer (Ed.), *Studies in mother-infant interaction.* New York: Academic Press, 1977.

Bruner, J. S., and Connolly, K. J. Competence: The growth of the person. In K. J. Connolly and J. S. Bruner (Eds.), *The growth of competence.* New York: Academic Press, 1974.

Cairns, R. B., Green, J. A., and MacCombie, D. J. The dynamics of social development. In E. C. Simmel (Ed.), *Early experiences and early behavior: Implications for social development.* New York: Academic Press, 1980.

Caplan, G. *Principles of preventive psychiatry.* New York: Basic Books, 1964.

Charlesworth, W. R. The role of surprise in cognitive development. In D. Elkind and J. H. Flavell (Eds.), *Studies in cognitive development: Essays in honor of Jean Piaget.* New York: Oxford University Press, 1969.

Chavez, A., Martinez, C., and Yaschine, T. The importance of nutrition and stimuli on child mental and social development. In J. Cravioto, L. Hambraeus, and B. Vahlquist (Eds.), *Early malnutrition and mental development.* Uppsalla, Sweden: Almquist and Wiksell, 1974.

Clarke, A. M., and Clarke, A. D. B. *Early experience: Myth and evidence.* London: Open Books, 1976

Clarke-Stewart, K. A. Interactions between mothers and their young children: Characteristics and consequences. *Monographs of the Society for Research in Child Development,* 1973, *38* (6–7, Serial No. 153).

Clarke-Stewart, K. A., VanderStoep, L. P., and Killian, G. A. Analysis and replication of mother-child relations at two years of age. *Child Development,* 1979, *50,* 777–793.

Cohen, L. B., DeLoache, J. S., and Strauss, M. S. Infant visual perception. In J. D. Osofsky (Ed.), *Handbook of infant development.* New York: John Wiley, 1979.

Cohen, S. E., and Beckwith, L. Preterm infant interaction with the caregiver in the first year of life and competence at age two. *Child Development,* 1979, *50,* 767–776.

Collins, A. H., and Pancoast, D. L. *Natural helping networks: A strategy for prevention.* Washington, D.C.: National Association of Social Workers, 1976.

Connolly, K. J., and Bruner, J. S. (Eds.). *The growth of competence.* New York: Academic Press, 1974.

Danish, S. J. Human development and human services: A marriage proposal. In I. Iscoe, B. L. Bloom, and C. C. Spielberger (Eds.), *Community psychology in transition.* New York: Halstead, 1977.

Danish, S. J., and D'Augelli, A. R. Promoting competence and enhancing development through life development intervention. In L. A. Bond and J. C. Rosen (Eds.), *Competence and coping during adulthood.* Hanover, N.H.: University Press of New England, 1980.

Danish, S. J., Smyer, M. A., and Nowak, C. A. Developmental intervention: Enhancing life-event processes. In P. B. Baltes and O. G. Brim, Jr. (Eds.), *Life-span development and behavior* (Vol.3). New York: Academic Press, 1980.

Eimas, P. D., Siqueland, E. R., Jusczk, P., and Vigorito, J. Speech perception in early infancy. *Science,* 1971, *171,* 303–306.

Eisenberg, R. B. Auditory behavior in the neonate. I. Methodological problems and the logical design of research procedures. *Journal of Auditory Research,* 1965, *5,* 159–177.

Finkelstein, N. W., and Ramey, C. T. Learning to control the environment in infancy. *Child Development,* 1977, *48,* 806–819.

Fraiberg, S. Intervention in infancy: A program for blind infants. *Journal of Child Psychiatry,* 1971, *10,* 381–405.

Goldberg, S. Social competence in infancy: A model of parent–infant interaction. *Merrill-Palmer Quarterly,* 1977, *23,* 163–177.

Goldberg, S. Premature birth: Consequences for the parent-infant relationship. *American Scientist,* 1979, *67,* 214–220.

Goldston, S. E. Defining primary prevention. In G. W. Albee and J. M. Joffe (Eds.), *Primary prevention of psychopathology,* Vol. 1: *The issues.* Hanover, N.H.: University Press of New England, 1977.

Gordon, T. Parent effectiveness training: A preventive program and its delivery system. In G. W. Albee and J. M. Joffe (Eds.), *Primary prevention of psychopathology,* Vol 1: *The issues.* Hanover, N.H.: University Press of New England, 1977.

Green, J. A., Gustafson, G. E., and West, M. J. The effects of infant development on mother–infant interactions. *Child Development,* 1980, *51,* 199–207.

Gunnar, M. R. Control, warning signals, and distress in infancy. *Developmental Psychology,* 1980, *16,* 281–289.

Gunnar-vonGnechten, M. Changing a frightening toy into a pleasant toy by allowing the infant to control its actions. *Developmental Psychology,* 1978, *14,* 157–162.

Gustafson, G. E., Green, J. A., and West, M. J. The infant's changing role in mother-infant games: The growth of social skills. *Infant Behavior and Development,* 1979, *2,* 301–308.

Haaf, R. A., and Bell, R. Q. The facial dimension in visual discrimination by human infants. *Child Development,* 1967, *38,* 893–899.

Harter, S. Effectance motivation reconsidered: Toward a developmental model. *Human Development,* 1978, *21,* 34–64.

Harter, S., and Zigler, E. The assessment of effectance motivation in normal and retarded children. *Developmental Psychology,* 1974, *10,* 169–180.

Held, R., and Hein, A. Movement-produced stimulation in the development of visually guided behavior. *Journal of Comparative and Physiological Psychology,* 1963, *56,* 872–876.

Hess, R. D. Social competence and the educational process. In K. J. Connolly and J. S. Bruner (Eds.), *The growth of competence*. New York: Academic Press, 1974.

Hoke, B. Promotive medicine and the phenomenon of health. *Archives of Environmental Health*, 1968, *16*, 269–278.

Hunt, J. McV. *Intelligence and experience*. New York: Ronald, 1961.

Hunt, J. McV. Intrinsic motivation and its role in psychological development. In D. Levine (Ed.), *Nebraska Symposium on Motivation* (Vol. 13). Lincoln: University of Nebraska Press, 1965.

Huntington, D. S. Supportive programs for infants and parents. In J. D. Osofsky (Ed.), *Handbook of infant development*. New York: John Wiley, 1979.

Jennings, K. D., Harmon, R. J., Morgan, G. A., Gaiter, J. L., and Yarrow, L. J. Exploratory play as an index of mastery motivation: Relationships to persistence, cognitive functioning, and environmental measures. *Developmental Psychology*, 1979, *15*, 386–394.

Jones, O. H. A comparative study of mother-child communication with Down's syndrome and normal infants. In D. Shaffer and J. Dunn (Eds.), *The first year*. New York: John Wiley, 1979.

Kagan, J. On class differences and early development. In V. H. Denenberg (Ed.), *Education of the infant and young child*. New York: Academic Press, 1970.

Kaye, K. Toward the origin of dialogue. In H. R. Schaffer (Ed.), *Studies in mother-infant interaction*. New York: Academic Press, 1977.

Kelly, G. A. *The psychology of personal constructs* (Vol. 1). New York: Norton, 1955.

Klein, D. C., and Goldston, S. E. (Eds.). *Primary prevention: An idea whose time has come*. Rockville, MD: ADAMHA, 1977. DHEW Publication No. (ADM)77-447.

Kohler, I. Experiments with goggles. *Scientific American*, 1962, *206*, 62–86.

Korner, A. F. Conceptual issues in infancy research. In J. D. Osofsky (Ed.), *Handbook of infant development*. New York: John Wiley, 1979.

Kuo, Z. Y. *The dynamics of behavior development: An epigenetic view*. New York: Random House, 1967.

Lamb, M. E. Social development in infancy: Reflections on a theme. *Human Development*, 1979, *22*, 68–72.

Laosa, L. M. Social competence in childhood: Toward a developmental, socioculturally relativistic paradigm. In M. W. Kent and J. E. Rolf, *Primary prevention of psychopathology*, Vol. 3: *Social competence in children*. Hanover, N.H.: University Press of New England, 1979.

Lazar, I., and Darlington, R. B. (Eds.). *Lasting effects of preschool*. Final report, HEW Grant 90C-1311 to the Education Commission of the States, 1978.

Lazarus, R. S. The stress and coping paradigm. In L. A. Bond and J. C. Rosen (Eds.), *Competence and coping during adulthood*. Hanover, N.H.: University Press of New England, 1980.

Levitt, M. J. Contingent feedback, familiarization, and infant affect: How a stranger becomes a friend. *Developmental Psychology*, 1980, *16*, 425–432.

Lewis, M., and Goldberg, S. Perceptual-cognitive development in infancy: A generalized expectancy model as a function of the mother-infant interaction. *Merrill-Palmer Quarterly*, 1969, *15*, 81–100.

Lewis, M., and Rosenblum, L. A. *The effect of the infant on its caregiver*. New York: John Wiley, 1974.

Mahrer, A. R., Levinson, J. R., and Fine, S. Infant psychotherapy: Theory, research, and practice. *Psychotherapy: Theory, Research and Practice,* 1976, *13,* 131–140.

Mason, W. A. Early deprivation in biological perspective. In V. H. Denenberg (Ed.), *Education of the infant and young child.* New York: Academic Press, 1970.

McCall, R. Exploratory manipulation and play in the human infant. *Monographs of the Society for Research in Child Development,* 1974, *39* (2, Serial No. 155).

Miller, G. A. Psychology as a means of promoting human welfare. *American Psychologist,* 1969, *12,* 1063–1075.

Murphy, L. B., and Frank, C. Prevention: The clinical psychologist. *Annual Review of Psychology,* 1979, *30,* 173–207.

Newson, J. An intersubjective approach to the systematic description of mother-infant interaction. In H. R. Schaffer (Ed.), *Studies in mother-infant interaction.* New York: Academic Press, 1977.

Newson, J. Intentional behavior in the young infant. In D. Shaffer and J. Dunn (Eds.), *The first year of life.* New York: John Wiley, 1979.

O'Keefe, A. An overview of the El Paso National Head Start Conference—Parents, children and continuity. *Head Start Newsletter,* 1977, 1–16.

Osofsky, J. D. (Ed.), *Handbook of infant development.* New York: John Wiley, 1979.

Packer, M., and Rosenblatt, D. Issues in the study of social behavior in the first week of life. In D. Shaffer and J. Dunn (Eds.), *The first year of life.* New York: John Wiley, 1979.

Papoušek, H. Conditioned head rotation reflexes in infants in the first months of life. *Acta Paediatrica,* 1961, *50,* 565–576.

Papoušek, H. Experimental studies of appetitional behavior in human newborns and infants. In H. W. Stevenson, E. H. Hess, and H. L. Rheingold (Eds.), *Early behavior: Comparative and developmental approaches.* New York: Wiley, 1967.

Papoušek, H. Individual variability in learned responses in human infants. In R. J. Robinson (Ed.), *Brain and early behavior.* London: Academic Press, 1969.

Papoušek, H., and Bernstein, P. The functions of conditioning stimulation in human neonates and infants. In A. Ambrose (Ed.), *Stimulation in early infancy.* London: Academic Press, 1969.

Papoušek, H., and Papoušek, M. Interdisciplinary parallels in studies of early human behavior: From physical to cognitive needs, from attachment to dyadic education. *International Journal of Behavioral Development,* 1978, *1,* 37–49.

Piaget, J. *The origins of intelligence in children.* New York: International Universities Press, 1952.

Piaget, J. *To understand is to invent: The future of education.* New York: Penguin Books, 1976.

Provence, S., and Lipton, R. C. *Infants in institutions.* New York: International Universities Press, 1962.

Ramey, C. T., and Finkelstein, N. W. Contingent stimulation and infant competence. *Journal of Pediatric Psychology,* 1978, *3,* 88–96.

Ramey, C. T., Hieger, L., and Klisz, D. Synchronous reinforcement of vocal responses in failure-to-thrive infants. *Child Development,* 1972, *43,* 1449–1455.

Ramey, C. T., Sparling, J. J., and Wasik, B. H. Creating social environments to facilitate language development. In R. Schiefelbusch and D. Bricker (Eds.), *Early language intervention.* Baltimore: University Park Press, 1979.

Ramey, C. T., Starr, R. H., Pallas, J., Whitten, C. F., and Reed, V. Nutrition, response-contingent stimulation, and the maternal deprivation syndrome: Results of an early intervention program. *Merrill-Palmer Quarterly*, 1975, *21*, 45–53.

Richards, M. P. The development of psychological communication in the first year of life. In K. J. Connolly and J. S. Bruner (Eds.), *The growth of competence.* New York: Academic Press, 1974.

Richards, M. P. Effects on development of medical interventions and the separation of newborns from their parents. In D. Shaffer and J. Dunn (Eds.), *The first year of life.* new York: John Wiley, 1979.

Riegel, K. F. Toward a dialectical theory of development. *Human Development*, 1975, *18*, 50–64.

Riksen-Walraven, J. M. Effects of caregiver behavior on habituation rate and self-efficacy in infants. *International Journal of Behavioral Development*, 1978, *1*, 105–130.

Roberts, C. A. Psychiatric and mental health consultation. *Canadian Journal of Public Health*, 1970, *51*, 17–24.

Rosenthal, M. The study of infant-environment interaction: Some comments on trends and methodologies. *Journal of Child Psychology and Psychiatry*, 1973, *14*, 301–317.

Rossetti Ferreira, C. M. Malnutrition and mother-infant asynchrony: Slow mental development. *International Journal of Behavioral Development*, 1978, *1*, 207–219.

Sameroff, A. J. Early influences on development: Fact or fancy? *Merrill-Palmer Quarterly*, 1975, *21*, 267–294. (a)

Sameroff, A. J. Transactional models in early social relations. *Human Development*, 1975, *18*, 65–79. (b)

Sameroff, A. J. Concepts of humanity in primary prevention. In G. W. Albee and J. M. Joffe (Eds.), *Primary prevention of psychopathology*, Vol. 1: *The issues.* Hanover, N.II.: University Press of New England, 1977.

Sameroff, A. J., and Chandler, M. J. Reproductive risk and the continuum of caretaking casualty. In F. D. Horowitz, M. Hetherington, S. Scarr-Salapatek, and G. Siegel (Eds.), *Review of child development research* (Vol. 4). Chicago: University of Chicago, 1975.

Schaefer, E. S. Need for early and continuing education. In V. Denenberg (Ed.), *Education of the infant and young child.* New York: Academic Press, 1970.

Schaffer, H. R. (Ed.). *Studies in mother-infant interaction.* New York: Academic Press, 1977. (a)

Schaffer, H. R. *Mothering.* Cambridge: Harvard University Press, 1977. (b)

Schaffer, H. R. Acquiring the concept of dialogue. In M. H. Bornstein and W. Kessen (Eds.), *Psychological development from infancy.* New York: Erlbaum, 1979.

Schneirla, T. C. Behavioral development and comparative psychology. *Quarterly Review of Biology*, 1966, *41*, 283–302.

Seligman, M. *Helplessness: On depression, development, and death.* San Francisco: Freeman, 1975.

Shure, M. D., and Spivack, G. *Problem solving techniques in childrearing.* San Francisco: Jossey-Bass, 1978.

Sigel, I. E., and Cocking, R. R. *Cognitive development from childhood to adolescence: A constructivist perspective.* New York: Holt, Rinehart and Winston, 1977.

Silverman, P. R. *Mutual help groups: A guide for mental health workers.* Rockville, MD: ADAMHA, 1978. DHEW Publication No. (ADM)78-646.

Sroufe, L. A., and Waters, E. The ontogenesis of smiling and laughter: A perspective on the organization of development in infancy. *Psychological Review,* 1976, *83,* 173–190.

Sroufe, L. A., and Wunsch, J. A. The development of laughter in the first year of life. *Child Development,* 1972, *43,* 1326–1344.

Stern, D. N. A micro-analysis of mother–infant interaction behavior regulating social contact between a mother and three-and-a-half-month-old twins. *Journal of the American Academy of Child Psychiatry,* 1971, *10,* 501–517.

Stern, D. N. Mother and infant at play: The dyadic interaction involving facial, vocal, and gaze behaviors. In M. Lewis and L. A. Rosenblum (Eds.), *The effect of the infant on its caregiver.* New York: John Wiley, 1974.

Stern, D. N., Beebe, B., Jaffe, J., and Bennett, S. L. The infant's stimulus world during social interaction: A study of caregiver behaviours with particular reference to repetition and timing. In H. R. Schaffer (Ed.), *Studies in mother-infant interaction.* New York: Academic Press, 1977.

Stone, L. J., Smith, H. T., and Murphy, L. B. (Eds.). *The competent infant: Research and commentary.* New York: Basic Books, 1973.

Task Force on Prevention. G. Albee, coordinator. *Report to the President's Commission on Mental Health* (Vol.4). Washington, D.C.: U.S. Government Printing Office, No.040-000-00393-2, 1978.

Tizard, B. Do social relationships affect language development? In K. J. Connolly and J. S. Bruner, *The growth of competence.* New York: Academic Press, 1974.

Trevarthen, C. Descriptive analyses of infant communicative behavior. In H. R. Schaffer (Ed.), *Studies in mother-infant interaction.* New York: Academic Press, 1977.

Ulvund, S. E. Cognition and motivation in early infancy: An interactionist approach. *Human Development,* 1980, *23,* 17–32.

Wachs, T. D. The relationship of infants' physical environment to their Binet performance at 2½ years. *International Journal of Behavioral Development,* 1978, *1,* 51–65.

Wachs, T. D., Uzgiris, I. C., and Hunt, J.McV. Cognitive development in infants of different age levels and from different environmental backgrounds: an explanatory investigation. *Merrill-Palmer Quarterly,* 1971, *17,* 283–317.

Wagenfeld, M. O. The primary prevention of mental illness. *Journal of Health and Social Behavior,* 1972, *13,* 195–203.

Watson, J. S. The development and generalization of contingency awareness in early infancy: Some hypotheses. *Merrill-Palmer Quarterly,* 1966, *12,* 123–135.

Watson, J. S. Smiling, cooing and "The Game." *Merrill-Palmer Quarterly,* 1972, *18,* 323–340.

Watson, J. S. Perception of contingency as a determinant of social responsiveness. In E. B. Thoman (Ed.), *Origins of the infant's social responsiveness.* New York: Erlbaum, 1979.

Watson, J. S., and Ramey, C. T. Reactions to response-contingent stimulation in early infancy. *Merrill-Palmer Quarterly,* 1972, *18,* 219–229.

Weikart, D. P., and Lambie, D. Z. Early enrichment in infants. In V. H. Denenberg (Ed.), *Education of the infant and young child.* New York: Academic Press, 1970.

White, B. L. An experimental approach to the effects of experience on early human behavior. In J. P. Hill (Ed.), *Minnesota Symposium on Child Psychology* (Vol. 1). Minneapolis: University of Minnesota Press, 1967.

White, B. L. The initial coordination of sensorimotor schemas in human infants—Piaget's ideas and the role of experience. In D. Elkind and J. H. Flavell (Eds.), *Studies in cognitive development*. New York: Oxford University Press, 1969.

White, R. W. Motivation reconsidered: The concept of competence. *Psychological Review,* 1959, *66,* 297–333.

White, R. W. Competence as an aspect of personal growth. In M. W. Kent and J. E. Rolf (Eds.), *Primary prevention of psychopathology,* Vol. 3: *Social competence in children.* Hanover, N.H.: University Press of New England, 1979.

Yarrow, L. J., Pedersen, F. A., and Rubenstein, J. L. Mother-infant interaction and development in infancy. In P. H. Leiderman, S. R. Tulkin, and A. Rosenfeld (Eds.), *Culture and infancy: Variations in human experience.* New York: Academic Press, 1977.

Yarrow, L. J., Rubenstein, J. L., and Pedersen, F. A. *Infant and environment: Early cognitive and motivational development.* New York: Halstead, 1975.

The Breadth of Development:
An Alternative Perspective on Facilitating Early Development

Dale Goldhaber

I have spent the last 12 years trying to understand the significance of early experience on development. The interest began as a graduate student when I wrote a term paper on the critical period hypothesis. More recently I attempted to examine the influence of early experience from the perspective of a life-span developmental psychology. In this paper (Goldhaber, 1979) I argued that beneficial early experience is a necessary but not a sufficient condition for full development. As such beneficial early experience should not be viewed as some form of immunization against deleterious life experience nor should attempts to accelerate the apparent rate of development during early childhood be seen as bestowing upon the individual some form of permanent advantage. Rather the necessary experiences of early childhood are those that help the child consolidate the emerging abilities of language and other forms of representation and those that extend the use of these abilities into increasingly wider areas of inquiry. In other words, the necessary experiences of early childhood are those that extend the breadth of development. If these statements are true, as I believe they are, what implications do they have for defining the life experience during infancy and early childhood that seems most likely to enhance present and future development?

When I think about the goal of experiences that influence development, I immediately think of Robert White's (1959) concept of competence. When I think of what makes individuals competent, I think of Piaget's (1952) concepts of adaptation and equilibrium; of individuals who can deal with a variety of situations, who are aware of themselves as agents of change, and who can take strategies developed in one setting and use them in another. In short, I think of individuals whose breadth of development is so wide as not to be easily toppled by new experiences.

Are there ways in which we can increase the likelihood that individuals can achieve such competence? In what way can the process begin with young children? For the past 15 years psychologists and educators have been trying to influence the lives of young children through various intervention programs (e.g. Gordon, 1969; Gray and Miller, 1967; Karnes and Hodgins, 1969; Palmer and Siegel, 1977; Weikart, 1967). Although these programs differ in many respects they have five common characteristics.

Characteristics of Traditional Early Intervention Programs

The first characteristic is that these programs were designed as interventions rather then preventions. This is an extremely important distinction because it immediately narrowed the focus of the efforts. The intervention became a set of procedures designed to increase the probability of a desired nonpresent behavior becoming present or of a nondesired behavior that was present being extinguished. The desirability of the behavior and whether it was considered appropriate at a particular age typically reflected the norms of the culture and quite often the academic requirements of the school system.

The second common characteristic is that these programs reflected a learning-theory oriented view of growth and development. As such, these intervention programs were and are primarily skill-oriented, and each tends to emphasize one behavioral domain. Interventions focusing on perception, for example, taught visual discriminations; those focusing on cognition taught children how to sort shapes or colors; those that focused on social development taught taking turns; and so on.

The third characteristic, also consistent with a learning-theory view, is that the interventions were vertical. Once children mastered simple visual discriminations they attempted more complex ones; once they could sort colors or shapes they were trained to sort other colors and shapes; once they were able to take turns they learned to share. Rarely did they go from visual discrimination to sharing to shapes and colors. The designers of each intervention program believed that they had found the key to development. The program had solved Hunt's (1961) problem of the match.

The fourth characteristic is that not all behavioral domains seemed created equal. Those that had direct impact on academic skills were most valued. Even programs such as Head Start, which as Zigler (Zigler and Trickett, 1978) has pointed out many times were intended to influence many aspects of a child's life, were spoken of and evaluated primarily in terms of their ability to influence measures of achievement.

The fifth characteristic is that only factors external to the individual were viewed as determining the scope and magnitude of the intervention. As such the extent of the intervention was considered dependent on factors external to the child, and intervention soon came to be equated with acceleration. The more basic question—even if the rate of development within a domain can be accelerated, should it be?—was rarely asked.

The impact of these intervention programs is still equivocal. From the original Westinghouse report on Head Start (Cicirelli, 1969) to Bronfenbrenner's (1975) analysis of intervention programs to the more recent report of the Consortium of Developmental Continuity by Lazar and colleagues (Lazar, Hubbell, Murray, Rosche, and Royce, 1977), no clear, consistent picture of the impact of these intervention efforts has emerged. Even when substantial impact is found, as in the consortium finding that the effect of infant and preschool intervention programs were "manifested in either a reduced probability of being held back in grade, or being assigned to a special education class" (Lazar et al., p. 27), one is still left with the question as to how the intervention impact could lie dormant for three or four years before becoming visible. I believe that these programs have not lived up to their expectations because they were based on a narrow view of human growth and development. A more appropriate strategy is to view development in the broader sense. Such a strategy rests on three assumptions.

Assumptions of a Developmental Perspective on Early Development

The first assumption is that learning is not development. Thus, procedures designed to influence learning are not necessarily appropriate to influence development. For example, we can define a set of procedures to extinguish a learned response. Development, however, is assumed to be irreversible and therefore not extinguishable. When we talk about learning, we do so with reference to what is learned, to the information or skills that have been acquired. When we talk about development, we are describing a level of functioning which conceivably can be directed at any content area. Development is described across domains and within levels; learning across levels and within domains. We only need turn to textbooks written from a child-development or a child-psychology perspective to see this difference. Development has its roots in the biological structure of the species; learning has its roots in the cultural structure of the environment.

The second assumption is that development is a lifelong process involving qualitative reorganization of people's understanding of their physical and social worlds and those individuals' places in those worlds.

The third assumption is that procedures designed to facilitate development should be consistent with our definition of development. More specifically, they must be consistent with the elements of rate, sequence, level, organization, and utilization. Although rate of development is variable between individuals and between settings, few of us are likely to confuse the words of the 2-year-old with those of the 4-year-old or the representational work of the 5-year-old with that of the 10-year-old. Sequence also seems relatively invariable and, in fact, is increasingly viewed as a reflection of our biological motivation (Scarr-Salapatek, 1976). Development is not, however, inevitable. Few of us function at the top levels of Kohlberg's (1964), Piaget's (Piaget and Inhelder, 1969), Loevinger's (1966), or Maslow's (1954) hierarchies. And those of who get there, do so only for limited times in limited situations. On the other hand, all human environments seem sufficient to facilitate development through the sensory-motor and preoperational stages.

Organization reflects the wholeness of development. It is what the developmentalists turn to when they try to convince the learning theorists that the whole is greater than the sum of its parts. In the Piagetian sense, organization is reflected in the coordination of actions and, eventually, thoughts. It is these coordinations that eventually allow children to go beyond the limits of their immediate perceptual experiences: to know the rattle is under the blanket, that the two glasses have the same amount of water, that not all little things float, and that certain things just have to be so. From the perspective of personality theorists such as White (1972), organization is a necessary prerequisite of competence. Utilization is the element that distinguishes the developmentalist from the maturationist. It concerns the extent to which an individual is able to realize that an operation is appropriate to a particular situation and is then able to use it effectively.

A Cognitive Developmental Perspective on Early Facilitation

From these assumptions, development becomes a very broad-based notion, a notion that is not only concerned with children's cognitive growth but with their social, moral, and aesthetic selves as well.

A focus on breadth of development is not a new idea. Uzgiris (1976), for example, has suggested that a "different way of thinking about individual differences might be to consider the domain or even specific content in which an individual excels as well as the solidity of that excellence" (p. 166). She thinks that the breadth of development over diverse tasks may predict differences in one's openness to developmental change.

Kohlberg and Mayer (1972) stress the importance of helping the child explore the limits of a level of functioning. They say that "the child who has never explored the limits of concrete logical reasoning and lives in a world determined by arbitrary unexplained events and forces will see the limits for the partial solution of concrete logic as set by intangible forces rather than looking for a more adequate logic to deal with unexplained problems" (p. 491).

Flavell and Wohlwill (1969) believe that there may actually be an inverse relationship between training in vertical progression and in horizontal transfer. They believe that such horizontal transfer is most likely to occur through the child's spontaneous unprogrammed experience. Wohlwill (1970), in particular, believes that an emphasis on horizontal transfer and on a broad context of experience in cognitive development in early childhood leads to young children functioning optimally under conditions relatively devoid of structure.

Until fairly recently statements such as these of Uzgiris, Kohlberg, Flavell, and Wohlwill were the stuff of discussion sections. We knew very little about how knowledge in one field was extended to other closely related fields or, as Inhelder, Sinclair, and Bovet (1979) put it, how to make possible extension of fields of operativity.

However, research on the interrelationships of diverse behaviors within stages (Uzgiris, 1973; McCall, 1976), research on the cause of the asynchronies or decalages frequently reported in the literature (Fisher, 1974), and an increased emphasis on the functional or constructivist aspects of Piagetian theory (Forman and Kuschner, 1977; DeVries, 1978; Reid, 1978) are providing new insights into the structural organization of stages, the transitions between stages, and the extension of children's fields of operativity.

How has the new perspective on Piagetian theory come about? Historically we have classified Piaget as a maturationist. He frequently insisted that he was an interactionist but we keep on telling him he was mistaken.

The problem is that for Piaget the four stages—sensory-motor, preoperational, concrete operational, and formal operational—are primarily descriptors of levels of organization. Although they each define the structures that are operational at a particular point in time; in and of themselves they provide little insight into how one gets from one stage to another or the extent to which the child is able to make use of stage-related properties. For many, however, the stages are the theory. As Lovell and Shayer (1978) noted, such a narrow view of the theory reduces development to a sequence of stages. The stages in turn are reduced to a set of logical structures, and the logical structures are reduced to a set of specific tasks which are in turn taught in order to produce cognitive development.

This is an unfortunate interpretation of the theory because, as DeVries (1978) argued, the tasks were never meant to be more than the context in which the development of the structure of thought was studied. The Piagetian tasks, such as conservation of mass, are merely indicators of a level of function. Teaching conservation as means of influencing cognitive development has about as much validity as teaching a child what to do with a sealed, addressed, stamped envelope found on the ground as a means of influencing intelligence. In fact, it probably has less validity. We are probably more likely in our day-to-day lives to be confronted with a letter on the ground than a playdough pancake on our plate.

Furthermore, a narrow focus in the stage-related aspects of Piaget's theory has resulted in the frequent demonstrations of asynchronous stage development—the observation that a child does not approach all situations at the same level of functioning—being taken as evidence questioning the validity of the entire theory. Piaget's viewing such asynchronies as mere decalages or temporal displacements has only compounded the misinterpretation.

Research on Within-Stage Task Relationships

The more recent work on the stage concept has searched for evidence of structural organization in infants and preschoolers and has interpreted the asynchronies not as blemishes but rather as a means to study the extent to which development in one domain influences development in another. McCall's (1976; McCall, Hogarty, and Hurlbert, 1972) reanalysis of the Gesell test administered to children in the Fels Longitudinal Study at 6, 12, 18, and 24 months is a fine example. McCall's intent was to determine the possibility of observing patterns or clusters of items on the Gesell at each of the four testings. At 6 months he found a cluster of behaviors that all had the quality of Piaget's circular reactions. He labeled the quality as "visually guided explorations of perceptual contingencies" and noted that they "all describe manipulations that produce some clear contingent perceptual consequences" (McCall, 1976, p. 113). As examples of this visually guided exploration, McCall (1976) mentioned reaching for a dangling ring, lifting an inverted cup, banging a spoon on the table, and splashing in the tub.

What is most important about McCall's data is the documenting of relationships between diverse behavioral domains. By 12 months this cluster of visually-guided exploratory behaviors had developed into a mixture of sensory-motor and social imitation plus rudimentary vocal-verbal behavior. Within this cluster are behaviors that are typically seen as reflecting fine motor skills—putting a cube in a box, imitating the ringing of a bell, building a block tower of two or three cubes—as well as items reflecting simple verbal skills and social interactions. Examples of these behaviors include waving goodbye, playing peek-a-boo or pat-a-cake, or saying bye-bye or hello.

McCall believes these findings imply that "social-verbal behavior and imitation of fine motor behavior are related activities, and it seems reasonable that the child who develops the tendency to imitate does so in a social context, playing reciprocal sensorimotor and vocal-verbal imitation games with his parents" (1976, p. 113).

The clusters were also evident at the 18- and 24-month testings. They increasingly reflected verbal behavior, and by 24 months the dominant theme of these behaviors had become grammatical fluency and production. The interdependency of sensory-motor, imitation, and language behavior helps explain, for McCall, their transition pattern between 6 and 24 months. He sees these diverse behaviors organized into two common purposes or themes: "The first is the reduction of perceptual-cognitive uncertainty. The child takes in information about the world and frequently checks on the validity of that information. During the first year he explores the attribute of objects—their size, color, weight, plasticity, and function. Later he discovers there is something else to be learned about objects and events: they have names, locations and attributes and are possessed by certain people" (1976, p. 117).

The second theme evolves out of the first. In the process of reducing perceptual-cognitive uncertainty, infants, make an important discovery—they have an influence on their environment—the beginning of White's concept of affectance. As McCall puts it: "At first the child manipulates objects as if he were asking 'What can this object do?" Later after he is more familiar with the nature of the object, the emphasis shifts from what the object can do to what he can do with the object. When language is available, he may simply describe his affectance behaviors in the manner of a verbal circular response" (1976, p. 117).

This pattern of interdependence between behavior domains is also evident in Bell's (1970) finding of a strong relationship between the quality of infant–mother attachment and the development of object and person permanence. Bell notes that "a harmonious relationship between mother and infant seems to be the precondition for eliciting the type of interest in the baby which Piaget hypothesized so pervasively affects the development of sensorimotor intelligence" (p. 309).

Even more extensive research on cognitive organization in young children is the work of Uzgiris (1973, 1976, 1977). Using the Infant Psychological Development Scales (IPDS) constructed with Hunt, she followed 12 infants longitudinally between the ages of 1 month and 2 years. She found not only interrelations between tasks on different scales of the IPDS but, perhaps of more importance, found pattern interdependence between tasks. That is, she found that advance in sequence on one task is often dependent on advance in sequence on tasks in other scales. For example, advancement in sequence on the object relations in space scale, which is designed to assess infants' understanding of the spatial arrangement between objects located in their immediate surroundings or moving through familiar space, seemed highly dependent on advancement on the object permanence scale (which consists of items such as obtains a partially covered object, obtains an object hidden under a number of superimposed screens, or obtains an object hidden with an invisible displacement under one of these screens). "Specifically, 11 of 12 infants began to search for a partially covered object before they began to follow the trajectory of a dropped object moving rapidly through space. A week after beginning search for a partially covered object, 7 of 12 infants were following the dropped object" (Uzgiris, 1973, p. 194). The sequential relations seem reciprocal since advancement on the construction of object relations in space scale was found to precede the achievement of the highest level in object concept development (searches under the last screen for a hidden object with successive invisible displacements and reverses if object is not there).

In addition to the sequential dependences between object permanence and object relations, Uzgiris found other significant relationships between the development of means scale (visually directed grasping, use of support, use of stick) and object permanence. The correlation, for example, between age for beginning search for a hidden object under one of three screens and making use of the observed relationship that one object serves as a support for another was .71. In addition, relationships were found between operational casuality and object relations in space. In considering her findings, Uzgiris (1973) suggests that "attempts to facilitate progress in some branch of development should not be limited to enhancement of opportunities to engage in activities clearly related to that branch of development. At certain levels, advance in another branch of development may be necessary to facilitate further progress" (pp. 201–202).

The work of McCall and Uzgiris is important for two reasons. First, each provides ample evidence of the organizational qualities of early cognitive development and the extent to which development in one domain is dependent on development in others. For instance, the reported interdependence between sensorimotor development and early language acquisition provides new insights into our understanding of early language development. Second, they support the hypothesis that operations may not emerge at a particular stage but rather what emerges is the level at which a particular operation can function effectively. For example, instead of conceiving of conservation as an ability that emerges with concrete operations, conservation becomes an ability less influenced by perceptual transformations at the concrete operational level. More generally, the ability to conserve is the ability to acknowledge invariance. In this sense, the rattle under the blanket is no less a measure of conservation than glasses of water.

Research on Developmental Asynchronies

The hypothesis that operations do not emerge at a particular stage but rather become increasingly invariant to extraneous cues has prompted a number of studies examining the conditions that cause asynchronous development. These studies are making more apparent the interactional nature of Piagetian theory and have led to an increased interest in the functional or constructivist aspects of the theory. One of the clearest statements of this view is that of Fisher (1977).

It is not enough to consider only the organism (that is the child's intellectual level) when trying to explain Piaget's stages. The environment (that is the task) makes an equally important contribution to the child's performance. I would propose that the best way to deal with this interaction is to view the child as trying to solve the problem posed by the task. His performance on a particular task is then determined jointly by his cognitive level and the difficulty of the task because these two factors together determine how well he can understand the problem posed by the task. Consequently stages of cognitive development are best understood as stages of problem solving. (p. 2)

Fisher uses the seriation task to illustrate his hypothesis. We typically think of seriation as one of the tasks used to note the passage of a child from preoperation to concrete operational thought. He points out that timing of this passage is highly dependent on the task used to mark it—namely a series of sticks differing from each other in terms of millimeters. If we consider other possible ways of measuring seriation, it is possible to demonstrate it with toddlers—using nesting cups—as have Greenfield, Nelson, and Saltzman (1972) and with preschoolers using sticks differing markedly in length, as Piaget himself did. If we use logical propositions as of the A>B C variety, however, seriation is not demonstrated until adolescence, as Inhelder and Piaget (1958) showed. The point is that the ability to seriate lies in the interaction of the individual's developmental level and the task demands of the situation.

A more general treatment of the operation eliciting power of task-related characteristics is offered by Flavell and Wohlwill (1969). For any given task, they define a number of factors that influence the likelihood that the operation, if functional, will in fact be called into play, and its end product be translated into the desired output. These factors include "the stimulus materials and their familiarity, the manner of presentation of the relevant information and the amount of irrelevant information from which it has to be abstracted, the sheer magnitude of the information load placed on the child in dealing with the problem, and the role played by memory and sequential processing of information" (p. 99). The reader is referred to Pascual-Leone for a more elegant treatment of the interaction of task-related characteristic and cognitive level (Pascual-Leone, Goodman, Ammon, and Subelman, 1978; Scardamalia, 1977; Toussaint, 1974).

The increased emphasis on the interactional nature of Piagetian theory has led some researchers to look for possible environmental correlates of cognitive growth. Hunt's (1977) cross-sectional comparisons of the development of object construction in different childrearing settings and Wachs's (1976) longitudinal study on the relationship of home environments to cognitive intellectual development are two examples of attempts to relate environmental circumstances to Piagetian development. Hunt compared five samples of infants. Three were from Athens, Greece. One of these was home-reared, the second reared in an orphanage with an infant–caregiver ration of 3 to 1, and the third in an orphanage with an infant–caretaker ration of 10 to 1. The other two samples were infants from a parent and child center in Illinois and a group reared in middle-class homes in Massachusetts. Infants in each setting were tested on a series of increasingly difficult displacements. As expected the mean age for successful solution of the displacement increased as the difficulty of the task increased. This was true in all five settings. A more important finding was that the "standard deviations for the ages at which the home-reared children reached the upper levels of object construction are even larger than the standard deviations for those in the Municipal Orphanage (10/1 ratio) and much larger than those for the children at Matera" (p. 45). Hunt concluded that such data provide very substantial support for the hypothesis that environmental circumstances have a very significant influence on the mean age at which children evidence specific developmental levels.

Wachs (1976) followed a sample of infants for approximately 3½ years, and during that time he collected naturalistic observations on each child, tested the infants on the IPDS at 3-month intervals, and had parents complete the Purdue Home Stimulation Inventory monthly. He was able to establish clear relationships between rearing conditions and cognitive development. In analyzing the many association patterns, Wachs also found "four major classes of experience that seem particularly relevant to early cognitive development" (p. 24). The first class of experience concerned the predictability or regularity of the environment. Among other things, it showed a strong positive association with the development of object permanence. The second class of items concerned the adequacy of stimulation. Adequacy was defined in terms of amount of stimulation, degree of stimulation, variability of stimulation, the extent to which a stimulation activity (e.g., a toy) produced audio-visual feedback, and degree of restraint to seek stimulation. The third class of items, measuring the presence of intense stimulation, correlated negatively with cognitive growth. The fourth class of items, measuring verbal stimulation, showed relatively little impact on development. Those verbal items that did show a positive association were mostly found during the latter part of the second year.

Of Wach's data, I find particularly interesting the information that the one item found to be more consistently and significantly related to cognitive development was degree of restraint to seek stimulation. It argues strongly for the importance of the breadth of developmental experiences on facilitating cognitive growth.

Research on Constructivist Early Childhood Education Programs

The research by McCall, Uzgiris, Hunt, and Wachs provides strong support for the hypothesis that the facilitation of development is best accomplished through an emphasis on breadth. There is another source of support. It is the research examining the functional or constructivist aspects of Piagetian theory and in particular the early childhood education programs that have been developed within the constructivist model. Most prominent in this effort have been Sigel (1979), Forman and Kuschner (1977), DeVries (1978), and Kamii and DeVries (1978). Although the models have been primarily used with normal children, my colleagues and I (Goldhaber and Goldhaber, 1980; Goldhaber, Goldhaber, Ishee, and Thousand, 1980) have successfully used the Forman curricula with children with special needs.

Constructivist programs place great importance on the distinction Piaget makes between types of knowledge. Physical knowledge consists of actions on objects which leads to knowledge of the objects themselves. Through such experiences, children are able to learn the properties of objects in their environment. Logico-mathematical knowledge consists of actions on objects which introduce into the object characteristics not inherent. Number is the most obvious example. Social knowledge comes from interaction with people. It consists of both arbitrary social conventions and moral norms agreed upon by coordination of points of view. To these three, the Forman model adds a fourth—self-knowledge. As a result of the coordination of all sources of knowledge the child gradually differentiates the self as a unique object and later as a unique personality (Forman and Kuschner, 1977).

The process of development (of which the stages serve as indicators) becomes the child's construction of knowledge. And the task of the educator becomes the facilitation of this constructive process. This facilitation takes the form of maximizing the child's opportunities to create and coordinate many relationships. It is from these coordinations that the more formal operational systems later develop. The different models have devised a number of learning encounters which attempt to capitalize on the child's spontaneous interest. The children's interests motivate them to act upon experiences that are necessary for the construction of knowledge. When, however, knowledge is taught directly, as in attempts to teach classification or conservation, children are denied the opportunity to construct the relationships for themselves. As a result, physical and logico-mathematical knowledge is reduced to social knowledge. And because it is understood as social knowledge, it is arbitrary, and not easily assimilated into existing cognitive structures.

Conclusions and Implications

What conclusions can we draw about the nature and course of early development and what implications do these have for those designing and implementing programs influencing early development?

The first conclusion is that structural organization is evident at all developmental levels. The research on patterns of infant development makes clear that such diverse behaviors as sensory-motor coordinations, imitation, and early language development are quite interrelated. Further, although the logic of action eventually comes to be replaced by the more flexible logic of thought, it is still no less a logic. The 12-month-old who shows great surprise when a train goes into the tunnel and the clown comes out is showing no less a sense of logical necessity than the 12-year-old who wonders what is wrong with you when you ask if changing the ball into a pancake changes its weight.

The second conclusion is that the presence of an organizational structure does not guarantee its functioning. For children to make use of particular operations they must be able to comprehend the situation and then invent a solution or action based on that comprehension (Kamii, 1975). Effective construction seems dependent on the developmental level of the child and environmental circumstance.

The third conclusion is that to ensure that an experience has a relatively lasting impact on the child, it is not only necessary to demonstrate the presence of the new behavior but also to allow the new behavior to be assimilated into existing cognitive structures. In other words, there needs to be time for consolidations as well as time for emergence. An obvious corollary is that there must already be present such a cognitive structure. Without such a structure, assimilation is impossible and regression likely. Inhelder et al. (1974) note that regression occurs when the subject only momentarily establishes certain coordinations suggested by specific situations—the reasoning remains strictly local, it cannot be generalized to other situations and is probably not accompanied by the feeling of logical necessity.

From this review, it is possible to draw five conclusions. They concern the scope of programs influencing early development, the content of the programs, the training of individuals to administer these programs, evaluation of these programs, and whether this perspective is relevant to special children—those who need intervention rather than prevention.

Scope of Programs Influencing Early Development

The first implication of a cognitive-developmental perspective on early development is that programming must be broadly based and integrated. It must exist in a social context. It must not resemble the assembly-line model typical of a physical examination or the manner in which specialized services are often administered to exceptional children.

Although we are developing a greater appreciation of the range of developmental services and experiences beneficial to children, we are not yet very sensitive to the importance of the integration of these services and experiences. This integration is necessary to ensure the relative permanence of our efforts. Failure to provide this integration will result in learning that remains strictly local and temporary.

To accomplish this integration, greater cooperation will be necessary between agencies, professionals within agencies, and between agencies and families. For example, rather than the speech pathologist or physical therapist removing the exceptional child from the classroom for short, intensive interventions, these individuals could serve as consultants to the classroom teacher or parent. The intervention would then be integrated into the ongoing daily routines and through the communication between adults, each could become more aware of the significance and problems of the other role (see Goldhaber [1980] for a more complete treatment of this topic).

The Content of the Programs

In a sense there is no content to a Piagetian-based constructivist early childhood program—at least not in the traditional sense of the word; there are no lists of skills to be mastered, competencies to be attained, no box of 3 × 5 cards filled with interesting activities, no kit or package to buy. The content is a set of ideas or guidelines and is limited only by the individual's understanding of the theory and its translation into practical activities. These guidelines stress the importance of activities that provide the young child with feedback, the importance of materials that are transformable, the importance of helping children represent their experiences through word, gesture, sight, or sound, the importance of the child using different actions on the same object and using the same object for different functions. In general it stresses the importance of children gaining an understanding of what has to happen to create a desired end and how they can use themselves to make it happen.

The Training of Individuals to Administer the Programs

Do we all have to become Piagetian scholars to successfully implement a Piagetian-based program? Fortunately, the answer is no. Surely there must be individuals involved in these programs who have a formal knowledge of the theory and of its possible applications. But Piaget was not an inventor, he was a discoverer. Piaget did not invent the four stages of development any more than Darwin invented evolution. Rather what Piaget and Darwin each did was to take a set of observations and organize them in such a way that certain patterns and sequences became apparent. Many parents and teachers routinely demonstrate the behaviors they observe. There is nothing particularly technical about them. They do not require highly specialized instruction to learn. When we try to increase day-to-day interactions between parent and child we develop programs that focus on what the child cannot do rather than what the child can do, and these programs will probably have little long-lasting impact on the development of the child. Programs, on the other hand, that point out the significance of the infants' and preschoolers' behavior, that focus on the strengths rather than on the weaknesses in children's behavior, that point out the importance of the everyday interactions between adults and children, and that do not see facilitation as something that occurs 15 minutes a day, 3 days a week, and lives in a kit, will be doing the most to facilitate development. When we point out to parents the number of ways in which their children are competent, we are telling them that the number of ways in which they are competent, and as any learning theorist will tell you, such positive reinforcement is likely to increase parent involvement.

Program Evaluation

We seem to be entering a decade of accountability—where administration defines the bottom line in terms of skills mastered, IQ points gained, and so forth. In such an atmosphere, Piagetian programs are not likely to thrive. We are barely beginning to understand the nature of the organization of cognitive structure. We are a long way from knowing how to measure the influence of activities in one domain or another, much less predicting the direction and degree of influence of one on another. This is an area that deserves much greater research emphasis.

Exceptional Children

At the beginning of this paper I made the point that prevention is not the same as intervention. Specifically, intervention programs are almost always designed to deal with an already defined problem or need.

Does a Piagetian program have anything to offer exceptional children? The answer is yes, and as empirical support I would refer you to our pilot study and the more complete work of Reid (1978) at University of Texas, Dallas, and Meisel (1979) at Tufts. Observation of exceptional children in our 2-month pilot project showed that the exceptional children increased their use of language, lengthened the average amount of time they chose to spend in an activity, and showed no difference when compared with our nonexceptional children in their level of task involvement and level of use of materials. The value of a Piagetian approach is that it reminds us that the exceptional child functions no less as a coordinated, self-regulated whole than the nonexceptional child (Reid, 1978) and that the impact of the child's handicapping condition is partially dependent on the nature and structure of the environment.

Kohlberg (1968), in concluding his paper on a cognitive-developmental view of early childhood, stated that "the Piagetian approach does not generate great optimism as to the possibility of preschool acceleration of cognitive development or of compensation for its retardation nor does it lead to a rationale in which such acceleration or compensation is especially critical during the preschool year" (p. 1059). The past 12 years have shown us that Kohlberg might be right about the probability of creating formal operational 3-year-olds but quite wrong about Piagetian theory providing a rationale for influencing development. It might not lead to formal operational preschoolers but I would take a Renaissance preschooler any day.

References

Bell, S. M. The development of the concept of object as related to infant-mother attachment. *Child Development,* 1970, *41,* 291–311.
Bronfenbrenner, U. Is early intervention effective? In J. Hellmuth (Ed.), *Exceptional infants* (Vol. 3). New York: Brunner/Mazel, 1975.
Cicirelli, V. G. Project Head Start, a national evaluation: Summary of the study. In D. G. Hayes (Ed.), *Brittanica review of American education* (Vol. 1). Chicago: Encyclopedia Brittanica, 1969.

DeVries, R. Early education and Piagetian theory—Application vs. implication. In J. Gallagher and J. Easley (Eds.), *Knowledge and development* (Vol. 2). New York: Plenum, 1978.

Fisher, K. W. *Cognitive development as problem solving: The meaning of decalage in seriation tasks.* Paper presented at Fifth Annual Interdisciplinary Conference on Structured Learning, Philadelphia, 1977.

Flavell, J. H., and Wohlwill, J. F. Formal and functional aspects of cognitive development. In D. Elkind and J. H. Flavell (Eds.), *Studies in cognitive development.* New York: Oxford University Press, 1969.

Forman, G. F., and Kuschner, D. S., *The child's construction of knowledge: Piaget for teaching children.* Monterey, CA: Brooks/Cole, 1977.

Goldhaber, D. E. Does the changing view of early experience imply a changing view of early development? In L. Katz (Ed.), *Current topics in early childhood education* (Vol. 2). Norwood, N.J.: Ablex Publishers, 1979.

Goldhaber, D. E. Child care services and public policy: A new perspective. *Children and Youth Services Review,* 1980, *2,* 369–384.

Goldhaber, D. E., and Goldhaber, J. Mainstreaming preschoolers: A cognitive-developmental perspective. Submitted to *Journal of Early Childhood of the Council of Exceptional Children,* 1980.

Goldhaber, D. E., Goldhaber, J., Ishee, N., and Thousand, J. *Working with developmentally diverse preschoolers.* Paper presented at the World Assembly of the World Organization for Preschool Educators, Quebec City, Quebec, Canada, 1980.

Gordon, I. J. *The Florida parent education model.* Gainesville, FL: Institute for Development of Human Resources, 1969.

Gray, S., and Miller, J. Early experience in relationship to cognitive development. *Review of Educational Research,* 1967, *37,* 475–493.

Greenfield, P. M., Nelson, K., and Saltzman, E. Embedded clauses and manipulating seriated cups: A parallel between action and grammar. *Cognitive Psychology,* 1972, *3,* 291–310.

Hunt, J. McV. *Intelligence and experience.* New York: Ronald Press, 1961.

Hunt, J. McV. Sequential order and plasticity in early psychological development. In M. H. Appel and L. S. Goldberg (Eds.), *Topics in cognitive development.* New York: Plenum, 1977.

Inhelder, B., and Piaget, J. *The growth of logical thinking from childhood to adolescence.* New York: Basic Books, 1958.

Inhelder, B., Sinclair, H., and Bovet, M. *Learning and the development of cognition.* Cambridge: Harvard University Press, 1974.

Kamii, C. One intelligence indivisible. *Young children,* 1975, *30,* 228–237.

Kamii, R., and DeVries, R. *Physical knowledge in preschool education: Implications of Piaget's theory.* Englewood Cliffs, N.J.: Prentice-Hall, 1978.

Karnes, M., and Hodgins, A. The effects of a highly structured preschool program on the measured intelligence of culturally disadvantaged four-year-old children. *Psychology in the Schools,* 1969, *6,* 89–91.

Kohlberg, L. Development of moral character and moral ideology. In M. L. Hoffman and L. W. Hoffman (Eds.), *Review of child development research* (Vol. 1). New York: Russel Sage Foundation, 1964.

Kohlberg, L. Early education: A cognitive development view. *Child Development,* 1968, *39,* 1013–1063.

Kohlberg, L., and Mayer, R. Development as the aim of education. *Harvard Education Review,* 1972, *42,* 449–497.

Lazar, I. J., Hubbell, V. R., Murray, H., Rosche, M., and Royce, J. *The persistence of preschool effects.* DHEW Publication No. (OHDS) 78-30129, 1977.

Loevinger, J. The meaning and measurement of ego development. *American Psychologist,* 1966, *21,* 195–206.

Lovell, K. and Shayer, M. The impact of the work of Piaget on science curriculum development. In J. M. Gallagher and J. A. Easley (Eds.), *Knowledge and development* (Vol. 2). New York: Plenum, 1978.

Maslow, A. H. *Motivation and personality.* New York: Harper and Row, 1954.

McCall, R. B. Toward an epigenetic conception of mental developments in the first three years of life. In M. Lewis (Ed.), *Origins of intelligence.* New York: Plenum, 1976.

McCall, R. B., Hogarty, P. S., and Hurlbert, N. Transitions in infant, sensory-motor development and prediction of childhood IQ. *American Psychologist,* 1972, *27,* 728–749.

Meisel, S. J. Special education and development. In S. J. Meisel (Ed.), *Special education and development.* Baltimore, MD: University Park Press, 1979.

Palmer, F. H., and Siegel, R. J. Minimal intervention at ages two and three and subsequent intellectual changes. In M. C. Day and R. K. Parker (Eds.), *The preschool in action* (2nd ed.). Boston: Allyn and Bacon, 1977.

Pascual-Leone, J., Goodman, D., Ammon, P., and Subelman, I. Piagetian theory and neo-piagetian analysis as psychological guides in education. In J. Gallagher and J. A. Easley (Eds.), *Knowledge and development* (Vol. 2). New York: Plenum, 1978.

Piaget, J. *The origins of intelligence in children.* New York: International University Press, 1952.

Piaget, J., and Inhelder, B. *The psychology of the child.* New York: Basic Books, 1969.

Reid, D. K. Genevan theory and the education of exceptional children. In J. M. Gallagher and J. A. Easley (Eds.) *Knowledge and development,* (Vol. 2): *Piaget and education.* New York: Plenum, 1978.

Scardamalia, M. Information processing capacity and the problem of horizontal decalage. *Child Development,* 1977, *48,* 28–37.

Scarr-Salapatek, S. An evolutionary perspective on infant intelligence: Species patterns and individual variations. In M. Lewis (Ed.), *Origins of intelligence.* New York: Plenum, 1976.

Sigel, I. E. Consciousness raising of individual competence in problem solving. In M. W. Kent and J. E. Rolf (Eds.), *Primary prevention of psychopathology* (Vol. 3): *Social competence in children,* Hanover, N.H.: University Press of New England, 1979.

Toussaint, N. A. An analysis of synchrony between concrete-operational tasks in terms of structured and performance demand. *Child Development,* 1974, *45,* 992–1001.

Uzgiris, I. C. Patterns of cognitive development in infancy. *Merrill-Palmer Quarterly,* 1973, *19,* 181–205.

Uzgiris, I. C. Organization of sensorimotor intelligence. In M. Lewis (Ed.), *Origins of intelligence.* New York: Plenum, 1976.

Uzgiris, I. C. Some observations on early cognitive development. In M. N. Appel and L. S. Goldberg (Eds), *Topics in cognitive development* (Vol. 2). New York: Plenum, 1977.

Wachs, T. D. Utilization of a Piagetian approach in the investigation of early experience effects. *Merrill-Palmer Quarterly,* 1976, *22,* 11–31.

Weikart, D. C. (Ed.) *Preschool intervention: A preliminary report of the Perry pre-school project.* Ann Arbor, MI: Campus Publications, 1967.

White, R. W. Motivation reconsidered: The concept of competence. *Psychological Review,* 1951, *68,* 297–333.

White, R. W. *The enterprise of living.* New York: Holt, Rinehart, and Winston, 1972.

Wohlwill, J. F. The place of structured experience in early cognitive development. *Interchange,* 1970, *1,* 13–27.

Zigler, E., and Trickett, P. K. IQ Social competence and evaluation of early childhood intervention programs. *American Psychologist,* 1978, *33,* 789–797.

Developmental Discontinuities:
An Approach to Assessing Their Nature

Ann M. Clarke

Two unrelated streams of work, starting at the turn of the century, have made a powerful and ongoing impact upon our model of human development. Both stressed continuities in development, whether through genetic factors or through the formative role of the early environment. The first stream—Galton, Pearson, Spearman—led to the explicit statement that the IQ was constant. At the same time Freud and his followers suggested that affective development was fixed for good or ill in the first few years, to be modified, if at all, by later psychotherapy.

I have been asked to write about discontinuities, and although my husband and I were among the first to discuss this topic (Clarke and Clarke, 1972, 1977), I should make it clear that I neither deny nor underestimate the continuities that exist; accounting for them is more difficult; some *discontinuities* are likely to be genetically caused, and in other cases we lack adequate measuring tools to determine in a precise way developmental patterns.

Developmental discontinuity, whether for individuals or groups, may best be defined under a number of headings:

●The emergence of an entirely new characteristic not present earlier, for example, the onset of schizophrenia, stammering, or formal reasoning.

●The disappearance or inhibition of an habitual characteristic, for example, the disappearance of crawling as a preferred mode of mobility, loss of a school phobia, the burning out of an emotional disorder of childhood.

●A significant shift in the ordinal position of an individual (let us say arbitrarily by a standard deviation or more) on a second or later assessment of status on a particular characteristic, for example, a large IQ increment or decrement, a large change in degree of extraversion at adolescence. Such a shift would normally imply either a change in the level or relative level of the characteristic (Clarke, 1978).

I acknowledge with gratitude the help and support which my husband, Alan Clarke, has provided in the preparation of this paper.

•Reflecting the point immediately above, a significant change in the test-retest correlation for groups, implying large changes in ordinal position for at least some subjects in the sample. A change in average *level* for the sample may or may not be implied.

Such discontinuities may be sudden and large, or slow and small, with everything in between these extremes. They may occur in response to environmental change, or they may arise within some environmental constancy. Thus we shall be looking both at discontinuities in relation to environmental change and also in the more-or-less constant micro-environment. A constant micro-environment should not be construed as a static one—obviously the social environment changes as a young child matures. But certain socioeconomic and psychological factors within a family and neighborhood can meaningfully be viewed as predictable. Contrast this usual rearing situation, however, with the effects of rescue on a socially isolated child, and it is clear that a real distinction between constant and inconstant environments can validly be made.

Apart from these brief introductory remarks, this paper will be divided into three sections: first, some problems central to measurement and evaluation; second, empirical research; and third, concluding discussion. A vast and indigestible amount of material could be packed into the allotted space, but instead, the empirical data will merely be exemplified.

Some Problems Concerned with Measurement

Two problems should be outlined. The first is really strategic or philosophical. If your model of development stresses continuities, you do not search for discontinuities. Hence although some popular stage theories are really discontinuity theories, remarkably little notice has been taken of their implications. Take, for example, the vast number of longitudinal correlational studies of various human characteristics, particularly IQ. Early papers by Nemzek (1933) and Thorndike (1940) summarized several hundred studies on this theme. They showed: (1) that preschool tests had little, if any, long-term predictive value; (2) that at all ages, the longer the test-retest time interval, the lower the correlation, that is, the greater the change of ordinal position of individuals. Recently updated literature analyses confirm these findings (McAskie and Clarke, 1976; Jensen, 1980). We can assume that the correlation between ages 3 to 5 with adult intelligence is around 0.4, increasing to around 0.7 in middle childhood (6 to 9 years). By contrast, the correlation for height between age 6 and adulthood is 0.8; a commensurate correlation for IQ is only attained in late adolescence. With height one is measuring the same dimension in early childhood as later, but with cognitive skills one is assessing *qualitatively* different behaviors in these two life periods. Thus it can be noted that it is not possible from any early behavioral measures during the period of considerable brain growth to predict adult ability to think abstractly (except in rare, extreme cases). This appears to represent a real discontinuity both in quality and in the individual's ordinal position of cognitive functions between preschool and later. An analogy might be with the metamorphosis of the butterfly—is the sequence caterpillar, chrysallis, butterfly to be regarded as evidence for continuity or discontinuity?

The second problem relates to difficulties in comparing levels of individual performance of psychological characteristics across time and space as a result of one or more of the following factors: (1) inadequate standardization of an instrument; (2) differences in the content of tests; and (3) secular trends (McAskie and Clarke, 1976; Jensen, 1980). To track cognitive or social development across the life span using either longitudinal or cross-sectional data always involves changing the measuring device along the line. Our task in assessing continuities or discontinuities is not helped by the fact that our tools are subject to often considerable errors of measurement. Please note, I am *not* referring to test bias.

My generation slowly discovered that the 1937 Stanford-Binet had different means at different ages, but, worse still, standard deviations that varied between 12 and 20 points. These errors ensure that a *constant* IQ for a bright or retarded child would, for example, appear grossly *inconstant* between ages 6 and 12, by as much as 24 points. The even greater horrors in the standardization of the 1916 Binet have been buried in the mists of time and have to be seen to be believed. We carried out a recent exhumation and with great difficulty secured from across the Atlantic the original standardization data. There can be no doubt that adolescent and adult IQs are seriously underestimated (e.g., Mitchell, 1941) and that IQ levels (though not correlations) in some of the still widely quoted nature-nurture papers (e.g., Skodak and Skeels, 1949) are in need of reinterpretation. A number of earlier and more sophisticated researchers, however, appreciated this problem and fiddled the CA denominator. Nor do our difficulties with this test stop after the first two revisions. The recent Texas Adoption Study (Horn, Loehlin, and Willerman, 1979) used the 1960 norms for younger children and ended up having to subtract 7 points from each IQ. Scarr and Weinberg (1976), using the 1972 norms, apparently avoided this problem.

Note that these problems are important in considering *level* of performance but are relatively unimportant in studies where only *ordinal position* is evaluated, as Outhit (1933) so elegantly demonstrated.

But level of performance is often crucially important in developmental psychology. To have to rely solely on correlations is hampering, to say the least.

Nor is it only IQ where there may be measurement difficulties. Take the assessment of that many-splendored thing, personality. Here the problems are that: (1) many personality tests consist of self-report—what individuals *say* they are or do (whereas cognitive tests assess what they actually do); (2) much of the information on child characteristics relies on ratings which tend to have a much lower reliability; and (3) there is a degree of situational specificity to personality expression. This is notably less than the situationists imply but more than could be predicted from trait theories. Attempts to identify basic and early expressions of temperament that would hold up over time have been similarly unsuccessful (Thomas and Chess, 1977).

Empirical Research

The prevention of psychopathology involves understanding its causes and assessing the efficacy of intervention programs. Psychopathology is concerned with deviant development, which in turn involves a focus on the nature and causes of human differences.

This is by no means to deny the importance of commonalities in development such as those which Piaget has investigated, nor the fact that nature and nurture are essential and interlocking processes. It may well also be that heritability indices are a latter-day philosopher's stone: In any case their sample dependence leads to widely different estimates, some of which have been collated by Vandenberg (1971) in connection with twin studies. But it has appeared to me that some psychologists, in their urgent desire to get away from painful, politically emotive issues of individual differences, have hoped that if they focused their attention on process models of development such as Piaget's, the differences would go away. Unfortunately, however, when various subgroups of the American and British populations were assessed on Piagetian tasks, the disparities across social classes (or ethnic subgroups) were, if anything, greater than on conventional IQ tests. Teachers and social workers are still going to have to cope with children whose characteristics vary enormously; these cannot be obscured.

In attempt to make sense of a great deal of apparently controversial material, which has vexed those interested in developmental abnormalities for years, I have undertaken detailed analyses of studies in the following areas:

• studies of infants adopted soon after birth
• studies of later adopted children
• case studies of children rescued from severe deprivation
• studies of cumulative deficit
• social factors affecting attainment and adjustment
• the outcome of experimental intervention programs, notably those by Skeels and by Heber and Garber (the Milwaukee project).

They will be briefly considered, one by one.

Early Adoption

The many studies of very early adopted children show quite uniformly: (1) average or above average intellectual status; (2) correlations with the natural parent's status; and (3) low correlations with the adopted parent's status, which can often be accounted for by (4) evidence of selective placement. In interpreting the first point, too rarely is account taken of selective factors that determine which children are considered for adoption and the timing of adoption. However, there is a great deal of evidence, acknowledged in the Scarr and Weinberg (1976) transracial study that these are important in interpreting the outcomes of early and later adoptions. As you may know, I do not believe that there is any reason to assume that lack of secure and stimulating early environment has by itself negative implications for later development, provided there follows a total ecological change into a greatly superior environment (Clarke and Clarke, 1976). These points will be illustrated by referring in the first instance to two studies that have had a seminal and probably distorting effect on our view of early development.

Behind many attempts to help disadvantaged children and behind some of the thinking on importance for later development of early environmental events looms the figure of that great humanist Harold Skeels. He and his colleague Marie Skodak are best known for two research projects: one reported the outcome for a large sample of infants adopted in the first six months of life whose mothers were said to be of low intelligence (Skodak, 1939; Skodak and Skeels, 1945; Skodak and Skeels, 1949); the second (Skeels, 1966) was entitled, "Adult Status of Children with Contrasting *Early* Life Experiences" (present author's italics). It will be assumed that readers are familiar with both studies, but that, unlike ourselves, they have not spent weeks pursuing all the relevant documents and combing through them to establish whether the implications attributed by the authors and many later commentators are necessarily justified.

Probably all the important points can be made by reference to the 1966 paper. This contrasted the fortunes in adult life of 13 young children in the Iowa Soldiers' Orphan Homes in the 1930s, supposedly rehabilitated in an institution for the mentally retarded, with a group who remained in the orphanage. This gives evidence of very considerable and intensive screening by the various adoption agencies, no doubt reflecting the requirements of potential parents, of *all* children who were adopted in Iowa during the relevant period. It is clear from the various papers on the early adopted children that there was selective placement; common sense demands that there was likely to be very careful selection *into* adoption in the first place. And this is in fact very well documented:

Since study homes or temporary care homes were not available to the state agency at that time, the choice for children who were not suitable for immediate placement in adoptive homes was between, on the one hand, an unstimulating, large nursery with predictable mental retardation or, on the other hand, a radical iconoclastic solution, that is, placement in institutions for the mentally retarded in a bold experiment to see whether retardation in infancy was reversible. . . . Children whose development was so delayed that adoptive placement was out of the question remained in the orphanage. (Skeels, 1966, p.7)

At the ages when adoptive placement usually occurred, nine of the children in the contrast group had been considered normal in mental development. All 12 were not placed, however, because of different circumstances: 5 were withheld from placement simply because of poor family histories, 2 because of other health problems and one because of possible mental retardation. (Skeels, 1966, p.11)

The contrast-group members remained in the orphanage until placement. One was returned to relatives, but in most instances the children were eventually transferred to an institution for the mentally retarded as long-term protected residents. A few of the contrast group had been briefly approved for adoptive placement, and two had been placed for short periods. None was successful, however, and the children's decline in mental level removed them from the list of those eligible for adoption. (Skeels, 1966, p.12)

While it is true that the very incomplete histories of the biological families of the two groups showed relatively little difference, it is also apparent that none of these children was eligible for placement in adoptive homes before the age of 6 months. It further appears from the honestly reported medical histories, that among the 12 contrast children there were more with possible neural damage than in the experimental group.

It is evident from Skeels's (1936) first paper that (1) the Bureau of Welfare required that a child remain in a foster home at least 12 months before adoption was permitted, and (2) on February 1, 1934 a policy was established whereby no child could be adopted until a psychological examination had been made.

As already noted, examination of the standardization of the 1916 Stanford Binet makes clear that it underestimated the IQs of adults and that, therefore, we have no way of accurately estimating the intelligence level of biological mothers of adopted children in Iowa in the 1930s (see Mitchell, 1941). My conclusion from all I have collated is that in the early adoption study the biological mothers were in the average range. I also conclude that an unknown number of children were returned by the adopting homes as unsuitable. All of which adds up to a highly selected sample of infants who became the subjects of the world's most famous adoption study.

Shall we return to the children who, at Skeel's request, were sent as house guests to the Glenwood State School after varying periods in the orphanage? Of the 13, 11 surmounted the obstacle race into adoptive homes and were not returned; 2 failed and remained in the institution for the mentally retarded. Both of these women were later discharged and at the time of follow-up were in modest jobs, one of them having married. The remaining 11 adoptees were on the whole more succesful. It should also be noted that all of these children had spent time in the orphanage whose facilities for infants were to say the least, very meager; they were then moved into an institution for retarded people where, according to Skeels, they were actively encouraged to make a close relationship with one person, and then at ages varying from 13 months to 82 months, averaging 37 months, all but two were removed from these loving mother figures and placed in adoptive homes to start making relationships all over again. On the whole, however, the outcome in adult life was good. For my money this progress was very marginally due to the early life experiences and massively due to the later prolonged period of security in permanent homes.

Meanwhile, the 12 contrast children had failed in the obstacle race into adoption and remained in the orphanage, with the exception of one boy (case 19). His ancestry was relatively impeccable, but he had a hearing loss and his IQ was, during the critical period, on a downward course. However, having survived the orphanage for 8 years, during the latter period being given special educational help, he was transferred to a residential school for the deaf where he made good all-round progress and completed 12th grade. At follow-up in adulthood he was totally atypical of the contrast group, more closely resembling the better members of the experimental group. Surely his progress was related both to his natural endowments and his circumstances in later life?

Late Adoption

What might some of the seminal factors be in determining outcome for late adoptees? Kadushin (1970) has sensitively documented his views, based on his own and other research workers' experiences as he described a cohort of late-adopted children removed from deplorable circumstances adapting to the social and academic expectations of their new homes.

It is true that in this study, as in other adoption studies, there was selection: Nobody with an IQ below 80 was offered. Nevertheless the fact remains that these children came from very low status families and many of them had had an incredibly rough time; they had been removed from their parents by court order and had been in several foster homes. "Outcome was positively related to parents' acceptance of the child, in their perception of him as a member of the family, and negatively related to self-consciousness by parents regarding adoptive status" (Kadushin, 1970, p.210).

Kadushin did not feel the need to offer evidence on the IQs of his late-adopted children. He felt it was sufficient to look deeply into the social and emotional adjustment of the children to their new parents and the outcome in terms of achievement at school. In seeking to identify the factors responsible for the resilience which so many children have shown in recovery from earlier traumas, he offers two. First, of course, the security of the home and the relationships within it, but in addition and very important, he suggests that the wider social context plays a significant part in the recovery process. He points out that these children had made *two* important shifts in moving from their own seriously disadvantaged backgrounds via foster homes to the adoptive contexts. They made a change from homes that offered little in the way of meeting their needs in terms of affection, acceptance, support, understanding, and encouragement to the adoptive homes that offered some measure of these essential psychic supplies. They also changed from deprived lower-class, multi-problem contexts to respectable, status-conscious, middle-class homes.

The child "now receives messages which proclaim his acceptability, and support, reinforce, and strengthen whatever components, however limited, of self-acceptance he has been able to develop as a result of whatever small amount of affection he received in his former home. The effect of positive parent-child relationships within the home are now buttressed by social relationships outside the home rather than vitiated by the contradiction between the acceptance of the lower-class child in the lower-class home and his rejection by the community" (Kadushin, 1970, p.222).

My own conclusion is that older children adapt towards the academic and behavioral norms of their domestic community whatever these may be. They may adapt up or they may adapt down, but the general ecology in which children are reared has almost certainly an important impact on their achievement and their adjustment: Their motivation is bound to be affected as goals change.

Case Studies of Children Rescued from Severe Deprivation

There are a few well-documented case studies of children rescued from conditions far more deprived and depraved than those which are normally considered in studies of deprivation. I am aware that the outcome is not equally happy in all cases, but hope I may be forgiven for not diverting from my course to contrast Genie, for example, with Isabelle or the Koluchova twins. My purpose here is to present evidence that we must take into account in considering developmental discontinuity. Many of you will already be familiar with the history presented by Mason (1942) and Davis (1947) of a 6-year-old child, Isabelle, rescued from life-long isolation with a deaf-mute mother. When discovered she was rachitic, without speech, and apparently severly retarded. She received prolonged specialist treatment and at follow-up when she was 14 was regarded as normal.

The Czechoslovakian twins documented by Koluchova (1972, 1976) were reared first in an institution, then with a maternal aunt until the age of 18 months. They were then isolated and cruelly treated in the home of their father and stepmother. On discovery at the age of 7 they were severly rachitic, without speech, emotionally disturbed, and had IQs of around 40. A prolonged specialist rehabilitation program which included placement at the age of 9 in a most carefully selected adoptive home resulted in recovery into cognitive, academic, and emotional normalcy.

Recently because of our known interest in cases of this kind we were approached by a research worker, Angela Roberts of Manchester University, who is an unusually qualified nurse. She spent a period in Bogota, Colombia, associated with a missionary orphanage that catered for a small group of abandoned illegitimate babies or infants given up because their parents could not cope. The illegitimate were usually the babies of young teenage servants and sometimes were literally foundlings. One little boy, Adam, was abandoned at 4 months and first received into a reformatory for girls. Our colleague visited him there and describes the conditions as appalling. His main diet was a watery vegetable soup and porridge, and he remained in a bleak, bare, windowless room in perpetual darkness, unless the door was open.

On admission to the mission orphanage Adam, aged 16 months, weighed only 12 lbs., 12 ozs. He had the physical signs of nutritional marasmus, his head was infested, he had scabies, a fungal rash, and numerous sores. His abdomen was grossly distended. Emotionally he was completely withdrawn; he could not sit, crawl, or walk. His development appeared similar to that of a 3-month infant. A local doctor diagnosed him as an extremely malnourished, mentally retarded spastic. By 23 months of age his weight was 23 lbs., he could sit up from a prone position, could stand holding furniture, could imitate two words together, and could feed himself with a spoon. A month later he could stand without support for a few seconds and could walk around his cot holding on with one hand. At 26 months, 10 months after admission, he weighed 26 lbs., took his first independent steps, had improved emotionally and in other ways, and at 32 months was adopted by a North American family. There were, of course, problems, but by the age of 5 Adam was essentially average both mentally and physically. At the age of 7¾ Adam is in the second grade and is evaluated by his teacher as an average 7-year-old, who is showing signs of specific talents.

Case studies of this kind illustrate in a tragic but dramatic way the effect of physical and social deprivation on developing humans, together with later recovery granted very special help and complete removal from the depriving circumstances. Some of you may wonder if I believe their recovery to be complete? Might they be even more able and stable had they not been subjected to these dreadful experiences? The answer of course is that I cannot be sure, but as some kind of Popperian I think we have here two alternatives, either to face the possibility that this is an hypothesis which is unfalsifiable or to make a stab at a solution. If we follow the psychoanalytic argument I think we will find that none of us is functioning at an optimal level—whatever that might be. My tentative solution is as follows: One should be able to make an actuarial prediction of the probable outcome for deprived children had they been reared in more normal circumstances with biological relatives (in the case of the Koluchova twins by their simple-minded father and mother who died). Sibling controls offer a potentially helpful solution but the data are not always available.

Studies of Cumulative Deficit

This familiar concept seems to have had its roots in a study by the Englishman, Gordon (1923), who found that canal-boat children averaged an IQ of 87 at age 6 and of 60 at age 12. The correlation between age and IQ was −0.76. Subsequently considerable research has been carried out, much of it in the United States, with controversy about the cause of declining IQs in children reared in disadvantaged circumstances.

Jensen (1974, 1977) has published two studies using older and younger sibling comparisons. The first, in California, found a significant age decrement in verbal but not in nonverbal IQ among black elementary school children. This difference averaged only 2 IQ points for an average sibling age discrepancy between about 19 and 31 months in the age range

5 to 12. Jensen raises the possibility that this small decrement may reflect reading differences on the verbal test.

The second study took place in rural Georgia and again used older and younger sibling comparisons. Significant and substantial linear IQ decrements, both verbal and nonverbal, between 5 and 16 years occurred in blacks but not in whites. There was an average decrement of 1.62 verbal IQ points per year and 1.19 nonverbal IQ points, over the age range 6 to 16. Jensen believes that an environmental explanation seems reasonable in this case. Kamin (1978), while not claiming to invalidate the notion of cumulative deficit, raises the possibility that the younger siblings may have been responding to general social and educational improvements that were taking place during the relevant period.

Heber's (1968) first study in Milwaukee seems to me to offer impressive cross-sectional evidence for cumulative deficit. Among the important factors to which he and his colleagues drew attention was that socioeconomic status is a rather poor guide to the familial processes that result in cumulative deficit. It will be recalled that he was able to differentiate between families living in the same slum, showing an average considerable deficit occurring in children whose mothers' IQs lay below 80 but no deficit among the children whose mothers' IQs lay above 80.

I would like to draw some conclusions from the material I have presented so far. It seems to me that studies of early-adopted children rather clearly show genetic effects and fail to show commensurate correlations with the rearing environment after account has been taken of selective placement. This is not altogether surprising in view of the selection both of infants and of adopting families. There is one French adoption study, however, which is an exception. Schiff, Duyme, Dumaret, Stewart, Tomkiewicz, and Feingold (1978) employed an entirely novel method that I hope will be followed by others. They searched the files of six public adoption agencies to find children of lower-class origin adopted into high-status homes who also had a sibling or half-sibling reared by the biological mothers. There are some problems with the presentation of the data, which make me cautious in interpreting the findings. However 32 adopted children were located, born to mothers and fathers who were unskilled workers; only 20 siblings were found, reared by their own mothers. The 20 home-reared children had average IQs of 94.5 and the 32 adoptees of 110.6, or on another test 95.4 and 106.9 respectively. In terms of school attainment the authors state that the two groups were typical of their rearing environments. Certainly the home-reared children were very much more likely than their adopted siblings to have presented educational problems. Only 2 out of 20 adopted had repeated a grade or been in a special class, whereas 13 out of 20 home-reared si-

blings had. None of the adopted had IQs below 85 and only 5 lay between 85 and 102. Among their disadvantaged siblings, 3 had IQs below
85 and only 5 were above 102 (Schiff, personal communication). This
study clearly needs replication for, among other things, the extent to
which such adopted children are accelerated by the positive features of
the environment or the home-reared depressed by negative aspects remains unclear.

My second conclusion is that cumulative deficit among socially disadvantaged families is a very real phenomenon. It appears to affect a minority of developing children. Taking the data together there appears to be
good evidence for the social environment operating as a threshold
phenomen. The majority of the children growing up in an advanced
nation almost certainly lie above that threshold; for them the physical
and social environment is sufficiently adequate for genetic effects to
show up as major causes of differences. Below the threshold it seems
likely that there are various degrees of deficit which will be related to the
severity of family pathology. There is as yet little direct evidence for this:
I present it simply as a hunch. However if we were to accept varying
degrees of pathology leading to varying degrees of deficit, the chances
are that we may have to think in terms of a substantial minority of our
children who may be subject to effective environmental deprivation.

My third conclusion is that late-adopted children represent a different
sample in terms of family background to the early adopted and that removing those reared in very adverse conditions to superior homes results
in normal development.

Attainment, Adjustment and Intervention Programs

The question of creating discontinuity through intervention with socially
disadvantaged children is exceedingly important. Here may I say that despite the evidence recently published by Willerman, Horn, and Loehlin
(1977) suggesting that achievement is no more subject to social influences
than is the IQ, a great deal of other evidence persuades me that this may
not be the case. Admittedly some of it comes from studies of the gifted,
with particular reference to the over representation of first-born children
in areas of academic distinction, which are beyond the scope of this
paper. However a recent longitudinal study by Rutter, Maughan, Mortimore, and Ouston (1979) conducted in inner London schools serving be-
low-average adolescents provides evidence of a very significant differential influence of schools on attainment and adjustment after allowance has
been made for preentry differences in verbal reasoning and parental status. School variables that appeared to be irrelevant to outcome were
those indices related to material factors, for example, size or age of

school or amount of resources. Variables that were found to be important include the balance of intellectual intake (but not social or ethnic), academic emphasis and teacher behavior, and positive attitudes among the staff toward their pupils. This study shows how schools may differentially contribute to discontinuities in those areas of competence that society most values; both family and school process variables are likely to affect outcome.

So far as intervention with the disadvantaged is concerned, the majority of programs so far have been made available to preschool children whose IQs as already noted, are not usually more than minimally predictive of cognitive status in later life. Furthermore, advantages in IQ for experimentally treated children are usually lost fairly rapidly (Bronfenbrenner, 1974; Zigler and Trickett, 1979).

These points are examplified in the two recent reports of the Consortium for Longitudinal Studies (Lazar, Hubbell, Murray, Rosche, and Royce, 1977; Lazar and Darlington, 1978). The major finding was that before inception into these specially designed, high-quality programs, the treatment and control children did not differ in IQ. At age 6 treatment children scored significantly higher than controls and this superiority continued for at least 3 school years after the end of the preschool programs. At the time of the latest follow-up in adolescence, however, there was no significant difference between treatment and control children on WISC-R scores for the vast majority of these projects. Very sensibly the researchers, perhaps influenced by Edward Zigler, gathered data on school achievement. They found that children who had attended preschool were only about half as likely as control children to be attending special education classes. They were also less likely to be retained in grade. However on achievement test scores, although there was a significant difference between mathematics scores of treatment and control children, the reading scores did not differ. Furthermore, although I do not wish to devalue the importance of the work and the care with which the follow-up was conducted, we are dealing here with differences among children for whom the general level is low. The Consortium monitored the long-term outcome of programs that were limited in the amount of time devoted to the children and indeed to their families, and there was, in the end, no difference shown between one kind of excellent program and another. Nor was there any relation between outcome and age of entry to the preschool program or time spent within it. Although evaluation of the admittedly limited gains is hazardous, it seems likely that the mediating mechanism may well have been the mothers' contacts with intelligent, informed, and devoted people who encouraged somewhat higher aspirations for the children than they otherwise would have

had. Perhaps even longer support for these families and enrichment programs for the children as they go through school might result in an even
better outcome.

   One of the most imaginative and courageous experiments was started
in Milwaukee in the mid 1960s (e.g., Garber and Heber, 1977, 1978;
Heber, 1968; Heber, Garber, Harrington, Hoffman, and Falender, 1972).
This program was designed to provide maximum intervention short of
removing the children altogether from their families. The intervention
effectively started at the birth of the children included in the experimental
group in that those who were later to stimulate and enrich the infants
were in contact with their mothers. Formal intervention started at the
age of 3 months on a full-day basis and lasted until the children entered
school at the age of 6. From 24 months to 72 months the experimental
group maintained an advantage over the control subjects of between 20
and 34 IQ points. Intervention terminated at school entry, which was at
the mean age of 72 months. At this point the experimental group's mean
IQ was 120.7 (SD = 11.2) compared to the control group's mean IQ of
87.2 (SD = 12.8), a difference of over 30 IQ points. The authors of this
program have repeatedly enjoined us not to overinterpret these IQ values
per se, for both experimental and control groups were subjected to a program of testing such as no children in any other longitudinal study have
experienced. Thus Heber and Garber caution that test-taking skills for
both groups have been enhanced. What is to be viewed as of significance
is the differential in performance between these two groups. However I
would like to comment that Ramey and Campbell (1979) presented results from a somewhat similar long-term intervention program, the
Abecedarian Project, (Ramey, Collier, Sparling, Loda, Campbell, Ingram, and Finkelstein, 1976), which showed much less striking IQ differences (12 points at age 4 and 8 points at age 5) than the Milwaukee
project and furthermore their control group was at a similar level to the
Milwaukee controls. There could be a number of explanations for these
disparities which include: A situation in which the Abecedarian Experimental Group did not reach the dizzy heights of the Milwaukee children
perhaps because they were tested less often or because they did not have a
maternal habilitation program, but the control children appear remarkably similar to the repeatedly tested Milwaukee controls, perhaps because
they had nutritional supplements, although my inclination is to reject
this as an explanation.

   Garber and Heber (1978) have followed the children for nearly 4 years
past intervention and in the last report the experimental group had a
mean IQ of 105 as compared to the control group mean of 85. Thus there
still continued to be a 20-point gap reduced from an earlier maximum of

over 30, between these groups and the experimental group continued to be above the national average. The picture is very much less rosy for scholastic achievement. On the Metropolitan Achievement Test the experimental group was significantly superior to the control group on all subtests through the first 2 years. For the first year the distribution of the experimental group approximates the national profile, while the performance of the control group was markedly depressed. The performance of the experimental children since then has further declined, first to the lower level of the city of Milwaukee and then to the still lower one of their inner-city schools. It is perhaps small comfort that they remain one grade ahead of the controls and are significantly superior in reading (Garber, personal communication).

Although the difference in outcome as measured on standardized intelligence tests between the Abecedarian and Milwaukee programs remain to be resolved, we cannot but accept the evidence in terms of scholastic achievement as an indication that Heber's enormously important and expensive intervention project has failed to safeguard its participants against deficit in those skills required for success in school. It is possible that later intervention would have been more effective; or that whatever the timing of intervention, subtle processes within the family and neighborhood will always determine major outcomes in attainment and adjustment. On the other hand, possibly new strategies of intervention for selected groups of high-risk families may be required; once again my advocacy would be for long-term intensive support by specially qualified teams. It is highly unlikely that the pervasive effects of severe environmental deprivation can be counteracted without exceptional effort by exceptional people. And, finally, it would be well to remember that as yet we have no evidence from adoption studies concerning the potential outcome for children selected as being at serious risk for mental retardation, as the participants in the Milwaukee project were.

Conclusions

From the evidence reviewed, buttressed by data beyond the scope of this paper, I make the following conclusions. First, there exist natural discontinuities under normal conditions of development, although inadequacies of our measuring instruments make it difficult to monitor these with precision. Such changes also occur in some deviant conditions (e.g., many cases of reactive behavior disorders or juvenile delinquency). In some other cases discontinuities appear rarely (e.g., serious conduct disorders in late childhood) or very rarely (e.g., childhood autism) or not at all (e.g., moderate to profound retardation). It is often difficult to establish the extent to which continuities are intrinsic or represent an environmental feedback effect that maintains and strenghtens earlier deviancy. Children are to a significant extent, active agents in creating their own environments, and hence their behavior.

Second, there is substantial reason to postulate a biological trajectory from which individuals may deviate when environmental deprivation is severe, but to which they will return when these stresses are removed or significantly diminished.

Third, there is also a social trajectory determined within broad limits by accident of birth and alterable by chance or design. Normally the two trajectories are interlocking, but in studies of deviant development they may not be so. The two trajectories are helpful conceptually in explaining apparently spontaneous recovery from deprivation. The idea is derived from the work of the British geneticist, Waddington (1957; 1966), who has drawn attention to a "self-righting tendency" which pushes deprived children towards normality whenever circumstances allow. Perhaps this represents the most optimistic finding in the whole field of discontinuities from pathology. In addition, as we and others have shown (Clarke and Clarke, 1974), the majority of earlier identified mild mental retardates merge into the working-class community in adulthood, partly as a result of prolonged social learning and adjustment and partly as a result of relief from educational pressures. And even studies of multiproblem families, of which the British research of Tonge, James, and Hillam (1975) seems outstanding, indicate that at least half the children escape the intergenerational cycle of disadvantage, especially females who "marry out". But each generation, while losing members to normality, recruits further replacements anew. We know very little about the mechansims of these natural discontinuities. They probably include genetic factors, modeling behavior especially in a normal adult work environment, and chance opportunities or misfortunes to which individuals react differentially. It does not take much imagination to assume that the number and variety of lucky chances are disproportionately distributed in middle-class social environments, as may also be the abilities required to exploit them.

Fourth, studies of adopted children give us considerable encouragement concerning the outcome for disadvantaged children who experience total ecological change even at a relatively late date, although so far we lack evidence on the adoptive outcome for children selected as at risk for mild retardation. Selective processes into adoption appear to be rather thorough, although of recent years an increasing number of families have proved willing to adopt deviant or potentially deviant children.

Fifth, some preschool intervention programs yield evidence for limited later benefit which may be in large measure attributable to changed attitudes and motivations on the part of the parents. This applies to the Milwaukee project as it does to the Consortium studies.

Sixth, accelerating young children in terms of cognitive skills appears relatively easy but of little later consequence. We do not as yet know what the outcome might be of acceleration starting at later stages of development and await the results of the second phase of the Abecedarian project, as well as further developments in Haywood's work (1979) based on Feuerstein's Instrumental Enrichment program, which appears to have been successful in Israel (Feuerstein, Rand, Hoffman, and Miller, 1980). Part of the evidence suggests that such a policy might be more successful in that after the age of 6 the biological trajectory is sufficiently advanced to make children potentially more receptive to social and educational intervention. However, conflict between the domestic social trajectory and the aims of even modest intervention programs may be an uneven battle. The best hope may in the end prove to be for ecological change to be encouraged by informed, responsible and caring citizens.

Seventh, in my country at least, it appears that social processes within schools contribute differentially to the outcome for inner-city adolescents in terms of achievement and adjustment, although Rutter (1980) is cautious about the extent to which these findings can be generalized to the United States.

Eighth, I believe there is evidence to suggest that the effects of serious environmental disadvantages are very hard indeed to shift permanently within the context of their origin and that as yet we do not understand how to proceed. I do not believe that the disappointing long-term outcomes of preschool intervention programs necessarily demonstrate that powerful genetic factors are overwhelming influences on the deviant academic and social development of these children, although it would be imprudent to discount them. I also believe that we have learned a great deal from those research workers who have mounted and monitored the programs.

It seems clear that unless intervention is greatly prolonged, or possibly total, then effects tend to fade, either very considerably or entirely. In the latter case they will also tend to swing over into deficit, intellectually, scholastically, and emotionally. While some brief interventions appear to promote desirable discontinuities, they have to be perpetuated over many, many years if their effects are not to be swamped by adverse social forces bearing upon individuals; for these life is an anti-Head Start program. It is important to realize, however, that potentially the disadvantaged have a greater range of possible phenotypic outcomes than is normally apparent. But the practical, ethical, and political difficulties of promoting on a large scale a psychologically healthier society are very considerable. To have potential solutions or part-solutions is one thing; to put them into practice is another. However, I have one practical suggestion to make. The Abecedarian program includes provision for one phase in which children will receive preschool day care to be followed by further support both in the home and in the school for a few years after the age of 6. At present it is not envisaged that this support will continue into adolescence, and I suggest that it could be important to do this experimentally within the context of this well established program.

The final general point which an examination of the literature has forced upon me is that the whole of life-span development is important and some of the principles which I have discussed in the context of childhood deviance appear to be equally relevant to adult development.

References

Bronfenbrenner, U. *A report on longitudinal evaluations of pre-school programs,* (Vol. 2), *Is early intervention effective?* Washington, D.C.: DHEW Publications No. (OHD) 74-25, 1974.

Clarke, A. D. B. Presidential address: Predicting human development: Problems, evidence, implications. *Bulletin of the British Psychological Society,* 1978, *31,* 249–258.

Clarke, A. D. B., and Clarke, A. M. Consistency and variability in the growth of human characteristics. In W. D. Wall and V. P. Varma (Eds.), *Advances in educational psychology.* London: University of London Press, 1972.

Clarke, A. M., and Clarke, A. D. B. (Eds.). *Mental deficiency: The changing outlook* (3rd ed.). London: Methuen, 1974.

Clarke, A. M., and Clarke, A. D. B. (Eds.). *Early experience: Myth and evidence.* London: Open Books, 1976.

Clarke, A. M., and Clarke, A. D. B. Problems in comparing the effects of environmental change at different ages. In H. McGurk (Ed.), *Ecological factors in human development.* Amsterdam: North-Holland Publishing Co., 1977.

Davis, K. Final note on a case of extreme isolation. *American Journal of Sociology,* 1947, *52,* 432–437.

Feuerstein, R., Rand, Y., Hoffman, M. B., and Miller, R. *Instrumental enrichment: An intervention program for cognitive modifiability.* Baltimore: University Park Press, 1980.

Garber, H., and Heber, R. The Milwaukee Project: Indications of the effectiveness of early intervention in preventing mental retardation. In P. Mittler (Ed.), *Research to practice in mental retardation* (Vol. 1). Baltimore: University Park Press, 1977.

Garber, H., and Heber, R. *The efficacy of early intervention with family rehabilitation.* Paper delivered at the Conference on Prevention of Retarded Development in Psychosocially Disadvantaged Children. Madison, Wisconsin, 1978.

Gordon, H. *Mental and scholastic tests among retarded children.* (Education Pamphlet 44, Board of Education, London). London: HMSO, 1923.

Haywood, H. C. *Modification of cognitive functions in slow-learning adolescents.*

Paper presented at the Fifth Congress of the International Association for the Scientific Study of Mental Deficiency. Jerusalem, August 1979.

Heber, R. The role of environmental variables in the etiology of cultural-familial mental retardation. In B. W. Richards (Ed.), *Proceedings of the First Congress of the International Association for the Scientific Study of Mental Deficiency*. Reigate, England: Michael Jackson, 1968.

Heber, R., Garber, H., Harrington, S., Hoffman, C., and Falender, C. *Rehabilitation of families at risk for mental retardation*. Progress Report, Madison: University of Wisconsin, 1972.

Horn, J. M., Loehlin, J. C., and Willerman, L. Intellectual resemblance among adoptive and biological relatives: The Texas Adoption Project. *Behavior Genetics*, 1979, *9*, 177–201.

Jensen, A. R. Cumulative deficit: A testable hypothesis? *Developmental Psychology*, 1974, *10*, 996–1019.

Jensen, A. R. Cumulative deficit in IQ of blacks in the rural South. *Developmental Psychology*, 1977, *13*, 184–191.

Jensen, A. R. *Bias in mental testing*. London: Methuen, 1980.

Kadushin, A. *Adopting older children*. New York: Columbia University Press, 1970.

Kamin, L. A positive interpretation of apparent "cumulative deficit". *Developmental Psychology*, 1978, *14*, 195–196.

Koluchova, J. Severe deprivation in twins: A case study. *Journal of Child Psychology and Psychiatry*, 1972, *13*, 107–114.

Koluchova, J. A report on the futher development of twins after severe and prolonged deprivation. In A. M. Clarke and A. D. B. Clarke (Eds.), *Early experience: Myth and evidence*. London: Open Books, 1976.

Lazar, I., Hubbell, V. R., Murray, H., Rosche, M., and Royce, J. *The persistence of preschool effects: Analysis and final report*. The Consortium on Developmental Continuity, Washington, D.C.: DHEW Publication No. (OHDS) 78-30130, 1977.

Lazar, I., and Darlington, R. B. *Lasting effects after preschool: Further analyses of longitudinal studies*. The Consortium for Longitudinal Studies, Washington D.C.: DHEW Publication No. (OHDS) 79-30178, 1978.

Mason, M. Learning to speak after six and one half years of silence. *Journal of Speech Disorders*. 1942, *7*, 295–304.

McAskie, M., and Clarke, A. M. Parent-offspring resemblances in intelligence: Theories and evidence. *British Journal of Psychology*, 1976, *67*, 243–273.

Mitchell, M. B. The Revised Stanford-Binet for adults. *Journal of Educational Research*, 1941, *34*, 516–521.

Nemzek, C. L. The constancy of the IQ. *Psychological Bulletin*, 1933, *30*, 143–168.

Outhit, M. C. A study of the resemblance of parents and children in general intelligence. *Archives of Psychology*, 1933, *23*, 1–60.

Ramey, C. T., and Campbell, F. A. *Educational intervention for children at risk for mild retardation. A longitudinal analysis*. Paper presented at the Fifth Congress of the International Association for the Scientific Study of Mental Deficiency, Jerusalem, August 1979.

Ramey, C. T., Collier, A. M., Sparling, J. J., Loda, F. A., Campbell, F. A., Ingram, D. L., and Finkelstein, N. W. The Carolina Abecedarian project: A longitudinal and multidisciplinary approach to the prevention of developmental retardation. In T. Tjossem (Ed.), *Intervention strategies for high-risk infants and young children.* Baltimore: University Park Press, 1976.

Rutter, M. School influences on children's behavior and development: The 1979 Kenneth Blackfan Lecture, Children's Hospital Medical Center, Boston. *Pediatrics,* 1980, *65,* 208–220.

Rutter, M., Maughan, B., Mortimore, P., and Ouston, J. *Fifteen thousand hours: Secondary schools and their effects on children.* London: Open Books, 1979.

Scarr, S., and Weinberg, R. A. IQ test performance of black children adopted into white families. *American Psychologist,* 1976, *31,* 726–739.

Schiff, M., Duyme, M., Dumaret, A., Stewart, J., Tomkiewicz, S., and Feingold, J. Intellectual status of working-class children adopted early into upper-middle-class families. *Science,* 1978, *200,* 1503–1504.

Skeels, H. M. Mental development of children in foster homes. *Journal of Genetic Psychology,* 1936, *49,* 91–106.

Skeels, H. M. Adult status of children with contrasting early life experiences: A follow-up study. *Monographs of the Society for Research in Child Development,* 1966, *31,* (105), 3.

Skodak, M. Children in foster homes. *University of Iowa Studies in Child Welfare,* 1939.

Skodak, M., and Skeels, H. M. A follow-up study of children in adoptive homes. *The Journal of Genetic Psychology,* 1945, *66,* 21–58.

Skodak, M., and Skeels, H. M. A final follow-up study of one hundred adopted children. *The Journal of Genetic Psychology,* 1949, *75,* 82–125.

Thomas, A., and Chess, S. *Temperament and development.* New York: Brunner/Mazel, 1977.

Thorndike, R. L. 'Constancy' of the IQ. *Psychological Bulletin,* 1940, *37,* 167–186.

Tonge, W. L., James, D. S., and Hillam, S. M. *Families without hope: A controlled study of 33 problem families.* British Journal of Psychiatry Special Publication No. 11. Ashford, Kent: Headley Brothers, 1975.

Vandenberg, S. What do we know today about the inheritance of intelligence and how do we know it? In R. J. Cancro (Ed.), *Intelligence: Genetic and environmental influences.* New York: Grune and Stratton, 1971.

Waddington, C. H. *The strategy of genes.* London: George Allen and Unwin, 1957.

Waddington, C. H. *Principles of development and differentiation.* New York: Macmillan, 1966.

Willerman, L., Horn, J. M., and Loehlin, J. C. The aptitude-achievement test distinction: A study of unrelated children reared together. *Behavior Genetics,* 1977, *7,* 465–470.

Zigler, E., and Trickett, P. K. The role of national social policy in promoting social competence in children. In M. W. Kent and J. E. Rolf (Eds.), *Primary prevention of psychopathology,* Volume 3: *Social competence in children.* Hanover, N.H.: University Press of New England, 1979.

Early Experience, Interactive Systems, and Brain Laterality in Rodents

Victor H. Denenberg

The Study of Behavioral Development: Causal Versus Systems Approach

Our concern in this volume is with the topic of behavioral development, as is indicated by the volume's title, *Facilitating Infant and Early Childhood Development*. Thus, it is a profound irony that the philosophical basis upon which most researchers in this field have built their careers now acts as a major intellectual and emotional barrier blocking attempts to gain an understanding of the deeper structure underlying developmental processes. The philosophical basis I am referring to is the Aristotelian approach of subdivision and classification coupled with causal attribution. Since this system has existed for more than 2,300 years, it is apparent that it satisfies something very powerful in the human mind (or, at least, in many Western minds).

However, a rigid adherence to simple cause-effect thinking prevents us from advancing conceptually in our understanding of behavioral development and also results in our asking questions that lead to theoretical deadends. Three examples will suffice to illustrate this point. Some researchers have asked whether there are direct causal connections between events in early life and later behavior. Only one with an Aristotelian philosophy would seek such linear connections and then, having failed to find them, arrive at the conclusion that early experiences are myths (Clarke and Clarke, 1976). A second example is the pseudo-argument about continuities and discontinuities in behavior. Continuity is defined as the ability to predict, usually using the correlation coefficient (Clarke and Clarke, 1976; Kagan, 1976; Sameroff, 1975). I have shown elsewhere (Denenberg, 1979) that the correlation coefficient, as typically used by researchers, is an insufficient statistic because it is not sensitive to interactional effects over time. Of course there must be continuity since we are linked to our past by genetic heritage, individual history, and cultural content. But continuity does not demand predictability—that is a logical

The preparation of this paper was supported, in part, by NIH Grant No. HD-12948 from the National Institute of Child Health and Human Development.

fallacy. Here, again, one sees the Aristotelian heritage of looking for linear cause-effect relationships. Finding none, the researcher concludes that
there must be a "discontinuity," and fails to realize that a more sophisticated model can readily account for both sets of findings. The third example is the futile, and seemingly endless, argument as to the relative
contribution of heredity and environment to intelligence. The Aristotelian model of classification (heredity and environment) is employed with
the attempt to associate each separately and additively with the outcome
variable of intelligence. (The pervasiveness of Aristotelian thinking is
highlighted by the opening comments of the biographer of Aristotle in
the 1959 *Encyclopaedia Britannica,* Sir Ernest Barker, who suggested that
Aristotle's interests in physiology and zoology may have been a hereditary contribution from his father, who was a physician.)

Heuristic as the Aristotelian approach has proven to be, it is also con-
stricting. As the various fields of science advanced in methodology, measurement, and theory about their respective disciplines, it became apparent that the Aristotelian model was not sufficient to account for the
known information and that other models, or paradigms, had to be developed. The best example is probably the marked changes in the concepts and theories of physics as represented by the work and thinking of
such great figures as Copernicus, Galileo, Newton, and Einstein. In the
field of biology, Weiss (1969) has done a masterful and scholarly job of
showing that causal thinking is insufficient to account for the development of the nervous system.

A number of proposals have been made with respect to new
paradigms to replace the cause-effect model. One well known and
influential paradigm has been that of Bertalanffy (1969), who created
the field of general systems theory to deal with the problem of what he
calls organized complexity. He states, "Organisms are organized
things, with respect to both structure and function, exhibiting
hierarchical order, differentiation, interaction of innumerable processes,
goal directed behavior, negentropic trends, and related criteria. About
these the mechanistic approach . . . is silent. . . . The conventional
categories, concepts and models of physics and chemistry do not deal
with the organismic aspects that I have mentioned. They seem to leave
out just what is specific to living things and life processes; and new
categories appear to be required" (p. 58). Thus, understanding the
properties and principles of "wholes" or organization is the objective of
general systems theory.

Bunge (1979) has dealt with the problems of a systems approach from
a philosophical perspective in his book, *A World of Systems.* Although he
does not care for Bertalanffy's systems philosophy, in part because of the
lack of rigor, Bunge is a firm believer in the concept of system per se.

Some of his basic assumptions about the nature of systems can be understood from the following quote: "An assumption of this book . . . is that there are no stray things: that every thing interacts with other things, so that all things cohere forming systems. . . . Every concrete thing is either a system or a component of a system. . . . Another assumption is that systems come in Chinese boxes or nested systems. Hence, given any system but the world, one may expect to find that it is part of some supersystem" (p. 245).

Note that one goes to a more complex model (systems approach) only after finding that a simpler model (causal analysis) does not work. All of us would clearly prefer to be able to use simple causal thinking in designing our experiments and interpreting the findings. Note also how seductive causal thinking is: if it works we are able to make predictions, an invaluable asset in the applied fields of child study; and it often suggests underlying mechanisms, thus offering us opportunity for theoretical advancement. I suspect it is because of these advantages, plus the fact that we have grown up in an intellectual climate which espouses Aristotelian thinking, that we are so loathe to give up the ghost, even though the body is beginning to decay.

However, give up the ghost we must if we are to advance. I submit that the assumptions of Bunge's I quoted above represent the minimum intellectual scaffolding needed to begin to construct interesting and relevant data bases with theoretically meaningful facades. The key phrase in Bunge's set of assumptions is " . . . that every thing *interacts* with other things . . . " (emphasis added). It is now time for researchers to deal with interactions at a conceptual level as an inherent property of systems, rather than think of them simply as statistical nuisances resulting from a particular type of experimental design involving the analysis of variance.[1]

[1]The so-called Transactional Model of Sameroff and Chandler (1975; Sameroff, 1975), which is widely cited as the next step beyond interaction, is fatally flawed and not a model at all. They start out with two examples of their Main Effect Model, one from a nativist perspective and the other from a nurturist viewpoint. Each model yields one main effect (constitution and environment, respectively) and no interaction. What they call their Interactional Model is actually a main effects model in which both environment and constitution are significant main effects acting independently and additvely, with both making equal contributions to the person's outcome. There is definitely *no* interaction in this model. It is not apparent why they call this an interactional model. Having falsely rejected the idea that an interactional model is of value, they then propose a Transactional Model, which is an odd chaining of constitutional and environmental events over time (the prior two "models" do not contain a time dimension). At best this can be depicted as an interactional model involving the three dimensions of constitution, environment, and time. However, this too is inadequate since it is necessary to specify what occurs in time if one is to begin to understand the dynamics of behavioral development. A series of experiments using the latter approach are in the literature. See Denenberg (1970, 1977, 1979) for reviews and theoretical discussions.

My purposes in this paper are: (1) to review some old research studies which led me to accept the necessity of adopting an interactional approach to the study of behavioral development; (2) to indicate their implications for theorizing about developmental processes; (3) to present some very recent findings concerning the interaction of early experiences and brain dynamics, including laterality effects; and (4) to consider their implications.

Developmental Studies of Behavioral Interaction

Experimental Studies

My first hint of the pervasiveness of interaction came in a paper I published in 1959 on an experiment in which mice were initially conditioned at 25 days under .2, .5, or .8 ma shock. When 50 days old, the mice were extinguished and then reconditioned using .2, .5, or .8 ma shock in a completely balanced design. Control subjects, who had not been conditioned at 25 days, were conditioned for the first time at 50 days. The results (Denenberg, 1959) are shown in Figure 1. The important thing is that the curves are not parallel (in analysis of variance parlance there is an interaction between early and late shock levels.)

These data made me wonder what would happen if animals were given similar shock at different ages in infancy. Figure 2 shows the results of such an experiment. In infancy mice were given no shock but were placed into the shock apparatus (0.0 ma.), .1, .3, or .5 ma shock. The shock was given when the animals were 2 to 3 days old (designated by Roman numeral I in Figure 2), 8 to 9 days old (II), or 15 to 16 days old (III). A fourth group was neither shocked nor handled (C). When adult, the mice were given avoidance learning training, and the figure shows the mean number of avoidance responses made by the various groups. It is not necessary to consider these findings in detail. Suffice it to say that most of the significance occurred in the interactions.

These two studies were with mice. In 1961 we did an experiment with rats in which pups were handled for the first 10 days of life, the second 10 days, or the first 20 days, while controls were not undisturbed (Denenberg and Karas, 1961). Body weights were obtained at weaning. When adult approximately half the rats in each group were given avoidance learning training while the others were left undisturbed. Body weights were obtained at the end of the avoidance training schedule. The weaning and adult weight data are shown in Figure 3. At weaning the 11-20 group weighed significantly less than the control or 1-10 group, and Group 1-20 weighed significantly less than the other three groups. However, this pattern is not seen in adulthood (Adult Control group). Even

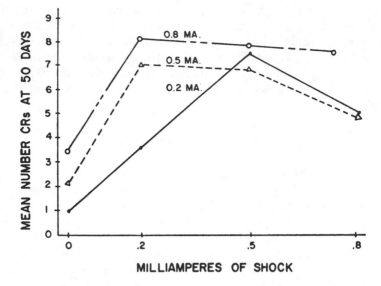

Figure 1. 50-day conditioning scores for three shock levels as a function of shock levels in infancy. From Denenberg (1959).

more interesting, note how the imposition of a stressful task in adulthood (avoidance training) yields an opposite pattern. Thus, we see again an interaction between early experience and adult experience.

Finally, in Figure 4 we see the results of an experiment in which rats were given different intensities of electric shock on Day 2 or Day 4 of life and were then given avoidance learning training in adulthood (Denenberg, 1964). Here there is an interaction between age of administration of shock and shock intensity.

Conclusions

First, since there were significant interactions between early and late experiences in these studies, the data were not consistent with the hypothesis that the effects of early experiences are irreversible—which is an assumption underlying the critical period hypothesis. In 1962 I drew the general conclusion that "there may be as many critical periods as there are combinations of independent-variable parameters and dependent-variable measures. It appears to be more fruitful to study the functional relationships among these variables than to isolate specific critical periods in development" (Denenberg, 1962, p. 815).

A second conclusion was to suggest that the effects of early experi-

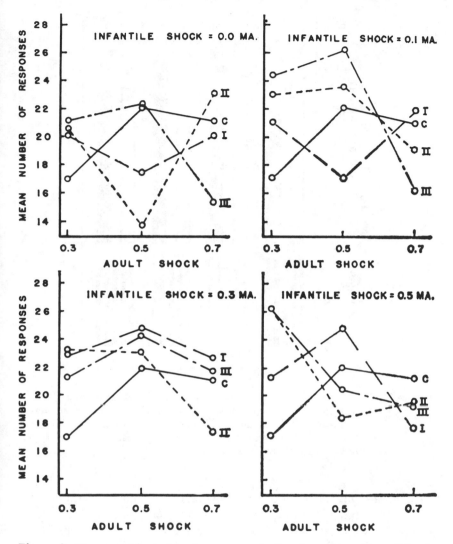

Figure 2. Mean avoidance learning score as a function of intensity of shock given during adulthood for each critical period. Each level of shock given during infancy is graphed separately. The Roman numerals refer to the critical periods when shock was administered in infancy: (I) 2–3 days; (II) 8–9 days, (III)15–16 days. From Denenberg and Bell (1960).

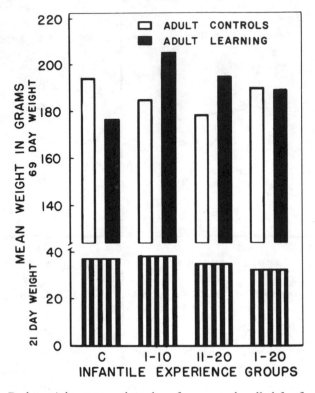

Figure 3. Body weight at 21 and 69 days for groups handled for first 10 days, the second 10 days, or the first 20 days of life; and for a nonhandled control group. The 69-day weights are further classified with respect to whether the rats were tested for avoidance learning in adulthood. From Denenberg and Karas (1961).

ences are not invariant, since later experiences are able to modify earlier ones. Thus, in the Denenberg and Bell study (1960), we concluded "that the age at which stimulation occurs and the magnitude of stimulation during infancy and adulthood, singly or in combination, are major parameters which affect learning scores. Whether the stimulated mice will learn more or less rapidly than the controls is a function of particular combinations of these three variables" (p. 228).

In light of these data and conclusions, which were in the literature in the early 1960s, it was quite startling to read, in 1976, such statements as the following: "There remains, however, one theory which is peculiarly resistant to change: that the environment in the early years exerts a

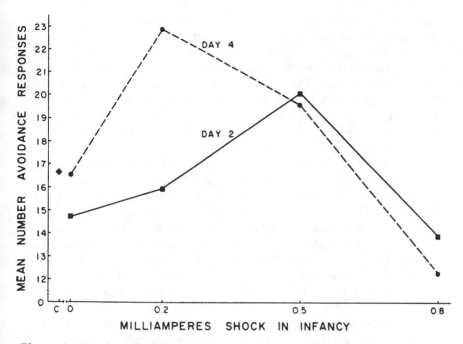

Figure 4. Number of avoidance learning responses in adulthood as a function of infantile shock intensity on Day 2 or Day 4 of life. From unpublished data of Kline and Denenberg as cited in Denenberg (1964).

disproportionate and irreversible effect on a rapidly developing organism, compared with the potential for later environmental influences" (Clarke and Clarke, 1976, p. ix). Or consider this statement: "The critical-period hypothesis maintains that for selected response systems, there is a period of time during which a system is being elaborated most rapidly. Particular environmental events have a strong effect on the system during that special interval, so strong that the resultant dispositions may be difficult or impossible to alter in the future" (Kagan, 1976, p. 98).

The Clarkes and Kagan then go on to show that there is not much evidence supporting the critical period hypothesis. They are, of course, correct.[2] However, this was known, in principle, 15 years earlier from studies with animals. At the pace that modern science moves, this

[2]This does not mean that critical periods do not exist. They are well documented for sensory and perceptual processes. This also appears to be true for first language acquisition. However, in the areas of learning, emotional behavior, and reactivity to stress, the animal research has not found delimited critical periods.

means these researchers are three to five generations behind the times. This is surely the path of intellectual extinction.

From the above comes my next conclusion. Those doing research on developmental behavioral processes with humans generally ignore the animal literature. The basis for this appears to be the belief that the principles of evolution and the concept of a comparative science do not apply to the human species. This is clearly stated by Clarke and Clarke (1976, p. 15): "It seems obvious that the role of early experience in animals is entirely different from in man. With 'nature, red in tooth and claw,' if learning is to play a part in development, it must do so very quickly. . . . Studies of animal behaviour will therefore not be included in this book. This is not to say that they may not offer useful hypotheses, particularly if they are concerned with the lower primates, which may be applied to human data." This is the kind of statement one would have expected from a Victorian gentleman in the post-Darwinian era rather than from serious modern-day researchers.[3]

To end on a positive note, the final conclusion from the data presented above is to suggest that we need to study interactions in order to gain insight and understanding about how development proceeds. Thus, let me now turn to a description of some of our current research in which we have been studying the interactions between early experiences and brain laterality.

Developmental Studies of Brain-Behavior Interaction

Background

Our initial study was to test the hypothesis that the effects of early experiences are asymmetrically distributed between the two hemispheres (Denenberg, Garbanati, Sherman, Yutzey, and Kaplan, 1978). We selected two early experience variables to manipulate: handling and environmental enrichment. Handling consists of removing the pups from the nest cage, leaving the mother in the cage, and placing the pups singly into tin cans where they remain for 3 minutes, after which they are returned to the nest box. This procedure is repeated from the first day of life until Day 20. The pups are weaned on Day 21. Handling has multiple effects upon the later behavior and physiology of the rat. A general conclusion is that handling makes animals less emotional, more explora-

[3]The titles of all publication in the journals *Development Psychology* and *Child Development* were examined for the 5 year period of 1975–1979 inclusive to see how many papers dealt with animal studies. There were 12 animal papers in *Development Psychology*, 7 with primates, 3 with rodents, and 2 with chicks. *Child Development* published 2 papers, 1 on primates and the other on chicks.

tory, and modifies their hypothalamic-pituitary-adrenal axis (Denenberg, 1964, 1967, 1969c, 1975, 1977; Denenberg and Zarrow, 1971).

The second variable, environmental enrichment, was administered between 21–50 days of age. It consists of placing 12 rats into a large cage containing food, water, a variety of "playthings," and a shelf upon which they can climb (Rosenzweig, Bennett, and Diamond, 1972). Animals reared in these environments are superior in problem solving and perceptual tasks and show differences in the weight, thickness, and chemistry of the brain as well (Bennett, 1976; Greenough, 1976; Rosenzweig et al., 1972). Exposure to this environment also reduces the rat's emotional reactivity (Denenberg, 1969c). During this same time interval, control animals are reared in groups of two or three in standard laboratory cages.

Open-Field Activity

The end point used to test these animals in our first experiment was activity in the open field. They were tested for 3 minutes daily for four successive days. This task has been shown to measure both emotional reactivity and exploratory behavior, as defined by factor analysis within the behavioral level and by convergent validity between the behavioral and physiological levels (Denenberg, 1969b; Whimbey and Denenberg, 1967a, 1967b).

Our procedure for determining whether the effects of the early experiences were asymmetrically distributed was to intervene surgically: four male litter-mates had (1) a right neocortical ablation, (2) a left neocortical ablation, (3) a sham operation, or (4) no surgery. After recovering, they were tested in the open field. We found that the sham and non-surgical groups did not differ, and their data were pooled to yield a control group with intact brains. Table 1 summarizes the data.

The interpretation of these data, with respect to laterality and brain dynamics, is based upon the modeling and analysis by Denenberg (1980). There are two rules, however, which are the bases for the interpretations. The first rule is that if a behavior is reduced or disappears following a lesion, conclude that the lesioned area controls that behavior via an activation mechanism. The classic example is that speech disappears after Broca's area is lesioned. The second rule is that if, after a lesion, the behavior appears or increases in magnitude, conclude that the behavior is controlled by the non-lesioned hemisphere and that the lesioned part acts to inhibit the behavior (Denenberg, 1981). For example, injury of the left hemisphere results in the occurrence of a set of emotional behaviors called "catastrophic reactions" (Gainotti, 1972).

The results in Table 1 confirmed our hypothesis, but in a somewhat

Table 1 Open-Field Activity as a Function of Early Experience and Adult Brain Lesion

Days 1–20	Days 21–50	Intact Controls	Right Brain Intact	Left Brain Intact
NH	LC	8.90	27.64	22.33
NH	EE	9.91	27.08	32.89
H	LC	12.51	17.91	36.27
H	EE	17.52	20.42	3.00

NOTE: NH, nonhandled; LC, laboratory cage; H, handled; EE, enriched environment.
SOURCE: Denenberg et al. 1978.

more complex way than we had anticipated. First of all, there is no evidence that nonhandled rats have a lateralized brain, whether they get enrichment after weaning or not. Both handled groups are lateralized but with differing dynamics. For those handled and then placed into standard laboratory cages at weaning, there is greater open-field activity associated with the left hemisphere when the two lesion groups are compared. Since the non-lesioned animals have scores similar to those of littermates with only an intact right hemisphere (i.e., lesioned left hemisphere), the conclusion is that the left hemisphere is being inhibited by the right brain when the two hemispheres are coupled in the intact animal. In contrast, when enrichment is combined with handling, the conclusion is that greater open-field activity is associated with the right hemisphere than the left, and the right hemisphere also controls behavior in the intact brain.

These data are saying several things to us. Firstly, handling, alone or jointly with enrichment, is able to induce lateralization in the brain of the rat. Second, it is possible to increase the behavioral activity of either the right or left hemisphere, depending upon the prior early experience regimen. And third, the right hemisphere is involved in both situations, either as an inhibitor of the left, or as the dominant controller of the intact brain.

Open-field activity measures the dimensions of emotional reactivity and exploratory behavior. We have other findings indicating that each dimension can be lateralized by early experiences (Denenberg, Hofmann, Garbanati, Sherman, Rosen, and Yutzey, 1980; Garbanati, Sherman, Rosen, Hofmann, Yutzey, and Denenberg, 1981; Sherman, Garbanati, Rosen, Hofmann, Yutzey, and Denenberg, 1980). In this paper I will only discuss data concerning the emotionality dimension. In addition to the open-field experiment, we have investigated emotional behavior by means of a taste aversion study, and by examining muricide. These will be described next.

Taste Aversion

Very powerful conditioned emotional responses can be formed in animals by associating certain kinds of novel stimuli with subsequent visceral upset caused by stomach poisoning (Garcia, Hankin, and Rusiniak, 1974). In the rat the association of sweetened milk with poisoning induced by an injection of lithium chloride will result in strong aversive behavior by the animal when it is next presented with the milk (Denenberg et al., 1980; Weinberg, Smotherman, and Levine, 1978). The subjects in this experiment were male rats that had been handled or not disturbed in infancy. When adult, they were trained to drink from a bottle containing sweetened milk. After the second day of milk consumption, they were injected with lithium chloride to induce a visceral disturbance, or with saline, as a control for the effects of the injection and stomach loading. They were then placed back onto a 24-hour water regimen, were given brain surgery 25 days later, and were tested for retention of the taste aversion response four weeks later. Therefore, these animals had been given one association between the sweetened milk and the stomach poisoning while their brains were intact, and were not exposed to the sweetened milk again until more than 50 days later, after neocortical ablations. Thus, the question asked by this design is: If handled and nonhandled rats learn a conditioned fear response with an intact brain, and one hemisphere is subsequently destroyed, what is the nature of the retention of the remaining hemisphere?

In the Denenberg et al. (1980) paper these data were presented as curves. In order to keep this set of data parallel with data in Tables 1 and 3 the mean amount of milk ingested during the last 6 days of testing is given in Table 2. Only the data from the lithium chloride injection are reported here. There was also a significant effect from the saline injection, but that is not relevant to this discussion. Those data are described in detail in Denenberg et al. (1980).

There were no differences among the three nonhandled groups. However, all three handled groups differed from each other. Those with an intact right hemisphere (left-brain lesion) ingested the least amount of milk during the retention trials, thus indicating that they had the greatest amount of fear associated with the sweetened milk. The finding that those with intact brains consumed the largest amount of milk is of special interest since it indicates that the intact brain exceeds the behavior of either hemisphere. One can account for this by assuming that each hemi-

Table 2 Amount of Milk Consumed (ml) after Lithium Chloride Injestion as a Function of Handling in Infancy and Adult Brain Lesion

Days 1–20	Intact Controls	Right Brain Intact	Left Brain Intact
NH	23.9	23.7	23.8
H	28.7	21.7	25.6

SOURCE: Denenberg et al., 1980.

sphere acts to inhibit the fear response of the other. In that sense, then, the whole brain is less "afraid" than either of its component parts.

Muricide

Muricide, or mouse killing, is a spontaneous species-specific behavior which is not dependent upon food deprivation for its occurrence. We selected this behavior as another measure of the emotional reactivity of the rat (Garbanati et al., 1981). We used the identical design as depicted in Table 1: Rats were handled or not disturbed in infancy; at weaning approximately half of each group were placed into enriched environments while the others were group housed in standard laboratory cages. All animals were maintained alike after 50 days of age. When adult, they had brain surgery, and several months thereafter they were tested for muricide. The incidence of killing is summarized in Table 3.

In the standard laboratory rat (i.e., Nonhandled in infancy and reared in a Laboratory Cage after weaning) there is no evidence of laterality. However, the single-hemisphere groups had a significantly lower incidence of muricide than the intact-brain group. This leads to the conclusion that when the two hemispheres are coupled, they act to facilitate the killing behavior of the intact brain.

There are no significant effects among the three brain groups in the Nonhandled Enrichment condition, even though the means suggest that the left hemisphere is more likely to kill than the right.

There is a significant effect for those Handled and then reared in Laboratory Cages with the right hemisphere having a higher muricide rate than the left. Since in the intact animal the incidence of mouse killing is similar to what was found for those with only an intact left brain, the conclusion is that the left hemisphere inhibits the killing response of the right hemisphere when the two are coupled.

Finally, no significant differences were found among the groups reared

Table 3 Incidence of Muricide as a Function of Early Experiences and Adult Brain Lesion

Days 1–20	Days 21–50	Intact Controls	Right Brain Intact	Left Brain Intact
NH	LC	96.0	75.0	68.8
NH	EE	79.4	73.7	94.7
H	LC	78.0	94.6	67.6
H	EE	62.9	61.1	57.1

SOURCE: Garbanati et al., 1981.

under the combination of Handling and Enrichment. However, there was an interaction between the site of the lesion and the early experience variables. Lesioning the right hemisphere of the Nonhandled Enriched group resulted in a 94.7 percent incidence of killing, not different from the 96.0 percent value found for the Nonhandled Lab Cage control; but adding the experience of handling to this condition dropped the percentage to 57.1, a significant reduction. Similarly, lesioning the left hemisphere of the Handled Lab Cage group did not influence the incidence of killing (94.6 percent), while the addition of enrichment to handling reduced the percentage significantly (61.1 percent).

Conclusions

First, in three separate experiments handling in infancy has acted to reduce the emotional reactivity of the left hemisphere, relative to the right. In the open–field study, handled rats with an intact left brain were more active than those with only a right hemisphere. When taste aversion was investigated, handled rats that had a left hemisphere alone ingested more milk than those with only a right hemisphere, thereby revealing less conditioned fear. And in the muricide study, the handled left-hemisphere group had a lesser killing incidence than did the right-hemisphere group.

Second, in the taste aversion and muricide studies, the less emotional left hemisphere inhibited the more emotional right hemisphere when the two were coupled in the intact brain. In the open–field study there was also cross-hemispheric inhibition, but it went in the opposite direction, with the right hemisphere inhibiting the left. This leads to the conclusion that cross-hemispheric inhibition is a major feature of emotional behavior.

Third, the findings that the stronger emotional responses of handled animals are in the right hemisphere and that the two hemispheres interact via cross-hemispheric inhibition are similar in nature to what we know about brain laterality and emotional behavior in the human (for reviews, see Gainotti [1979] and Wexler [1980]). Clinical studies have found that "catastrophic reactions" and depressive responses occur when the left hemisphere is injured or temporarily immobilized (e.g., by an intra-carotid amytal injection), while injury or immobilization of the right hemisphere brings about an "indifference reaction" and euphoria (Gainotti, 1972; Perria, Rosadini, and Rossi, 1961; Rossi and Rosadini, 1967). The emotional response of those with left-hemisphere damage is greater than in those with damage to the right side of the brain and includes swearing, anxiety reactions, and tears. For an extended discussion on this issue, see Denenberg (1981).

Fourth, early experiences are able to induce brain asymmetry and will also modify the asymmetry already existing (i.e., for certain measures the standard laboratory rat already has a lateralized brain [Denenberg et al., 1980; Sherman et al., 1980]).

Fifth, our initial hypothesis, that the effects of early experiences are asymmetrically distributed in the brain, has been amply confirmed.

Facilitating Infant and Early Childhood Development: Implications and Speculations

Let me suggest several ways that the material I have discussed may be of value in relation to the topic of this volume. First of all, experiences in early life literally bring about changes in the manner that the rat's brain is organized. A number of years ago, neuroendocrinologists discovered that the function of the sex hormones in the prenatal or perinatal period was to organize the animal's brain, making it either a male or a female brain. Experience appears to play a similar organizing role, at least with respect to emotional behavior. These findings strongly imply that the brain of the human infant may also be influenced by its experiences during ontogeny, with the consequence that different kinds of brain organization may ensue.

There are actually a few sets of data with humans that support the suggestion I have just made. Recall that several Western researchers have found that lesions to the left hemisphere bring about a depressive reaction while right-brain lesions result in a euphoric response (Gainotti, 1972; Perria et al, 1961; Rossi and Rosadini, 1967). However, an opposite pattern has been found with Japanese subjects. Tsunoda and Oka (1976) studied native Japanese patients who had had their right and left hemispheres anesthetized by injections into the right or left carotid artery. All 44 patients showed euphoric reactions when the left hemisphere was anesthetized, and 5 patients also showed a depressive response to an injection into the right hemisphere.

Tsunoda (1973) has also reported another major difference between Japanese and Western brain organization with respect to processing of vowel sounds. Westerners process these sounds in their right hemispheres. However, with native Japanese these sounds are processed by the left brain. In contrast, Japanese whose native language is a Western one (English, Portugese, Spanish) process vowel sound in their right hemisphere, thus eliminating genetic factors as a determiner of this difference. Tsunoda (1973) points out that vowel sounds in Japanese are meaningful words which can be perceived categorically, and this may be part of the reason for the major difference in hemispheric site.

In a later paper Tsunoda (1978) presented verbal, emotive, animal, and mechanical sounds in a dichotic competition test. His subjects were Westerners, native-born Japanese, and Japanese whose mother tongue was a Western language. The general findings were that those whose native language was a Western one processed the vowel, animal, and emotive sounds in their right hemispheres, while the native-born Japanese processed these sounds in their left hemispheres.

These findings seem to indicate that language and cultural factors can significantly influence how the brain organizes emotional actions and perceptions and vowel processing. However, caution is needed. Though Tsunoda's work appears solid, there has not been an independent replication as yet, and that will be necessary before one can argue that there is a substantial relationship, in principle, between his work and our animal studies on early experience and brain laterality.

A second point is that one cannot use a learning model to interpret the effects of early experience (Clarke and Clarke, 1976). We have known for a long time that some early experiences are stressors which cause changes in the reactivity of the hypothalamic–pituitary adrenal system (Denenberg, Brumaghim, Haltmeyer, and Zarrow, 1967; Denenberg and Zarrow, 1971; Levine, 1969; Levine and Mullins, 1966; Zarrow, Campbell, and Denenberg, 1972). These new data tell us that early experiences are also affecting brain organization, thus modifying the most important biological substrate we possess. Therefore, a psychobiological model is necessary.

To return to a point I made in the introduction, these data require us to use an interactional framework for our models and theories. That is, we must think in systems terms rather than in linear cause–effect terms. To illustrate, note in Tables 1 and 3 that the combined effects of handling and environmental enrichment yield a configuration of findings which cannot be predicted from knowing the effects of each variable alone. These independent variables occur at different times in the animal's developmental history, thus imparting a dynamic quality to the temporal dimension over and above that due to maturational factors.

A derivative of the above comments is that different experiences may have different kinds of effects upon brain organization and behavior, as a function of what has occurred in the past and what will occur in the future.

The final point I wish to make is to repeat a conviction I expressed a number of years ago at the Minnesota Symposium on Child Psychology: "If real progress is to be made in understanding ontogeny of human development, I believe that it is absolutely necessary for those working with animals and those working with the human to collaborate in active research programs" (Denenberg, 1969a, p. 43).

And what if developmental researchers continue to ignore animal studies and the biological substrates of behavior? The following prophetic words are worthy of serious contemplation: "Specialists determined to remain within the boundaries of their own discipline remain irremediably short-sighted, because it is only through contact with other branches of scientific knowledge that real progress can be achieved. Without recourse to biology, logic and mathematics, developmental psychology can again only be descriptive" (Piaget and Inhelder, 1969, p. 148).

Summary and Conclusions

Research studies with animals in the late 1950s and early 1960s of the effects of early experience found significant interactions between early and late experiences. Such findings (1) are inconsistent with the hypothesis that the effects of early experience are irreversible—which is an assumption underlying the critical period hypothesis; and (2) suggest that the effects of early experiences are not invariant, since later experiences can modify earlier ones. Approximately 15 years later researchers studying humans came to the same general conclusion, and in doing so they criticized the animal research as being incorrect or not relevant. It is pointed out that this studied avoidance of information available in the animal developmental literature puts the student of human developmental processes three to five generations behind the leading edge of science, and may result in the intellectual extinction of this species of researcher.

An argument is advanced that the linear cause-effect paradigm must be abandoned in favor of a more complex and inclusive systems approach to the study of behavioral development.

Recent animal research has found that early experiences can markedly influence brain laterality. Some of the conclusions from these findings are: (1) hemispheric control of emotional behavior appears to be similar in animals and humans; (2) early life experiences may act to change the nature of brain organization; (3) a learning model is wholly inadequate for interpreting the effects of early experiences; and (4) a systems interaction perspective is needed to account for the animal data, thus strongly suggesting that a model of equal or greater complexity is necessary for an understanding of human development.

References

Bennett, E. L. Cerebral effects of differential experience and training. In M. R. Rosenzweig and E. L. Bennett (Eds.), *Neural mechanisms of learning and memory*. Cambridge, MA: MIT Press, 1976.

Bertalanffy, L. V. Chance or law. In A. Koestler and J. R. Smythies (Eds.), *Beyond reductionism*. Boston: Beacon, 1969.

Bunge, M. *Treatise on basic philosophy* (Vol. 4); *Ontology II: A world of systems*. Boston: D. Reidel, 1979.

Clarke, A. M., and Clarke, A. D. B. *Early experiences: Myth and evidence*. London: Open Books, 1976.

Denenberg, V. H. Interactive effects of infantile and adult shock levels upon learning. *Psychological Reports, 1959, 5,* 357–364.

Denenberg, V. H. An attempt to isolate critical periods of development in the rat. *Journal of Comparative and Physiological Psychology, 1962, 55,* 813–815.

Denenberg, V. H. Critical periods, stimulus input, and emotional reactivity: A theory of infantile stimulation. *Psychological Review, 1964, 71,* 335–351.

Denenberg, V. H. Stimulation in infancy, emotional reactivity, and exploratory behavior. In D. C. Glass (Ed.), *Neurophysiology and Emotion*. New York: Rockefeller University Press, 1967.

Denenberg, V. H. Animal studies of early experience: Some principles which have implications for human development. In J. P. Hill (Ed.), *Minnesota Symposium on Child Psychology*. Minneapolis: University of Minnesota Press, 1969. (a)

Denenberg, V. H. Open-field behavior in the rat: What does it mean? *Annals of the New York Academy of Sciences, 1969, 159,* 852–859. (b)

Denenberg, V. H. The effects of early experience. In E.S.E. Hafez (Ed.), *The behavior of domestic animals*. London: Bailliere, Tindall and Cassell, 1969. (c)

Denenberg, V. H. Experimental programming of life histories and the creation of individual differences. In M.R. Jones (Ed.), *Miami Symposium on the Prediction of Behavior: Effects of Early Experience*. Coral Gables, FL: University Miami Press, 1970.

Denenberg, V. H. Effects of exposure to stressors in early life upon later behavioral and biological processes. In L. Levi (Ed.) *Society, stress and disease: Childhood and adolescence* (Vol. 2) New York: Oxford University Press, 1975.

Denenberg, V. H. Interactional effects in early experience research. In A. Oliverio (Ed.), *Genetics, environment, and intelligence*. Amsterdam: Elsevier, 1977.

Denenberg, V. H. Paradigms and paradoxes in the study of behavioral development. In E. B. Thoman (Ed.), *Origins of the infant's social responsiveness*. Hillsdale, N.J.: Erlbaum Associates, 1979.

Denenberg, V. H. General systems theory, brain organization, and early experience. *American Journal of Physiology*, 1980, *283*, R3–R13; or *American Journal of Physiology Regulatory Integrative Comparative Physiology*, 1980, 7, R3–R13.

Denenberg, V. H. Hemispheric laterality in animals and the effects of early experiences. *Behavioral and Brain Sciences*, 1981, *4*, 1–49.

Denenberg, V. H., and Bell, R. W. Critical periods for the effects of infantile experience on adult learning. *Science*, 1960, *131*, 227–228.

Denenberg, V. H., Brumaghim, J. T., Haltmeyer, G. C., and Zarrow, M. X. Increased adrenocortical activity in the neonatal rat following handling. *Endocrinology*, 1967, *81*, 1047–1052.

Denenberg, V. H., Garbanati, J., Sherman, G., Yutzey, D. A., and Kaplan, R. Infantile stimulation induces brain lateralization in rats. *Science*, 1978, *201*, 1150–1152.

Denenberg, V. H., Hoffman, M., Garbanati, J. A., Sherman, G. F., Rosen, G. D., and Yutzey, D. A. Handling in infancy, taste aversion, and brain laterality in rats. *Brain Research*, 1980, *200*, 123–133.

Denenberg, V. H., and Karas, G. G. Interactive effects of infantile and adult experiences upon weight gain and mortality in the rat. *Journal of Comparative and Physiological Psychology*, 1961, *54*, 685–689.

Denenberg, V. H., and Zarrow, M. X. Effects of handling in infancy upon adult behavior and adrenocortical activity: Suggestions for a neuroendocrine mechanism. In D. N. Walcher and D. L. Peters (Eds.), *Early childhood: The development of self regulatory mechanisms*. New York: Academic Press, 1971.

Gainotti, G. Emotional behavior and hemispheric side of the lesion. *Cortex*, 1972, *8*, 41–55.

Gainotti, G. Affectivity and brain dominance: A survey. In J. Obiols, C. Ballus, E. Gonzalez Monclus, and J. Pujol (Eds.), *Biological psychiatry today*. Amsterdam: Elsevier, North-Holland Press, 1979.

Garbanati, J. A., Sherman, G. F., Rosen, G. D., Hofmann, M. Yutzey, D. A., and Denenberg, V. H. *Handling in infancy, brain laterality, and muricide in rats*. Unpublished manuscript, 1981.

Garcia, J., Hankin, W. G., and Rusiniak, K. Behavioral regulation of the milieu interne in man and rat. *Science*, 1974, *185*, 824–831.

Greenough, W. Enduring brain effects of differential experience and training. In M. R. Rosenzweig and E. L. Bennett (Eds.), *Neural mechanisms of learning and memory*. Cambridge: MIT Press, 1976.

Kagan, J. Resilience and continuity in psychological development. In A. M. Clarke and A. D. B. Clarke (Eds.), *Early experiences: Myth and evidence*. London: Open Books, 1976.

Levine, S. An endocrine theory of infantile stimulation. In A. Ambrose (Ed.), *Stimulation in early infancy*. London: Academic Press, 1969.

Levine, S., and Mullins, R. F. Hormonal influence on brain organization in infant rats. *Science*, 1966, *152*, 1585–1592.

Perria, L., Rosadini, G., and Rossi, G. F. Determination of side of cerebral dominance with amobarbital. *Archives of Neurology*, 1961, *4*, 173–181.

Piaget, J., and Inhelder, B. The gaps in empiricism. In A. Koestler and J. R. Smythies (Eds.), *Beyond reductionism*. New York: Macmillan, 1969.

Rosenzweig, M. R., Bennett, E. L., and Diamond, M. C. Brain changes in response to experience. *Scientific American*, 1972, *226*, 22–29.

Rossi, G. F., and Rosadini, G. Experimental analysis of cerebral dominance in man. In C. H. Millikan and F. L. Darley (Eds.), *Brain mechanisms underlying speech and language*. New York: Grune and Stratton, 1967.

Sameroff, A. J. Early influences on development: Fact or fancy? *Merrill-Palmer Quarterly*, 1975, *21*, 267–294.

Sameroff, A. J., and Chandler, M. J. Reproductive risk and the continuum of caretaking casualty. In F. D. Horowitz, M. Hetherington, S. Scarr-Salapatek, and G. Siegel (Eds.), *Review of child development research*. Vol. 4. Chicago: University of Chicago Press, 1975.

Sherman, G. F., Garbanati, J. A., Rosen, G. D., Hoffman, M., Yutzey, D. A., and Denenberg, V. H. Brain and behavior asymmetries in spatial preference in rats. *Brain Research*, 1980, *192*, 61–67.

Tsunoda, T. The characteristic pattern of cerebral dominance for vowel sounds found in second-generation Japanese. In M. Arslan and V. Ricci (Eds.), *Otorhinolaryngology*. Proceedings of the 10th World Congress. Amsterdam: Excerpta Medica, 1973.

Tsunoda, T. Logos and pathos: Difference in the mechanism of vowel sound and natural sound perception in Japanese and Westerners, and in regard to mental structure. *Journal of Dental Health*, 1978, *28*, 131–139.

Tsunoda, T., and Oka, M. Lateralization for emotion in human brain and auditory cerebral dominance. *Proceedings of the Japan Academy*, 1976, *52*, 528–531.

Weinberg, J., Smotherman, W. P., and Levine, S. Early handling effects on neophobia and conditioned taste aversion. *Physiology and Behavior*, 1978, *20*, 589–596.

Weiss, P. The living system: Determinism stratified. In A. Koestler and J. R. Smythies (Eds.), *Beyond reductionism*. Boston: Beacon, 1969.

Wexler, B. E. Cerebral laterality and psychiatry: A review of the literature. *American Journal of Psychiatry*, 1980, *137*, 279–291.

Whimbey, A. E., and Denenberg, V. H. Experimental programming of life histories: The factor structure underlying experimentally created individual differences. *Behaviour*, 1967, *29*, 296–314. (a)

Whimbey, A. E., and Denenberg, V. H. Two independent behavioral dimensions in open-field performance. *Journal of Comparative and Physiological Psychology*, 1967, *63*, 500–504. (b)

Zarrow, M. X., Campbell, P. S., and Denenberg, V. H. Handling in infancy: Increased levels of the hypothalamic corticotropin releasing factor (CRF) following exposure to a novel situation. *Proceedings of the Society for Experimental Biology and Medicine*, 1972, *141*, 356–358.

Plasticity in Development:
Implications for Intervention

Marian Sigman

The concept of plasticity is central to all biological and psychological studies of development. The concept signifies that the living organism can be modified by the environment. Any time we measure development or behavior of a subject in response to a stimulus, we are measuring plasticity.

Studies of infant development, whether concerned with normal or high-risk infants, frequently focus on the plasticity of infant behaviors in response to stimulation. All studies of infant learning and habituation measure short-term plasticity. In determining the nature of associations between rearing conditions and infant development, we assume that we are assessing a more stable outcome of the infant's plasticity. Investigations of infant development have been quite sophisticated in delineating environmental effects on the infant's behaviors over both short and extended time periods.

Thus, the concept of plasticity is critical for our understanding of early development. Furthermore, some degree of infant plasticity must be assumed as a basis for intervention. Intervention is only appropriate if the infant can be modified by the environment. What is needed for intervention is some small degree of continuity of development and a large degree of plasticity. The lack of continuity in development from infancy to adulthood is often lamented, and we are told that it is useless to intervene in a system that has so few links to later life. However, if continuity from infancy to later life were too strong there would be little room for change. The very plasticity of infancy may be partial justification for early intervention.

The purpose of this chapter is to examine the degree to which developmental plasticity has been demonstrated. I will review briefly what is

Much of the researcher reported in this chapter is the result of an enduring and enriching collaboration with Arthur Parmelee, Leila Beckwith, and Sarale Cohen. Data analyses were planned and implemented by Alan Forsythe and Linda Moody. The research was supported by NIH-NICHD Contract No. 1-HD-3-2776, "Diagnostic and Intervention Studies of High-Risk Infants" and continues to be supported by a grant from the W.T. Grant Foundation.

known about the effects of damage to the central nervous system, environmental influences on normal individuals and environmental remediations of brain damage. Based on the data of other investigators, I will argue that there is a significant degree of plasticity in the development of most infants. Furthermore, both the nature of this plasticity and its limitations in high-risk infants will be viewed from the perspective of our own longitudinal research.

In reviewing studies of environmental influence and remediation in children, the extensive literature on neurological and behavioral plasticity in animals will also be discussed. Many researchers have investigated behavioral and physiological plasticity in animals because there are fewer limitations on experimental design and methodology than in experiments with humans.

There are two major experimental limitations on studies of human children. First, in measuring environmental effects, individuals cannot be assigned randomly to treatment conditions. We can only assess the effects of varying rearing conditions on the individuals who have experienced these conditions. The assumption is often made that such individuals are similar at the time of birth. The empirical evidence invalidates this assumption. We know that poor people have babies who are sicker at birth; that schizophrenic and alcoholic mothers tend to have birth complications; that the mothers of infants in institutions have had less than optimal prenatal care. The assumption of random selection can never be made, and this limits our knowledge concerning infant plasticity.

Second, the effects of early trauma on the nervous system cannot be described precisely. In neurophysiological studies of animals or studies of brain-damaged adults, the exact localization of lesions can often be specified. In assessing the effects of early trauma, we can only assume that the nervous system may have been damaged. In those individuals who show deficits, some estimate can be made on the basis of the nature of the deficit and corroborating evidence from EEG's or EMI scans. However, this is always an imprecise localization of damage.

The random assignment of subjects to treatments and the localization of lesions is more precisely controlled in animal studies. On the other hand, the applicability of animal studies to the issue of plasticity in the human infant may be somewhat limited by the inferior cognitive capacities of animals.

Recovery from Lesions in the Central Nervous System

Animal Studies

The purpose of many animal studies has been to delineate the areas of localization of particular functions and the extent to which these functions can be served by alternate areas of the brain. In order to investigate functional localization, precise lesions are made in the central nervous system and a variety of behaviors and skills are assessed. Deficits in skills previously shown by the animal are attributed to the lesion and the area of the lesion is considered to be responsible for this function. Recovery of function is attributed to a number of mechanisms, usually involving either a substitution of neurological pathways or behavioral strategies.

Based on results from studies over many years, we have considered young animals less vulnerable since deficits from similar lesions have seemed less profound (Kennard, 1936, 1938; Rosner, 1974). The infant brain has been considered more plastic in that remaining tissue more easily assumes functions normally carried out by damaged regions.

There now appear to be several problems with the conclusions drawn from the comparative studies of recovery of function in immature and mature animals. First, disruption of function may be due to acute effects of surgery. Attribution of functions based on behavioral deficits may be erroneous. Recovery of functions may be the result of the animal's general recovery (Von Monakow, 1914) rather than any real plasticity in the nervous system. Young animals may simply recover more quickly from acute effects.

A second problem derives from the timing of the outcome assessments. If all animals are compared as adults, the immature animals will have had longer to recover from the effects of the surgery than the adults. On the other hand, some systems may not show deficits until the animal has matured. Goldman (1974) has identified deficits in animals whose functioning appeared normal at earlier ages following lesions in the dorsolateral frontal lobe. She suggests that the nervous system may have to mature for the deficit to become apparent.

The animal studies do show that recovery of function is possible but the mechanisms for this recovery are poorly understood. Four different mechanisms have been suggested (Goldberger, 1974): (1) equipotentiality, (2) vicarious function, (3) substitution, and (4) functional reorganization. The first two models postulate that a previously existing system takes over a new function, with the equipotentiality model rejecting the notion of localization (Lashley, 1938). Substitution refers to behavioral change whereas functional reorganization implies some reorganization of the nervous system. This has been attributed to the growth of collateral axons (Moore, Bjorklund, and Stenevi, 1971). However, there is little evidence that these new neural connections are functionally effective and some investigators even suggest that they may impede reorganization (Rosner, 1974). Thus, the basis for recovery of function is completely unknown and probably varies from one system to another.

To summarize, studies of recovery of function in brain-lesioned animals indicate that plasticity of function is common but the basis for this plasticity in brain or behavior is unknown. Furthermore, the effects of early lesions on maturing animals are virtually unknown from the research to date; most studies have used mature animals. In addition, the complexity of the behaviors affected is necessarily limited by the species of animal selected for study. The most sophisticated tasks explored are delayed response and discrimination learning in monkeys while most lesion studies measure much simpler learning tasks. In early intervention, our efforts are directed at enhancing relatively sophisticated cognitive skills and concepts, whose localization must be more diffuse. Thus, the experimental advantages of the animal model are somewhat offset by the inferior capacities of animals. For this reason, the results of animal studies may have only limited applicability for our understanding of plasticity in infant development.

Recovery from Brain Damage in Children

The studies of brain-lesioned animals are paralleled by investigations of recovery from brain damage in children and adults. Developmental differences have been investigated directly, particularly in the period since Lenenberg (1967) proposed a critical period for equipotentiality of the two hemispheres for language. This hypothesis generated a series of studies, most of which indicate that there is some specialization of the hemispheres at birth and that this lateralization is increased with experience.

In all investigations of brain-damaged children, substantial recovery is observed. Geshwind (1974) cites nearly 100 percent recovery from acquired aphasia in children. Although this figure is undoubtedly too high, most researchers report habitual improvement of childhood aphasia if the damage is not massive, and more substantial recovery than in adults. Furthermore, language develops in children in spite of very early left-hemispheric lesions (Hécaen, 1976).

There are several problems in understanding the data concerning recovery from brain damage in children. One difficulty stems from the nature of the data base. Many research reports use clinical observations so that the extensiveness and reliability of measures varies from one subject to another. A second major problem is the difficulty of localizing the actual lesion. In most cases, the lesion is attributed to one hemisphere based on observations of motor incoordination on one side of the child's body. However, there is no way of knowing the extent of the damage, the state of the other hemisphere, and whether the connections between hemispheres are intact.

To overcome some of these experimental problems, the abilities of children who have had either the left or right hemisphere removed have been compared. In most investigations, hemispherectomies have not resulted in any decrement in abilities. However, in all cases, the hemisphere was damaged previous to the operation, so that the child's functioning may have improved simply as a consequence of decreased seizure activity. In general the abilities of children missing the left hemisphere are similar to those of children missing the right hemisphere, although Dennis and Whitaker (1976) report a problem with syntax in two 10-year-old children whose left hemispheres were removed before language acquisition, and this was not observed in a 10-year-old whose right hemisphere had been removed.

Prenatal and Perinatal Disorders

The effects of central nervous system damage due to congenital malformations are frequently less benign than the effects of brain damage following early trauma. There is a high incidence of severe intellectual and physical disorders in children who suffer cranial meningoceles and encephaloceles in association with spina bifida conditions (Laurence and Weeks, 1971; Tew and Laurence, 1972). However, there are some children with these malformations who develop normally. Fishman and Polkes (1974) reported that 12 of 21 children suffering from hydrocephalus and myelomeningoceles or encephaloceles who were followed longitudinally scored within the normal range on developmental assessments at 18 months of age.

Variability in intellectual functioning is also limited in children suffering enzyme- and chromosome-based disorders, which are thought to create irreversible changes in the central nervous system (see Kopp and Parmelee, 1979). Children with untreated phenylketonuria or children whose dietary treatment is begun after 6 months of age show lower intellectual functioning than children whose retardation was prevented by early dietary treatment (Steinhausen, 1974). Furthermore, children who suffer from Down's syndrome, and other chromosomal abnormalities, do not show age-appropriate intellectual achievements no matter how they are reared. Thus, there is clearly a limit to the plasticity of development based partly on the nature and extensiveness of central nervous system dysfunction.

On the other hand, traumatic perinatal factors, such as preterm birth and associated complications, are correlated with a wide range of outcomes. Although the incidence of developmental disorders is greater in preterm infants (Caputo and Mandell, 1970; Davies and Stewart, 1975; Harper and Wiener, 1965; Hunt, 1981), many infants who experience postnatal medical complications develop normally. To some extent, early medical complications may cause only temporary dysfunction in the central nervous system although these temporary difficulties may have sustained effects in some rearing conditions. This issue will be discussed in more detail later in this chapter.

Effects of Early Experience on Development

A second source of information regarding developmental plasticity is the evidence concerning the effects of variations in rearing conditions on the development of normal animals and children. The studies of young animals and children have identified differential effects of varied rearing conditions on cognitive and behavioral characteristics of adults.

Animal Studies

Effects of sensory deprivation.
Investigations of the effects of early sensory deprivation on functional attributes have also provided evidence of neurophysiological plasticity. Hubel and Wiesel (1962; Wiesel and Hubel, 1965) discovered a sensitive period when appropriate visual experience must occur for the visual system to develop normally. The effects of monocular deprivation are more permanent than binocular deprivation. This may be because visual pathways compete for cortical sites during the sensitive period. With binocular deprivation, both eyes still have to form connections, whereas with monocular deprivation only one eye may be represented in all locations in the visual cortex, or only one set of neurons may be able to function.

The extent to which cortical cells are actually modified by experience is still undetermined. It is clear that raising kittens in a visual environment containing only vertical stripes produces a visual cortex sensitive only to these orientations and blind to horizontal stimuli (Blakemore and Cooper, 1970; Hirsh and Spinelli, 1970). Whether cortical cells are actually adjusted to verticality or those sensitive to horizontal orientations die off is open to question. However, several other studies have demonstrated that idiosyncratic visual experiences increase the number of cortical cells which are rare (Pettigrew and Freeman, 1973) or less frequently found (Spinelli and Jensen, 1979) in kittens who have normal experiences.

The significance of these results for studies of human development must be considered. The sensitive period for this type of plasticity is undoubtedly determined by central nervous system maturation. These findings have emerged from studies of the visual system in the cat, in which neural proliferation occurs postnatally. The human visual system is largely formed at birth. Furthermore, other species, such as rabbits, do not show the same sensitivity to visual deprivation.

Finally, the cortical cells studies in these visual deprivation studies are those located in the striate cortex. Principles governing the development of one system may not be applicable to another. Intervention efforts with infants are usually aimed at affecting cognitive processes, whose control must rest in association cortex. Thus, the type of sensitive period and plasticity demonstrated for the striate cortex and simple visual functions may not be applicable to our understanding of plasticity of higher-order behaviors.

Effects of general deprivation and enrichment.

Studies that have varied the overall level of stimulation and observed corresponding differences in the brains and behaviors of rats (Rosenzweig, Bennett, and Diamond, 1967) do seem to be relevant to our intervention efforts. Denenberg (1977) has identified clear effects of early handling on the behaviors of rats in novel situations. Some of the "enrichment" studies have been criticized on the grounds that all laboratory animals are more or less deprived since the laboratory situation is so much less complex than natural rearing conditions. On the other hand, the principle concerning variations in stimulus conditions would seem to hold, although increases in stimulation may not have beneficial effects beyond a certain level.

A more serious problem with these studies from our point of view is the question of species differences. Most studies have used either laboratory rats or mice, although one investigation with kittens has reported similar results. However, Sackett (1981) has pointed to startling differences in the effects of isolation on the subsequent social behaviors of rhesus monkeys and pigtail maeques. Even within a species, there were variations in effects for males and females. If it is difficult to generalize about an environmental effect from males to females of one species or from rhesus to pigtail maeques, then it is that much more difficult to know how such effects apply to human infants.

Effects of Early Experience on Children

The developmental studies of infants have followed three experimental design forms. First, a number of studies have compared the outcome of groups of infants reared in different environments. The early, classic studies using this paradigm, like those of Goldfarb (1943), Spitz (1945), and Dennis (1960) have shown poorer social, cognitive, and motor abilities in infants raised in institutions than in home-reared infants. One problem with this experimental paradigm has been mentioned in the introduction: Infants in institutions are likely to have had constitutional, prenatal, and perinatal histories different from those of infants reared with their families.

A second method for studying the effects of early experience has been the introduction of systematic modification in the practices and environments of the institutions. Hunt and his colleagues (Hunt, 1979) have been foremost in planning and implementing early intervention as an experimental technique for measuring plasticity in various developmental systems. These investigators and others (White and Held, 1966) report accelerations in the subjects' development as compared with control subjects. In addition, there appears to be some specificity in the impact of particular interventions on particular behavioral systems.

Although such studies clearly indicate that the behavior of infants reared in deprived environments can be affected by enrichment of these environments, the effects of increasing stimulation may not be continuous. Thus, extra amounts of caretaking may have beneficial effects on institution-reared infants but may not influence the child raised in an average expectable environment.

However, more recent investigations have indicated that the quality of the caretaking environment is related to the child's level of development even in home-reared children (Bradley and Caldwell, 1976; Clarke-Stewart, 1973; Wachs, Uzgiris, and Hunt, 1971). Furthermore, there is some specificity of effects in the home as well. Yarrow, Rubenstein, and Pederson (1975) have shown that the nature of the infant's inanimate environment affects the infant's motivation and cognitive capacities. The quality of the animate environment tends to influence the child's level of vocalizations. A recent study (Lewis and Coates, 1980) suggests that the important variable in the caregiving environment is not the overall level of stimulation provided by the caregiver but the extent to which the caregiver's responses are contingent to the infant's behaviors.

Thus, this current series of studies indicates quite clearly that the nature of the environment and, particularly, the nature of the caretaker–infant relationship, affects the infant's development. Of course one can still argue that the caretaker–infant relationship is influenced not only by the caretaker but by the infant as well. It is a shibboleth in our field that different infants elicit different responses. The effects of the caretaking environment on outcome may be partly a function of initial infant characteristics and, thus, evidence of continuity rather than plasticity. We will only be able to unravel the threads of this tangled relationship when we can identify similar infants in varying environments who have grown up differently or different infants who have grown up similarly.

Environmental Remediation of Brain Damage

Animal Studies

Since environmental enrichment seems to enhance adaptive behavior in normal animals, the effects of environmental variations on brain-lesioned rats are of considerable interest. Enriched environment, provided postoperatively, seems to enhance some of the skills of brain-lesioned animals (Finger, 1978). In several studies (Schwartz, 1964; Will, Rosenzweig, and Bennett, 1976) general learning abilities of subjects operated upon in infancy have been measured. It was found that rats permitted greater perceptual and motor exploration performed better than animals reared in individual or standard laboratory cages. In one of these studies, the rats with lesions raised in enriched environments performed better than nonlesioned animals reared in standard cages.

Thus, stimulating conditions seem to overcome some of the effects of brain lesions inflicted at both early and later ages (Will and Rosenzweig, 1976). On the other hand, Bland and Cooper (1969) reported no improvement in pattern discrimination after 11 months of postsurgical enrichment in rats who had lesions in the visual cortex. Finger (1978) suggests that the differences in results between various studies may arise from the nature of the task. Specific sensory tasks, with focal cortical involvement, may not be remediated by enriched environments. Such nonspecific enrichment may enhance the animal's general adaptive capacity which is reflected in more general learning tasks, a very important point for human intervention.

Remediation of Identified and Assumed Brain Damage in Children

The disorders of the brain-damaged child may be ameliorated by environmental intervention in a similar fashion. Although brain-damaged children are treated clinically with a variety of programs, almost no systematic research on experiential effects has been carried out. The majority of intervention studies have focused on children suffering sociocultural disadvantages. Many of these programs have accomplished long-term and short-term improvement, a function of the characteristic of both the program and the children enrolled (Miller and Dyer, 1975).

Mental retardation secondary to sociocultural deprivation is also modifiable. The classic study by Skeels (1966) and the Milwaukee study directed by Heber (1978) indicated that massive changes in the rearing milieu could alter cognitive deficits caused by early deprivation. Furthermore, there is a limited degree of plasticity in the development of children suffering genetically-based mental retardation. Down's syndrome children reared with their families are more competent than those reared in institutions (Stedman and Eichorn, 1964).

If the cognitive development of children with identified brain damage and mental retardation can be influenced by environmental rearing conditions, then the development of children who have suffered early medical and neurological complications must also be modifiable. In fact, the effects of preterm birth are modulated by social class variables (Drillien, 1964; Sameroff and Chandler, 1975). Preterm infants from poorer families tend to have more cognitive deficits than those from families with greater economic resources. Similarly, a variety of interventions in the nursery and the home have had beneficial effects on the development of preterm infants (Cornell and Gottfried, 1976; Scarr-Salapatek and Williams, 1973; Powell, 1974). In our own longitudinal study of preterm infants at UCLA, an understanding of the transactional processes between medical complications suffered by the infants and the environmental reaction has proved critical for describing early development.

Remediation of Early Medical Complications Experienced by Preterm Infants

To review our longitudinal study briefly, a risk-assessment system was developed that included measures of the infants at term through 9 months, with outcome assessments at 2 years and 5 years. We included a variety of pediatric, behavioral, and cognitive assessments carried out when the infant was between term and 9 months. We assumed that preterm birth itself might be relatively unimportant in influencing development, although the associated obstetric and medical complications might be critical. We included a neurological examination and several sleep polygraphs to ascertain the nature of the infant's neurological organization. Measures of attention, exploration of objects, and manipulative schema were used to assess early information processing. More standard developmental and cognitive measures were also administered. Home observations of the caregiver–infant interaction were carried out when the infants were 1, 3, and 8 months of age. The measures have been described in detail in Parmelee, Kopp, and Sigman (1976), and Sigman and Parmelee (1979).

Subjects were 126 preterm infants with a gestational age at birth of 37 weeks or less and a birth weight of 2,500 grams or less. Gestational age was calculated according to maternal report. All testing was carried out at conceptional ages with correction for the length of prematurity. Seventy-five infants were from families who were English-speaking, 37 infants were from Spanish-speaking families, and 14 infants were from bilingual families or families speaking other languages.

Medical complications were measured with several separate scales, one assessing obstetrical complications and the other recording illnesses and medical events throughout the first 2 years. Analysis of the results showed that obstetrical and postnatal medical complications were not individually related to Gesell scores at 24 months nor did these variables contribute significantly to best subsets generated from the measures in relation to Gesell developmental scores at 2 years. For the total sample, the only medical event scales that had any predictive power were the assessments of pediatric complications at 4 and 9 months.

We postulated that early medical complications might be related to later development in several complex ways. First, infants who were sick early in life might continue to suffer pediatric complications that would affect their overall development. A negative association between the number of pediatric complications suffered from 4 to 9 months of age and 9-month Gesell score has been identified for this sample (Littman and Parmelee, 1977). An indirect way in which the early complications suffered by the infant might have been linked to subsequent development would be through the environment (Beckwith and Cohen, 1978). The model, then, allows for medical complications to have both direct and indirect influences on development.

In order to test this hypothesized model, path analysis of the data from the entire sample was carried out. Path analysis is a method for relating variables to each other, both directly and indirectly, and assessing the degree of association between variables with standardized regression coefficients. For this hypothetical model, the variables used were the risk score based on assessments of postnatal and pediatric complications, observations of caregiver–infant interaction, and the Gesell score at 9 months. In all cases, a higher score represents fewer complications.

The path model and standardized regression coefficients are shown in Figure 1. Almost all the regression coefficients were significant links. The indirect path from postnatal complications through caregiver–infant interaction to outcome was much stronger then the direct path through medical complications. However, there was some influence by medical complications so that illness did deflate developmental progress to some extent. Thus, the results showed two different and opposing links between early illness and later performance. One reflected the remediation effect by the environment; the caregivers of sick babies interacted more than the caregivers of healthy babies, and the level of care did relate to the infant's later performance. On the other hand, sickness did tend to continue and finally depressed development to some extent. Early illness had no direct association with outcome because the two paths have opposite effects which cancelled each other out.

To illustrate the path analyses, the data can be shown for a single case.

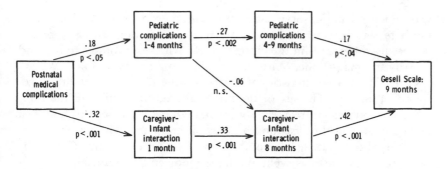

Figure 1. Path analysis for medical complications and caregiver–infant interaction to 9-month Gesell score. (Figures 1, 2, and 3 are reproduced by permission from M. Sigman, S. E. Cohen, and A. B. Forsythe. The relation of early infant measures to later development. In S. Friedman and M. Sigman (Eds.), *Preterm birth and psychological development*. New York: Academic Press, 1981.)

In Figure 2, the scores for one infant are presented with values standardized using the means and standard deviations of the entire sample for each measure. As Figure 2 shows, even with a low postnatal complications scale score, the infant performed better than the mean on the Gesell at 9 months. She did not perform as well as one might expect given the level of interaction nor as poorly as might be suggested by the nature of her pediatric complications.

In order to understand the effects of early illness on subsequent development, the environmental transactions between the infant and caregiver had to be considered not only for this infant but for the sample as a whole. Of course, there were infants for whom the developmental score was more strongly influenced by pediatric problems. Several children with serious physical complications, including three with moderate cerebral palsy, were included in the sample. An example of the path diagram for one infant with cerebral palsy is shown in Figure 3. For these infants, Gesell scores at 9 months tended to be more highly associated with the pediatric events scale than caregiver–infant interaction. This may not be so true at 5 years when the outcome measure involves fewer motor skills and more cognitive abilities. On the other hand, there are children in the sample who show unfortunate consistency and very limited plasticity over the first 5 years of life.

For the sample as a whole, our results show a naturally occurring remediation effect. We do not know what allows certain mothers to respond adaptively to their sick infant. We know that adaptive behavior was independent of social class; poor mothers were as responsive as mothers with greater financial resources. In addition, there were undoubtedly differences in the emotional capacities of mothers to respond to early trauma (Minde, Marton, Manning, and Hines, 1980).

Other infant characteristics also affected the caretaker's ability to respond optimally. The sex of the infant altered the timing of the caretaker's responses. Caretakers differentiated between healthy and sick female infants in the first month. This differentiation did not occur for males until they reached 4 months of age. Infant behaviors affected the caretaker's responses as well. We have reported a relationship between infant attention to inanimate stimuli in the laboratory and caregiver–infant interaction observed one month later at home (Sigman and Beckwith, 1980).

Whatever the mediating factors, it cannot be claimed that more effective caretaking was a function of a more responsive baby since the sicker babies received more attention. Furthermore, the effects of the intensified caretaking were beneficial. The caretakers' behavior may have ameliorated some of the infants' problems. Thus, any intervention which could strengthen this naturally occurring remediation might have salutary effects on the development of preterm infants.

Implications for Intervention

Based on this review of studies concerning developmental plasticity and our longitudinal study, several clinical implications can be drawn. First, the development of most infants shows plasticity and the individual's de-

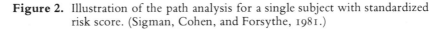

Figure 2. Illustration of the path analysis for a single subject with standardized risk score. (Sigman, Cohen, and Forsythe, 1981.)

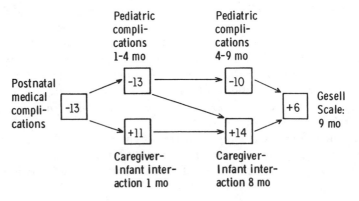

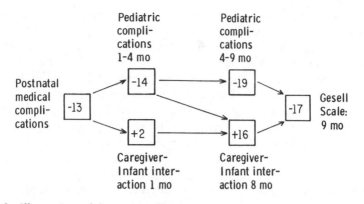

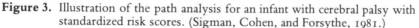

Figure 3. Illustration of the path analysis for an infant with cerebral palsy with standardized risk scores. (Sigman, Cohen, and Forsythe, 1981.)

velopmental progress is affected by early rearing experiences. These early experiences can ameliorate medical and neurological trauma suffered by the infant.

We believe that the earliest intervention with medically high-risk infants should be general, with the overall goal of facilitating the family's adaptation to the sick infant. As part of our research study, all infants received well-child care from one team of medical personnel and frequent supportive contacts in the early months with the same nurse. For many families, this type of medical support may have been adequate to allow the natural remediation effect described above.

On the other hand, some families may require more specialized forms of intervention (Bromwich, in press). For the sick infant, this intervention should still be fairly general, focusing on the caregiver–infant interaction. The results of our study show that the caregiver–infant interaction measures were the major early predictors of the infants' status (Sigman and Parmelee, 1979). We have argued elsewhere that continuity in the first 6 months of life may be carried by this interaction (Sigman, Cohen and Forsythe, 1981). Even if more sensitive infant assessment techniques are discovered, these marker variables will not be sufficient to guide intervention programs. Unless predictive factors can be tied to the developmental process, intervention plans should not focus too narrowly on specific deviations in the high-risk infant. This does not mean that children suffering particular handicapping conditions should not have their programs designed to suit their strengths and weaknesses. But the aim of the earliest intervention with high-risk infants should generally be toward improving interaction between child and principal caregivers.

However, intervention with high-risk infants may have to change focus in the latter part of the second year of life. Our data and that of many other investigators indicate that sociocultural factors begin to impact on the infant's development at 18 months to 2 years. For our sample, significant differences in the developmental scores of infants from English-speaking and Spanish-speaking families were found when the infants reached 25 months of age (Sigman, Cohen, Beckwith, and Parmelee, 1981). Before this age, differences between language groups were attributable to other social and demographic factors. However, by 2 years, the children from Spanish-speaking families scored much lower than the children from English-speaking families on the Bayley Mental Scale and language assessments, despite the fact that these were administered in Spanish by a Latino examiner. The significant differences between infants from Spanish-speaking families and infants from English-speaking families became even more dramatic when the children reached 5 years of age.

Thus, intervention efforts in the 2nd and 3rd year of life may need to focus on sociocultural differences even with medically high-risk infants. The fact is that the majority of preterm infants are born to poor and immigrant families. The consequences of these associated sociocultural factors need to be addressed in intervention with preterm infants.

Finally, the evidence on plasticity in childhood and adult years has an additional implication for intervention. Almost all research and clinical studies agree that there is significant plasticity in behavior at all ages. While the debate continues as to whether early plasticity is greater than that observed later in life, the capacity for recovery remains at all ages. This observation suggests that remediation can be attempted at all ages. If intervention is not planned in the early years, clinical treatment can be initiated in later childhood and adolescence.

On the other hand, the evidence of continued plasticity cuts both ways (Hunt, 1979). Our awareness of the individual's continued responsiveness to the environment should make us more conservative in our expectation that intervention for a brief period in early infancy will have long-term effects over time. We cannot anticipate that early intervention will be an inoculation against the trauma of all future environments. Although change brought about in the family may have more lasting effects, the family is also responsive to the greater milieu. With both child and family showing significant plasticity, intervention efforts must be sustained. Only by improving living and rearing conditions throughout childhood can we expect to promote continual developmental progress at the optimal level.

References

Beckwith, L., and Cohen, S. E. Preterm birth: Hazardous obstetrical and postnatal events as related caregiver–infant behavior. *Infant Behavior and Development,* 1978, *1,* 403–411.

Blakemore, C., and Cooper, G. F. Development of the brain depends on the visual environment. *Nature,* 1970, *228,* 467–468.

Bland, B. H., and Cooper, R. M. Posterior neo-decortication in the rat: Age at operation and experience. *Journal of Comparative and Physiological Psychology,* 1969, *69,* 345–354.

Bradley, R. H., and Caldwell, B. M. Early home environment and changes in mental test performance in children from 6 to 36 months. *Journal of Developmental Psychology,* 1976, *12,* 93–97.

Bromwich, R. M. *Working with parents and infants: An interactional approach.* Baltimore: University Park Press, in press.

Caputo, D. V., and Mandell, W. Consequences of low birth weight. *Developmental Psychology,* 1970, *3,* 363–383.

Clarke-Stewart, K. A. Interactions between mothers and their young children: Characteristics and consequences. *Monographs of the Society for Research in Child Development,* 1973, *38,* (6–7, Serial No. 153).

Cornell, E. H., and Gottfried, A. W. Intervention with premature human infants. *Child Development,* 1976, *47,* 32–39.

Davies, P. A., and Stewart, A. L. Low-birth-weight infants: Neurological sequelae and later intelligence. *British Medical Bulletin,* 1975, *31,* 85–91.

Denenberg, V. H. Assessing the effects of early experience. In R. D. Myers (Ed.), *Methods of psychobiology* (Vol. 3). New York: Academic Press, 1977.

Dennis, M., and Whitaker, H. A. Language acquisition following hemidecortication: Linguistic superiority of the left over the right hemisphere. *Brain and Language,* 1976, *3,* 404–433.

Dennis, W. Causes of retardation among institutional children: Iran. *Journal of Genetic Psychology,* 1960, *96,* 47–59.

Drillien, C. M. *The growth and development of the prematurely born infant.* Baltimore: Williams and Wilkins, 1964.

Finger, S. Environmental attenuation of brain-lesion symptoms. In S. Finger (Ed.), *Recovery from brain damage.* New York: Plenum Press, 1978.

Fishman, M. A., and Polkes, H. S. The validity of psychometric testing in children with congenital malformations of the central nervous system. *Developmental Medicine and Child Neurology,* 1974, *16,* 180–185.

Geshwind, N. Late changes in the nervous system: An overview. In D. G. Stein, J. J. Rosen, and N. Butters (Eds.), *Plasticity and recovery of function in the central nervous system.* New York: Academic Press, 1974.

Goldberger, M. E. Recovery of movement after CNS lesions in monkeys. In D. G. Stein, J. J. Rosen, and N. Butters (Eds.), *Plasticity and recovery of function in the central nervous system.* New York: Academic Press, 1974.

Goldfarb, W. Effects of early institutional care on adolescent personality. *Child Development,* 1943, *14,* 213–223.

Goldman, P. S. Plasticity of function in the CNS. In D. G. Stein, J. J. Rosen, and N. Butters (Eds.), *Plasticity and recovery of function in the central nervous system.* New York: Academic Press, 1974.

Harper, P., and Wiener, G. Sequelae of low birth weight. *Annual Review of Medicine*, 1965, *16*, 405–420.

Heber, R. Research in prevention of socio-cultural mental retardation. In D. G. Forgays (Ed.), *Primary prevention of psychopathology* (Vol. 2): *Environmental influences*. Hanover, N.H.: University Press of New England, 1978.

Hécaen, H. Acquired aphasia in children and the ontogenesis of hemispherical functional specialization. *Brain and Language*, 1976, *3*, 114–134.

Hirsh, H. U. B., and Spinelli, D. N. Visual experience modifies distribution of horizontally and vertically oriented receptive fields in cats. *Science*, 1970, *168*, 869–871.

Hubel, D. H., and Wiesel, T. Receptive fields binocular interaction and functional architecture in the cat's visual cortex. *Journal of Physiology*, 1962, *160*, 106–154.

Hunt, J. McV. Psychological development: Early experience. *Annual Review of Psychology*, 1979, *30*, 103–143.

Hunt, J. V. Predicting intellectual disorders in childhood for preterm infants with birthweights below 1501 grams. In S. Friedman and M. Sigman (Eds.), *Preterm birth and psychological development*. New York: Academic Press, 1981.

Kennard, M. A. Age and other factors in motor recovery from precentral lesions in monkeys. *American Journal of Physiology*, 1936, *115*, 138–146.

Kennard, M. A. Reorganization of motor function in the cerebral cortex of monkeys deprived of motor and premotor areas in infancy. *Journal of Neurophysiology*, 1938, *1*, 477–496.

Kopp, C. B., and Parmelee, A. H. Prenatal and perinatal influences on infant behavior. In J. D. Osofsky (Ed.), *Handbook of infant development*. New York: Wiley, 1979.

Lashley, K. S. Factors limiting recovery after central nervous system lesions. *Journal of Nervous and Mental Disorders*, 1938, *88*, 733–755.

Laurence, K. M., and Weeks, R. Abnormalities in the central nervous system. In A. P. Norman (Ed.), *Congenital abnormalities in infancy*. Oxford: Blackwell, 1971.

Lenenberg, E. H. *Biological foundations of language*. New York: Wiley, 1967.

Lewis, M., and Coates, D. L. Mother–infant interaction and cognitive development in twelve-week-old infants. *Infant Behavior and Development*, 1980, *3*, 95–105.

Littman, B., and Parmelee, A. H. Medical correlates of infant development. *Journal of Pediatrics*, 1978, *61*, 470–474.

Miller, L. B., and Dyer, J. L. Four preschool programs: Their dimensions and effects. *Monograph of the Society for Research in Child Development*, 1975, 40, (5–6, Serial No. 162).

Minde, K., Marton, P., Manning, D., and Hines, B. Some determinants of mother–infant interaction in the premature nursery. *Journal of the American Academy of Child Psychiatry*, 1980, *19*, 1–21.

Moore, R. Y., Bjorklund, A., and Stenevi, V. Plastic changes in the adrenergic innervation of the rat septal area in response to denervation. *Brain Research*, 1971, *33*, 13–35.

Parmelee, A. H., Kopp, C. B., and Sigman, M. Selection of developmental assessment techniques for infants at risk. *Merrill-Palmer Quarterly*, 1976, *22*, 177–199.

Pettigrew, J. D., and Freeman, R. D. Visual experience without effect on developing cortical neurons. *Science*, 1973, *182*, 599–601.

Powell, L. G. The effects of extra stimulation and maternal involvement on the development of low-birth-weight infants and on maternal behavior. *Child Development*, 1974, *45*, 106–113.

Rosenzweig, M. R., Bennett, E. L., and Diamond, M. L. Effects of differential environments on brain anatomy and brain chemistry. In J. Zubin and G. Jervis (Eds.), *Psychopathology of mental development*. New York: Grune and Stratton, 1967.

Rosner, B. S. Recovery of function and localization of function in historical perspective. In D. G. Stein, J. J. Rosen, and N. Butters (Eds.), *Plasticity and recovery of function in the central nervous system*. New York: Academic Press, 1974.

Sackett, G. P. A nonhuman primate model for studying causes and effects of poor pregnancy outcomes. In S. L. Friedman and M. Sigman (Eds.), *Preterm birth and psychological development*. New York: Academic Press, 1981.

Sameroff, A. J., and Chandler, M. J. Reproductive risk and the continuum of caretaking casualty. In F. D. Horowitz, M. Hetherington, S. Scarr-Salapatek, and G. Siegel (Eds.), *Review of child development research*, Vol. 4. Chicago: University of Chicago Press, 1975.

Scarr-Salapatek, S., and Williams, M. The effects of early stimulation on low-birth weight infants. *Child Development*, 1973, *44*, 94–101.

Schwartz, S. Effect of neocortical lesions and early environmental factors on adult rat behavior. *Journal of Comparative and Physiological Psychology*, 1964, *57*, 72–77.

Sigman, M., and Beckwith, L. Infant visual attentiveness in relation to caregiver–infant interaction and developmental outcome. *Infant Behavior and Development*, 1980, *3*, 141–154.

Sigman, M., Cohen, S. E., Beckwith, L., and Parmelee, A. H. Social and familial influences on the development of preterm infants. *Journal of Pediatric Psychology*, 1981, *6*, 1–13.

Sigman, M., Cohen, S. E., and Forsythe, A. B. The relation of early infant measures to later development. In S. Friedman and M. Sigman (Eds.), *Preterm birth and psychological development*. New York: Academic Press, 1981.

Sigman, M., and Parmelee, A. H. Longitudinal evaluation of the preterm infant. In T. M. Field, A. M. Sostek, S. Goldberg, and H. H. Shuman (Eds.), *Infants born at risk*. Jamaica, N.Y.: Spectrum, 1979.

Skeels, H. Adult status of children with contrasting early life experiences. *Monographs of the society for Research in Child Development*, 1966, *31*, 3.

Spinelli, D. N., and Jensen, F. E. Plasticity: The mirror of experience. *Nature*, 1979, *203*, 75–78.

Spitz, R. A. Hospitalism: An inquiry into the genesis of psychiatric conditions in childhood. *Psychoanalytic Study of the Child*, 1945, *1*, 53–74.

Stedman, D., and Eichorn, D. A comparison of the growth and development of institutionalized and home reared mongoloids during infancy and early childhood. *American Journal of Mental Deficiency*, 1964, *69*, 391–401.

Steinhausen, H. C. Psychological evaluation of treatment in phenylketonuria: Intellectual, motor, and social development. *Neuropaediatrie*, 1974, *5*, 146–156.

Tew, B. J., and Laurence, K. M. The ability and attainment of spina bifida patients born in South Wales between 1956 and 1962. *Developmental Medicine and Child Neurology*, 1972, *14*, 124–131.

Von Monakow, C. *Die lokalisation in der grosshin rinde und der abbau der funktiva durch korticale herde*. Wiesbaden: Bergmann, 1914.

Wachs, T. D., Uzgiris, I. C., and Hunt, J. McV. Cognitive development in infants of different age levels and from different environmental backgrounds: An exploratory investigation. *Merrill-Palmer Quarterly*, 1971, *17*, 283–317.

White, B. L., and Held, R. Plasticity of sensorimotor development in the human infant. In J. Rosenblith and W. Allinsmith (Eds.), *The causes of behavior: Readings in child development and educational psychology*. Boston: Allyn and Bacon, 1966.

Wiesel, T., and Hubel, D. H. Comparison of the affects of unilateral and bilateral eye closure on cortical unit responses in kittens. *Journal of Neurophysiology*, 1965, *28*, 1029–1040.

Will, B. E., and Rosenzweig, M. R. Effects de l'environment sur la recuperation fonctionnelle apres lesion cerebrales chez les rats adultes. *Biology of Behavior*, 1976, *1*, 5–16.

Will, B. E., Rosenzweig, M. R., and Bennett, E. L. Effects of differential environments on recovery from neonatal brain lesions measured by problem-solving scores and brain dimensions. *Physiology and Behavior*, 1976, *16*, 603–611.

Yarrow, L. J., Rubenstein, J. L., and Pedersen, F. A. *Infant and environment: Early cognitive and motivational development*. Washington, D.C.: Hemisphere, 1975.

PART II

Identification and Assessment of Risk

Introductory Notes

Given limitations in resources, primary prevention efforts have often been focused on populations that have been identified as "at risk" for problematic development. Although many authors in this book argue that preventive and promotive efforts should assume a broader scope than this, they acknowledge that an understanding of risk factors is central to our design and implementation of methods to facilitate development. The papers in this section are quite diverse, but, at the same time, each enlightens us about subtleties in the nature, identification, and assessment of risk, and its implications for prevention.

Within the context of considering the prevention of adverse developmental consequences of genetic and prenatal factors, Justin Joffe leads readers to reexamine the utility of current modes of conceptualizing risk. Historically, there has been an attempt to move away from global definitions of risk status (e.g., socioeconomic position) to a search for specific factors that are related to adverse developmental outcomes. While supporting (and, in fact, participating in) these efforts, Joffe illustrates the limits that this move can place on bringing us closer to effective prevention.

In an extensive review of the literature on human and subhuman development, Joffe examines genetic, chromosomal, prenatal, and perinatal factors which are associated with reproductive risk and deviant development. Although some writers have recently questioned whether prenatal and perinatal events produce deleterious effects in the absence of adverse postnatal circumstances, Joffe carefully examines these arguments, revealing, for example, that the very theoretical premises on which they are based provide support for the significant contribution of prenatal events.

Joffe proceeds with an analysis of the types of interventions that can reduce deviant developmental outcomes, and he discusses the extent to which they can be regarded as preventive measures. He distinguishes between postnatal interventions, high-risk approaches, and primary prevention with a detailed look at techniques in the last two categories. His analysis of the extent to which these techniques are preventive confirms Joffe's contention that knowing the causes of adverse development does not adequately explain what should be done for prevention. It is against this background that Joffe points out the need to consider the larger network of societal variables that encompass risk factors.

In the second paper Evelyn Thoman offers a behavioral model for assessing premature infants regarding their risk for the development of subsequent dysfunction. Premature birth has long been recognized as associated with an unusually high incidence of various kinds of developmental problems. Thus premature infants belong to one of the most widely identified "risk" groups, and they have been the targets of a large proportion of intervention programs, as seen in Part III of this book. However, a major difficulty which persists is that the population of premature infants is tremendously heterogeneous and demonstrates a wide range of developmental outcomes, a great many of which are positive even in the absence of intervention. Efforts to identify those particular infants who, in fact, have early subtle dysfunction and therefore might be targeted for intervention have not been particularly successful. Like Joffe in the previous paper, Thoman expresses concern about the consequent arguments for a lack of relationship between early events and later development since they tend to be used to excuse researchers from continuing attempts at such identification and hence prevention.

Elaborating on Sigman's review (Part I), Thoman discusses some of the most recent findings concerning the brain's plasticity during early development, and she emphasizes that the question is no longer *whether* there is plasticity, but rather *how* the incredibly complex brain reorganization comes about and is expressed functionally. She suggests that the trauma of premature birth is likely to be followed by quite distinctive reorganizational patterns for each infant. This accounts for the great variation in developmental outcome among premature infants.

In her thoughtful discussion of perennial problems in assessment of prematurely born infants, which integrates a number of methodological issues raised throughout this book, Thoman proposes several important criteria for a realistic assessment of developmental status. Arguing the need to move away from static instruments which "measure factors rather than babies or . . . organs rather than cerebral functioning," she contends that we must assess patterns of ongoing change in individuals, focus on develop*ing* rather than develop*ed* competence, and attend to indices of individual functioning rather than group means.

Thoman provides remarkable data on the feasibility of assessing the stability of infant behavioral state over time to reveal cerebral dysfunction and to identify infants in need of intervention and prevention. Her assessment, which clearly meets the stringent and challenging criteria she has proposed, is likely to have a major impact on the future of identifying infants at risk for developmental disorder.

Over the years, Elsie Broussard has effectively used maternal perception of the infant as a screening measure predicting risk of subsequent psychosocial disorders. More than a decade ago, she revealed a significant relationship between the absence of positive maternal perception of the neonate and subsequent psychosocial disorder in the child. Broussard begins her chapter with a brief overview of her longitudinal studies in the Pittsburgh First Born Project. She comments upon the usefulness of her Neonatal Perception Inventories (NPI) as a screening instrument and cautions us that such screening is only the first step, which needs to be followed by careful clinical assessment and evaluation of the level of need for intervention. Broussard reports her success in preventive intervention with infants (and mothers) labelled at risk using the NPI.

Suggesting that a mother's early perceptions of her infant reflect her own sense of well being, which is then reflected back to her child as the infant's first "mirror," Broussard illustrates these points through an extensive account of a mother–child relationship, and focuses on the boy's development through his first 5 years. Perceived by his mother as a "bad" and an "odd" infant, the child proceeds to display admirable cognitive and motor development. Yet Broussard points out that his characteristics of psychosocial disorder, although less apparent in traditional assessments, are nonetheless real. Through this study of a mother and child preoccupied with their own images and those of each other, Broussard demonstrates that our standard, "neat" indicators of risk and developmental disorder do not always adequately reveal an individual's developmental status; both interventions and assessments must be based upon a broader concept of development.

In the final paper in this section, Ann McGillicuddy-DeLisi and Irving Sigel examine the interplay of child development, parental constructs of child development, and parental teaching strategies. Although it has been established that parents can play a primary role in the development of their children's cognitive abilities, the authors emphasize the importance of this relationship in families of children with atypical development. They cite evidence that parents of children with learning disabilities often have different concepts of their own role as teacher and therefore have different attitudes toward, and tolerance of, their children's cognitive activities. Reiterating the constructivist perspective favored by Bond and

Goldhaber (Part I), the authors stress that parents' belief systems regarding child development and childbearing are constructed (and reconstructed) through their own experience with those around them. The authors present a path model of influences between family members which demonstrates the dynamics and complexity of this construction. Learning-disabled children give parents different feedback from other children which, in turn, affects parental constructs of child development and parental teaching strategies. Meanwhile the strategies that emerge are not necessarily those which optimally suit the needs of the atypical child. On the contrary, the strategies may lead to less intellectual challenge, thus compounding the child's learning difficulties.

In particular, McGillicuddy-DeLisi and Sigel focus on parents' use of distancing strategies with their children, behaviors which separate the child from the immediate environment in the cognitive sense and are thus the bases of the development of representational abilities and active inference. Since the authors' earlier work has demonstrated the manner in which such teaching strategies can promote children's cognitive skills, the use of distancing strategies with children with poorly developed cognitive abilities is particularly interesting.

McGillicuddy-DeLisi and Sigel describe their current study, which examines parental teaching strategies and beliefs about childrearing among families with learning-disabled children. They present an extensive case example of a 4½-year-old boy and his parents to illustrate the reciprocal nature of family influences and the relationship between parental beliefs and practices in each parent. Their case study illustrates some of their methods, data, and interpretations of effects as well as the consistencies and inconsistencies between data derived from groups versus individual cases.

Approaches to Prevention of Adverse Developmental Consequences of Genetic and Prenatal Factors

Justin M. Joffe

Both hereditary factors and prenatal events influence the survival and the development of organisms. The purpose of this chapter is to consider what steps can be taken to minimize the chances of genetic, chromosomal, maternal constitutional, and prenatal and perinatal environmental factors having deleterious effects on intrauterine and postnatal development. In order to explore the issues relating to preventing disorders of prenatal origin, it is necessary first to indicate the nature and assess the importance of genetic, chromosomal, prenatal, and perinatal factors that are associated with deviant development of various kinds and with reproductive risk. To provide such an overview two categories of influences are distinguished, namely genetic and chromosomal factors on the one hand and environmental events on the other.

Prenatal Influences

Genetic and Chromosomal Factors.

Almost 2,000 autosomal dominant and recessive and X-linked disorders had been catalogued by 1970 (McKusick, 1971), and the number had risen to 2,336 by 1975 (Elinson and Wilson, 1978). Individual disorders due to single gene defects are rare, but together they are estimated to affect about 1 percent of children born (Elinson and Wilson, 1978; Motulsky, Benirschke, Carpenter, Fraser, Epstein, Nyhan, and Jackson, 1976). Many of these conditions—which include galactosemia, maple syrup urine disease, Hurler's syndrome, genetic thyroid defects, and phenyl

I am very grateful to George Albee, Daryll Joffe, and Philip Kitcher for their helpful comments on an earlier draft of this paper. They are not responsible, of course, for misunderstandings that I still entertain. And also to Josephine F. Beach for her Herculean labors in retyping successive drafts of this paper.

ketonuria—are associated with mental retardation (Kopp and Parmelee, 1979; Nitowsky, 1975). Multifactorial or polygenic disorders may account for the largest number of genetically determined deviant outcomes. Brent and Harris (1976), on the assumption that these play a role in producing not only congenital malformations but also schizophrenia and manic-depressive disorders and susceptibility to various common adult disorders such as high blood pressure, diabetes, and arteriosclerosis, estimate that they may affect as many as 10 percent of *all births*.

As are genetic disorders, individual chromosomal disorders are infrequent. Their effects range from intrauterine death through severe malformations with or without mental retardation to sterility and mild intellectual impairment; some have no known clinical effects (Harris, 1975). The most common "chromosomal disease" is Down's syndrome with a frequency of about 1 in 600 births (Motulsky et al., 1976) but other less prevalent chromosomal abnormalities such as Turner's syndrome (1 in 5,000 births) can have dramatic effects on development. The overall incidence of chromosomal anomalies is estimated at about 6.7 per 1,000 births (Elinson and Wilson, 1978). Considerably more detailed treatment of genetic and chromosomal factors can be found in the volumes edited by Brent and Harris (1976) and by Milunsky (1975a).

How large a problem overall do genetic and chromosomal factors present for those concerned with development? It is difficult to provide exact estimates of the overall involvement of hereditary factors in developmental defects and susceptibility to dysfunction. Even if one limits one's attention to relatively clearcut outcomes such as birth defects, only rough approximations are available. It is estimated that about 25 percent of birth defects are the result of genetic transmission and chromosomal aberrations (Brent, 1976; Wilson, 1977a), an estimate that does not include anomalies due to genetic-environmental interactions. Generally accepted estimates of the incidence of congenital malformations run from 3 to 5 percent at birth, a rate which rises to about 10 percent when malformations ascertained from birth to 2 years of age are included. Given an annual total of a little over 3,000,000 births in the United States in recent years (National Center for Health Statistics [NCHS], 1978), these estimates imply that each year about 300,000 children are born with congenital malformations, amongst whom about 75,000 are malformed as the result of genetic or chromosomal factors. Genetic and chromosomal conditions constitute the second most frequent cause of death prior to one year of age (NCHS, 1978). Alarming as these figures may be, however, they seriously underestimate the scope of the problem with regard to prevention. In the first place, these figures should more accurately be termed prevalence rather than incidence figures since no estimate is possible of the extent of chromosomal damage in the approximately 50 percent of conceptuses that die within 17 days of fertilization before pregnancy is recognized (Hertig, Rock, and Adams, 1956), and it is probable that many defective conceptuses do not reach an age where their disorder is recognized. A majority of embryos and fetuses with chromosomal abnormalities are spontaneously aborted, and it is estimated that a minimum of 7 percent of all *recognized* pregnancies involve a conceptus with a chromosomal abnormality (Motulsky et al., 1976).

More important, as Slone, Shapiro, and Mitchell (1980) state in discussing the effects of prenatal chemical events, congenital malformations probably represent only the tip of the iceberg of hereditary or environmentally induced developmental anomalies because, in addition to malformations, genetic and chromosomal factors and environmental agents can produce prenatal and perinatal mortality, postnatal functional aberrations (biochemical, physiological, neurological, intellectual, and behavioral) and congenital neoplasms in addition to various reproductive disorders that are themselves associated with suboptimal neonatal outcomes.

In addition, the relevance of genetic and chromosomal factors to morphological and functional characteristics in the "normal" range is seldom explicitly considered, although chromosomally determined characteristics such as an individual's gender and genetically influenced characteristics such as temperament (Thomas, Chess, and Birch, 1968) and cognitive ability play a major role in modifying important features of the postnatal psychosocial environment. These aspects of prenatal influences will be discussed in more detail later.

Environmental Factors

In discussing environmental agents two overlapping categories need to be included, maternal characteristics and agents in the external environment. Maternal characteristics such as the development of the reproductive system or metabolic disorders are factors influencing the intrauterine environment of the conceptus. This can, in addition, be affected by agents in the maternal environment such as stressors and drugs. Furthermore, not only is the mammalian organism susceptible to the effects of an astonishing range of physical, chemical, and biological agents during the period from conception to birth, but for a complete understanding of outcome, events occurring prior to pregnancy and during the birth process itself have to be taken into account.

For many reasons, it is impossible to provide an exhaustive list of environmental agents that affect human development. In the first place, in the case of most of more than 1,000 agents that have been reported to be mutagenic, teratogenic, or carcinogenic in animals, evidence is simply unavailable on humans. Second, failure to recognize until recently that an agent may affect development even when encountered prior to conception either by the mother or the father has resulted in a paucity of evidence on the effects of agents prior to conception and on paternal drug effects. Third, if the effects of an agent are mild (for example, subclinical intrauterine growth retardation), the outcome may not even be recognized as anomalous (Redmond, 1979). Fourth, even in the case of clear structural malformations it is often difficult to establish a causal relationship between an agent and an outcome: identical outcomes can result from either genetic or environmental factors, and particular agents can produce a variety of outcomes (Barnes, 1968), probably as a result of variations in time and duration of exposure and of dosage or as a result of individual differences in susceptibility. The absence of a distinctive defect or pattern of defects, particularly in the absence of a large number of cases, means that a teratogenic agent is unlikely to be recognized (Wilson, 1977a). Even if an agent results in a distinctive defect, if the effect is found only in susceptible individuals, unless the defect is otherwise very rare, the relationship may not readily be detected (Redmond, 1979).

These difficulties in establishing that an agent affects development are exacerbated in the case of functional alterations and delayed effects (that is, those not manifested or ascertained at birth). Not only does delay in the manifestation of the condition mean that a prenatal event is less likely to be suspected, but, in the case of functional alterations, postnatal events can produce effects identical to both genetic factors and prenatal events. Animal experiments can be of only limited help in clarifying causal relationships because there are enormous species and strain differences in susceptibility.

Nevertheless, a listing of the types of agents that affect development helps to illustrate the scope of the problem (see Table 1). More details, including summaries of probable effects and references to supporting data can be found in Brent (1976, 1977), Catz and Yaffe (1976), Goldman (1980), Grabowski (1977), Wilson (1977a, 1977b), and Winick (1976).

In view of the difficulties involved in establishing that an agent affects development, the agents listed in Table 1, particularly drugs and chemicals, probably constitute a minimum estimate of relevant environmental variables, and it is probably appropriate to regard any drug or chemical as potentially embryo-toxic until it is demonstrated not to be: "The burden of proof must be on those who wish to believe that a drug is safe during pregnancy" (Redmond, 1979, p. 7). In Table 1 no attempt is made to identify sequelae associated with the agents listed. As discussed, effects depend on a number of other factors, perhaps the most important

Table 1 Environmental Causes of Developmental Defects

Radiation
Drugs and Hormones[a] (including obstetric medication)
Chemicals
Infections[b]
Maternal metabolic disorders
Pregnancy, labor, and delivery complications
Nutrition
Maternal stress and emotions
Intrauterine physical factors (e.g. uterine structure)
Miscellaneous (e.g. maternal hypoxia, mechanical trauma)

NOTE. The table includes both agents in the maternal environment (e.g. radiation, drugs, and chemicals) and maternal factors (e.g. metabolic disorders) that alter the intrauterine environment of the conceptus.
[a]Specific teratogens are discussed by Catz and Yaffe (1976), Goldman (1980), Wilson (1977a); agents causing intrauterine growth retardation by Redmond (1980); and effects of obstetric medication by Brackbill (1979).
[b]Specific agents are discussed by Wilson (1977b)

of which is the time the event is encountered. An overview of the periods during which the environmental agents can produce effects adds another dimension to one's appreciation of the scope of the problem presented by environmentally produced developmental defects.

Prior to conception.

Agents such as radiation and possibly some hormones and drugs can cause chromosome damage in sperm or ova and thus act as determinants of embryonic death or developmental defects well before conception. In the case of damaged ova such events could exert their effect decades in advance of fertilization since the development of human ova begins while the mother herself is a fetus. In the case of the sperm, the susceptible period is up to about 64 days prior to fertilization, the time required for maturation of a sperm cell (Goldman, 1980). Consequently, some proportion of chromosomal disorders are attributable to environmental events, including events long before the conception of the affected embryo.

In addition, agents acting prior to conception can affect development without apparently producing chromosomal damage. Drugs and chemicals administered to *males* have been associated with deleterious effects on their progeny in both experiments on animals (Table 2) and clinical investigations of humans (Table 3). There appears to be sufficient evidence to conclude that risks associated with maternal exposure to drugs and chemicals extend also to those ingested or encountered by the father. Three effects emerge with considerable consistency in the animal research: decreased litter sizes, decreased birth weights, and increased neonatal mortality. Similar effects have been reported in humans.

Table 2 Summary of Adverse Effects of Drugs and Chemicals Administered to Male Mammals, Prior to Mating, on their Progeny: Experimental Studies

Species	Effects	Reference and year
Lead		
Rabbit	Decreased litter size, birth weight, and survival	Cole & Bachhuber, 1914
Guinea pig	Decreased birth weight, survival, and weight gain	Weller, 1915
Rat	Decreased litter size, birth weight, and survival	Stowe & Goyer, 1971
Rat	Decreased learning ability—T-maze	Brady et al., 1975
Morphine		
Mouse	Decreased weight—$F_1 + F_2$ generations	Friedler, 1974
Rat	Decreased survival	Smith & Joffe, 1975
Methadone		
Rat	Decreased litter size, birth weight, and survival	Smith & Joffe, 1975 Joffe et al., 1976 Soyka et al., 1978a, b, 1980a
Ethanol		
Guinea pig	Intrauterine deaths, decreased post-natal survival ($F_1 - F_3$ generations)	Stockard, 1913
Mouse	No significant effects on sex ratio or prenatal mortality	MacDowell et al., 1926 a,b MacDowell & Lord, 1927 Durham & Woods, 1932
Guinea pig	No significant effects on birth weight, sex ratio, or prenatal or postnatal mortality	Durham & Woods, 1932
Mouse	Intrauterine deaths	Badr & Badr, 1975
Rat	Decreased litter size and fetal size	Klassen & Persuad, 1976
Caffeine		
Hamster	Skewing of sex ratio toward females	Weathersbee et al., 1975
Rat	Decreased birth weight of males, decreased survival	Soyka et al. (un-published)
Propoxyphene		
Rat	Decreased survival	Soyka et al. (un-published)
Thalidomide		
Rabbit	Decreased birth weight, decreased litter size survival, increased malformations	Lutwak-Mann, 1964 Lutwak-Mann et al., 1967

SOURCE: Joffe, 1979.

Table 3 Summary of Adverse Effects of Drug Exposure on the Reproductive Performance of Men

Agent	Effects	Reference and year
Lead	Increased spontaneous abortions, neonatal mortality	Paul, 1860
	Reduced family size	Chyzzer, 1908
	Increased spontaneous abortions	Rudeaux, 1910
	Increased spontaneous abortions, still-births, neonatal mortality	Reid, 1911
Anesthetic gases	Increased spontaneous abortions, congenital anomalies	Ad Hoc Committee, 1974
	Increased spontaneous abortions	Cohen et al., 1975
Cigarettes	Increased incidence of low-birthweight (LBW) infants, increased neonatal mortality, and congenital anomalies in LBW infants	Yerushalmy, 1971
Caffeine	Increased reproductive loss (spontaneous abortions, stillbirths, premature births)	Weathersbee et al., 1977

SOURCE: Soyka and Joffe, 1980b

Factors operating prior to conception can also operate through the mother to affect development. The quality of reproductive performance (as indicated by perinatal mortality, delivery complications, and prematurity) is associated with maternal height (Baird, 1949; Baird and Illsley, 1953; Thomson, 1959; Yerushalmy, 1967) with taller women having better outcomes—a relationship that holds across social classes (Baird, 1964). The relationship between height and reproductive performance may be mediated by the association of height with health and general physique (Thomson and Billewicz, 1963) and with pelvic development (Bernard, 1952) and possibly with other changes in the reproductive and endocrine systems. Although there may be some genetic contribution to height differences, secular changes in populations and differences between immigrants and native stock indicate that nutrition plays a major role (see Birch and Gussow, 1970, Ch. 5). In addition, in epidemiological studies of anencephaly and spina bifida, in which an inverse relationship between maternal stature and rates of anencephaly has been demonstrated, rates are unrelated to the social class of the father but significantly related to the social class of the maternal grandfather (Carter and Evans, 1973) and peaks of occurrence were found to be due largely to births to women who were themselves born during periods of severe economic depression (Baird, 1974). Emanuel (1976) suggests that epidemiological data are consistent with growth disturbance during childhood being perhaps the major environmental influence on the occurrence of anence-phaly and spina bifida. In short, nutritional deficiencies during the development of the mother may affect the development of her offspring by affecting her reproductive competence.

Animal research suggests that it may not be possible to compensate for such effects in a single generation. Cowley and Griesel (1966) maintained rats on low-protein diets from weaning until their offspring were weaned; the offspring were placed on rehabilitation diets at weaning (with some attenuation of the effects on growth, development, and behavior) and then mated to produce a third generation. The offspring of mothers that had been adequately fed while growing to maturity and producing young were lighter at birth, showed developmental lags (incisor eruption, unfolding of pinnae, eye opening, righting response), and made more errors than controls on a maze-learning task at maturity.

In addition to rendering the mother less biologically competent to provide her unborn child with an optimal prenatal environment, factors operating prior to pregnancy could obviously affect her competence to do so psychosocially, making her less informed about, or able to cope with, potential hazards or the need for adequate care.

Zygotic and early embryonic period (fertilization to gastrulation).
During the first 3 weeks of human gestation the embryo is relatively resistant to teratogenesis. The most likely effect, if any, of environmental agents during this period is death of the embryo with subsequent abortion, but if it survives it is not generally deformed although some evidence indicates that some chemicals and drugs and possibly radiation can produce nonfatal teratogenic effects during this period (see Goldman, 1980; Joffe, 1969, p. 64).

Embryonic period.
From 4 to 9 weeks of gestation the embryo is highly susceptible to teratogens and to lethal effects of toxic agents. Anomalies produced by an agent are likely to differ according to the exact time of administration, since different organs are susceptible at different times. Different agents can produce similar morphological effects either by interfering in the same way with organ formation or by acting on different developmental processes of which the normal progress of each is necessary for a normal outcome. With increasing age both individual organs and the embryo as a whole become increasingly resistant to teratogenic influences, and larger doses of drugs, chemicals, hormones, or radiation are needed to produce effects. These generalizations are derived principally from research on the effects of radiation, drugs, chemicals, and hormones on

morphological development, including the development of the nervous system. It is probable, but not established, that they apply also to other agents and to other adverse developmental outcomes that may or may not be accompanied by morphological anomalies.

Fetal period.

The period from 9 weeks of gestation to birth is largely one of growth and development and because organogenesis is completed prior to the fetal period teratogenesis in the strict sense cannot occur (Wilson, 1965). However, growth retardation of the fetus as a whole or of particular organs, damage to organs, prematurity or abortion, and alterations of function can result from environmental agents encountered during the fetal period. Sequelae such as growth retardation and functional changes are precisely the ones that are least likely to be noticed or to be regarded as anomalous unless the effects are extreme. Consequently these effects of environmental agents are likely to be underestimated unless they are specifically sought in carefully controlled studies (Redmond, 1979).

Many of the agents listed in Table 1 can produce effects if encountered during the fetal period, with the retarding effects of drugs and hormones on intrauterine growth being among the best documented in humans (Redmond, 1979). Intrauterine growth retardation is associated with increased perinatal morbidity and mortality, and surviving small-for-date infants are at greater risk of impaired postnatal development.

Intrapartum period.

The period from the onset of labor to the emergence of the neonate in the extrauterine world is not unique in terms of vulnerability to environmental agents but is worth delineating as a separate period since it is one of altered probability of exposure to environmental agents such as obstetric medication and hypoxia-producing events. In the course of a comprehensive and careful review of available evidence on effects of obstetric medication on infant behavior, Brackbill (1979) summarized the evidence as follows: "Drugs given to mothers during labor and delivery have subsequent effects on infant behavior . . . . The direction of the effect is consistent across studies in showing behavioral degradation or disruption. No study has demonstrated functional enhancement following obstetrical medication" (p. 109). She found that behavioral effects were not transient, being found in some cases in infants of 1 year of age, and that the most pronounced defects was seen in areas of cognitive function and gross motor abilities.

As in the case of genetic and chromosomal factors, it is difficulty to assess the extent of the involvement of prenatal environmental factors in deviant development. About 10 percent of developmental defects (principally malformations) are estimated to be caused by environmental agents (Brent, 1976; Wilson, 1977a). However, the causes of about two-thirds of all defects are at present unknown, and it seems likely that many of these will turn out to be attributable to multiple causes with environmental components. Teratogenic effects of a drug, for example, may be dependent on other environmental agents (such as temperature, diet, or stress), maternal factors (such as age and parity), other pharmacological agents, or maternal or fetal genetic factors (Fraser, 1977). In addition, estimates do not include any allowance for prepregnancy environmental influences on reproductive function. Unless a large proportion of defects is attributable to spontaneous errors in development, environmental factors will probably turn out to have a causal role in over 60 percent of malformations.

In any event, as was pointed out in relation to genetic factors, congenital malformations are only one of the more obvious adverse consequences of prenatal events, which can also result in perinatal mortality and morbidity and a wide range of adverse delayed and functional effects.

Do Prenatal and Perinatal Events Matter?

In light of the information outlined in the previous sections the question may seem rhetorical. However, doubts have been expressed about the long-term importance of functional effects of prenatal and perinatal events, and thus the question merits attention. Should the answer be "no", the subsequent discussion of prevention would be superfluous.

The position discounting the important of prenatal and perinatal events has been based on the argument that in the absence of adverse postnatal circumstances the effects of prenatal and perinatal events are, at worst, transient. It has been most forcefully and systematically presented by Sameroff (1975, 1977; Sameroff and Chandler, 1975), who, after reviewing studies of perinatal factors such as anoxia, prematurity, and delivery complications, stated:

There is a serious question as to whether a child who has suffered perinatal trauma but shows no obvious physical damage, is at any greater risk for later deviancy, either neurological, perceptual, or intellectual, than a child who has not suffered perinatal trauma. In the studies reviewed, the effects of social status tended to reduce or amplify intellectual deficits. In advantaged families infants who had suffered perinatal complications generally showed minor residual effects, if any, at follow-up. Many infants from lower social class homes with identical histories of complications showed significant retardations in later functioning. Socio-economic status appears to have much stronger influence on the course of development than perinatal history. (Sameroff, 1975, p. 274)

The first sentence alone would constitute a very strong dismissal of the importance of prenatal and perinatal factors but the position is qualified by the rest of the statement. Nevertheless the statement as a whole deemphasizes the importance of prenatal and perinatal events to a degree that is unwarranted for a number of reasons.

First, and most obviously, many prenatal events—drugs, radiation, malnutrition, and so forth—*do* produce physical damage and consequently are important both insofar as they directly affect the child's abilities and functioning and as they are indirectly responsible for producing changes in the child's environment. The child's family environment, for example, may be modified by the stress of having a child with a birth defect, and the child's altered abilities may change the way he or she is perceived and treated.

Second, the question might be raised as to the extent that the data indeed support the position that effects of prenatal and perinatal events wane and are consistently related to later development only in the presence of poor postnatal circumstances. To consider this question it is not necessary to reevaluate all the studies reviewed by Sameroff and Chandler (1975): They question the validity of several studies that produced findings contrary to their position. These can be set aside and attention given instead to findings of two major longitudinal studies that they discuss in support of their position.

The first of these was an extensive study of children in St. Louis who suffered perinatal conditions likely to produce anoxia (Corah, Anthony, Painter, Stern, and Thurston, 1965; Graham, Ernhart, Thurston, and Craft, 1962; Graham, Matarazzo, and Caldwell, 1956; Graham, Pennoyer, Caldwell, Greenman, and Hartman, 1957). These children showed deficits on five measures of physiological and behavioral responsivity (measures of maturation level, visual responsiveness, irritability, muscle tension, and pain threshhold) obtained during the first few days of life (Graham et al., 1957) and scored lower than controls on a number of tests of cognitive function at the age of 3 (as well as showing more positive neurological signs and some personality differences), although they did not score lower on tests of perceptual–motor functioning at this age (Graham et al., 1962). However, at 7 years of age they did not show significant differences from controls in IQ and scored significantly less well on only 2 of 21 cognitive and perceptual measures (Corah et al., 1965). These findings are in accord with several others on the effects of anoxia (see, for example, Tizard, 1978; Sameroff and Chandler, 1975). It seems possible that the nature of the mammaliam birth process may have resulted in selection for organisms that are relatively resistant to transient anoxia. Perhaps humans, with the prolonged labor that may have been a consequence of selection for increased brain size, would need to be particularly resistant to perinatal anoxia or capable of compensating for its effects later. Whatever the explanation, although the studies do not shed much light on the question of the role of postnatal factors, the position that the effects of perinatal events are relatively transient appears to be defensible with regard to perinatal anoxia, provided it is not sufficiently prolonged to result in brain damage.

However, to what extent is the position generally true? The findings of a second extensive longitudinal study, that of the children of Kauai, Hawaii are the ones that Sameroff (1977) views as supporting the position that "perinatal complications taken alone do not appear to be consistently related to later physical and psychological development; only when combined with and supported by persistently poor environmental circumstances do such infants show later deficiencies" (p. 47). In this long-term investigation of all 698 children born on Kauai in 1955, data collection was begun in the prenatal period and the children's progress assessed at various ages over a period of nearly two decades, with almost 90 percent of the 698 children tested at 17 to 18 years of age and even higher percentages at 20 to 24 months and at 10 years (Werner, Bierman, and French, 1971; Werner, Bierman, French, Simonian, Connor, Smith and Campbell, 1968; Werner, Simonian, Bierman, and French, 1967; Werner and Smith, 1977). The investigators have presented information on relationships between perinatal factors and assessments at each age as well as information on relationships between assessments carried out at different ages. The extensive findings and analyses constitute a treasure trove of information on development and, at the same time, virtually defy brief summarization and make differences in interpretation unsurprising.

The Kauai findings indicate that there was a clear overall relationship between the rated severity of perinatal complications and physical status and intellectual development (as assessed by the Cattell Infant Intelligence Scale and observations) at 20 to 24 months of age. The effects of perinatal complications on intellectual status were more pronounced in the children of parents who were poor, had little education, or were unstable.

At age 10, "differences found between children with various degrees of perinatal complications and those without perinatal stress were less pronounced than at age 2 . . . . The effect of family environment was even more powerful than was apparent at age 2 and accounted for more of the variance in IQ than the degree of perinatal stress" (Werner and Smith, 1977, p. 32); however, "children considered in need of long-term mental health services at age 10 had twice as high an incidence of *moderate* perinatal stress (16 percent) as controls matched by age, sex, SES, and ethnicity and twice as high an incidence of severe perinatal stress as the total 1955 cohort (4 percent)" (Werner and Smith, 1977, p. 32–33). In addition, the analyses of information collected at age 18 revealed durable effects of perinatal complications on a number of characteristics. Although no significant differences between groups with different degrees of perinatal stress were found on a number of personality and scholastic achievement tests, among those who had experienced severe perinatal stress, 4 out of 5 of the 18-year-olds "still had significant behavior, learning, and physical problems in late adolescence . . . . The incidence of mental retardation was 10 times, the incidence of significant mental health problems was 5 times, and the incidence of significant physical handicaps was slightly more than twice that found in the total population of 18-year-olds" (p. 33). Among those who had experienced moderate perinatal stress there were no differences from the total population in significant physical health problems or overall delinquency rates, but there was "a greater incidence of mental retardation, significant mental health problems, and sociopathic (acting-out) behavior, especially among girls in adolescence" (Werner and Smith, 1977, p. 33). These findings are summarized in Table 4.

Unlike the findings on anoxia, the Kauai findings indicate that on many measures, including some of those obtained at 18 years of age, effects of perinatal events were not transient, regardless of postnatal environmental factors, although in other cases effects *were* exacerbated by adverse postnatal circumstances. Overall, the Kauai data seem to indicate that perinatal complications are related to later physical and psychological development *especially*—rather than only—when combined with and supported by persistently poor environmental circumstances, a position that suggests a more important role for perinatal complications in deficiencies at all ages than Sameroff's (1975 1977; Sameroff and Chandler, 1975) analyses imply.

It should be stressed that by claiming a more important role for prenatal variables I do not mean to imply that generally poor environmental circumstances are not important. Sameroff's position is a valuable reminder of the importance of socioeconomic and other demographic variables and that a "monoetiologic" (Nuckolls, Cassel, and Kaplan, 1972, p. 431) model of causation is unlikely to be useful in analyzing the role of prenatal and perinatal factors in development. Stating that prenatal and perinatal factors are also important is not to ignore this, nor to claim that their occurrence is unrelated to variables such as socioeconomic status or to predict a one-to-one relationship between prenatal events and later outcomes. We neither expect nor find that all offspring of mothers encountering a particular agent end up with a particular disorder or that all

Table 4 Problems at Ages 17-18 among Youth with Perinatal Stress
(percentage)

Problem	Total 1955 Cohort (N=698)	Youth with Moderate Perinatal Stress (N=69)	Youth with Severe Perinatal Stress (N=14)
All problems	36.0	33.0	79.0
Mental retardation	3.0	6.0	29.0
Physical handicaps	6.0	6.0	14.5
Mental health problems[a]	3.0	9.0	14.5
Delinquency	15.0	17.0	21.5
Teenage pregnancies	6.0[b]	14.0[b]	0

[a] Schizoid, paranoid, obsessive-compulsive.
[b] Percentage of females.
SOURCE: Werner and Smith, 1977, p. 34 (Reproduced by permission of University Press of Hawaii).

infants with a disorder had mothers who encountered the agent. And this remains true even if we take into account variations in the timing and amount of the agent. We still have to consider environmental circumstances—the "social allies" (Rosen, 1975, p. 28) of disease—and individual make-up. Since these variables are all related, forming a complex web of interacting factors, it is hardly surprising that the broader, enduring variables are the best predictors of outcome, as in the Kauai study and in the investigation of determinants of IQ at age 4 in the Collaborative Perinatal Project (Broman, Nichols, and Kennedy, 1975).

Even if it were clearly the case that prenatal and perinatal factors had only limited effects in the absence of adverse postnatal events there are two reasons why this would not diminish their importance in development. First, there is considerable evidence to indicate that the incidence of hazardous prenatal and perinatal events is higher among the poor and among oppressed ethnic minorities. Some of this evidence is inferential. For example, blacks in the United States are more likely to have babies at ages when complications of labor are more prevalent and to have poor obstetric care during pregnancy; the latter implies that prenatal and perinatal problems are less likely to be diagnosed and treated and is, in any case, associated with higher rates of prematurity (Birch and Gussow, 1970, Chs. 4 and 7). Furthermore, insofar as outcomes such as birth weight and perinatal mortality are indicative of adverse prenatal events, a mass of evidence indicates that such events occur more frequently among the disadvantaged: stillbirths, neonatal deaths, birth weight, and prematurity are clearly related to family income, father's occupation, and other measures of socioeconomic status (Birch and Gussow, 1970, Chs. 2 and

3). In addition there is more direct evidence: Pasamanick, Knobloch, and Lilienfeld (1956) reported that while the rate of complications of pregnancy was only 5 percent in the white "upper economic fifth" it was 14.6 percent in the "lower economic fifth" and 50.6 percent in the nonwhite group. Furthermore, nutrition during pregnancy is likely to be less adequate among the poor (Birch and Gussow, 1970, Ch. 6). In other words, it is precisely those groups—the poor, the disadvantaged—who are least likely to be able to provide ameliorating postnatal environments who suffer higher incidences of hazardous prenatal events.

There is a second reason for arguing that prenatal and perinatal events would be of considerable significance even if their effects waned in the absence of adverse postnatal environmental circumstances. Briefly, the reason is that the prenatal events themselves may indirectly help to provide just such postnatal circumstances. Aside from the reasonable possibility that a stressful pregnancy might affect the mother's (and father's) care and treatment of the infant, the effects of the prenatal events on the infant's functioning and behavior are likely themselves to alter the way it is treated—the child's characteristics are themselves important determinants of his or her psychosocial environment. Indeed, this is precisely the point made by Sameroff and Chandler (1975) in their argument that development should be conceptualized as a process of *transactions* between the child and the environment and one which was made about animal development even before such a model was proposed for human development (Joffe, 1969, pp. 22–23). Perhaps surprisingly, the possibility that offspring characteristics might affect parental behavior was considered—and demonstrated—in research on animals (Ressler, 1962; Young, 1965) well before it was generally discussed in relation to human development. An interesting "taxonomy" of genotype-environment correlations suggested by Plomin, Defries, and Loehlin (1977) might be adapted to provide a systematic approach to phenotype-environment interactions of the sort involved in parent–infant relationships.

A good example of how, in the context of the transactional model, even transient effects of prenatal events might impair development is provided by Ferreira (1978), who analyzed the way in which malnutrition might interact with socioeconomic conditions to impair mental development:

The family in a deprived social environment is usually burdened with socioeconomic and health problems. In these circumstances, the child will rarely find in its immediate environment a person available and prepared to "syntonize", i.e., to tune in to him, and to be stimulating and responsive to his behavior. At the same time, children born in this environment, because of malnutrition and other ailments, will often be biologically less able to be stimulating and responsive to the caregivers. These children show apathy, irritability, and loss of interest in the social environment. Their behavior is often more disorganized and less predictable than that of the controls, requiring a special effort from those who interact with them to achieve syntony and synchrony with them. The combination of these conditions, acting throughout the child's early years, creates a cycle of interactional deprivation, which inhibits its intellectual development. (p. 207)

In contrast to the situation of the biologically vulnerable child in the deprived environment, Ferreira suggests that the child of normal prenatal development born into the same environment will be better able to elicit a 'healthy transaction", and the impaired child in a favorable environment has a better chance of having parents who can make the necessary effort to respond to the child in a way that compensates for the initial effects of the adverse prenatal and perinatal events.

In brief, Sameroff and Chandler's (1975) transactional model of development itself suggests that adverse conditions and hazardous prenatal and perinatal events might have considerable significance for development even if the direct effects of such conditions and events were transient.

Before turning to a discussion of issues relating to prevention of adverse outcomes it should be noted that the perspective in which prenatal and perinatal factors have been viewed thus far is one of prevention of defects rather than promotion of optimal development. Much concern has focused on avoiding adverse effects, very little on whether prenatal development takes place in an environment that fosters even more favorable outcomes than usual. Should we reach a point where our "control" group is not one defined by the absence of adverse conditions during prenatal life but rather by the presence of favorable conditions—those optimizing neonatal status and functioning—it may emerge that the children who experience hazards have lost more than we thought and that the rebound that sometimes occurs in favorable postnatal environments does not bring the children to the level of functioning that we might assume them to have been capable of reaching. If such is the case we will have to give greater weight to the primary prevention of prenatal hazard than we currently do. As long as we think we can compensate postnatally for the consequences of prenatal disadvantage, there is a danger that we will not give sufficient attention to prenatal development.

Prevention

In this section some of the approaches to intervening to reduce the incidence of deviant outcomes of prenatal origin—death, malformations, stunting of growth, functional aberrations—will be considered. Issues of *what* can be done are often inseparable from questions about *how* they should be done and questions of desirability are linked with both of these, but the focus in this section is primarily on characterizing types of interventions that could reduce deviant outcomes and discussing the extent to which they can be regarded as preventive measures. Three general approaches to the task, distinguishable initially largely by the time at which they are implemented, are diagrammed in Figure 1. The first is postnatal intervention which, in principle, could be applied generally or could be restricted to groups considered to be at high risk for deviant development on the basis of measures of neonatal status or on the basis of factors (for example, socioeconomic status) that are associated with an increased probability of the child encountering circumstances that lead to less than optimal development. Depending on the nature of the risk factors the interventions might be intended to do one or both of the following:

●To interrupt the causal chain linking already encountered events to undesirable outcomes or to compensate for their effects; this might be classified as prevention of sequelae or early treatment.

●To obviate the child's encountering events that might not be conducive to optimal development, or to improve the child's ability to cope with such events in a manner that does not deflect such development.

Postnatal approaches are essential for continued optimal development in even the healthiest of neonates, and until such time as we have intervened with complete success prior to birth, postnatal measures to minimize the anticipated deleterious effects of adverse prenatal events—to treat them, to prevent their sequelae—will be essential. Since we may always have a residue of unpreventable neonatal outcomes for which we will need to implement ameliorative postnatal programs, concern for definitional purity (see Kessler and Albee, 1975; Bloom, 1980) may have to take a back seat to practical concerns. Postnatal interventions are the subject of detailed consideration elsewhere in this volume and will not be further discussed here.

In any case, intervention prior to birth is obviously more attuned to the notion that the purpose of primary prevention is to obviate negative events and promote positive ones (Bloom, 1980), *not* "to reduce or contain already manifest deficits" (Task Panel on Prevention, 1978, p. 1833).

Even limiting our concern to interventions prior to birth we are left with at least two general approaches: We can consider ways of minimizing the likelihood of adverse neonatal outcomes in the presence of threatening prenatal events—roughly characterizable as "high-risk ap-

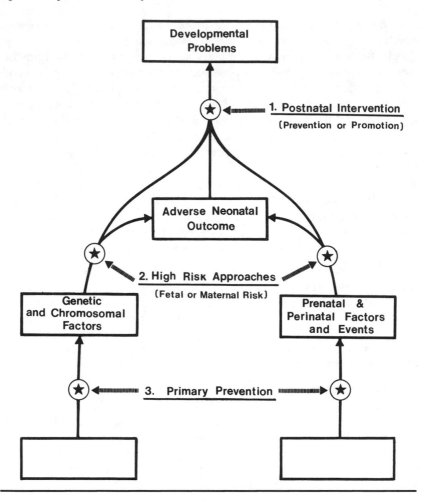

Figure 1. Approaches to prevention of adverse outcomes of prenatal and genetic factors.

proaches"—as well as ways of preventing the occurrence of such events (see Figure 1). In any case, we will see, once again, that distinctions between prevention and treatment are not straightforward. In considering each approach, three questions underlie the discussion. What kinds of techniques are available—that is, what can we do? How effective are these techniques—in particular, to what extent are they *preventive?* And how do we know when, or to whom, to apply them?

High-Risk Approaches

Similar general principles apply to prenatal intervention whether the disorders are of genetic or nongenetic origin and for this reason, and because many prenatal problems are of unknown or multifactorial origin, genetic and environmentally determined disorders will not be considered separately. Despite the risk of oversimplification, a rough distinction between the techniques and the treatments used when the concern is with identifying sick embryos or fetuses as opposed to identifying sick mothers is of some help in organizing a discussion of these approaches. In fact, of course, the two categories overlap and many of the matters discussed in the section on fetal disorders are relevant to prenatal disorders in general.

Fetal disorders.

Ingalls (1953), in discussing what he termed "preventive prenatal pediatrics", wrote:

The nearly insurmountable obstacle to clinical study of prenatal sickness arises in the fact that the patient voices no complaint, remembers nothing about his illness, hides himself from view, and puts off his visit to the doctor until the last possible moment. (p. 34)

This statement illustrates what are still unique difficulties in dealing with problems in perinatal development, although technical progress since the 1950s has made the unborn organism far less inaccessible than it was when Ingalls wrote. The development of procedures of visualizing the fetus using indirect techniques such as sonography and improved radiographic methods or direct ones such as fetoscopy, and the concurrent development of procedures of obtaining samples of fetal tissue and blood or of amniotic fluid (Golbus, 1978; Kushnick, 1979), have made it more difficult for fetuses to hide themselves from view. Advances in our ability to read the messages in amniotic and fetal fluids and cells and in maternal blood and urine have helped provide the fetus with a voice. We have, in fact, entered an era where a variety of fetal disorders, including neural tube defects and biochemical disorders of metabolism, have been, or are capable of being, diagnosed prenatally (Golbus, 1978; Kushnick, 1979; Milunsky and Atkins, 1975).

Aside from the need for technical and scientific advances to make the techniques safer, more accurate, cheaper, and capable of detecting even more disorders, we need to consider two problems of some importance. The first is the question of what is to be done when congenital disorders are detected—and is it prevention?—and the second relates to efficient and effective use of our technology. How do we know when to resort to prenatal diagnosis?

JUSTIN M. JOFFE

When prenatal diagnosis detects genetic or other prenatal disease, few options are available. The first, intrauterine therapy, is at present available in only a limited number of disorders. Therapy can take the form of preventing toxic changes in maternal physiology (as, for example, in dietary control in maternal phenylketonuria), of intrauterine fetal transfusion (as treatment in cases of rhesus incompatibility), and of prevention of toxic changes in the fetus (as, for example, in the use of intrauterine corticosteroids to treat congenital adrenal hyperplasia) (Hsia, 1975). Compared with postnatal treatment these approaches have the advantage of being applicable early enough to prevent changes that may be irreversible if left until after birth (Hsia, 1975). However, they are clearly no different in principle from postnatal interventions and even though they comprise earlier and potentially more effective treatment, they do not constitute prevention of the conditions themselves.

The second option in the event of prenatal diagnosis of fetal disorder is abortion. Although this is clearly primary prevention of the chronic stress that may be experienced by parents and family of an affected child, when the focus is on the condition itself, whether abortion is regarded as primary prevention or not is a matter of definition. It can reduce the prevalance of a disorder but does not affect incidence, unless one adopts birth as the point at which incidence is determined. Although it obviously prevents the birth of an infant with a given condition, it does not prevent the occurrence of the condition. Furthermore it is possible that detection and abortion of affected fetuses could result in an increase in the number of abnormal genes in the population as a whole since parents may tend to replace affected fetuses with normal infants, about two-thirds of whom will be unaffected carriers of the condition (Harris, 1975). In the case of many congenital disorders abortion is, at present, the only method available to avoid the birth of an affected child. An intriguing alternative approach is contained in the suggestion that we find ways of improving the natural mechanisms that already result in the discarding of a large proportion of damaged embryos (Fraser, 1978; Smithells, 1978), an approach that Warkany (1978) has termed "terathanasia". When prenatal diagnosis *excludes* the possibility that the fetus is defective, its findings could be said to constitute primary prevention since they eliminate a source of parental apprehension and anxiety that might affect development.

A problem that presents other kinds of difficulties for practical application of prenatal diagnosis and from the point of view of obviation or prevention of the conditions rather than their treatment is related to decisions about the circumstances in which prenatal diagnosis should be used. One possibility is to attempt to implement prenatal diagnosis universally. Such an approach would encounter formidable technical, economic, service delivery, psychological, legal, and ethical obstacles (many of which are discussed in the volume on preventing genetic disease and mental retardation edited by Milunsky, 1975a). The more practicable approach is to use prenatal diagnostic techniques only when there are a priori reasons to suspect genetic or congenital abnormalities. At present, indications for undertaking prenatal diagnosis include the following (Kushnick, 1979):

•For chromosomal abnormalities: advanced parental age, chromosomal abnormalities in a parent; previous chromosomally abnormal child or abortus

•For metabolic diseases: known maternal metabolic disorders; both parents known carriers; mother known or suspected carrier of X-linked disorder; previous affected child.

•For neural tube defects: raised maternal alpha-fetoprotein; previous affected child.

•For erythroblastosis: Rh negative mother.

The presence of indicators of these kinds defines a pregnancy in which the risk of a child with significant impairment is substantially greater than it is in the population at large. As indicated, if the aim is primary prevention, prenatal diagnosis, for whatever reason it is carried out, has limitations. Even its effective use as a method of secondary prevention is compromised as long as issues relating to the availability of adequate medical attention and the resources and knowledge to seek it remain unresolved. In addition, there are somewhat different implications for prevention depending on the kind of risk indicator which determines that diagnostic methods are invoked.

Indicators like parental age and manifest metabolic disorder offer the best possibility for prevention since they provide a way of identifying couples at risk before the birth of an affected child. Age of parents and, for some disorders, ethnicity (sickle cell anemia, Tay-Sachs disease, and so forth) can provide indications of risk before the disorders have appeared in the family. Recognized metabolic disorders in a family, although no strictly "pre-proband" indicators, at least are potentially capable of indicating risk before an affected child is born to the couple. By contrast, when risk indicators that depend on the prior birth—or miscarriage—of an affected child are relied upon, "only limited reduction in the overall postnatal incidence of the disease could be expected" (Kaback, 1975, p. 95), since the majority of cases of genetic disease tend to occur in families without a previous history of the disorder.

The final category of risk indicators includes such things as knowledge that the parents are carriers of a genetic disorder or knowledge of correlates of fetal defects, such as raised maternal serum alpha-fetoprotein. Discussion of these indicators can be recursive: unless we rely on post-proband identification of at-risk couples, with its attendant drawbacks, or screen entire populations (and this may be feasible for some disorders: see Scriver and Laberge, 1978), we need to determine on the basis of what indicators (of possible possession of deleterious genes) we will look for indicators (of prenatal disorder).

These questions as to whom to apply techniques are important not only in the context of prenatal diagnosis but also for using pre-proband identification techniques to obviate the *conception* of children with genetic disorders, a topic that will be discussed in the section on primary prevention.

Maternal risk factors.
The rationale of an approach to prevention based on maternal risk factors is that through adequate prenatal care to reduce the occurrance of disorders of pregnancy or labor or through identification and subsequent treatment or management of such disorders, adverse neonatal outcomes can be avoided or the severity of the disorders reduced. There is no shortage of risk factors that can be used to identify high-risk pregnancies: For example, McNeil and Kaij (1977) list 20 criteria used to identify obstetric risk groups in need of specialist care in the Swedish health system; Meier (1975) identifies 26 risk factors spanning maternal variables and complications during pregnancy and delivery; and Chez, Haire, Quilligan, and Wingate (1976), in the course of their comprehensive review of the relationships between prenatal and perinatal factors and adverse neonatal outcome, provide a table that contains a total of 69 pregnancy risk factors (not counting 19 fetal-maternal and neonatal factors).

A list of the categories of variables other than fetal-maternal and neonatal ones that Chez et al. (1976) present illustrates the variety of factors that can be involved in this approach:

•socioeconomic factors (for example, father's occupation, housing conditions, minority status, early prepregnancy malnutrition)

•demographic factors (for example, maternal age, weight, familial genetic disorder, poor obstetric history)

•maternal medical factors (for example, lack of prenatal care, toxemia, hypertensive disorders, mental retardation, emotional disturbance)

•placental and membrane factors (for example, vaginal bleeding, placental insufficiency, abruptio placentae)

•labor and delivery factors (for example, premature labor, prolonged labor, high mid-forceps delivery).

It seems clear that the efficacy of interventions based on the presence of risk factors of these kinds is dependent upon their being obviated entirely or treated as early as possible. This in turn depends upon the availability of prenatal care that people can afford and a recognition by consumers of the need to seek such care as early as possible. In practice it is just those groups that are at highest risk on socioeconomic criteria—the poor, the unmarried, the oppressed minorities—who are least likely to seek early care, as well as those least likely to receive adequate care when they do (Birch and Gussow, 1970). Experience in Sweden indicates that such problems may arise even when services are readily available; according to McNeil and Kaij (1977), "the women who do not take advantage of the [parent education] classes are to a large extent the very ones who need the most help—the young, the poorly informed, and foreigners" (p. 99).

In the event that risk factors are recognized, a variety of medical and "psycho-obstetric" (McNeil and Kaij, 1977) interventions are available to reduce the probability of miscarriage of embryonic or fetal damage. Depending on the nature of the condition, intervention may take the form of evaluating the condition of the embryo or fetus (perhaps followed, if indicated, by treatment or abortion) or implementing one or other form of medical management of the condition. Given the diversity of the risk factors involved, it is difficult to provide an overall characterization of the preventive status of the approach. Much depends on the nature of the risk factors.

When maternal medical or placental or membrane factors are involved, the approach can be said to constitute primary prevention insofar as the conditions can be corrected and the potential threat to the unborn child expeditiously removed; the only qualification would pertain to the question of whether the condition itself could have been prevented through earlier intervention. When the measures are palliative, as with medical or obstetric disorders that can only be ameliorated or their consequences monitored to enable treatment to be instituted expeditiously—perhaps maternal diabetes and placenta praevia constitute examples of such disorders—the approach might be termed partial prevention. When the maternal risk factors result in prenatal examination of the fetus and subsequent fetal therapy or abortion, the approach, as discussed earlier, constitutes early treatment. Similarly, when labor and delivery factors are involved, interventions will often have to be directed at neonatal amelioration of the effects on the infant.

Socioeconomic and demographic risk factors are different from the other factors considered, both in the sense of being antecedents of other risks and in being unamenable to alteration by the types of techniques used to deal with complications of pregnancy and delivery. Demographic variables may predict a greater probability that complications will occur but variables like family income, maternal age or stature, and poor obstetric history are not treatable in the same way as medical disorders. Aspects of this dilemma will be discussed later.

Primary Prevention

In discussing high-risk approaches we mostly considered methods of ameliorating or eliminating the early consequences of genetic and chromosomal factors on the one hand and prenatal and perinatal factors and events on the other. These approaches cannot be considered to be primary prevention insofar as they deal with disorders after their occurrence: in many cases the very presence of high-risk groups constitutes evidence that primary prevention measures have either not been implemented or have failed.

If we are actually to prevent risk—that is, to eliminate the occurrence of conceptuses with chromosomal and genetic disorders, women who are reproductively incompetent, the occurrence of prenatal and perinatal events that harm the unborn child—we need to identify and eradicate the factors that result in their occurrence or to alter those exposed to them in a way that makes them immune to the effects. In brief, we have to identify and control the *causes of the causes,* the events and conditions that fill the empty boxes in Figure I. Causal chains are long and complex, and it is in the nature of scientific inquiry to be selective about which links to investigate in detail. In addition, causal chains tend to acquire more and more interlinking strands as one moves away from the effect one wishes to understand, making it less likely, and certainly more difficult to demonstrate, that earlier links constitute necessary and sufficient conditions for the occurrence of the "effect". Consequently, once important links are identified, there is a tendency to concentrate study on subsequent links rather than antecedent ones, so that the "causes of the causes" are relatively neglected.

The subsequent discussion attempts to demonstrate the greater effectiveness of directing more effort at dealing with earlier links, first briefly in considering genetic and chromosomal disorders and then at more length in considering environmentally related prenatal and perinatal factors and events.

Genetic and chromosomal disorders.

We know a considerable amount about the antecedents of chromosomal and genetic disorders. Some chromosomal abnormalities (and genetic mutations) are the result of environmental agents, which are considered in the next section. In other cases we can identify causally relevant variables, those that may not constitute immediate antecedents of chromosomal abnormalities, but that are predictive of an increased likelihood of such abnormalities. An obvious example is the relationship between maternal and paternal age and Down's syndrome (Abroms and Bennett, 1979), with considerably increased risk of chromosomal nondisjunction in older parents. Intervening to ensure that people confine child bearing to their lower risk years would presumably constitute a preventive measure although recent decreases in mean age of child-bearing women in England, Canada, the United States, and other industrialized nations (Holmes, 1978) have not, however, been accompanied by a decreased incidence of Down's syndrome, possibly indicating an improvement in ascertainment or a biological change (see Bennett and Abroms, 1979). It is interesting to note that such an approach, despite its apparent simplicity, has many ramifications. At the very least, to be maximally effective, it requires widespread educational measures and the availability (and acceptability) of contraceptive measures; it is little use telling women over 35 not to have babies unless steps have been taken to ensure that they have had the number of children they want before then (and unless they have the means of preventing further conceptions and the willingness to use them). Ensuring that a desired family size is attained during the optimal years for childbearing in turn depends in part on socioeconomic conditions and on social support services since family planning is affected by a couple's ability to afford the loss of income resulting from interruption of work and by the question of whether or not there are affordable and adequate alternatives to one member rearing the child rather than being employed outside the home.

We know enough to prevent a great many genetic disorders too. We can, as yet, do little, even if we wish to, about the ultimate causes of genetic defects, mutation, and natural selection, but we could, in many cases, take steps to deal with the proximate cause of genetically affected embryos, the mating of genetic carriers. People affected with dominant genetic disorders or X-linked ones pose a threat to their offspring regardless of the genotype of their mate, while individuals heterozygous for some autosomal recessive disorder (unaffected carriers) pose a threat only if their mate is also a carrier (Reilly, 1975). Provided such individuals can be identified, intervention to reduce the incidence of genetic disorders is possible, with the potential efficacy of intervention substantially greater in cases in which identification can be made prior to the birth of an affected child (as was discussed earlier). At present, only one preventive method is available in such cases, the prevention of reproduction—either the abortion of the conceptus or the prevention of conception. In principle, such an approach could be extremely effective: "Mass screening for genetic disease, when coupled with appropriate mating prohibitions, could permit the reduction of all identifiable disorders to mutation level in a single generation" (Reilly, 1975, pp. 430–431). Aside from technical and economic considerations (Harris, 1975), mass screening (and effective use of the information obtained) poses a variety of legal questions (Reilly, 1975). In addition, the design and implementation of programs to reduce the frequency of "deleterious" genes—negative eugenics—through voluntary or compulsory restrictions on procreation raise troubling ethical issues, the difficulties of which are exacerbated by geographic, ethnic, and class-related concentrations of certain genes and by lack of knowledge of what constitutes eugenic improvement (Lappé, 1975). Similar issues arise, though less pointedly, in attempts to apply the same preventive method on a smaller scale, through the use of genetic counseling (Milunsky, 1975b). At present, expanded availability of genetic counseling in conjunction with increased public awareness of its role probably represent the least controversial approach to the primary prevention of genetic disorders. In combination with improved techniques of identification and mass screening it has the potential to reduce markedly the incidence of such disorders.

Environmental factors and events.

In abstract terms, the process of prevention can be stated very simply: once the damaging agent is identified, any one of three actions can be taken to prevent its effects—removal of the agent, strengthening the host to increase resistance to the agent, or preventing contact between agent and host (Roberts, 1970). In the case of deleterious prenatal and perinatal environmental factors and events, we have a great deal of knowledge about the agents involved. This knowledge takes two apparently disparate forms: information about factors that cause adverse outcomes (see Table 1) and information about variables correlated with such outcomes. In neither case does the information alone seem to enable us to determine ways of removing agents, strengthening the host, or preventing contact between agent and host. In each case we seem to have to do something further with the information to design prevention programs. The remainder of this paper will briefly examine the form that these attempts take and argue that the "causes" are less relevant to prevention than the correlated variables and that the reluctance to deal directly with these variables is based on misconceptions.

First, then, we examine the prenatal "causes" of adverse development. Table 1 lists categories of causes and we can provide detailed lists of agents in each category, yet these do not, in themselves suggest what can be done. The problem seems to result from the fact that exposure to any of the agents in Table 1 could arise in many different ways, each involving multiple determinants. In practice, what we seem to do to design prevention programs is to look for these determinants—in effect, to identify the causes of the causes. We might, for example, inquire about why a pregnant woman took a prescription drug during pregnancy, and identify among the causes failures in medical education; ignorance of the patient (of the risk or of the fact that she was pregnant); too-ready reliance on chemical solutions to problems of living (in the case of a tranquilizer, say) in both doctor and patient; the overconcern of the pharmaceutical industry with profit; the unavailability, inaccessibility, or unaffordability of alternative means of dealing with problems for which the tranquilizer was resorted to; and so on. The number and scope of "prevention programs" suggested by even a casual analysis of this kind is dizzying and could involve anything from revising the medical school curriculum and increasing the number of public service messages in the media to nationalizing the pharmaceutical industry.

This kind of approach is nothing if not fruitful and does offer potential benefits, but they may be slow in coming and each program may in itself be able to show only negligible results. As Fraser (1978) suggested about the prevention of teratogenic effects, "no one preventive measure will bring about a dramatic drop in frequency. . . . We must keep on chipping away . . . ; each small decrease in the burden will be vitally important to some families, and the cumulative effect will be eventually visible" (p. 398). The practical difficulties of obtaining funding for programs that only chip away are substantial; many otherwise admirable programs will founder on the fiscal rocks given their low expectations of benefits in relation to costs. In attempting to prioritize programs we will be in danger of spending the little that is available for prevention (Albee, 1979) on pilot projects.

Parenthetically, this approach represents something of a methodological paradox. Normally, compounded variables correlated with a particular outcome are subjected to further dissection, by experimental study whenever possible, to identify "causal variables" entangled in the correlations. Yet it seems that to develop effective prevention programs we may have to go from the kinds of physical, chemical, and biological variables we have already identified to the larger network of variables that encompass them.

The second approach, which starts with the larger, correlated variables usually suggests programs that are indistinguishable from those arrived at by the first, but the process differs. In this approach, we start with the demographic variables that correlate with the outcome we wish to prevent, those variables encompassed by answers to questions about who does and does not suffer from a given condition and when and where the condition is or is not found. When we do this, we find that our best predictors are global and complex variables like ethnic group and socioeconomic status. With regard to prenatal factors, for example, the variables in the Collaborative Perinatal Project (Broman et al., 1975) with the highest correlations with IQ at age 4 were socioeconomic index and mother's education (there was also a 13 point IQ difference between black and white children) and in the Kauai study (Werner and Smith, 1977) low level of maternal education and low standard of living were among the key predictors of poor developmental outcomes at 2 years and of learning and behavior problems at 10 and 18.

What do we do with such information? The short answer is, anything but deal with the factors identified. We claim that the only proper use of such data is to look for variables within the demographic correlates that account for the effects and that it is misguided to consider that prevention might best be served by dealing with them directly. They can be unravelled in plausible ways. For example: "The poor woman having a baby may be at risk because of her age, her nutritional status, her probable poor growth, her excessive exposure to infection in the community which she inhabits, her poor housing, and her inadequate medical supervision, as well as because of complex interactions between these and other potentially adverse influences" (Birch and Gussow, 1970, p. 175). Such unravelling is useful in suggesting prevention programs: we can design programs to improve prenatal care in urban ghettos; to provide vitamin supplements for poor women; to reduce drug abuse; and so on. These are very much the kinds of programs suggested by the first approach, in which the reasons people are exposed to the proximate causes of poor developmental outcomes are analyzed.

An interesting question arises, however. Since the broad demographic variables seem to encompass something closer to ultimate causes, and since we seem to be better able to design prevention programs when we deal with causes of causes, why do we choose the middle ground? Why do we ask: What is it about poverty that produces increases in birth defects, prematurity, perinatal death, instead of designing programs to prevent poverty?[1] Why do we ask, what is it about powerlessness that produces breakdown, misery, and violence, instead of trying to redistribute power?

We seem to be given three reasons why we should leave the broader variables alone: They are not the real causes of the problems, we are not

[1] For example: "The important question . . . is: in what way do adverse socio-economic conditions produce the disorders of pregnancy and delivery?" (Joffe, 1969, p. 269). I was writing at the time about methodological issues but cannot now defend the narrowness of focus that makes analysis of the variables entwined in socioeconomic status *the* important question.

competent to deal with them, and it would not solve the problem if we did. The first reason has to do with a particular concept of what constitutes a causal relationship and implies that attempting to deal with global factors is scientifically misguided. For example:

Efforts at prevention will not succeed . . . unless we establish specific interventions that work on the causes of specific kinds of psychopathology. . . . Without an understanding of causes, we are in the position of relying on serendipity—surely a poor substitute for the solid knowledge that research can provide—or relying on vague hopes that broad, often unsubstantiated social action programs will automatically decrease the rate of mental illness by correcting social woes and increasing the general psychological well-being. Arnhoff (1975) noted, "Somewhere along the line, a problem as old as man, that of mental illness, was absorbed into the pursuit of global mental health" (p. 1281). It is this confusion of objectives that has led some workers to formulate the issue of primary prevention in terms of eliminating poverty, slums, and economic insecurity—among other commendable but nebulous proposals. (Erlenmeyer-Kimling, 1977, p. 86)

It seems that we think we have two kinds of variables: the "real causes"—things like drug abuse, marital problems, lack of parenting skills—that we can deal with as professionals, and the global and nebulous factors, like poverty, ignorance, and powerlessness that we know correlate with the causes but do not themselves constitute causes. The dichotomy is misleading in implying that the variables we can deal with have a unique scientific status—it cloaks our bias and ignorance in a scientific rationalization.

In fact, the "real causes" do not appear to be quite as different from "mere correlations" as we seem to find it convenient to believe, and if this is the case, we cannot be excused on scientific grounds from dealing with the correlated variables. This is not the place to undertake a philosophical disquisition of the nature of causation. However, it is pertinent to point out that the distinction between "genuine causes" and "merely correlated" variables is more complex than seems to be appreciated by many of those who wish to make this kind of distinction with a view to de-emphasizing the kinds of variables the importance of which I want to stress. If one takes the simplest approach, that variables have to be individually necessary and sufficient in order to be regarded as causal, one will find that very few causes have been identified in the biological and social sciences—or even in physics for that matter. In many cases we cannot claim that what we regard as a causal variable is either necessary or sufficient. In fact, we appear to recognize a causal relationship when we see that in the presence of a particular factor the probability of a certain outcome is increased and we have no reason to believe that both are dependent on a third variable. Given these considerations, brief as they may be, unless one has evidence that both are due to a third (genetic?) variable, there is no reason not to say that poverty and powerlessness (see Albee, 1980) cause disease—and birth defects.

Variables like age, ethnic group, socioeconomic status, education, housing conditions, and so on are not second-class scientific variables and attending to them may, in fact, enable us to design more effective prevention programs than we can when we give all our attention to *mere causes*.

The second reason we are given why we have no business with social reform is that we have no particular competence in this area and that involving ourselves in the arena of social reform detracts from our credibility and effectiveness as professionals. For example:

Instead of focusing narrowly on the environmental stressors that are likely to be amenable to the intervention of mental health specialists with community decision makers, they become preoccupied by such major and global problems as poverty and racial prejudice, and they embark themselves on quixotic remedial campaigns as revolutionaries and social agitators. Unfortunately, they are no more skilled in social action than in community mental health practice; on the one hand they make inflated rhetorical promises about putting the bad world right which eventually bring inevitable discredit, or they lead inept marches on City Hall on behalf of the downtrodden, and get repudiated both by their disappointed clients and by the municipal authorities who pay their salaries. In any event, primary prevention for which they have ostensibly been fighting, gets a bad name. (Caplan, 1978 p. 10).

Indeed we may have no special competence as professionals to solve social problems—even if we do seem to be able to identify them—but the modesty we assume when talking about poverty and injustice seems to be put aside when we attempt to influence public policy to achieve what we claim as professional goals. Do we not claim special competence in identifying needs and implementing solutions when it comes to influencing legislation or acquiring funding for prevention programs of other kinds? Is it that we define as within our professional sphere those actions and aims that we approve of, while those we disapprove of are "political"? Furthermore, with whom do we lose credibility when we attempt remedial campaigns? It seems that our inaction, rather than action, in the social arena is more likely to compromise the credibility of our efforts as professionals. Or do we believe that our efforts as professionals excuse us from working for social change? If primary prevention is to have any hope of success, it needs a more committed stance than that represented by an "I gave at the office" philosophy.

The third reason we are given why we should not attack social evils is that even if we succeeded we would not have eradicated deviance, unhappiness, or the birth of infants with impaired potential. This, too, may be true, but there are reasons to believe that this approach will achieve more than piecemeal one-small-problem-at-a-time approaches. If we are realistic, we acknowledge that each proximate cause is the outcome of complex interactions of variables and that, as Vance (1977) pointed out, "the greater the number of relevant interactions, the smaller the groupings for which a single treatment will be appropriate" (p. 208). If this is so, then either we resign ourselves to designing myriads of low-payoff prevention programs or we lay siege to the broader variables that encompass the complex interacting variables. Dealing with variables like socioeconomic status and ethnicity deals simultaneously with factors giving rise to hazardous prenatal and perinatal events, those enhancing susceptibility to such events, and those that ensure postnatal conditions that at best fail to alleviate the consequences of prenatal hazards and at worst exacerbate their efforts. In addition, the broader variables are also more promising in terms of the timing of intervention. They exert their effects earlier than the proximate causes of adverse neonatal outcomes so their eradication has a greater change of obviating problems before they occur. A further advantage to putting emphasis on prevention that can be achieved through attention to demographic variables is that the approach encompasses both prevention and promotion: Removal of the global causes of dysfunction at the very least should result in a population with the means and the desire to pursue improved function. Removing external barriers strengthens people and provides conditions in which they can direct their strength toward the removal of further barriers.

None of this is to argue that social change will solve all the problems but rather that without such change much of whatever else we do may be futile. We will have to do it over and over again. Social change may not be sufficient, but it is necessary. Even if social change brought equitable programs to prevent genetic disease, reduce reproductive incompetence, and minimize environmental hazards, we would still be left with an apparently irreducible minimum of developmental defects. The perspective of primary prevention might be defined as never concluding that the minimum has been reached.

References

Abroms, K. I., and Bennett, J. W. Parental age and Trisomy-21. *Down's Syndrome*, 1979, 2, 6–7.

Ad Hoc Committee on the Effect of Trace Anesthetics on the Health of Operating Room Personnel. Occupational disease among operating room personnel: A national study. *Anesthesiology,* 1974, *41,* 321–340.

Albee, G. W. The prevention of prevention. *Physician East,* April 1979, 28–30.

Albee, G. W. Politics, power, prevention, and social change. In J. M. Joffe and G. W. Albee (Eds.), *Prevention through political action and social change,* Vol. 5: *Primary prevention of psychopathology.* Hanover, N.H.: University Press of England, 1980.

Arnhoff, F. N. Social consequences of policy toward mental illness. *Science,* 1975, *188,* 1277–1281.

Badr, F. M., and Badr, R. S. Induction of dominant lethal mutation in male mice by ethyl alcohol. *Nature,* 1975, *253,* 134–136.

Baird, D. Social class and foetal mortality. *Lancet,* 1949, *1,* 1079–1083.

Baird, D. The epidemiology of prematurity. *Journal of Pediatrics,* 1964, *65,* 909–924.

Baird, D. Epidemiology of congenital malformations of the central nervous system in (a) Aberdeen and (b) Scotland. *Journal of Biosocial Science,* 1974, *6,* 113–137.

Baird, D., and Illsley, R. Environment and childbearing. *Proceedings of the Royal Society of Medicine,* 1953, *46,* 53–59.

Barnes, A. C. The fetal environment: Drugs and chemicals. In A. C. Barnes (Ed.), *Intrauterine development.* Philadelphia: Lea and Febiger, 1968.

Bennett, J. W., and Abroms, K. I. Changing perspectives on Down's syndrome. *Journal of the Louisiana Medical Society,* 1979, *131,* 305–307.

Bernard, R. M. The shape and size of the female pelvis. (Transactions of the Edinburgh Obstetrical Society) *Edinburgh Medical Journal,* 1952, *59,* 1–16.

Birch, H. G., and Gussow, J. D. *Disadvantaged children: Health, nutrition and school failure.* New York: Harcourt, Brace, and World, 1970.

Bloom, M. A working definition of primary prevention related to social concerns. *The Journal of Prevention,* 1980, *1,* 15–23.

Brackbill, Y. Obstetrical medication and infant behavior. In J. D. Osofsky (Ed.), *Handbook of infant behavior.* New York: Wiley, 1979.

Brady, H., Herrera, Y., and Zenick, H. Influence of parental lead exposure on subsequent learning ability of offspring. *Pharmacology, Biochemistry and Behavior,* 1975, *3,* 561–565.

Brent, R. L. Environmental factors: Miscellaneous. In R. L. Brent and M. I. Harris (Eds.), *Prevention of embryonic, fetal, and perinatal disease.* DHEW Pub. No. (NIH) 76-853. Washington, D.C., 1976.

Brent, R. L. Radiations and other physical agents. In J. G. Wilson and F. C. Fraser (Eds.), *Handbook of teratology.* Vol. 1: *General principles and etiology.* New York: Plenum, 1977.

Brent, R. L., and Harris, M. I. Summaries. In R. L. Brent and M. I. Harris (Eds.), *Prevention of embryonic, fetal, and perinatal disease.* DHEW Pub. No. (NIH) 76-853. Washington, D.C., 1976.

Broman, S. H., Nichols, P. L., and Kennedy, W. A. *Preschool IQ: Prenatal and early developmental correlates.* Hillsdale, N.J.: L. Erlbaum Associates, 1975.

Caplan, G. *The primary prevention of mental disorders in children: Developments during the period 1962–1977.* Lecture, University of Leuven, Belgium, May 26, 1978.

Carter, C. O., and Evans, K. Spina bifida and anencephalus in Greater London. *Journal of Medical Genetics,* 1973, *10,* 209–234.

Catz, C. S., and Yaffe, S. J. Environmental factors: Pharmacology. In R. L. Brent and M. I. Harris (Eds.), *Prevention of embryonic, fetal, and perinatal disease.* DHEW Pub. No. (NIH) 76-853. Washington, D.C., 1976.

Chez, R., Haire, D., Quilligan, E. J., and Wingate, M. B. High risk pregnancies: Obstetrical and perinatal factors. In R. L. Brent and M. I. Harris (Eds.), *Prevention of embryonic, fetal, and perinatal disease.* DHEW Pub. No. (NIH) 76-853 Washington, D.C., 1976.

Chyzzer, A. Des intoxications per le plumb se presentant dans le ceramique en Hongrie Budapest XLIV, Chir. Presse, 1908, 906. (Quoted by Weller, 1915).

Cohen, E. N., Brown, Jr., B. W., Bruce, D. L., Cascorbi, H. F., Corbett, T. H., Jones, T. W., and Whitcher, C. E. A survey of anesthetic health hazards among dentists. *Journal of the American Dental Association,* 1975, *90,* 1291–1296.

Cole, L. J., and Bachhuber, L. J. The effect of lead on the germ cells of the male rabbit and fowl. *Proceedings of the Society for Experimental Biology and Medicine,* 1914, *12,* 24–29.

Corah, N. L., Anthony, E. J., Painter, P., Stern, J. A., and Thurston, D. L. Effects of perinatal anoxia after seven years. *Psychological Monographs,* 1965, *79,* 3 (Whole No. 596).

Cowley, J. J., and Griesel, R. D. The effect on growth and behavior of rehabilitating first and second generation low protein rats. *Animal Behaviour,* 1966, *14,* 506–517.

Durham, F. M., and Woods, H. M. Alcohol and inheritance: An experimental study. *Medical Research Council Special Report Series.* London: H.M.S.O., No. 168, 1932.

Elinson, J., and Wilson, R. W. Prevention. In *Health, United States, 1978.* U.S. Department of Health, Education and Welfare. DHEW Pub. No. (PHS) 78-1232. Hyattsville, M.D., 1978.

Emanuel, I. Problems of outcome of pregnancy: Some clues from the epidemiologic similarities and differences. In S. Kelly, E. B. Hook, D. T. Janerich, and I. H. Porter (Eds.), *Birth defects: Risks and consequences.* New York: Academic Press, 1976.

Erlenmeyer-Kimling, L. Issues pertaining to prevention and intervention of genetic disorders affecting human behavior. In G. W. Albee and J. M. Joffe (Eds.), *Primary prevention of psychopathology,* Vol. 1: *The issues.* Hanover, N.H.: University Press of New England, 1977.

Ferreira, M.C.R. Malnutrition and mother-infant asynchrony: Slow mental development. *International Journal of Behavioral Development,* 1978, *1,* 207–219.

Fraser, F. C. Interactions and multiple causes. In J. G. Wilson and F. C. Fraser (Eds.), *Handbook of teratology,* Vol. 1: *General principles and etiology.* New York: Plenum, 1977.

Fraser, F. C. Future prospects—clinical. In J. W. Littlefield, J. DeGrouchy, and F.J.G. Ebling (Eds.), *Birth defects. Proceedings of the fifth international conference, Montreal, Canada, 21–27 August 1977.* Amsterdam: Excerpta Medica, 1978.

Friedler, G. Morphine administration to male mice. Effects on subsequent progeny. *Federation Proceedings,* 1974, *33,* 515.

Golbus, M. S. Prenatal diagnosis of genetic defects—where it is and where it is going. In J. W. Littlefield, J. DeGrouchy, and F.J.G. Ebling (Eds.) *Birth defects. Proceedings of the fifth international conference, Montreal, Canada, 21–27 August 1977.* Amsterdam: Excerpta Medica, 1978.

Goldman, A. S. Critical periods of prenatal toxic insults. In R. H. Schwarz and

S. J. Yaffe (Eds.), *Drug and chemical risks to the fetus and newborn.* New York: A. R. Liss, 1980.

Graham, F. K., Ernhart, C. B., Thurston, D. L., and Craft, M. Development three years after perinatal anoxia and other potentially damaging newborn experiences. *Psychological Monographs,* 1962, *76,* 3 (Whole No. 522).

Graham, F. K., Matarazzo, R. G., and Caldwell, B. M. Behavioral differences between normal and traumatized newborns: II. Standardization, reliability, and validity. *Psychological Monographs,* 1956, *70,* 21 (Whole No. 428).

Graham, F. K., Pennoyer, M. M., Caldwell, B. M., Greenman, M., and Hartman, A. F. Relationship between clinical status and behavior test performance in a newborn group with histories suggesting anoxia. *Journal of Pediatrics,* 1957, *50,* 177–189.

Grabowski, C. T. Atmospheric gases: Variations in concentration and some common pollutants. In J. G. Wilson and F. C. Fraser (Eds.), *Handbook of teratology,* Vol. 1: *General principles and etiology.* New York: Plenum, 1977.

Harris, H. *Prenatal diagnosis and selective abortion.* Cambridge, Mass.: Harvard University Press, 1975.

Hertig, A. T., Rock, J., and Adams, E. C. A description of 34 human ova within the first 17 days of development. *American Journal of Anatomy,* 1956, *98,* 435–459.

Holmes, L. B. Genetic counseling for the older pregnant woman: New data and questions. *New England Journal of Medicine,* 1978, *298,* 1419–1421.

Hsia, Y. E. Treatment in genetic diseases. In A. Milunsky (Ed.), *The prevention of genetic disease and mental retardation.* Philadelphia: W. B. Saunders, 1975.

Ingalls, T. H. Preventive prenatal pediatrics. *Advances in Pediatrics,* 1953, *6,* 33–62.

Joffe, J. M. *Prenatal determinants of behavior.* Oxford: Pergamon, 1969.

Joffe, J. M. Influence of drug exposure of the father on perinatal outcome. In L. F. Soyka (Ed.), *Clinics in perinatology,* Vol. 6, No. 1: *Symposium on pharmacology.* Philadelphia: W. B. Saunders, 1979.

Joffe, J. M., Peterson, J. M., Smith, D. J., and Soyka, L. F. Sublethal effects on offspring of male rats treated with methadone. *Research Communications in Chemical Pathology and Pharmacology,* 1976, *13,* 611–621.

Kaback, M. M., Heterozygote screening for the control of recessive genetic disease. In A. Milunsky (Ed.), *The prevention of genetic disease and mental retardation.* Philadelphia: W. B. Saunders, 1975.

Kessler, M., and Albee, G. W. Primary prevention. *Annual Review of Psychology,* 1975, *26,* 557–591.

Klassen, R. W., and Persaud, T.V.N. Experimental studies on the influence of male alcoholism on pregnancy and progeny. *Experimental Pathology,* 1976, *12,* 38–45.

Kopp, C. B., and Parmelee, A. H. Prenatal and perinatal influences on infant behavior. In J. D. Osofsky (Ed.) *Handbook of infant development.* New York: Wiley, 1979.

Kushnick, T. Antenatal diagnosis. In H. A. Kaminetzky, L. Iffy, and J. J. Apuzzio (Eds.), *New techniques and concepts in maternal and fetal medicine.* New York: VanNostrand Reinhold, 1979.

Lappé, M. Can eugenic policy be just? In A. Milunsky (Ed.), *The prevention of genetic disease and mental retardation.* Philadelphia: W. B. Saunders, 1975.

Lutwak-Mann, C. Observations on progeny of thalidomide-treated male rabbits. *British Medical Journal,* 1964, *1,* 1090–1091.

Lutwak-Mann, C., Schmid, K., and Keberle, H. Thalidomide in rabbit semen. *Nature*, 1967, *214*, 1018–1020.

MacDowell, E. C., and Lord, E. M. Reproduction in alcoholic mice: Treated males. Study of prenatal mortality and sex ratios. *Archiv fur Entwicklungsmechanik der Organismen*, 1927, *110*, 427–449.

MacDowell, E. C., Lord, E. M., and MacDowell, C. G. Heavy alcoholization and prenatal mortality in mice. *Proceedings of the Society for Experimental Biology and Medicine*, 1926, *23*, 652–654. (a)

MacDowell, E. C., Lord, E. M., and MacDowell, C. G. Sex ratio of mice from alcoholized fathers. *Proceedings of the Society for Experimental Biology and Medicine*, 1926, *23*, 517–519. (b)

McKusick, V. A. *Mendelian inheritance in man. Catalogs of autosomal dominant, autosomal recessive, and X-linked phenotypes* (3rd ed.). Baltimore: The Johns Hopkins Press, 1971.

McNeil, T. F., and Kaij, L. Prenatal, perinatal, and post-partum factors in primary prevention of psychopathology in offspring. In G. W. Albee and J. M. Joffe (Eds.), *Primary prevention of psychopathology*, Vol. 1: *The Issues*. Hanover N.H.: University Press of New England, 1977.

Meier, J. H. Early intervention in the prevention of mental retardation. In A. Milunsky (Ed.), *The prevention of genetic disease and mental retardation*. Philadelphia: W. B. Saunders, 1975.

Milunsky, A. (Ed.). *The prevention of genetic disease and mental retardation*. Philadelphia: W. B. Saunders, 1975. (a)

Milunsky, A. Genetic counseling: Principles and practice. In A. Milunsky (Ed.), *The prevention of genetic disease and mental retardation*. Philadelphia: W. B. Saunders, 1975. (b)

Milunsky, A., and Atkins, L. Prenatal diagnosis of genetic disorders. In A. Milunsky (Ed.), *The prevention of genetic disease and mental retardation*. Philadelphia: W. B. Saunders, 1975.

Motulsky, A., Benirschke, K., Carpenter, G., Fraser, C., Epstein, C., Nyhan, W., and Jackson, L. Genetic diseases. In R. L. Brent and M. I. Harris (Eds.), *Prevention of embryonic, fetal, and perinatal disease*. DHEW Pub. No. (NIH) 76-853. Washington, D.C., 1976.

National Center for Health Statistics. *Facts of life and death*. U.S. Dept. of Health, Education and Welfare. DHEW Pub. No. (PHS) 79-1222. Hyattsville, MD., 1978.

Nitowsky, H. M. Heterozygote detection in autosomal recessive biochemical disorders associated with mental retardation. In A. Milunsky (Ed.), *The prevention of genetic disease and mental retardation*. Philadelphia: W. B. Saunders, 1975.

Nuckolls, K. B., Cassel, J., and Kaplan, B. H. Psychosocial assets, life crisis, and the prognosis of pregnancy. *American Journal of Epidemiology*, 1972, *35*, 431–441.

Pasamanick, B., Knobloch, H., and Lilienfeld, A. M. Socioeconomic status and some precursors of neuropsychiatric disorders. *American Journal of Orthopsychiatry*, 1956, *26*, 594–601.

Paul, C. Archives generales de Medecine, 1860, *1*, 513. (Quoted by Weller, 1915).

Plomin, R., DeFries, J. C., and Loehlin, J. C. Genotype-environment interaction and correlation in the analysis of human behavior. *Psychological Bulletin*, 1977, *84*, 309–322.

Redmond, G. P. Effect of drugs on intrauterine growth. In L. F. Soyka (Ed.), *Clinics in Perinatology*, Vol. 6, No. 1: *Symposium on pharmacology*. Philadelphia: W. B. Saunders, 1979.

Reid, G. Report of the Departmental Commission on the dangers attendant on the use of lead. Quoted by T. Oliver, Lecture on lead poisoning and the race. *British Medical Journal*, 1911, *1*, 1096–1098.

Reilly, P. The role of law in the prevention of genetic disease. In A. Milunsky (Ed.), *The prevention of genetic disease and mental retardation*. Philadelphia: W. B. Saunders, 1975.

Ressler, R. H. Parental handling in two strains of mice reared by foster parents. *Science*, 1962, *137*, 129–130.

Roberts, C. A. Psychiatric and mental health consultation. *Canadian Journal of Public Health*, 1970, *51*, 17–24.

Rosen, G. *Preventive medicine in the United States 1900–1975: Trends and interpretations*. New York: Science History Publications, 1975.

Rudeaux, P. La Clinique, 1910. Quoted by Thompson in *The occupational diseases*. New York: Appleton, 1914.

Sameroff, A. J. Early influences on development: Fact or fancy? *Merrill-Palmer Quarterly of Behavior and Development*, 1975, *21*, 267–294.

Sameroff, A. J. Concepts of humanity in primary prevention. In G. W. Albee and J. M. Joffe (Eds.), *Primary prevention of psychopathology*, Vol. 1: *The issues*. Hanover, N.H.: University Press of New England, 1977.

Sameroff, A. J., and Chandler, M. J. Reproductive risk and the continuum of caretaking casualty. In F. D. Horowitz, M. Hetherington, S. Scarr-Salapatek, and G. Siegel (Eds.), *Review of child development research*, Vol. 4. Chicago: University of Chicago, 1975.

Scriver, C. R., and Laberge, C. Genetic screening. An outlook en route. In J. W. Littlefield, J. DeGrouchy, and F.J.G. Ebling (Eds.), *Birth defects. Proceedings of the fifth international conference, Montreal, Canada, 21–27 August 1977*. Amsterdam: Excerpta Medica, 1978.

Slone, D., Shapiro, S., and Mitchell, A. Strategies for studying the effects of the antenatal environment on the fetus. In R. H. Schwarz and S. J. Yaffe (Eds.), *Drug and chemical risks to the fetus and newborn*. New York: A. R. Liss, 1980.

Smith, D. J., and Joffe, J. M. Increased neonatal mortality in offspring of male rats treated with methadone or morphine before mating. *Nature*, 1975, *253*, 202–203.

Smithells, R. W. Future prospects: Environmental factors. In J. W. Littlefield, J. DeGrouchy, and F.J.G. Ebling (Eds.), *Birth defects. Proceedings of the fifth international conference, Montreal, Canada, 21–27 August 1977*. Amsterdam; Excerpta Medica, 1978.

Soyka, L. F., and Joffe, J. M. Influence of concurrent testosterone on the effects of methadone on male rats and their progeny. *Developmental Pharmacology and Therapeutics*, 1980, *1*, 182–188. (a)

Soyka, L. F., and Joffe, J. M. Male mediated drug effects on offspring. In R. H. Schwarz and S. J. Yaffe (Eds.), *Drug and chemical risks to the fetus and newborn*. New York: A. R. Liss, 1980. (b)

Soyka, L. J., Joffe, J. M., Peterson, J. M., and Smith, S. M. Chronic methadone administration to male rats: Tolerance to adverse effects on sires and their progeny. *Pharmacology, Biochemistry and Behavior*, 1978, *9*, 405–409. (a)

Soyka, L. F., Peterson, J. M., and Joffe, J. M. Lethal and sublethal effects on the progeny of male rats treated with methadone. *Toxicology and Applied Pharmacology*, 1978, *45*, 797–807. (b)

Stockard, C. R. Effect on the offspring of intoxicating the male parent and transmission of the defects of subsequent generations. *American Naturalist*, 1913, *47*, 641–682.

Stowe, H. D., and Goyer, R. A. The reproductive ability and progeny of F_1 lead-toxic rats. *Fertility and Sterility*, 1971, *22*, 755–760.

Task Panel on Prevention. *President's Commission on Mental Health* (Vol. 4). Washington, D.C.: U.S. Government Printing Office, No. 040-000-00393-2, 1978.

Thomas, A., Chess, S. and Birch, H. *Temperament and behavior disorders in children.* New York: New York University, 1968.

Thomson, A. M. Maternal stature and reproductive efficiency. *Eugenics Review*, 1959, *51*, 157–162.

Thomson, A. M., and Billewicz, W. Z. Nutritional status, physique and reproductive efficiency. *Proceedings of the Nutrition Society*, 1963, *22*, 55–60.

Tizard, J.P.M. Pre-natal and perinatal factors. In J. W. Littlefield, J. DeGrouchy, and F.J.G. Ebling (Eds.), *Birth defects. Proceedings of the fifth international conference, Montreal, Canada, 21–27 August 1977.* Amsterdam: Excerpta Medica, 1978.

Vance, E. T. A typology of risks and the disabilities of low status. In G. W. Albee and J. M. Joffe (Eds.), *Primary prevention of psychopathology*, Vol. 1: *The issues.* Hanover, N.H.: University Press of New England, 1977.

Warkany, J. Terathanasia. *Teratology*, 1978, *17*, 187–192.

Weathersbee, P. S., Ax, R. L., and Lodge, J. R. Caffeine-mediated changes of sex ratio in Chinese hamsters, *Cricetulus griseus. Journal of Reproduction and Fertility*, 1975, *43*, 141–143.

Weathersbee, P. S., Olsen, L. K., and Lodge, J. R. Caffeine and pregnancy: A retrospective study. *Postgraduate Medicine*, 1977, *62*, 64–69.

Weller, C. V. The blastophthoric effect of chronic lead poisoning. *Journal of Medical Research*, 1915, *33*, 271–293.

Werner, E. E., Bierman, J., and French, F. *The children of Kauai: A longitudinal study from the prenatal period to age ten.* Honolulu: University Press of Hawaii, 1971.

Werner, E. E., Bierman, J. M., French, F., Simonian, K., Connor, A., Smith, R., and Campbell, M. Reproductive and environmental casualties: A report on the 10 year follow-up of the children of the Kauai pregnancy study. *Pediatrics*, 1968, *42*, 112–127.

Werner, E. E., Simonian, K., Bierman, J. M., and French, F. Cumulative effect of perinatal complications and deprived environment on physical, intellectual and social development of preschool children. *Pediatrics*, 1967, *39*, 490–505.

Werner, E. E., and Smith, R. S. *Kauai's children come of age.* Honolulu: University Press of Hawaii, 1977.

Wilson, J. G. Embryological considerations in teratology. *Annals of the New York Academy of Sciences*, 1965, *123*, 219–227.

Wilson, J. G. Embryotoxicity of drugs in man. In J. G. Wilson and F. C. Fraser (Eds.), *Handbook of teratology*, Vol. 1: *General principles and etiology.* New York: Plenum, 1977. (a)

Wilson, J. G. Environmental chemicals. In J. G. Wilson and F. C. Fraser (Eds.), *Handbook of teratology*, Vol. 1: *General principles and etiology.* New York: Plenum, 1977. (b)

Winick, M. Maternal nutrition. In R. L. Brent and M. I. Harris (Eds.), *Prevention of embryonic, fetal, and perinatal disease.* DHEW Pub. No. (NIH) 76-853. Washington, D.C., 1976.

Yerushalmy, J. Biostatistical methods in investigations of child health. *American Journal of Diseases of Children*, 1967, *114*, 470–476.

Yerushalmy, J. Relationship of parents' cigarette smoking to outcome of pregnancy—implications as to the problem of inferring causation from observed observations. *American Journal of Epidemiology*, 1971, *93*, 443–456.

Young, R. D. Influence of neonatal treatment on maternal behavior: A confounding variable. *Psychonomic Science*, 1965, *3*, 295–296.

A Biological Perspective and a Behavioral Model for Assessment of Premature Infants

Evelyn B. Thoman

Premature birth is the single most prevalent perinatal abnormality, and the sequelae to prematurity remain a central concern from both the medical and social points of view. Clearly, this is a segment of the population for which the possibility for facilitating early development is great. In terms of outcome, individuals born prematurely range from those with severe abnormalities to those who are physically and emotionally healthy and intellectually superior, so that not all prematurely born infants are in need of facilitation or intervention once they have become stabilized following the trauma of early birth.

There is no question about the ongoing needs of infants with obvious physical impairment or neurological abnormalities. The persisting problem is that a large, but undetermined, percentage of those premature infants who appear to become stabilized in early infancy go on to have developmental dysfunction at a later age. Despite growing evidence that early intervention *can* prevent later emotional and cognitive disorders, and despite the enormous amount of attention and effort that has been dedicated to screening, assessment, and prediction, the remarkable lack of success in identifying those infants who may have subtle dysfunction at an early age has led some to conclude that prediction from early infancy is not possible (Meier, 1973). In fact, some have even deduced that early events, particularly in the premature infant prior to full gestational age, are not even related to later development.

Such conclusions have major political and social implications for continued efforts at identifying those infants who may have subtle dysfunction at an early age with more serious implications for later development. Most of us agree that these efforts must continue. It is apparent, however, that we need new paradigms and different approaches to iden-

The preparation of this paper was supported, in part, by NIH Grant No. HD-12948 from the National Institute of Child Health and Human Development, The William T. Grant Foundation, The Spencer Foundation, and the Connecticut Research Foundation.

160   EVELYN B. THOMAN

tifying these infants and considering their needs for intervention. A reformulation of the issues may lead to different questions, with more meaningful and practical answers.

Any reformulation must take into account the complexities of development, normal and abnormal. We still know very little about behavioral development during the preterm period, how prematurely born infants compare with full-terms at comparable gestational ages, or the implications for later development of the differences that may be due to prematurity. For example, in a recent study (Booth, Leonard, and Thoman, 1980), we found that the sleep-wake organization of prematurely born infants was, in some ways, delayed when compared with full-term infants and, on some measures, their state organization was more advanced. Thus, we concluded that the premature infants could not be described as being either delayed or advanced as a function of their differential perinatal history. Rather, their state behaviors are differently organized. These differences can be viewed as handicaps only to the extent that they are maladaptive, and this is certainly not necessarily the case in all prematurely born infants. Yet if we insist on the full-term infant as being the normal comparison against which any deviation is abnormal, we will surely not understand the developmental progress of premature infants. This specific population requires a great deal more study to elaborate the nature of behavioral and biological characteristics of these infants that may constitute adequate or inadequate adaptation to extrauterine life.

Assessment and prediction for any infant must take into account the nature of development in general, variations in the developmental course of a specific risk group of infants, and the developing status of the individual infant. Assessment will undoubtedly have to be more complex than we would wish in order for it to be meaningful for the purpose of identifying developmental difficulties at a very early age. These ideas will be expanded in the present chapter.

Our own perspective on early development and the concerns of early assessment has evolved from many years of study of normal infants. Since 1972, we have focused primarily on a longitudinal study of infants beginning on the day after the baby is born and continuing through the first year of life. Some of the details of the observational procedure will be described in a later section. It will serve here to mention that the intensive observations during the infants' first 5 weeks after birth have provided data for examining the early adaptation of the infant as an individual and as a social being.

The observational procedures for this project were originally designed for full-term infants. Prematurely born infants have also been included in the project, and some of these have been observed during the preterm period (Booth et al., 1980; Davis, 1980). Although all of the full-term babies were normal following delivery and during the early weeks of life, some of them did show developmental dysfunction at a later age (Thoman, 1980a, 1981a; Thoman, Acebo, Dreyer, Becker, and Freese, 1979; Thoman and Becker, 1979) including sudden crib death (Thoman, Miano, and Freese, 1977). We were able to identify behavioral patterns from post hoc analyses of social interaction and sleeping and waking states, including respiration and apnea, which were the prelude to these unfortunate developmental events. These patterns have subsequently been validated by being used for prediction of later dysfunction in other babies (Thoman and Becker, 1979; Thoman, Denenberg, Sievel, Zeidner, and Becker, 1981; Thoman et al., 1977).

The demonstrated potential of the parameters and procedures of the longitudinal study for identifying infants with subtle cerebral dysfunction has suggested their applicability for early assessment. We are proposing a behavioral model for assessment that is derived from the principles of our major longitudinal study without requiring the many hours of direct observation of the baby. The result is, we believe, a practical assessment program that reflects a recognition of the biological and behavioral changes that are occurring during the early weeks of life.

Consideration of an assessment procedure for prematurely born infants must take into account the unique nature of their development, especially during the preterm period. Recent studies of prenatal brain development have yielded some dramatic evidence for early neural plasticity that may have either positive or negative effects, and these findings are most relevant to a rationale for our assessment strategy for premature infants.

Plasticity of the Brain During Early Development

In terms of outcome, premature infants can be divided very roughly into two major groups: those infants with physical or neurological abnormalities that are apparent during the preterm period and persist thereafter; and a second and larger group of babies who may be stabilized sometime after birth and appear to be without neurological dysfunction. Some of the latter group go on to develop normally while others show mild to severe developmental disability. One notion why apparently normal infants later become abnormal is that they have "minimal brain damage". The concept as such provides no real explanatory account, and its use has created major concerns because of the possibility of labeling children who have unexplained behavioral deficits which vary widely in the nature of their expression and in the degree of maladaptiveness. In addition, the term implies that the degree of brain damage is simply and directly related to the degree of dysfunction. Recent reports of research on brain development indicate that the term is a simplistic one and its implications are erroneous. They provide a new perspective on this issue by offering a biological basis for the wide range of developmental outcomes following perinatal and early postnatal trauma.

"As the human brain develops in utero it gains neurons at the rate of hundreds of thousands a minute. One problem of neural biology is how the neurons find their place and make the right connections" (Cowan, 1979, p. 113). This quotation highlights the current interest among neurobiologists in the search for mechanisms that account for the plasticity of brain organization, particularly during early development. It should be emphasized that the issue is not *whether* there is plasticity but rather how brain modifications come about and how any modification may be expressed functionally, at both the neurophysiological and the behavioral levels. These basic biological questions are not necessarily fully comprehensible to those of us interested primarily in behavior. the neurobiologists, however, offer generalizations about brain organization that are highly relevant to understanding behavioral development.

The principle of interest is that the developing brain is an extremely plastic structure, with some regions "hard-wired" while others are open to a variety of influences, both intrinsic and environmental. The manner in which the brain responds was the focus of recent reports by Cowan, (1979), Lynch and Gall (1979), and Schneider (1979), and these have proven invaluable in our efforts to achieve a perspective on the early biobehavioral development of the prematurely born infant.

Lynch and Gall (1979) summarized a number of studies which have established that the anatomical structure of the brain is plastic in that it can show a remarkable degree of reorganization under certain circumstances. What is most important for our interests is the evidence that the brain is capable of generating entirely new circuitry. The "final architecture of the brain reflects interactions between its neuronal and glial constituents as well as between the organism and its environment. . . . The still evolving concept of anatomical plasticity provides a possible (and at least partial) explanation for the flexibility and adaptability of behavior. . . . If we accept the idea that the environment of the neonate can influence the number of dendritic branches and spines, it would hardly be surprising that early experiences might produce profound and lasting behavioral consequences" (p. 139). Supporting studies are cited including those by Rosenzweig, Bennett, and Diamond (1972) which have established that the physical size of brain areas can be influenced by the degree of environmental complexity experienced by the organism (Bennett, 1976; Diamond, 1967).

Schneider (1979) discusses the effect of early brain lesions and relates the findings from both animal and human studies to the early brain and behavioral development in prematurely born infants. He points out that it is difficult to judge how common early brain damage actually is during the prenatal period in humans since obvious behavioral signs such as the type seen in the cases of adult injury may not be found because of neuronal compensation. Additionally, "neural pathological study of brains could not easily uncover morphological signs of very early focal damage, since if lesions occur before a certain age they will not cause glial scar (Schneider, 1973; Sumi and Hager, 1968); the only morphological trace may be a quantitative change in sizes of certain structures, perhaps some alterations in cytoarchitectural details, and most importantly some anomalies in axonal pathways and connections that would not be evident in the absence of experimental tracing methods" (p. 574–575).

Given the traumatic nature of the birth of any prematurely born infant, it is reasonable to assume an impact on the central nervous system. It is also reasonable to assume that the preterm period is a time of additional stress, requiring adaptations to an external environment at a time when the normal infant rests securely within the mother's uterus. The evolutionary process designed infants for survival after a 40-week gestation period. Thus, according to the biological principles cited above, it should be expected that the brain organization of any prematurely born infant would differ from that of an infant born at term—a consequence of both intrinsic and extrinsic factors that interact in a very complex fashion over time.

These notions are elaborated by Schneider (1973) in an article entitled, "Is it really better to have your brain lesion early? A revision of the 'Kennard Principle'." The "Kennard Principle" refers to the generalization that the earlier the lesion the greater is the sparing of function. This principle was derived from numerous experiments with animals demonstrating that the behavioral effects of lesions differ according to the age when they are inflicted. Although the findings have been confirmed by observations of brain-injured human subjects, numerous exceptions to this rule have also been reported, and Schneider agrees with Teuber (1971) that the "Kennard Principle" is deceptively simple. In fact, it has been found that some functions appear to be more impaired after an early lesion. For example, "children who have suffered early damage to the cerebral hemispheres may show little of the specific sensory or motor impairments seen in cases of cortical injury in adulthood, but they commonly suffer from a harder-to-define cognitive retardation which is not a characteristic effect of later injury" (p. 557). These findings have led Woods, Teuber, and Schneider to a hypothesis that may have considerable generality in explaining the wide variety of early lesion effects in humans. Rather than the earlier the lesion the greater the sparing of function, they propose: "The earlier the lesion, the greater the reorganization of neural mechanisms underlying behavior" (Woods, personal communication to Schneider).

Schneider (1979) cites experimental neuroanatomical findings obtained over the last decade in experiments with animals which have lent credence to this notion. In addition, Schneider's own research provides evidence for reorganization of brain connections after lesions in the visual system soon after birth, and he is able to demonstrate changes in neuronal connections underlying behavioral changes. After lesions, they found redirected growth of axonal pathways interrupted before the development was completed and a spreading of axon terminal arbors over a larger-than-normal territory. "These findings not only underscore the importance of a basic understanding of the phenomena of neuronal development and plasticity, but they also lead us to specific expectations about the consequences of prenatal, perinatal, and early postnatal brain injury in human beings" (p. 558).

These ideas are extended, and environmental influences are more clearly implicated, by Cowan (1979) with respect to the nature of the neuronal connections that may develop following early lesion.

Considering the distances over which many neurons move in the course of development, it is perhaps not surprising that during their migration some cells are misdirected and end up in distinctly abnormal positions. Such neuronal misplacements . . . have long been recognized by pathologists as a concomitant of certain gross disorders in brain development, but it is not generally appreciated that even during normal development a proportion of the migrating cells may respond inappropriately to the usual directional cues and end up in aberrant locations. . . . It is significant that the majority of such misplaced neurons appear to be eliminated during the later stages of development. (p. 173–174).

Thus it is now recognized that many structures and tissues in the brain are sculptured by highly programmed phases of cell death in the normal developing organism; and the same principle applies following a lesion. "The ability of the brain to reorganize itself in response to external influences or to localized injury is currently one of the most active areas in neurobiological research" (p. 133).

Schneider (1979) points out that changes in brain structure may occur as the result of the workings of developmental cellular mechanisms, irrespective of whether the result is functionally adaptive. The nature of the changes and their consequences for behavior vary with the site of the lesion and with the age when the damage is incurred. These consequences may range from functional sparing, nearly complete or very partial, to functional retardation or even bizarre behavioral abnormalities. In many instances, however, the changes in reorganization are sufficient to escape identification until a later age.

In summary, it appears that the recovery and early development of the prematurely born infant may involve more or less extensive reorganization of damaged neural circuitry; and it should be expected that the developmental consequences will be the result of complex interactions within the brain of each individual baby and the environmental circumstances provided for the infant. Thus, the presence and degree of brain damage may not be directly related to the presence or degree of disability at a later age. It is not surprising, then, that Denhoff (1980) reports preliminary findings from CAT-scan studies of children reveal no relation between apparent brain damage and their cognitive dysfunction.

Given that the reorganization process is more or less distinctive for each individual baby, it is understandable that the population of premature infants shows such a range of developmental outcome. The ongoing developmental process reflects wide variations in the characteristics of their nervous systems, both neurophysiologically and functionally, in interaction with the wide variations in environmental circumstances.

The neuroanatomical literature cited provides overwhelming support for the expectation that the environment of the premature infant is important at every age and stage. The ongoing task is to identify optimal environments and forms of stimulation for those who are developing adequately and to determine the most supportive environments and stimuli for those with demonstrable deficits. A major task, however, is that of identifying those infants who are in need of special supportive intervention where the need is not apparent from medical assessment or traditional assessment procedures.

Perennial Problems in the Assessment of Prematurely Born Infants

Even for full-term infants, a general issue is the lack of predictive potential from emotional or intellectual assessments throughout the first year of life (Honzik, 1976; Lewis, 1973; Thoman, 1981a). This serious problem was the focus of a conference sponsored by the President's Committee on Mental Retardation (Meier, 1973). The basic tenet for this conference was the assumption that the earlier the intervention the greater the potential for effectiveness. Meier (1973) reviewed the prevailing assessment procedures and the scales which have been designed to assess intellectual and cognitive functioning in infants. He concluded that, although the major concern is for intellectual and cognitive functioning, most items on tests for neonates are based on, and consequently biased toward, sensory-motor functioning, and they are therefore more highly related to subsequent sensory-motor development than to intellectual development.

Sensory-motor development may correlate statistically with subsequent cognitive functioning when the data for large groups of normal children are reviewed. However, Meier appropriately emphasizes that this fact only contributes to confusion in the field, since an illicit judgment is frequently made that a statistical correlation is the same as a cause-effect relationship. Difficulty in eye-hand coordination, basic reflexes, or achievement of gross and fine motor developmental milestones may or may not reflect disturbance of lower brain functions as well as higher cortical functioning. Nevertheless, it is quite possible for an individual with severe sensory-motor problems to have totally intact higher cortical processes as demonstrated by an intellectually bright quadriplegic or a child with cerebral palsy. Conversely, a given child may be seriously impaired intellectually but be physically well-coordinated and up to par in gross and fine motor milestones—"the all-brawn-no-brain syndrome is an exaggerated description of this" (Meier, 1973, p. 96).

There are other aspects of early assessment approaches that account for their general inadequacy for identifying the individual infant with neurological dysfunction. Parmelee and Haber (1973) reviewed the development of the concept of the "risk infant" and described recent longitudinal studies that have attempted to define the degree of risk for sequelae including sensory and motor deficit and/or mental handicap in children. Early efforts were aimed at identifying specific items that would place an infant at risk, including genetic factors and events during pregnancy and the early postnatal period. Correlations between single perinatal or postnatal events and later disabling sequelae have been very low in several large prospective studies (Buck, Gregg, Stavraky, Subrahmaniam, and Brown, 1969; Niswander, Friedman, Hoover, Pietrowski, and Westphal, 1966; Parmelee and Haber, 1973; Parmelee, Sigman, Kopp, and Haber, 1976; Sameroff and Chandler, 1975). Unfortunately, there is very little information concerning the degree of risk for any specific item, and many of these as isolated events carry very low risk for the future of the infant. In all follow-up studies of risk factors, a broad spectrum of outcomes has been obtained. It is such findings that have led some to conclude that intellectual dysfunction is not predictable in infancy.

Clusters of pregnancy and perinatal events have been found to be more predictive than single events; but even with these, there has been a wide distribution of outcomes ranging from normal to superior, regardless of the type of measure used (Parmelee et al., 1976). The cluster approach assumes that any of a number of risks can be considered additively, such that a sufficient number may be of sufficient seriousness as to place the infant at risk for serious sequelae. The hope remains that with more information about the degree of risk related to specific perinatal items, a risk level can be derived. And, in fact, some of these studies have demonstrated the possibility of predicting outcome for *groups* of infants.

A major issue for the reliance on risk factors for prediction is that any relationship found between a single event or even any combination of events can only predict outcome for a group of infants "on the average". Thus, the correlational approach gives little information on any *individual* baby. This limitation applies to scales that have been devised for scoring prenatal, perinatal, and postnatal factors. For example, the Prechtl scale (1968) allows for weighting of single events and clusters of events, and gives a rating of the relative degree of insult to which an infant may have been exposed as an initial handicap. It is not designed, however, to assess neurological dysfunction, rate of neurological recovery of function, or how the baby as an individual is coping with this handicap. The problem of predicting the outcome of individuals on the basis of pregnancy and perinatal problems has not been solved. It is simply not possible to know the infant's developmental status from the infant's prior exposure to risk factors or even the infant's prior distress conditions. As each infant has had an individual pattern of early trauma, each will show an individual course in central nervous system compensation. This is the point we repeatedly return to. Additionally, the correlational strategy for prediction from one age to another must assume linearity in developmental changes. This issue is addressed in this book in the chapter by Denenberg.

A step toward assessing developmental change was made by Parmelee and his collaborators in a longitudinal study that used successive assessments over the first year of life. The purpose was to have, over age, a more reliable determination of factors to the infant's risk status—thus, their notion of "Cumulative Risk Score" (Parmelee, 1979; Parmelee et al., 1976). This approach reasonably assumes that the infant may move in the direction of greater or less risk over age and that prediction will increase with increasing information on the factors that may be involved in the infant's developmental course, including biological and social conditions.

I should like to take the next step and to propose criteria by which a realistic and practical assessment procedure should be designed; then the specific application of these procedures to premature infants will be suggested.

Criteria for Realistic Assessment of Developmental Status

We agree with Meier (1973) that it is *not* necessary to conclude that reliable assessment and prediction is impossible with young infants simply because prediction has been generally unsuccessful. As indicated in the previous section, assessment procedures have been used as static instruments, either to measure factors rather than babies or to measure organ rather than cerebral functioning. These and a number of other problems are taken into account in the following criteria which are the minimal considerations for a practical assessment program for premature infants, although the principles involved are not limited to this population of infants.

In view of the dramatic neurobiological changes that are occurring during the preterm period in the prematurely born infant, a meaningful picture of the infant's functional status must come from indications of the nature of the *ongoing changes*—assessment of the developing competence of the infant rather than of competence demonstrated at a single point in time. Therefore, the major criterion we propose for an assessment procedure is that of repeated tests or measurement. As Wohlwill (1973) and Thoman and Becker (1979) point out, process assessment questions cannot be answered from a single observation or a single test. Whether the infant is in the hospital or in the home, there is ongoing interaction between the infant and the environment, and brain organization and behavior are in the process of organizational changes. Assessment must be designed to sample these changes.

Closely related to the issue of repeated measures for assessing the infant's changing biological status is the concern for reliability. This issue has received too little attention. Measures obtained at one age cannot be expected to correlate with outcome measures at another age unless the measures at both ages are reliable. Therefore, repeated observations are also necessary to obtain a quantitative statement of the error of measurement. This error is likely to be much greater in a population of subjects who are highly variable in their performance, and one would expect preterm infants to be more variable than infants at full-term.

The final criterion that we propose is that the functioning or performance of the individual infant be assessed. This is a statement that is all too obvious to most clinicians but seems to have evaded the attention of experimental researchers determined to assess factors rather than babies and to relate these factors to the mean developmental outcome of groups of babies rather than investigating the developmental trajectory of individual babies. There are few risk factors which are so severe in their impact on the infant that all infants exposed to that risk factor are destined to be abnormal. This is clearly not the case with prematurely born infants. Since it is not feasible to provide intervention for all infants in any particular risk group, false positive identification leads to unnecessary expenditure of resources and false negatives lead to the failure to intervene for a baby in need. Thus it is imperative that we find ways to assess the functioning status of individual infants as the basis for a decision on intervention, rather than basing decisions on probability statements which apply to a category of babies.

A Strategy for Assessing Functional Status of Infants

A State Stability Index Derived from the Study of Full-Term Infants

Of the first 20 subjects in our Connecticut Longitudinal Study, there was a higher than expected incidence of morbidity. This was the case despite the fact that subjects were enrolled and maintained in the study only if there were no prenatal, perinatal, or postnatal complications for mother or baby. And all babies were within the normal range based on the Prechtl Risk Scale (1968). Post hoc analyses of some aspects of the data proved to be very enlightening. The respiration and apnea data for a baby who died of Sudden Crib Death provided us with a predictive model for prolonged apnea, and this model has been validated by predicting prolonged apnea in two other babies. Likewise, the model has found support in studies from other laboratories (Baker and McGinty, 1979, Hoppenbrouwers, Hodgman, Harper, McGinty, and Sterman, 1977). Post hoc analyses were also made on the respiration and apnea data of a baby with infantile seizures and EEG hypsarrhythmia. The data revealed highly erratic levels of respiration and apnea over weeks 2 to 5, and these data have been described in a previous report (Thoman and Becker, 1979). One common characteristic of the deviant babies was extreme variability in measures over successive weeks. Taking this into account, and the common knowledge that instability is of general concern clinically, we became interested in the possibility of using stability as an indicator of functional status.

A concern for stability led us to focus on behavioral states as the basic dimension of interest for early assessment. The rationale for this choice has a wide base of support. First, my own studies of infants during the early weeks of life (Thoman, 1975a, 1975b, 1980a, 1981b) have led me to view states as the convergent expression of the interaction of the infant's endogenous status and the various forms of exogenous stimulation provided from the environment, primarily in the form of caregiving activities of the parent. The infant's states of alertness, drowsiness, fussing, crying, or sleeping provide cues to the caregiver, or mother, to which she responds by feeding, changing, performing soothing activities, or simply enjoying holding and talking to the baby. The state of the baby during the course of these maternal ministrations will mediate the nature of the response the baby makes. For example, the situation wherein the baby is crying and the mother picks up him or her and rocks and sings to the baby, who then becomes quiet and alert, is very different from one in which the baby is fussing and drowsy and the mother picks up him or her to rock. In this latter case, the baby may quiet and go to sleep. Thus the state during an intervention determines the state that ensues. And then the state that ensues—in these instances, alerting or sleeping—constitutes a response to the maternal behaviors. The intimate ongoing exchange between an infant and caretaker is a process that is expressed in the ongoing state behaviors of the infant.

We have found that erratic state organization in the infant is associated with erratic organization of maternal activities on the part of the mother (Thoman, 1980b, 1981a; Thoman et al., 1979; Thoman, Becker and Freese, 1978). Thus, states reflect the interlacing process of the mother–infant relationship and a basic reflection of the infant's adaptive functioning. Behavioral states are assumed to be an expression of fundamental processes in the central nervous system, and deviations in patterns of state organization have been associated with known neurological deficits. Autistic children show a delay in development of sleep patterns (Tanguay, Ornitz, Forsythe, and Ritvo, 1976); newborn small-for-gestational-age infants show an immature EEG, and some also have abnormal EEG components (Schulte, Hinze and Schrempf, 1971); retarded children have delayed development in patterns of eye movements during sleep (Petre-Quadens, De Lee, and Remy, 1971); children with PKU or hypothyroidism show deviations in sleep patterns (Petre-Quadens et al., 1971; Lenard and Schulte, 1974); infants with bilirubinemia have slower breathing during sleep states (Theorell, Prechtl, and Vos, 1974); and babies with brain malformation and/or chromosomal anomalies are poor sleepers (Monod and Guidasci, 1976).

Since behavioral and electrophysiological measures of state discriminate between normal and abnormal infants under many circumstances, we are proposing that state measures would also prove to be useful in assessing the functional status of premature infants.

During the home observations for Longitudinal Study, the baby's behavioral states are recorded throughout any observation. Thus it is possible to describe the baby's states in any social context or when the baby is alone. However, only when the baby is alone, usually in the crib, is it possible to discriminate the sleeping as well as the waking states. It was hypothesized that stability in the infant's state organization over the early weeks of life should provide a clue to the functional status of the baby's central nervous system.

In a prospective study, a State Stability Index was calculated for individual babies, using the first 22 subjects enrolled in the Longitudinal Project. The index was designed to indicate the consistency in state organization over 4 successive weeks. For each week a profile, or set of scores, was obtained for each child based on the percentage of time spent in each of the behavioral states when the baby was alone. State stability, or consistency of state profiles, across the 4 weekly observations was measured by an analysis of variance procedure applied to each baby individually, as follows: Because the percentage scores for each week's profile sum to 100 percent for each week, there is no Between Weeks variation; there are only two sources of variance: Between States (with 5 df) and the interaction of States × Weeks (with 15 df). Under these circumstances, the more similar the profiles from week to week, the larger will be the Between States mean square and the smaller will be the mean square for States × Weeks. Thus when there is high profile similarity, the F ratio obtained by dividing the Between States mean square by the States × Weeks mean square will be very large. Similarly, when the intra-infant profiles vary from week to week, the F-ratio will be relatively small.

For each infant this F ratio was obtained and used as a *descriptive* statistic to indicate relative degree of profile consistency. It is necessary to emphasize that the F ratio is not being used in its usual manner as an inferential statistic to test the null hypothesis that there are no significant differences among the behavioral states of an infant. Instead, the F ratio is used descriptively as a single number to describe how parallel the 4 profile curves are for each infant. Thus the term State Stability Index. This statistical approach was developed by Denenberg (Thoman et al., 1981) without knowledge of either the medical history or the medical or behavioral outcome of the infants in the study. Denenberg and Zeidner had not been involved in the observations of the infants, and only the state data from the observations on weeks 2 to 5 were made available to them. They were only aware that one baby in the sample of subjects had died of sudden infant death syndrome (SIDS) (Thoman, 1977; Thoman et al., 1977).

The F values for the 22 subjects ranged from 3.1 to 304.9. Figure 1 presents the 4 babies with the lowest State Stability Indices and the 4 babies with the highest Stability scores. It can be seen that babies A, B, C, and D have profiles with considerable discrepancy over the 4 weeks, whereas the profiles for the remaining four babies show a remarkable degree of consistency from week to week.

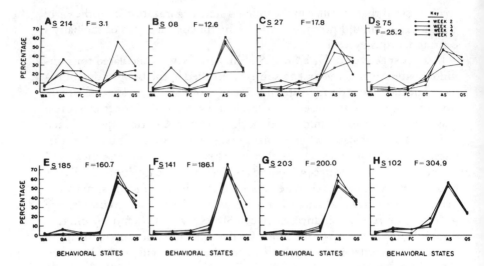

Figure 1. Behavioral state profiles while the baby is alone during a 7-hour observation day on Weeks 2, 3, 4, and 5. Infants A, B, C, and D are the four infants with the lowest profile stability index; Infants E, F, G, and H, on the bottom row, had the highest state stability scores. Along the X-axis are the behavioral states, and the Y-axis is the percentage of time in each state. WA: Walking Active; QA: Quiet Alert; FC: Fuss or Cry; DT: Drowse or Transition; AS: Active Sleep; QS: Quiet Sleep.

Validation of the State Stability Index came from relating the developmental outcome of each infant in the study to the individual Stability score. The complete results have been reported elsewhere (Thoman et al., 1981). It will suffice here to summarize the outcome for the 4 babies with the lowest Stability scores: Baby A in Figure 1 appeared medically normal until approximately 30 months, when he was diagnosed as having aplastic anemia (a disease with congenital contributions of an unknown nature); Infant B had no known medical disturbance initially, but at 6 months he developed infantile seizures, with hypsarrythmia of the EEG. Baby C died of SIDS at 3 ½ months with no prior indication of any medical disturbance; and Baby D is not known to have any severe medical difficulties but has had emotional problems which could reasonably be considered an expression of hyperactivity, and it has been impossible for the psychometrician to complete developmental assessment even at 2 ½ years. Each of these children was under the care of competent physicians during the early months of life and serious problems were not suspected until the ones described above occurred. It should also be noted that none of the babies with Stability Indices above the median level has shown any evidence of intellectual deficit or other major disorder.

This study was the original application of the State Stability Index. Subsequently, the index has been found to relate to other aspects of immaturity or disorganization during the early weeks (Becker and Thoman, unpublished). These findings suggested its usefulness for the assessment of the functional status of premature infants.

The State Stability Index for Premature Infants

The State Stability Index provides us with a model for the assessment of functional status of an infant. We propose a regime of behavioral observations that will permit the calculation of a State Stability Index for the purposes of assessment. Preliminary observations of premature infants (Thoman and Davis, unpublished; Thoman, Waite, and Shafer, unpublished) indicate that 4 successive weekly observations would serve during the preterm period as well as during the postterm age.

The model for assessment of the premature infant would include the following: Observations of prematurely born infants on 4 successive weeks while the baby is still in the hospital, after the baby has become stabilized. From these observations an F value (for stability) can be calculated. Then, after the baby has been discharged, or at fullterm gestational age, whichever comes later, an additional 4 weeks' observations would be made in the home. From these observations, another F ratio can be calculated.

This model for successive determination of stability in state organization is an approach that has not been used for assessment. The approach fulfills the criteria set forth for realistic assessment: repeated observations that not only permit the measures of stability but also permit the determination of reliability of individual measures; and evidence for developmental change over each time period. Most importantly, the use of the Stability Index permits the assessment of the functional status of individual babies. Figure 2 presents an overview of this model for assessment. The F ratio, or Stability score, can be calculated for the preterm period for each individual infant, and this value can be compared with a baseline group of premature infants of the same gestational age.

We are currently collecting data to provide a normative range for Stability scores for premature infants. For example, preliminary data obtained from three premature infants at 38 to 41 weeks of age indicated State Stability scores ranging from 8.4 to 44.4. As expected, these levels are lower than the median for full-term infants from weeks 42 to 45. These early Stability scores ranked the 3 premature infants in the same

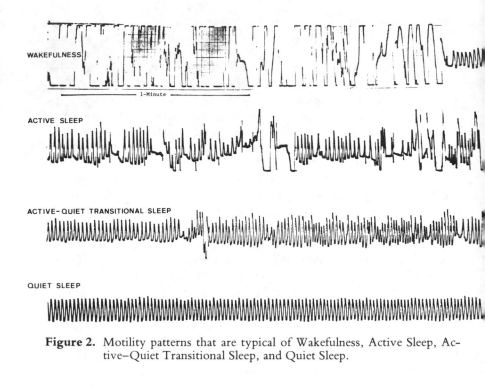

Figure 2. Motility patterns that are typical of Wakefulness, Active Sleep, Active–Quiet Transitional Sleep, and Quiet Sleep.

order as their Prechtl (1968) score for risk status. Thus, at the early age, the stability of the infant's state organization reflects the severity of the early trauma, although environmental events have had an interactive impact, if we accept the biological perspective presented earlier. The environmental-organism interaction should be even more profound by the postnatal assessment of state stability. Thus, the F ratio for the later age will provide an indication of whether the infant's state organization is becoming more stable over time—within the infant's given environment—or whether there is a decrease in stability. Greater instability during the postterm period will be the clearest evidence for the need for intervention.

A Methodology to Permit Continuous Observations for State Stability Assessment

The Longitudinal Project suggested the model of successive observations of behavioral states and the determination of a State Stability Index. The many hours of direct observation of state, however, is obviously not a feasible procedure for assessing large numbers of babies. To meet the criterion of feasibility, we propose a major modification in methodology, one which has also derived from observations made during the course of the Longitudinal Project.

Observations of sleep states, in the home or in the hospital, are accompanied by a recording of the infant's respiration from a pressure-sensor placed under the infant's crib pad. From many years of processing these analog recordings, which indicate not only respiration but motor movements as well, we have found the the motility patterns can be used to reliably judge the infant's behavioral sleep states and wakefulness (Thoman and Zeidner, 1979; Thoman, Zeidner, and Denenberg, unpublished). Figure 3 presents examples of the analog patterns that are produced by variations in the infant's motility. Minimal movement occurs during periods of apnea, when the respiration signal is absent and the very small deflections of the recorder pen are produced by heartrate. Respiration signals are apparent only during periods when there are no gross body movements. Figure 3 illustrates the patterns of analog signals that are typical for infant motility during wakefulness, active sleep, active-quiet transitional sleep, and quiet sleep. The overall distinctiveness of these patterns is readily apparent. There are also more subtle distinctions in the records that are meaningful in making state judgments. For example, during active sleep, in addition to the characteristic irregular respiration, there may be intermittent periods of squirming or writhing, which produce large and relatively slow-onset signal deflections. In quiet sleep, and sometimes in active sleep, jerks or startles occur, and these are very sudden movements that produce very sharp-peaked deflections. Generalized twitching of active sleep produces sharp-peaked signals as well, but of a lower amplitude.

We now have a sensor-mattress from which patterns of the baby's motility can be recorded. The patterns can be analyzed, and the ongoing behavioral states can be discriminated by visual inspection. We are in the process of adapting a computer program to automate analyses of these signals. With this advance, it will be possible to obtain 24 hours of data on an infant's wakefulness and sleep states. The procedure will then make it possible to collect an enormous amount of data on each infant's behavioral states not only without the necessity of direct observation but also without the necessity for physical intervention to obtain the recordings. Nothing has to be attached to the baby for this purpose, as the recording from the sensor-mattress proceeds continuously throughout an observation day. In addition to state signals, the analog pattern indicates periods of time when the infant is removed from the crib.

The final feasibility consideration is the miniature Medi-log recorder, which makes it possible to collect 24 hours of data on a single small cassette. This small recorder can easily be beside or under the crib in the hospital or home for 24-hour monitoring.

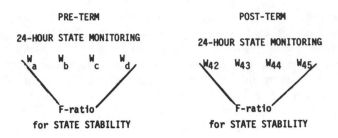

Figure 3. Model for assessment of stability of sleep-and-waking states of prematurely born infants: weekly monitoring over two successive age periods.

Concluding Comments

The clinical assessment approach I have described is based on growing evidence that premature infants have suffered a variety of CNS insults and that their recovery may involve more or less reorganization of damaged neural circuitry. Developmental outcome ranges from severe dysfunction to individuals who are truly superior intellectually and emotionally. Their recovery, however, reflects variations in neural organization following the early insults. Despite this heterogeneity in etiology and outcome, it should be possible to assess the functional status of prematurely born infants if changes in organization over time are taken into account.

The proposed strategy approaches this problem with a perspective that behavioral adaptation is a dynamic process to be studied temporally and with a recognition that the behavioral functioning of the infant in any caretaking environment, in the hospital or in the home, expresses the infant–environment interactions.

A most important consideration for this clinical application of the State Stability Index is that the procedures are designed to assess the individual baby. This is in contrast to an objective of assessing the effects of any specific risk factors, which must be interpreted in terms of main effect or mean outcome for a group. The individual focus is an obvious necessity for a clinical procedure.

While attempting to meet the requirements for a reliable and valid assessment procedure, we have not overlooked the feasibility issue. The procedures proposed involve minimal human participation. It should be noted that the complexity of recording the data processing for these procedures does not approach that required for physiological or electrophysiological recording. At the same time—and a major consideration for our purposes—the recordings do not involve intervention with, or instrumentation of, the baby. Our basic premise is that we should be able to demonstrate the efficacy of this assessment procedure and that the monitoring device and recording system should be appropriate for recording large numbers of babies in any intensive care nursery or in the home.

Successful determination of dysfunction during the very early weeks offers the possibility of individualized intervention that can be limited to those infants in a high-risk population whose disability is subtly expressed at this very early age but with the possibility for disabling sequelae. Under these circumstances, early intervention can represent an efficient allocation of medical, educational, and family resources by concentrating efforts in the direction where they can result in the greatest savings of human potential.

References

Baker, T. L., and McGinty, D. J. Sleep apnea in hypoxic and normal kittens. *Developmental Psychobiology,* 1979, *12,* 577–594.

Bennett, E. L. Cerebral effects of differential experience and training. In M.R. Rosenzweig and E. L. Bennett (Eds.), *Neural mechanisms of learning and memory.* Cambridge, MA: MIT Press, 1976.

Booth, C. L., Leonard, H. L., and Thoman, E. B. Sleep states and behavior patterns in preterm and fullterm infants. *Neuropediatrics,* 1980, *11,* 354–364.

Buck, C., Gregg, R., Stavraky, K., Subrahmaniam, K., and Brown, J. The effect of single prenatal and natal complications upon the development of children of mature birth-weight. *Pediatrics,* 1969, *43,* 942.

Cowan, W. M. The development of the brain. *Scientific American,* September 1979, 113–133.

Davis, D. H. *The social competency of premature infants discharged from the hospital prior to forty weeks conceptional age.* Master's Thesis, University of Connecticut, 1980.

Denhoff, E. *Early differential diagnoses of neurologically impaired and environmentally deprived infants.* Paper presented at the Conference on Follow-up of low birth weight infants, Brown University Medical School, Providence, R.I., June 1980.

Diamond, M. C. Extensive cortical depth measurements and neuron size increases in the cortex of environmentally enriched rats. *Journal of Comparative Neurology,* 1967, *131,* 357–364.

Honzik, M. P. Value and limitations of infant tests: An overview. In M. Lewis (Ed.), *Origins of intelligence: Infancy and early childhood.* New York: Plenum Press, 1976.

Hoppenbrouwers, T. T., Hodgman, J. E., Harper, R. M., McGinty, D. J., and Sterman, M. B. Respiratory rates and apnea in infants at high and low risk from sudden infant death syndrome (SIDS). *Clinical Research,* 1977, *25,* 189A.

Lenard, H. G., and Schulte, F. J. Sleep studies in hormonal and metabolic diseases of infancy and childhood. In O. Petre-Quadens and J. D. Schlag (Eds.), *Basic sleep mechanisms*. New York: Academic Press, 1974.

Lewis, M. Infant intelligence tests: Their use and misuse. *Human Development* 1973, *16*, 108–118.

Lynch, G., and Gall, C. Organization and reorganization in the central nervous system: Evolving concepts of brain plasticity. In F. Falkner and J. M. Tanner (Eds.), *Human growth*, Vol. 3. New York: Plenum, 1979.

Meier, J. *Screening and assessment of young children at developmental risk*. The President's Committee on Mental Retardation, DHEW Publication No. (OS) 73–90, 1973.

Monod, N., and Guidasci, S. Sleep and brain malformation in the neonatal period. *Neuropediatrics*, 1976, *7*, 229–249.

Niswander, K. R., Friedman, E. A., Hoover, D. B., Pietrowski, H., and Westphal, M. Fetal morbidity following potentially anoxigenic obstetric conditions. I Abruptio placentae. II Placenta previa. III Prolapse of the umbilical cord. *American Journal of Obstetrics and Gynecology*, 1966, *95*, 838.

Parmelee, A. H. General discussion. In E. B. Thoman (Ed.), *Origins of the Infant's Social Responsiveness*. Hillsdale, N.J.: Lawrence Erlbaum Associates, 1979.

Parmelee, A. H., and Haber, A. Who is the "risk infant?" In H. J. Osofsky (Ed.), *Clinical obstetrics and gynecology*. New York: Harper and Row, 1973.

Parmelee, A. H., Sigman, M., Kopp, C. B., and Haber, A. Diagnosis of the infant at risk for mental, motor or sensory handicap. In T. Tjossem (Ed.), *Intervention strategies for high-risk infants and young children*. Baltimore, M.D.: University Park Press, 1976.

Petre-Quadens, O., DeLee, C., and Remy, M. Eye movement density during sleep and brain maturation. *Brain Research*, 1971, *26*, 49–56.

Prechtl, H.F.R. Neurological findings in newborn infants after pre- and paranatal complications. In *Aspects of prematurity and dysmaturity*. Nutricia Symposium, Groningen, 1967; Leiden, Stenfert Kroese NV, 1968.

Rosenzweig, M. R., Bennett, E. L., and Diamond, M. C. Chemical and anatomical plasticity of brain: Replications and extensions. In J. Gaito (Ed.), *Macromolecules and behavior*, (2nd Ed.). New York: Appleton-Century-Crofts, 1972.

Sameroff, A. J., and Chandler, M. J. Reproductive risk and the continuum of caretaking casualty. In F. D. Horowitz, M. Hetherington, S. Scarr-Salapatek, and G. Siegel (Eds.), *Review of child development research*, Vol. 4. Chicago, IL: University of Chicago Press, 1975.

Schneider, G. E. Early lesions of superior colliculus: Factors affecting the information of abnormal retinal projection. *Brain, Behavior and Evolution*, 1973, *8*, 73–109.

Schulte, F., Hinze, G., and Schrempf, G. Maternal toxemia, fetal malnutrition, and bioelectric brain activity in the newborn. *Neuropediatrics*, 1971, *2*, 439–460.

Sumi, S. M., and Hager, H. Electron microscopic study of the reaction of the newborn rat brain to injury. *Acta Neuropathalogica*, 1968, *10*, 324–335.

Tanguay, P. E., Ornitz, E. M., Forsythe, A. B., and Ritvo, E. R. Rapid eye movement (REM) activity in normal and autistic children during REM sleep. *Journal of Autism and Childhood Schizophrenia*, 1976, *6*, 275–288.

Teuber, H. L. Mental retardation after early trauma to the brain: Some issues in search of facts. In C. R. Angel and E. A. Bering, Jr. (Eds.), *Physical trauma as an etiological agent in mental retardation*. Bethesda, MD: National Institutes of Health, 1971.

Theorell, K., Prechtl, H.F.R., and Vos, J. E. A polygraphic study of normal and abnormal newborn infants. *Neuropediatrics*, 1974, *5*, 279.

Thoman, E. B. How a rejecting baby affects mother-infant synchrony. In *Parent-infant interaction*. New York: Associate Scientific Publishers, 1975. (a)

Thoman, E. B. Sleep and wake behaviors in neonates: Consistencies and conquences. *Merrill-Palmer Quarterly*, 1975, *21*, 295–314. (b)

Thoman, E. B. Earlier behavioral development of an infant who died of SIDS. In *Sudden Infant Death Syndrome Research Program of the National Institute of Child Health and Human Development*. Washington, D.C.: U.S. Department of Health, Education, and Welfare, 1977.

Thoman, E. B. Infant development viewed within the mother-infant relationship. In E. Quilligan and N. Kretchmer (Eds.), *Perinatal medicine*. New York: John Wiley and Sons, 1980. (a)

Thoman, E. B. Disruption and asynchrony in early parent-infant interactions. In D. B. Sawin, R. C. Hawkins II, L. O. Walker, and J. H. Penticuff (Eds.), *Exceptional infant IV: Psychosocial risks in infant-environment transactions*. New York: Brunner-Mazel, 1980. (b)

Thoman, E. B. Early communication as the prelude to later adaptive behaviors. In M. J. Begab, H. C. Haywood, and H. L. Garber, (Eds.), *Psychosocial influences in retarded performance*, Vol. II: *Strategies for improving competence*. Baltimore, MD: University Park Press, 1981. (a)

Thoman, E. B. Affective communication as the prelude and context for language learning. In R. L. Schiefelbusch and D. Bricker (Eds.), *Early Language: Acquisition and intervention*. Baltimore, MD.: University Park Press, 1981. (b)

Thoman, E. B., Acebo, C., Dreyer, C. A., Becker, P. T., and Freese, M. P. Individuality in the interactive process. In E. B. Thoman (Ed.) *Origins of the infant's social responsiveness*. Hillsdale, N.J.: Lawrence Erlbaum Associates, 1979.

Thoman, E. B., and Becker, P. T. Issues in assessment and prediction for the infant born at risk. In T. Field, A. Sostek, S. Goldberg, and H. H. Shuman (Eds.), *Infants born at risk*. New York: Spectrum, 1979.

Thoman, E. B., Becker, P. T., and Freese, M. P. Individual patterns of mother-infant interaction. In G. P. Sackett (Ed.), *Observing Behavior* Vol. I: *Theory and Applications in Mental Retardation*, Baltimore, MD: University Park Press, 1978.

Thoman, E. B., Denenberg, V. H., Sievel, J., Zeidner, L. P., and Becker, P. State organization in neonates: Developmental inconsistency indicates risk for developmental dysfunction. *Neuropediatrics*, 1981, *12*, 45–54.

Thoman, E. B., Miano, V. N., and Freese, M. P. The role of respiratory instability in SIDS. *Developmental Medicine and Child Neurology*, 1977, *19*, 729–737.

Thoman, E. B. and Zeidner, L. P. Sleep-wake states in infant rabbits: Profiles from motility monitoring. *Physiology and Behavior*, 1979, *22*, 1049–1054.

Wohlwill, J. F. *The study of behavioral development*. New York: Academic Press, 1973.

Primary Prevention of Psychosocial Disorders:
Assessment of Outcome

Elsie R. Broussard

The longitudinal studies of Pittsburgh First-Borns, begun in 1963, are epidemiological studies which focus on the "Silent majority" of newborns—those healthy, full-term infants born without physical defect who traditionally have not been considered at high risk for psychosocial disorder.

Throughout the history of the Pittsburgh First-Born Project we have been concerned with measurement of the adaptive potential of the infant–mother system and the subsequent psychosocial development of the infants over time. This paper reviews selected aspects of the longitudinal studies of the Pittsburgh First Borns; provides a clinical study of one infant's development during the first 5 years of life, and discusses some issues regarding assessment.

Instrument of Measure

In 1963 Broussard developed the Neonatal Perception Inventories (NPI) to measure the maternal perception of the newborn as compared with her concept of the average infant. The NPI provide a measure of the adaptive potential of the mother–infant unit during the first month of life.

The NPI may be viewed as a projective measure. The mother is presented with a set of ambiguous stimuli—the "Average Baby" and "Your Baby"—upon which she projects her concept of what most babies are like and her expectation of what her newborn will be like. Understandably these concepts vary from mother to mother and are influenced by her life experiences. The NPI score is obtained by determining the discrep-

This research was supported by grants from the Benedum Foundation, Buhl Foundation, Amelia Miles Foundation, Pittsburgh Foundation, Staunton Farm Foundation, through private donations, and the General Research Support Grant No. 5451, NIH. The author wishes to acknowledge the assistance of Margaret Gillick in reviewing the data from which the case of Justin was assembled.

ancy between the mother's rating of her own infant and the average baby. If a mother rates her baby as better than average, her perception is considered positive and the infant low risk. If she does not rate her baby as better than average, her perception is considered negative and the infant at high risk for subsequent psychosocial disorder.

Prospective Study of 1963 Cohort

Inventories were administered to 318 mothers delivering healthy, full-term, first-born infants during a specified 2½-month period. All socio-economic and racial groups were included.

Follow-up studies were designed to test the hypothesis that maternal perception of the 1-month-old infant would be related to the child's subsequent psychosocial development.

Findings

At age 4½, 120 of the original 1963 population were evaluated by one of two child psychiatrists who had no knowledge of the NPI ratings.

At age 10½, 104 of the first-borns were evaluated by one of three different psychiatrists who had no knowledge of the NPI risk rating or of the previous evaluation conducted at age 4½. At each age more infants classified as high risk at 1 month of age were diagnosed as having emotional disorders than were those who were at low risk. (At 4½, $p <$ .00002; at 10½, $p <$ .01) The details of the follow-up studies have previously been reported and are not repeated here (Broussard, 1976a; Broussard, 1976b; Broussard and Hartner, 1970, 1971)

At age 15, 99 of the children were evaluated by one of four psychiatrists who did not know the risk ratings of the children. Again a significant association ($p <$ .007) was present between the NPI risk rating at 1 month and the psychiatric rating at age 15 (Broussard, 1981). The odds ratio indicated that 1-month-old infants who were considered to be high risk were 5½ times more likely to have psychosocial disorders at age 15 than those 1-month-old infants who had been considered low risk.

Examination of the data for those 42 children who were evaluated at all of the three ages revealed that 27 percent of the low-risk children were found free of disorder at each time point. *None* of the high-risk children were found to be free of disorder at all three evaluations. Of the low-risk children, 15 percent had some disorder at each of the time points versus 63 per cent of the high-risk children (Broussard, in press). The presence of a positive maternal perception during the first month of life does not guarantee that there will be no difficulties in the child's subsequent development. The *absence* of a positive maternal perception of the neonate is associated with a very high rate of subsequent psychosocial disorder.

The NPI do not predict the precise nature of the psychosocial disorder. The complexity of human development makes such predictive specificity impossible. The NPI can serve to screen for potential failures in psychosocial adaptation stemming from disorders in the earliest mother–infant relationships, disorders that may exist undetected at an early stage. It is essential to view the NPI as a screening measure to predict the adaptive potential of a given mother–infant pair. Screening is the first step. The next is to conduct a careful clinical assessment of the adaptive potential of a specific mother–infant pair and establish the level of need for intervention.

Preventive Intervention Program

In 1973 Broussard selected a second population of 281 healthy first-borns and screened these using the NPI. Intervention was offered to half of the high-risk infants and not the other half who served as a comparison group. This was an outreach program and as such constituted an attempt at primary prevention. Infants had not been referred to us by an agency nor had parents asked for help.

The characteristics of mothers of infants at high risk have been reported elsewhere (Broussard, 1977, 1979, in press). We noted that many mothers lacked confidence in themselves, had poor self-esteem, and seemed depressed and anxious. They often lost their infants from their perceptual field and had difficulty in moving from dyadic to triadic relationships.

The technique of preventive intervention which we used has been previously reported (Broussard, 1977, Broussard and Cornes, 1981) and is beyond the scope of this paper. Broussard telephoned each mother, whom had been randomly selected, and asked if she wished to participate in the first-born program being offered for first-time parents. The program was described as an opportunity for parents to talk with other parents and staff about their concerns regarding childrearing.

It is not feasible to tell parents of a healthy, full-term first-born that their infant is considered a high risk for subsequent emotional difficulty. This might have the potential for establishing a self-fulfilling prophecy— that is, the mother's already negative perception of her newborn might be compounded by such a prediction. In addition, this would fail to take into account the multiplicity of life variables with impact on development that may modify the effect of the negative maternal perception, such as the presence of other family members, various support systems, or some unique capacity within the infant.

Of the 39 mothers in the experimental group, 17 elected to participate in the intervention program. Intervention contacts consisted of an initial individual interview with one or both parents, participation in mother–infant group meetings, and home-based intervention. Dr. Cleon Cornes and I served as co-leaders for two groups, each composed of 7 or 8 mothers and their infants. Groups met every other week for 1½ hours, beginning when the infants were 2 to 4 months of age and continuing until they were 3½ years old. Home visits were made by child development specialists. During the process of intervention, we actively observed the functioning of the mother–infant pair and intervened with each individual dyad according to our understanding of their developmental needs. This understanding influenced our timing as well as the nature of the interventions. We used basic principles of child development and knowledge of the parenting process to guide our responsiveness to changing parent and infant needs.

Throughout the project, we continually monitored the developmental progress of the infants. In order to measure the impact of the intervention, formal evaluations were conducted when the infants were 1 and 2½ years old.

The details of the evaluation procedure have been previously reported (Broussard, 1979).

Evaluations Findings at Age 2½

At age 2½ years, 68 subjects [25 low-risk and 43 high-risk (13 intervention, 12 intervention refused, and 18 comparison)] were evaluated. The entire evaluation interview was observed via a one-way-vision mirror and notes recorded by an observer-rater. The interview consisted of (1) a period of free play for the mother and infant; (2) administration of the Bayley tests; (3) observation of child's reaction to mother leaving room with examiner present; (4) observation of the mother and child reunion.

An observer-rater, who had no knowledge of the 1-month NPI rating or of the group membership of the children, rated the children on 15 single-item graphic scales that were then grouped into 8 clinical clusters: (I) separation-individuation process (Mahler); (II) confidence; (III) implementation of contacts with the nonhuman environment; (IV) aggression; (V) affective balance; (VI) investment in use of language for communication; (VII) coping; and (VIII) play.

A two-way multivariate analysis of variance for the four groups and sex was performed. The test for the equality of group mean vectors yielded an F ratio of 2.84 ($p < 0.0001$). All of the univariate F tests were significant. The individual group means for each of the clusters were compared and in all cases the low-risk and intervention groups had the lowest scores (low scores reflect more optimal functioning). The comparison and the intervention-refused groups had similar scores, with both groups having scores considerably higher than those of the first two groups. The test for interaction between group and sex was not significant (multivariate F ratio = 1.57, p > 0.05). (Results of an evaluation of 59 children ranging in age from 4 years, 8 months to 5 years, 2 months will be subsequently reported.)

It must be recognized that the results given are for groups of children. Within the intervention group, there were varying degrees of success. The goals of our intervention were to foster the infant's optimal psychosocial development by working within the mother–infant system.

The mother's early perception of her newborn seems to reflect her own sense of well-being. Mothers of infants at high risk have negative self-images that appear to be projected on to their infants. They seem unable to believe that what they have created is of value. The negative self-images of mothers of infants at high risk are not identical. In each there is a different source, resulting in different ranges of adult behavior.

The importance of looking and being seen, of having self reflected back, is crucial for a child. The mother is a child's first mirror. A thousand times a day, through each interaction, mothers reflect to their children the realities of self and life as they see them. There are times when some mothers' views of the world and self are distorted, and so the mirror they hold up to their children is also distorted. Either way, this mirroring process is the cornerstone of development. The origins of precursors of self-esteem, self-love, and of omnipotence can be discerned within the mother–infant field. The mother constitutes the major portion of the infant's mechanisms for maintaining what later we would call self-esteem. Her own experiences of well-being and self-regard are significant for the way in which she provides for her infant. Stability is maintained within the mother–infant field by way of the mother's reliable, predictable, consistent care. When the mother lacks empathy the child may experience her unpredictable behavior as being turned "on and off". When there is failure in the empathic mirroring function of the mother, the infant may develop a problem in acquiring a sense of continuity of his or her self (Bach, 1975). This failure may later be manifested as a narcissistic personality disorder.

In Ovid's version of the legend of Narcissus, Echo sees Narcissus wandering in the woods and falls in love with him. Narcissus rejects her love and in her grief she wastes away so that only her voice remains. Those who saw what happened prayed: "So may he himself love and not gain the thing he loves." Nemesis, goddess of retribution, heard their prayers. One day Narcissus came upon a clear pool with silvery bright water. When he drank, he was captivated by the reflection of his own beautiful form. As Ovid writes:

Oh fondly foolish boy, why vainly seek to clasp the fleeting image. What you seek is nowhere, but turn yourself away and the object of your love will be no more. That which you behold is but the shadow of a reflected form and has no substance of its own. With you it comes, with you it stays and it will go with you if you can go. (pp. 42–43)

This was his tragedy—that he loved, and did not gain what he loved. The legend of Narcissus, a tale ever old and ever new holds within it the kernels of living truth, the enchantment of the mirror image and the mystery of our need to know ourselves. The dynamics in this legend can be seen in the story of *Justin's Reflection*.

Justin, product of a normal pregnancy and delivery, was a normal, healthy 7 lb. 2 oz., first-born male infant born to white, married, Catholic parents when his mother was 23 and his father was 22.

The ongoing assessment of Justin's developmental milestones gave no cause for alarm. Mother reported smiling at 1 month. At 4 months staff observed him vocalizing and bringing his hands to midline. When placed in a prone position, he elevated his head and shoulders and attempted to push his knees up under his body. At 6 months he sat alone, then went from sit to prone and into a bridging position. He crawled at 7 months and at 8½ months he played "pat-a-cake" and waved "bye". By 9½ months he walked competently. At 1 year he scored 128 on the Bayley Scale of Mental Development and scored 111 on the Psychomotor Development Index. His speech development was precocious. At 13 months he correctly identified his body parts when mother requested him to show her his nose, ears, and so forth. At 18 months Justin's vocabularly was large and he spoke in short sentences (e.g., "Dump truck is broken.").

Six days prior to his fifth birthday, Justin came to our office for assessment of his psychosocial development. The central method of data collection was to observe the child's behavior directly in a relatively unstructured situation in the presence of his mother. To keep the mother occupied, yet accessible to the child during this period, she was seated at a table at the end of the office and asked to complete the Parental Attitude Research Instrument (PARI) (Schaefer and Bell, 1958). The child was told, "You can play with any of the toys you want to while Mommy and I do some work. When I finish my work, we'll do some things together." The examiner then sat and made a detailed written recording of the child's play. This included the sequential recording of those toys he touched, how he manipulated them, play themes, spontaneous conversation of mother and child, the child's demeanor, fine and gross motor movements, general kinesics, expressions and affects, and the mother–child verbal and nonverbal interactions during the evalution.

Free play of 25 minutes duration was followed by a 25-minute semistructured interview with the child. The toys, which occupied one corner of the office, were arranged in an identical location and angle prior to each interview. During the 25 minutes of free play, conversation initiated by the child was responded to in a nondirective fashion. The investigator initiated conversation only if the child became overwhelmingly anxious, and the silence was judged to be psychonoxious. In such a case, the investigator could offer some support by structuring the child's activity into play in a minimally directive fashion, such as by repeating that the child could play with the toys. When a child chose not to play, again, no comment was made by the investigator, unless the child was overwhelmingly anxious.

Transition to the structured interview was accomplished by asking the child to choose a crayon and draw a person (Goodenough). The Complete-A-Man (Binet) and the Information subtest of the Wechsler Preschool and Primary Scale of Intelligence were also administered. Justin's scores on all three tests indicated that his mental development was in the superior range. One could conclude that Justin was a very "competent" child and that the intervention was successful. Yet we did not consider this to be a successful outcome. A chronological review of other observations during Justin's first 5 years of life illustrates our concern.

The Neonatal Perception Inventories were administered on the second postpartum day when I invited Mrs. J to participate in the project. At that time her perception of Justin was negative. Mrs. J again completed the NPI during a home visit when Justin was 1 month old. Her perception of him remained negative. On the basis of the NPI, the adaptive potential of this mother-infant pair was considered to be in jeopardy, and Justin was viewed as an infant at risk for subsequent psychosocial disorder. Signs of distress with the mother–infant system were already evident. Mrs. J said the baby was "bad" because he cried a lot and had a "sleep problem". He could not be put down unless he was already asleep. The pediatrician suggested use of a pacifier and prescribed medicine at 2½ weeks to help him sleep. Mother said the baby did not like the pacifier so she fed him each time he cried. Mrs. J was clearly interested in giving good care to her son and devoted a great deal of time to his wellbeing. She frequently spoke to him and held him close. Signs of Justin were everywhere—rattles and foam toys on the floor, an infant seat, a bounce seat, an automatic swing, a play pen with toys on the side.

She described the first few weeks at home as hectic, saying she was unable to get anything done around the house. When asked if she had help from anyone, she replied that she had help from her mother and husband for the first 4 days. She added, "It really didn't help and I'd rather not have had any." She was critical of the hospital nurses who advised against using lotion on the diaper area and thought Justin's mild diaper rash could have been prevented if she had not listened to their advice. She made several comments about the baby being "odd"—having "odd" sleeping habits and an "odd" way of looking at television, seeming to prefer football games.

When Justin was 3 ½ months old, his mother visited the office to consider participation in a parent–infant group. She left her son at home, fearing that he might be "bad". Mrs. J reported that Justin had gained weight rapidly and weighed 16 pounds. Fearful that his rapid weight gain would result in his lagging developmentally, she said she was trying to teach him to roll over. She also confided that although Justin was named after his father, she chose to call him by a nickname which his father considered to be "sissy".

During this visit, Mrs. J alluded to difficulty between herself and her husband. Mr. J accused her of being babyish and spoiled. He suggested that she change her hairstyle to one which was more mature. Mrs. J defended herself against his accusations and criticized her husband's sister for being shy and overly dependent. She complained her husband was too dependent and his own father, comparing Mr. J unfavorably with her own father who "could do anything". There was also some conflict about where they should live. Mr. J wanted to move so they would not be so near her family, and she did not want to live too near his.

The following week, Mrs. J attended a mother–infant group for the first time. Again she left Justin at home, fearing he would be "bad". She inquired if it were possible to train a child to be right-handed and told how each time her son reached for an object with his left hand, she moved it near his right. Justin was sleeping from midnight to 10:00 a.m. and napping twice a day. Mrs. J said he really liked to be around people and was beginning to whimper if she walked out of his sight.

Mrs. J first brought Justin to the mother–infant group meeting when he was 4¾ months old. He seemed somewhat sober and visually explored the other people in the room. His mother held him in her lap throughout the 1½-hour-long meeting and entertained him with an assortment of toys she had brought.

His mother came alone to the next group meeting, commenting that she left Justin at home because she was afraid he would be "bad". She brought pictures of him to show the others and spoke glowingly about his many accomplishments and her ability to provide good mothering care. She spoke in much detail about his appetite and the special foods she prepared. We were impressed with her struggles with dependency as evidenced by her comments and interactions with others as she simultaneously reported how efficiently she coped and how clever her son was. We wondered if she left Justin at home in order to have more time to establish an image of herself as the competent mother before submitting her child to the scrutiny of others.

At 6 months, Mrs. J again brought Justin to the group. He was sitting unsupported but seemed to be a very unhappy, solemn baby. He often attempted to be close to his mother, but she rarely permitted him to be close to her. Repeatedly she substituted toys for herself, and even when she held him she rarely looked at him. Once, when he fussed, she held him to the mirror and talked to him while looking into the mirror. She was critical of Justin, calling him "old sobersides" when he did not smile as a staff member took a Polaroid snapshot. Mrs. J also said she was anxious for him to get teeth, adding, "That's a milestone to be proud of."

Mrs. J frequently looked at her image in the observation mirror and often seemed to speak to her own reflection in the mirror although ostensibly talking to others. She often had an appearance of being "on stage" when telling stories, smiling broadly as she described some funny antic of Justin's.

Mrs. J began to bring Justin regularly to group, and said that she was glad to bring him so he could get used to other babies and learn to be more friendly.

At 7 months Mrs. J held another child and teased Justin saying, "Look, I have another baby." Justin was very unhappy and began to fuss—Mrs. J commented that she felt her husband was too close to his mother. She advised another mother, "If you let babies be dependent on you while they are little, they will be more independent when they are older." Mrs. J repeatedly engaged with other infants in the group in ways which invariably elicited protests from her son. On one occasion she said to him, "I know you're jealous." Then she told the group, "This is a mild reaction. He really screams when my husband and I get close in front of him."

It seemed to the staff there was something seductive in the way in which Mrs. J took on the posture of loving mother by bestowing gifts of attention and love on other children in the group while being unavailable to her own child who was watching. Justin's predominant affect was one of sadness, and he was most often in a "low key" mood. At times when his mother showered him with attention, he responded with many smiles.

We were concerned that Mrs. J's lack of empathy for Justin and her unpredictable behavior would be experienced by him as being turned "on and off". On one occasion when he was just learning to walk, his mother called him to her. His face had an expression of utter delight as he approached her. Each time he neared reunion with her, she backed further away until he seemed so frustrated that he sat on the floor and began to cry.

As Justin's walking skills improved, he did begin to explore the environment, moving some distance from his mother. His attempts to return to her according to his own needs were often thwarted by her lack of availability. The observers noted that Mrs. J sought closeness to Justin according to her needs—rather than permitting him to initiate a return to her when he needed it. There were repeated instances when Justin would approach his mother, stand at her knees, tug at her knees, signaling a wish for interaction. Mrs. J was often oblivious to his presence or would somewhat mechanically briefly pat his head without visual engagement, focusing on other adults or children in the group and often looking at her own reflection in the mirror. The emotional refueling which Justin sought from his mother seemed just beyond his reach. Upon occasion when his mother did not respond he would sit solemnly at her feet, often mouthing a toy.

Excerpts from the record of a home visit at 1 year are revealing. Mrs. J asked Justin to show the home visitor first one toy and then the other. Each time she asked him to bring her an object to show the interviewer or herself, he would obediently comply. She initiated a game of peek-a-boo, coaxing him to continue the game although he had lost interest. She was lavish with smiles and tokens of appreciation for his competence in his activities. As soon as he stopped the peek-a-boo game, he got down onto the floor, assuming a position that looked as though he were wanting to do a somersault. His mother asked if he wanted to so a somersault and gave him a slight push, helping him to roll over. As he stood up he smiled broadly and beamed at his mother as she clapped. Then, Mrs. J said, "You didn't do it as well as you usually do," explaining that he did not hold his head steady. It was evident that Mrs. J had the capacity to provide much gratification to her son at times and yet to be exceedingly disappointing at others. From time to time during that home visit Mrs. J seemed momentarily to lose sight of the interviewer, Justin, and everything else in the room as she became distracted by her own image in the wall mirror of the living room.

Justin's aggression was channeled in numerous ways. When Justin was 13 months old, mother embraced another child in the group and Justin reached over and pinched that child's arm. Later again when that same child approached his mother and threatened to intrude between him and his mother, Justin grimaced and put his hands around the child's neck in an aggressive way. Mrs. J told Justin to kiss the child; instead he hit her. He became somewhat more resistant to his mother's continual demands for compliance, and he resisted toilet training, which Mrs. J began at 14 months.

Mrs. J maintained a meticulously neat apartment with nothing out of place. The home visitor noted that when Justin was 18 months old he, also, was preoccupied with cleanliness as he drank a cup of orange juice. Each time he sipped, he replaced the cup very carefully into the middle of a coaster. Then he would back off, rub the front of his shirt saying "spill" or look at the carpet saying "messy". Although he had not spilled a drop he was apparently checking to see if he had. His mother said she thought he was too preoccupied with things being messy. He remained very close to his mother during the entire visit only leaving her when she instructed him to go and fetch something to show the interviewer. Mrs. J had him bring her a book and she pointed to pictures while he correctly identified the objects in the book. He had an extensive vocabulary and understood appropriately almost everything said to him. He imitated many many words that his mother said to him, even multisyllabic words of great difficulty. With a tone of pride, Mrs. J said, "He can say anything." She instructed Justin to get his dump truck to "show the lady". He did so and attempted to open the door of the truck. When it did not readily open, he said "Dump truck is stuck." Mrs. J affirmed that he was now saying sentences. Although some of his words were spontaneous, the majority were in response to questions that his mother asked. Mother and child demonstrated a series of routines where Mrs. J asked repeated questions and he answered them all, such as, "What happens when it rains?" Justin said, "Drips." Mother said, "What do we do with the teapot?" Justin said, "Pour."

At times when his mother spoke directly to the home visitor, Justin tried to regain her attention by talking very loudly to her with a tone of urgency in his voice. He also leaned on his mother's knees, placing his body between her and the home visitor. Mrs. J said Justin followed her from room to room and did everything with her. For example, when she makes the bed, he gets on the other side of the bed and pulls the sheet up at the same time that she does. Mrs. J so closely directed his play that he showed very little initiative of his own. At one point his mother directed Justin to go into his room and show the home visitor how he could ride his rocking horse. He complied and competently mounted a rather large rocking horse without any assistance. The rocking horse faced a large mirror and he gazed at himself in the mirror as he rocked. Mrs. J entered the room and stood by him also staring into the mirror. The two of them remained like this for some time with Justin bouncing up and down on this horse and staring in the mirror, and his mother standing next to him also staring in the mirror. Even though the home visitor was in the same room, neither of them seemed to be aware of her presence.

Mrs. J confided to the home visitor that her husband was upset with her because he said Justin was a mama's boy. She added that she also wondered about it. She said that he had moved farther away from her today during the visit than he had ever done before.

The behavior that we observed in the home situation was very similar to what we observed in the group meetings. At 21 months Justin was not moving into increased social interaction with the other children in the group. Rather he remained isolated and sought physical closeness and attention from his mother. He was a solemn child closely bound to his mother. On one occasion he brought a book to her indicating he would like her to read it to him. She permitted him to sit beside her in the chair and began to point to pictures. Another child soon approached and Mrs. J immediately focused on the other child. Justin pointed to the book and insistently said, "Me, me." Mrs. J then spoke to another adult, and Justin turned and hit at the other adult.

Often when Justin brought a toy to his mother indicating a wish to play with her, she would take the toy and play with it herself. Thus, she did not facilitate or help him to expand upon his play. For example, when Justin was 22 months, he asked his mother to play catch with him, tossing her a foam block. She caught it and rather than returning it to him she began to ask, "What color is this?" and then proceeded to have him point to and identify different colored blocks. She then quizzed him on the color of his pants and his shirt sleeve. With some encouragement from staff, Mrs. J again began to play catch with Justin. Justin threw the block and his mother did not catch it. Justin said, "Missed it." His mother indignantly replied, "I didn't miss it, you have to throw it to me carefully." She then terminated the game.

When Justin was 2½ he visited the office for an evaluation and became engrossed with toys while his mother chatted with the examiner during the initial phase of a free play situation. In spite of suggestions of a skillful examiner that he bring some of the toys to the table to begin the Bayley test, he resisted and was unable to make a smooth transition to the table. His mother pleaded with him but he resisted. Finally she picked him up and sat him in the chair. Then Mrs. J aggressively poked his cheek with a toy shark. He recoiled saying, "Don't make him bite me." The lack of synchrony between this mother and child was striking at this time. Justin became fascinated with one of the Bayley test items, a pair of scissors. He enjoyed playing with them and had great trouble relinquishing them when it was time to proceed to the next test item. He said he wanted to "color and snip". Mrs. J told him to give her the scissors, he resisted, and she took them. He pleaded for their return. She promised to return the scissors if he would cooperate with the tester. An intense struggle between Mrs. J and Justin followed. Then the examiner gave him a picture card and asked him to name the item. Mrs. J was intrusive, directing how to hold the picture card so she could also see. He snatched the card from her and knocked some blocks onto the floor. He then turned his back to his mother so she could not see and shared the picture card with the examiner.

Later during the evaluation process, Mrs. J was asked to leave the room briefly. In her absence Justin turned his aggression to the examiner, approaching her with a pair of pliers and wanting to snip her hair and poke her face. When the examiner suggested going to "find mommy", he said "I ain't coming." The examiner opened the door and Mrs. J returned. He avoided his mother and continued his snipping on the furniture with pliers. Next, he approached his mother and pulled her hair with the pliers. Thus we saw an ascendence of aggression and oppositional behavior. During Justin's process of individuation, Mrs. J had repeatedly interfered with his autonomous functioning both at group and during home visits. Her interference in his play efforts was so frequent that she literally smothered him with unnecessary verbal directives and actively took over to do the play activities herself. These were not attempts to play with Justin; instead Mrs. J repeatedly took away from him the objects that interested him and forced him into the passive role of watching her. There was lack of empathy on Mrs. J's part, and Justin tried for many months to resist her intrusions. However, her dogged persistence seemed to win out, and Justin became unwilling to initiate his own interactions with play materials, insisting that the home visitor or his mother build something that he could then copy. When this was resisted by the home visitor he would try to copy a picture of a construction from the box containing the materials.

During this same period, struggles continued with toilet training. Justin had a period of withholding bowel movements which his mother said the pediatrician said was psychological. He prescribed laxatives which his mother said she hated to give him; instead she chose to give enemas.

When the children were 2 years of age we implemented a change in the intervention format. Whereas the infants and mothers had previously met in the same room, for 1½ hours, we initiated discrete groups. After a brief period of joint activity in the familiar room, the leaders and mothers would leave and meet in an adjacent room, apart from the children, and then rejoin them for a brief period prior to departing. The children remained in the familiar room under the supervision of several staff members. Soon after the division into the two discrete groups, we noted Mrs. J's interest in attending diminished.

When Justin was 2 years, 9 months old, they came to the group after an absence of several months. The home visitor, who had visited Justin since he was 18 months old, tried to help him feel more comfortable explaining where new toys were. He did not make eye contact with her, although he seemed to listen. She encouraged him to join the other children, whom he had known for some time, but he remained alone. He sat on the floor surrounded by toys but was unable to play or join the group. He watched the children from a distance. Soon he rejoined his mother, who explained she was going across the hall, and he looked very sad. He seemed near tears when she kissed him goodbye. He shadowed his home visitor while she attempted to offer structure and support. The home visitor had to leave the room briefly and, although other familiar staff were available, his distress mounted. Upon her return he burst into tears and could not be comforted. His distress was very intense and he cried loudly, calling for his mother. Justin was taken across the hall to see his mother and they returned. Mrs. J remained with Justin for some time to comfort him. He continued to be distressed and said he wanted to go home. When he seemed somewhat comforted, his mother said she was going back across the hall. Unable to cope with the threat of a brief separation, Justin again burst into tears and his mother remained with him.

Following this episode, Mrs. J and Justin did not return to group meetings, although his mother continued to permit the home visitor to visit at home until Justin was 3½ at which time the intervention ended. Mrs. J said she did not want Justin to be frightened by being away from her. It was the opinion of the staff that the separation from Justin was also threatening to Mrs. J.

At age 5 Justin, accompanied by his mother, returned for evaluation. Justin was a handsome, slender boy; he was dressed in very short briefs and a sleeveless, low-necked shirt. His movements were graceful and somewhat effeminate.

Mrs. J's difficulty with empathy for Justin had been interspersed with seductive and erotic interchanges. We observed Justin draw a picture of a woman and discuss various body parts with his mother, who giggled at his questions. When Justin was asked to draw a person and had difficulty with drawing the extremities, his mother suggested he look into the observation mirror. As he did so, he lifted his briefs exposing half of his hip region. Both he and Mrs. J giggled at this.

At times Justin and his mother appeared fascinated with each other. At other times considerable aggression was apparent in their relationship. Mrs. J and Justin sat facing a mirror. He aimed a toy gun and whispered, "I'm going to shoot those mirrors. I'm gonna shoot 'em." First he shot at his own reflection in the mirror and then at his mother's Throughout the 5-year evaluation Justin was often so captivated by his own reflection in the mirror that his playing and interactions with people were seriously disrupted. He preened and posed and many of his body gestures resembled those of contestants in a body builder contest. When the examiner began to question Justin he continued to look at himself in the mirror and did not turn to face her at all. The evaluation was being videotaped with a camera located behind the observation as well as with a remote-control camera located in the playroom. As the interview progressed, we began to film Justin's reflection directly from the mirror—with the remote-control camera pointed at the mirror. His fascination with his image and his inability to engage with the examiner was striking.

Just prior to his departure, Justin was told we would show him the TV pictures that had been taken and he was shown the remote control camera in the room (which was at a right angle to the camera behind the observation mirror). Immediately he went to that camera and began to smile and wave. As he posed, he glimpsed his reflection in the mirror and once again, like Narcissus, gazed at his mirror image, losing interest in the remote camera. He did not know there was also a camera behind the mirror. Thus on videotape we have dramatic documentation of Justin's fascination with his image.

The sense of continuity of self depends on the regularity of events, the expectability of satisfactions, and the tolerability of frustrations. When these are absent the infant may later develop an impaired sense of self. The sum total of conscious and unconscious sensing of oneself is responsible for the cohesiveness of self, for its continuity over time, and for the way in which the essential sense of continuity and sameness in the midst of developmental changes is retained. We have come to know difficulties in these areas as narcissistic disorder.

Mrs. J had difficulty in providing age-appropriate gratifications and frustrations for Justin. She was inconsistent, intrusive, and unduly projected onto him aspects of her own images and needs. When a woman has not experienced good mothering and a pleasurable infancy with her own mother, she may be hampered in her ability to provide good mothering for her child. Mrs. J told us she would not turn to her mother for any help. Her relationships with others were superficial. Her ability for empathy was impaired and reflected in relation to her husband and son.

The unevenness in Justin's self feelings, both omnipotent and helpless, which was expressed in his fantasy life and his relationships is character-istic of narcissistic disturbance. Recalling Justin's early attempts to make contact with his mother and his frustrations within the relationship, raised the question; What was the function of the mirror for him? Was it "not me", "part me" or "me" to Justin? If the mirror represented mother and "part me", how could it be given up? It became part of his shared experience and necessary to complete himself. Unfortunately, the mirror could not bring him into true personal fulfilling relationship.

During the first 3½ years of Justin's life, there were 105 contact hours (38 group meetings and 30 home visits). A subsequent publica-tion will deal with the interventions used within this specific mother–infant system and discuss the implications for technique. It is not possi-ble to say what Justin's development would have been without the intervention. It is also true that the group of children who received intervention were functioning more optimally at age 2½ when com-pared with those infants at high risk who did not have intervention. With regard to Justin, however, we felt saddened that more progress had not been accomplished. There remained a split between his fund of intellectual knowledge and his ability with autonomous functioning, the quality of his interpersonal relationships, his self-esteem, and joy in existence.

Justin's uneven development illustrates not only a need for refining techniques of intervention but also the importance of using a variety of measures in evaluating outcome—we need to look beyond "I.Q." and "Competence".

References

Bach, S. Narcissism, continuity and the uncanny. *International Journal of Psycho-Analysis,* 1975, *56,* 77–86.

Broussard, E. R. Evaluation of televised anticipatory guidance to primiparae. *Community Mental Health Journal,* 1976, *12,* 203–210. (a)

Broussard, E. R. Neonatal prediction and outcome at 10/11 years. *Child Psychia-try and Human Development,* 1976, *7,* 85–93. (b)

Broussard, E. R. Primary prevention program for newborn infants at high risk for emotional disorder. In D. Klein and S. Goldston (Eds.), *Primary prevention: An idea whose time has come.* Washington, D.C.: U.S. Government Printing Office, 1977.

Broussard, E. R. Assessment of the adaptive potential of the mother-infant sys-tem: The Neonatal Perception Inventories. *Seminars in Perinatology* (Vol. 3) (1), January, 1979.

Broussard, E. R. Prospective longitudinal study of first-born neonates. In E. Er-lenmeyer-Kimling, B. Bowhenrend, and N. Miller (Eds.), *Life span research on the prediction of psychopathology.* (In press)

Broussard, E. R., and Cornes, C. C. Identification of mother-infant systems in distress: What can we do? *Journal of Preventive Psychiatry*, 1981, *1*, 119–132.

Broussard, E. R., and Hartner, M.S.S. Maternal perception of the neonate as related to development. *Child Psychiatry and Human Development*, 1970, *1*, 16–25.

Broussard, E. R., and Hartner, M.S.S. Further considerations regarding maternal perception of the first-born. In J. Helmuth (Ed.), *Exceptional infant: Studies in abnormalities* (Vol. 2). New York: Brunner-Mazel, 1971.

Ovid, *Metamorphoses III*, quoted in G. Nielsen, *Studies in self confrontation*. Copenhagen: Munksgaard Publishers, 1962.

Schaefer, E. S., and Bell, R. Q. Development of a parental attitude research instrument. *Child Development*, 1958, *29*, 339–361.

Effects of the Atypical Child on the Family

Ann V. McGillicuddy-DeLisi and Irving E. Sigel

Many investigations of the family environment have shown that parents play a primary role in the development of children's cognitive abilities. Parental childrearing practices or parenting styles have been found to be related to children's IQ scores, achievement, and verbal ability in a number of studies (Bayley and Schaefer, 1964; Brophy, 1970; Freeberg and Payne, 1967; Hess and Shipman, 1965; Hurley, 1959; Jones, 1972; Marjoribanks, 1979; Moss and Kagan, 1958; Norman, 1966; Radin, 1974; Rolcik, 1965). Although these studies have been conducted on normally developing children, there is some evidence that a similar relationship between parental attitudes or practices and children's abilities exists, and may even be augmented, in the case of a learning-disabled child. For example, intervention programs with disadvantaged and handicapped children often fail when there is a lack of parental involvement in a manner that influences childrearing practices (Starr, 1971) and home-based programs seem to be more successful in effecting cognitive gains than traditional instruction programs (Shearer and Shearer, 1972). Positive changes in learning disabled children have often been cited as outcomes of parent intervention programs (Edgerly, 1975; Grilli, 1974; McWhirter, 1972).

Additional evidence indicates that parents of a learning disabled (LD) child may have different ideas about their role as a teacher, different tolerance levels or attitudes toward academic behavior, and so forth that may have a marked effect on the LD child's progress (Freeman, 1971; Wetter, 1972). Observations of parent–child interactions indicate that parents have a marked effect on the LD child's progress (Freeman, 1970; Wetter, 1972). Observations of parent–child interactions indicate that parents of LD children teach and manage their children differently from parents of normally developing children (Campbell, 1972; Doleys, Cartelli, and Doster, 1976; Wilson, 1975). The impact of having a learning-

Portions of this research program are supported by NIH Grant No. MH 32301 and by BEH Grant No. 443CH90187.

disabled child may affect the parents in such a manner that "negative" interactions occur, that is, varied stimulation, affection, and parental responses are not optimally provided so as to maintain a learning disabling condition.

The nature of reciprocal influences between parent and child may work to the disadvantage of the LD child (Abrams and Kaslow, 1976). That is, parents may be affected by the LD condition of their child in such a manner that fewer opportunities for the cognitive growth of the child are provided. In subsequent sections we shall present a theoretical rationale for differences between parents of learning-disabled children versus normally developing children relative to types of teaching and management strategies that have been found to have an impact on the child's level of cognitive functioning (Sigel, in press; Sigel, McGillicuddy-DeLisi, and Johnson, 1980). Strategies of parents with an LD child may not be optimal given the LD condition, and in fact may compound the child's difficulties by not providing an environment that is intellectually challenging. Parents' childrearing strategies are not to be construed as a cause of the child's disability, but rather parental styles of interaction are conceptualized as affected by feedback from the child's behavior. We hypothesize that differences in strategies of parents of LD children are manifestations of differences in parental beliefs about child development states and processes that are a result of feedback generated from interactions with LD versus non-LD children. With this framework, parents of an only child with a learning disability, for example, are expected to evidence a system of beliefs about child development that differs from beliefs of parents of an LD child who has non-LD siblings. Parents in the latter group have had more extensive and perhaps contradictory experiences with their LD and non-LD children, and these experiences are the bases from which belief systems are constructed by the parent. The ordinal position of the LD child in the family constellation is also of potential significance. If the LD child is the first-born, parents' beliefs are likely to be affected differently than if the LD child has an older normal sibling. Thus, the feedback network or reciprocal influences between children and parents is of paramount importance for providing an environment that enables the LD child to fulfill his or her intellectual potential.

The Significance of Parental Beliefs (Constructs of Child Development)

A basic premise of this research is that parental beliefs about children in general, and about the learning disabled child in particular, contribute significantly to parental teaching and managerial strategies. This premise is derived in part from the work of George Kelly (1955, 1963) who created a system known as Constructive Alternativism and in part from our own work into family influence on children's problem-solving abilities (Sigel et al., 1980). Kelly proposes that each individual formulates his or her own constructs through which the world is viewed. We propose that parents' beliefs about children, or constructs of child development, are used to categorize events and guide the parent's own behavior with respect to the child's progress and behavior just as Kelly's personal constructs are seen as the directing source of behaviors in interacting with any other person. Thus, the parents' constructions about the child are hypothesized to be a source of parental childrearing practices and parental childrearing goals with respect to their children, whether normal or learning disabled.

A principal assumption within such a framework is that parents, as active organisms, do not passively incorporate information to form a belief system. Rather, the parent builds from experience and systematizes the groupings of constructs so as to minimize psychological inconsistencies among these cognitive elements. Parents of an LD child in particular have experiences with a child that differ from their experiences with other children, from what they have been taught about children in general, and from what they remember of their own childhood. The environment produces both confirmation and disconfirmation of existing belief systems, but parents of an LD child are more likely to have experiences that are discrepant and challenge these world views which are derived from the norm. When this occurs, the entire system of general beliefs may be altered in order to accommodate new or discrepant constructs that have evolved on the basis of specific experiences.

Numerous studies have investigated parental attitudes toward an LD, physically handicapped, or mentally retarded child, but such investigations have tended to focus on acceptance–rejection patterns and perceived discrepancies between normal, special, and ideal children (cf. Worchel and Worchel, 1961); perception of the child's adjustment (cf. Wetter, 1972); overindulgence (cf. Wilson, 1975); authoritarian control (Freeman, 1971); and overprotectiveness (cf. Abrams, 1970). Empirical research relating parents' constructs of child development to childrearing practices has indicated a relationship between parental beliefs and particular teaching and managerial behaviors of parents of normally developing children (McGillicuddy-DeLisi, in press), but a great deal of additional research is needed in this area. What parents believe about the cognitive capabilities of the LD as well as of the normally developing child will be major influences on parental practices which ultimately influence the child's cognitive growth and development.

Parental Beliefs within the Context of Family Influences

This formulation of cognitive organization of parental construction systems leads directly to a nonrecursive[1] path model of family influence. Since belief systems are subject to change as a result of new experiences, the behaviors and abilities of children have potential impact on parental beliefs as information about the child's behaviors is incorporated into the existing belief system. When this occurs, the parental behaviors may change so as to be consistent with these modified beliefs. In our past research, data from 120 families of normally developing children were analyzed using a path model in which parent affects child and child affects parent (see Figure 1). For the most part, the relationships hypothesized were supported (Sigel et al., 1980). The model was subsequently modified to include effects of siblings on the target child, the effects of relationships among children in the family, and the effects of the marital relationship on parental childrearing beliefs and subsequent behaviors. In addition, there were some data from the previous study which indicated that mothers' beliefs may be differentiated according to a particular child's abilities within a more general framework of child development. Such a differentiation may be more marked for parents of learning-disabled children, and for this reason parental beliefs regarding the saliency of particular developmental processes for their child are included in the present model (see Figure 2). Such a model also implicates family structure variables such as number of children and ordinal position of the target child. The impact of these variables on the mutual influences within the family is our next consideration.

Interrelationships of Family Structure and Family Process

Past research on the effects of family structure on children's intellectual functioning indicates that family size is negatively related to intellectual achievement (Anastasi, 1956; Dandes and Dow, 1969; Lentz, 1927; Nisbet, 1953; Schooler, 1972a; Wray, 1971, Zajonc and Markus, 1975), although there is some indication that the effect is attenuated in upper income groups (Anastasi, 1959; Belmont and Marolla, 1973; Kennett and Cropley, 1970; Marjoribanks, Walberg and Bargen, 1975). Data presented by Marjoribanks and Walberg (1975) indicate that variance in amount of parent–child interaction with size of family can account for the relationship between family constellation and children's cognitive performances. Thus, there is some evidence that variation in intelligence

---

[1]The mathematical definition of "nonrecursive" differs from the usual meaning of the term. Nonrecursive in the mathematical sense implies bidirectionality.

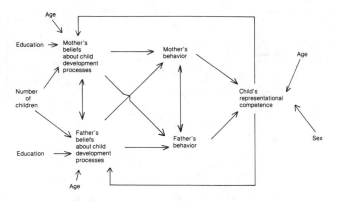

Figure 1. Path model of influences between parent and child.

with status or population characteristics could be due to different patterns and processes in the home environment.

The literature on birth order effects is equivocal (Adams, 1972; Hare and Price, 1969, Price and Hare, 1969; Schacter, 1963; Schooler, 1972b). A number of studies report that second-borns do better on intelligence tests than first-borns (Koch, 1954; Thurstone and Jenkins, 1929; Willis, 1924), or that there are no significant differences in intelligence with birth order (Schoonover, 1959). On the other hand, some studies show the opposite results (Altus, 1966; Chittenden, Foan, Zweil, and Smith, 1968; Eysenck and Cookson, 1970). There are some findings that family interaction systems account for variability in intelligence with birth order. That is, investigations of childrearing practices indicate that types of parental behaviors during interactions with the child vary with first- versus later-born children (Cicirelli, 1976; Hilton, 1967).

Information regarding the effect of the position of the atypical child in the family on either parents or children is minimal, but parental belief systems may be a critical moderating factor influencing how parents behave with each child in the family. The belief system may become differentiated relative to the ordinal position and sex of the children as subsequent births occur in the family. There are a number of possibilities for different reactions to the LD child as a function of that child's ordinal position. If the first-born evidences an LD condition and the second child does not, the second child may be "prized" because of his or her intactness. Or parents' experience with the first LD child may be a source of developmental landmarks for the parent, leading to overreaction to the achievements of their second, non-LD child. It is also conceivable, how-

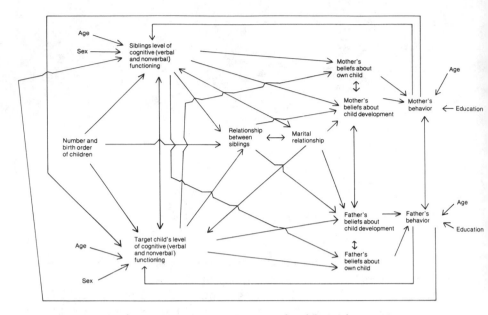

Figure 2. Path model of influences between family members.

ever, that parents may be intent on fostering the development of the LD child and believe that this child needs special help and attention, while normal children can fend for themselves. In the case of a second-born child who evidences a language disorder, the usual dethronement of the first-born may be more dramatic if parents take this approach. This may be due to the added demands and services required by the LD child. (In this sense, there can also be economic demands, e.g., private schools.)

Unless parents are truly unbiased in their hopes and plans for their male and female children, there may well be differences in how the parents will respond if the child involved is a boy or a girl or whether it is an only child, first-born or later-born child in the family constellation. Farber describes how older sisters were often expected to function as surrogate caretakers for the young retarded child (Farber and Jenne, 1963). Whether this is still true in the 1980s is an open question. Further, the view that males will have to be the breadwinners and so fulfill the traditional male role may well be a critical feature in influencing how a parent responds to the child with a language disorder. Where maleness is viewed traditionally, it might be expected that different plans, expectations, and acceptance of the child's difficulty would arise for male versus female LD children.

Parental beliefs may also affect the urgency with which parents seek professional help for their children. If the LD child is a first-born or an only child and the parent has had little experience with children, then the parent may not be certain as to cognitive benchmarks marking developmental progress or may not recognize certain symptoms as problems. They may be guided by constructions of normal development on the basis of their experiences only with an LD child. Yet, on the other hand, the parent may be disappointed and reject the first child who is not normal. This may well produce a family crisis as defined by Farber (1960). Having an LD child as the first-born provides a different experiential base (versus having a later-born LD child with older normal siblings), which would have differential effects on parental beliefs and practices for subsequent children.

In sum, entry of an LD child into a family upsets the equilibrium. Parents' expectations are affected and different patterns are set in play for later births in the case of a first-born LD child. How the parents react and cope with this event can be of momentous impact on *how* the LD child will develop.

Distancing Strategies and the LD Child

According to distancing theory (Sigel, 1970, 1971, 1972), representational abilities are derived in part by events that separate the child from the immediate environment in a cognitive sense. Distancing behaviors include classes of parental behaviors that "demand" that the child anticipate future actions or outcomes, reconstruct past events, employ his or her imagination in dealing with objects, events, and people, and attend to transformations of phenomena. It is our contention that such behaviors encourage children to make inferences actively, consider alternatives, and reach conclusions on their own.

The development of such competencies is influenced by the demands of the environment in addition to biological and maturational factors. On the assumption that the cognitive environment the parents provide through distancing behaviors will vary as a function of their constructions of the child's capability and development as well as the positon of an LD child in a family constellation, it is necessary to examine the relationship between parental constructs and types of parental teaching strategies, such as distancing, within the context of family size and ordinal position.

Parental distancing strategies focus in large part on the communicative environment the child lives in and emphasize parental practices that provide opportunities for children to think and represent on their own.

Parental distancing behaviors consist of inquiries that vary in the level of demand on the child to represent (cf. Sigel and Cocking, 1977; Flaugher and Sigel, 1980), that is, anticipate, reconstruct, or imagine. Empirical research indicates that parental behaviors do have an impact on the child's level of verbal ability (see Introduction). A learning-disabled child with a language disorder may be exposed to an environment that exacerbates the disability. That is, the child's verbal ability is likely to affect the quantity and quality of language behaviors of those around the child in a negative manner. Communicative overtures are likely to decrease in quantity and quality since the child has difficulty responding verbally to such overtures. This would limit the child's input experiences and demands for verbal participation. Yet children evidencing a language disorder represent a group with great potential for benefitting from parental distancing behaviors because they have intrinsic cognitive abilities which may be either enhanced or impeded in their development by parental practices.

We are currently collecting data from 120 families with a learning-disabled child with a language disorder in order to investigate the relationship between the child's communication disability and parental constructions and teaching practices. A language disorder is defined, for the purposes of this study, as a deficit in linguistic competence relative to existing levels of nonverbal intellectual and social development. Such a definition is applied without attention to the cause of the disorder, with the exception of physical handicaps since the presence of visible physical disabilities are likely to affect parents and siblings differently from disturbances of psychological processes involved in using and understanding language. Learning disabled children with a language disorder were selected for the following theoretical and practical reasons: (1) this group is likely to benefit the most from distancing experiences and yet, by the very nature of their disability, are not likely to be provided with a wide variety of experiences in the home environment; (2) early identification of family influence may provide a basis for embarking on remedial programs that focus on parent behaviors prior to elementary school entrance, hopefully preventing compounding of the child's learning problems; (3) limitations in the child's development of language are likely to be apparent in the child's speech and therefore are likely to be identified earlier than other specific learning disabilities; (4) when poor language development is not remediated early, it may have negative effects on peer relationships, social skills, school adjustment, and so forth, that is, the nature of the disability may lead to a set of negative outcomes that occur in spite of the child's basic intellectual abilities; and (5) language development is a full-time process, and a rich and primary source of language experience is in the functional communication of the family environment.

Beliefs and Behaviors of Parents of an LD Child

The models of family influences which we previously presented address two major research questions with respect to parents' adaptation to their LD child. First, it is proposed that experience with both LD and non-LD children influences parental constructions of children's development as well as their definition of optimal childrearing practices. Parents may hold that the cognitive processes of LD and non-LD children are similar or that developmental states and processes differ relative to non-LD and LD children. If parents refer to different types of developmental processes for their own LD child compared to normally developing children, it is likely that the belief system has become differentiated. Similarity of beliefs espoused for LD and non-LD children may be due to one of three factors: (1) the parent's belief system was sufficient to account for development of both language-impaired and non-LD children, and there was no necessity for modification after experience with the LD child; (2) the belief system has been modified so as to account for the development of children with and without language difficulties; or (3) the belief system is relatively impermeable, and the parent maintains prior beliefs that do not appear adequate in relation to the LD child's progress and capabilities. The last alternative is relatively easy to distinguish from the former two possibilities, as the parent is likely to deny the disability or else refer to the necessity of total remediation in order for the LD child to attain certain capabilities. A longitudinal investigation is necessary to distinguish between the first and second alternatives. The content of responses to interview probes that focus on self-reports of changes in beliefs provides some indication of which alternative is most plausible for the particular parent.

The second major research question focuses on the relationship between parental beliefs and parental practices. Although parental behaviors have been found to be related to parental constructs of developmental states and processes for families with normally developing children (McGillicuddy-DeLisi, in press), it is possible that such a relationship is disrupted by the presence of a disability in the child. That is, the child's problem may impose constraints, real or imagined by the parent, to such a degree that it seems impossible for the parent to act in accordance with beliefs, and the parent may not be aware that alternative strategies are available. For example, it may be necessary to focus attention on protecting the child from physical harm to a greater degree than is typical for a non-LD child. The parent may therefore engage in many structuring and management behaviors, essentially restricting the child's activity, in spite of a belief that children must explore and experiment on their own in order to attain particular abilities or concepts. Thus, an investigation of parental beliefs and behavior is necessary in order to establish whether previously reported findings that parents of LD children teach and manage their children differently from other parents (see Introduction) are due to differences in parental beliefs or are simply responses to the special needs and behavior of the LD child that do not stem from the parent's thinking about the child.

A case example which provides material related to these two research questions was selected to illustrate the reciprocal nature of family influences and the relationship between parental beliefs and practices. A three-child family in which the third-born child has a severe language production problem was selected because the parents have had experience with both LD and non-LD children. Material obtained from parent interviews and from observations of parent–child interactions will be presented in order to provide a view of the individuality of the family members, describe each parent's adaptation to the LD child, and demonstrate relationships between parent's beliefs and behaviors.

A Case Study

Rationale for Case Analysis

The use of case studies has a long and honorable history because "the case study is the technique par excellence for dealing with the individual as an individual in all his uniqueness" (Watson, 1963, p. 39). In our case, we substitute the term "family" for the term "individual". The rationale and justification for using a case study approach at this time overlaps with those of the traditional clinical approach because it provides qualitative descriptions of the family as well as confirmation of some results from empirical research.

The case study we shall present provides a qualitative perspective of the relationship of parental constructs, teaching strategies, and child behaviors. Where quantitative analysis of group data provides tests of our basic hypotheses, qualitative analysis creates the opportunity to tie together various aspects of family processes and provides an alternative mode of examining parent–child interactions. In this particular case, the case example serves as an exemplar in miniature of our concepts and methods.

Not every case selected will provide material to accomplish these goals. Since our primary research questions focus on the effect of experience with both LD and non-LD children on parental constructions and teaching strategies, a family with more than one child was chosen. Second, it was necessary to select a family in which the LD child showed a clear-cut instance of a language disorder.

Data Collection Methods

Each parent was interviewed to ascertain their beliefs about children in general and their own LD child in particular. They were also video-taped interacting with each of their children on two tasks. The content of the interview consisted of 12 vignettes that involved a parent teaching or managing the behavior of a child. The format of the interview consisted of four main parts relative to each vignette: (1) parents' preferred communication strategies and rationales for that strategy; (2) parents' predicted communication strategy for their LD child and associated rationales; (3) parents' predicted follow-up strategies and associated rationales; and (4) parents' beliefs about child development states and processes. The two parent–child interaction tasks were a story-telling task and paper-folding task. Each parent performed equivalent versions of the two tasks alone with each child. Interactions were videotaped through a one-way mirror.

Background of the Family

The target child, Jon, was 4 years, 4 months old at the time of testing and is the youngest of three boys. Both parents began to think there was a problem when the child reached age 2 years and was not speaking. At age 3 years, the child was evaluated at Children's Hospital in Philadelphia and an audiogram indicated normal hearing. The child has been diagnosed as communication-handicapped because of a neurological impairment and is currently enrolled in a 5-day-a-week special education preschool. He has speech therapy twice a week.

The parents have been married 12 years and are both Roman Catholic. The father is 33 years old, has a college degree, and earns over $31,000 a year as a roofing salesman. The mother is 33 years old, is a high school graduate, and is at home full-time. Both parents expressed interest in joining or forming some type of parent group, but they are not currently involved in any type of parent program.

Analysis of the Father's Beliefs and Behaviors

Mr. A's responses to the interview indicate that both his communication strategies and beliefs about child development are differentiated for areas of concept learning versus behavior control or socialization situations. He is inclined to advocate distancing or rational explanatory strategies when the focus is upon getting the child to understand an event, although direct authoritative approaches are advocated for management situations. However, Jon's ability level and behavior impose constraints on Mr. A's choice of communication strategies, requiring Mr. A to be more directive and didactic while teaching and more authoritarian in behavior management. The discrepancy between preferred strategies and strategies predicted for use with Jon will be apparent in the transcript of portions of the interview presented below.

Mr. A's responses to probes aimed at eliciting his beliefs about child development states and processes (* items) indicate that he thinks 4-year-olds are generally capable and have acquired an understanding of cause-effect, have a grasp of reality, understand rules, and are challenged by frustration. They learn many concepts and skills through experimentation and social interaction with peers. Feedback from others, notably parents, concerning appropriate behavior is important for socialization of the child. His view of the child is one of a relatively active, processing organism. Although Mr. A does not explicitly state that Jon is delayed in his development, he does imply that Jon is not as intellectually and emotionally mature as most 4-year-olds. Jon does have, however, a certain level of competency which Mr. A. attends to in his predicted interactions. He views social interactions with siblings and peers as a source of Jon's, as well as other children's, knowledge.

I = Interviewer   F = Father

VIGNETTE #1: Billy was playing with his Lincoln logs. A couple of logs wouldn't fit together and Billy started throwing them about the room.

I: What do you think is the best way for a parent to handle such a situation?

F: I think by asking him, "Billy, are you aware of what could happen by throwing those blocks around?" (*distancing as a preferred strategy*)

I: And why do you think this response is the best response in this situation?

F: I think it gives him a chance to think the situation through himself and realize the consequences of what could happen. (*cognitive goal for the child*)

I: Now if this were a real situation and you were the parent in it, how do you think you would respond?

F: Make him stop throwing the blocks initially. "Stop throwing your blocks Jon. You're gonna hurt somebody." (*rational authoritative predicted strategy*)

I: And why would you handle it that way?

F: Jon is rather independent and headstrong, very headstrong. He really tends to do what he wants to do when he wants to do it. Jon needs just certain guidelines or rules. (*constraint due to child; behavior management goal*)

I: And if that didn't work . . .

F: Probably take his blocks away from him. (*authoritarian behavior follow-up strategy*)

I: Why would you do that?

F: To prevent him from damaging or hurting his brothers or anything else in the room. (*physical goal*)

★I: These next few questions are about 4-year-olds in general. In answering them think about all 4-year-olds, not just your child. Do 4-year-old children understand the consequences their own actions may have? For example, do 4-year-olds know something could get broken if they throw things around?

★F: I think so. (*children capable of understanding cause-effect*)

★I: How does a child come to realize the consequences of his own behavior?

★F: I think it's a learned process he's developed with his parents.

★I: How?

★F: Depending how far they let him go. If he does something and consequently it reaches some goal that he wants, it's reinforced. I think he learns very quickly what type of consequences that behavior will bring. I guess through parental reinforcement of the act. (*feedback from parents*)

VIGNETTE #3: One day Jimmy's friend was invited to play. Jimmy had taken out only his Lego building set to play with in the living room. He wasn't sharing any of the pieces in the set with his friend.

I: What do you think is the best way for a parent to handle such a situation?

F: Say "How would your friend feel without having anything to play with" because really the toys are Jimmy's and at 4 years old, you know, the concept of sharing probably isn't always that easy. (*distancing preferred strategy*)

I: Why do you think this response is the best response in this situation?

F: Because I think the child can relate to how he might feel himself, you know, being invited to Jimmy's and not having anything to play with and maybe it's just not right for him not to share. (*cognitive goal*)

I: OK. If this were a real situation and you were the parent, how do you think you'd probably respond?

F: I think probably explain to him that he should be sharing his toys with his friend so that they'd both have something to play with. (*rational authoritative strategy*)

I: And why would you say that to him? What would you be hoping to accomplish?

F: Teach him how to share. Although that really hasn't been a prob-
    lem. (*social behavior goal*)

I: Let's say this time it is a problem (laugh) and that didn't work.
    What might you try next?

F: I would think perhaps ordering him to share. "Jon you have to
    share this with whoever's over, Jimmy, whatever, because if you
    don't we're going to take these toys away from you." (*threat; au-
    thoritarian behavior strategy*)

I: And why would you respond in that way?

F: Again, just to teach him that when you invite friends over, when
    you have people over, you just can't ignore the feelings of others
    and treat them rudely by not sharing with them. (*cognitive and social
    behavior goals*)

★I: Does a 4-year-old realize that someone else may be feeling differ-
    ently than he does?

★F: No, I don't think so. You know, unless you take the time to explain
    to him. (*children not particularly adept at role taking*)

★I: How do children come to realize that other people may feel some-
    thing differently than they do?

★F   You have to explain it to them. Teach them. Teach them. (*direct
    instruction from adults*)

★I: How would you do that?

★F: I think that when the situation occurs or someone maybe isn't
    feeling well or when there's something my 4-year-old wants to do
    but the other child just doesn't want to do, he wants to know why
    he doesn't. I don't know, maybe they explain it to each other. I
    think the children explain it to each other. (*curiosity, peer influence,
    observation*)

. . . . (later excerpt) . . . .

★I: Does Jon realize that someone else may be feeling differently than
    he does?

★F: I think so.

★I: How did he come to realize other people may feel something differ-
    ently than he does?

★F: Probably with the kids. I mean the way the kids were feeling gets to
    him. (*peer influence; empathy*)

. . . . (later excerpt) . . . .

★I: All right. Now let's talk about 4-year-olds in general. Is it impor-
    tant to correct misunderstandings or misconceptions a child may
    have about the real world?

★F: I, I think so. I think they can appreciate some situations that occur
    in the real world. (*children are capable at this age*)

*I: Where do these misconceptions come from?

*F: I think they just develop them themselves. I think they have certain thoughts that they expand upon themselves, and this in itself is good. I think that if they realize what is real as opposed to what they're just imagining, they can appreciate the differences between them. (*cognitive processes, generalization, imagination, discrimination*)

*I: Why do such ideas eventually change?

*F: I just think as they grow and develop they can appreciate and understand it better, through interacting with their friends. I think there's a lot of, um, situations that probably their friends teach them more than their parents do. (*maturation, peer influence*)

. . . . (later excerpt) . . . .

*I: What purpose does playing with others serve?

*F: They have a good time. I think it teaches the concept of sharing, the importance of the rights of others, probably doing things on team-like basis, in which they'd get together and help each other with toys. (*positive feedback, peer influence in cognition*)

*I: How does playing with others accomplish this?

*F: I think 4-year-olds probably force each other to understand what they want from each other.

VIGNETTE #9: One day Father was watching Sandy build with blocks. Sandy was trying to make a tall building by stacking the blocks one on top of the other, but the building kept falling down.

I: What do you think is the best way for a parent to handle such a situation?

F: How about telling me why you think the building keeps falling down?" (*distancing*)

I: And why do you think this response is the best one in this situation?

F: It gives the child a chance to think and to reason for itself why it's happening. (*cognitive goal*)

I: And if this were a real situation involving yourself and Jon, how do you think you'd handle it?

F: Probably "When you stack the blocks too high the top of the building will be shaky and fall down." (*rational authoritative*)

I: And why would you handle it that way?

F: I would think he himself would understand better being shown what was happening actually and the reason being tacked with it. He hasn't demonstrated a real ability to reason. But there are certain things we've explained to him and he can understand and this would probably be one of them. I think he would become less frustrated if he knew as he stacked, the building was going to get shaky and was going to fall down. (*constraints; cognitive goal*)

I: And if that didn't work what would you try next?

F: Probably stacking the blocks myself and show him as they got taller they become shakier. *(demonstration)*

I: And why would you do that?

F: Probably be easier for him to understand actually seeing it again and following step-by-step what was happening. *(cognitive goal)*

★*I:* What role do you think frustration may play in learning?

★*F:* I think due to frustration children are more apt to ask for explanations or more apt to reason explanations for themselves. I don't think I would keep frustration bottled up inside of them. It's going to come out one way or another.

★*I:* Is it ever OK to allow a child to become frustrated?

★*F:* Up to a point, yeh. I think by allowing them to be frustrated they start seeking answers to their own frustrations, start to reason themselves. *(self-regulation; cognitive processes)*

★*I:* With regard to 4-year-olds in general again, is it all right to allow a child to be independent instead of following a rule he or she actually follows?

★*F:* I think it's good to encourage a certain amount of independence.

★*I:* Why?

★*F:* I think eventually we all have to become very independent people. However we should realize that there are certain consequences too. These are hard and fast rules and there are certain things that are going to happen if we break them. *(feedback)*

★*I:* Does a 4-year-old know when to be independent and when to follow a rule?

★*F:* I think so. *(children are capable at this age)*

★*I:* How does a child come to know when to follow rules and when to be independent?

★*F:* I think when he starts to measure what he might gain by being independent and consequences by not following the rule. *(cognitive processes and feedback)*

★*I:* Does Jon know when to be independent and when to follow a rule?

★*F:* No. Jon knows when to be independent but he doesn't know when to follow a rule. At least at home. I think he does much better at school. *(Jon is not capable)*

★*I:* How will he come to know when to follow a rule and when to be independent?

★*F:* Hopefully we keep trying to reinforce the rules. Try to make him understand what's happening. *(feedback and cognitive processes)*

. . . . (later excerpt) . . . .

*I: We have some more "4-year-old in general" questions. Does a 4-year-old understand time?

*F: No, not to any great degree. I mean he has some basic concept. (*not capable*)

*I: Does a child know about an hour, tomorrow, a year?

*F: I think tomorrow. I don't an hour; I don't think they'd understand an hour to a great degree.

*I: How does a 4-year-old eventually come to understand about time?

*F: I guess just as they're growing. I think as you get older time just becomes less conceptual and more concrete: hours, days, minutes. (*maturation*)

*I: Do 4-year-olds plan what they want to do ahead of time?

*F: I really don't know. I guess perhaps to some degree they must understand, you know, now we watch and later we go, we're gonna go get ice cream, go to the movies. (*capable*)

*I: How does a child become able to plan?

*F: I think they can plan at 4, I don't think in a specific time frame. I think like I'm gonna watch TV for an hour and later, or after dinner . . . I think they set benchmarks in their day and then later get more concrete, say after lunch, after dinner initially, develop maybe into an hour after lunch. As they learn the concepts of time as in a clock, actually telling time. Probably in a more standardized routine, as in a school situation. (*structure of environment, differentiation*)

*I: Does Jon understand time?

*F: No. (*not capable*)

*I: How will Jon eventually come to understand time?

*F: I think we try and explain to him time. We show him clocks. We explain what's happening on the clock. We explain benchmarks in the day, after lunch, after school, after the kids coming home. I think it's a ways off before he really starts to get a firm understanding of time. (*direct instruction from adults, structure of environment*)

Thus, in Mr. A's view, 4-year-olds are generally capable of reasoning and thinking through the consequences of their behaviors, but Jon is not quite so competent. Jon cannot respond to the parent's distancing strategies, which are aimed at getting him to think or reason for himself. Jon is described as a headstrong, independent child. Consequently, Mr. A posits strategies that are more directive than he would prefer for other children. Data from our previous study of families (Sigel et al., 1980) indicated that parents' responses about how children develop (* items) and their rationales for communication strategies were better predictors of observed parental behaviors than the strategies predicted by parents dur-

ing the interview. The father's view of children in general as active processors who are able to think and reason on their own and his focus on
cognitive rationales for his communication strategies led us to predict
that he would indeed employ distancing strategies during an interaction
with Jon instead of using didactic, rational, authoritative approaches.

The transcript of portions of the parent–child interaction that follows
indicates that Mr. A's behavior with Jon is related to his child development beliefs and preferred strategies and goals. Yet many aspects of his
behavior do have a relationship to his description of ways he would interact with Jon. Mr. A interacted in a patient and benign way with Jon on
both the story and the paper tasks. When we first see Mr. A and Jon during the story task, Jon is playing with one of the toys deliberately left in
the room in order to note how parents deal with this natural type of dis-
traction. Mr. A asks Jon a series of questions that involve Jon in labelling
and locating objects or pictures. Jon responds both verbally and nonver-
bally. Jon's involvement in the story is short-lived, and Mr. A uses a
puppet as a means of getting Jon involved in the story.

Mr. A paces his efforts at getting Jon involved in the story. There are
relatively long periods where the father allows Jon to move around the
room and play with the distracting toys. The father uses a humoring
approach or gentle encouragement, often becoming involved himself
with one of the toys and using the toy to bring Jon back to the story. At
one point, Mr. A does insist that Jon attend to the story, physically
placing Jon on his lap and kissing him. As he reads the story, Mr. A
interjects some questions and reinforces Jon's efforts at articulating verbal responses. Mr. A's general demeanor is consistent throughout the
interaction, allowing Jon to become involved in other activities but then
capturing Jon's attention again and repeating or rephrasing previously
unanswered questions.

F = Father   J = Jon
  F: What's that? (pause) Huh?
  J: Uh. (J looks at fish toy)
  F: What that?
  J: Goo.
  F: Water? Fish?
  J: Fish.
  F: What's this? (point to book) (pause) A book?
  J: Book.
  F: Do you want to read the book? (J takes book and turns pages)
     Wait a minute. What's the book about? (J turns pages) It's about
     rainbows.

J: Yeah.

F: What's a rainbow? Do you know what a rainbow is? (J looks at toy) Here. Here's a rainbow (pointing). All different colors in the sky. (J looking at book) See it? (pointing) It goes all the way across.

J: Book. (turns pages)

F: Wait a minute. We gotta find out what it's all about.

J: Eh.

F: Start from the beginning?

J: No.

F: Noooo. Where do you want to start from, the end? (J points to page) That's a rainbow. (J looks at book and F reads for 3 seconds) Where's the rainbow, Jon? (J picks up toy and plays) Hey, wanta put this down and watch the rainbow? (J gives up toy) Where's the rainbow? (pause) Look. (J looks and F reads for 4 seconds)

J: Yeah.

F: Can we catch that rainbow? (J plays with toy) Where's the rainbow? (J points to book) Look. (J looks) Here's the rainbow.

J: Eh.

F: This is the rainbow. Up in the sky. Where's the fish? Do you see any fish in that picture?

J: Yep.

F: Where's the fish (J reaches for fish toy) There's a fish (pointing). Do you see any fish in that picture? (J playing with toy). Where's the fish in here? Do you see any fish in here? (toy) What's that?

J: Fish.

F: Fish.

J: Ish.

F: See, look. (Playing with toy, J looks) The fish is catching it. (J. laughs)

J: Goo.

F: (Reading for 4 seconds) How fast did that little boy run? (pause) What's this? (pointing)

J: Gook.

F: That's a rainbow. Do you like rainbows, Jon? (J gets up and gets puppet) Ut. Oh, who's that?

J: Buta.

F: What's his name?

J: Bwort.

F: (Using puppet) Where's the rainbow? Show Burt where the rainbow is. Where's the rainbow at? (J picks up page and turns) Nooo, it's right there.

J: (Pointing) Goo?

F: That's a little boy.

J: Goo?

F: (Reads) Where'd the rainbow go? Where did it go?

J: All go (using hands in gesture).

F: All gone.

J: Where's the rainbow? (J looks at book) There's the rainbow over here. (J shakes head) Where's the rainbow, over here? (J puts hands on ears, turns around, gets up) You don't like rainbows? (J gets another toy and looks at F) Come here. (J comes) What's that? (looking at book)

J: Tha.

F: (Using puppet) Jon, ehh, you want to read about the rainbow?

J: (Looks, kisses puppet on nose, laughs, touches head) Oooo

F: (With puppet) Shake hand, Jon. (J shakes hand) How do you do? (J looks at F) Shake my other hand. (J shakes hand) Not that hand, use the other hand. (F lifts puppet's hand) This one. (J shakes it) Hi Jon. My name's Burt. What's yours? (J puts finger in puppet's mouth, F makes puppet bite J's finger)

J: (Opens mouth of puppet) Goo, ge ahh et. Oo the.

F: (Using puppet) Do you want to read the book with me? (J laughs, bangs cash register) Do you want to read the book with me? (J laughs, hits puppet) I'd like you to read me the book.

J: (Laughs, hits puppet, laughs, looks at book, turns page) Goo. The goo?

F: (Using puppet) Oh, where is the rainbow? (J turning pages) Look. What's that, Jon?

J: Boo.

. . . . (later excerpt) . . . .

F: Look at this (whisper) (J, playing with toy, walks away) Come here. (puts puppet on hand) Come here, Jon, come here. (using puppet) Sit down, sit down. (J looks and laughs) Come here (points)

J: Ga! Ga!

F: OK. (J takes puppet and puts on) We're going to make Ernie, Burt—What's his name?

J: Bwur.

F: Burt? Is it Burt? (pause) Going to make him talk? (J uses puppet to play with water toy) Why don't you come over here and we'll read the story to Ernie.

J: (Laughs) A girl.

F: Do you want to read the story to Burt?

J: Girl. (looks at coffee, in mirror, laughs)

F: Come here. Come here. (J looking in mirror, laughs) Oh, you're getting ridiculous now. (J still looking in mirror, laughing) Come over here. (moves chair) Come to Daddy. (opens arms and J sits on F's lap, F kisses J and reads) Look. Look. (points) Would you like to sleep in a rainbow? (pause) See, this little boy. Little Jon is sleeping in the rainbow.

J: Nooo. (puts hand on eye, jumps up and down)

F: Turn the page (J turns page) One page at a time. How they're playing hide and go seek. Looking all around for the rainbow. Where's the rainbow hiding? (J turns pages) You're going the wrong way. Turn to the next page. (J turns page) Find out where the rainbow is hiding. (J points to picture) In the flower garden. All the flowers look like a rainbow.

J: A rainbow.

F: Rainbow. (kisses J)

After the story task, Mr. A and Jon participated in making a paper airplane, following steps displayed on a board. Mr. A attempts to get Jon involved, but Jon is restless and moves about. Mr. A makes an airplane not according to the model, but a simplified version. Failing to involve Jon in making a plane of his own, Mr. A encourages him to get involved in action with the plane. Eventually Jon becomes involved in throwing the plane.

When Mr. A interacts with his older non-LD son, he places higher levels of demands on him. He introduces the task to Greg as a complex one and asks him to try to make the paper bird. Mr. A attends to Greg's production and intervenes when Greg has trouble. While for Jon, Mr. A simplified the steps required for making an airplane, with Greg he assiduously follows the prepared model. Both Mr. A and Greg appear to have trouble making the bird and they check with each other whether each appears to the other to be doing the task correctly.

To summarize thus far, Mr. A uses many questions in his interaction with Jon and allows Jon to become involved in other activities tangential to the questions without confronting him. Mr. A modifies the inquiry approaches to engage Jon and encourages Jon to verbalize whenever possible. The pacing of demands is slow and consistent with Jon's limited ability to attend and to tolerate frustration. The contrast is marked with his older son, where Mr. A allows and encourages Greg to try to accomplish the task on his own and does not take the role of the expert who knows how to complete the task. When Greg errs he does intervene, ask-

ing him if he thinks a particular aspect is correct. Mr. A appears to place
appropriate demands to think and to represent on each child, given their
different levels of capability. Mr. A is warm and supportive with both
children. His inquiries with Jon focus on encouraging labelling, observing, and attending. His inquiries with Greg focus on encouraging him to
propose alternatives, evaluate consequences, and plan ahead.

Analysis of the Mother's Beliefs and Behaviors

Mrs. A differs from her husband in her preferred communication strategies and goals. She advocates rational authorative strategies for teaching
items and direct authoritative strategies for child management. Her rationales tend to focus on the child's motivation, frustration, and affective
state as well as on cognitive aspects of the child. There is less discrepancy
between Mrs. A's preferred and predicted strategies than was the case for
Mr. A as she tends to propose rational explanations or direct authoritative strategies as ways to behave in general and with Jon. Mrs. A, as her
husband, characterizes Jon as limited in understanding of many events
and manifesting little control of his emotional expressiveness. Since Jon
has difficulty communicating, he is somewhat perplexing to Mrs. A. At
times he does not seem to comprehend, while at other times he seems to
understand even communication directed toward his older siblings.

Mrs. A's responses to questions concerning beliefs about child development processes indicate that the source of developmental achievements resides in large part in parental guidance, verbal instruction, and
repetition as well as in the child's own observation and experimentation.
Jon is at a particular disadvantage with respect to developmental achievements when viewed from this perspective. She is not sure how he will
come to realize other's feelings unless he begins to communicate. Perhaps, one hopes, through repetitive verbal instruction he will acquire an
understanding of rules and time as is the case for other children. In contrast to Mr. A's beliefs, adults (particularly parents) are seen by Mrs. A as
exerting a greater influence over development than peers.

I = Interviewer   M = Mother

VIGNETTE #1: Billy was playing with his Lincoln Logs. A couple of
logs wouldn't fit together and Billy started throwing them about the
room.

I: What do you think is the best way for a parent to handle a situation
    like this one?
M: I guess, "Since you're having trouble with the blocks, why don't
    you put them away and play with another toy." (*diversion as a pre-
    ferred strategy*)

I: Why do you think that's the best way for a parent to handle the situation?

M: Well, in the question it said the logs wouldn't fit and he was getting a, you know, little annoyed cause they wouldn't fit. So you don't think he was really doing it, you know, viciously. It's just that his temper got to him and he just couldn't take it any more and just threw the blocks and I just think that this would be the best thing to do. *(affective goal)*

I: Let's say this is a real situation involving you and Jon. How do you think you'd probably respond with him?

M: With Jon? I would say, "Jon, don't throw the blocks. I'll help you with it if you want. We'll sit down and see why they don't fit." That's what I would do with Jon. *(rational authoritative and demonstration strategies)*

I: OK. And why would you handle it that way with him?

M: Because he, his ability to do this isn't that of what another 4-year-old would do so he has a lot of trouble, you know, fitting things together and understanding how it happens, so you have to explain it to him and sit down and help him with it. *(constraints due to disability; cognitive goal)*

I: Let's say this didn't work and Jon was still throwing the Lincoln Logs around the room. What do you think you'd try next?

M: Oh, let's see. I think with Jon I would say, "OK, Jon, let's just put the blocks away and we'll play with something else right now." *(diversion)*

I: And why would you handle it that way at this point in the situation?

M: This is hard. (laugh) Um, basically I think because he wouldn't stop, he would just continue on wanting to do this even if he wasn't able to do it. He would still throw the blocks and, you know, not understand the whole thing so I would just point-blank say, "Let's put the blocks away and do something else." *(affective; behavior management goals; constraints)*

★I: The next few questions are about 4-year-olds in general.

★M: OK.

★I: In answering them, think about all 4-year-olds and not just your child. Do 4-year-old children realize the consequences their own actions may have? For example, do 4-year-olds know that something could get broken if they throw things around?

★M: Yes they do. *(capable at this age)*

★I: How does a child come to realize the consequences of his or her own behavior?

★M: Well, I think it's probably from earlier, like at 1, 2, and 3, "Don't touch this, you get hurt." You know, this type of thing, "You're

gonna fall if you climb." And I think by 4 they probably know what's right and what's wrong and what's going to happen to them. Of course, there are, you know, some things they're gonna try anyway, but I think a regular normal 4-year-old would know the dangers after all this time of you saying, "No no, don't touch." (direct instruction from adults; repetition)

VIGNETTE #3: One day Jimmy's friend was invited over to play. Jimmy had taken out only his Lego building set to play with in the living room. He wasn't sharing any of the pieces in the set with his friend.

I: What do you think is the best way for a parent to handle a situation like this one?

M: You have to share your toy with your friend when he comes to play. (direct authoritative)

I: Why is that the best response?

M: Well, because the other child, you've invited him over to play with you and he doesn't have any of his own toys and the child shouldn't be selfish and they should learn to share the toys. Why is it the best one? Well, every child has to learn to share, um, and that's the way you would do it I suppose. (behavior management goal)

I: Let's say this was a real situation and it was Jon who wasn't sharing his building set with a friend he had invited over. How do you think you'd handle it?

M: With Jon. OK, with Jon. Well, with Jon, let's see. I don't think he's at the point of sharing yet, even though he's 4. But I think with him, if he was playing and someone wanted to share, I think his idea would be that they were taking it away, I don't know why but that's what he does. He thinks that that's taking away. So I'd have to sit with him and say, you know, "You have some and he has some" and that's how I'd have to handle it with Jon. (rational authoritative; child constraints)

I: Why would you handle it that way with Jon?

M: Because he hasn't come to the point, the idea and understanding of sharing yet. Although we're working on that. I want him to realize that the person is not taking the things away or if the other child is playing with it that doesn't mean he can't play with it also. (affective and cognitive goals)

I: Let's say that this didn't work and he still wasn't willing to share. What do you think you might try next?

M: I guess I would tell him that if he doesn't share his toys then that friend can't come and play with him any more because that friend doesn't like it when you're not sharing. (threat)

I: Why would you handle it that way at this point?

M: Because he likes to play with other children. He's at that right now. He enjoys other children. He's just getting into playing with things whereas he didn't do anything before. If there was another child there he just ignored him and just did as he pleased so I think maybe it might stick in his head that if I don't share this, my Mom is going to send him home and then I won't have anyone to play with. It might not work again but that's what I'd try next. (*affective and cognitive*)

★I: Does a 4-year-old understand that someone may be feeling something differently than he or she does?

★M: Oh I think so. (*capable at this age*)

★I: And how do children come to that point, come to realize that other people may feel something differently than they do?

★M: Maybe by looking at their expressions on their face, or the way they talk. Like you're saying feeling sad or happy things like this, in this respect. Well, I think that any 4-year-old, usually, a normal 4-year-old can look at, say their parents and tell when they're happy and when they're not happy just by the expression on their face or the tone that they use when they're speaking to them. (*observation*)

. . . . (later excerpt) . . . .

★I: Does Jon realize someone else may be feeling differently than he does?

★M: No, it's Jon's way or no way (laugh). If I live through this, I am going to live through anything. I am convinced. I am really convinced.

★I: How do you think he'll eventually come to realize that other people may feel something differently than he does?

★M: I don't know. Hopefully, the understanding, you know, just watching, learning, and listening. But he doesn't listen and he doesn't watch. But hopefully this will come. Unless he starts to talk to one of us, to anyone, that may be a possibility, we haven't given up. Then he could communicate and you could communicate back and it would all make sense. Hopefully. (*observation, verbal communication/instruction*)

VIGNETTE 9: One day Father was watching Sandy build with blocks. Sandy was trying to make a tall building by stacking the blocks one on top of the other, but the building kept falling down.

I: What do you think is the best response for a parent to make?

M: Explaining it, you know, if you stack the blocks too high, the building's going to get shakey and fall down. (*rational authoritative*)

I: And why is that the best response?

M: Well, it's a simple explanation. That's one reason that this is going to happen and the child might understand it better. (*cognitive goal*)

I: Let's say it was Jon. What do you think you'd try with him?

M: Now that's a good question 'cause he doesn't take, you know, that type of thing. He'll sit there and keep on trying and they'll keep on falling. Well, with Jon I might sit down and I might put a few on the top and say to him, "When it gets too high, it's gonna fall down." As simple as possible. (*rational authoritative and demonstration*)

I: Why would you handle it that way?

M: Basically, the understanding. Because he can't communicate to me. He can't say to me, "Well, how come Mommy? How come it's falling down?" I'd say to him, I'd try to explain in the simplest possible way so hopefully that'll work. (*constraints; cognitive goal*)

I: And let's say it doesn't work . . .

M: And if it doesn't work maybe I would just let him experiment. Let him sit there and keep on putting them on top and as they just keep falling maybe it will get to him that that's why it keeps falling down. This is the reason, you know, this is really the reason, why, you know, too many on the top, they're falling down. (*nonintervention*)

I: Why would you handle it that way at this point?

M: With Jon? Basically, the understanding. He hasn't really gotten to the 4-year-old understanding yet, and the point with no talking, noncommunication, he'd have to, maybe he's just learning for himself that this is what's happening. (*constraints, cognitive goal*)

★I: What role do you think frustration plays in learning?

★M: Frustration. I think it plays a big part. The child is so frustrated he just, you know, nothing seems to work. He just is a total loss. The whole thing, I'm giving up. I don't care.

. . . . (later excerpt) . . . .

★I: Is it all right to allow a child to be independent instead of following a rule that he or she usually follows?

★M: I think, to a point, yes. I think it's good for them to show their independence as long as they can't get hurt doing it or you can't foresee them getting hurt doing it.

★I: Why is it OK to sometimes allow a child to be independent rather than follow a rule?

★M: They have to learn on their own sometimes, what's good for them and what's not good for them and the only way they can do that is by experimenting and trying it themself. As long as you know that nothing really drastic is going to happen to them. I think it's a really good thing to let them explore and learn what life is all about, you know, they can't constantly have your supervision all the time. (*experimentation, manipulation of environment*)

*I: Does a 4-year-old know when to be independent and when to follow a rule?

*M: Some children do. I would say yes. Greg, for one, at 4 years old was very independent, my oldest son was not.

*I: How does a child know when to follow a rule and when it's OK to be independent?

*M: Only by being put in a situation where they have to decide, you know, for themself what's the thing to do. (*exposure*)

. . . . (later excerpt) . . . .

*I: Does Jon know when to be independent and when to follow a rule?

*M: Sometimes. I tell you, it's like this kid is not the same kid. There are times when you are not even talking to him, and you're talking to maybe Greg or Jeff, and he will do what you're asking them to do. I mean if you say, "Greg, will you please pick that up, honey, and put it in the garbage," Jon goes, picks it up and puts in the garbage. I mean I think that's an independent act, you know, on his part, the way he is.

*I: But sometimes instead of following a rule, one or the other, would he sometimes be independent rather than following the rule at a particular time?

*M: No, he would be more apt to do as he pleases than doing what he's supposed to be doing at a certain time. I would say yes and no on that. I would have to. There would be no other reason, no other way to answer it. I can't say he's completely closed out to everything because he isn't, he does understand quite a bit and he does listen and he does do things you tell him to do. But not always.

*I: How do you think he'll eventually come to know when to follow a rule and when to be independent?

*M: Probably just repetition. You know, repetition, over and over again. Saying the same thing over and over, no, yes, no, and hopefully this will work. (*direct instruction, repetition*).

. . . . (later excerpt) . . . .

*I: We have some more "4-year-old in general" questions. Does a 4-year-old understand time?

*M: I don't know. I would say maybe during the day, they would understand like, it's time to go to school, it's time to come home, time to eat. But I don't know about a day, a week, a month. I don't think that they would be, how can I explain this. I just don't think they would understand that amount of time. I think their daily routine would be time that they would understand, but not anything in the future. (*not capable*)

*I: How does a 4-year-old eventually come to understand about time?

★*M*: I guess repetition, things you do and the things you tell them. From learning from parents, just explaining, in two more days, in three more days, this type of thing. (*direct instruction and repetition*)

. . . . (later excerpt) . . . .

★*I*   Up to now, we've been talking about 4-year-olds in general. And there are a lot of differences between different children, so now we want to know about your child Jon in particular. Does Jon understand time?

★*M*: Jon doesn't understand time at this point. (*not capable*)

★*I*:   How do you think he'll eventually come to understand about time?

★*M*: By showing him, telling him, maybe putting something in front of him and saying, "When this is over" or "When this is done." Very simple and keep saying it over and over. (*direct instruction and repetition*)

Mrs. A's focus is on protecting Jon from harm, attending to his affective state, and coping with frustration levels that result from his lack of understanding. Consequently, it was expected that she would engage in more task structuring behaviors and didactic teaching strategies. Although she thinks that children learn through verbal instruction and repetitions she does not have confidence that such a characterization fits Jon. This does not provide her with alternative strategies, and she is likely to focus on providing support for Jon. She is not inclined to focus on challenging his intellectual capabilities with inquiry approaches.

As the transcript below indicates, Mrs. A tends to be warm and physical, accompanying her holding and hugging with verbal direction. Her approach, however, does not help Jon attend to the story. She responds to nearly every effort Jon makes toward moving away from the story task by constantly trying to hold his attention. In spite of these difficulties, Mrs. A retains her calm and warmth. Jon, however, is engaged very briefly in the story, about 3 seconds at a time. Jon does utter some distinctive words, but his few verbalizations tend to be distractive rather than interactive—"No", "no", and "mama".

M = Mother   *J* = Jon

M: OK. Come here. (J walks to table) I've got this neat book. Look. (J looks) Look at these little boys in here. (J walks out door) Come here. Wait, you can't go out. (M gets up and gets J) Come on. (J laughs) Ah, ha? (M has J in arms) OK, come on. Let's close this up. (closes and locks door, still holding J)

J: Ohhh. (laughing)

M: Ohhh. Oh, ho, ho. (still holding J)

J: Ohhh. (laughing)

M: Now. You don't know what I've got here (tries to put J in chair) Come on. All right. Put your feet down. (J laughing, sits down on M's lap with M's assistance) Look at this. Can we see this? Look. (J looks) Let's turn the pages. (J grabs book) Wait a minute. (M tries to take book) Wait, wait, wait, wait. (M gets book) OK. Look. (M puts J in chair next to hers, reads for 2 seconds) Where's that rock, Jon? (J moves out of seat, M hold him) Wait, wait, wait. Come on. Lookit. Look it this little boy. He's looking for that rock. (M points to picture)

J: Naw.

M: Look where that is. (M points) Let's turn the page. (M turns page and reads from book, "Is this one your mommy?")

J: Nooo.

M: (Reads "Is this one your daddy?")

J: Nooo.

M: (Reads, "Ah, there are lots of things I can do with a nice rock like you")

J: Me? (points to book)

M: Yeah.

J: Ah me. (gets up in chair)

. . . . (later excerpt) . . . .

(J sees self in mirror)

M: Listen, Jon. Jon. Listen. (J is laughing at his reflection) Sh. Come on. (M holds J and holds his hand away from his head) Settle down. (J laughs louder and puts hands to cheek; M reads 1 second while J laughing and trying to see self in mirror) Wait a minute, ut oh. (J squirms in M's lap, still laughing) Jon. Are you looking at yourself? Is that what's the matter? You see your funny face? (J is laughing) OK, let's finish this book. (M reads 5 seconds, J is laughing) Look. (Reads, "You can put it in your pocket" and puts J's hand in pocket) OK. Shh. Listen. Listen. (Reads "Would you feel important sitting on his desk?")

J: Nooo.

M: Nooo? OK. Look at this one (M turns page and reads; J stands up) Ut, oh, wait a minute. Listen, Listen to me. Jon, sit down and be a good boy.

J: Ooo, oh.

M: OK?

J: Good.

M: All right. But you're not being good, you're being silly. (J points to mirror) I know. You see yourself. Mommy and Jon.

J: Mom-mie. (points to self, then M)

M: Mommy and Jon. OK?

J: Heeee.

M: All right. (holds J's hands) Let's finish this book up. (reads)

J: (Sees self in mirror again) Mama, mama.

M: What. (chuckles and hugs and kisses J) All right. Let's look. (looks at book) A boat, Jon. Look. (M points to book) He's playing with a boat. See? (J looks) See and with the water. (J stand up, looks in mirror, laughing) OK. (M pulls J down, reads one second, J takes book) OK. Listen to me. (restraining J) Listen to me. Listen. We're almost done with this (J sits but looks away).

J: Oooo.

M: OK. We're almost done with the book. (reads 3 seconds) Oh.

J: Oooh. (looks at M)

M: OK. Turn the page for me. (M turns page; J covers eyes with hands; mother reads 5 seconds)

J: I kime it.

M: You want to climb that? No. (no time for J to respond; M continues reading, holding J with one hand and turning pages).

J: Ar. (repeats last sound mother read)

M: Are. OK. Let's . . . (J starts to put hands on book; M holds J's hands) Oh, look Jon. (M reads 4 seconds) Want to wave goodbye to the rock? (M waves J's hand, releases it, J turns page) All done.

J: All ga.

M: All done. (J closes book) OK? Did you like the story?

J: No.

The paper-folding task with Jon was a disaster. Jon refused to attend at all, continually moving about the room, climbing on the table, and so forth. The mother finally took Jon on her lap, held his hands and made a boat while Jon tried to pull his hands away, and deliberately looked away from the product.

Mrs. A's behaviors with Greg, the older sibling, expressed her belief in children's need for guidance and adult instruction. She began constructing the whale herself at the outset. As soon as Greg began his model, she intruded and fixed a fold. However, when Greg disagreed with her, she accepted this without apparent difficulty and watched with interest as Greg quickly completed the task. Mrs. A's behavior with each of her children reveals warmth and support with minimal task orientation and intellectual stimulation.

Summary: Mr. and Mrs. A agree about Jon's level of ability and behaviors. Jon's performance level on a battery of tasks, as well as his behavior during the two interactions with each of his parents, suggests that their perspective of Jon's ability level is accurate. The WPSSI was adminis-tered to Jon, and he was given four tasks, each of which focused on a different type of representational thinking and required no verbalization on Jon's part. Jon's WPSSI score was 60. He scored slightly higher on the performance subtests than on verbal subtests. The representational thinking tasks involved memory, seriation, a reaction time mental rota-tion task, and a Piagetian anticipatory imagery task. Jon's performance on the memory and seriation tasks was below the level expected by chance and he failed to pass a criterion test for the mental rotation task. However, Jon's performance on the Piagetian anticipatory level con-sisted of transposition errors, which is characteristic of many preschool-age children. During the testing situations, Jon was often restless and dis-tractable. Thus, his behavior in the testing situations was similar to that expressed in interactions with his parents.

The parents agree on their descriptions of Jon's *level* of development. Their beliefs about child development *processes* and their behaviors with Jon, however, were very different. The father's construct system appears broad enough to account for achievements of both his LD and non-LD children. Mr. A stimulates each child intellectually by asking questions. The content of the questions varies for each of his children and serves to encourage representational thinking appropriate for each child's level of development. For example, Mr. A asks Jon to label objects in the room and pictures of objects in the story, whereas he asks Greg, Jon's non-LD sibling, to anticipate possible outcomes and propose alternative ways to build a bird. Mr. A allows both children to explore and experiment, which is consistent with references to such processes during the inter-view. His use of humor and participation in the tasks at the child's level of interest rather than taking an expert or authority stance are consistent with his view that friends "may teach them more than parents do" through mutual exchange of ideas, helping each other, and forcing each other to understand.

Mrs. A's emphasis on adult guidance, verbal instruction, and repeti-tion as processes of development cause her to be somewhat perplexed about Jon's cognitive development. While Mr. A approaches Jon from the point of view of what he is capable of understanding, albeit a lower level than most 4-year-olds, Mrs. A characterizes Jon more often in terms of what he cannot understand. Her beliefs do not provide her with many alternative strategies to encourage Jon's intellectual development. As a result, she tends to focus on his affective state and on protecting him from frustration and physical harm. Her repertoire of behaviors for in-teracting with Jon is largely limited to child-management and task-struc-turing behaviors since Jon does not respond very well to her didactic methods and her verbal repetition. Mrs. A's behavior with Greg also indicates a limited range of teaching strategies, although the restriction is less severe because Greg responds to verbal communications. She intrudes into Greg's paper folding and after he reprimands her, she becomes relatively passive, limiting her involvement to watching him with interest.

Jon's behavior during the interactions with each of his parents provides some support for our hypotheses regarding the utility of distancing strategies with a child who has a language disability. First, Mr. A's use of an inquiry approach directed at Jon's level of cognitive ability did result in increased verbalizations and increased attempts at verbalization on Jon's part. It is interesting to note, in fact, that many of Jon's verbalizations toward his mother were responses to questions she read from the story rather than to questions posed by his mother. Second, the father's use of distancing communication strategies also served to engage and maintain Jon's interest. This was facilitated by the father's strategy of allowing the child to become involved in other activities and then redirecting Jon's attention through an interaction related to the target activity. The father accomplished his cognitive goals independently of the specific activity set up by the experimental situation. Although Jon became involved in other activities, Mr. A chose to use these as vehicles for distancing with Jon. Mrs. A, on the other hand, remained tied to the specific task and engaged Jon (or failed to do so) through repeated suggestions and commands.

Integration and Implications

Our conceptual framework and the place of this study in the larger schema of investigations of family interrelationships have been described. Taking the argument that an atypical child can create disequilibrium in the family system, we have focused on how parents adapt to such an unanticipated event and how childrearing patterns are affected. By providing a single case as an exemplar of our research, we have illustrated some of our methods, the kind of data gathered, and our interpretation of possible effects of the LD child on the parents' constructions of the child and teaching strategies. We provided a glimpse of our research aimed at understanding the complexities of family interaction.

Analysis of the case study in terms of effects on parental beliefs and practices provides the opportunity to compare the case results with previous empirical findings of our study (Sigel et al., 1980). In addition, the case study provides insights into how parents adapt to an LD child and suggests issues that are relevant for intervention programs, particularly the question of helping parents consider the range of options they have in dealing with their LD child.

The results of the case study are generally consistent with findings of our previous large-scale research. A causal analysis of the path model presented in Figure 1 yielded a strong causal connection between parental level of education and parental beliefs (1) that children learn through experimentation, their own internal congitive processes, self-regulation feedback from the environment and (2) that children develop in stages (variables comprising a principal component used in the path analysis). Mr. A, a college graduate, expressed such beliefs more often than his wife, a high school graduate, and it is possible that educational level is affecting beliefs about child development more than experience with the child or that an interactive effect between education and parenting experience exists. Findings from the previous study also indicated that parents' references to child-development processes in general and childrearing goals associated with strategies posited during the interview were better predictors of observed parental behaviors than the parents' predicted communication strategies. This was certainly the case for Mr. A, who stated at one point during the interview that he could not ask Jon a question because Jon is nonverbal. Yet Mr. A does ask Jon questions, he also allows Jon to explore and experiment, and he attempts to stimulate Jon cognitively. This behavior is consistent with his expressed beliefs and cognitive goals underlying his rationales for communication strategies.

There were, however, several inconsistencies between the case analysis and findings from the previous study. Mother's and father's beliefs were correlated across the large sample ($r = .44$) and Mr. and Mrs. A do not evidence very much similarity in their references to child-development constructs. This inconsistency with prior findings might be due to differential adaptation of the mother and father to the LD child, or it may be due to selecting a single case out of a sample in which parents' beliefs will be found to correlate. In addition, fathers' beliefs in the previous study were found to be better predictors of their behaviors than mothers' beliefs were of their behaviors. In the present case, the mothers' behaviors did appear to be consistent with their focus on parental guidance and protection and the child's affective state.

The case example does tend to confirm our hypotheses that parents are affected by the LD child as well as our hypothesis concerning the usefulness of distancing strategies with a child who has a language handicap. The interview data for both parents revealed that they do feel that possible strategies for interacting with Jon are limited by his language problem. The mother appears somewhat more constrained than the father in coping with the problem because of her belief system. Rational authoritative and direct authoritative statements directed toward the child are the teaching strategies consistent with a view that children acquire knowledge through direct instruction from adults. Mrs. A refers to such strategies for each of 12 interview vignettes. Mr. A, on the other hand, refers to distancing strategies, demonstration and participation, and non-intervention in addition to authoritative and authoritarian strategies. He tends to vary his preferences and predictions with the content of the item (cognitive, social, or behavior management). Mr. A's belief about child-development processes (references to feedback, curiosity, observation, peer influence, generalization, cognitive processes, self-regulation, differentiation) may be broad enough to encompass alternative strategies to enhance cognitive development. It is possible that if Mrs. A could become aware of alternative options, including distancing strategies, her interactions with Jon would consist, not of as much behavior management, but of more interactions that challenge Jon to verbalize and interact in a reciprocal exchange. We have proposed, however, (McGillicuddy-DeLisi, 1980), that parent education that focuses on teaching alternative behaviors may produce only short-term changes. That is, if beliefs are indeed a source of parental behavior, parents must first become aware of their system of beliefs and be aware that alternative interpretations of the process of development are possible. Focus on parental reconceptualization of how children learn will reduce the possibility that parents reject or resist the introduction of new behaviors or modify information concerning alternative strategies in such a manner that no change is really produced. The child will then be viewed from a perspective that includes the development of all children through many years of growth, thus providing the parent with a basis for generating alternative strategies even after their own child has passed through one stage or phase and the previously learned strategies are no longer appropriate or applicable.

Essentially, then, we contend that changes in belief systems provide the cognitive readiness on the part of the parents to assimilate new ideas and strategies which should produce more options for the parents in interacting with their LD child.

References

Abrams, J. C. Parental dynamics: Their role in learning disabilities. *Reading Teacher*, 1970, *23,* 751–755;760.

Abrams, J. C., and Kaslow, F. W. Learning disability and family dynamics: A mutual interaction. *Journal of Clinical Child Psychology*, Spring, 1976, 35–40.

Adams, B. N. Birth order: A critical review. *Sociometry*, 1972, *35,* 411–439.

Altus, W. D. Birth order and its sequelae. *Science*, 1966, *151*, 44–49.

Anastasi, A. Intelligence and family size. *Psychological Bulletin*, 1956, *53*, 187–209.

Anastasi, A. Differentiating the effects of intelligence and social status. *Eugenics Quarterly*, 1959, *6*, 84–91.

Bayley, N., and Schaefer, E. S. Correlations of maternal and child behaviors with the development of mental abilities: Data from the Berkeley Growth Study. *Monographs of the Society for Research in Child Development*, 1964, *29* (6, Serial No. 97).

Belmont, L., and Marolla, F. A. Birth order, family size and intelligence. *Science*, 1973, *182*, 1096–1101.

Brophy, J. E. Mothers as teachers of their own preschool children: The influence of socioeconomic status and task structure on teaching specificity. *Child Development*, 1970, *41*, 79–94.

Campbell, D. M. Interaction patterns in families with learning problem children (Doctoral dissertation, Boston University, 1972). *Dissertation Abstracts International*, 1972, *33*, 1783B. (University Microfilms No. 72–25, 252).

Chittenden, E., Foan, W. Zweil, D., and Smith, J. School achievement of first- and second-born siblings. *Child Development*, 1968, *39*, 1223–1228.

Cicirelli, V. G. Mother-child and sibling-sibling interactions on a problem-solving task. *Child Development*, 1976, *47*, 588–596.

Dandes, H. M., and Dow, D. Relation of intelligence to family size and density. *Child Development*, 1969, *40*, 629–640.

Doleys, D. M., Cartelli, L. M., and Doster, J. Comparison of patterns of mother-child interaction. *Journal of Learning Disabilities*, 1976, *9*, 371–375.

Edgerly, R. F. The effectiveness of parent counseling in the treatment of children with learning disabilities (Doctoral dissertation, Boston University) *Dissertation Abstracts International*, 1975, *36*, 1301A. (University Microfilms No. 75–20, 920).

Eysenck, H. J., and Cookson, D. Personality in primary school children: 3—Family background. *British Journal of Educational Psychology*, 1970, *40*, 117–131.

Farber, B. Family organization and crisis: Maintenance of integration in families with a severely mentally retarded child. *Monographs of the Society for Research in Child Development*, 1960, *25* (1, Serial No. 75).

Farber, B., and Jenne, W.C. Family organization and parent-child communication: Parents and siblings of a retarded child. *Monographs of the Society for Research in Child Development*, 1963, *28* (7, Serial No. 91).

Flaugher, J., and Sigel, I.E. *The parent-child interaction observation coding system.* Princeton, N.J.: Educational Testing Service, 1980 (revision of 1977 coding manual).

Freeberg, N.E., and Payne, D.T. Parental influence on cognitive development in early childhood: A review. *Child Development*, 1967, *38*, 65–87.

Freeman, M.A. A comparative analysis of patterns of attitudes among mothers of children with learning disabilities and mothers of children who are achieving normally (Doctoral dissertation, Northwestern University, 1970). *Dissertation Abstracts International*, 1971, *31*, 5125A. (University Microfilms No. 71–10, 115)

Grilli, R. W. The effects of counselor-learning disabilities specialist co-led parent discussion groups on parental attitudes toward their children's development and on selected personality variables of parents and their children. *Dissertation Abstracts International*, 1974, *35*, 1978A. (University Microfilms No. 74-20, 432)

Hare, E. H., and Price, J. S. Birth order and family size: Bias caused by changes in birth rate. *British Journal of Psychiatry*, 1969, *115*, 647–657.

Hess, R. D., and Shipman, V. C. Early experience and the socialization of cognitive modes in children. *Child Development*, 1965, *36*, 869–886.

Hilton, I. Differences in the behavior of mothers toward first- and later-born children. *Journal of Personality and Social Psychology*, 1967, *7*, 282–290.

Hurley, J. R. Maternal attitude and children's intelligence. *Journal of Clinical Psychology*, 1959, *15*, 291–292.

Jones, P. Home environment and the development of verbal ability. *Child Development*, 1972, *43*, 1081–1087.

Kelly, G. A. *The psychology of personal constructs*. New York: Norton, 1955.

Kelly, G. A. *A theory of personality*. New York: Norton, 1963.

Kennett, K. F., and Cropley, A. J. Intelligence, family size and socio-economic status. *Journal of Biosocial Science*, 1970, *2*, 227–236.

Koch, H. L. The relation of primary mental abilities in five- and six-year-olds to sex of child and characteristics of his sibling. *Child Development*, 1954, *25*, 209–223.

Lentz, R. Relation of IQ to size of family. *Journal of Educational Psychology*, 1927, *18*, 486–496.

Marjoribanks, K. *Families and their learning environments*. London: Routledge and Kegan Paul, 1979.

Marjoribanks, K., and Walberg, H. J., Ordinal position, family environment and mental abilities. *Journal of Social Psychology*, 1975, *95*, 77–84.

Marjoribanks, K., Walberg, H. J., and Bargen, M. Mental abilities: Sibling constellation and social class correlates. *British Journal of Social and Clinical Psychology*, 1975, *14*, 109–116.

McGillicuddy-DeLisi, A. V. The role of parental beliefs in the family as a system of mutual influences. *Family Relations*, 1980, *29*, 41–47.

McGillicuddy-DeLisi, A. V. The relationship between family configuration and parental beliefs and practices. In L. Laosa and I. E. Sigel (Eds.), *The family as a learning environment*. New York: Plenum, in press.

McWhirter, J. Influencing the child: A program for parents. *Elementary School Guidance and Counseling*, 1972, *7*, 26–31.

Moss, H. A., and Kagan, J. Maternal influences on early IQ scores. *Psychological Reports*, 1958, *4*, 655–661.

Nisbet, J. Family environment and intelligence. *Eugenics Review*, 1953, *45*, 31–40.

Norman, R. D. The interpersonal values of parents of achieving and non-achieving gifted children. *Journal of Psychology*, 1966, *64*, 49–57.

Price, J. S., and Hare, E. H. Birth order studies: Some sources of bias. *British Journal of Psychiatry*, 1969, *115*, 633–646.

Radin, N. Observed maternal behavior with four-year-old boys and girls in lower-class families. *Child Development*, 1974, *45* 1126–1131.

Rolcik, J. W. Scholastic achievement of teenagers and parental attitudes toward and interest in schoolwork. *Family Life Coordinator*, 1965, *14*, 158–160.

Schachter, S. Birth order, eminence and higher education. *American Sociological Review*, 1963, *28*, 757–768.

Schooler, C. Birth order effects: Not here, not now. *Psychological Bulletin,* 1972, *78,* 161–175. (a)

Schooler, C. Childhood family structure and adult characteristics. *Sociometry,* 1972, *35,* 255–269. (b)

Schoonover, S. M. The relationship of intelligence and achievement to birth order, sex of sibling, and age interval. *Journal of Educational Psychology,* 1959, *50,* 143–146.

Shearer, M. S., and Shearer, D. E. The Portage Project: A model for early childhood education. *Exceptional Children,* 1972, *39,* 210–217.

Sigel, I. E. The distancing hypothesis: A causal hypothesis for the acquisition of representational thought. In M. R. Jones (Ed.), *Miami Symposium on the Prediction of Behavior: Effect of early experiences.* Coral Gables, FL: University of Miami Press, 1970.

Sigel, I. E. Language of the disadvantaged: The distancing hypothesis. In C. S. Lavatelli (Ed.), *Language training in early childhood education.* Urbana, IL: University of Illinois Press, 1971.

Sigel, I. E. The distancing hypothesis revisited: An elaboration of a neo-Piagetian view of the development of representational thought. In M. E. Meyer (Ed.), *Cognitive learning.* Bellingham, WA: Western Washington State College Press, 1972.

Sigel, I. E. The relationship between parents' distancing strategies and children's representational thinking. In L. Laosa and I. E. Sigel (Eds.), *The family as a learning environment.* New York: Plenum, in press.

Sigel, I.E., and Cocking, R.R. *Cognitive development from childhood to adolescence: A constructivist perspective.* New York: Holt, Rinehart and Winston, 1977.

Sigel, I.E., McGillicuddy-DeLisi, A.V., and Johnson, J. *The effects of spacing and birth order on problem solving competence of preschool children.* Final report to NIH under grant number Ro1 H1686, Washington, D.C., January 1980.

Starr, R.H., Jr. Cognitive development in infancy: Assessment, acceleration, and actualization. *Merrill-Palmer Quarterly,* 1971, *17,* 153–185.

Thurstone, L.L., and Jenkins, R.L. Birth order and intelligence. *Journal of Educational Psychology,* 1929, *20,* 640–651.

Watson, R.I. *The clinical method in psychology.* New York: Wiley, 1963.

Wetter, J. Parent attitudes toward learning disability. *Exceptional Children,* 1972, *38,* 490–491.

Willis, C.B. The effects of primogeniture on intellectual capacity. *Journal of Abnormal and Social Psychology,* 1924, *18,* 375–377.

Wilson, L.R. Learning disability as related to infrequent punishment and limited participation or delay of reinforcement tasks. *Journal of School Psychology,* 1975, *13,* 255–264.

Worchel, T., and Worchel, P. The parental concept of the mentally retarded child. *American Journal of Mental Deficiency,* 1961, *65,* 782–788.

Wray, J.D. Population pressure on families: Family size and child spacing. In R. Revelle (Ed.), *Rapid population growth: Consequences and policy implications* (Vol. 2). Baltimore, MD: Johns Hopkins University Press, 1971.

Zajonc, R.B., and Markus, G.B. Birth order and intellectual development. *Psychological Review,* 1975, *82,* 74–88.

PART III

Programs for Prevention and Promotion

Introductory Notes

In this section we are provided with some examples of how theories of development have been translated into specific programs intended to obviate developmental problems and to facilitate optimal development. The studies described by no means exhaust the range of efforts in this area and the findings of a number of well known and important programs, such as Head Start[1] and the work of the Consortium on Longitudinal Studies[2] are not covered here.

The authors who describe their programs in this section share, implicitly or explicitly, a large portion of the conceptual approach described in the first part of the book and it is, consequently, particularly interesting to see how diverse are the specific programs that can result from these shared assumptions. The diversity seems partly to be due to the investigators giving different weight to different aspects of the multidimensional developmental model, partly due to the need to fit the concepts to specific conditions, and partly due to the inventiveness of the program designers—facilitating infant and early childhood development still relies a great deal on art and intuition as well as on conceptual models.

The first three papers provide more insight into how concepts become translated into programs than answers to the question, "Does it work?", because most of these programs are at an early stage. Klaus Minde, Nancy Shosenberg, and Peter Marton, like all the authors, clearly recognize the interactional or transactional nature of the mother–infant (or parent–infant) relationship and provide an example of a program that economizes on effort by directing its attention to a high-risk group, low birthweight infants. Furthermore, the program makes use of specially

1. See, for example, Zigler, E., and Valentine, J. *Project Head Start: A legacy of the war on poverty.* New York: Free Press, 1979.
2. See, for example, Lazar, I., and Darlington, R.B. (Eds.). *Lasting effects of preschool.* Final report, HEW Grant 90C-1311 to the Education Commission of the States, 1978.

trained peers as teachers on the grounds that those who have themselves experienced the problem are more readily accepted as teachers than are health professionals. The program incorporates features of both support groups and educational approaches. Mothers who participate in these groups once a week for 2 to 3 months after the birth of their premature infants showed, a year later, a higher degree of personal autonomy and more changes in their attitudes toward work and in relationships with others; they displayed more social interaction with their children and a greater ability to demonstrate affection, which Minde and his co-workers interpret as a reflection of their improved self-concept.

Sharing concerns about their feelings and difficulties in coping with a premature infant, obtaining information about the needs of their infants, and receiving assistance in solving practical problems and using community resources was, it seems, good for mothers. The improved self-esteem and sense of autonomy appear to have been responsible for changes in mother–infant interaction that are likely to have been good for the babies, although direct evidence of developmental benefits is not presented in this report.

The next paper, by Virginia Rauh, Barry Nurcombe, Paul Ruoff, Al Jette, and David Howell, also focuses on low birthweight infants and their parents. Following a review of the literature on developmental characteristics of low birthweight infants from a number of perspectives, the authors present the rationale, aims, and methods of their intervention program and speculate on likely outcomes. Why is the low birthweight infant at developmental risk? Rauh and her co-authors discuss the literature on six possible sources of risk to low birthweight babies: family bonding, stimulus deprivation, deficits in the infant's capacity to elicit care, the problems of parents adjusting emotionally to the birth of their premature infant, medical complications, and the association of low birthweight with adverse socioeconomic conditions. As in Minde's work, we see the futility of any effort that involves isolating the infant or the caregivers as the target of the intervention: We have to deal with a complex and dynamic relationship between infant and caregivers.

The Vermont Project, as a result, places considerable emphasis on enhancing mother–infant interactions using a pediatric nurse to train individual mothers prior to, and for the months after, the premature baby's discharge from the hospital. This aspect of the program is more formal and systematic than it is in Minde, Shosenberg, and Marton's work, but, in its use of a health professional and in working with mothers individually, does not provide the support-group component of Minde's program. Thus the results will be doubly interesting, not only will they provide information on the developmental effects of a carefully and systematically formulated intervention effort but they may, by being compared with those of Minde and his co-workers, provide insights into the contribution of a support group to the mother's self-concept and the baby's development.

The program described by Jay Belsky and Joanne Benn, although it shares much of the conceptual approach of the previous two programs, differs from them in at least one important respect; the authors' concern is not with any kind of special or high-risk group, such as premature infants, but with infants in general. In addition to emphasizing the importance of recognizing the dynamic aspect of infant–caregiver interactions, the authors add two further points: "The newborn period is a special time for *all* families", and the family is a social unit made up of "several individuals and relationships in addition to the mother–infant dyad." Although neither of these additional points is unfamiliar to the authors of the two previous papers, Belsky and Benn explicitly integrate these notions into the intervention program.

Belsky and Benn work on the assumption that early infant–mother contact is effective only "to the extent that it reveals the complexity and intriguing nature of the infant and thereby seems to stimulate the parents' fascination with the baby. Once the parents' interest is captured, interaction will occur and, in most cases, sensitive and growth-promoting parent–infant relations will develop." This leads directly to their designing a program intended to foster parental awareness and promote interaction. Their method of doing so is to use the Brazelton Neonatal Behavioral Assessment Scale to highlight the complexity of the baby for the parents. Belsky and Benn present evidence suggesting that this technique can engage parental attention and influence maternal behavior, but they have, as yet, no data to report on the developmental outcomes. The technique, however, does seem to offer promise, as Belsky and Benn suggest, of not only providing a screening procedure for detecting potentially adverse relationships but also of constituting a relatively simple, inexpensive, and nonstigmatizing method of facilitating parent–infant interactions and, as a consequence, of facilitating infant development. This might be particularly beneficial if most formal evaluations of infants were used as opportunities to sensitize parents to the "skills and limits" of their children, as Belsky and Benn suggest. Indeed, this proposal is potentially of more value than any particular intervention program in itself, because it detaches the notion of facilitating infant development by enhancing parent–infant interaction from any specific program or instrument.

The last two papers in this section present a considerable amount of information on the effects of a variety of intervention techniques. Tiffany

Field presents data from a series of studies on the effects of early compensatory experiences on groups of infants considered at risk for one or more of several reasons, including early respiratory distress syndrome (RDS), prematurity, socioeconomic status, being the weaker (lighter) of a pair of twins, or being born to a teen-age mother. The first study she describes made use of infants born in the same hospital at different times to examine the effects of changes in technology and hospital practice on development up to the age of 4. Scores on Bayley Scales at 1 to 2 years and IQs and social quotients at 4 years were significantly higher in more recent RDS survivors than in earlier ones. The second study reports on the apparently beneficial effects of providing supplemental nonnutritive sucking experience for infants in a newborn intensive care unit. The third reports the unexpected finding that lower birthweight twin fared better over the first year of life than their larger, healthier twin. The fourth discusses the less surprising fact of developmental disadvantages in infants of poorer (and teen-age) mothers; the fifth the beneficial effects of interventions (similar to Belsky and Benn's) with low income teen-age mothers; and the sixth the effects of a more extensive parent-training program. The seventh compares a home-based intervention program with a center-based program.

The group of studies taken together constitute powerful evidence for the preventive effects of interventions early in the lives of infants considered at risk. Even relatively simple and inexpensive techniques can be remarkably beneficial, particularly those that are focused on the parent rather than aimed directly at the infant. The studies demonstrate a point made earlier at a theoretical level: that the rate of return on an intervention investment is much greater if the intervention increases the parents' transactional skills, presumably because the effects of changing a parent have pervasive effects on the child and persist well beyond the end of the formal intervention.

The final paper in this section, by Craig Ramey, David MacPhee, and Keith Yeates, presents an extensive account of a theoretical model of development with particular reference to developmental retardation, together with data on the findings of the first 8 years of a program designed to prevent mild mental retardation. The General Systems Model, which was discussed by Denenberg in Part II, provides the framework for their work; it appears much more capable of capturing the complex and dynamic nature of developmental processes than models with simpler notions of causation. Ramey and his collaborators clarify the model and consider its implications for the important questions of where interventions can be made and on what they should be focused. The detailed theoretical analysis in the first third of this paper can be read on its own as a valuable description of a major theoretical perspective on development and intervention strategies.

Much of the remainder of the paper describes the design and implementation of the Carolina Abdecedarian Project, a major longitudinal project based on their theoretical model. This project involves providing systematic developmental day care for infants and children at high risk for school failure; the families of these children, in common with those in a control group, also have social and medical services made available to them as well as nutritional supplements for the children. In accordance with the guiding theory, results are presented at various "levels"—that of the child, the caregiver, the family, and the neighborhood; eventually effects at the level of society will also be examined. In addition to presenting data attributable to the effects of the program on children's cognitive, linguistic, social, and affective development, and on parental education and income, the authors take pains to present an analysis and discussion of the complex ways in which effects are mediated.

Ramey, MacPhee, and Yeates' comprehensive discussion of theory and research echoes the theme of this volume as a whole in that it explicitly discusses how programs are developed from theory and how information from intervention programs is both relevant to practical concerns and useful for evaluating and modifying theoretical frameworks.

The Effects of Self-Help Groups in a Premature Nursery on Maternal Autonomy and Caretaking Style 1 Year Later

Klaus K. Minde, Nancy E. Shosenberg, and Peter L. Marton

Introduction

The recent literature suggests that parents of premature infants find it more difficult to look after their infants than do parents whose children were born following a normal gestation (Brown and Bakeman, 1980; Goldberg, 1978; Klaus and Kennell, 1976; Minde, 1980). The question of why this is so has been of interest to a number of investigators. Some have reported these infants' apparent lack of responsiveness to be a source of distress and consequent maladaptation for their parents. (Als and Brazelton, 1980; Field, 1979). Others have pointed out that difficulties in the mothers' past life or a lack of early intimate contact between mothers and their infants influence later maternal caretaking abilities (Hunter, Kilstrom, Kraybill and Loda, 1978; Minde, Marton, Manning, and Hines, 1980a). In addition, a number of authors have emphasized that many mothers of premature infants perceive themselves as having failed in their biological role to bear a "complete" infant (Kaplan and Mason, 1960; Seashore, Leifer, Barnett, and Leiderman, 1973). Consequently they feel inadequate and depressed and often see themselves as personally responsible for the early birth of their infant (Shosenberg, 1980). It appears that, although there is presently no clear agreement about the relative contribution of any of the above-mentioned factors for later parenting disorders, all authors who have written about this area agree that the birth of such a small infant is an extremely stressful event for any parent.

The assistance given to the families of these babies by physicians or other health care professionals has often been determined by whichever

This work was supported by grant number 606-1360-44A National Health and Welfare Canada and the Laidlaw Foundation. It could not have been done without the support of Dr. P. R. Swyer, Director, Department of Perinatology, The Hospital for Sick Children, and all the staff of wards 7F and 7G.

deficit an author assumed to be operative. For example, investigators who have stressed the inadequate postnatal environment of these infants have typically provided extra stimulation to them (Masi, 1979). Others who felt that the premature birth had prevented the parents of such infants from forming a stable bond gave mothers an opportunity to have ready access to their infants after birth (Klaus and Kennell, 1976; Leiderman and Seashore, 1975).

Although both types of intervention have been shown to benefit these infants initially, any long-term effects on both the infants and the parent–child relationship have been found to be associated with a continuing active involvement of the mother in the treatment process. For example, the best results of infant stimulation programs have been obtained when mothers were taught, and then themselves carried out, the suggested stimulation programs both in the hospital and later at home (Chapman, 1979; Rice, 1977; Scarr-Salapatek and Williams, 1973). It is possible and likely that the execution of these stimulation programs, in addition to benefiting the infant, also gave these mothers the feeling of competence; that is, that they were needed, important, and did a good job.

Similarly, early maternal visiting may have affected later caretaking behavior not primarily because of the establishment of a stronger early mother–infant bond but because these initial visits allowed mothers to handle their infants more and consequently increased their feelings of competence (Seashore et al., 1973). It is of interest to note that the above-mentioned studies either did not provide any long-term follow-up or the initial differences in the mothers' behaviors toward their premature infants disappeared after 1 month at home.

Although the above interventions were compatible with the notion that the maternal caretaking changes were caused primarily by inadvertently improving the self-esteem or the feeling of autonomy of the mothers of these very small infants, at least initially, the authors of these studies never mention this possibility. In addition, both types of program seem to have one other potential shortcoming. They only provide parents with *either* short-term specific emotional support (Klaus and Kennell, 1976; Leiderman and Seashore, 1975) *or* practical suggestions in regard to their infant's special needs (Field, 1979; Rice, 1977; Scarr-Salapatek and Williams, 1973). In contrast our own clinical experience had suggested to us that families of such high-risk infants were in need of both emotional and practical support for the task of parenting such small infants.

In an attempt to see the effect of such comprehensive care, we evaluated an intervention program in which peer-oriented, self-help groups served to assist the parents of premature infants. We chose this approach because of the following:

●our wish to avoid labeling parents as patients

●our clinical impression, supported by the work of Dumont (1974), Caplan (1974), and Powell (1975), that parents would be more accepting of supportive teaching from peers than from health professionals

●the evidence reported by Bronfenbrenner (1975) that the most successful long-term enhancement of the reciprocal mother–infant interaction is brought about by regular contact of mothers with specially trained peers during the first 3 years.

Subjects

Our study sample consisted of 57 very low birthweight infants and their mothers, assigned to experimental (N=28) and control groups (N=29) on the basis of their time of admission to the hospital. A more detailed discussion of our methodology can be found in previous publications (Minde, Shosenberg, Marton, Thompson, Ripley, and Burns, 1980b). In short, the selection criteria were as follows: for infants, birthweight less than 1,501 grams; singleton birth; weight appropriate for gestational age; absence of physical malformation and of serious medical complications, such as respiratory distress requiring ventilatory assistance or convulsions, at 72 hours of age; and for parents, their intent to keep the infant; ability to speak English; and domicile within 15 miles of The Hospital for Sick Children. The sample thus constituted a group of very small premature infants who had a relatively good medical prognosis and were unlikely to have suffered gross cerebral damage. The background characteristics of this sample are described in Table 1.

Setting

The study was conducted in the Neonatal Intensive Care Unit of The Hospital for Sick Children in Toronto, Canada. This unit has an annual admission of about 1,300 infants, about 350 of which weigh less than 1,500 grams and 110 less than 1,000 grams at birth. It has a nursing staff of approximately 150, placing it among the largest neonatal units in North America. Parental visiting and stimulation of the infants by parents are actively encouraged by all staff.

Method

All parents assigned to the experimental group were met by the group coordinator (N.S.) at the time of their first visit to the hospital and informed about the availability of the group. Each group consisted of 4 to 5 families who met once weekly for 90 to 120 minutes for 7 to 12 weeks following the birth of their infant, together with the group coordinator who was an experienced neonatal nurse and with a "veteran

Table 1 Background Data

Mothers	Experimental N = 28	Controls N = 29
Marital Status		
Married	21	23
Single	4	6
Other	3	0
Parity		
Primipara	15	15
Multipara	13	14
Previous spontaneous abortions		
One	5	13
More than one	5	3
Socioeconomic class		
One, two	4	6
Three	8	8
Four, five	16	15

Infants		
Sex		
Female	17	14
Male	11	15
Birthweight		
Mean	1142	1144
SD	215	249

mother". The veteran mother had similarly had a small baby in the nursery during the previous 9 to 12 months and was known for her general sensitivity and integrity. She was seen as the official animator of each group.

The initial objective of the groups was to provide the parents with a forum within which they could talk about their intense feelings of fear, guilt, and depression about having given birth to such a small baby. Once they had shared these feelings with each other and, as a consequence, begun to trust each other, the parents were exposed, with the help of specific resource personnel, to more didactic materials. These included films and slide presentations highlighting the developmental and medical needs of premature infants. Assistance was also provided for such concrete tasks as getting babysitters, finding better accommodations, or applying for unemployment benefits. Finally, the families were made familiar with local community resources for family support, and much time was spent on discussing issues such as working mothers, the role of the father in infant care, and the way parents can become emotionally available to their infants. In addition, the group coordinator was also available to the parents between group meetings to answer questions about specific medical problems of their infant and to provide individual support. About 60 percent of the parents made use of this opportunity at one time or another.

Parents in the group received only the routine ward care.

Summary of Previously Reported Results

In a previous publication (Minde et al., 1980b) we reported some findings suggesting that the 28 families who participated in these groups visited their infants significantly more in hospital than did the 29 control parents. They also touched, talked to, and looked at their infants in the en face position more during their visits (see Figures 1 and 2) and on a rating scale rated themselves as more confident in taking care of their infants at the time of discharge. Three months after discharge of the infants, group mothers continued to show more involvement with their babies during feedings (see Figures 3 and 4) and were more concerned about their general development.

In a follow-up study 1 year later, which included all but 2 of the original sample of 57 families, we again found significant differences between the mothers who had participated in the group meetings and their controls (Minde, Shosenberg, and Thompson, in press). For example, a statistically significant 69 percent of the mothers in the experimental group perceived the development of their infants at an age corrected for their gestation and adjusted their expectations accordingly. Only 37 percent of the control mothers did so. The experimental mothers at 1 year also gave their infants significantly more floor space to play, disciplined them less, and in general were more free in expressing concerns they had about them. When observed during a routine feed, the experimental mothers were also found to spend less time feeding their children, instead allowing them to feed themselves more. During a play session these mothers also vocalized and played more with their infants. We interpreted these findings to mean that the experimental mothers gave their infants more general freedom and stimulation and judged their competence more appropriately to their biological abilities.

During these same observations the infants of the experimental families in turn spent significantly more time sharing food with their mothers during their meals and during the play sessions played more and touched their mothers more frequently. When the infants were reunited with their mothers after a 5-minute separation, the experimental mothers hugged and kissed their infants significantly more. In contrast the control mothers showed their joy at reunion by doing many instrumental tasks with their babies, such as changing their diapers or combing their hair.

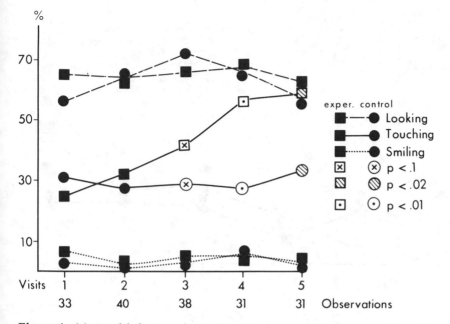

Figure 1. Maternal behavior observed in the nursery during one weekly visit over 5 weeks.

These results suggested to us that the experimental mothers were more socially stimulating with their infants and shared their feelings with them more easily. Their children reciprocated by showing more social and independent behaviors such as general playing, food sharing, and self-feeding.

Although these data suggest a significant relation between maternal group participation and various objectively measured maternal behaviors in the nursery and later at home, we did not know to what extent this group experience had altered the relationship between the mother's level of involvement with her infant and her own previous life experiences. Thus, in our previous work we had observed that mothers who were highly active during their initial visits tended to remain very active during later visits to the nursery as well (Minde et al., 1980a). Likewise mothers who showed little activity during the initial observations continued to do so later on. In order to understand this phenomenon more clearly, we had arbitrarily placed mothers who scored above the median on more than 75 percent of all maternal behaviors during all their visits in a "high" activity category. Mothers who ranked below the median on 75 percent of all maternal behaviors during all observations were put in the

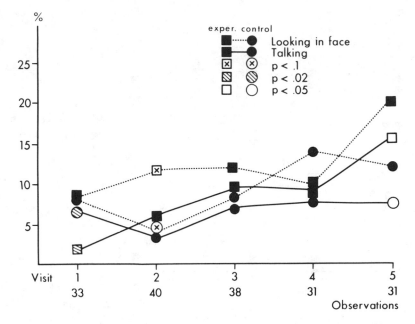

Figure 2. Maternal behavior observed in the nursery during one weekly visit over 5 weeks.

"low" activity category. If a mother fitted neither of the extreme group-ings she was designated as a "medium" activity mother. In our previous work some 20 percent of all mothers turned out to be "high" mothers, 35 percent were "low" mothers and 45 percent fell into the "medium" activity group.

In order to understand possible connections between these rather per-sistent behavior patterns and maternal background variables, we had suggested that these early parent–child interactions could be a reflection of a variety of factors that might include (1) the caretaker's personal mothering experiences, modified by later relationships with peers and spouses; (2) the experiences associated with the premature child in ques-tion during the pregnancy, delivery, and early postnatal period; (3) eco-nomic and social factors; (4) the behavior of the infant and; (5) a combi-nation of any of the above.

To investigate these possibilities, we divided the information obtained from a semi-structured psychiatric interview, which was given to each family 4 weeks after the birth of their infant by a child psychiatrist (K.M.) into three categories, each representing a different cluster of po-tential maternal background factors.

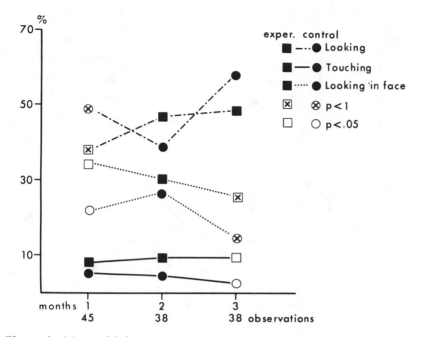

Figure 3. Maternal behavior observed during feedings 1 to 3 months after discharge from hospital.

Psychological Factor

This factor took in all those variables that are typically seen as the necessary precursors of later parenting ability—relationship with own father and mother and with father of the infant; previous psychiatric history; present emotional support from own family, friends, and father of the infant; interest in seeking knowledge about prematurity and its associated conditions.

Factor Related to Present Pregnancy

This included all the events that might facilitate or hinder the attachment of a mother to her infant, such as the presence and number of previous abortions or miscarriages; complications during present pregnancy or delivery; the ability to hear, see, or touch the infant after birth; and the prognosis and support given by the physician during first 48 hours after birth.

Factor Related to Social Conditions

This consisted of variables that reflected more general environmental and cultural parental experiences which in the literature have been found to

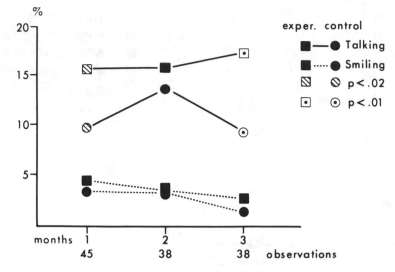

Figure 4. Maternal behavior observed during feedings 1 to 3 months after discharge from hospital.

be associated with differences in the caretaking patterns of individuals. Specifically, we mean socioeconomic class, marital status, and ethnicity.

After the psychiatric interview, individual items recorded were rated on either a 3-point scale (favorable, neutral, unfavorable) or a 2-point scale (present, absent). In order to quantify these ratings for each item, events judged favorable were given a score of plus 1, those unfavorable were scored as minus 1, and neutral events received a score of 0. The scores on the 18 items were then summed to yield a composite risk score for each family which could range from −17 (all items unfavorable) to +17 (all items favorable).

When we assigned to each experimental and control mother an activity level as determined by her behavior during her nursery visits, and compared this with her total composite background score, using analysis of variance, marked differences between the experimental and control groups appeared.

Table 2 shows that "low" activity mothers in the control group had a much lower composite score on the psychiatric interview than had "medium" and "high" mothers. This confirms the results of our previous study in which we did not attempt any intervention (Minde et al., 1980a). Furthermore, the table shows that, in contrast to the control mothers, the psychiatric sum score did not differentiate the various activ-

Table 2 Global Risk Scores of Group and Control Mothers

	High (N=9)	Medium (N=16)	Low (N=3)
Group			
Mean	3.2	2.6	2.0
S.D.	5.5	3.2	6.2

	High (N=5)	Medium (N=15)	Low (N=9)
Controls			
Mean	7.6	4.2	−1.5
S.D.	3.6	4.7	6.1

Source	SS	df	MS	F
Groups	7.06	1	7.06	0.32
Activity level	189.9	2	95.0	4.24[xx]
Interaction	114.4	2	57.2	2.55[x]
Within cell	1141.3	51	22.4	

[x] $= p < .10$
[xx] $= p < .05$

ity groupings among the experimental mothers. This suggests that the participation in the group in some way altered the characteristics of a mother's interactional activity which we had been able to predict in the control mothers from some of their background experiences. This finding is not due to an initial sampling bias as the total grand sum score of all activity groups among experimental and control mothers was not different (experimental 2.72: control 3.02) but may indeed reflect a genuine shift in the experimental mothers' behavior toward their infants.

In order to define more clearly the relative association of each background variable with the three levels of general maternal activity we used the statistic lambda B to compute group differences for each of the 17 background items collected during the psychiatric interview.

In our sample we found that in the control group all the combined psychological factors predicted maternal behavior best (53 percent accuracy in prediction), while in the experimental group none of these three major background factors predicted above 24 percent. In the control group, the mother's relationship with her own mother, her own father, and the father of the infant were the highest predictors (57 percent, 57 percent and 24 percent respectively), while in the experimental group the best predictor (23 percent) was the presence of a previous abortion in the mother's obstetrical history (see Table 3).

Although the results from the control mothers again replicate data

Table 3 Relationship of Maternal Background Variables to Maternal Activity Level

	λB	Percentage in activity group with favorable score		
		High	Medium	Low
Relationship with mother				
Control	.57	80	80	11
Group	.0	71	53	67
Relationship with father				
Control	.57	80	69	0
Group	.0	57	29	67
Relationship with father of infant				
Control	.24	100	67	22
Group	.08	71	67	83
Previous abortion				
Control	.0	60	47	33
Group	.23	43	67	85
Assistance from father of infant				
Control	.29	100	53	33
Group	.23	71	60	67

from our previous study (Minde et al., 1980a), they also raise the question why in the experimental mothers the traditional factors predicting maternal activity level did not do so.

A further scrutiny of our clinical data revealed that the experimental group had only three low activity mothers (11 percent), while there were nine (32 percent) such mothers in the control group. Conversely, the control group had five high activity mothers (18 percent), while the experimental group had nine (33 percent). (See also Table 2.) The one previously unrecorded difference in the background of these two groups was that the experimental "high" mothers, although they did not usually have a satisfactory relationship with their own parents, all remembered at least one significant adult (a teacher, a neighbor, or an in-law) who had been "good to them" over a fairly extended period and had given them the feeling of being a worthwhile human being. Two of the three "low" experimental mothers, however, during the psychiatric interview could not remember anyone whom they had regarded as a source of self-esteem.

This may suggest that mothers who had any sort of positive interpersonal relationship of a certain duration in their past can "make use" of other such potential positive relationships later on. This ability to compensate for the lack of early parental warmth through later relationships with other significant adults has been cited by Rutter as one characteristic found in those who cope well in adulthood, despite a history of early deprivation (Rutter, 1979).

While these clinical data may indeed reflect some of the underlying readiness that allowed the group mothers to relate more actively to their infants, it does not explain the actual psychological changes which brought about the more active behavior in these mothers during the first year of their infants' life. In an attempt to look for a possible source of such a change, a number of variables specifically related to the mothers' economic, social, and psychological wellbeing were extracted and analyzed from our clinical data. We first considered the possibility that the experimental mothers had experienced a significant improvement in their external life as shown by their economic circumstances and had more time and energy available to stimulate their infants. However, a comparison of the economic conditions of both control and experimental mothers between the time of their infant's birth and the first birthday showed no difference between the groups (see Table 4).

The table clearly shows that although the majority of mothers stayed the same, about 35 percent in each group either improved or went down economically, but there was no difference in this pattern for each group.

There was also no variation in the improvement of housing in the two groups as defined by more bedrooms or by an increase in other housing amenities (see Table 5).

Educationally there were also no changes between the groups. Only four experimental and two group mothers had seriously enquired about furthering their education, but none had in fact done so.

We next considered the possibility that the experimental mothers had experienced a significant improvement in their interpersonal relationships as this in turn could have generalized to the care they provided their infants. When we enquired about any changes the mothers had felt in their relationships with members of their own family or with the husband or the father of the premature infant, we found that the experimental mothers indeed reported significantly more often that they had experienced a positive change in their relationship with one or more significant persons in their life (see Table 6).

The individual clinical summaries of those mothers who had reported an improvement in their relationships with others important to them also showed that five experimental mothers versus none in the control group had left their husbands or companions during the past year. Although such a separation is usually seen as a sign of deteriorating mental health, it seemed that in all these cases the woman had deserted a man who had been physically abusive to her or who had a history of severe alcoholism or who had a criminal record. This suggested to us that some of our

Table 4 Economic Situation of Mothers at
One Year

	Worse	Unchanged	Better
Group	2	17	9
Control	5	20	4

$X_2 = 3.59$ $df = 2$ $p < .2$

Table 5 Housing of Mothers at One Year

	Worse	Unchanged	Better
Group	2	17	9
Control	4	17	8

$X_2 = 0.74$ $df = 2$ NS

Table 6 Changes in Mother's Relationship
with Significant Others at One Year

	Worse	Unchanged	Better
Group	2	11	15
Control	10	13	6

$X^2 = 9.79$ $df = 2$ $p < .01$

mothers had become more self-sufficient and more autonomous in their actions in that they insisted on safeguarding their needs and those of their infants with fewer compromises. In order to verify this clinical impression we devised a global 5-point rating for autonomy. The descriptions of each point of this rating were derived from the work of Lozoff (1973), Anderson (1973), and Baker-Miller (1976) and private discussions between Minde and 20 women actively engaged in contemporary women's issues.

The following descriptions for a rating of 1, 3, and 5 on the global autonomy score were finally agreed upon, with a rating of 2 and 4 falling in between.

● 1 = A woman who has been chronically abused either in her working or in her personal relationships since her childhood. She does not report awareness of any alternatives to this type of life, or she thinks that they do not apply to her.

● 3 = A woman who has established herself in some area of her life, such as a job or volunteer activity, but who uses the potential advantages this gives her primarily either to maintain a basically dependent status quo or to identify with and hence adopt the traditional model of male independence.

• 5 = A woman who has established herself in some area of her life and has acknowledged or overcome the guilt induced by this step. Nevertheless she is aware of her femaleness and in that sense has demonstrated an authenticity which in turn has allowed her to avoid copying the traditional male model of independence. Furthermore, she can give up outward signs of independence such as a job for some time to look after an infant or other significant person in her life or is able to tolerate the attachment of her child to surrogate caretakers.

Taking these criteria, the two senior authors independently rated all mothers on the clinical transcripts of the initial and 1 year follow-up psychiatric interviews.

Table 7 shows the results of these ratings and indicates that a significantly higher number of group mothers were seen to have achieved a positive change in their autonomy during the first year of their infants' life.

This differential change was not related to any initial differences in the degree of autonomy between the groups since both groups initially had very similar autonomy scores with group mothers scoring a mean of 2.4 (S D 0.83) and control mothers 2.5 (S D 0.86). Furthermore, the control mothers showed no change in their mean score after 1 year (mean: 2.5, S D 0.82) while the experimental mothers increased their mean autonomy score to 3.0 (S D 0.92). The changes in the autonomy scores of the experimental mothers can therefore not be seen as a result of regression to ward the mean. In fact, some further data appear to validate this concept of autonomy, especially since they were arrived at independently of the global autonomy score. Table 8 shows that more group than control mothers had not returned to work at the 1 year interview (7 group and 5 control mothers had never worked and were therefore excluded from the analysis). Since all but two group mothers who returned to work did so after their infant was 7 months old and the return to work in neither group was associated with socioeconomic class, number of children at home, and the high, medium, or low activity status of the mother, these figures may well indicate yet again, that the group mothers in this study had become more autonomous and consequently more free to choose their own lifestyle.

Discussion

The present study indicates that women who 1 year earlier took part in a peer self-help group following their premature infants' birth differ from

Table 7 Changes in Maternal Autonomy at One Year

	No change or decrease	Increase
Group	16	12
Control	25	4

$X^2 = 5.95$ $df = 1$ $p < .02$

Table 8 Mothers Return to Work within One Year

	Yes	No
Group	12	9
Control	8	16

$X^2 = 2.75$ $df = 1$ $p < .1$

a control group on a number of behaviors. In particular they show a higher degree of personal autonomy, a particular attitude towards their work, and positive changes in their relationships with other people. Although these findings are obviously not based on hard data, especially since our definition of autonomy may not be shared by others, we can speculate that this sense of maternal autonomy may also have been responsible for some of the changes we found in the behavior of these same mothers with their infants in our previous reports on the results of this self-help group experience. The increased social behavior of both mothers and infants during the observations at 1 year, as well as the increased ability of our group mothers to demonstrate their affection and concern for their infants which was seen during the early home visits and at 1 year, can be interpreted as a direct result of this changed self-concept of these women. This would also confirm some of the recent writings of Baker-Miller (1976) who states that autonomy and personal authenticity do not automatically imply lessening in activities traditionally associated with maternal caretaking behavior. In fact, the gain in autonomy, according to this writer, may allow a woman to utilize her interpersonal abilities and sensitivities with more ease and less conflict and in this sense make her into a more caring mother.

The question arises why this type of self-help experience should have had such a global impact upon these mothers. Even though a clear answer to this question is obviously not yet possible, we hypothesize that this group contact allowed us to take care of these families in a way that went beyond the "biomedical" model of traditional medicine. This traditional model, which applies the classical Western scientific "factor analytic" approach to medicine, basically assumed the "science" alone will finally deal with all the problems of both the body and the mind. In contrast, Engel (1977, 1980) in some important recent papers has presented an alternative model of medical care and called it the biopsychosocial model. This model sees "illness" and "distress" as disturbances in a complex integrated system. A particular illness is then seen at the same time as a component of a higher disturbance or a system, in the same way that a person is a component of his or her family or of society at large, as well as of lower systems such as the organs of a person which are made of cells. Engel states that the system-oriented clinicians will be aware that their primary task is the identification and characterization of the constituent components of the system they have to deal with. They will then intervene at the system(s) level most appropriate for the disorder at hand but will always remain conscious of changes within other systems which may affect the future process of the disorder.

It is clear that an awareness and understanding of these systems is especially important in medical conditions that affect the whole ecology of a person. For example, any type of chronic illness or physical handicap would have important repercussions on the total life of an individual and consequently he or she would be affected by the reactions of those sharing his/her life. Similarly, prematurity is a condition affecting far more than the biology of the infant (Als and Brazelton, 1980; Field, 1977; Frodi, Lamb, Leavitt, Donovan, Neff, and Sherry, 1978; Klaus and Kennell, 1976; Shosenberg, 1980). For example, some mothers may have precipitated their premature labour by not availing themselves of proper prenatal care for other than medical reasons. Others may find themselves depressed and anxious following the birth of such an infant, which compromises their ability to look after such a baby. In addition, there is good evidence that the future biological, social, and psychological functioning of these infants to a large extent depends on systems other than those associated with the specific biological impairment of the infant. In fact, the biological impairment that can be measured at birth is a very poor predictor of the future general functioning of these infants, while the attitudes in child-care practices of their primary caretakers are significantly correlated with later functioning in these areas (Cohen and Beckwith, 1979; Fitzhardinge, 1976; Littman, 1979; Sigman and Parmelee, 1980).

In summary, we feel that the self-help groups constituted one practical application of Engel's biopsychosocial model. The infants were given exemplary traditional medical care during their hospitalization, although at the same time their parents were allowed initially to mourn the loss of their hoped for full-term infants and to deal with other areas of this emotional crisis. In addition, they could all share concerns about both medical care and feelings with each other, such as their difficulties in providing their infants with breast milk and in getting clarified potentially confusing information from staff, to mention just two commonly encountered issues. Hence the groups allowed care to go on at various systems levels and converted a potentially very disorganizing and disintegrating experience into one which taught these parents competence and self-reliance.

In keeping with this model we argue that parents were able and willing to learn through videotapes, slides, and lectures about the common characteristics and problems of their infants only after their initial emotional crisis had been dealt with through group discussions and private meetings with the group coordinator. This approach, in our estimation, gave them a sense of mastery, especially since their interest and concerns were appreciated and reinforced by the professional staff and, later on, by their infants. The veteran parents (in five groups both the father and the mother acted as veterans) were crucial agents in this process as they could bridge the gap between the "professional" and the "patient" and communicate our concern and interest in the various systems implicated in this life crisis and also model a sense of potential mastery for the new parents. Since some sort of awareness in the various ecological systems influencing human behavior and development is an important aspect of any positive interpersonal relationship, we hypothesize that the increase in the group mothers' autonomy may be a direct result of our systems-oriented treatment program, although a replication of our study in another setting is clearly warranted.

An indication of this program's potentially long-term impact on the autonomy of these women has been the recent formation of the Toronto Perinatal Association. This organization of parents who initially benefited from these group meetings continues to make self-help groups available for families with premature infants in our hospital and has also become increasingly involved in the shaping of future perinatal service in Ontario.

References

Als, H., and Brazelton, T. B. A new model of assessing behavioral organization in preterm and full term infants. *Journal of the American Academy of Child Psychiatry*, 1980, *20*, 239–263.

Anderson, J.V. Psychological determinants. *Annals of New York Academy of Sciences*, 1973, *208*, 185–193.

Baker-Miller, J. *Toward a new psychology of women*. Boston: Beacon Press, 1976.

Bronfenbrenner, U. Is early intervention effective? In B. Z. Friedlander, G. M. Sterritt, and G. E. Kirk (Eds.), *Exceptional infant assessment and intervention*. New York: Brunner/Mazel, 1975.

Brown, J., and Bakeman, R. Relationships of human mothers with their infants during the first year of life: Effects of prematurity. In R. Bell and W. Smotherman (Eds.), *Maternal influences and early behavior*. New York: Spectrum, 1980.

Caplan, G. *Support systems and community mental health*. New York: Behavioral Publications, 1974.

Chapman, J.S. Influence of varied stimulation development of motor patterns in the premature infant. In *Newborn Behavioral Organization: Nursing Research and Implications*. The National Foundation March of Dimes Birth Defects: Original Article Series, Vol. 15, Alan R. Liss Inc. 1979.

Cohen, S.E., and Beckwith, L. Preterm infant interaction with the caregiver in the first year of life and competence at age two. *Child Development*, 1979, *50*, 767–776.

Dumont, M. Self-help treatment programs. *American Journal of Psychiatry*, 1974, *131*, 631–635.

Engel, G.L. The need for a new medical model: A challenge for biomedicine. *Science*, 1977, *129*, 129–136.

Engel, G.L. The clinical application of the biopsychosocial model. *American Journal of Psychiatry*, 1980, *137*, 535–544.

Field, T.M. Effects of early separation, interactive deficits, and experimental manipulations on infant–mother face-to-face interaction. *Child Development*, 1977, *48*, 763–771.

Field, T.M. Interaction patterns of preterm and term infants. In T. M. Field, A. M. Sostek, S. Goldberg, and H. H. Shuman (Eds.), *Infants born at risk*. New York: Spectrum, 1979.

Fitzhardinge, P. Follow-up studies on the low birth weight infant. *Clinics in Perinatology*, 1976, *3*, 503–516.

Frodi, A., Lamb, M., Leavitt, L., Donovan, W., Neff, C., and Sherry, D. Fathers' and mothers' responses to the faces and cries of normal and premature infants. *Developmental Psychology*, 1978, *14*, 490–498.

Goldberg, S. Prematurity: Effects on parent–infant interaction. *Journal of Pediatric Psychology*, 1978, *3*, 137–144.

Hunter, R.S., Kilstrom, N., Kraybill, E.N., and Loda, F. Antecedents of child abuse and neglect in premature infants: A prospective study in a newborn intensive care unit. *Pediatrics*, 1978, *61*, 629–635.

Kaplan, D.M., and Mason, E.A. Maternal reaction to premature birth viewed as an acute emotional disorder. *American Journal of Orthopsychiatry*, 1960, *30*, 539–547.

Klaus, M.H., and Kennell, J.H. *Maternal–Infant bonding*. Saint Louis: C. V. Mosby, 1976.

Leiderman, P.H., and Seashore, M.J. Mother–infant neonatal separation: Some delayed consequences. In Ciba Foundation Symposium No 33. *Parent Infant Interaction*. New York: Elsevier, 1975.

Littman, B. The relationship of medical events to infant development. In T. M. Field, A. M. Sostek, S. Goldberg, and H. H. Shuman (Eds.), *Infants born at risk*. New York: Spectrum, 1979.

258   KLAUS K. MINDE ET AL.

Lozoff, M.M. Fathers and autonomy in women. *Annals of New York Academy of Sciences*, 1973, *208*, 91–97.

Masi, W. Supplement stimulation of the premature infant. In T. M. Field, A. M. Sostek, S. Goldberg, and H. H. Shuman (Eds.), *Infants born at risk*. New York: Spectrum, 1979.

Minde, K. Bonding of parents to premature infants: Theory and practice. In P. Taylor (Ed.), *Monographs in Neonatology Series*. New York: Grune and Stratton, 1980.

Minde, K., Marton, P., Manning, D., and Hines, B. Some determinants of mother–infant interaction in the premature nursery. *Journal of the American Academy of Child Psychiatry*, 1980, *19*, 1–21. (a)

Minde, K., Shosenberg, N., Marton, P., Thompson, J., Ripley, J., and Burns, S. Self-help groups in a premature nursery—a controlled evaluation. *Journal of Pediatrics*, 1980, *96*, 933–940. (b)

Minde, K., Shosenberg, N., and Thompson, P. Self-help groups in a premature nursery—infant behavior and parental competence 1 year later. In E. Galenson and J. Call (Eds.), *Frontiers of infant psychiatry*. New York: Basic Books, in press.

Powell, L.F. The use of self-help groups as supportive reference communities. *American Journal of Orthopsychiatry*, 1975, *45*, 756–762.

Rice, R. Neurophysiological development in premature infants following stimulation. *Developmental Psychology*, 1977, *13*, 69–76.

Rutter, M. Invulnerability or why some children are not damaged by stress. In S. J. Shamsie (Ed.), *New directions in children's mental health*. New York: S.P. Medical and Scientific Books, 1979.

Scarr-Salapatek, S., and Williams, M.L. The effects of early stimulation on low birthweight infants. *Child Development*, 1973, *44*, 94–101.

Seashore, M.J., Leifer, A.D., Barnett, C.R., and Leiderman, P.H. The effects of denial of early mother–infant interaction on maternal self-confidence. *Journal of Personal and Social Psychology*, 1973, *36*, 369–378.

Shosenberg, N. Self-help groups for parents of premature infants. *Canadian Nurse*, 1980, July–August, 30–33.

Sigman, M., and Parmelee, A.H. Longitudinal evaluation of the preterm infants. In T. M. Field, A. M. Sostek, S. Goldberg, and H. H. Shuman (Eds.), *Infants born at risk*. New York: Spectrum, 1979.

The Vermont Infant Studies Project:
The Rationale for a Mother–Infant Transaction Program

Virginia A. Rauh, Barry Nurcombe, Paul Ruoff, Al Jette, and David Howell

A remarkable number of small infants, who formerly might have perished, are now surviving as a result of advances in perinatal medical care. They are a vulnerable group, characterized by (1) diagnosed medical disorders of known etiology carrying well-known expectancies for developmental delay; and/or (2) a history of troublesome perinatal events suggestive of biological insult, carrying a high probability of later developmental delay. Some babies are born prematurely, some are small for their gestational age, and some fall into both categories. Low birthweight is known to be associated with aberrant biological and psychosocial development (Caputo, Goldstein, and Taub, 1979; Davies, 1975; Drillien, 1961; Eaves, Nuttall, Klonoff, and Dunn, 1970; Fitzhardinge and Steven, 1972; Knobloch, Rider, Harper, and Pasamanick, 1956; Lubchenco, Delivera-Papadopoulos, and Searles, 1972; Lubchenco, Horner, Reed, Hix, Metcalf, Cohig, Elliott, and Bourg, 1963; Parmelee and Schulte, 1970; Wiener, Rider, Oppel, and Harper, 1968). The disproportionately high incidence of parenting disorders in the low birthweight population has been reported and has aroused considerable concern (Fanaroff, Kennell and Klaus, 1972; Green and Solnit, 1964; Hunter, Kilstrom, Kraybill, and Loda, 1978; Klein and Stern, 1971; Leifer, Leiderman, Barnett, and Williams, 1972; Rubin, Rosenblatt, and Balon, 1973; Shaheen, Alexander, Truskowsky, and Barbero, 1968; Stern, 1973; Thoman, 1975).

The low birthweight itself may be a result of intrauterine insults, such as subnutrition, infection, placental circulatory insufficiency, and antepartum hemorrhage. All of these conditions are more likely to occur in poor, socially stressed, adolescent women. The baby, stunted as a result of premature labor, intrauterine growth retardation, or both, is vulnera-

This research has been made possible by National Institute of Mental Health Grant #1 RO1 MH 32924-01.

ble to a variety of specific peri- and postnatal medical complications. These may include perinatal asphyxia, respiratory distress, apneic episodes, hypoglycemia, jaundice, and cerebral hemorrhage—conditions that have implications for psychosocial as well as physical development. It is generally agreed that an infant's emotional and social development are powerfully affected by prenatal, perinatal, and postnatal environmental factors, just as survival and subsequent physical health are affected by prenatal, perinatal, and postnatal medical factors.

The primary prevention of excess mortality and morbidity in this population is based on knowledge of what constitutes and, indeed, causes intrauterine insult. Secondary prevention has brought about major advances in neonatal intensive care and regionalized systems of health care delivery. The primary prevention of poor parenting and poor developmental outcome must be based on knowledge of the prenatal, perinatal, and postnatal factors associated with optimal parent–infant relationships and child development. Secondary prevention involves identification of an "at risk" population and remedial efforts to stimulate the child or enhance the parent–infant relationship in some way.

A Review of the Literature on Intervention

Intervention with low birthweight infants has included a variety of primary and secondary preventive approaches. This work stems from many theoretical perspectives on the nature and causes of parenting failures and the psychosocial and developmental maladjustments of the child.

Faulty Bonding

One theory holds that early separation and the lack of physical contact between parents and low birthweight infants somehow results in faulty bonding and attachment (Barnett, Leiderman, and Grobstein, 1970; Carlsson, Fagerberg, and Horneman, 1978; de Chateau, 1979; Field, 1977; Hales, 1977; Kennell, Gordon, and Klaus, 1970; Klaus and Kennell, 1970; Leifer et al, 1972; Powell, 1974; Ringler, Kennell, Jarvella, Navojosky, and Klaus, 1975; Seashore, Leifer, Barnett, and Leiderman, 1973). Many of these investigators postulate the existence of a sensitive period; thus, intervention most often consists of additional, earlier, or multimodal contact between mother and infant. Outcome is generally evaluated in terms of maternal affectionate behaviors (manifested during interactions such as feeding), maternal attitudes, and the child's sensorimotor and cognitive development (Field, 1977; Rice, 1977). Although many of the studies report significant "improvements" in these areas, most fail to differentiate stimulation dimensions from maternal contact variables.

Furthermore, small numbers of subjects, lack of adequate follow-up, lack of full-term comparison groups, and failure to control for medical complications characterize many studies.

Stimulus Deprivation

The so-called extra or optimal stimulation programs represent a large volume of work with confusing and contradictory implications. For the most part, they are based on an environmental deprivation model or on some modification thereof. Mother–infant interaction is neither the target of the intervention nor its goal, making the results difficult to relate to attachment theory. Outcomes are most often measured by weight gain, amount of crying, activity level, duration of apneic episodes, visual exploratory behavior, and short-term mental and motor development of the infant (Barnard, 1975; Freedman and Boverman, 1966; Hasselmeyer, 1964; Kattwinkel, Nearman, Fanaroff, Katona, and Klaus, 1975; Katz, 1971; Korner, Kraemer, Faffner, and Casper, 1975; Kraemer and Pierpoint, 1976; Measel and Anderson, 1979; Scarr-Salapatek and Williams, 1973; Solkoff, Weintraub, Yaffe, and Blase, 1969; White and Labarba, 1976).

In general, experimental results are inconsistent and difficult to replicate because of failure to control for differences in level of stimulation in the nursery environment (consisting of noise, lights, medical intrusion, nursing routines, and so forth). Most would now agree that the extra uterine environment is probably not "under" stimulating. The sensory input of today's typical intensive care nursery is more likely to be excessive, unstructured, and noncontingent. The sensory deprivation model has limited usefulness in light of the more sophisticated concept of the appropriateness of the stimulation rather than the amount (Thoman, 1975).

Deficits in the Capacity of the Infant to Elicit Care

A third major approach emphasizes the contribution of the infant to the subsequent parent–child relationship (Bell, 1974; Greenberg, Rosenberg, and Lind, 1973; Klein and Stern, 1971; Lewis, 1972; Osofsky and Danzger, 1974; Thomas, Chess, and Birch, 1968). It has been clearly documented that individual differences exist in infants' capacities to elicit social interaction (Brazelton, 1979; Brazelton, Koslowski, and Main, 1971; Condon and Sander, 1974; Korner, 1971; Lester and Zeskind, 1979; Stern, 1973). Special subgroups over represented among abused children include the mentally handicapped and the blind (Fraiberg, 1974; Schmitt and Kempe, 1975). Most low birthweight infants do not have serious physical abnormalities but certainly do contribute to the parent–infant relationship with their unique patterns of state regulation and visual attentiveness (Dreyfuss-Brisac, 1970; Kopp, Sigman, and Parmelee, 1975; Parmelee, Wenner, Akiyama, Schultz, and Stern, 1967; Prechtl, Theorell, and Blair, 1973). The preterm infant has not yet achieved integrated physiologic and motoric functioning (Als, Tronick, and Lester, 1977; Als, Lester, and Brazelton, 1979). The full-term but underweight infant may spontaneously shift from lethargy to irritability over a period of weeks (Als. Tronick, and Adamson, 1976). These infant behaviors bewilder and frustrate parents and may elicit uncertainty in caretaking even under the most optimal conditions (Campbell and Wilson, 1976; Gorski, Davison, and Brazelton, 1979).

A closely related line of research that has developed somewhat independently emphasizes contingency experience (Ainsworth and Bell, 1974; Beckwith, Cohen, Kopp, Parmelee, and Marcy, 1976; Clarke-Stewart, 1973; Lewis and Goldberg, 1969; Ramey, Starr, Pallas, Whitten, and Reed, 1975; Yarrow, Rubenstein and Pederson, 1975). According to this model, the unpredictable or unresponsive infant engages the parent in cycles of ineffective interaction resulting in parental feelings of failure.

Perhaps no one would argue with the notion that individual differences exist at birth and that even low birthweight infants can be characterized on the same dimensions (i.e., alertness, crying behavior, soothability). The contribution of infants to their own social experiences must be considered in any longitudinal research, but the interaction of infant temperament (responsiveness, for example) and parents' response is complex. First, not all difficult infants elicit anxiety and rejection from their caretakers. The caretaker's response depends upon perception of the infant, sensitivity to the infant's signals, predetermined (to some degree) child-care attitudes, and present level of adjustment. These factors are being increasingly considered in assessment of infant–caregiver fit. Second, the stability of effects needs further investigation. That is, some associations between infant behavior and aspects of caregiving disappear over time depending upon the sex of the infant (Kagan and Klein, 1973). The stability of the effects of early experience may be mediated by characteristics of the infant. Siqueland (1973) found that interventions with premature infants in the first few weeks of life changed the babies so that they thereby evoked more responsive interaction from the mother.

Assessment of infant contribution is critical, but such investigation must consider parental or environmental response factors as well.

The Emotional Crisis of Prematurity
Premature delivery has been described as a crisis requiring profound emotional adjustment by the parents (Benfield, Leib, and Reuter, 1976;

Caplan, 1968; Caplan, Mason, and Kaplan, 1965; Cramer, 1976; Kaplan and Mason, 1960; Littman and Wooldridge, 1976). Kaplan and Mason have suggested that mothers of premature infants must deal with the following issues:

- preparing for possible loss (anticipatory grief)
- acknowledging failure to deliver a full-term infant
- resuming the process of relating to the infant
- learning how the premature infant differs from a full-term infant
- understanding the infant's special needs.

Unresolved issues affect a parent's capacity both to relate to the infant and to make use of any intervention program. The timing of interventions must be highly individualized, and the approach must be sensitive to a particular parent's emotional adjustment. Few programs have sufficient flexibility to meet these needs.

It seems likely that difficulty experienced in adjustment and delay in establishing effective parent–infant interaction are exaggerated by medical complications such as prolonged time on a respirator, severe apneic episodes, and infection requiring isolation. Yet a recent study shows that prenatal and perinatal medical complications do not predict later parental activity levels (Minde, Marton, Manning, and Hines, 1980). Although the association has not been studied systematically, medical complications may function as encumbrances to infant responsiveness and parental feelings of "efficacy" and may well have far-reaching and complicated effects on parent–child relationships (Beckwith and Cohen, 1978; Goldberg, 1977).

Medical Complications

This approach stresses the impact of pre-, peri-, and postnatal medical complications on long-term developmental outcome of premature and small-for-gestational-age infants (Broman, Nichols, and Kennedy, 1975; DiVitto and Goldberg, 1979; Field, Dempsey, and Shuman, 1979; Fisch, Bilek, Miller, and Engel, 1975; Fitzhardinge, Pape, Arstikaitis, Boyle, Ashby, Rowley, Netley, and Swyer, 1976; Gottfried, 1973; Marriage and Davies, 1977; McNeil and Wiegerink, 1971; Parmelee and Haber, 1973; Sepkaski, Coll, and Lester, 1977; Smith, Flick, Ferriss, and Sellmann, 1972). Although this work rarely considers interactional or psychosocial adjustment dimensions, it has enabled researchers to identify the relative usefulness of various indices of risk in predicting future development. It is apparent that prematurity alone does not necessarily lead to developmental delay (Douglas and Gear, 1976), that later performance of the smallest infants is not always the poorest, and that healthy premature tend to have very good developmental outcomes (Caputo and Mandell, 1970; Sostek, Quinn, and Davitt, 1979). Some results indicate that risk status cannot be established simply on the basis of obstetric and perinatal medical complications but must include continuing developmental assessments of the child (Littman, 1979; Sigman and Parmelee, 1979). A recent intervention study by Bromwich and Parmelee (1979) has attempted to enhance the quality of parent–infant interaction while controlling for medical complications by assigning cumulative "risk" scores. They report a short-term effect on interaction but no long-term effect on cognitive development (the study is still in progress). The cumulative "risk" score is assigned at 9 months of age and is weighted by 4-, 8-, and 9-month assessments. This approach greatly improves prediction of later risk but necessarily postpones intervention until late in the first year of life.

Although studies of the effects of individual medical factors have been valuable, the major contribution from this area lies in the consideration of groups of "high-risk" medical events (often using a multiple regression approach). Certain predictors account for a larger proportion of the variance in outcome when considered in combination with other factors. Using this method, the best predictions take into account more than individual medical events; they include later developmental assessments as well (Bromwich and Parmelee, 1979). Given a constellation of medical complications, certain later experiences have a modifying effect on outcome. Bromwich and Parmelee (1979) incorporated 4-, 8-, and 9-month assessments of medical and cognitive development into a risk score. The fact that repeated assessments (not included in previous studies) improve prediction suggests that medical factors interact significantly with environment and are of limited usefulness when considered alone.

Adverse Childrearing Environment

A major research area relates the poor outcome of low birthweight infants to environmental factors, primarily socioeconomic ones (Bronfenbrenner, 1975; Drillien, 1964; Greenberg, 1971; Sameroff, 1975; Sameroff and Chandler, 1975; Tulkin, 1977; Tulkin and Cohler, 1973; Wallace, 1970; Werner, Bierman, and French, 1971; Wiener, 1970; Wiener, Rider and Oppel, 1965). Characterization of infant experience by such a global variable as socioeconomic status obscures the specific aspects of the environment which are operative (Beckwith et al., 1976). Investigators differ as to how social class affects development. Some report that lower socioeconomic childrearing environments are at least as stimulating as upper socioeconomic environments, but that the stimuli are less predictably patterned (Tulkin, 1972; Wachs, Uzgiris, and Hunt, 1971). Others report that lower and upper socioeconomic status children do not differ on amount of affective physical contact received (Lewis and Wilson, 1972). Cohen and Beckwith (1976) suggest that upper socioeconomic status infants are exposed to more reciprocal and face-to-face stimulation. Environmental factors, other than demographic variables, found to affect outcome include abnormal previous life experiences of parents (Hunter et al., 1978; Kempe and Helfer, 1972; Schneider, Helfer, and Pollock, 1972) and stresses during the prenatal period (Bibring, 1959; Bibring, Dwyer, and Huntington, 1961; Cohen, 1979; Gunter, 1963; McDonald, 1968; Sugarman, 1977). Stott (1973) found that low socioeconomic status was not related to poor outcome in terms of child morbidity, if there were no prenatal tension but that severe prenatal stress was more common in mothers of low social class. Williams, Williams, Griswold, and Holmes (1975) report that life stress is not related to pregnancy outcome (birthweight and severity of perinatal medical complications) in a low medical risk middle-class population but suggest that multiple life changes may be a factor in low birthweight outcome of pregnancy in lower socioeconomic groups.

It is likely that environmental factors interact in a complex manner making them difficult to control in research designs. Socioeconomic status is merely a marker for a whole cluster of attributes. Deficits in one area may be compensated for by positive experiences in another, suggesting a kind of *redundancy* in behavioral development. The real lesson to be learned from the wide range of work in this area is that intervention could be expected to be successful through a variety of mediating processes.

Although an attempt has been made to compare research efforts, interventions tend to defy classification by conceptual base because they vary on treatment mode, target of intervention, indices of risk, and length of follow-up. The sheer complexity (number of assessments, professional contacts, and services provided) of some programs makes it difficult to generalize from or replicate the programs. It is extremely important to be clear about the use of the term "risk factors". Who is at risk for which outcomes at which points in time? The most recent studies suggest that "risk" status should be assigned on the basis of summary scores rather than single factors, thus taking into consideration repeated assessments. This raises the serious question of stability of effects, a question which threatened to undermine the preschool efforts (Headstart, for example) because it was not adequately addressed prior to program implementation. The significance of any intervention depends upon its timing; in the case of low birthweight, it is tempting to assume the primacy of early experience over the course of a lifetime. When immediate effects are no longer apparent, are they no longer operative? How long do we wait to measure outcome?

Some projects screen for or identify a so-called high-risk group which then receives an intervention. Whether or not the indices of risk are valid, the method produces homogeneous groups. Homogeneity decreases within group variance and maximizes the chances of finding significant differences between single main effects. Since there is pressure to publish significant results, a homogeneous sample is preferable. There are, however, a number of low birthweight infants who do not have severe medical complications or extremely deprived home environments, and yet whose parents are equally in need of intervention and support. These "normal" tiny infants are seldom selected for study and yet may contribute heavily to the higher incidence of learning disabilities and other more moderate behavioral disturbances in the low birthweight population as a whole.

Rationale of Intervention

It is apparent from the above review that a number of factors affect premature and small infants' chances of realizing their social and developmental potential. Influences are both early and continuing—there is a dynamic equilibrium between child and environment (Sameroff, 1975). Infants who have experienced ante- or perinatal adversity in the form of medical complications may not necessarily be doomed to poor outcome if their subsequent environment encourages positive development. Similarly adults who have experienced sociocultural deprivation or family alienation do not necessarily fail as parents, if their present environment and relationships are supportive.

Infants and parents are continually modifying each other's behavior, but how successful interactions differ from destructive patterns is not fully understood. The sensorimotor development of preterm infants is thought to be differentially influenced by studies of mother–infant interaction (Ainsworth and Bell, 1974; Beckwith et al., 1976; Clarke-Stewart, 1973). The ingredients of effective interactions seem to include positive feelings, a certain degree of interest or involvement, and some ability of both partners to respond to each other. Bromwich (1976) suggests that a positive affective relationship between parent and child provides a healthy incentive for future interactions and, in fact, may be the necessary base on which parenting skills are built (Bromwich and Parmelee, 1979). Parenting skills also require some degree of sensitivity in reading and responding to infant behaviors (Goldberg, 1977; Gorski et al., 1979). Parents and infants seem to enjoy social interactions when there is some sort of mutually satisfying and reciprocal feedback going on in the system. Initially unresponsive parents may be engaged in more productive interaction if they are helped to enjoy their infants, recognize cues, and respond effectively. The Vermont group contends that these sensitivities and behaviors can be learned and are so inherently reinforcing as to lead to new behaviors.

For those unfamiliar with premature infants, a brief behavior description will be helpful. Als et al. (1979) proposed that there is a hierarchy of levels of organization in a developing infant. Preterm infants have not yet achieved integrated functioning or control over autonomic, motoric, and state regulation. Such infants can respond, but often the effort required is disorganizing and exhausting. They spend most of their time maintaining internal stability and are less available for social response early on. Gorski et al. (1979) call this the "in-turning" or physiologic stage, during which respirations, posture, and movements are poorly coordinated and controlled. An infant may appear tremulous and may tire easily when handled. "Coming out", or the first active response to the environment, usually occurs while the infant is still hospitalized. Parents receive more feedback now and can take an active part by learning the unique capacities of their individual babies. That is, infants can respond socially when they are supported and stabilized by their environments rather than when stressed and overstimulated. The final stage is termed "reciprocity" and entails full participation of the infants in social interactions such as modulated attention, visual following, and touching. At each phase of development, parents can be involved and their expectations geared to real emerging capacities.

Low birthweight infants may frustrate their parents because they tend to be unpredictable and unresponsive. They bring to the relationship:

●a disorganized, unstable, and unique behavioral repertoire composed of reflexes, different levels of tolerance to different stimuli, fleeting periods of alertness, and weak self-regulating capacities (Als et al., 1979; Gorski et al., 1979)

●the likelihood of medical complications, often entailing feeding tubes, monitors, intravenous lines, ultraviolet lights, and blindfolds—all of which function as encumbrances to parent–infant interaction.

Parents of low birthweight infants may fail to relate to their children because they often feel helpless, estranged, ineffective, and upset. They bring to the relationship:

●an inaccurate, possibly negative, perception of their infants' capacities and needs (Broussard 1979; Field, Widmayer, Stringer, and Ignatoff, 1980)

●a high level of anxiety, stemming from their grief response to an emotional crisis, inability to mother the baby, and their inexperience in handling fragile infants (Thoman, Turner, Leiderman, and Barnett, 1970; Thoman, 1975)

●a set of expectations and attitudes based on previous life experiences and sociocultural values (Minde, Marton, Manning, and Hines, 1980).

We, of the Vermont Studies Project, believe that low birthweight infants are more vulnerable than normal infants to disorganized caretaking and poorly prepared parents. The needs of the infant can be identified and met as well as possible by parents who have been taught to recognize behavioral cues. Parents who have learned to enjoy their infants and elicit some responses will feel more attached, effective, and confident. Intervention is therefore directed at the interactional experiences of the parent–child system.

Aims of the Vermont Infant Studies Project

Information gathering
The Vermont Project seeks to investigate the individual and collective relationship between *antecedent risk factors* (birthweight; gestational age; size for gestational age; sex; obstetric and perinatal complications, infant state organization), *intermediate factors* (socioeconomic status; social stress; inanimate environment and home stimulation; parental psychopathology, confidence, perception of the infant, acceptance of parenting role, and locus of control; quality of mother–infant interaction) and *outcome variables* (Infant cognitive-motivational development and temperament; parental adjustment).

Intervention
The Vermont Project seeks to develop and implement a program that will facilitate parent–infant bonding, enhance parental adjustment to caretaking, and provide the low birthweight infant with the motivational basis for later learning. An intermediate goal, *enhancement of mother–infant interaction,* is the focus and vehicle of the Mother–Infant Transaction Program (MITP). The MITP is an individualized, experiential program delivered by a pediatric nurse for 7 days prior to the infant's discharge and including 4 home visits in the first 3 months after discharge. The MITP teaches the mother according to the following behavior progression to (adapted from Bromwich, 1976):

- enjoy her infant
- be sensitive to the infant's behavioral cues and social signals
- respond to the cues promptly, effectively, and appropriately while maintaining infant organization and stability
- engage in reciprocal and mutually satisfying exchanges with the infant
- introduce new play and stimulation appropriate to the infant's organizational and developmental level

Mothers are recruited shortly after delivery but do not actually begin the program until their own infants are recuperating and in a stable medical condition. Prior to that, all mothers are encouraged to view and touch their infants. All parents have access to routine nursery social services, such as assistance with finances, lodgings, and breastpumping. There is no emphasis on "extra" stimulation; the focus is on transactions that occur naturally in the course of daily care. Each mother moves at her own pace, according to her own behavioral progression. Techniques of interaction (arousal, engagement, and consolation) are based on the stages of behavioral organization in the high-rise neonate as proposed by Als (Als et al., 1976) and Gorski (Gorski et al., 1979). An outline of MITP content appears in Appendix I. Because of the experimental nature of this research, the recipients of the intervention program are randomly selected from all those who are eligible.

Evaluation

The Vermont Project seeks to evaluate the effects of the MITP in a controlled fashion, over 12 months, in terms of the following:

- the quality of the mother-infant interaction—behavioral events are recorded with the Datamyte, a portable electronic continuous event recorder (Sidowski, 1977). Analysis utilizes frequencies, durations, sequences, and conditional probabilities.
- the infant's cognitive development and temperament—outcome measures include the Bayley Mental and Motor Development Scales (Bayley, 1969), Uzgiris-Hunt Scales of Psychological Development (Uzgiris and Hunt, 1975), and the Carey Infant Temperament Scale (Carey, 1970; Carey and McDevitt, 1977).
- parental adjustment, self-confidence, and perception of the baby—assessment utilizes the Taylor Manifest Anxiety Scale (Taylor, 1953); Broussard Infant Perception Inventory (Broussard and Hartner, 1970); Seashore Self-Confidence Scale (Seashore et al., 1973); and a semistructured interview (developed and piloted by this group).

Standardized measures have been chosen whenever possible. Administration and scoring is done by "blind" evaluators.

Sample

From the population of infants weighing less than 2,200 grams at birth and requiring intensive care at the Medical Center Hospital of Vermont over an 18 month period, two groups of 40 infants each will be randomly selected. One group receives intervention (E_1), the other does not (C_1). A second control group (C_2) of 40 normal full-term infants born at 38 weeks or later and weighing 2,500 grams or more at birth will be randomly selected and tested on all measures.

The following criteria are applied to all subjects: mothers must be over 15 years, duration of intensive care must be 10 days or more, the birth must be a single birth (twins excluded), parents must live inside a 60-mile radius of Burlington to allow access, infant must be free of severe congenital anomaly or severe neurological damage, and there must be a spouse or equivalent figure in the home.

Random assignments to groups is intended to control for variables such as socioeconomic status, infant temperament, infant behavioral state organization, gestational age, birthweight, size for gestational age, prior social stress, maternal psychopathology in response to the crisis of prematurity, maternal locus of control, and obstetric and perinatal complications. To confirm random distribution of these factors, the following measures will be applied to all cases: the Brazelton Neonatal Assessment Scale (Brazelton, 1973), the Research Obstetric Scale (ROS) (Zax, Sameroff, and Babigian, 1977), the Taylor Manifest Anxiety Scale (Taylor, 1953), the Rotter Locus of Control Questionnaire (Rotter, 1966), and a scale developed for this project and designed to record medical factors that function as encumbrances to parent–infant contact. Random assignment of mother–infant pairs to experimental (E_1) and control (C_1) groups is achieved by the toss of a coin.

An extremely high-risk group, low birthweight infants born to single, adolescent mothers, is excluded because there is an insufficient number of births in the Burlington, Vermont, area to make up 2 full groups of 20 who receive the intervention and 20 who do not. However, those who are included represent a substantial group with a variety of birthweights, medical complications, and parental characteristics, all of whom require some form of intervention.

Hypothesized Outcomes

In general, it is hypothesized that the experimental group, E_1, will demonstrate more favorable outcome than the controls, C_1, C_2, and C_3, in the following dimensions, at the times indicated:

- maternal interaction style (4, 6, and 12 months adjusted gestational age)—promptness/appropriateness; effectiveness in consoling and engaging in social interaction
- maternal personality (4, 6, and 12 months adjusted gestational age)—anxiety; perception of infant; adjustment to mothering role; self-confidence in mothering role
- paternal personality (4, 6, and 12 months adjusted gestational age)—anxiety; perception of infant
- infant outcome (6 and 12 months)—temperament; cognitive/motivational development.

Discussion: Caveats and Future Directions

The Vermont Project offers an individualized learning experience to a wide range of mothers, with varying socioeconomic status, life experiences, and coping skills. We anticipate that the population of infants served will differ substantially in medical complications, degree of physiological and motor organization, and size for gestational age. The program is not aimed at the primary prevention of premature delivery or intrauterine growth retardation, nor is it our purpose to identify high-risk mother–infant dyads and intervene with them.

It is our contention that even under the most supportive of circumstances, the task of parenting a low birthweight infant is stressful enough to justify immediate intervention. That this intervention should focus on daily mother–infant interaction follows directly from the notion that interactive styles and maternal activity levels are predictive of later infant development. Since the mother's interactive style and her level of activity with the baby influence development (Ainsworth and Bell, 1974), we have made the daily interaction of mother and infant the pivot of our program. The program does not attempt to compensate for previous adverse life experiences or to eradicate familial and environmental deficiencies.

Although the intervention program does not specifically involve fathers on a daily basis, we do not wish to neglect the father's role in early infancy. Many fathers are participating in sessions when they are available, and we are keeping a careful record of their involvement. In general, a father who chooses to be involved has a close and supportive relationship with his spouse, as described by her in the 6-month interview. Mothers are encouraged to share what they are learning with their husbands and any other significant caretakers. Since fathers are also participating in the majority of measures, we are monitoring differences and changes. Indirectly, we are hoping to positively affect fathers' adjustment and perception of the infant. Although patterns of interaction between father and infant undoubtedly have an impact on the infant's social and cognitive development, direct observations are not a part of this project. Hopefully, a future phase can include this component.

The Vermont Project currently plans to follow the adjustment and development of our subjects for 1 year, although it is hoped that funds will be obtained to follow the original cohort until they enter school. Vermont is particularly suitable for longitudinal studies because it has a stable, relatively homogeneous, and accessible population.

Although it is too soon to report any findings, the program has been well-received by mothers with very different experiences and educational backgrounds. We have designed the program so that it could be replicated by a trained nurse without great expense, and applied to the management of all low birthweight infants and their families.

References

Ainsworth, M. D. S., and Bell, S. M. Mother-infant interaction and the development of competence. In K. J. Connolly and J. S. Bruner (Eds.), *The growth of competence*. New York: Academic Press, 1974.

Als, H., Lester, B. M., and Brazelton, T. B. Dynamics of the behavioral organization of the premature infant: A theoretical perspective. In T. M. Field, A. M. Sostek, S. Goldberg, and H. H. Shuman (Eds.), *Infants born at risk*. New York: Spectrum, 1979.

Als, H., Tronick, E., and Adamson, L. The behavior of the full-term yet underweight newborn infant. *Developmental Medicine and Child Neurology*, 1976, *18*, 590–602.

Als, H., Tronick, E., and Lester, B. The Brazelton Neonatal Behavioral Assessment Scale (BNBAS). *Journal of Abnormal Child Psychology*, 1977, 5, 214–231.

Barnard, K. *A program of stimulation for infants born prematurely*. Seattle: University of Washington Press, 1975.

Barnett, C. R., Leiderman, P. H., and Grobstein, R. Neonatal separation, the maternal side of interactional deprivation. *Pediatrics*, 1970, *45*, 197–205.

Bayley, N. *Bayley Scales of Infant Development*. New York: Psychological Corporation, 1969.

Beckwith, L., and Cohen, S. E. Pre-term birth: Hazardous obstetrical and postnatal events as related to caregiver-infant behavior. *Infant Behavior and Development*, 1978, *1*, 4–21.

Beckwith, L., Cohen, S. E., Kopp, C. B., Parmelee, A. H., and Marcy, T. G. Caregiver-infant interaction and early cognitive development in preterm infants. *Child Development*, 1976, *47*, 579–587.

Bell, R. A. Contributions of human infants to caregiving and social interaction. In M. Lewis and L. A. Rosenblum (Eds.), *The effect of the infant on its caregiver*. New York: Wiley, 1974.

Benfield, D. G., Leib, S. A., and Reuter, J. Grief response of parents after referral of the critically ill newborn to a regional center. *The New England Journal of Medicine*, 1976, *294*, 975–978.

Bibring, G. Some considerations of the psychological processes in pregnancy. *Psychoanalytic Study of the Child*, 1959, *14*, 113–121.

Bibring, G., Dwyer, T. F., and Huntington, D. S. A study of the psychological processes in pregnancy of the earliest mother-child relationship. II: Methodological considerations. *Psychoanalytic Study of the Child*, 1961, *16*, 9–24.

Brazelton, T. B. Neonatal Behavioral Assessment Scale. *Clinics in developmental medicine*. Philadelphia: J. B. Lippincott, 1973.

Brazelton, T. B. Behavioral competence of the newborn infant. *Seminars in perinatology*, 1979, *3*, 35–44.

Brazelton, T. B., Koslowski, B., and Main, N. The origin of reciprocity in the mother-infant interaction. In M. Lewis and L. Rosenblum (Eds.), *The effect of the infant on its caregiver* (Vol. 1). New York: Wiley, 1971.

Broman, S. H., Nichols, P.L., and Kennedy, W. A. *Preschool I.Q.: Prenatal and early developmental correlates*. New Jersey: Lawrence Erlbaum Associates, 1975.

Bromwich, R. M. Focus on maternal behavior in infant intervention. *American Journal of Orthopsychiatry*, 1976, *46*, 439–446.

Bromwich, R. M., and Parmelee, A. H. An intervention program for pre-term infants. In T. M. Field, A. M. Sostek, S. Goldberg, and H. H. Shuman (Eds.), *Infants born at risk: Behavior and development*. New York: SP Medical and Scientific Books, 1979.

Bronfenbrenner, U. Is early intervention effective? In B. Z. Friedlander, G. M. Sterritt, and G. E. Kirk (Eds.), *Exceptional Infant* (Vol. 3). New York: Brunner/Mazel, 1975.

Broussard, E. R. Assessment of the adaptive potential of the mother-infant system: The Neonatal Perception Inventories. *Seminars in Perinatology*, 1979, *3*, 91–100.

Broussard, E. R., and Hartner, M. S. Maternal perception of neonate as related to development. *Child Psychiatry and Human Development*, 1970, *1*, 16–34.

Campbell, S. K., and Wilson, J. Planning infant learning programs. *Physical Therapy*, 1976, *56*, 1347–1357.

Caplan, G. Patterns of parental response to the crisis of premature birth: A preliminary approach to modifying mental health outcome. *Psychiatry*, 1968, *23*, 365–375.

Caplan, G., Mason, E. A., and Kaplan, D. M. Four studies of crisis in parents of prematures. *Community Mental Health Journal*, 1965, *1*, 149–161.

Caputo, D. V., Goldstein, K. M., and Taub, H. B. The development of prematurely born children through middle childhood. In T. M. Field, A. M. Sostek, S. Goldberg, and H. H. Shuman (Eds.), *Infants born at risk: Behavior and development*. New York: SP Medical and Scientific Books, 1979.

Caputo, D. V., and Mandell, W. Consequences of low birthweight. *Developmental Psychology*, 1970, *3*, 363–383.

Carey, W. B. A simplified method for measuring infant temperament. *Journal of Pediatrics*, 1970, *77*, 188–201.

Carey, W. B., and McDevitt, S. C. *Infant Temperament Questionnaire*. Revised profile and scoring sheet, 1977. Available from authors.

Carlsson, S. G., Fagerberg, H., and Horneman, G. Effects of amount of contact between mother and child on the mother's nursing behavior. *Developmental Psychobiology*, 1978, *11*, 143–150.

274 VIRGINIA A. RAUH ET AL.

Clarke-Stewart, K. A. Interaction between mothers and their young children: Characteristics and consequences. *Monographs of the Society for Research in Child Development, 38* (6–7, Serial No. 153), 1973.

Cohen, R. L. Maladaptation to pregnancy. *Seminars in Perinatology,* 1979, *3,* 15–24.

Cohen, S. E., and Beckwith, L. Maternal language in infancy. *Developmental Psychology,* 1976, *12,* 371–372.

Condon, W. S., and Sander, L. W. Neonate movement is synchronized with adult speech: Interactional participation and language acquisition. *Science,* 1974, *183,* 99–101.

Cramer, B. A mother's reactions to the birth of a premature infant. In M. W. Klaus and J. H. Kennell (Eds.), *Maternal infant bonding.* St. Louis: Mosby, 1976.

Davies, P. A. Low birthweight infants: Neurological sequelae and later intelligence. *British Medical Bulletin,* 1975, *31,* 85–91.

deChateau, P. Effects of hospital practices in synchrony in the development of the infant-parent relationship. *Seminars in Perinatology,* 1979, *3,* 45–60.

DiVitto, B., and Goldberg, S. The effects of newborn medical status on early parent-infant interaction. In T. M. Field, A. M. Sostek, S. Goldberg, and H. H. Shuman (Eds.), *Infants born at risk: Behavior and development.* New York: SP Medical and Scientific Books, 1979.

Douglas, J. W. B., and Gear, R. Children of low birthweight in the 1946 cohort: Behavior and educational achievement in adolescence. *Archives of Diseases in Childhood,* 1976, *51,* 820–826.

Dreyfuss-Brisac, C. Ontogenesis of sleep in human prematures after 32 weeks of conceptual age. *Developmental Psychobiology,* 1970, *3,* 91–121.

Drillien, C. M. A longitudinal study of the growth and development of prematurely and maturely born children. VII. Mental development from two to five years. *Archives of Diseases of the Child,* 1961, *36,* 233–240.

Drillien, C. M. *The growth and development of the prematurely born infant.* Edinburgh: Livingston, 1964.

Eaves, L. C., Nuttall, J. C., Klonoff, H., and Dunn, H. C. Developmental and psychological test scores in children of low birth weight. *Pediatrics,* 1970, *45,* 9–20.

Fanaroff, A. A., Kennell, J. H., and Klaus, M. H. Follow-up of low birthweight infants—the predictive value of maternal visiting patterns. *Pediatrics,* 1972, *49,* 288–290.

Field, T. M. Effects of early separation, interactive deficits, and experimental manipulation on infant-mother face-to-face interaction. *Child Development,* 1977, *48,* 763–772.

Field, T. M., Dempsey, J. R., and Shuman, H. H. Developmental assessments of infants surviving the respiratory distress syndrome. In T. M. Field, A. M. Sostek, S. Goldberg, and H. H. Shuman (Eds.), *Infants born at risk: Behavior and development.* New York: SP Medical and Scientific Books, 1979.

Field, T. M., Widmayer, S. M., Stringer, S., and Ignatoff, E. Teenage, lower-class, black mothers and their preterm infants: An intervention and developmental follow-up. *Child Development,* 1980, *51,* 426–436.

Fisch, R. O., Bilek, M. K., Miller, L. D., and Engel, R. R. Physical and mental status at 4 years of age for survivors of the respiratory distress syndrome. *Journal of Pediatrics,* 1975, *86,* 497–503.

Fitzhardinge, P. M., Pape, K., Arstikaitis, M., Boyle, M., Ashby, S., Rowley, A., Netley, C., and Swyer, P. R. Mechanical ventilation of infants of less than 1,501 gm birthweight: Health, growth, and neurologic sequelae. *Journal of Pediatrics*, 1976, *88*, 531–541.

Fitzhardinge, P. M., and Steven, E. M. The small-for-date infant. II. Neurological and intellectual sequelae. *Pediatrics*, 1972, *50*, 50–57.

Fraiberg, S. Blind infants and their mothers: An examination of the sign system. In M. Lewis and L. A. Rosenblum (Eds.), *The effect of the infant on its caregiver*, New York: John Wiley and Sons, 1974.

Freedman, D. G., and Boverman, H. The effects of kinesthetic stimulation on certain aspects of development in preterm infants. *American Journal of Orthopsychiatry*, 1966, *36*, 223–224.

Goldberg, S. Social competence in infancy: A model of parent-infant interaction. *Merrill-Palmer Quarterly of Behavior and Development*, 1977, *23*, 163–177.

Gorski, P. A., Davison, M. F., and Brazelton, T. B. Stages of behavioral organization in the high-risk neonate: Theoretical and clinical considerations. *Seminars in Perinatology*, 1979, *3*, 61–72.

Gottfried, A. W. Intellectual consequences of perinatal anoxia. *Psychological Bulletin*, 1973, *80*, 231–242.

Green, M., and Solnit, A. Reactions to the threatened loss of a child: A vulnerable child syndrome. *Pediatrics*, 1964, *34*, 58.

Greenberg, M., Rosenberg, I., and Lind, J. First mothers' rooming-in with their newborns: Its impact upon the mother. *American Journal of Orthopsychiatry*, 1973, *43*, 783–788.

Greenberg, N. H. A comparison of infant-mother interactional behavior in infants with atypical behavior and normal infants. In J. Hellmuth (Ed.), *Exceptional Infant* (Vol. 2). New York: Brunner/Mazel, 1971.

Gunter, L. M. Psychopathology and stress in the life experience of mothers and premature infants: A comparative study. *American Journal of Obstetrics and Gynecology*, 1963, *86*, 333–340.

Hales, D. M., Lozoff, B., and Sosa, R. Defining the limits of the maternal sensitive period. *Developmental Medicine and Child Neurology*, 1977, *19*, 454–461.

Hasselmeyer, E. G. The premature neonate's response to handling. *Journal of American Nurses' Association*, 1964, *2*, 15–24.

Hunter, R. S., Kilstrom, N., Kraybill, E. N., and Loda, F. Antecedents of child abuse and neglect in premature infants. *Pediatrics*, 1978, *61*, 629–635.

Kagan, J., and Klein, R. E. Cross-cultural perspectives on early development. *American Psychologist*, 1973, *28*, 947–961.

Kaplan, D. N., and Mason, E. A. Maternal reactions to premature birth viewed as an acute emotional disorder. *American Journal of Orthopsychiatry*, 1960, *30*, 539–552.

Kattwinkel, J., Nearman, B. S., Fanaroff, A. A., Katona, P. G., and Klaus, M. Apnea of prematurity. *Journal of Pediatrics*, 1975, *85*, 588–592.

Katz, V. Relationship between auditory stimulation and the developmental behavior of the premature infant. *Nursing Research*, 1971, *7*, 103–117.

Kempe, C. H., and Helfer, R. E. (Eds.). *Helping the battered child and his family*. Philadelphia: Lippincott, 1972.

Kennell, J. H., Gordon, D., and Klaus, M. The effects of early mother-infant separation on later maternal performance. *Pediatric Research*, 1970, *4*, 473–474.

Klaus, M. H., and Kennell, J. H. Mothers separated from their newborn infants. *Pediatric Clinics of North America*, 1970, *17*, 1015–1037.

Klein, M., and Stern, L. Low birthweight and the battered child syndrome. *American Journal of the Diseases of Childhood*, 1971, *122*, 15–18.

Knobloch, H., Rider, R., Harper, P., and Pasamanick, B. Neuropsychiatric sequelae of prematurity. *Journal of the American Medical Association*, 1956, *161*, 581–585.

Kopp, C. B., Sigman, M., and Parmelee, A. H. Neurological organization and visual fixation in infants at 40 weeks conceptual age. *Developmental Psychobiology*, 1975, *8*, 165–170.

Korner, A. F. Individual differences at birth: Implications for early experience and later development. *American Journal of Orthopsychiatry*, 1971, *41*, 608–619.

Korner, A. F., Kraemer, N. C., Faffner, M. E., and Casper, L. M. Effects of waterbed flotation on premature infants: A pilot study. *Pediatrics*, 1975, *56*, 361–367.

Kraemer, L. I., and Pierpoint, M. E. Rocking waterbeds and auditory stimuli to enhance growth of preterm infants. *Journal of Pediatrics*, 1976, *88*, 297–299.

Leifer, A. D., Leiderman, P. H., Barnett, C. R., and Williams, J. A. Effects of mother-infant separation on maternal attachment behavior. *Child Development*, 1972, *43*, 1203–1218.

Lester, B. M., and Zeskind, P. S. The organization and assessment of crying in the infant at risk. In T. Field, A. M. Sostek, S. Goldberg, and H. H. Shuman (Eds.), *Infants born at risk*. New York: Spectrum, 1979.

Lewis, M. State as an infant-environment interaction: An analysis of mother-infant interaction as a function of sex. *Merrill-Palmer Quarterly*, 1972, *18*, 95–122.

Lewis, M., and Goldberg, S. Perceptual-cognitive development in infancy: A generalized expectancy model as a function of mother-infant interaction. *Merrill-Palmer Quarterly*, 1969, *15*, 81–100.

Lewis, M., and Wilson, C. D. Infant development in lower-class American families. *Human Development*, 1972, *15*, 112–127.

Littman, B. The relationship of medical events to infant development. In T. M. Field, A. M. Sostek, S. Goldberg, and H. H. Shuman (Eds.), *Infants born at risk*. New York: Spectrum, 1979.

Littman, B., and Wooldridge, P. Caring for families of high-risk infants. *The Western Journal of Medicine*, 1976, *124*, 429–433.

Lubchenco, L. D., Delivera-Papadopoulos, M., and Searles, D. Long-term follow-up studies of prematurely born infants. II. Influence of birthweight and gestational age on sequelae. *Journal of Pediatrics*, 1972, *80*, 509–512.

Lubchenco, L. D., Horner, F. A., Reed, L. H., Hix, I. E., Metcalf, D., Cohig, R., Elliott, H. C., and Bourg, N. Sequelae of premature birth. *American Journal of Diseases of Childhood*, 1963, *106*, 101–114.

Marriage, K. J., and Davies, D. A. Neurological sequelae in children surviving mechanical ventilation in the neonatal period. *Archives of Diseases in Childhood*, 1977, *52*, 176–182.

McDonald, R. L. The role of emotional factors in obstetric complications: A review. *Psychosomatic Medicine*, 1968, *30*, 222–237.

McNeil, T. F., and Wiegerink, R. Behavioral patterns and pregnancy and birth complication histories in psychologically disturbed children. *Journal of Nervous and Mental Disease*, 1971, *152*, 315–323.

Measel, C. P., and Anderson, G. C. Nonnutritive sucking during tube feedings: Effect upon clinical course in premature infants. *Journal of Obstetrics, Gynecologic and Neonatal Nursing*, 1979, *8*, 265–272.

Minde, K. K., Marton, P., Manning, D., and Hines, B. Some determinants of mother–infant interaction in the premature nursery. *Journal of the American Academy of Child Psychiatry*, 1980, *19*, 1–21.

Neal, M. Vestibular stimulation and developmental behavior of the small premature infant. *Nursing Research Reports*, 1968, *3*, 2–5.

Osofsky, J. D., and Danzger, B. Relationships between neonatal characteristics and mother-infant interaction. *Developmental Psychology*, 1974, *10*, 124–130.

Parmelee, A. H., and Haber, A. Who is the "risk infant"? In H. J. Osofsky (Ed.), *Clinical obstetrics and gynecology*. New York: Harper and Row, 1973.

Parmelee, A. H., and Schulte, F. J. Developmental testing of pre-term and small-for-date infants. *Pediatrics*, 1970, *45*, 21–28.

Parmelee, A. H., Wenner, W. H., Akiyama, Y., Schultz, M., and Stern, E. Sleep states in premature infants. *Developmental Medicine and Child Neurology*, 1967, *9*, 70–77.

Powell, L. F. The effect of extra stimulation and maternal involvement on the development of low-birthweight infants and on maternal behavior. *Child Development*, 1974, *45*, 106–113.

Prechtl, H. F. R., Theorell, K., and Blair, A. W. Behavioral state cycles in abnormal infants. *Developmental Medicine and Child Neurology*, 1973, *15*, 606–617.

Ramey, C. T., Starr, R. H., Pallas, J., Whitten, C. I., and Reed, V. Nutrition, response-contingent stimulation, and the maternal deprivation syndrome: Results of an early intervention program. *Merrill-Palmer Quarterly*, 1975, *21*, 45–54.

Rice, R. Neurophysiological development in premature infants following stimulation. *Developmental Psychology*, 1977, *13*, 69–76.

Ringler, N. M., Kennell, J. H., Jarvella, R., Navojosky, B. J., and Klaus, M. H. Mother-to-child speech at two years—effect of early postnatal contact. *Journal of Pediatrics*, 1975, *86*, 141–144.

Rotter, J. B. Generalized expectancies for internal vs. external control of reinforcement. *Psychological Monographs*, 1966, *80*, Whole No. 609, 1–28.

Rubin, R. A., Rosenblatt, C., and Balon, B. Psychological and educational sequelae of prematurity. *Pediatrics*, 1973, *52*, 352–363.

Sameroff, A. J. Early influences on development: Fact or fancy? *Merrill-Palmer Quarterly*, 1975, *21*, 267–294.

Sameroff, A. J., and Chandler, M. J. Reproductive risk and the continuum of caretaking casualty. In F. D. Horowitz (Ed.), *Review of child development research* (Vol. 4). Chicago: University of Chicago Press, 1975.

Scarr-Salapatek, S., and Williams, M. L. The effects of early stimulation on low birthweight infants. *Child Development*, 1973, *44*, 94–101.

Schmitt, B. D., and Kempe, C. H. Neglect and abuse of children. In V. C. Vaughan and R. J. McKay (Eds.), *Nelson textbook of pediatrics*. Philadelphia: Saunders, 1975.

Schneider, C., Helfer, R. E., and Pollock, C. The predictive questionnaire: A preliminary report. In C. H. Kempe and R. E. Helfer (Eds.), *Helping the battered child and his family*. Philadelphia: Lippincott, 1972.

Seashore, M. J., Leifer, A. D., Barnett, C. R., and Leiderman, P. N. The effects of denial of early mother-infant interaction on maternal self-confidence. *Journal of Personality and Social Psychology*, 1973, *26*, 369–375.

Sepkaski, C., Coll, C. G., and Lester, B. M. *The effects of high-risk factors on neonatal behavior as measured by the Brazelton Scale.* Paper presented at the biennial meetings of the Society for Research in Child Development, New Orleans, 1977.

Shaheen, E., Alexander, D., Truskowsky, M., and Barbero, G. Failure to thrive—a retrospective profile. *Clinical Pediatrics,* 168, 7, 255–264.

Sidowski, J. B. Special report section—observational research methods: Portable event recording systems. Observational research: Some instrumented systems for scoring and storing behavioral data. *Behavior Research Methods and Instrumentation,* 1977, 9, 403–404.

Sigman, M., and Parmelee, A. H. Longitudinal evaluation of the preterm infant. In T. M. Field, A. M. Sostek, S. Goldberg, and H. H. Shuman (Eds.), *Infants born at risk.* New York: Spectrum Books, 1979.

Siqueland, E. R. Biological and experiential determinants of exploration in infancy. In L. J. Stone, J. T. Smith, and L. B. Murphy (Eds.), *The competent infant.* New York: Basic Books, 1973.

Smith, A. C., Flick, G. L., Ferriss, G. S., and Sellmann, A. H. Prediction of developmental outcome at seven years from prenatal, perinatal, and postnatal events. *Child Development,* 1972, 43, 495–507.

Solkoff, N., Weintraub, D., Yaffe, S., and Blase, B. Effects of handling on the subsequent development of premature infants. *Developmental Psychology,* 1969, 1, 765–769.

Sostek, A. M., Quinn, P. D., and Davitt, M. K. Behavior, development and neurologic status of premature & fullterm infants with varying medical complications. In T. M. Field, A. M. Sostek, S. Goldberg, and H. H. Shuman (Eds.), *Infants born at risk.* New York: Spectrum, 1979.

Stern, L. Prematurity as a factor in child abuse. *Hospital Practice,* 1973, 117–123.

Stott, D. H. Follow-up study from birth of the effects of prenatal stresses. *Developmental Medicine and Child Neurology,* 1973, 15, 770–787.

Sugarman, M. Paranatal influences on maternal-infant attachment. *American Journal of Orthopsychiatry,* 1977, 47, 407–421.

Taylor, J. A. A personality scale of manifest anxiety. *Journal of Abnormal Social Psychology,* 1953, 48, 285–290.

Thoman, E. B. Development of synchrony in mother-infant interaction in feeding and other situations. *Federation Proceedings,* 1975, 34, 1587–1592.

Thoman, E. B., Turner, A. M., Leiderman, P. H., and Barnett, C. R. Neonate-mother interaction: Effects of parity on feeding behavior. *Child Development,* 1970, 41, 1103–1111.

Thomas, A., Chess, S., and Birch, H. G. *Temperament and behavior disorders in children.* New York: New York University Press, 1968.

Tulkin, S. R. An analysis of the concept of cultural deprivation. *Developmental Psychology,* 1972, 6, 326–339.

Tulkin, S. R. Social class differences in maternal and infant behavior. In P. H. Leiderman, S. R. Tulkin, and A. Rosenfeld (Eds.), *Culture and infancy: Variations in the human experience.* New York: Academic Press, 1977.

Tulkin, S. R., and Cohler, B. J. Child-rearing attitudes and mother-child interaction in the first year of life. *Merrill-Palmer Quarterly,* 1973, 19, 95–106.

Tulkin, S. R., and Kagan, J. Mother-child interaction in the first year of life. *Child Development,* 1972, 43, 31–41.

Uzgiris, I. C., and Hunt, J. M. *Assessment in infancy: Ordinal scales of psychological development.* Chicago: University of Illinois Press, 1975.

Wachs, T. D., Uzgiris, I.C., and Hunt, J. M. Cognitive development in infants of different age levels and from different environmental backgrounds: An explanatory investigation. *Merrill-Palmer Quarterly,* 1971, *17,* 283–317.

Wallace, H. M. Factors associated with perinatal mortality and morbidity. In E. M. Gold (Ed.), *Clinical obstetrics and gynecology.* New York: Harper and Row, 1970.

Werner, E. E., Bierman, J. M., and French, F. E. *The children of Kauai: A longitudinal study from the prenatal period to age ten.* Honolulu: University Press of Hawaii, 1971.

White, J., and Labarba, R. The effects of tactile and kinesthetic stimulation on neonatal development in the premature infant. *Developmental Psychology,* 1976, *9,* 569–577.

Wiener, G. The relationship of birthweight and length of gestation to intellectual development at ages 8–10 years. *Journal of Pediatrics,* 1970, *76,* 694–699.

Wiener, G., Rider, R. V., and Oppel, W. Correlates of low birthweight: Psychological status at 6–7 years of age. *Pediatrics,* 1965, *35,* 431–444.

Wiener, G., Rider, R. V., Oppel, W. C., and Harper, P. A. Correlates of low birthweight: Psychological status at eight to ten years of age. *Pediatric Residents,* 1968, *2,* 110–127.

Williams, C. C., Williams, A., Griswold, M. S., and Holmes, T. H. Pregnancy and life change. *Journal of Psychosomatic Research,* 1975, *19,* 123–129.

Yarrow, L. J., Rubenstein, J., and Pedersen, R. *Infant and environment: Early cognitive and motivational development.* New York: John Wiley and Sons, 1975.

Zax, M., Sameroff, A. J., and Babigian, H. M. Birth outcome in the offspring of mentally disordered women. *American Journal of Orthopsychiatry,* 1977, *47,* 218–230.

Appendix 1

Outline of Mother–Infant Transaction Program*

DAY 1. *Introduction:* Getting acquainted with the baby

DAY 2. *Homeostatic Systems:* How the baby feels
- Respiration
- Facial movement
- Skin circulation
- Visceral activity
- Automatically mediated movement

DAY 3. *Motor System:* How the baby moves
- Posture
- Tone
- Movement

DAY 4. *State Observation and Regulation:* How the mother can enhance organization
- Predominant states
- State changes
- Consolability

DAY 5. Attention-Interaction System: How the mother can engage her baby and sustain an interaction
- Attention and alertness
- Responsivity

DAY 6. *Recognizing and Responding to Cues:* Facilitating daily care
- Waking
- Changing
- Feeding
- Bathing

*Details of the program are available from the authors.

DAY 7. *Initiating Activity:* Getting ready for play at home
- Alerting
- Timing and methods

FIRST HOME VISIT. *Consolidation and Adjustment* (3 days after discharge)

SECOND HOME VISIT. *Mutual Enjoyment Through Play* (2 weeks after discharge)
- Visual
- Auditory
- Tactile

THIRD HOME VISIT. *Temperamental Patterns* (1 month after discharge)
- Activity level
- Rhythmicity
- Approach-withdrawal
- Adaptability
- Intensity
- Thresholds
- Mood
- Distractibility
- Attention span

FOURTH HOME VISIT. *Review of Program and Termination*

Beyond Bonding:
A Family-Centered Approach to Enhancing Early Parent-Infant Relations

Jay Belsky and Joanne Benn

Since the late 1960s, there has been a virtual explosion in research on the parent–infant relationship, with much of it geared toward identifying those aspects of parenting which foster optimal infant functioning. Although the majority of this work has centered on the mother–infant dyad, recently investigators have begun to direct attention to the role of the father during infancy. As we intend to demonstrate in the course of this chapter, this inclusion of father in the study of infancy has dramatic implications for both our understanding of early parent–child relationships and the design of early intervention programs.

Despite the vast quantity of research examining the characteristics and consequences of the early parent–child relationship, the results of these observational studies can be summarized in fairly brief compass. This is because the major findings of this body of literature are surprisingly consistent. Specifically, in the realm of cognitive/motivational functioning, detailed studies of mother–infant interaction highlight the positive role played by attentive, warm, stimulating, responsive, and nonrestrictive mothering in fostering intellectual development (Beckwith, 1971; Beckwith, Cohen, Kopp, Parmelee, and Marcy, 1976; Carew, Chan, and Halfar, 1975 Clarke-Stewart, 1973, 1978; Engel and Keane, 1975; Lewis and Goldberg, 1969; Rubenstein, 1967; Tulkin and Covitz, 1975; Wachs, 1976; Yarrow, 1976; Yarrow, Rubenstein, and Pedersen, 1975). The positive influence of similar maternal styles has also been noted with respect to healthy social and emotional development (Clarke-Stewart, 1975). Infants whose mothers are nurturant, responsive to their needs, and accepting of their limits as immature organisms tend to develop secure attachments to their caregivers and to be cooperative and communicatively skillful (Ainsworth, 1973; Ainsworth, Bell, and Stayton, 1971; Stayton, Hogan, and Ainsworth, 1971). In brief, it is sensitive mothering, evidencing appropriate responsiveness to infant cues, that fosters optimal development.

The significance of such a caregiving style has recently been underscored by several studies demonstrating that one of the products of maternal sensitivity, a secure infant–parent attachment, forecasts skill in problem solving and peer competence when children are 2 and 5 years of age (Arend, Gove, and Sroufe, 1979; Matas, Arend, and Sroufe, 1978; Sroufe, 1979). Block and Block (1979) have shown, moreover, that the kinds of skills assessed during the preschool years by Sroufe and his students are conceptually and empirically related to competence displayed across a wide variety of contexts during the elementary school years. These findings strengthen the argument that sensitivity is *the* influential dimension of mothering in infancy. It not only fosters healthy psychological functioning during this developmental epoch but it also lays the foundation upon which future experience will build.

Less explicit conclusions can be drawn from the relatively recent literature on fathering. The one characteristic of fathering that has emerged repeatedly as being influential, however, is general paternal involvement; this has been so whether investigators have focused upon social and emotional relations with father (Kotelchuck, 1975; Pedersen and Robson, 1969; Ross, Kagan, Zelazo, and Kotelchuck, 1972; Spelke, Zelazo, Kagan, and Kotelchuck, 1972) or upon cognitive/motivational development (Belsky, 1980a; Clarke-Stewart, 1978; Pedersen, Rubenstein, and Yarrow, 1979; Wachs, Uzgiris, and Hunt, 1971). There is some suggestion that a father's play behavior may be particularly influential (Parke, 1978), that he may exert greater influence on sons than on daughters (Pedersen et al., 1979), and that he may influence his children by drawing them into a world beyond an intimate relationship with the mother (Belsky, 1980a).

It is important to point out that research on parental influences on infant development is limited in several ways. Most critical is the fact that almost all data summarized above are from correlational studies. And the fact that many of these investigations are longitudinal means that they cannot guarantee the identification of actual cause-and-effect relations. Simply because measures of association are calculated between assessments of parental behavior and infant functioning at different points in time does not ensure that the first measure caused the second, as many reports imply. This criticism applies to investigations using cross-lag panel correlational strategies (e.g., Clarke-Stewart, 1973), since there is some indication that such techniques are inappropriate for drawing conclusions regarding causality (for an extended discussion of this issue, see Rogosa, 1979).

Despite this serious methodological weakness, there are good reasons to believe that the conclusions drawn regarding parental influences on infant development are sound and will be substantiated as more definitive analyses are carried out in future studies. Interpretations of the data have credibility for three reasons: the results of the correlational studies done to date have been remarkably consistent (even across divergent samples and data collection strategies); some findings have been confirmed by experimental analyses (e.g., Belsky, Goode, and Most, 1980; Riksen-Walraven, 1978; Ramey and Finkelstein, 1978; Watson and Ramey, 1972); and, most important, they make theoretical sense. Sensitive caregiving enables the infant to develop the trust that the world is a warm and caring place that functions in an orderly manner. The fact that it is also responsive teaches children that their actions have consequences, thus motivating subsequent activity. Restrictions, in contrast, squelch the curiosity that motivates learning and that thrives in a stimulating environment. Thus, it is not surprising that it is infants whose caregivers are sensitive to their cues, responsive to their actions, stimulating, and not too restrictive whom the literature identifies as most likely to develop optimally during the first years of life.

Although the available data do not definitively demonstrate that caregiving patterns during infancy are the sole or even primary determinants of later functioning, they do suggest that to the extent that parental sensitivity and involvement can be promoted, healthy psychological development in the early years may be enhanced. As we consider family intervention efforts, then, our concerns center on the question: "Can sensitivity and involvement be promoted and, if so, when might efforts at enhancement prove most successful?" Recent research in pediatrics and developmental psychology suggests that the newborn period may represent a time when caregiving can be positively influenced.

Early Mother–Infant Contact: A Critical Appraisal

Drawing upon observations that certain animals exhibit complex, species-specific patterns of mother–newborn interaction (Rheingold, 1963; Rosenblatt and Siegel, 1975) and upon data indicating that when these patterns are disturbed in some species through the separation of mother and newborn subsequent caregiving failure often results, a group of investigators at Case Western Reserve University initiated a series of researches to explore the characteristics and consequences of early mother–neonate contact among humans (Hales, Lozoff, Sosa, and Kennell, 1977; Kennell, Jerauld, Wolf, Chesler, Kreger, McAlpine, Steffa, and Klaus, 1974; Klaus, Jerauld, Kreger, McAlpine, Steffa, and Kennell, 1972; Klaus, Kennell, Plumb, and Zuehlke, 1970; Ringler, Kennell, Jarvella, Navojosky, and Klaus, 1975). Noting that standard hospital practices resulted in minimal contact between mother and newborn, Klaus,

Kennell, and their colleagues modified the established procedures to allow mothers to have their naked infants with them for approximately an hour shortly after delivery and for several hours daily thereafter. Randomly assigned control groups experienced the usual practice in American hospitals—a glance at their baby shortly after birth; a short visit 6 to 12 hours after birth for identification purposes, and then 20 to 30 minute visits for feeding every 4 hours during the day.

The results of these early experiments are in line with much of the animal research. First, mothers of full-term babies in the extended contact group showed an "orderly progression of behavior" (Klaus et al., 1970; Klaus, Trause, and Kennell, 1975). Starting with fingertip touch on the infants' extremities, the mothers proceeded in 4 to 8 minutes to massage the babies' trunks with their palms. Mothers in the extended contact group also showed a remarkable increase in the time spent in the "en face" position after only 4 to 5 minutes of contact.

Second, when mother–infant dyads were observed feeding at 1 month, the mothers in the extended-contact group showed significantly more soothing, fondling, and eye-to-eye-exchange (Klaus et al., 1972). At 1 year these same mothers evidenced *what might be considered more maternal behaviors* when seen in the physician's office for the infant's regular check-up. They not only were more likely to stand beside their babies on the examining table, but they also more frequently soothed them when they cried (Kennell et al., 1974). Further, during an interview, mothers in the extended contact group expressed greater inclination to pick up their infants when they were distressed and more reluctance and anxiety about leaving the baby in someone else's care (Klaus et al., 1972).

While these findings clearly suggest that early contact may enhance the quality of the mother-infant relationship, additional follow-up data on these families leads us to question the enduring nature of these early effects. Although many cite Ringler et al.'s (1975) investigation of maternal verbal behavior 2 years postpartum as evidence of the long-lasting positive influence of early contact (Klaus and Kennell, 1976; Kennell, Voos, and Klaus, 1979), we have reason to question this interpretation. It is simply not clear to us why using more adjectives and words per preposition, and fewer commands and content words, diagnoses an enhanced parent–child relationship as Ringler et al. (1975) suggest. Moreover, it is not clear how many statistical comparisons were made in this investigation before these potentially chance early-contact/regular-contact group differences emerged from the statistical analyses reported.

In addition to the reports by Klaus, Kennell and their colleagues concerning a group of Cleveland mother–baby pairs, a number of other investigations of early contact has been found to be positively related to a variety of measures of the early mother–infant relationship, including physical affection during the first feeding interaction (Gaulin-Kremer, Shaw, and Thoman, 1977), during breast feeding on the second and fourth postpartum days (Carlsson, Fagerberg, Horneman, Hwang, Rodholm, Schaller, Danielsson, and Gundewall, 1978), and during mother–infant interaction on the third postpartum day (Hales et al., 1977); the maintenance of breast feeding through 2 months of age (Winters, 1973; Sousa, Barros, Gazalle, Begeres, Pinheiro, Menezes, and Arruda, 1974; both cited in Kennell et al., 1979) and through the first year of life (Sousa, Kennell, Klaus, and Urrutia, 1977; deChateau, 1976); and to maternal affectional behavior (e.g., kissing, fondling, and looking en face) in the home at 3 months postpartum and infant crying, smiling, and laughing at this time (deChateau and Wiberg, 1977).

Several more recent attempts to replicate the original Cleveland studies, however, cast doubt upon the potency of early skin-to-skin contact in the postpartum period. In a follow-up study of one report cited earlier, Carlsson, Fagerberg, Horneman, Hwang, Larsson, Rodholm, Schaller, Danielsson, and Gundewall, (1979) observed 50 of 62 mother–infant pairs initially seen during the first postpartum week when infants were 6 weeks of age. No significant differences were discerned between dyads randomly assigned to various early contact treatments on 18 individually coded maternal–infant behaviors or on summary measures based on conceptual and statistical clusterings of those individual behavior scores. Moreover, interviews with mothers regarding breastfeeding, father involvement, and caretaking failed to reveal any early-contact effects. These results led the investigators to question both the reliability and the magnitude of experimental/control group differences in other early contact studies (Schaller, Carlsson, and Larsson, 1979). In fact, Schaller et al. observed that only 3 of 35 behavior categories revealed group differences in deChateau and Wiberg's (1977) work, raising the strong possibility that early contact effects may be merely statistical artifacts (chance results), as we suggested earlier.

In another recent study focusing on the long-term effects of early mother–infant contact, Ottaviano, Campbell, and Taylor (1979) examined the quality of mother-infant attachment when infants were 1 year of age. Results indicated that 25 infants who had received extra contact during the postpartum period were no more likely to be classified as securely attached to their mothers when seen in the Ainsworth and Wittig (1969) Strange Situation than were a group of 15 infants who received regular postpartum contact. Neither did mothers randomly assigned to the early contact treatments appraise their infant's temperaments differently during the eighth postpartum month (Campbell, Maloni, and Taylor, 1979). Regardless of time of initial mother–infant contact, infants were equally likely to be categorized as easy or difficult to care for on the basis of maternal responses on the Carey Scales of Infant Temperament (Carey, 1970)

These "nonresults" seem especially important in light of the fact that some group differences favoring the early-contact dyads were discerned in this investigation during observations of feeding interaction when the study subjects were 2 days and 1 month of age (Taylor, Taylor, Campbell, Maloni, and Dickey, 1979). The fact, though, that such positive effects were restricted to mother–male infant dyads, were not corroborated by maternal perceptions of her infant or expressed concern for her child during the first postpartum month, and did not translate into any discernible benefits for the child in the latter half of the first year of life (see above), leads us to question the ultimate significance of early contact even in studies reporting positive effects.

The Process of Influence

What remains unclear in all the aforementioned research, whether showing positive or no effects of early contact, is the actual or hypothesized *process* by which early contact is presumed to facilitate maternal sensitivity and involvement and, ultimately, infant development. Klaus and Kennell (1976) propose a process they have termed "bonding" which is reminiscent of Lorenz's (1957) notion of imprinting. Specifically, they argue that there may exist a species-wide sensitive period during which mothers are physiologically primed to psychologically attach themselves to, or invest themselves in, their newborns. In support of this claim they cite the earlier-summarized evidence from animal research demonstrating that when goats and sheep are separated from their newborns immediately after parturition, they will refuse to provide the care required to ensure survival during subsequent encounters with their offspring (Hersher, Moore, and Richmond, 1958; Moore, 1968; Rosenblatt, 1965).

Much criticism has been directed against such an explanation. Lozoff (1977), for example, has pointed out that throughout 99 percent of our evolutionary history, humans have lived in hunting and gathering societies in which early contact of the variety believed to promote bonding could not have been the norm. Indeed, she notes that current evidence on primitive societies indicates that during the newborn period, and especially the immediate postpartum period, mothers and babies are often routinely separated. Such observations raise doubts about both the necessity and the species-wide nature of early mother–infant contact and bonding.

Consideration of Gibson's (1969) theory of perceptual learning and development not only suggests that nonbiological and noninstinctual processes may account for some of the observed effects of early and extended contact but, in so doing, that alternative procedures can be deployed in the newborn period to facilitate parental sensitivity to, and involvement with, the infant. At the core of Gibson's theorizing is the assumption that stimuli contain information that must be "picked up" if they are to be perceived. The process by which information is picked up is gradual and entails the recognition of "distinctive features" of the stimulus, that is, its most information-rich aspects. Opportunity to actively engage stimulus materials facilitates perceptual learning by revealing these "distinctive features".

When this model of perceptual learning is applied to the early contact data, it suggests that opportunity for early contact with the newborn may initiate a process of parental familiarization or orientation which heightens awareness of the distinctive features of the newborn. In this regard, it is interesting to note that descriptions of mother–infant interaction during early contact emphasize the systematic manner in which mothers explore the bodies of their naked newborns (Klaus et al., 1970, 1975). At a more intrapsychic level, the clinical work of Greenberg and Morris (1974) indicates that early paternal contact across the baby's first 3 days of life enhances father's preoccupation with and interest in, the child. More specifically, strong feelings of attraction, elation, and self-esteem seem to derive from fathers' visual and tactile contact with the infant and their ability to identify the baby's distinct characteristics.

From a Gibsonian point of view, it can be argued that mothers are actually engaging in a process of perceptual learning in the course of early contact which heightens awareness of the complex nature of the newborn, which subsequently translates into maternal sensitivity in caring for the infant. In other words, sensitivity is derived from an understanding and appreciation of the young infant which itself is fostered by early contact. This discussion does not presume, of course, that sensitivity is derived solely from a heightened awareness of the complex nature of the newborn. Undoubtedly, other factors influence the development of sensitivity also (e.g., maternal personality).

In sum, what the above analysis suggests is that is is not skin-to-skin contact per se that is potentially influential—as emphasized by Klaus and Kennell (1976)—but rather that it is what transpires during early contact: namely, perceptual learning that is fostered by mother–infant *interaction*. Both conceptual and empirical support can be found for this contention. In evaluating the care of all newborns, Barnett, Leiderman, Grobstein, and Klaus (1970) proposed that a "continuum of interactive deficit" characterizes the range of experiences of mothers during the newborn period. In the case of the incubated high-risk neonate, the deficit is large. In the case of the normal infant this deficit is small. The fact that such a deficit, however limited, is created through the course of standard maternity care, which routinely separates mother and newborn in the immediate postpartum period, may account for some of the positive effects of the aforementioned studies of early contact and bonding.

At an empirical level, a recent analysis of the "process" of intervention in the original Cleveland investigation (Kennell et al., 1974) provides evidence to support this interactional model of the so-called bonding phenomenon under discussion. Upon examining still photos taken every 30 seconds during the skin-to-skin contact episodes and audio tape recordings of these sessions, Trause (1977) identified two subgroups *within* the experimental group (i.e., the early contact group). Mothers in one subgroup, who might be appropriately labeled the "functional experimentals", remained awake throughout the early contact session. In contrast, mothers in the other subgroup (the "nonfunctional experimentals") fell asleep. Not surprisingly, these latter mothers touched, looked at and spoke to their babies less during the experimental contact period. Subsequently these mothers engaged in less en face and fondling behavior during the 1 month follow-up observation of a feeding session than did their counterparts who remained awake and interacted more with their newborns during the initial contact episode. In fact, these "nonfunctional" experimental mothers were not significantly different from the control mothers who received no early contact with their newborns in the immediate postpartum period. Thus, the widely reported difference between early contact and control groups seems to have been a function of the subgroup of experimental mothers who remained awake and interacted with their babies.

In view of some of the previously mentioned long-term benefits associated with early contact at 1 year (Kennell et al., 1974), it is important to note that these experimental subgroup differences extended beyond the 1-month assessment. At the 12-month follow-up, Trause (1977) found that the mothers who displayed more fondling behavior at 1 month were more likely to soothe their distressed infants during their babies' physical examinations. Additionally, those mothers who engaged in more en face interaction during the 1-month feeding assessment talked to their 1 year olds more frequently during a free play laboratory assessment of mother–infant interaction. Thus, it appears that the interaction that took place during the initial early contact phase of the experiment, and not the skin-to-skin contact per se, was what was influential during these immediate postpartum "bonding" sessions.

Additional support for this conclusion comes indirectly from one of the most impressive studies to date that has attempted to enhance positively the development of the mother–infant relationship by modifying hospital maternity care. O'Connor, Vietze, Hopkins, and Altemeier (1977) and O'Connor, Sherrod, Sandler, and Vietze (1978) reported experimentally manipulating rooming-in to be associated with a decreased incidence of parenting failure. Specifically, only one case of child maltreatment was reported among 143 low-income mother–infant pairs randomly assigned to room-in, as compared with 9 cases among 158 dyads provided with traditional nursery care which separated mother and baby except during scheduled feedings. Since rooming-in affords mother and baby extended periods of time together, and thus extra time to interact and "get to know" one another, it seems reasonable to argue that the group differences discerned in this investigation were a function of the minimal interactive deficit experienced by the rooming-in dyads.

The fact that O'Connor et al. (1977, 1978) could show such pronounced effects of rooming-in, which does not guarantee close physical contact in the first hour of life, suggests to us that we are not dealing with a critical period phenomenon of the kind which Kennell and Klaus believed to exist. This is not to say, however, that parents cannot be assisted in developing optimal relationships with their children in the first hours or days of life. We believe they can, but we do not believe such assistance is mandatory for the development of healthy parent–infant relationships or must come at a certain delimited time. In all likelihood, if the appropriate strategies of intervention can be identified, parents will prove susceptible to influence when their children are a variety of ages. The contribution of Kennell and Klaus that we consider to be most important is the attention they draw to one of these periods—the neonatal period.

Critical Life Events as Opportunities for Enhancement: The Case of the Neonatal Period

Recent work in both community and life-span developmental psychology suggests that the newborn period, and the transition to parenthood more generally, may be an optimal time for effecting change in the family. This is because this time period qualifies as a major life transition, that is, a period of life involving stress and requiring significant alteration in customary life patterns (Holmes and Rahe, 1967; Hultsch and Plemons, 1979), including both role transition and status change (Antonovsky and Kats, 1967; Myers, Lindenthal, Pepper, and Ostrander, 1972). Consider here the fact that the life event defined by the transition to parenthood involves commitment to bear and raise a child, high levels of physical and psychological investment associated with pregnancy and delivery, and the real and symbolic changes that accompany the addition of a small, relatively helpless, and extremely demanding new member to the family unit. There are also the real changes that undoubtedly occur in day-to-day living and require adjustment. From everyone's perspective, then, be they mother, father, husband, wife, or infant, the process of adding a new member to the family represents an event of some magnitude.

The notion of process should be underscored, here, as it must be recognized that while the transition to parenthood is eventful, and actually occurs rather abruptly, the experience of parenthood is not shortlived. Indeed, it is irrevocable. This life event thus qualifies as a process event, since it extends over a rather lengthy period of time.

The deeper implications of the birth of a new baby, especially for first-time parents, is revealed by a related concept, that of "marker event". As LeMasters (1957) noted in the first transition-to-parenthood study, this family experience represents for many the final step into adulthood, with requirements of lifelong responsibility. It is no wonder, then, that Guttman (1975) observed that across cultures parenthood often plays a pivotal role in the life span, giving shape and meaning to a variety of tasks of adulthood. Consider, for example, the implications of becoming a parent for Freud's two-component model of psychological wellbeing—love and work. For some couples the shared creation of life tightens bonds of love, intimacy, and commitment, while for others it no doubt weakens or possibly even destroys such emotional ties. Like marriage, work too can be affected by the transition to parenthood. Parents may strive to increase their productivity, gain promotions on the job or merely maintain the security of their employment to guarantee an adequate standard of living for their dependent offspring. In the home, parenthood may stimulate changes in the division of labor (Lamb, 1978), which may not always prove mutually acceptable to husband and wife.

This appraisal of the transition to parenthood demonstrates that this life event is of some significance to both individual and family functioning. Serious consideration of the changing demographics of the American population suggests that it is also of consequence to the communities in which we live and to our way of life. If present trends continue, life spans will remain lengthy and birth rates will remain low. Consequently, the years to come will be marked as a time when fewer and fewer young will be available to provide for the care and economic wellbeing of the ever-increasing number of aged. We must be alert to the fact, then, that the societal cost of "wasting" human resources will increase, with risk of irreparably weakening our nation for when the quality of children's care is comprised, the tendency is to produce unproductive adults who become burdens rather than resources to their communities. From an intervention standpoint, our obligation should be self-evident: to support families as they add new members and, by so doing, enhance the developmental experience that children will have as they grow up.

This imperative demands an entirely new way of looking at life events as they influence mental health. Indeed, disease models which stress the debilitating nature of life events (Dohrenwend, 1973; Dohrenwend and Dohrenwend, 1974, Holmes and Rahe, 1974; Holmes and Masuda, 1974) must be abandoned in favor of perspectives that envision developmental opportunity in transitions throughout the life course. Danish (1977) and others have offered such a perspective, as they view life events as critical opportunities to restructure the life course and thereby stimulate growth. Enhancement, or optimization, rather than prevention or remediation becomes the focus or goal of intervention (Baltes and Danish, 1980; Baltes, Reese, and Nesselroade, 1979; Danish, 1977; Danish and D'Augelli, 1980; Danish, Smyer, and Nowak, 1980). And experiences become universally available rather than being restricted to a select few— usually the at risk or already damaged. Stigmatization is thereby avoided, and one of the greatest roadblocks to effective intervention is removed.

While this analysis of life events and the transition to parenthood suggests that the newborn period may represent an ideal time for promoting individual and family functioning, it happens to be the case that most interventions at this time are neither enhancement-oriented nor family-focused. The usual strategy is to deal with special populations of children in hopes of preventing later problems (e.g., stimulation programs for low birthweight infants) and to direct efforts solely towards the mother–infant dyad (e.g., mother–infant bonding). In what follows, we describe a program of intervention that recognizes that: (1) the newborn period is a special time for *all* families, not just those with infants at risk for developmental problems; and (2) that the family is a social unit comprising several individuals and relationships in addition to the mother–infant dyad. Our approach to intervention in the newborn period can be characterized, then, as both family-centered and enhancement oriented.

An Alternative Approach to Intervention in the Newborn Period

The preceding analysis of life events as focal points for intervention efforts and the work on bonding reviewed earlier draws attention to the newborn period as a time for attempting to influence family functioning. However, our critical analysis of the process of influence in bonding studies leads us to believe that more is required than mere skin-to-skin contact or time together if we hope to foster healthy parent–infant relations at this time. Indeed, it is our working hypothesis that such early experience in the hospital is only effective to the extent that it reveals the complexity and intriguing nature of the infant and, thereby, serves to stimulate the parent's fascination with the baby. Once the parent's interest is captured, interaction will occur and, in most cases, sensitive and growth-promoting, parent–infant relations will develop. Infant competence, we know, is a natural consequence of such processes.

If this analysis is valid, there is reason to believe that procedures designed specifically to foster parent–neonate interaction and to promote parental awareness of the complexity and distinctive features of the newborn should serve to enhance parent–infant relations and infant development. The work we are presently carrying out is designed to test this assumption. Before describing it, we report the results of several intervention efforts that have adopted an approach similar, but not identical, to that which we are presently testing. All this work, like our own, draws upon the Brazelton Neonatal Behavioral Assessment Scale (BNBAS) (Brazelton, 1973) as a tool for highlighting the complexity of the newborn. For those unfamiliar with the exam, the BNBAS comprises some 47 items (27 behavioral and 20 reflex) geared toward eliciting reflex, orienting, and interactive responses from the neonate. Items include, for example, shaking a rattle to see if the baby can habituate to redundant auditory stimulation; disturbing the child to determine its ability to quiet itself; and moving a bright object across the infant's visual field to see if it can track.

In two early studies Kang (1974) and Ryan (1973) employed demonstrations of related BNBAS test items to inform mothers of the capabilities of their newborns. Both investigators reported that mothers who had observed a neonatal assessment in the first 2 weeks of their infants' lives were more positively oriented toward their babies when the child was 1 month of age than were mothers who had not had such experience. Given the limited size of experimental and control groups in these two studies ($n = 5$), as well as limitations in data analysis and methodology, and the complete absence of any follow-up past the first month of life, the results can only be considered suggestive of the potential positive impact that maternal exposure to the Brazelton exam may have on the subsequent development of the caregiver–infant relationship.

In a more complex study conducted by Anderson (1979), 30 mothers either (1) observed their infants being assessed on the Brazelton (demonstration group); (2) were verbally informed of the nature of the exam and of their infants' performance (information only group); or (3) received instruction on the selection and purchase of infant furnishings (control group). Given the potential for Hawthorne effects in this kind of experimental research, the nature of the "treatment" administered to the control group is important, and indeed represents a strength of the study, since it controls for the potential influence of simply providing something extra or special to mothers in the other two groups. Pre- and postintervention comparisons of maternal reciprocity during a feeding session revealed that although the demonstration group displayed less reciprocity than did the control group on the baby's second day of life (pretest), these experimental mothers exceeded the controls at the post-test evaluation conducted in the infant's own home approximately 9 days later. Despite the fact that the change in reciprocity scores across the two testings was greater for the demonstration group than for the information-only group, the difference between these two groups was not statistically reliable.

Unfortunately, the value of Anderson's work is undermined by methodological shortcomings and inadequately reported data. For example, comparisons between the information-only and the control group were not reported by the investigator, and since only F ratios without accompanying mean scores were presented in her written report, it is impossible to determine the functional significance of any group differences—whether statistically reliable or not. Furthermore, because this study, like the Kang (1974) and Ryan (1973) work, fails to provide any information on parent–infant interaction beyond the first month of life, it is impossible to determine how long-lasting the effects of these interventions might be or how they might be modified by parents' and infants' subsequent experience.

The studies reported above, like our own work, deal with low-risk families. Widmayer and Field (1980) have recently tested the possibility that a Brazelton-based intervention could be employed as a tool of secondary prevention with high-risk families. In an effort to enhance the sensitivity of low-income teenage mothers to the interactional skills of their preterm infants, a group of mothers, who had observed their babies being assessed on the Brazelton exam in the hospital, were asked to perform a modified version of that procedure called the Mothers' Assessment of the Behavior of her Infant (MABI) (Field, Dempsey, Hallock, and Shuman, 1978) at 1-week intervals from birth through the first postnatal month. A second group was also asked to administer the MABI, but without prior demonstration of the Brazelton assessment. Mothers of 10 preterm infants and 10 full-term infants who completed a scale designed to assess their knowledge of developmental milestones and their attitudes toward childrearing served as control subjects in this study.

To assess the effect of the interventions, videotapes of 2 minutes of mother–infant interaction during a feeding session and face-to-face play were studied. Although the MABI-only group performed better than the preterm controls on several measures of mother–infant interaction, the group that both observed their infants' assessments on the Brazelton exam *and* used the MABI were found to differ from all groups, including the MABI-only group. Mothers in this dual-treatment group talked more to their infants, attended more regularly to their gaze signals, and utilized more physical activity in interacting with them. In addition, infants whose mothers had received the Brazelton-plus-MABI treatment gazed at their mothers more, vocalized more, and used more animated facial features than those in the other preterm groups.

In another study of high-risk infants, Eyler (1980) followed 31 mother–infant pairs in which the infants were at risk for perinatal medical complications (including prematurity) during the 1-month period in which the infants remained hospitalized. Assessments of these infants on a modified version of the Brazelton exam administered at approximately 3 days, 2 weeks, and 4 weeks postnatally showed them to be depressed and flat, with weak motoric processes, little activity, and poor response to stimuli. Despite these interactional deficits, demonstrations of the first two assessments, stressing infant strengths and capabilities, were provided to 16 mothers randomly assigned to an experimental-treatment group.

Although participation in this program failed to alleviate negative maternal attitudes and intense concerns about the wellbeing of the preterm infants for any of the mothers, those parents who had observed the Brazelton demonstrations were more likely to call or visit the hospital and were less likely to drop out of the research program. Most important, mothers who had been assigned to the experimental treatment displayed higher rates of mother–infant interaction in the form of looking at and talking to their infants. Further, these mothers were more than twice as likely to include efforts to elicit reflexes which they had seen demonstrated in the Brazelton assessment in their interactions with their offspring.

Considered together, the Widmayer and Field (1980) and Eyler (1980) studies strongly suggest that the Brazelton exam can be successfully employed to encourage the provision of sensitive care to infants at risk for developmental delay. We feel compelled to say "suggests" rather than "demonstrates" because we are concerned about the generalizability of the results of these studies. Although Widmayer and Field (1980) have shown that exposure to the Brazelton exam influences maternal behavior during a short episode of videotaped interaction, no evidence exists to date that behavior in this context is related to caregiving in the child's everyday home environments. A similar criticism can be made of the Eyler (1980) assessment. In our minds, the effectiveness of any intervention is demonstrated in the field, under naturalistic conditions, or via procedures known to portray accurately individual differences in such contexts, since it is only here that the effects of an intervention truly matter. Our point is not to minimize the real contribution of the work but rather to inject a note of caution. In evaluating intervention efforts, investigators need to be certain that they are not simply carrying out successful training studies in which individuals are taught how to behave under certain circumscribed conditions. The fact that the Eyler subjects were especially likely to display behaviors from the Brazelton exam during evaluation assessments alerts us to this possibility.

Beyond the Mother–Infant Dyad

In all the work reviewed above, whether concerning the effects of immediate postpartum contact, rooming-in, or exposure to the Brazelton exam, interventions have been directed toward mothers and infants. Most likely as a consequence, follow-up assessments to evaluate the impact of these experimental modifications of hospital maternity care have focused solely upon this mother–child relationship. This is not unusual among interventions geared to promote healthy parenting styles and optimal infant development. Like those experimental programs summarized above, other interventions dealing with older infants have failed to consider the father as a parent whose behavior can affect the infant's development (e.g., Kessen, Fein, Clarke-Stewart, and Starr, 1975; Lambie, Bond, and Weikart, 1974; Levenstein, Kochman, and Roth, 1973; Rice, 1977; Scarr-Salapatek and Williams, 1973).

The relative dearth of experimental efforts geared toward influencing paternal behavior is not surprising given the neglect that the role of fatherhood has received during the infancy years by basic researchers, for only recently has fathering during the first 2 years of life received much systematic empirical attention (see Parke, 1978, for review). Data accumulated to date suggest that despite relatively low levels of participation in parenting (in comparison with mothers), fathers do influence their infant's socioemotional and cognitive/motivational development (Belsky, 1980; Clarke-Stewart, 1978; Pederson et al., 1979; Pedersen and Robson, 1969; Spelke et al., 1973; Wachs et al., 1971). These findings clearly suggest that efforts to influence paternal behavior could prove beneficial to infant functioning. To our knowledge, only two efforts have been made to influence the father–infant relationship in the newborn period and assess the effects of the experimental programs implemented.

In a first-of-a-kind study, Parke, Hymel, Power, and Tinsley (1979) presented to a group of fathers a videotape of father–infant interaction which highlighted neonatal perceptual and social competencies and parental play styles and caregiving techniques. Observations of structured 10-minute feeding and 10-minute play sessions revealed that fathers who viewed the tapes engaged in significantly more "stimulate feed" behavior—in the newborn period and during 3-week and 3-month follow-up assessments—and spoke to their infants more during play sessions than did their control counterparts. Furthermore, evaluations of fathers' knowledge of infants' perceptual capacities revealed that the experimental intervention increased paternal understanding of babies. Fathers in the experimental group also expressed less resentment and concern about the disruptive impact of the infant on their lives.

Myers (1980) took a most logical and necessary step by extending the use of the Brazelton-type demonstrations described earlier in an intervention aimed at the father–infant relationship. Forty-two middle-class primiparous couples were randomly assigned to one of three groups: a mother-only treatment group, a father-only treatment group, and a control group. Parents in each of the experimental groups were taught to perform most of the Brazelton items as "simple games and exercises to get to know the baby better", while control parents briefly chatted with the researcher about their baby. For both treatment groups, the skill training was positively linked to knowledge of infant behaviors during the 1st and 4th weeks postpartum, as well as to reports of greater parental confidence along with satisfaction with the infant. Interestingly, although 10-minute observations of mother–infant and father–infant behavior in the hospital revealed no treatment effects, the treatment was positively related to greater paternal involvement in the form of caretaking behavior at the 4-week follow-up.

In sum, these studies not only suggest the value of stimulating perceptual learning in parents during the early postpartum period, but also they illustrate the value of including fathers in intervention efforts directed at that important phase of family development.

A Family Approach

It is of interest to note that these experimental efforts to influence the father–infant relationship evidence the same conservatism that characterizes recent studies of father–infant interaction. That is, in the same way that basic scientists studying this "second" parent–infant dyad have applied to father methods and procedures initially employed to study mothers (Belsky, 1980b), practitioners intervening with fathers have merely permutated mother–infant interventions by substituting one parent (i.e., father) for another (i.e., mother). Thus, whether we consider basic or applied science, the recent inclusion of fathers in the study of early development seems to have had only a modest impact. In fact, we believe that these efforts have failed to recognize the real significance of considering the father. As we have argued elsewhere (Belsky, 1980b), the very inclusion of fathers in the study of infancy does more than create an additional parent–infant relationship: It transforms the mother-infant dyad into a family system comprising marital as well as parent–infant relations.

Serious consideration of this analysis suggests that the most effective means of influencing parent–infant relations and thereby promoting infant development may not entail simply treating the mother–infant or father–infant relationship. Indeed, we believe that an intervention which focuses simultaneously on the mother–infant, father–infant, and husband–wife relationships, and thereby treats the family as a system of interdependent relationships, may prove most effective in enhancing parent–infant relations and family functioning in the newborn period.

In order to test this proposition, we are using items culled from the Brazelton Neonatal Assessment to assist parents in "getting to know" their newborns. Specifically, a trained examiner, serving as facilitator, guides mother/wife and father/husband in eliciting from their infant a series of behaviors that together serve three functions: (1) highlight intriguing behaviors that disappear as the baby develops (e.g., stroking bottom of baby's foot results in toes curling up, rather than down; the stepping and placing reflexes which make it look like the baby is trying to walk); (2) reveal neonatal competencies that parents may not realize the newborn possesses (e.g., capacity to track a moving visual stimulus; capacity to habituate or shut out a disturbing, redundant sound); and (3) identify domains of functioning that will show gradual improvement in skill over time (e.g., capacity to support own head when pulled to sit). In sum, by directing parents' attention to a wide array of skills and reflexes, we hope to increase parents' fascination with, sensitivity to, and involvement with their infants.

Moreover, by treating mother/wife–father/husband–infant as an interactive system, we hope to promote general family functioning. To achieve this end, we have designed our intervention procedure to encourage husband–wife communication and reinforce father–mother teamwork. For example, before directing a parent to elicit the Babinski reflex from his or her infant, we ask the wife about what would happen if she tickled her husband's foot. After some laughter, the usual response from husband or wife is that his toes would curl downward. Having set the stage for a violated expectancy, we have the father stroke the bottom of the infant's foot and direct the mother to tell her husband what happened. Usually, both parents are surprised by their infant's strange behavior (the toes fan upward), and they share a laugh together.

As another illustration, during the habituation items we have one parent stimulate the sleeping infant with a rattle or flashlight while the other describes the baby's responses and counts the "trials" before the baby stops responding. Having demonstrated neonatal habituation behaviorally, we ask the parents what they are capable of shutting out and remind them that, like most couples, they probably have learned to habituate to each other at times!

We feel it important to stress that our work differs from all that previously described. In addition to our *joint* treatment of mother and father, the attentive reader will have recognized that our work is as a facilitator of family interaction, not an examiner. Since we strongly believe that the baby belongs to its parents, and that all too often professionals forget this, we guide parents in interacting with *their* infants. Ours is an active-involvement strategy rather a passive-involvement approach in which parents merely watch an examiner interact with *their* baby.

Since we hypothesize that treating the family system is more effective than treating a single parent–infant relationship, we have designed our work so that we can test this assumption. Specifically, we are comparing the family functioning of families in which only mother received the guided interaction with those in which both parents *jointly* participate in the intervention. We have not permuted our design to include a father-only group because of concerns regarding sample sizes.

The operative word in the preceding paragraph was *family* functioning. Since we believe we are treating the family system, we are making every effort to evaluate the multiple components of this system. And since, as noted earlier, we believe the merits of an intervention can only be evaluated by the real world behavior of people in their natural habitats, we are conducting naturalistic observations of family interaction. Thus, at 1-, 3-, and 8-months postpartum, specially trained observers are going into homes to record mother–infant, father–infant *and* husband–wife interactions. Because we are concerned about the *enduring* impact of our efforts to enhance family functioning we have purposefully extended our evaluations beyond the first month of life.

After this build up, we are sorry to say, and a bit embarrassed to admit, that there are no data to report as yet. Our project has only just begun, with just a few of our families having reached the third postpartum month. Nevertheless, we do have expectations. For example, we are predicting that both mothers and fathers will be more involved in interacting with their infants if they received the family treatment. Moreover, we expect that couples experiencing this treatment will spend more time talking about the baby. Finally, we are hypothesizing that such families will interact more as a three-person system, rather than as a system composed of independent dyads. Thus, we expect mother/wife, father/husband, and infant to be more involved in joint, family-focused interaction if they experienced the family intervention. The mother-only-treatment families, we suspect, will spend more time in independent mother–infant, father–infant, or husband–wife interactions.

The work we have just described grows out of that reviewed in this paper. The bonding work of Kennell, Klaus, and their followers alerted us to the potential significance of early interaction for the development of parent–infant relations and to the newborn period as a time for intervention. Recent thinking in community and life-span developmental psychology enhanced our understanding of this life event (for infant and parents) as a time for intervention by underscoring the meaning of the transition to parenthood as a significant life event. Finally, recent research on the father–infant relationship sensitized us to the need to consider the family as a system of interdependent relationships. When considered together, these sources of influence made it evident to us that the Brazelton exam, when modified to create an interactional process between parent and infant, might serve to sensitize parents to their infants and serve as a focus for enhancing family functioning.

Conclusions

In a recent discussion of developmental interventions, Danish, Smyer, and Nowak (1980) contrast two approaches to service delivery that Rappaport and Chinsky (1974) refer to as the "waiting mode" and the "seeking mode". In the waiting mode, the expert waits passively for others to request help. Like Danish et al., we see this approach as severely limited by its emphasis on the identification and treatment of disease, rather than the promotion of healthy functioning. Moreover, we are concerned that in the waiting mode expertise is hoarded by a select group of professionals and dispensed only upon request.

In our mind the seeking mode, in which the helper seeks out individuals needing help, is equally limited. Specifically, we are concerned with any mental health service or intervention that is overzealous in its efforts to give away its product; for anytime a program focuses its efforts on searching for a clientele, it runs the risk of putting the interests of the helper above those of the helped.

As in any dialectic, the bridge between thesis and antithesis (i.e., synthesis) often represents the optimal position, and for this reason we see the need to synthesize the most beneficial aspects of both modes of service delivery described above. This can be accomplished, we believe, when many people are exposed to opportunities for enhancement at a time when they are most likely to take advantage of them. This is the context in which we view our program.

Since birth is a time when families may initiate contact with the helping professions, services offered in the newborn period are available to a large number of families. And since the Brazelton-based intervention we are offering is relatively inexpensive, it could be provided on a universal basis as part of standard maternity care. This would avoid the stigmatizing process that often accompanies special programs directed toward special populations. In our minds, this is an extremely important point, since so many services today, by virture of their selectivity, label users as problem people.

It should be noted also that widespread implementation of the service we have described would require no new army of intervenors. To the extent that any intervention requires additional cadres of helpers, we view it as fatally flawed. In these inflationary times innovative strategies of intervention must be amenable to service delivery systems that are already in place. Since obstetrical, pediatric, and public health nurses could easily be trained to assist families in "getting to know" their newborns, we consider the program described earlier as not only hopeful, but realistic. The only major change that would be required is that the traditional nursing clientele and function would need to be redefined. The patient would no longer be the mother and baby, but the family, and the goal of nursing would not be simply health care, but family support.

The services we have described could also serve a useful screening function. For example, a parent observed interacting with a baby in a way that engenders concern might subsequently be visited at home for additional observation and intervention by the same individual who initially served as facilitator. If this home contact failed to alleviate the original concern, then the facilitator could return once more, this time accompanied by a public health nurse who would be handed the function of building supports for the family. Note that this strategy of watching and helping would develop naturally out of standard maternity care and ensure continuity in service delivery. Indeed, if such follow-up visits by a facilitator were routinely made (as in several European nations, e.g., the Netherlands), stigmatization of the family in need would be minimized. In fact, it would be only upon subsequent contacts that a family would be receiving anything special and by then, hopefully, sufficient trust would have developed to assure acceptance of continued support.

In essence, what we are describing is a process by which all families would be routinely "caught" in a family-support "net" as they pass through the birthing period. Most would be "weaned" from this support relatively quickly, with others holding on until both the family and the support system judged them to be ready to steer their own course.

The model of family support we have just outlined is illustrative of a strategy of intervention that could be implemented at a variety of life junctures other than the newborn period. These life events, like the transition to parenthood, would be times when families routinely make contact with the community at large. The child's entry into school or day care readily come to mind as additional examples, that is, periods in which all families could pass through a support net, with only those who really require special assistance holding on, or being held on to. Again, universal contact with the service would help avoid the stigma that often accompanies involvement with a supportive agency.

An innovative, though relatively unnoticed program, operated out of a well-baby clinic in New York City, alerts us to the fact that other opportunities exist for catching families in a supportive service web. In providing guidance to parents interacting with their preschoolers during the long hours waiting in a well-child clinic, Morris (1974) successfully created a support structure where one naturally fit but had never before existed. Her creative work demonstrates that family support nets, which large numbers of families could filter through, need not be tied solely to major events.

Indeed, on the basis of extrapolations from our own work, we see no reason why most formal evaluations, be they medical, psychological, or scholastic, could not be transformed into opportunities to sensitize parents to the skills and limits of their children. Note that such modifications of test procedures could stimulate a shift away from unnecessarily competitive emphases, which are of little value in the early childhood years, to recognition of the family's role in promoting early development. To do this successfully, of course, intervention efforts would need to highlight family strengths, not underscore weaknesses, and thereby promote the beneficial aspects of a child's early experience.

The point we are trying to make is that opportunities exist for developing inexpensive, nonstigmatizing, and effective enhancement programs that would be used by families at those times when large segments of the childrearing population are expected to come into contact with what could be a widespread family support system. Before rushing out to disseminate such programs, we need to recognize that humility, caution, and respect for science should be integral components of every interventionist's tool box. Programs must be based on a firm understanding of the phenomenon of concern and serious evaluations of helping efforts are absolutely essential. Proponents of a particular program (and here we include ourselves) must be willing to accept negative results and must be sensitive to the potential that all interventions have for generating unintended negative consequences. In this regard, we believe that in proselytizing bonding so widely, Kennel and Klaus unwittingly damaged some individuals and families; we have met mothers deeply concerned about the ultimate quality of their relationships with their children because they were denied the early contact experience because of their caesarean deliveries. In this regard, Campbell and Taylor (1979) have recently commented that:

It is troubling to contemplate that as the public may come to regard early contact as an important requirement for mental health, those mothers who must be separated from their infants for reasons beyond their control may be burdened by guilt and, furthermore, may initiate a self-fulfilling prophecy of negative interactions with the infant. (p. 8)

Although it is difficult to imagine an intervention that has absolutely no negative side effects, it is nevertheless the interventionist's responsibility to be ever alert to them. In the brief period of time that we have offered our modest experimental intervention, we have discovered that our goals are not always realized. Sandra was a pregnant teenager, whom the first author observed spanking her 2-month-old niece during a prenatal interview. When queried about her motivations, she expressed the opinion that the baby understood the cause and reasons for the discipline. In this context it became easy for us to understand what went wrong when we offered Sandra the Brazelton intervention we have described. While we intended to demonstrate both the competencies and limitations of her newborn baby, it was not our intent to suggest to Sandra that her 2-day-old infant could understand the meaning of her demands. Yet this is exactly the effect we had when we assisted this young mother in discovering that when she spoke softly to her newborn he could hear her and would alert to the human voice. The distinction between hearing and understanding was beyond Sandra's own capacity, so we erred in the manner in which we presented our intervention.

Although it is doubtful that any lasting damage was done, we became, through this episode, ever aware of the caution that must be exercised before proselytizing a program. Our purpose in this chapter, then, has been to share ideas and discuss a family-centered enhancement program that we are evaluating. We discourage the reader from viewing our approach, or any other for that matter, as a panacea for the primary prevention of psychopathology.

References

Ainsworth, M.D.S. The development of infant-mother attachments. In B. Caldwell and H. Ricciuti (Eds.), *Review of child development research* (Vol. 3). Chicago: University of Chicago Press, 1973.

Ainsworth, M.D., Bell, S., and Stayton, D. Individual differences in strange-situation behavior of one year olds. In H.L. Schaffer (Ed.), *The origins of human social behavior*. New York: Academic Press, 1971.

Ainsworth, M.D.S., and Wittig, B. Attachment and exploratory behavior of one year olds in a strange situation. In B. M. Foss (Ed.), *Determinants of infant behavior*, IV. London: Metheun and Co. Ltd., 1969.

Anderson, C. *Informing mothers about the behavioral characteristics of their infants: Effects on mother-infant interaction*. Paper presented at the biennial meetings of the Society for Research in Child Development, San Francisco, March 1979.

Antonovsky, A., and Kats, R. The life crisis history as a tool in epidemiological research. *Journal of Health and Social Behavior*, 1967, *8*, 15–21.

Arend, R., Gove, P., and Sroufe, L. Continuity in early adaptation: From attachment theory in infancy to resiliency and curiosity at age five. *Child Development*, 1979, *50*, 950–959.

Baltes, P.B., and Danish S.J. Intervention in life span development and aging: Issues and concepts. In R. R. Turner and H. W. Reese (Eds.), *Life-span developmental psychology: Intervention*. New York: Academic Press, 1980.

Baltes, P.B., Reese, H.W., and Nesselroade, J.R. *Life-span developmental psychology: Introduction to research methods*. Monterey: Brooks/Cole, 1977.

Barnett, C., Leiderman, H., Grobstein, R., and Klaus, M. Neonatal separation: The maternal side of interactional deprivation. *Pediatrics*, 1970, *45*, 197–205.

Beckwith, L. Relationships between attributes of mothers and their infants' IQ scores. *Child Development*, 1971, *42*, 1083–1097.

Beckwith, L., Cohen, S., Kopp, C.B., Parmelee, A.H., and Marcy, T.G. Caregiver-infant interaction and early cognitive development in preterm infants. *Child Development*, 1976, *47*, 579–587.

Belsky, J. A family analysis of parental influence on infant exploratory competence. In F. Pedersen (Ed.), *Observational studies of the father-infant relationship*. New York: Praeger Special Studies, 1980 (a)

Belsky, J. Early human experience: A family perspective. Under editorial review, 1980. (b)

Belsky, J., Goode, M., and Most, R. Maternal stimulation and infant exploratory competence: Cross-sectional, correlational, and experimental analyses. *Child Development*, 1980, *51*, No. 4.

Block, J., and Block, J. The role of ego control and ego-resiliency in the organization of behavior. In W.A. Collins (Ed.), *Minnesota Symposia on Child Psychology* (Vol. 13). New York: Lawrence Erlbaum, 1979.

Brazelton, T.B. *Neonatal behavioral assessment scale*. National Spastics Society Monograph, Philadelphia: J.B. Lippincott, 1973.

Campbell, S., Maloni, J., and Taylor, P. *Early contact and maternal perceptions of infant temperament*. Paper presented at the biennial meetings of the Society for Research in Child Development, San Francisco, March 1979.

Campbell, S. and Taylor P. Bonding and attachment: Theoretical issues. *Seminars in Perinatology*, 1979, *3*, 3–13.

Carew, J., Chan, I., and Halfar, C. *Observed intellectual competence and tested intelligence: Their roots in the young child's transactions with his environment*. Paper presented at the biennial meetings of the Society for Research in Child Development, Denver, March 1975.

Carey, W.B. A simplified method of measuring infant temperament. *Journal of Pediatrics*, 1970, *77*, 188–194.

Carlsson, S., Fagerberg, H., Horneman, G., Hwang, P., Rodholm, M.,

Schaller, J., Danielsson, B., and Gundewall, C. Effects of amount of contact between mother and child on the mother's nursing behavior. *Developmental Psychobiology*, 1978, *11*, 143–150.

Carlsson, S., Fagerberg, H., Horneman, G., Hwang, P., Larsson, K., Rodholm, M., Schaller, J., Danielsson, B., and Gundewall, C. Effects of various amount of contact between mother and child on the mother's nursing behavior: A follow-up study. *Infant Behavior and Development*, 1979, *2*, 209–214.

Clarke-Stewart, K.A. Interactions between mothers and their young children: Characteristics and consequences. *Monographs of the Society for Research in Child Development*, 1973, *38* 6–7 (Serial No. 153).

Clarke-Stewart, K.A. And daddy makes three: The father's impact on mother and young child. *Child Development*, 1978, *44*, 466–478.

Danish, S.J. Human development and human services: A marriage proposal. In I. Iscoe, B.L. Bloom, and C.C. Spielberger (Eds.), *Community psychology in transition*. New York: Halsted Press, 1977.

Danish, S.J., and D'Augelli, A.R. Promoting competence and enhancing development through life development intervention. In L.A. Bond and J.C. Rosen (Eds.), *Competence and coping during adulthood*. Hanover, N.H.: University Press of New England, 1980.

Danish, S., Smyer, M., and Nowak, C. Developmental intervention. In P. Baltes and O. Brim (Eds.), *Life-span development and behavior* (Vol. 3). New York: Academic Press, 1980.

deChateau, P. *Neonatal care routines, influences on maternal and infant behavior and on breast feeding*. Umea, 1976, Umea University Medical Dissertation, New Series, No. 20.

deChateau, P. and Wiberg, B. Long term effect on mother-infant behavior of extra contact during the first hour post partum II. Follow-up at three months. *Acta Paediatrica Scandinavica*, 1977, *66*, 145.

Dohrenwend, B.S. Social status and stressful life events. *Journal of Personality and Social Psychology*, 1973, *28*, 225–235.

Dohrenwend, B.S., and Dohrenwend, B.P. (Eds.), *Stressful life events: Their nature and effects*. New York: Wiley, 1974.

Engel, M., and Keane, W. *Black mothers and their infant sons: Antecedents, correlates and predictors of cognitive development in the second and sixth year of life*. Paper presented at the Society for Research in Child Development, Denver, April 1975.

Eyler, F.D. *Assessment and intervention with mothers and their premature newborns*. Paper presented at the International Conference on Infant Studies, New Haven, March 1980.

Field, T., Dempsey, J., Hallock, N., and Shuman, H. Mothers' assessments of the behavior of their infants. *Infant Behavior and Development*, 1978, *1*, 156–167.

Gaulin-Kremer, E., Shaw, J., and Thoman, E. *Mother-infant interaction at first prolonged encounter: Effects of variation in delay after delivery*. Paper presented at the biennial meetings of the Society for Research in Child Development, San Francisco, March 1977.

Gibson, E.J. *Principles of perceptual learning and development*. New York: Appleton-Century-Crofts, 1969.

Greenberg, M., and Morris, N. Engrossment: The newborn's impact upon the father. *American Journal of Orthopsychiatry*, 1974, *44*, 520–531.

Guttman, D. Parenthood: A key to the comparative study of the life cycle. In N. Datan and L.H. Ginsberg (Eds.), *Life-span developmental psychology: Normative life crises.* New York: Academic Press, 1975.

Hales, D., Lozoff, B., Sosa, R., and Kennell, J. Defining the limits of the maternal sensitive period. *Developmental Medicine and Child Neurology,* 1977, *19,* 454–461.

Hersher, L., Moore, A., and Richmond, J. Effect of post-partum separation of mother and kid on maternal care in the domestic goat. *Science,* 1958, *128,* 1342.

Holmes, T.H., and Masuda, M. Life changes and illness susceptibility. In B.S. Dohrenwend and B.P. Dohrenwend (Eds.), *Stressful life events: Their nature and effects.* New York: Wiley, 1974.

Holmes, T.H., and Rahe, R.H. The social readjustment rating. *Journal of Psychosomatic Research,* 1967, *11,* 213–218.

Hultsch, D.K., and Plemons, J.K. Life events and life span development. In P.B. Baltes and O.G. Brim, Jr. (Eds.), *Life-span development and behavior* (Vol. 2). New York: Academic Press, 1979.

Kang, R. *The relationship between informing both parents of their infants behavioral response patterns and the mother's perception of the infant.* Unpublished Master's Thesis, University of Washington, August, 1974.

Kennell, J., Jerauld, R., Wolf, L., Chesler, R., Kreger, N., McAlpine, W., Steffa, M., and Klaus, M. Maternal behavior one year after early and extended postpartum contact. *Developmental Medicine and Child Neurology,* 1974, *16,* 172.

Kennell, J., Voos, D., and Klaus, M. Parent-infant bonding. In J. Osofsky (Ed.), *Handbook of infancy.* New York: Wiley, 1979.

Kessen, W., Fein, G., Clarke-Stewart, K.A., and Starr, S. *Variations in home-based infant education.* Final report to the Office of Child Development, Grant #OCD-CB-98, August 1975.

Klaus, M., Jerauld, R., Kreger, N., McAlpine, W., Steffa, M., and Kennell, J. Maternal attachment: Importance of the first postpartum days. *New England Journal of Medicine,* 1972, *286,* 460–463.

Klaus, M., and Kennell, J. *Mother-infant bonding.* St. Louis: C.V. Mosby, 1976.

Klaus, M., Kennell, J., Plumb, N., and Zuehlke, S. Human maternal behavior at the first contact with her young. *Pediatrics,* 1970, *46,* 187–192.

Klaus, M., Trause, M., and Kennell, J. Does human maternal behavior after delivery show a characteristic pattern? In Ciba Foundation Symposium No. 33. *Parent-infant interaction.* New York: Elsevier, 1975.

Kotelchuck, M. *The nature of the child's tie to the father.* Unpublished doctoral dissertation, Harvard University, 1972.

Lamb, M. Influence of the child on mental quality and family interaction during the prenatal, perinatal, and infancy periods. In R. Lerner and G. Spencer (Eds.), *Child influences on marital and family interaction: A life-span perspective.* New York: Academic Press, 1978.

Lambie, D., Bond, J., and Weikart, D. *Home teaching with mothers and infants.* Ypsilanti, MI: High/Scope Educational Research Foundation, 1974.

LeMasters, E.E. Parenthood as crisis. *Marriage and Family Living,* 1957, *19,* 352–355.

Levenstein, P., Kochman, A., and Roth, B. From laboratory to real world: Service and delivery of the mother–child home program. *American Journal of Orthopsychiatry,* 1973, *43,* 72–78.

Lewis, M., and Goldberg, S. Perceptual-cognitive development in infancy: A generalized expectancy model as a function of mother–infant interaction. *Merrill-Palmer Quarterly*, 1969, *15*, 81–100.

Lorenz, K. The nature of instinct. In C.H. Schiller (Ed.), *Instinctive Behavior.* New York: International Universities Press, 1957.

Lozoff, B. *The sensitive period: An anthropological view.* Paper presented at the biennial meeting of the Society for Research in Child Development, New Orleans, March 1977.

Matas, L., Arend, R., and Sroufe, L. Continuity in adaptation in the second year: The relationship between quality of attachment and later competence. *Child Development,* 1978, *49*, 547–556.

Moore, A. Effects of modified maternal care in the sheep and goat. In G. Newton and S. Levine (Eds.), *Early experience and behavior.* Springfield, IL: Thomas, 1968.

Morris, A. Conducting a parent education program in a pediatric clinic playroom. *Children Today,* November/December 1974, 11–14.

Morris, A.G. Parent education for child education being carried out in a pediatric clinic playroom. *Clinical Pediatrics,* 1973, *12*, 235–239.

Myers, B.J. *Fathers and mothers of newborns: An intervention to improve parenting.* Paper presented at the Southeastern Conference on Human Development, Alexandria, Virginia, April 1980.

Myers, J.L., Lindenthal, J.J., Pepper, M.P., and Ostrander, D.K. Life events and mental status: A longitudinal study. *Journal of Health and Social Behavior,* 1972 *13,* 398–406.

O'Connor, S., Sherrod, K., Sandler, H., and Vietze, P. The effect of extended post-partum contact on problems with parenting: A controlled study of 301 families. *Birth and The Family Journal,* 1978, *5,* 231–234.

O'Connor, S., Vietze, P., Hopkins, J., and Altemeier, W. *Post-partum extended maternal-infant contact: Subsequent mothering and child health.* Paper presented at the biennial meetings of the Society for Research in Child Development, San Francisco, March 1979

Ottaviano, C., Campbell, S., Taylor, P. *Early contact and infant-mother attachment at one year.* Paper presented at the biennial meetings of the Society for Research in Child Development, San Francisco, March 1979.

Parke, R. Perspectives in father-infant interaction. In J. Osofsky (Ed.), *Handbook of infancy.* New York: Wiley, 1978.

Parke, R., Hymel, S., Power, T., and Tinsley, B. Fathers at risk: A hospital-based model of intervention. In D. Sawin, R. Haskins, L. Walker, and J. Penticuff (Eds.), *Psychosocial risks in infant-environment transactions,* New York: Brunner-Mazel, 1980.

Pedersen, F., and Robson, K. Father participation in infancy. *American Journal of Orthopsychiatry,* 1969, *39,* 466–472.

Pedersen, F., Rubenstein, J., and Yarrow, L. Infant development in father-absent families. *Journal of Genetic Psychology,* 1979, *135,* 51–61.

Ramey, C., and Finkelstein, N. Contingent stimulation and infant competence. *Journal of Pediatric Psychology,* 1978, *3,* 89–96.

Rappaport, J., and Chinsky, J. Models for delivery of service from a historical and conceptual perspective. *Professional Psychology,* 1974, *5,* 42–50.

Rheingold, H. (Ed.). *Maternal behavior in mammals.* New York: Wiley, 1963.

Rice, R. Neurophysiological development in premature infants following stimulation. *Developmental Psychology,* 1977, *13,* 69–76.

Riksen-Walraven, J. Effects of caregiver behavior on habituation rate and self-efficacy in infants. *International Journal of Behavioral Development*, 1978, *1*, 105–130.

Ringler, N.M., Kennell, J.H., Jarvella, R., Navojosky, B.J., and Klaus, M.H. Mother-to-child speech at 2 years: Effects of early postnatal contact. *Journal of Pediatrics*, 1975, *86*, 141–144.

Rogosa, D. Causal models in longitudinal research: Rationale, formulation and interpretation. In J. Nesselroade and P. Baltes (Eds.), *Longitudinal research in the study of behavior and development*. New York: Academic Press, 1979.

Rosenblatt, J. The basis of synchrony in the behavioral interaction between the mother and her offspring in the laboratory rat. In B.M. Foss (Ed.), *Determinants of Infant Behavior* (Vol. 3). London: Metheun, 1965.

Rosenblatt, J., and Siegel, H. Hysterectomy-induced maternal behavior during pregnancy in the rat. *Journal of Comparative Physiological Psychology*, 1975, *89*, 685–670.

Ross, G., Kagan, J., Zelazo, P., and Kotelchuck, M. Separation protest in infants in home and laboratory. *Developmental Psychology*, 1975, *11*, 256–257.

Rubenstein, J. Maternal attentiveness and subsequent exploratory behavior. *Child Development*, 1967, *38*, 1089–1100.

Ryan, L. *Maternal perception of neonatal behavior.* Unpublished Master's Thesis, University of Washington, August 1973.

Scarr-Salapatek, S., and Williams, M.L. The effects of early stimulation on low birthweight infants. *Child Development*, 1973, *44*, 94–101.

Schaller, J., Carlsson, S., and Larsson, K. Effects of extended post-partum mother-child contact on the mother's behavior during nursing. *Infant Behavior and Development*, 1979, *2*, 319–324.

Sousa, P., Barros, F., Gazalle, R., Begeres, R., Pinheiro, G., Menezes, S., and Arruda, L. *Attachment and lactation.* IXV Congresso Internacional de Pediatrica, Buenos Aires, Argentina, 1974.

Sousa, P., Kennell, J., Klaus, M., and Urrutia, J. The effect of early mother-infant contact on breast feeding, infection and growth. In Ciba Foundation Symposium No. 45 *Breast feeding and the mother.* New York: Elsevier, 1977.

Spelke, E., Zelazo, P., Kagan, J., and Kotelchuck, M. Father interaction and separation protest. *Developmental Psychology*, 1973, *9*, 83–90.

Sroufe, L. The coherence of individual development. *American Psychologist*, 1979, *34*, 834–841.

Stayton, D., Hogan, R., and Ainsworth, M. Infant obedience and maternal behavior: The origins of socialization reconsidered. *Child Development*, 1971, *42*, 1057–1069.

Taylor, P., Taylor, F., Campbell, S., Maloni, J., and Dickey, D. *Effects of extra contact on early maternal attitudes, perceptions and behaviors.* Paper presented at the biennial meetings of the Society for Research in Child Development, San Francisco, March 1979.

Trause, M. *Defining the limits of the sensitive period.* Paper presented at the biennial meetings of the Society for Research in Child Development, New Orleans, March 1977.

Tulkin, S., and Covitz, F. *Mother-infant interaction and intellectual functioning at age six.* Paper presented at the biennial meetings of the Society for Research in Child Development, Denver, April 1975.

Wachs, T. Utilization of a Piagetian approach in the investigation of early experience effects: A research strategy and some illustrative data. *Merrill-Palmer Quarterly*, 1976, *22*, 11–30.

Wachs, T., Uzgiris, I., and Hunt, J. Cognitive development in infants of different age levels and from different environmental backgrounds. *Merrill-Palmer Quarterly*, 1971, *17*, 283–317.

Watson, J., and Ramey, C. Reactions to response-contingent stimulation in infancy. *Merrill-Palmer Quarterly*, 1972, *18*, 219–227.

Widmayer, S.M., and Field, T.M. Effects of Brazelton demonstrations on early interactions of preterm infants and their teenage mothers. *Infant Behavior and Development*, 1980, *3*, 79–89.

Winters, M. *The relationship of time of initial breastfeeding.* Unpublished Master's Thesis, University of Washington, 1973.

Yarrow, L. *The origins of mastery motivation.* Paper presented at the annual meeting of the American Academy of Child Psychiatry, Toronto, Canada, October 1976.

Yarrow, L., Rubenstein, J., and Pedersen, F. *Infant and Environment.* New York: Wiley, 1975.

Infants Born At Risk:
Early Compensatory Experiences

Tiffany M. Field

Infants born at risk are generally considered at risk for developmental problems due to reproductive casualties, caretaking casualties, or both. Examples of infants on the reproductive casualty continuum, first defined by Pasamanick and Knobloch (1966), include those born with congenital disorders such as the mentally retarded and cerebral palsied and those who are born too soon or too small. On the not necessarily separate caretaking casualty continuum—described by Sameroff and Chandler (1975)—are infants who may experience developmental problems secondary to being parented by adults stressed by emotional or socioeconomic problems. These might include infants born to lower socioeconomic-status (SES) mothers or teenage mothers. Infants at risk because of both reproductive and caretaking casualties are, for example, preterm infants of teenage mothers, twins, and infants born to schizophrenic mothers.

Although retrospective studies of developmentally handicapped children ranging from those who are profoundly retarded to those who are abused reveal a number of reproductive and caretaking casualties in the histories of their subjects (e.g., a heightened incidence of prematurity among handicapped and abused children) the prospective studies of the last couple of decades on these same casualties reveal a surprisingly less negative picture. For example, among the population of infants born prematurely IQ scores may frequently appear in the low end of the normal distribution, speech and hearing deficits are more common than in the larger population, and behavior problems as well as learning disabilities are more frequent. But the incidence of severe handicapping conditions is very often less than 10 percent, even among the very small, very premature infants. That is not to say that speech and hearing deficits, be-

This research was funded by Grants #OHD90C1358 and OHD90C176471 to Tiffany Field. I would like to thank the infants and mothers who participated in these studies, and Lou De Stefano, Ed Ignatoff, Lisa Lubin, Cynthia Neuman, Shelly Payne, Wendy Stone, Sharon Stringer, Susan Widmayer, and Jacquelyn Zagursky for their assistance with data collection.

havior disorders, or learning disabilities are not morbidity problems, but merely that the more severe pathologies we might have predicted from the earlier retrospective studies appear to be infrequent.

Neonatologists may be correct when they claim that both mortality and morbidity are on the decline. They are not correct in concluding from normal 4-year IQ scores that there is no morbidity associated, for example, with respiratory distress syndrome (RDS), since 4 years is too soon to know how a child will fare in school, particularly inasmuch as children with learning disabilities typically have reasonably normal IQ scores. But they are correct in noting that severe neurological or intellectual problems are infrequent sequelae of RDS.

How is it, then, that so many infants survive and succeed despite reproductive or caretaking casualties: for example, the 600 gram infant experiencing a couple of months on assisted ventilation and other assorted treatments or the low birthweight twin born fourth to a lower SES teenage mother? These are the infants who once did not survive either because the technology was not available to save them or because in some places such children were killed. Some very recent phenomena, which are already to some extent taken for granted but which may serve as compensatory or facilitating influences for vulnerable infants, include our relatively new intensive care technology, modern birthing and lying-in practices, recent emphases on parenting and parent education, early intervention strategies, and even the recently popular longitudinal follow-ups of infants born at risk. All of these, from the most sophisticated intensive care technology to merely being a subject in a longitudinal research project, may compensate for insults of reproductive and caretaking casualties.

This chapter describes a number of examples of data which demonstrate these compensating influences. Among these studies are (1) a comparison between early survivors and later survivors of RDS, illustrating the varying effects of different intensive care technologies; (2) effects of supplemental stimulation on preterm RDS infants; (3) a comparison between low birthweight twins and their normal weight co-twins among discordant pairs and the apparent compensating treatment provided for the weaker twin; (4) a comparison of preterm infants born to middle versus lower SES parents to illustrate stressful and nonstressful parenting effects; (5) the effects of a very minimal parent-training intervention; and (6) more extensive parent-training interventions for infants at risk because of both reproductive and caretaking casualties, that is, preterm infants born to lower SES teenage mothers. These separate studies are presented to illustrate the potential compensatory influences of postnatal environments on infants born at risk because of reproductive and caretaking casualties.

Study 1: Developmental assessments of more recent survivors versus earlier survivors of RDS. Effects of changing technology and hospital practices

This study involved a comparison between earlier and more recent survivors of RDS to determine whether infants born at the same hospital, with similar neonatal histories, but who were born at different time periods when different forms of treatment were being used, were any different on developmental measures (Field, Dempsey, and Shuman, 1979).

Method

Subjects

The sample was comprised of 42 preterms including 21 earlier survivors and 21 more recent survivors of Type 1 idiopathic respiratory distress syndrome. Most of the children were later born, and sex was evenly distributed in the groups, with 14 males and 7 females in each. These groups did not differ on traditional birth measures (gestational age, birthweight, birth length, head circumference, and Apgar scores) nor did they differ on neonatal history data including bilirubin levels, PO_2 and pH levels, and number of apnoeic spells. Mean birth measures can be seen in Table 1. The earlier survivors averaged 2.6 days intermittent negative pressure respiration and 37 days intensive care, and the more recent survivors 2.9 days intermittent positive pressure ventilation (IPPV) and 44 days intensive care. The earlier sample was born in 1973 and the more recent sample in 1975, both groups to mothers who were the same SES (middle-class), education (high school) and age range (22–32 years).

Procedure

The infants from these groups were not matched, although several neonatal measures were analyzed to determine the comparability of the samples. In addition to making comparisons of the groups on the traditional birth measures and medical data, the Obstetric and Postnatal Complications Scales of Littman and Parmelee (1978) were used.

The Obstetric Complications Scale is comprised of optimal or nonoptimal pregnancy events such as infection, bleeding, and hypertension, of obstetric events such as duration of labor and delivery medication, and of birth events including the onset of respiration and Apgar scores. The Postnatal Complications Scale is an assessment of the infant's postnatal course including items that reflect an increased risk of mortality and morbidity. Among these are postnatal complications such as hyperbilirubinemia, convulsions, and metabolic and temperature disturbances.

Table 1 Means for Neonatal Measures of Earlier and Recent RDS
Survivors

Dependent Measures	Earlier RDS Survivors (N=21)	Recent RDS Survivors (N=21)
Gestational age (weeks)	32	32
Birthweight (grams)	1,778	1,733
Obstetric Complication Scale[a]	76	78
Postnatal Complication Scale[a]	61	66
Duration of intensive care (days)	37	44

[a]See text.

The children were assessed annually during their first 2 years of life
with the Bayley Scales of Infant Development (Bayley, 1969) by two
separate groups of testers. A correction for the prematurity of the RDS
subjects was made in order that developmental scores could be figured at
equivalent postconceptional ages (gestational age plus age from birth).
When the subjects were 4 years of age, they were given the following
assessments: (1) a Stanford-Binet IQ (Terman and Merrill, 1972) or the
McCarthy Scales; (2) the Vineland Social Maturity Scale (Doll, 1965),
which is a list of age-related developmental milestones such as washing
self, dressing self, and helping with household tasks; and (3) the Beha-
vior-Problem Checklist (Quay and Peterson, 1975), which is a questionnaire composed of several assessments of developmental habits, including a number of symptoms that correlate with minimal brain dysfunction such as hyperactivity, distractability, short attention span, irritability, impulsiveness, specific fears, and unclear speech (Gross and Wilson,
1974).

Results

Multivariate and univariate analyses of variance on the perinatal data of
these groups yielded no significant differences (see Table 1 for means).

A 2(group) × 2(sex) multivariate analysis performed on the group of
Bayley Developmental assessments yielded significant differences in
Bayley scores (see Table 2). Univariate analyses on each of the Bayley
assessments suggested that the more recent survivors of RDS received
superior scores on both Bayley mental and motor scales at both 1 and 2
years.

Analyses of the 4-year data revealed continuing differences favoring
the more recent survivors of RDS on IQ scores, social quotient and behavior problem measures (see Table 3).

Table 2 Means for 1- and 2-year Assessments of
Earlier and Recent RDS Survivors

Dependent Measures	Earlier RDS Survivors (N=21)	Recent RDS Survivors (N=21)
1-year scores		
Bayley Mental	78	89*
Bayley Motor	74	80*
2-year scores		
Bayley Mental	80	95*
Bayley Motor	78	90*

*$p < .001$ (Earlier v. Recent survivors).

Discussion

Although other studies on more recent survivors of RDS suggest that our "technology" is saving sicker newborns (Fitzhardinge, Pape, Arstikaitis, Boyle, Ashley, Rowley, Nettley, and Swyer, 1976; Johnson, Malachowski, Grabstein, Welsch, Daily, and Sunshine, 1974), none of these studies compared earlier and more recent groups born and treated at the same hospital. The differences between our samples may relate to advances made in perinatal medicine and hospital practices. As some have claimed, recent technology may be reducing morbidity as well as perinatal mortality. The data suggest perinatal differences between the earlier and more recent survivors of RDS only on types of treatment (the recent group receiving IPPV) and on duration of intensive care (the recent group remaining in intensive care for a slightly longer period). The better outcome of the recent group may relate to IPPV being a superior form of treatment to their slightly longer period of intensive care. Unfortunately, these variables are confounded with changes in hospital practices.

Among the hospital practices which changed over the 2-year period separating the birth dates of these two groups were the following (1) the nurseries became less sterile and more interesting for infants, families and staff; for example, they featured rocking chairs, colorful decorations, mobiles, bassinette propping, and infant swings; (2) handling and breastfeeding were encouraged, and a private room was recently made available for those contacts; (3) parents' involvement was more actively encouraged, and a comparison of visiting patterns suggested that the parents of the more recent group, although geographically as distant from the hospital, visited their infants more often than the earlier group; (4) home visits preceding and following the infant's discharge were more

Table 3 Means for 4-year Assessments of Earlier and Recent RDS Survivors

Dependent Measures	Earlier RDS Survivors (N=21)	Recent RDS Survivors (N=21)
Stanford-Binet I.Q. or McCarthy General Cognitive Score	103	112**
Vineland Social Quotient	121	125*
Behavior Problem Checklist	20	14**
Number of Minimal Brain Dysfunction Symptoms	12	9

*p < .05
**p < .01

frequent; and (5) pediatric visits were more closely monitored, and earlier referrals were made to the recently developing early infant stimulation programs.

Another potential contributor to the developmental differences of these two groups is the treatment effect of research. Single assessments (the Bayley Developmental Scales) were made only once a year on the earlier sample, while the more recent sample was given multiple assessments every 4 months during the first year. The Hawthorne effect or the influence of the researcher-subject relationship may have contributed to these differences (Goldberg, 1979). Parents' involvement and attempts at enriching their infants' environments may have been inadvertently inspired or reinforced by our fairly intensive research program. The multiplicity of factors which could have contributed to developmental differences between our earlier and more recent RDS groups leaves us with a somewhat confusing but promising picture.

Study 2: Providing supplemental nonnutritive sucking stimulation: Effects of a behavioral treatment on intensive care unit neonates

The results of Study 1 were interpreted as the effects of improved medical technology and a more humane intensive care unit (ICU) environment. The present study investigated the effects of providing a behavior treatment in the form of supplemental nonnutritive sucking stimulation for ICU neonates. The thesis was that providing very small, sick, preterm neonates the opportunity to suck on a pacifier during tube feedings might be an effective treatment facilitating recovery, weight gain, and earlier hospital discharge. Sucking during tube feedings may increase peristalsis and secretion of digestive fluids, enhancing mixing, propulsion, absorption of nutrients, and expulsion of waste, and thus facilitate not only the initiation but also the completion of the gastrointestinal cycle (Measel and Anderson, 1979).

This model is supported by findings that sucking improves digestion, prevents abdominal distention (Miller and Dymsza, 1963), promotes normoglycemia, decreases crying (Grant, Vidyasagar, and Anderson, 1978; Lambesis, Vidyasagar, and Anderson, 1976), improves oxygenation (Burroughs, Asonye, Anderson-Shanklin, and Vidyasagar, 1978), and increases rest (Grant, et al., 1978; Lambesis et al., 1976), thereby promoting weight gain, earlier oral feedings, and a shorter hospital stay.

Field (1978a) has noted that during nonnutritive sucking, preterm infants exhibit more stable organization of behavioral state and show fewer episodes of crying and cogwheel-like limb movements. In addition, following the onset of nonnutritive sucking, infants will alert, make eye contact, and track the movement of the examiner's face as assessed on the Brazelton Neonatal Behavior Scale (Brazelton, 1973).

Method

Subjects

The sample consisted of 33 infants admitted to the newborn intensive care unit with birthweights less than 1,800 grams, gestational age less than 35 weeks, and free from major congenital anomalies, chromosomal abnormalities, oropharyngeal problems, and conditions known to be incompatible with life. There were 17 babies in the control group consisting of 7 males and 10 females and 16 babies in the treatment group consisting of 8 males and 8 females. After gestational age was assessed by the Dubowitz method, subjects were assigned to groups using a stratified random sampling technique to ensure that the groups were similar on mean gestational age and birthweight. The two groups were similar on neonatal characteristics as can be seen in Table 4.

Procedure

Infants in the treatment group were given a pacifier during all tube feedings. Pacifiers were the various size amber, red, and blue nipples manufacturered by Ross Laboratories, stuffed with a 2 in = 3 in gauze for resistance. The infant received the largest nipple that could be tolerated. Infants were given the pacifiers whether or not they made an effort to suck. Infants in both groups were allowed to have a pacifier at any time other than tube feedings depending on customary ICU practice, but only the treatment babies received the pacifier during tube feedings.

Data collected from the medical records included weight at first tube

Table 4 Means for Neonatal Measures of Infants Assigned to Nonnutritive Sucking Treatment and Control Groups

	Treatment	Control
Gestational Age (weeks)	32	32
Birthweight (grams)	1,269	1,339
Apgar score	8	7
Obstetric Complication Scale[a]	84	74
Postnatal Complication Scale[a]	64	66

[a]See text.

feeding, discharge weight, first tube feeding, last tube feeding, first bottle feeding, number of tube feedings, number of days in the ICU and cost of the hospital stay. The Obstetric Complications Scale (OCS) and the Postnatal Factors Scale (PNF) (Littman and Parmelee, 1978) were used to assess the obstetric and postnatal factors affecting the infants. The Brazelton Neonatal Behavioral Assessment Scale was administered to each infant, upon being placed in an open crib, to compare the two groups on the four a priori behavioral dimensions.

Finally, the infants were observed during a bottle feeding just prior to discharge. A number of infant behaviors including alertness, eye contact, physical activity, persistence in sucking, regurgitation, vocalization, and fussiness were observed using a time sample unit coding system. In addition, the amount of intake and length of feeding time were recorded. Nurse behaviors observed included feeding position, the amount of bottle jiggling, and other stimulation-to-feed behaviors. Of interest here was whether infants receiving the nonnutritive sucking stimulation treatment might be more organized, easier-to-feed babies.

The data were analyzed by analysis of covariance with weight at first tube feeding as the covariate.

Results

The clinical outcome variables can be seen in Table 5. The adjusted means are presented. It appears that the group means on these variables are falling in the predicted direction. Namely, the treatment group started bottle feeding 2 days earlier, they required 37 fewer tube feedings, and they averaged 24 grams greater weight gain. In addition, the treatment infants were hospitalized 3 days less than the control group and their hospital cost was approximately $2,000 less than that of the control group (Ignatoff and Field, 1980).

The adjusted means on the Brazelton clusters are presented in Table 6.

Table 5 Adjusted Means for Clinical Measures of Nonnutritive Sucking. Treatment and Control Infants

	Treatment	Control
First tube feed to first bottle feed (days)	26	28
Number of tube feedings	296	333
Weight change (grams)	729	705
Hospital stay (days)	51	54
Intensive care	39	39
Minimal care	12	16
Hospital cost (dollars)	19,766	21,521

Surprisingly, the control group performed significantly better ($p < .05$) on Cluster II (motoric processes). The other clusters were not significantly different.

Discussion

To understand the difference observed on the motoric process dimension of the Brazelton we looked at the seven items that comprise that dimension: number of deviant reflexes, motor tone, activity, pull-to-sit, motor maturity, defensive reaction, and hand-to-mouth activity. It seems that in deriving the cluster score the "deviant reflex" item is heavily weighted, and the control group did, in fact, have fewer deviant reflexes: an average of 4.1 for the treatment group and 3.1 for the control group. One of the predicted effects of nonnutritive sucking is increased rest. Perhaps the treatment babies took longer to wake up when being examined and were therefore in a lower state at the time the reflex items were administered. This might contribute to the hypotonic reflexes observed in the treatment group as compared with the stronger reflexes of the control group. The treatment babies actually had higher scores on 4 out of the 7 items of the motoric process cluster. Notably, the difference on the hand-to-mouth item approached significance with the treatment group performing more optimally. The more optimal hand-to-mouth behavior of the treatment group may be a direct effect of being provided additional nonnutritive sucking experience, since sucking on a nipple may generalize to hand sucking. Coding of later nurse–infant bottle feeding observations revealed that the control infants regurgitated more often, consumed less volume of formula per feeding, and elicited more bottle jiggling and stimulation-to-feed behavior from the nurses, suggesting that the infants receiving nonnutritive sucking during earlier tube feedings were easier-to-feed babies during later bottle feedings (Stringer and Field, 1980).

Table 6 Mean Brazelton Scores for Non-nutritive Sucking Treatment and Control Infants

	Treatment	Control
Interaction	2.5	2.3
Motor	2.4	2.0
State organization	1.7	1.9
Response to stress	1.6	1.3

The treatment group means on the clinical measures suggest that this may be a cost-effective intervention for preterm ICU neonates. They gain more weight, go home sooner, and cost someone less money. However, the considerable variability of ICU neonates suggests that larger samples of neonates need to be assessed to determine the reliability of these effects and ensure that there are no undesirable side effects of providing nonnutritive sucking during tube feedings.

Study 3: Discordant twin pairs: Bigger is not always better, or parents may prefer the tiny one

Some say supplemental stimulation should be provided in the ICU; others claim those neonates get enough stimulation in the ICU and even more when they go home. The results of the present study came as a complete surprise. The study investigated discordant twin pairs, that is, pairs of twins in which one twin was small weight-for-date and the other normal weight-for-date. Since the literature suggests that being born too small may have adverse effects on development—indeed worse effects than being born too soon (Nelligan, Kolvin, Scott, and Garside, 1976)—we predicted that small-for-date twins would fare worse than their normal weight co-twins. In fact, the opposite occurred: the smaller, sicker twin fared better over the first year of life (Field and Widmayer, 1980).

Method

Subjects

The sample was composed of 36 twins (22 of them preterm) who were discordant on birth weight by at least 15 percent ($M = 25$ percent discordance). This sample was drawn from a larger group of 158 monozygotic and same-sex dizygotic twins of lower SES mothers. Ethnicity was 52 percent black, 18 percent white, and the remaining pairs Hispanic or Haitian. The mothers averaged 24 years of age and most were multiparous.

Procedure

All twins were assessed at the neonatal stage and at 3 and 12 months (corrected age). Measures at birth were the traditional birth measures (gestational age, birthweight, Apgar scores, and Ponderal Index [PI] of appropriate weight for length). Other neonatal measures were Brazelton assessments, and the Obstetric and Postnatal Complications Scales adapted by Littman and Parmelee (1978) from the Prechtl complication scales.

Assessments made at 3 to 4 months corrected age at our interaction lab included growth measures (length and weight), blood pressures, feeding, and face-to-face interactions between the twins and their mothers (and occasionally fathers). These were videotaped and coded for infant gaze aversion and mother verbal activity as well as rated according to our interaction rating scales (IRS) which include ratings of eye contact, facial expressions, vocalizations, and contingent responsivity (Field, 1980).

At 12 months growth measures, blood pressure, and Bayley scale performance were assessed. The mothers completed questionnaires on temperament (Colorado Temperament scale: Rowe and Plomin, 1977), a twin confusability scale (Wilson, Brown, and Matheny, 1971), and a twin zygosity "guesstimate" scale (Nichols and Bilbro, 1966) to assess the degree to which twins are perceived as similar or different and the accuracy with which their perceptions match the separate zygosity determinations made by blood typing. Finally, floor play interactions of both twins together with their mother were videotaped and coded for durations of time. Various social behaviors were observed for evaluating the twins' language environment and development.

Results

If one were to use the traditional birth measures data to predict later performance, the prediction would favor the normal birthweight twin of the discordant pairs (Table 7). However, on the basis of the Brazelton data in Table 8, one would make a different prediction. A number of the Brazelton scores surprisingly favor the low birthweight twin in the case of the term pairs. Term pairs perform more optimally, as one might predict, than the preterm pairs. Within the preterm pairs, there is matching performance between low and normal birthweight co-twins except in the case of the motor score which favors, again surprisingly, the low birthweight twin.

Although these data came as a surprise it should be noted that most of

Table 7 Mean Neonatal Measures of Higher and Lower Birthweight Twins among Discordant Term and Preterm Pairs

	Term		Preterm	
	High	Low	High	Low
Birthweight (grams)	3,025	2,372**	1,920	1,421**
Birth length (cms)	50	49	45	42*
Head circumference (cms)	34	32*	31	29*
Apgar score	8	6*	6	4*
Discordance rate		22%		28%

*p < .05
**p < .001

Table 8 Mean Brazelton Measures of Higher and Lower Birthweight Twins among Discordant Term and Preterm Pairs

	Term		Preterm	
	High	Low	High	Low
Interaction	2.5	2.3*	2.7	2.7
Motor	2.3	2.1*	2.3	2.0**
State organization	2.0	2.3**	2.3	2.3
Response to stress	1.9	1.6*	1.7	1.7

*p < .05
**p < .01

the scores are lower than average. Because these are not low PI babies, however, we should not have formulated expectations based on the lesser Brazelton performance of the low weight for length neonates reported by Als, Tronick, Adamson, and Brazelton (1976). The equivalent, and in some cases, better performance of the low birthweight twins is, nonetheless, perplexing. Perhaps these small babies are not growth deprived in the same way that low weight for length babies are, or the effects at least are not manifested in neonatal behavior as they are in low PI babies. Or perhaps the Brazelton examiner does not relate to these babies as small-for-length, obviously growth deprived infants but rather as very small twins in accordance with an expectation that twins are usually smaller neonates. Their smallness may have unwittingly elicited compensatory maneuvers in the Brazelton examiners as has been reported for mothers. Even though examiners could not make comparisons, since separate examiners assessed the small and average twins of each pair, they may have worked harder to elicit optimal peformance from the smaller twins.

The prediction, then, on birth data alone would be poorer later interactions of the low birthweight twins, and the prediction based on the Brazelton neonatal data and reports in the literature on compensatory tendencies of mothers of discordant twins might predict equivalent or better performance of the low birthweight twin. Again, the data surprisingly support the latter prediction as can be seen in Figures 1 and 2 on face-to-face interactions filmed when the infants were 3 months.

Figure 1 shows less infant gaze aversion and more maternal verbal activity for the low birthweight infants and their mothers. Figure 2 shows more optimal face-to-face interaction summary scores for the low birthweight infants of both term and preterm groups and for their mothers. These scores summarize the performance on a number of ratings which comprise our interaction rating scale derived from microanalyses of some 200 mother–infant interactions (Field, 1980).

Although we have seen only three discordant pairs at 12 months, their data are again a surprise as can be seen in Table 9. The scores of two term discordant pairs suggest more optimal Bayley mental and motor performance as well as Bayley behavioral extraversion and cognitive ratings for the low birthweight discordant twin. The scores on the preterm twin pair suggest equivalent performance of the low and normal birthweight co-twins. The floor play interaction data also favored the low birthweight twin.

Were this trend to continue at one year our data would support the findings indicating that the low birthweight twin is at no additional risk for developmental delays, but not the findings of several other studies that suggest delays of the low birthweight twin. One possible explanation of the discrepancies in the literature may be that others have assessed small-weight-for-length of low PI twins, who might be expected to show delays based on longitudinal data on low PI singletons. Another possibility relates to their use of less conservative measures of discordance, that is, calling twins discordant when they are only 5 to 10 percent discordant, a weight difference which may not even be noticed by mothers. Still another possibility is that these early developmental scores may be inconsistent or discontinuous with later IQ scores such that the low birthweight twins only show delays at a later age.

In any case, the data suggest that early risk factors (e.g., low birthweight for singletons) may not generalize to twins. At-risk twins may be treated differentially by parents than at-risk singletons. Mothers, for example, may strive to provide compensatory treatment for the smallest infant.

In addition, the data suggest that the sicker twin who remains in the hospital longer is not necessarily at risk for parenting disorders because of early separation. Another recent study on twins by Bauer (1977) suggests that the sicker twin who required intensive care for a number of

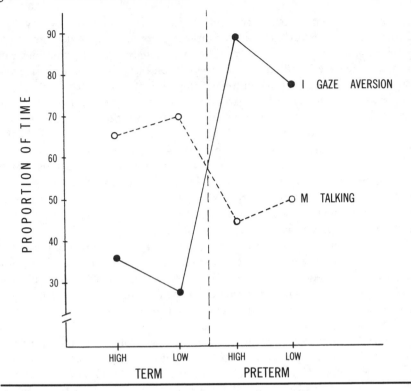

Figure 1. Proportion of time 3-month-old infants gaze averted and mothers talked to higher and lower birthweight twins among discordant pairs during face-to-face interactions.

medical complications including RDS, experienced accelerated development of both motor and mental developmental milestones compared with the healthy co-twin. Bauer's (1977) data and the data of this study suggest that risk factors for singletons may not generalize to twins. Parents may provide compensatory treatment for the smaller, sicker twin, and by having more optimal early interactions may contribute to more optimal development.

A separate literature on early parent–twin relationships offers observational, interview, and anecdotal data suggesting that the mother of twins is more affiliated with the smaller, weaker twin at least during the first year (Allen, Greenspan, and Pollin, 1976; Allen, Pollin, and Hoffer, 1971; Gifford, Murawski, Brazelton, and Young, 1966). This early affiliation or differential treatment by the parent may serve as a compensatory mech-

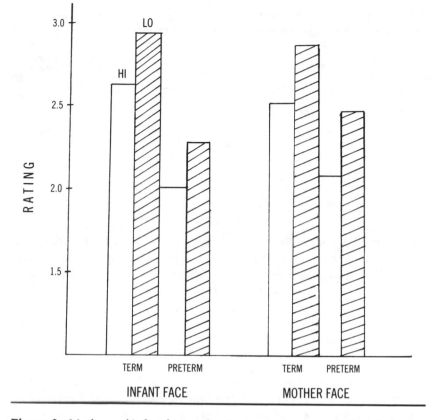

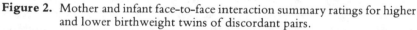

Figure 2. Mother and infant face-to-face interaction summary ratings for higher and lower birthweight twins of discordant pairs.

anism to facilitate matching development of the low birthweight and normal birthweight co-twins. This possibility was raised only after our collection of twin data, which surprised us by failing to support our a priori prediction that the low birthweight twins of discordant pairs would fare more poorly on early interactions and developmental assessments.

Study 4—Comparisons between preterm infants born to middle and lower SES, teenage mothers: Home environments may compensate

The preterm infant born to a teenage, lower SES mother might be at considerable risk because of the cumulative effects of adolescent parent-

Table 9 Sample Bayley Scores for 12-month Assessments of Higher and Lower Birthweight Twins among Discordant Term and Preterm Pairs

	Discordance	Mental	Motor	Behavior Extraversion rating	Cognitive rating
Term twins					
Harv-High	28%	91	117	7	26
-Low		122	134	9	31
Brop-High	21%	119	111	12	25
-Low		128	122	17	34
Preterm twins					
Schu-High	21%	119	92	14	23
-Low		119	92	9	24

ing, low SES conditions, and developmental delays associated with prematurity. Since teenage mothers of middle SES appear, themselves, to fare better, so might their infants. The purpose of this study was to compare preterm infants born to teenage mothers of middle and lower SES backgrounds (Field, 1980).

Method

Subjects

The sample was 20 lower SES, black teenage mothers, and their preterm infants and 20 middle SES, white teenage mothers, and their preterm infants. Ethnicity was confounded with socioeconomic status since the available lower SES dyads were black and the available middle SES dyads were white. The teenage mothers were <19 years and the preterm infants were <37 weeks gestation and weighed <2500 grams at birth.

Procedure

The infants were assessed at birth on the Brazelton Neonatal Behavioral Assessment Scale, and the traditional birth measures and postnatal complication data were collected. The infants and their mothers were then seen at 4-month intervals over the first year for assessments of their interactions and infants' growth and development.

Results

As can be seen in Table 10, the only differences between the neonates were the higher Ponderal Index and the more optimal Brazelton interaction scores of the middle SES Neonates.

At 4 months (Table 11) there were no differences on the Denver

Table 10 Means for Neonatal Measures of Infants Born to Middle and Lower SES Teenage Mothers

Measures	Middle SES	Lower SES
Neonatal		
Gestational age (weeks)	35	35
Birthweight (grams)	2,410	2,347
Ponderal Index	2.41	2.27*
Apgar score	7.9	7.4
Postnatal Complication Scale[a]	128	121
Brazelton		
Interaction	2.3	2.6*
Motor	2.6	2.7
State	2.4	2.5
Stress	2.1	2.0

[a]See text.
*$p < .05$

Developmental Scale. However, the interaction ratings of both mother and infant were more optimal for the middle SES dyads. In addition, the middle SES mothers assigned more optimal temperament ratings to their infants. At 8 months (Table 11) and 1 and 2 (Table 12) years, the middle SES infants received higher Bayley mental scores, although no group differences occurred for the Bayley motor scale scores. In addition, the middle SES infants received more optimal temperament and behavior ratings and had a longer mean length of utterance during floor play interactions at 1 and 2 years (Table 12).

Discussion

Infants born to lower SES as opposed to middle SES mothers received lower Ponderal Indexes suggesting that they were less appropriate weight for length. This may have contributed to their less optimal Brazelton interaction scores, since the latter have been reported previously for small-for-length infants by Als et al. (1976). Lesser interaction skills at birth may have also mediated the less optimal interaction scores of the infants at 4 months. Like the lower SES infants of the Lewis and Wilson (1972) study, these infants were less vocal, less expressive, and less animated. Similarly, the lower SES mothers engaged in less verbal activity (Bee, VanEgeren, Streissguth, Nyman, and Lockie, 1969; Kilbride, Johnson, and Streissguth, 1977; Tulkin and Kagan, 1972), contingent responsivity (Lewis and Wilson, 1972), infantized behavior and game-playing (Field and Pawlby, 1980).

As implied by the transactional model of Sameroff and Chandler

Table 11 Means for 4- and 8-month Measures of
Infants Born to Middle and Lower SES Teenage
Mothers

Measures	Middle SES	Lower SES
4 months		
Denver Developmental	29	31
Face-to-Face interaction		
Mother	1.7	1.3**
Infant	1.8	1.5*
Temperament	3.4	3.8*
8 months		
Bayley		
Mental	101	94**
Motor	97	98
Temperament	3.1	3.6*

*$p < .05$
**$p < .01$

(1975), the lower SES infants' lower Ponderal Indexes and interaction skills at birth may have contributed to the mothers' lesser responsivity during interactions and lower temperament ratings of these infants at 4 months. These, in turn, may have contributed to the infants' lower Bayley mental scores, less optimal behavior ratings, and shorter MLU of later assessment periods.

Study 5—A mini-intervention for preterm infants and their lower SES, teenage mothers: Effects of Brazelton demonstrations

Since the lower SES teenage mothers of the previous study treated their infants like baby dolls who could not see or hear but merely feed, cry, and wet their pants, this study was directed at showing them the amazing skills of the newborn. We hoped that by demonstrating the infants' skills to the teenage mother, she in turn, might be verbally more responsive to her infant. The vehicle we used was the Brazelton scale since that assessment is routinely made on the preterm infants at our hospital and consequently might serve as a cost-free intervention (Widmayer and Field, 1980).

Method

Subjects

Thirty preterm infants born to teenage, lower SES, black mothers were randomly selected from our normal nurseries. The mothers were <19

Table 12 Means for 1- and 2-year Measures of Infants Born to Middle and Lower SES Teenage Mothers

Measures	Middle SES	Lower SES
1 year		
Bayley		
Mental	104	99*
Motor	97	98
Language—MLU	1.4	1.0*
2 years		
Bayley		
Mental	111	102**
Motor	102	99
Language—MLU	1.7	1.2**
Behavior rating	31.2	140.7**

*$p < .05$
**$p < .01$

years and their preterm infants were <37 weeks gestation and <2500 grams birthweight, but free of medical complications requiring intensive care. The preterm infants were randomly assigned to a control group, a Brazelton demonstration group and Mother's Assessment of the Behavior of her Infant (MABI) group. The groups were similar on all birth measures and Brazelton scores at the neonatal stage.

Procedure

The MABI group mothers were asked to administer independently the mother's version of the Brazelton assessment (Field, Dempsey, Hallock, and Shuman, 1978) at birth and at 1 week intervals during the first month. The Brazelton group received a demonstration of the Brazelton and completed the MABI. We speculated that the Brazelton demonstration would provide modeling of the ways in which the mother might elicit optimal interactive behaviors of the infant which would then be practiced and reinforced by her periodic administration of the MABI. The control mothers were asked to complete a weekly assessment of developmental milestones and childrearing attitudes to control for a Hawthorne effect. Mothers were paid for the return of these assessments.

Home visits were made at 1 month to administer a second Brazelton, and to film feeding and face-to-face interactions. At 4 months the infants' growth and development was assessed, interactions were again filmed and mothers assessed their infants' temperament. At 12 months the infants and their mothers were revisited in their homes. At this time

growth measurements were taken, the Bayley scales of infant development were administered, and videotapes of the mothers and their infants
in floor play sequences were made.

Results

At 1 month the Brazelton demonstration group infants received more
optimal interactive process scores than did the infants of the control
group (Table 13). A repeated measures analysis of variance on the Brazelton Neonatal and Brazelton 1-month assessments suggested that Brazelton demonstration group infants showed a significant improvement on
Brazelton interaction scores over the first month.

Group comparisons on our feeding interaction scale suggested that
only the mothers' rating differed. As can be seen in Figure 3, the Brazelton and MABI mothers received more optimal ratings than the control
mothers. Group comparisons on our face-to-face interaction rating scale
suggested that both mothers and infants of the Brazelton and MABI
groups received more optimal ratings than the mother–infant dyads of
the control group (Field, 1980).

Also, as can be seen in Figure 4, Brazelton and MABI mothers vocalized to their infants a lesser proportion of the time than did mothers of
the control group. Infants of the control group averted their gaze a
greater proportion of the time than did the Brazelton infants.

Four Months

At 4 months there were no group differences on infant or mother feeding
interaction ratings. However, both mother and infant face-to-face interaction ratings favored the MABI and Brazelton dyads (Figure 5). In addition, the MABI and Brazelton infants gaze averted less of the time than
did infants in the control group and their mothers engaged in more verbal activity.

Twelve Months

At 12 months, although the Brazelton infants were heavier and taller
than the control group, these differences were not significant.

As may be seen in Table 14, the Brazelton infants received significantly
higher scores on the Bayley Mental Scale. The Bayley motor scores of
the Brazelton group also approached significance as compared with the
motor scores of the control group.

Discussion

The results of this study suggest that the introduction of an easy and
comparatively brief intervention such as a Brazelton demonstration to

Table 13 Means for 1-month Brazelton Measures of Preterm Control, MABI and Brazelton Demonstration Infants

Brazelton Scale	Control	MABI	Brazelton
Interaction	2.4	2.2	1.6*
Motor	2.1	2.0	1.8
State organization	1.8	1.7	1.8
Response to stress	1.3	1.0	1.2

*$p < .05$

teenage, lower SES mothers may be an effective method of fostering more optimal interactions between these young women and their preterm infants. It may be that the mothers become more sensitive to the unique abilities of their infants, more interested in observing this development closely, and more active in encouraging them to realize their potential over the first weeks and months.

The Brazelton group mothers were unanimous in their amazement that their newborn infants were capable of following their mothers' moving faces, orienting to the sounds of their voices, and, in general, being so aware of their environment. They were then encouraged to rediscover these behaviors of their preterm infants on their own as they completed the MABIs weekly.

Not surprisingly, perhaps, the teenage mothers of the Brazelton group continued to perceive their infants as more receptive to sensory and verbal stimulation and may have provided more optimal levels of these than did the mothers of the preterm control group, resulting in higher Bayley scores at 1 year. It appears that use of the Brazelton and MABI may be a cost-effective intervention for teenage mothers within the first few days following delivery of their preterm infants.

Study 6—The effects of a more extensive parent-training program on preterm infants and their lower SES teenage mothers: A home-based intervention.

Since the study on lower SES teenage mothers and their preterm infants suggested that this group was at particular risk for delayed development because of the combined effects of premature delivery and lower SES teenage parenting and since the previous study suggested that these mothers can benefit from intervention, this study investigated the effects of a more extensive parent-training program for these mothers (Field, Widmayer, Stringer, and Ignatoff, 1980).

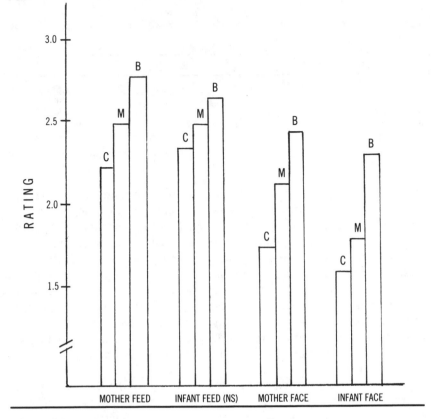

Figure 3. Mean ratings on 1-month feeding and face-to-face interactions of Brazelton demonstration (B), MABI (M), and control (C) groups of infants and mothers.

Intervention programs typically mounted for teenage mothers focus on
the prenatal and delivery periods and cease at the point at which the
need for intervention appears to be most critical. Intervention programs
for preterm infants, not necessarily born to teenage mothers, have
typically provided supplemental stimulation, but usually cease again
shortly after the neonatal period. As far as we know, intervention
programs have not been established specifically for the preterm infants
of teenage mothers. However, the separate literatures on preterm
infants and teenage parenting suggest that these two risk factors may
interact to place the infant at even greater risk, and thus at greater need
for intervention.

The present study provided a home-based, parent-training interven-

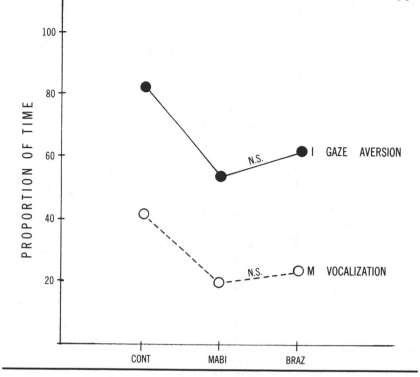

Figure 4. Proportion of time control, MABI and Brazelton demonstation infants gaze averted and mothers vocalized during 1-month, face-to-face interactions.

tion for lower SES, black teenage mothers and their preterm infants. Their development was then compared to nonintervention control dyads.

Method

Subjects

Subjects were 60 preterm infants and their lower SES, black teenage mothers. Subjects were recruited by seeking volunteers for an intervention program. Half of the dyads were then randomly assigned to an intervention and half to a control group. The teenage mothers were <19 years and the preterm infants <37 weeks gestation and <2500 grams birthweight. A series of neonatal assessments including traditional birth measures, Brazelton assessments, and postnatal complications revealed

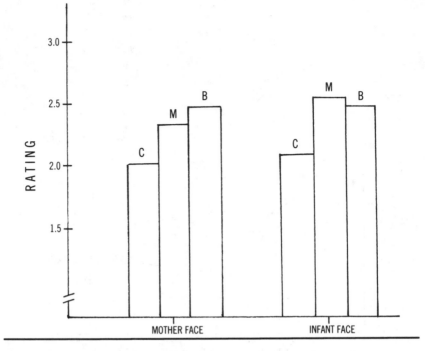

Figure 5. Mean ratings on 3-month, face-to-face interactions of Brazelton demonstration (B), MABI (M), and control (C) groups of infants and
mothers.

no initial differences between the infants randomly assigned to intervention and control groups.

Procedure

Two procedures were used: intervention and assessments. Intervention
consisted of home visits made by two-person teams including a trained
interventionist and a teenage, black female work/study student. Home
rather than clinic visits were made after high-school hours to minimize
sample attrition. Although approximately one-third of the infants of
teenage mothers were cared for by grandmothers or other relatives during the teenage mother's school hours, designating the teenage mother as
secondary caregiver, the literature on teenage parenting suggested we
should target the at-risk teenage mother in our interventions (Badger,
1980; DeLissovoy, 1973; Tjossem, 1976).

Home visits were made biweekly for approximately ½ hour per visit

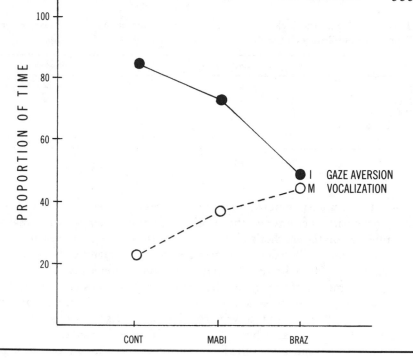

Figure 6. Proportion of time control, MABI, and Brazelton demonstration infants gaze averted and mothers vocalized during 3-month, face-to-face interactions.

and were designed to achieve the following goals: (1) to educate the mothers on developmental milestones and childrearing practices; (2) to teach the mothers exercises and age-appropriate stimulation for facilitating sensorimotor and cognitive development of their infants; and (3) to facilitate mother–infant interactions in the interest of developing communication skills and fostering harmonious mother–infant relationships.

Developmental milestone tables, general ideas for facilitating these milestones, and instructions on plotting growth measurements and developmental milestones were given to the mother when she was enrolled in the program. The training in caretaking practices and sensorimotor/cognitive and interaction exercises was the same for all subjects of a given age (postconceptional age to adjust for prematurity) in the interest of keeping the treatment condition fairly standardized. The caretaking, sensorimotor, and interaction exercises were graded developmentally. For each 2-week period a group of these exercises was given to the mother.

Table 14 12-month Bayley Scores of Preterm Control, MABI and Brazelton Demonstration Infants

	Control	MABI	Brazelton
Mental	97	122	127*
Motor	96	108	118
Behavior			
Extraversion	13	15	14
Cognitive	29	24	30

*$p < .001$

The interventionist demonstrated the exercises (approximately five exercises per visit), then invited the mother to try the exercises and finally commented on the mother's performance of the exercises. On each exercise card a photo illustrates the exercise, since the reading skills of this population are often limited. A very short explanation is given of the exercise, the amount of time it should be practiced daily (usually 5 minutes for a total 25 to 30 minutes of exercise time per day) and a time chart on which the mother is asked to write the time she starts and stops the exercise each day and whether her baby successfully performed this exercise. During the subsequent visit the interventionist asked the mother to perform the exercises to determine whether she had been working on these throughout the intervening weeks.

Most of the sensorimotor exercises were adapted from Brazelton, Denver, and Bayley scale test items, and most of the interaction exercises were taken from research on infant games (Field, 1978b; 1979a; Sroufe and Wunsch, 1972). Examples of exercises for the first month include the following: (1) demonstration of cradled feeding position, sponge bath, and lotion rub; (2) the animate and inanimate visual and auditory items taken from the Brazelton scales; and (3) rocking and singing lullaby. Examples of exercises for 2 to 4 months are: (1) passive exercise of infant's limbs and pulling infant to standing position on lap; (2) tracking, reaching, and grasping items adapted from the Denver and Bayley scales; (3) face-to-face interaction games; and (4) imitating infant's sounds and mirror play. Examples of exercises for 4 to 5 months are: (1) demonstrating spoon and finger feeding and bath tub play; (2) holding, shaking, banging, and search items adapted from the Bayley scale; (3) sitting, rolling, and precrawling exercises; (4) face-to-face interaction games such as peek-a-boo or tell-me-a-story, and imitation and mirror play. For most of the exercises, special toys or objects were constructed since piloting revealed limited availability of toys, other than household items, in most of these lower-income homes.

Assessments were made at 4-month intervals over the first year. These included assessments of mother–infant interactions; infant growth and development; and mothers' developmental expectations, childrearing attitudes, and assessments of infant temperament.

Results

As can be seen in Table 15, the intervention group faired more optimally at 4 months on weight, length, Denver developmental scores, and face-to-face interaction ratings. Their mothers also performed more optimally during interactions, and expressed more realistic developmental expectations and less punitive childrearing attitudes. In addition, the intervention mothers rated their infants more optimally on infant temperament. At 8 months the intervention mothers again assigned more optimal temperament ratings to their infants, and their infants performed more optimally on the Bayley mental and motor scales (Table 16). Finally, at 12 months (Table 16) the intervention infants were heavier and longer than control infants. Although their Bayley motor scores did not differ, they received higher mental scores. In addition, their mothers again rated their temperaments as being less difficult. Interaction measures also revealed more verbal activity on the part of the intervention mothers and more play on the part of both intervention mothers and their infants.

Discussion

Many of the apparent effects of intervention were not surprising since the intervention group had been provided training on a number of exercises adapted from infant assessments (e.g., the Denver, Bayley, and Interaction scales) which also served as the dependent or criterion reference measure. Other differences between intervention and control groups (e.g., growth differences) received no direct training and thus cannot be as readily attributed to the intervention.

Although the growth differences between intervention and control infants are difficult to interpret, they may be a secondary effect of the more adequate stimulation the intervention infants appeared to be receiving during their more optimal face-to-face interactions. Several have reported relationships between supplemental stimulation and calorie intake/weight gains (Cornell and Gottfried, 1976; Masi, 1979). In addition, although it is not clear whether infant temperament was only perceived as more optimal or in fact was more optimal, the supplemental stimulation may have contributed to more optimal temperament and, in turn, to more optimal growth by a relationship between less colic and more intake.

An important caveat for these fairly dramatic benefits of a very low

Table 15 Means for 4-month Measures of Lower SES Teenage Offspring Assigned to Control and Intervention Groups (all differences significant at $p < .001$)

Measures	Control	Intervention
Weight (grams)	6,003	6,730
Length (cms)	64	67
Denver Developmental	31	35
Face-to-face interaction		
Mother	1.7	2.5
Infant	2.0	2.5
Infant temperament[a]	4.0	2.0
Developmental expectations	3.3	7.2
Childrearing attitudes[a]	4.1	3.1

[a]Lower score is optimal

cost intervention is that the results may derive simply from increased contact of a supportive nature with these mothers, that is, a Hawthorne effect. Although the control mothers received periodic phone calls, they were not routinely visited because of funding constraints. Although the intervention mothers did not enthusiastically endorse this exercise program, the mere continual contacts with health care professionals may have provided the necessary support system for the developmental gains noted.

Study 7—A comparison between a home-based and a center-based intervention for infants of lower SES teenage mothers.

The home-based, parent-training intervention program just presented clearly facilitated the infants' growth and development but did not appear to alter the teenage mothers' socioeconomic or educational status. The purpose of this study was to provide a more comprehensive intervention, a center-based, parent-training program that might facilitate the teenage mothers' status, and the effects of this center-based program were then compared with those of a home-based program like the one just described.

Method

Subjects

Subjects were 60 term infants and their lower SES, black teenage mothers. Subjects were recruited by seeking volunteers for an intervention program. One-third of the dyads were then randomly assigned to a control group, a home-based, or a center-based intervention group.

Table 16 Means for 8- and 12-month Measures of Lower SES Teenage Offspring Assigned to Control and Intervention Groups

Measure	Control	Intervention
8 months		
Bayley		
Mental	101	110*
Motor	111	115
Infant temperament	3.8	2.7*
12 months		
Weight (grams)	10,187	10,350*
Length (cms)	71	74
Bayley Mental	105	114**
Toddler temperament rating	3.7	2.2**
Interaction measures		
Mother language	43	63**
Infant play	43	56*
Mother play	35	52**

*$p < .05$
**$p < .01$

Neonatal assessments including traditional birth measures, Brazelton assessments, and postnatal complications revealed no initial differences between the infants randomly assigned to intervention and control groups.

For the center-based program an infant nursery was established for all-day care of infants, and the stimulation package used in the home-based program was incorporated in the curriculum of this nursery. The infants' teenage mothers were employed as part-time teacher aide trainees in the nursery during the 20 hours per week following or preceding their school hours. The teenage mothers were paid the minimum wage by CETA for their infant nursery teacher aide training. Thus, the teenage mothers received free day care for their infants, a paid job, training, and an incentive to continue schooling. In addition, they experienced modeling of parenting skills by teachers and by middle SES adult mothers whose infants also attended the nursery.

Infants and mothers were assessed at 4-month intervals on mother–infant interactions; infant growth and development; and mothers' developmental expectations, childrearing attitudes, and assessments of infant temperament.

Results

As can be seen in Table 17 both home- and center-based groups benefited from the interventions. The infants receiving intervention were heavier

Table 17 Means for 12-month Measures of Home- and Center-based Intervention Groups

	Control	Home	Center
Weight (grams)	8,626	10,279**	11,024**
Length (cms)	71	76*	78*
Head circumference (cms)	45	46	47
Bayley Mental	106	108	119*
Bayley Motor	102	111*	119**
Work/School	.23	.36	.70**
Recidivism	.17	.07	.00**

*p < .05
**p < .01

and taller at 1 year. The center-based infants performed more optimally on the Bayley mental scale and both intervention groups received better Bayley motor scores. The mothers appeared to benefit most from the center-based intervention as manifested by a greater return-to-school-or-work rate and a lower rate of recidivism or repeat pregnancy.

Discussion

The apparent growth advantage of the nursery infants may be explained by the active nutritional component of the nursery intervention including lectures by a nutritionist, active involvement in the WIC program providing free dairy products, pediatric consults for babies who had apparent milk allergies and modeling of feeding interactions by teachers and middle SES mothers attending the program. The greater gains on the Bayley mental scale by the center-based infants may relate to the considerable language stimulation provided in the center-based program.

The most salient effects of this program appeared to be the higher rate of girls returning to work or school and the lower rate of girls with repeat pregnancies. Because the costs associated with this program—support of the teenage mother teacher aides and tuition monies paid by the middle SES working mothers—are largely covered by CETA, the benefits would appear to exceed the costs.

Summary

There appear to be a number of compensating factors that may attenuate anticipated developmental problems, although we might expect morbidity problems associated with reproductive casualties such as preterm delivery, low birthweight, or complications such as RDS or might predict caretaking casualties associated with teenage, lower SES parenting.

The comparison between earlier and more recent survivors of RDS suggests that medical technology and new neonatal care practices may facilitate more optimal development in addition to reducing mortality. Newer forms of ventilation, parent education, prettier nurseries, and increased parent visiting may all mediate more optimal development.

A simple intervention such as providing a pacifier during tube feedings appears to contribute to fewer feedings, smoother bottle feedings, and probably happier parents for both lower hospital costs and easier to feed babies at discharge.

The smaller, sicker, preemie twin does not appear to be rejected by his or her parents, rather he or she appears to be specially treated. Although we do not know whether parents do, in fact, treat this twin differently, the data suggest some compensation has occurred for the twin to excel in some areas during infancy despite the disadvantage at birth.

The power of parenting is further suggested by the dramatic developmental effects of simply showing mothers the skills of the newborn on a Brazelton. The teenage mother, through education and support posthospitalization, not only appears to change her attitudes and developmental expectations but also her interactive behaviors with her infant. Many of the reported effects are suggestive of a transactional phenomenon whereby teaching parents other ways or altering their perceptions, attitudes, and behaviors appears to mediate developmental strides in their infants, which, in turn, reinforce and elicit more of the parenting skills necessary for fostering development.

Thus some infants born at risk appear to escape the gross insults of reproductive and caretaking casualties, perhaps because there are these compensatory experiences. There are, however, a number who do not experience these, as well as others who fail despite compensatory treatment. In addition, there are the unknown effects of being treated specially. While the low birthweight twin out performs his/her normal birthweight co-twin, parents anecdotally report the weaker twin as more difficult to manage behaviorally. Our RDS sample at 4 years achieved normal IQ scores but were extremely difficult to test because of limited attention span, restlessness, and hyperactivity. Some suggest that learning disabilities are mediated by early behavioral problems such as restlessness and hyperactivity. Thus a very large question is whether our treatments—the compensatory experiences we provide such as supplemental stimulation, enriched environments, parent training and, in general, very special treatment of the high-risk infant which are reducing mortality and serious morbidity—also mediate undesirable later childhood behaviors such as being a "brat" or writing backwards. The neonatologist's and psychologist's concerns too often cease with healthy weight gains and normal IQ scores, while the more subtle uninvestigated problems may remain with parents, teachers, and the child.

References

Allen, M., Greenspan, S., and Pollin, W. The effect of parental perceptions on early development in twins. *Psychiatry,* 1976, *39,* 65–71.

Allen, M. G., Pollin, W., and Hoffer, A. Parental birth and infancy factors in infant twin development. *American Journal of Psychiatry,* 1971, *127,* 1597–1604.

Als, H., Tronick, E., Adamson, L., and Brazelton, T. B. The behavior of the full-term yet underweight newborn infant. *Developmental Medicine and Child Neurology,* 1976, *18,* 590–594.

Badger, E. Effects of parent education program on teenage mothers and their offspring. In K. Scott, T. Field, and E. Robertson (Eds.), *Teenage parents and their offspring.* New York: Grune and Stratton, 1980.

Bauer, C. Effects of neonatal intensive care: A follow-up study of multiple births. *Pediatric Research,* 1977, *11,* 374.

Bayley, N. *Manual for the Bayley Scales of Infant Development.* New York: Psychological Corporation, 1969.

Bee, H. L., VanEgeren, L. F., Streissguth, A. P., Nyman, B. A., and Lockie, M. S. Social class differences in maternal teaching styles and speech patterns. *Developmental Psychology,* 1969, *1,* 726–734.

Brazelton, T. B. *Neonatal Behavioral Assessment Scale.* London: Spastic International Medical Publications, 1973.

Burroughs, A. K., Asonye, I. O., Anderson-Shanklin, G. C., and Vidyasagar, D. The effect of nonnutritive sucking on transcutaneous oxygen tension in non-crying preterm neonates. *Research in Nursing and Health,* 1978, *1,* 69–75.

Cornell, E. M., and Gottfried, A. W. Intervention with premature human infants. *Child Development,* 1976, *47,* 32–39.

DeLissovoy, V. Child care by adolescent parents. *Children Today,* 1973, *2,* 22–25.

Doll, E. A. *Vineland Social Maturity Scale.* Minnesota: American Guidance Service, 1965.

Field, T. *Effects of providing preterm infants a pacifier during Brazelton examinations.* Unpublished manuscript, University of Miami, 1978. (a)

Field, T. The three Rs of infant-adult interactions: Rhythms, repertoires, and responsivity. *Journal of Pediatric Psychology,* 1978, *3,* 131–136. (b)

Field, T. Games parents play with normal and high-risk infants. *Child Psychiatry and Human Development,* 1979, *10,* 41–48. (a)

Field, T. Interaction patterns of high-risk and normal infants. In T. Field, A. Sostek, S. Goldberg, and H. H. Shuman (Eds.), *Infants born at risk.* New York: Spectrum, 1979. (b)

Field, T. Interactions of preterm and term infants with their lower and middle class teenage and adult mothers. In T. Field, S. Goldberg, D. Stern, and A. Sostek (Eds.), *High-risk infants and children: Adult and peer interactions.* New York: Academic Press, 1980.

Field, T., Dempsey, J., and Shuman, H. Developmental assessments of infants surviving the respiratory distress syndrome. In T. Field, A. Sostek, S. Goldberg, and H. Shuman (Eds.), *Infants born at risk.* New York: Spectrum, 1979.

Field, T., Dempsey, J., Hallock, N., and Shuman, H. H. Mothers' assessments of the behavior of their infants. *Infant behavior and development*, 1978, *1*, 156–167.

Field, T., and Pawlby, S. Early face-to-face interactions of British and American working- and middle-class mother-infant dyads. *Child Development*, 1980, *51*, 250–253.

Field, T., and Widmayer, S. *Infant twin-mother interactions: Bigger is not always better*. Paper presented at the International Conference on Infant Studies, New Haven, Connecticut, April 1980.

Field, T., Widmayer, S., Stringer, S., and Ignatoff, E. Teenage, lower class black mothers and their preterm infants: An intervention and developmental follow-up. *Child Development*, 1980, *51*, 426–436.

Fitzhardinge, P. M., Pape, K., Arstikaitis, M., Boyle, M., Ashby, S., Rowley, A., Nettley, C., and Swyer, P. R. Mechanical ventilation of infants of less then 1,501 gm birthweight: Health, growth, and neurologic sequelae. *Journal of Pediatrics*, 1976, *88*, 531–541.

Gifford, S., Murawski, B. J., Brazelton, T. B., and Young, G. C. Difference in individual development within a pair of identical twins. *International Journal of Psychoanalyses*, 1966, *47*, 261–268.

Goldberg, S. The pragmatics and problems of longitudinal research with high-risk infants. In T. Field, A. Sostek, S. Goldberg, and H. H. Shuman (Eds.), *Infants born at risk*. New York: Spectrum, 1979.

Grant, A. R., Vidyasagar, D., and Anderson, G. C. The effect of self-regulatory sucking upon behavioral state in restless newborn infants. Unpublished manuscript, University of Florida, Gainesville, 1978.

Gross, M. B., and Wilson, W. C. *Minimal brain dysfunction*. New York: Brunner/Mazel, 1974.

Ignatoff, E., and Field, T. *Effects of nonnutritive sucking during tube feedings on the clinical course and behavior of ICU preterm neonates*. Paper presented at the International Conference on Infant Studies, New Haven, Connecticut, April 1980.

Johnson, J. D., Malachowski, N. C., Grabstein, R., Welsch, D., Daily, W. J. R., and Sunshine, P. Prognosis of children surviving with the aid of mechanical ventilation in the newborn period. *Journal of Pediatrics*, 1974, *88*, 272–276.

Kilbride, H. W., Johnson, D. L., and Streissguth, A. P. Social class, birth order and newborn experience. *Child Development*, 1977, *48*, 1686–1688.

Lambesis, C. C., Vidyasagar, D., and Anderson, G. C. The effects of surrogate mothering upon physiologic stablization of the transitional newborn. In G. C. Anderson and B. Raff (Eds.), *Newborn behavioral organization: Nursing research and implications*. National Foundation/March of Dimes. *Birth Defects: Original article series* (Vol. 15). New York: Liss, 1979.

Lewis, M., and Wilson, C. D. Infant development in lower-class American families. *Human Development*, 1972, *15*, 112–127.

Littman, B., and Parmelee, A. H. Medical correlates of infant development. *Pediatrics*, 1978, *61*, 470–474.

Masi, W. Supplemental stimulation of the premature infant. In T. Field, A. Sostek, S. Goldberg, and H. H. Shuman (Eds.), *Infants born at risk*. New York: Spectrum, 1979.

Measel, C. P., and Anderson, G. C. Nonnutritive sucking during tube feedings: Effect upon clinical course in premature infants. *Journal of Obstetric, Gynecologic and Neonatal Nursing*, 1979, *8*, 265–272.

Miller, S. A., and Dymsza, H. A. Artificial feeding of neonatal rats. *Science,* 1963, *141,* 517–518.

Neligan, G. A., Kolvin, I., Scott, D. Mcl., and Garside, R. F. *Born too soon or born too small.* Philadelphia: J. B. Lippincott, 1976.

Nichols, R. C., and Bilbro, W. C. The diagnosis of twin zygosity. *Acta Genetica,* 1966, *16,* 265–275.

Pasamanick, B., and Knobloch, H. Retrospective studies on the epidemiology of reproductive casality: Old and new. *Merrill-Palmer Quarterly,* 1966, *12,* 7–26.

Quay, H., and Peterson, D. R. *Manual for the behavior problem checklist.* Miami: University of Miami Press, 1975.

Rowe, D. C., and Plomin, R. Temperament in early childhood. *Journal of Personality Assessment,* 1977, *41,* 150–156.

Sameroff, A. J., and Chandler, M. J. Reproductive risk and the continuum of caretaking casualty. In F. D. Horowitz, M. Hetherington, S. Scarr-Salapatek, and G. Siegel (Eds.), *Review of child development research* (Vol. 4). Chicago: University of Chicago Press, 1975.

Sroufe, L. A., and Wunsch, J. P. The development of laughter in the first year of life. *Child Development,* 1972, *43,* 1326–1344.

Stringer, S., and Field, T. *Effects of nonutritive sucking stimulation on preterm infants' feeding performance.* Paper presented at the International Conference on Infant Studies, New Haven, Connecticut, April 1980.

Terman, L. M., and Merrill, M. A. *Stanford-Binet Intelligence Scale.* Boston: Houghton-Mifflin, 1972.

Tjossem, T. D. Early intervention: Issues and approaches. In T. D. Tjossem (Ed), *Intervention strategies for high-risk infants and young children.* Baltimore: University Park Press, 1976.

Tulkin, S., and Kagan, J. Mother-child interaction in the first few years of life. *Child Development,* 1972, *43,* 31–41.

Widmayer, S., and Field, T. Effects of Brazelton demonstrations on early interactions of preterm infants and their mothers. *Infant Behavior and Development,* 1980, *3,* 79–89.

Wilson, R. S., Brown, A. M., and Matheny, A. P. Emergence and persistence of behavioral differences in twins. *Child Development,* 1971, *32,* 1381–1398.

Preventing Developmental Retardation:
A General Systems Model

Craig T. Ramey, David MacPhee, and Keith Owen Yeates

> Seek simplicity and distrust it.
> —Alfred North Whitehead

The Historical Context

Developmental retardation can be defined in terms of deficits in intellectual functioning and adaptive behavior that occur in the course of ontogeny. The developmental retardation of concern in this chapter is not that caused primarily by genetic defects, teratogens, or injury, although they may be present to some degree in developmentally retarded children. Our concept of developmental retardation shares much in common with the American Association of Mental Deficiency (AAMD) (Grossman, 1973) definition of psychosocial retardation but differs in several important aspects. According to the definition adopted by American Association of Mental Deficiency, a person is considered retarded if (1) his or her IQ score is below 70; (2) other positive indicators exist such as the presence of other retarded family members; and (3) the individual in question has a history of maladaptive behavior in ecologically valid situations (cf. Brooks and Baumeister, 1977). We take issue with the AAMD definition of psychosocial retardation on two scientific points. First, an IQ of 70 as the criterion for retardation is arbitrary. Although such cutoff points must be established as administrative guidelines for therapeutic or custodial planning, they do not represent the kinds of positive diagnostic signs that should define a discrete syndrome, and, further, they imply more precision than the score warrants. Second, insisting on the presence

This research was supported, in part, by grants from the National Institute of Child Health and Human Development and the Bureau of Education for the Handicapped, Office of Education. We are indebted to Marie Butts, Pam McPherson, Nancy Daniels, and John Bernard for editorial assistance in preparing the manuscript.

of other retarded individuals in the family presupposes a constellation of characteristics that should be empirically determined rather than established by a priori definition.

Our working criterion for developmental retardation is, therefore, somewhat different from that in the AAMD classification manual. We define developmental retardation as any significant impairment in ecologically valid assessments of cognitive and adaptive functioning which is known to be preventable. We think this definition is preferable for scientific purposes because (1) it avoids presently arbitrary cutoff points; (2) it focuses research attention on alterable processes governing development; (3) it does not establish by fiat what is essentially an empirical issue; and (4) it permits cultural relativism in diagnosis. However, because this proposed working definition is akin to the classification scheme currently used for placement decisions, a brief discussion of the epidemiology of psychosocial retardation is necessary to establish further the historical context of this chapter.

Psychosocial Retardation and the Concept of Risk

Baroff (1974) reviewed the scientific literature on the epidemiology of mental retardation and concluded that approximately 89 percent of all retardation can be considered as mild. Although the exact percentage of mildly retarded persons in the total mentally retarded population may be debated, it seems safe to assume that the mildly retarded outnumber all other mentally retarded persons combined. Furthermore, Stein and Susser (1963) have estimated that 75 percent of all retarded persons have no clear-cut physiological pathology, and it seems likely that even more than 75 percent of the mildly retarded are free of major biological dysfunction. Thus, the largest segment of individuals classified as mentally retarded may be considered mildly impaired and without organic involvement.

If biological dysfunction is not the obvious cause of mild developmental retardation (as it almost invariably is for more severe forms), then perhaps the social ecology of the mildly retarded will provide clues to causal pathways by indicating which segments of society are most *at risk* for the condition. By *risk* we mean a substantiated, empirical relationship demonstrating that individuals who possess particular attributes have a greater likelihood of being classified as developmentally retarded than persons who do not possess those attributes. Risk is therefore an actuarial concept pertaining to groups with identifiable characteristics and is probabilistic in nature.

Currently there is general agreement that social class membership predicts psychosocial retardation. The report of a correlation between social class status and IQ, however, does not address many important issues. The most important are the accuracy of predictions for purposes of individual identification and the specification of the psychological mechanisms involved in incidence. Even though mild retardation is strongly associated with lower social class status, not all or even most lower-class individuals can be classified as mentally retarded. Begab (1978) has estimated that only about 10 percent of the poor in the United States would be considered as mentally retarded. Thus, to improve the identification process within the most at-risk population, further specification is necessary to identify which subsets of parents are more likely to give birth to a biologically intact child who at some point is classified as developmentally retarded for psychosocial reasons. One strategy to accomplish this end is to look for correlations between measures of intellectual and social adaptation *within* the lower social classes. Given that psychologists, sociologists, and educators have reported correlations between social class and many other attributes, surprisingly little is known about the correlates of IQ and other measures of social adaptation within a given social class and particularly within the lower classes.

Variables that have been related to developmental retardation (presumably of a psychosocial nature) within the lower classes include: maternal IQ (Heber, Dever, and Conry, 1968; Ramey, Farran, and Campbell, 1979); family disorganization; a room ratio of two or more persons; and five or more children (Birch, Richardson, Baird, Horobin, and Illsley, 1970). Thus, at least some clues can be used to guide more refined and extensive epidemiological studies.

We know from our own early intervention work in North Carolina (e.g., Ramey and Campbell, 1979a), as well as from the research of others (e.g., Bayley, 1965; Knobloch and Pasamanick, 1953) that it is during the second year of life that social class differences become evident in cognitive functioning. Prior to 12 months of age, measurable cognitive deficits have not been reliably detected. Whether the failure to identify significant differences before 12 months is a function of the insensitivity of our measuring instruments is, at present, not established. Nevertheless, if early intervention is to prevent developmental retardation, then the earlier that identification can occur the better. The main task is to develop risk indicators for the prenatal or early infancy period if psychosocial retardation is to be prevented rather than remediated.

One approach to early prediction has been direct assessments of the child. Measures of the child's performance during early infancy, however, have not been highly predictive of the child's subsequent intellectual status. Further, high-risk indices such as the one reported by Ramey and Smith (1977) require costly interviews and family assessments and may be limited to use in research and in predicting group rather than individual status.

Another approach to prediction has focused on assessments of the child's early environment. These measures have yielded more encouraging screening results. Work by Elardo, Bradley, and Caldwell (1975) using the Home Observation for the Measurement of the Environment (HOME) has indicated significant prediction of both later IQ and school achievement from assessments of the home made during infancy. More recently, Frankenburg, Coons, Van Doorninck, Goldstein, Berrenberg, and Moriarty (1977) have developed a brief questionnaire based on the HOME that parents can complete by themselves in settings such as waiting rooms at physicians' offices or at social service agencies. Frankenburg's measures are highly correlated with Caldwell's HOME scores and also predict subsequent child status. This questionnaire approach appears to be a very promising lead for screening home environments. Assessing children's home environments, however, requires that the children to be screened have contact with the agency doing the screening. Many of the children most likely to yield positive screening results will go unseen by relevant agencies because their families do not seek or receive services for their young children (Birch and Gussow, 1970). In order to cast the net more widely, a first-line screening device that includes information on all children in a given geographical area is necessary. Following the identification of high-risk children, subsequent multiphasic screening and assessment of a more refined nature may assist families and professionals in providing services to needy children on a more cost-effective basis.

Recently we have been exploring the efficacy of information available from standard birth certificates as a possible first-line screening mechanism (Ramey, Stedman, Borders-Patterson, and Mengel, 1978). In a retrospective study of 1,000 randomly sampled first-grade children, we found that the top six variables which discriminated between children who were successfully achieving in school, and children who were failing were (in order of importance): (1) race; (2) having an older sibling who had died; (3) educational level of the mother; (4) birth order; (5) legitimacy; and (6) the month that prenatal care began. At this point we regard these characteristics as marker variables rather than as causal ones in the processes of development. As marker variables, they help identify populations with elevated risk levels, but they do not necessarily indicate which psychological mechanisms require intervention.

We are now attempting to refine our first-line screening precision by generating separate prediction equations for different racial and educational groups (Finkelstein and Ramey, 1980; Ramey and Finkelstein, 1981). The goal of this research is to make our prediction equations more precise and, ultimately, to increase our initial ability to detect high-risk infants at a more reasonable cost. A preliminary finding from our current efforts is particularly intriguing. Discriminant function equations for blacks and whites reveal different factors to be important for predicting intellectual status or school achievement within the two racial groups, even though the two equations are about equally discriminative for school success or failure. For the black children in the group (N=290), the three most important factors, in order of importance, were education of the mother, birth order, and the month that prenatal care began. For the white children (N=631), the three most important factors were whether there were previous live births who had subsequently died, education of the mother, and maternal age. Thus, there was overlap between the two samples on only 1 of the 3 most important discriminators between school success and school failure. This would suggest that the same risk factors may enter prediction equations differently for different populations. In sum, the need for early intervention is not necessarily predicted by the same variables in different subgroups in the population.

Form and Focus of Prevention Programs

After finding high-risk children, the next step is to have a program to offer them. On an elementary level, the type of program that professionals offer depends on what they believe needs changing. Yet the range of potential etiological agents of psychosocial retardation is very large (Ramey and Gallagher, 1975), and little consensus exists as to the relative importance of specific agents (Begab, 1981). Consequently a wide range of intervention efforts have taken place. Although relatively few are aimed toward mental retardation per se and even fewer are targeted specifically at prevention, the programs present a range of stances on what the best type of intervention might be, that is, what form and focus intervention efforts should take.

Intervention efforts have ranged in breadth from attempting to influence a large set of developmental domains, such as the Head Start programs (Zigler and Valentine, 1979), to programs designed primarily for one developmental process, such as the reading skills program of Wallach and Wallach (1976). Projects also have ranged in intensity from minimal to nearly full-time contact, and in scope from short-term to decade-long efforts. For example, the Ypsilanti Perry Preschool Project (Schweinhart and Weikart, 1981) enrolled 3 to 4 year olds who spend 2 ½ hours per day during the school year in the program, while the Milwaukee Project (Garber and Heber, 1977) enrolled infants who spend 8 hours a day, 52 weeks a year in the program. Nevertheless, little evidence exists for the relative effectiveness of any one program or group of programs over any other (Mann, Harrell, and Hunt, 1976). The only major finding is that more structured programs seem to achieve greater gains—at least in cognitive growth—than do more play-oriented programs (Bronfenbrenner, 1975). Furthermore, while some evaluation studies find greater gains in IQ scores in more intense and lasting programs (Stedman, Anastasiow, Dokecki, Gordon, and Parker, 1972), we do not know whether it is the *intensity* or *length* of prevention efforts that is important in producing lasting change. A definitive answer to these important issues awaits closer and continuing scientific scrutiny. We have little data, at present, to indicate that any particular intervention program is singularly more effective than others.

Effectiveness of Prevention

In many ways, the cost-effectiveness and the manner in which intervention is implemented depend on continuing scientific inquiry into the relative efficacy of various preventive strategies. Applied scientists must be concerned with public accountability. The proof of effectiveness appears, at first glance, to be deceptively simple: decide what needs changing, implement a program, and then measure to see if the program changed the target variable(s). Unfortunately, this simplistic conception masks great complexity. First, most interventions are designed to produce changes in more than one developmental domain. Second, scientists must allow for possible unintended consequences, both positive and negative. Third, there is little consensus concerning the most effective tools for measuring development. Finally, investigators must follow their subjects longitudinally in order to determine if their program produces lasting, meaningful gains. Thus, difficulties in deciding what to measure and how to measure it, plus the need for follow-up, make proving effectiveness an arduous task.

The initial obstacle is deciding what to measure. Even this decision is problematic. In general, intervention efforts have the broad goal of improving development or preventing a decline in functioning. The word *development,* though, encompasses an extensive range of possibilities so that selecting the most appropriate variables for study is quite difficult. Most studies have focused on cognitive growth, as measured by IQ tests, while other programs have preferred to use achievement tests to measure success in school. Cognitive growth and school success, though, are only two benchmarks of successful adaptation and they by no means epitomize "development". In another domain, namely adaptive behavior, one is faced with the difficulty of defining what is adaptive. While some programs have focused on school behavior, scant attention has been paid to behavior in the home or neighborhood. What is adaptive for a child in a school setting may well be maladaptive in the home or neighborhood. Measures of social adjustment have the same difficulty. Finally, little if any attention has been paid to the domains of personal adjustment, motivation, or mental health (Begab, 1981). The potential areas of change, intended or not, are numerous, and some have been barely explored. Scientists must press for measurement of more than cognitive growth and move to a more balanced assessment of developmental domains.

Better assessment, however, is limited by the adequacy of the measurement tools. Unfortunately, techniques for assessment are often imprecise, invalid, or even nonexistent. In the realm of cognitive development, the IQ test has been the method of choice. Although IQ scores have been bemoaned for their unreliability, their invalidity for minority children, their lack of predictive validity, and their lack of information, among other things (Stedman et al., 1972), they remain the psychologist's best all-around assessment instrument for general intellectual development. Substitutes have been suggested, such as measures developed from a Piagetian framework (e.g., Elkind, 1969). These measures, however, have also been criticized because of their limitations in predicting success in school (Wallach and Wallach, 1976). Thus, measures of cognitive development, which are perhaps the most widely developed and used, are not fully adequate. Measures of school success, though, have not fared much better. Achievement tests often contain as many items requiring reasoning ability as they do items requiring the skill supposedly being measured (Stedman et al., 1972). Instruments in other domains are even less adequate and too frequently are nonexistent. Attempts at measuring adaptive behavior are scarce (see Schaefer, 1981), and tools for measuring motivation or personal adjustment are practically nil. At present, the best policy may be to measure the domains of interest using the best techniques available and, if possible, to employ multiple measures of any given construct. The need for psychometrically sound and ecologically valid instruments for measuring development is among the most pressing today and, unfortunately, one of the most neglected.

Nevertheless, scientists need to press ahead with research, even with the problems of deciding what to measure and how to measure it. A problem that goes beyond measurement though, and that is essential to the issue of effectiveness, is the need for continuous longitudinal study. Adequate follow-up of children who have been in preventive efforts is the only effective way to investigate potentially lasting benefits (e.g., Gallagher, Ramey, Haskins, and Finkelstein, 1976). The importance of follow-up is underscored by the findings that many of the initial benefits of intervention disappear after children leave the programs (Bronfenbrenner, 1975). Furthermore, the possibility of "sleeper effects" (Kagan and Moss, 1962)—effects that become obvious only after intervention ends—requires long-term follow-up, even into adolescence and adulthood. But longitudinal study is not without hazards. Repeated measurements have long been recognized as producing, for example, regression artifacts and practice effects. In addition, the measurement of change is difficult and sometimes misleading (Cronbach and Furby, 1970). Finally, attrition of subjects as well as experimenter makes it difficult to maintain experimental validity or even to complete many investigations. Thus, just conducting longitudinal research is fraught with problems.

The lucky investigators are those who think they know what should be measured, have several reliable and valid ways to do so, and can guarantee that their subjects will remain accessible. Unfortunately, such birds are rare indeed. The fact is that effectiveness is difficult to prove or disprove and professionals concerned with accountability are faced with a host of obstacles. The press for increased and long-term measurement necessitates the development of more satisfactory instruments and more sophistication with valid measures of change.

A General Systems Model

Although technical limitations have hampered the development of preventive programs, our limited models for general developmental processes have been an even greater hindrance. During the decade when intervention was seen as a vehicle for social change, the prevalent attitudes were that children of poverty lived in an inadequate environment and that the early environment was the critical factor in later intellectual growth. These assumptions about the nature of development translated into prevention strategies that emphasized instruction in cognitive skills, with the aim of "inoculating" the child against further privation. Sameroff (1979) has noted that a medical model such as this assumes a unitary relationship between environmental deprivation (the "pathogen") and school failure (the "disease").

As a number of reports have shown (e.g., Zigler and Valentine, 1979), the intentions of earlier social policies were laudable but rested on tenuous assumptions about the processes of development. For example, hereditarian proponents (e.g., Jensen, 1969; 1981) have attributed differences between developmentally retarded, socially disadvantaged children and middle-class children to the global wellspring of genetics without postulating either specific genetic mechanisms or adequately acknowledging genotype-environment interactions, which are the hallmark of modern behavioral genetics (e.g., Schneirla, 1966; Gottlieb, 1976) and particularly the genetics of development (e.g., McClearn and DeFries, 1973). Environmentalists have been equally vague in identifying causal models, frequently emphasizing only one developmental domain such as language (e.g, Bernstein, 1970), mother–child interactions (e.g., Hess and Shipman, 1965), or anomie (e.g. Ogbu, 1978) as the major agent.

The skepticism about simple models of development culminated in several seminal review papers, including those by Clarke and Clarke (1976) and Sameroff (1975). Both monographs argued: (1) that development involves the action of complex regulatory processes (environmental and constitutional); and (2) that later outcomes have multiple causes with the result that there are few isomorphic continuities in development. Additional challenges to traditional assumptions also forced researchers to consider more complex models of development. Some of the trends that have crept into current theorizing include bidirectionality of infant–caregiver effects (Bell, 1968, 1971; Harper, 1971), Bronfenbrenner's (1977) ecology of human development, and a concern for competence-related outcome measures rather than a single criterion such as an IQ score (McClelland, 1973; Zigler and Trickett, 1978). In brief, researchers came to appreciate the complex nature of development.

The crowning blow to the Main Effects and Interactional models of development was Sameroff's (1975) Transactional Model. In this model, Sameroff argued that the child modifies the environment at the same time the surround is acting on the child.[1] Constitutional factors are partially responsible for individual differences in behavior (e.g., temperamental variables such as reactivity or sociability) and for the ability to compensate following insult (see Parmelee and Michaelis, 1971, and Sameroff, 1979, for a discussion of self-righting tendencies). Environmental variables affect, among other things, the biological integrity of the organism, morphological characteristics, and what is learned. When the two—the continuum of reproductive casualty and the continuum of caretaking casualty—are interwoven in development, intellectual deficits may be amplified or reduced.

In some respects, the Transactional Model is incomplete since the intervening variables are left unspecified. For instance, the "continuum of caretaking casualty", translated into psychological variables, would go

---

[1] While we recognize that Sameroff misconstrued the Interactional Model and failed to deal with some issues in the Transactional Model (see Denenberg, this volume), it is noteworthy that his papers (Sameroff, 1975; Sameroff and Chandler, 1975) influenced the field to think in terms of multiple rather than linear causation. From a statistical or experimental design point of view, Sameroff's discussion of the Main Effects, Interactional, and Transactional Models clearly is flawed. In terms of the zeitgeist, however, the Transactional Model represented a break from the past in that more complex models were seen as necessary for a complete understanding of developmental phenomena.

beyond social class and parental education to include patterns of dyadic interaction, modes of communication, and teaching strategies. In this way, the notion of a "supportive environment" (cf. Yarrow, Rubenstein, and Pedersen, 1973) is defined in terms of specific behaviors that can be examined for their contribution to later competencies or deficits. Ultimately, the task is to construct a model of development that specifies the variables and processes constituting a supportive environment and that defines the desired product of our endeavors, be it adaptation to the environment (Parmelee, Kopp, and Sigman, 1976) or social competence (Zigler and Trickett, 1978). In the next section, we will discuss a variation on General Systems Theory (Bertalanffy, 1975; Miller, 1978) that attempts to do justice to the demands of this task.

The General Systems Model

At this point we need to introduce some of the concepts of General Systems Theory that are the core of our approach.

The emergent principle.

The developing child can be viewed as one product of a system of units that interact. According to Miller (1978), "The state of each unit is constrained by, conditioned by, or dependent upon the state of other units. The units are coupled" (p. 16). The behavior of a system emerges out of the interaction of the components such that there are multiple causes rather than unitary causes.

Levels of analysis.

Living systems have different levels of complexity and functioning, as Bronfenbrenner (1977) has pointed out. Further, complex interactions can occur *within* each level as well as *across* levels such that, for example, societal processes can influence functioning at the level of the family. Other implications might include: assessment of risk status must consider the level at which the variables operate, and intervention may have consequences across levels.

Range of stability.

Each variable within a system has a range of stability (Miller, 1978) that is maintained in equilibrium by transactions with the environment and the system. Any variable that forces the system beyond its range of stability is called a stress, producing strain in the system. According to Miller, living systems have a limited repertoire of strategies to deal with stress: (1) altering the system by learning new skills; (2) altering the environment; (3) withdrawing to a more favorable environment; or (4) changing what the organism defines as stable. A corollary of the notion of equilibrium is much like Werner's (1957) orthogenetic principle, "A living organism maintains itself in a state of highest organization [and] during differentiation an organism passes from states of lower to higher heterogeneity" (Bertalanffy, 1975, p. 46). When combined with self-regulatory strategies, one is then able to identify the "competent" individual in terms of adaptive functioning and level of organization.

Regulatory mechanisms.

In the human, cybernetic processes operate to regulate behavior. In terms of development, this means that there is constant feedback and regulation so that the child continuously adapts to the environment. However, in cases where self-regulatory mechanisms are unable to cope with strain on the system, disorder or maladaptive behavior may result as in child abuse (Belsky, 1980), schizophrenia (Meehl, 1962), or retarded growth (Tanner, 1963), unless outside resources are called upon.

The active organism.

This principle suggests that development is characterized by plasticity since adaptation occurs in the presence of changing demands. Furthermore, the child is seen as an active (rather than reactive) agent, eliciting responses from the environment at the same time that he or she is adapting to its demands.

   In general, Systems Theory is not a true theory as traditionally defined by the ability to explain and predict. Rather, it is a perspective or paradigm (Kuhn, 1962) in which the many components of the system interact to produce strong, *synergistic* effects. The usefulness of this approach rests in the ability to see new relationships between variables and in the flexibility to wed different theories about component processes to each other so as to explain behavior.

Ontogenetic Processes

Ontogeny usually is taken to mean changes that occur over the life span of an individual organism. In the General Systems Model, though, ontogeny can occur at all levels of analysis (see Figure 1). Therefore, one can speak of change in the family (as measured by marriage, child bearing, and family crises, to mention a few), the development of neighborhoods (from the moving of neighbors to urban decay), and the rise and fall of societies and civilizations. Implicit in this more general use of ontogeny is the notion that the historians of different levels will be affiliated with disciplines as diverse as developmental psychology, sociology, and anthropology.

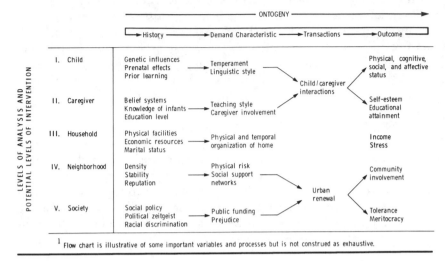

A GENERAL SYSTEMS MODEL FOR INQUIRY INTO DEVELOPMENTAL RETARDATION [1]

[1] Flow chart is illustrative of some important variables and processes but is not construed as exhaustive.

Figure 1. A General Systems Model, illustrating developmental paths at different levels of analysis.

Several terms in the General Systems Model need further clarification. By the *history* of the component, we mean the effects of previous transactions that are not manifested as observable behavior. This may be thought of as the probability of an action given the history of the individual. History at the different levels can be thought of in terms of genotypes, teratogenic effects, and learning (the child); general knowledge of child development, and attitudes and beliefs that have been inculcated by society and upbringing (the caregiver); the social status of the family; the reputation of a neighborhood; and the social policy and values advocated by a society. Historical variables are assumed to mediate or influence behavior but they cannot be observed directly. Thus, a central issue in studying behavior is to determine how "history" (e.g., socioeconomic status) is related to action (e.g., teaching strategies, language, the organization of the inanimate environment).

In the domain of psychopathology, a process approach would inquire how it is that these etiological factors act on development, via their expression as concrete behaviors and actions, or *demand characteristics*. Research on risk factors in the infant, for example, has found that the mother's childhood health history is a significant predictor of her infant's postnatal condition; the process is presumed to involve the viability of the ovum as affected by diet and disease (Birch and Gussow, 1970).

Transactions, as used in the General Systems Model, imply an interactional process that is bidirectional. The most commonly used illustration would be interactions between the infant and caregiver. The behavior of each participant can be attributed to proximal (cf. Patterson, 1974; Bakeman and Brown, 1977) and distal determinants. Distal determinants of interaction include general expectancies about the partner's behavior (the individual's history) as well as the demand characteristics of the partner. For instance, infant characteristics such as cuddliness (Schaffer and Emerson, 1964), temperament (Thomas, Birch, Chess, Hertzig and Korn, 1963), predominant state (Wolff, 1966), and physical attractiveness, including cry sounds (Zeskind, 1980), shape the caregiver's behavior to the infant. Similarly, the caregiver's demand characteristics include the warmth of the individual, the function of the interaction (play or caregiving), and the current mood of the mother or father. At another level, transactions between the neighborhood and society, through the mechanism of revenue sharing, would result in urban renewal. It is important to note that transactions can occur between any two or more levels as well as within levels. An exemplar of an interlevel transaction might be the role of television as a mediator between society and the child or family; an intralevel process might include the interaction of cognition and arousal to produce an affective state (Rothbart, 1973). The point is that a myriad of relationships between components are possible, leaving the attribution of cause in rather murky waters.

Finally, the endpoint of this stream of cause and effect would include a number of *outcome* variables that also must be measured in an ecologically valid manner. Here, the emphasis is on instruments that are appropriate to the questions being asked. In the case of developmental retardation, we would want to know about the competence of the child in a number of settings, about the ability of the child to adapt to the environment, and at another level about how supportive the environment is. These global, ill-defined terms must be translated into valid assessment instruments in order to do justice to the complexity of development. In retrospect, it is apparent that developmental pathology can be caused by any number of factors, both within the organism (e.g., temperamental variables, limited self-righting strategies), within the dyad, and at the level of societal norms, as well as others. When these intra-, inter-, and supracomponent processes are combined, the inadequacy of simplistic models becomes all too evident.

Our conceptual model for developmental retardation contains two major process components that illustrate the interplay of ontogenetic history and transactions with the environment. These components concern the functioning of subgroups within the society (*sociocultural difference com-*

ponent) and the child's contingency history (*reinforcement-motivational component*). In the past, each has been perceived as a competing explanation for developmental retardation. The General Systems Model, however, views them as complementary processes that act at somewhat different levels of analysis.

Sociocultural Difference Component

A growing body of epidemiological literature suggests that individuals from the lower socioeconomic strata are most at risk for retarded intellectual and adaptive behavior (Ramey and Finkelstein, 1981). Poor individuals with minority group status are particularly likely to develop educational handicaps during the public school years (Ramey et al., 1978b; Richardson, 1975; Mercer, 1977). We now think that the sociocultural component operates through three primary mechanisms. First, disadvantaged sociocultural subgroups may learn complex modes of intellectual and social adaptation but learn ones *not valued* by the larger culture. Linguistic style is a good example. Baratz and Baratz (1970), for instance, argued that lower-class black dialect was as complex as standard English and that is was different from standard English but not inherently deficient. Second, sociocultural subgroups may learn modes of functioning *specifically disapproved* of by the larger society. For instance, aggressive or assertive interactions—particularly in the school system—may be construed as disrespectful and problematic behaviors even when there is no apparent damage. Third, the larger society may form stereotypes of sociocultural subgroups and actively or unwittingly but *systematically discriminate* with respect to intellectual and adaptive opportunities to the point of creating a self-fulfilling prophecy. A recent study by Haskins, Walden, and Ramey (1980) concerning ability-grouping in kindergarten and first grade illustrates this point. In assigning children to high- or low-ability groups within their classrooms, teachers reported using their own informal observations of the child's ability and teacher-made tests. None of the other factors assessed, including standardized tests, teacher recommendations, the child's interest in school work, or information about the child's home or background were reported as influential in teachers' placement of children in ability groups. To the extent that the teacher is biased in attitudes or incorrect in assessments of children's abilities, though, the child's performance will be affected. In summarizing the results of the ability grouping study, Haskins et al. noted that:

These teachers' beliefs about differences between students in the two (high and low) groups were clearly reflected in their instructional techniques. Thus, teachers more often kept low-group students together while sitting with them. They also used more control statements, more disciplinary statements, and more positive reinforcement with low-ability groups. Finally, teachers not only engaged in more total blocks (of time) for instruction with low-ability students, they also gave them relatively more drill and less new subject matter. (p. 20)

To the extent that personal bias may operate in assignment to ability groups, the structure of those groups seems likely to nurture their disadvantage through reduced exposure to new material and a social stigma that fosters a lower self-concept. This point leads us into the second major process component of our model that is important throughout the developmental period, especially during infancy.

Reinforcement-Motivational Component

It is our contention that high-risk children are reared in an environment with inadequate or inappropriate contingencies (Wachs, Uzgiris, and Hunt, 1971). This, in turn, has been implicated as a cause of lowered effectance motivation and reduced success in mastery situations. Further, the deficient contingency history is asserted during infancy and can be observed during the second year of life. Support for this thesis accrues from two converging lines of our research. The first aspect is a set of laboratory contingency experiments that are analogs of some components of adult–child interactions. The second line is a set of direct observations of mother–infant dyads from high-risk and general population backgrounds.

Experimental evidence.

Finkelstein and Ramey (1977) and Ramey and Finkelstein (1978) have reported a series of four experiments suggesting that increased amounts of response-contingent stimulation during the first year of infancy enhances subsequent learning performance when treated infants are compared with yoked controls. Ramey and Finkelstein (1978) presented a two-component model for the processes thought to underlie the strength of transfer. The components are contextual similarity between the treatment and transfer environments, and the extent to which there has been the development of an attentional strategy linking one's own responses to available external stimulation. These findings are consistent with earlier reports by Watson and Ramey (1972) and with Lewis and Goldberg's (1969) idea of a generalized expectancy for effectiveness that derives from the responsiveness of the mother to her infant's behavior.

Observational evidence.

For over a decade, researchers have speculated that maternal responsiveness to infants' operant behaviors (such as smiling and vocalizing) is a major determinant of the infant's subsequent cognitive and social development. Such a proposition, however, is not contradictory to Bell's (1968, 1971) notion that the infant is a determinant of parental behaviors as well. Two major types of information are relevant to caregiver–infant interactions and developmental retardation. The first type of evidence concerns the interactional differences between low-risk dyads (typically middle-class) and high-risk dyads (e.g., from poverty environments). Lewis and Wilson (1972), Ramey and Mills (1975), Tulkin and Kagan (1972), and others have reported social class differences in mother–child interaction during infancy (cf. a review by Ramey, Farran, Campbell, and Finkelstein, 1978). It has always been unclear from comparative social class research, however, whether the observed behavioral differences were causally related to cognitive growth or whether they were merely correlates of social class status, of little importance to subsequent development. Therefore, a different argument is becoming increasingly influential in implicating caregiver–child interactions as causally important. This second type of evidence concerns variations in parenting style within high-risk (typically lower-class) dyads. Clarke-Stewart, Vander-Stoep, and Killian (1979) and Ramey et al. (1979) have reported positive correlations of substantial magnitude between stimulating, interactive, and responsive behaviors and children's cognitive development during the first 3 years of life within disadvantaged samples. Thus, the dimension of responsivity, viewed from a reinforcement-motivational perspective, has increased plausibility.

Implications of the Model

There are several major implications of our model, both for normal development and for the prevention of pathology. In general, the overriding conclusion must be that a complex process like development demands a multivariate, multilevel, interdisciplinary approach. It is worth repeating that the first principle of Systems Theory is that behavior is a product of the entire system. Components studied in isolation may yield some information about processes, but behavior cannot be explained by the action of isolated parts. For instance, some individuals assert that environmental deprivation is primarily one of impoverished physical surroundings while others counter that the social world of maternal language and teaching strategies is responsible for later deficits. From a systems perspective, though, the primary mission is to discover how these variables act in concert to produce a given outcome. A supportive social environment coupled with impoverished physical circumstances may lead a child down a different path from a child reared in a physically adequate home environment by an abusive or neglecting parent.

This brings us to a second implication of the General Systems Model: different environments may lead to qualitative or quantitative differences in outcome. Stated differently, there may be different *paths* to the same outcome, or the same process may occur but at different *levels*. In findings to be reported later in this chapter, we have found that both alternatives may occur when one group of at-risk infants is placed in an experimental daycare program, and another serves as an educationally untreated control group.

A major hurdle in preventing developmental retardation is the translation of abstract and general models, such as ours, into an effective intervention strategy. Two implications of the General Systems Model speak to the design of intervention programs. The first is a corollary of the level of analysis principle: In order to prevent later pathology, we must identify components of the system where intervention *can* occur. For instance, proposed remedies for breaking the "cycle of poverty" have included preschool programs (the level of the child); a guaranteed annual income (the level of the family); urban renewal and job programs (the neighborhood); and civil rights laws that foster the establishment of a true meritocracy (the society).

The crucial question, though—and the second implication of the model—is where intervention *should* be focused. Ideally, one would want a prevention strategy that produces powerful, permanent effects with a minimum of money and effort. Invoking a cost-effectiveness criterion, we may find that some loci in the system produce greater effects than others. Furthermore, we can infer from the emergent principle that intervention at several points may produce synergistic effects (i.e., more dramatic changes than prevention aimed at isolated components). For example, Bronfenbrenner (1975) reviewed the effects of early intervention programs and concluded, among other things, that: (1) center-based programs with cognitive curricula produced greater gains than play-oriented programs; (2) parent intervention yielded benefits that extended to younger siblings and to the attitudes and feelings of the parents; and (3) families who are under the most economic and psychological stress are the ones least likely to become involved in an intervention program.

What this suggests is that a *combination* of approaches may be the most effective. These might include quality daycare, family education, and social services that move the family into a broader social support network. The goal of prevention should be to provide a supportive environment for the child, a rearing atmosphere where the needs of the child are attended to with a maximum of flexibility, and resources on the part of the caregivers. This sensitivity of the caregiver to the child is constrained by time, economics, education, and societal norms (Sameroff, 1979), so that prevention components geared to supporting the family may indirectly benefit the child. A major task for the future is to identify those components of a "supportive environment" that are most amenable to effective intervention.

At the core of Systems Theory is the idea of interactive influences, that is, all properties of complex systems have multiple causes rather than single causes. Thus, intervention may initiate a series of *ripple effects* or unintended consequences, either positive or negative. One of the unfortunate byproducts of simplistic cause-effect theories of development was that evaluations of the Head Start program were cast solely in terms of intellectual-gain scores. As the Lazar consortium (Lazar and Darlington, 1978) was to discover, early interventions have a number of ripple effects including parent satisfaction and involvement, health-related benefits, a lower drop-out rate in high school, and fewer cases of delinquency. On the other hand, intervention may have undesirable side effects: the parents may abdicate responsibility for the child, aggressiveness in social interactions with peers may increase (Schwarz, Strickland, and Krolick, 1974), and the parents' philosophy or style of childrearing may clash with that of the intervention program. In brief, the General Systems Model cautions us to be aware of the consequences of tampering with one aspect of the system when we are most interested in its overall functioning.

Another implication of the General Systems Model is that modifiability and learning tend to strike a balance over time (cf. Bateson, 1979). Although the infant is viewed as a dynamic individual, constantly adapting to changes in the environment, learning and hierarchical organization of behavior patterns are also taking place. This interplay of plasticity and learning has crucial significance for the timing of intervention and for the reversibility its effects. Clarke and Clarke (1976), in discussing this issue, liken development to a wedge where there is "a greater potential responsiveness during early life . . . tailing off to little responsiveness in adulthood" (pp. 271–272). From a systems perspective, then, early intervention (during the period of greatest sensitivity) must be coupled with continuous enrollment to ensure continuity and the learning of adaptive behavior patterns not demanded at earlier periods. Early and prolonged enrichment is even more critical in those cases where the individual's self-righting tendencies (intrinsic plasticity, if you will) or ability to learn are impaired.

One final implication of the model concerns general strategies for conducting an intervention program. Recall that equal emphasis is placed on the contribution of the infant to its own development and on the characteristics of the environment. As a consequence, the most effective prevention will capitalize on the unique capabilities of any given individual (the supportive environment theme) while emphasizing transactions that are most effective in fostering later competence. Therefore, curriculum development (what is most effective for infants in general) and research on learning styles (what is most suited to a particular infant) go hand in hand to exploit individual strengths and overcome weaknesses. Although this implication may seem so obvious as to be a time-worn adage, its full realization depends on a comprehensive knowledge of child development, a flexible and individually tailored curriculum, an intimate acquaintance with each child's abilities, and an active program of research directed at discovering what works for given categories of child characteristics. With such a tack, we may be able to make progress in our efforts to prevent the insidious effects of development gone awry.

The Carolina Abecedarian Project

The Carolina Abecedarian Project is a two-pronged attack on the forces affecting the growth of high-risk children. At a secondary level, within the framework established in Figure 1, intervention occurs at the level of the family for both experimental and control groups. Thus, the availability of social services for the family and medical services and nutritional supplements for the children are common to both groups. These provisions were included to reduce potential Hawthorne effects in the experimental group and to ensure the delivery of a set of services already guaranteed, in principle, to all members of our society. Recent preliminary reviews of social services used by the Abecedarian families (Ramey and Dempsey, 1979) and documented illnesses of the Abecedarian children (Ramey and Dubinsky, 1979) revealed no substantial differences between the experimental and control group families or their children. These interventions were aimed at the socioeconomic and physical survival of our children and their families. In some sense, these services control for alternate explanations of group differences in intellectual and adaptive functioning. More important, we believe these services to be so vital to normal growth and development that it was ethically indefensible to withhold services from the control group.

The *primary level* of intervention is what differentiates our experimental and control groups. At this level, individual children receive direct educational programming through the mechanism of systematic, developmental daycare, as described in subsequent sections. A word of justification is in order concerning the form and focus of our preventive efforts. While parents are encouraged to be actively aware of their children's experiences and to visit the center and participate in its functioning, no systematic attempt is made to teach parenting skills. As in most other daycare centers, parent participation is generally sporadic.

We chose to focus our educational efforts on the child for several reasons. First, it was already clear in 1971 (when pilot work for the Project began) that at least modest cognitive success with child-centered approaches was feasible. The work of Klaus and Gray (1968), Weikart (1967), and Robinson and Robinson (1971) figured prominently in our decisions. Second, there was a growing realization that parent-focused programs were having great difficulty working successfully with the most disadvantaged or at-risk families (cf. Bronfenbrenner, 1975; Stedman et al., 1972). Third, daycare was rapidly growing as a social institution in this country. If we were successful, then we could anticipate more opportunities to reach other disadvantaged families through a mechanism that was, in principle, a downward extension of the public schools. Fourth, we felt that operating our own daycare facility would give us better control over the treatment process. Finally, early and continuing daycare of high quality would constitute an intensive treatment regimen for what seemed to be an intractable set of social problems faced by the families. We did not begin by assuming that daycare was the best or the most powerful treatment. Rather, it represented a prevention-oriented mechanism which looked promising and worthy of serious interdisciplinary pursuit.

Admission of Families

The Carolina Abecedarian Project began in 1972 as an attempt to intervene with infants and children believed to be at high risk for school failure. Families were referred to the project through local hospitals, clinics, the County Department of Social Services, and other sources. Once families had been identified as potentially eligible, the nursery supervisor visited them in their homes to explain the program and to determine whether the family appeared to meet selection criteria. If so, mothers were invited for an interview and psychological assessment.

During the interview, which typically occurred in the last trimester of pregnancy, demographic information about the family was obtained, and mothers were assessed with the Wechsler Adult Intelligence Scale (WAIS) (Wechsler, 1955). Final determination of eligibility was made following this visit. Criteria for selection included maternal IQ, family income, parent education, intactness of family, and seven other factors that were weighted and combined to yield a single score called the High-Risk Index (see Ramey and Smith, 1977, for details). Only families at or above a predetermined cutoff score were considered eligible. Selected characteristics of all families admitted to the Experimental and Control groups are summarized in Table 1. As can be seen, well over half the families are headed by females; average earned income is less than $1,500; and the mothers have about a 10th grade education with a mean IQ of approximately 85. Over 95 percent of all children in the project can be classified as black. A recent study of 1,000 first grade students in North Carolina indicated that race and maternal educational level (less than 10th grade) are strongly associated with school failure (Ramey et al, 1978b). Thus, the families in the Abecedarian project appear to be at high risk for school failure and psychosocial retardation.

We admitted four cohorts of families between 1972 and 1977. The oldest children are now over 7 years of age and have entered the public schools; the youngest children are approximately 3 years of age. Of 122 families judged to be eligible and invited to join the program, 121 families accepted the condition of random assignment to the Experimental or Control group. When these 121 families were assigned to groups, 116 or 96 percent accepted their group assignment. Of these 116, 3 children have died and 1 child has been diagnosed as retarded because of organic etiology.[3] Not counting these 4 children, we have a base sample of 112 children and families. Of these 112 biologically normal children, including 57 Experimentals and 55 Controls, 8 have dropped out of our sample as of September 1, 1978. One child was adopted out of the area, 2 children withdrew for personal reasons, and 5 moved out of the area. Thus, not counting attrition by death or biological abnormality, 93 percent of our sample is intact after 6 years. This represents a sample attrition rate of 1.18 percent per year. Most of the results to be reported in this chapter are derived from analyses on the first half (first two cohorts) of the sample during their first 5 years of development.

The Abecedarian Daycare Program

The largest component of the Abecedarian project is the systematic, developmental, and educational daycare service that the experimental children receive. The daycare program has been developed with the hypothesis in mind that "relative inferiority in the areas of language development and motivation to learn are particularly detrimental to normal development" (Ramey and Gallagher, 1975, p. 45). The experiences of our experimental group children are planned to foster language

---

[3]In comparison with Chapel Hill and North Carolina, the infant mortality rate in our sample (25.9 per thousand) is quite high. Between 1974 and 1978, the infant mortality rate for whites in Chapel Hill was 9.3; for nonwhites in Chapel Hill it was 10.9; and for all individuals in North Carolina, the rate was 17.6 per thousand (North Carolina Vital Statistics, 1978). The infant mortality rate in the Abecedarian sample is 2.78, 2.38, and 1.47 times higher (respectively) than the figures from the general population, attesting to the high–risk status of these infants.

Table 1 Demographic Data by Experimental and Control Groups

Group	N	Female-headed Family (percentage)	Mean Income	Mother's Education (in years)	Mean Maternal IQ	Percent Black Families (percentage)
Experimental	58	81	$1,534	10.33	84.33	97
Control	54	63	$1,370	10.04	83.89	100
Totals	112	72	$1,455	10.19	84.22	98

development and to promote appropriate and adaptive social behavior. The daycare setting is operated with these goals in mind so as to provide environments that, as Harms and Cross (1978) have detailed, are predictable and promote self-help, supportive and facilitate social-emotional adjustment reflective of the child's age, ability, and interest, and varied in activities.

Children begin attending the center as young as 6 weeks of age; attendance must begin by age 3 months. The center operates from 7:45 a.m. to 5:30 p.m. each weekday for 50 weeks per year. Transportation to and from the center is provided for the children. The center cares for children on various parts of two floors of a four-story research building. The setting for the children are structured so as to be age and developmentally appropriate. Generally, children are grouped according to age with sections for infants, toddlers, and so on. For example, prewalking infants are cared for in a two-room suite, with one room for sleeping and one room for play and curriculum activities. Toys are arranged so as to be available to creeping infants. Infant seats with attractive toys suspended over them often are used for younger infants when they are not engaged in formal teaching, feeding, or changing. Prop pillows which permit free use of hands in babies unable to sit alone are also used. Teachers, throughout the day, participate actively with and talk to the infants (for more detailed descriptions of the center and the childrens' settings, see Ramey and Campbell, 1979a; Ramey and Haskins, 1981; and Ramey, McGinness, Cross, Collier, and Barrie-Blackley, in press). The goals of environments such as these, even in infancy, are to promote independence and self-help while enriching relevant developmental domains such as language and concept attainment.

An important part of the implementation of any preventive effort, of course, is the staff. In the Abecedarian project, 12 teachers and assistants, aided by three administrative staff members, are responsible for providing the educational program for children. The typical teacher/child ratio is between 1:3 and 1:6. Teaching staff vary in their level of formal training (averaging 7 years of direct experience) but all have demonstrated skill and competencies in working with young children. Staff development is a critically important and ongoing process. Of particular importance is the language training program that seeks to help teachers develop childrens' communication skills through strategies based on current research in adult–child verbal interaction.

We have attempted to define an approach to language development that goes beyond linguistic forms to the development of an elaborated code. In doing so, we have agreed with a position similar to that of the Duchess in Alice in Wonderland: "Take care of the sense and the sounds will take care of themselves." The focus of our effort to date has been to promote a particular *kind* and *amount* of verbal interaction between teacher and daycare pupil. Much of our language work is derived from the frameworks developed by Tough (1976) and Blank (1973). The kind of verbal interaction encouraged is largely modeled on what a middle-class mother establishes with her child; the *amount* is higher, perhaps more like what a tutorial hour might afford. Because our daycare effort is competing with extensive experience in another type of linguistic environment (the home), we have assumed that it cannot be as casual and diluted as the normal family interaction. To foster certain types of linguistic functioning in the child's repertoire, therefore, we are trying to provide a large number of practice opportunities.

The language intervention approach that has been adopted rests on several assumptions:

- The acquisition of *communicative competence* is the primary goal.
- The notion of communicative competence is *multifaceted,* implying competencies in at least three interrelated dimensions:
—social (pragmatic) competence (*language use*)
—representational competence (level of abstraction)
—linguistic competence (language structure—syntax/semantics)
- The child acquires communication skills mainly through interaction with adults who are effective communicators, particularly in interactions in which the child is able and motivated to engage the adult in dialogue.

Thus, the language development approach is focused at the level of "critical skills" (i.e., successful communication in situations where the child really wants to communicate), with the awareness that there are specific prerequisites for success. Teachers learn to apply the approach in any potential interaction with children. In this way, they can capitalize on those situations and activities that happen to motivate individual children. In addition, teachers can use the approach in planning cohesive sequences of class activities and projects according to particular needs and constraints.

Teachers are given inservice training and consultative help in assessing children's needs, setting objectives, planning and implementing activities that will stimulate particular kinds of communication, and in evaluating their own interactions with the children. Our theoretical framework and a more detailed treatment of the language experiences can be found in a paper by Ramey, McGinness, Cross, Collier, and Barrie-Blackley (in press).

Other opportunities for staff development include consultant-run workshops and the encouragement of further education in child-related areas. The goal and, we hope, the result of these opportunities is the provision of a staff that provides a variety of human contacts for the children while having gained a relatively unified and systematic approach toward the prevention of developmental retardation.

Beyond a comfortable, constructive environment and competent, creative staff, though, is the need for a curriculum that meets the needs of at-risk children. Although unstructured activities play an important role in Abecedarian daycare, standard curricula ensure a continuity of intervention that spontaneous interactions cannot guarantee. The curricula used in the Abecedarian project have been developed to provide a systematic but individualized educational experience for the children. The infant curricula, which are designed to meet the goals expressed earlier, grew out of the following: (1) Piagetian developmental theory; (2) known developmental facts; (3) parental value judgments; and (4) professional value judgments. Although the curricula continue to be refined, they can be at present roughly divided into those for infants and toddlers (newborns to 3 year olds) and those for young children (3 to 4 year olds). The division reflects both the growing efficiency of children in the use of language and the increasing importance of peer and adult interaction in fostering adaptive social behavior.

The infant curricula that are used in the Abecedarian project are the Carolina Infant Curriculum and the Task Orientation Curriculum, developed by Sparling and Lewis (1979). These curricula consist of over 300 items in language, motor, social, and cognitive areas (see Ramey et al. in press (b), for a more complete description). Each item is described in a guide sheet that sets forth a goal, the means to accomplish the goal, and the usefulness of the particular skill. Children are taught both in one-to-one interactions and, with increasing age, in small groups. Individual prescriptions of items are written for each child every 2 to 3 weeks, with a typical prescription containing 2 to 6 items. Teachers keep a developmental chart for each child to assist in providing a suitable match between child status and items selected; new items are chosen or old ones continued based on a given child's progress. This process helps to document the variety and quality of each child's curriculum experience while also providing a sense of continuity in the application of the curriculum. The program is formally applied up to a child's third birthday. The goal of the infant curricula is to enrich early development in several realms and to prepare the children for the more structured educational curricula they will partake of after their third year.

After the children reach 3 years of age, they begin to receive more structured educational curricula. The curricula continues to promote active child participation and independence and to provide a good deal of variety while giving the children a systematic exposure to areas such as science, math, and music. The formal cognitive curricula, which teachers can draw on as it best benefits the individual needs of a given child, include the GOAL math program (Karnes, 1973), the Peabody Early Experiences Kit (Dunn, Chun, Crowell, Dunn, Avery, and Yachel, 1976), Bridges to Reading (Greenberg and Epstein, 1973), and for the 4 year olds the Wallach and Wallach (1976) reading program. The daily schedule of 3 and 4 year olds is a mixture of structured and unstructured activities, outside and inside play, and rest times. The daily schedule also allows for the use and reinforcement of adaptive social behavior which is encouraged through the use of a program called *My Friends and Me* (Davis, 1977), a social curriculum designed to make children aware of their feelings and emotions and of appropriate responses to these feelings. Large-group, small-group, and solitary activities are scheduled, with active teacher participation and an emphasis on independence and appropriate peer interaction. The children also are prepared for the transition to public school with an increasing emphasis on sustained on-task behavior and personal responsibility. The infant and early childhood curricula, in toto, provide a systematic yet individually responsive experience for at-risk children so that relevant domains of development are enriched and sustained and the children are prepared to cope with the educational and social demands of public school.

Results from the Carolina Abecedarian Project.

In summarizing results from the Abecedarian Project, we will use the concept of levels of analysis and transactions of units discussed earlier and included as components in Figure 1. Specifically, we will present data from the level of the child, the caregiver, the family, the neighborhood, and society. We also will briefly summarize some data relevant to transactions of selected units.

Effects at the Level of the Child

History.

The specific purpose of the Abecedarian Project was to intervene at the level of the individual or, in terms of the General Systems Model, to modify the "history" of the infant so as to sever the relationship between poverty and retarded intellectual development. Since infants were randomly assigned to the daycare and control groups, effects on other aspects of the system ultimately can be attributed to this manipulation. Changes in the development of the infant, though, can be caused by direct influences such as the acquisition of concepts or by indirect processes involving changes in motivation or the stimulus properties ("demand characteristics") of the infant. The direct influences of daycare on cognitive and social outcomes will be considered in a later section. Now we will turn our attention to other, more subtle consequences of infant daycare.

Demand characteristics.

Several sources of information suggest that the Abecedarian Project has been successful in altering the stimulus properties of the child. Two studies have used behavioral ratings on the Infant Behavior Record (IBR) of the Bayley Scales of Infant Development. In a study by Ramey and Campbell (1979a), the IBR items from ratings of Cohorts 1 and 2 at 6, 12 and 18 months were factor analyzed, resulting in two factors labeled goal-directed behavior and social confidence (responsiveness to the examiner and happiness versus fearfulness). Infants attending daycare were rated as more socially confident than controls at all three ages; by 18 months, center-attending infants scored significantly higher than control children on the goal-directedness dimension. Finally, it was found that the fearfulness item showed the greatest degree of group difference at all ages and, further, that this item was uncorrelated with concurrent performance on the mental scale. Thus, daycare seems to have modified the infants' social behaviors in a manner that permits them to adjust to new situations and novel people more rapidly than infants who have not experienced our daycare.

MacPhee and Ramey (1980) extended these findings in their analysis of the Infant Behavior Record data for all four cohorts. Factor analysis of IBR items at 3, 6, 9, 12, 18, and 24 months revealed four factors: task orientation (attention span and goal-directed behaviors); cooperativeness (emotional tone, cooperativeness, and response to the examiner); activity level; and sociability. The first two factors are similar to Ramey and Campbell's (1979a) factors. Infants attending daycare were significantly more cooperative than controls at all ages except 9 months. Furthermore, differences in task orientation in favor of the daycare group emerged at 18 months ($p < .001$) and continued to be found at 24 months ($p < .002$). To foreshadow later discussion, a summary temperament variable—comprising scores on all four factors—was related both to performance on the mental scales of the Bayley and to the mother's involvement with her child.

Additional support for the effects of daycare on the child's demand characteristics is furnished by Finkelstein and Wilson (1977) and Finkelstein (in press). Their results suggest that the daycare-attending, high-risk children are as interested in peers and as friendly and cooperative as more advantaged middle-class age mates. Contrary to other research findings (e.g. Schwarz et al., 1974), daycare children were not more aggressive or more selfish as a result of having to share the teacher's attention with other children. The daycare children in the Finkelstein and Wilson study also appeared to be more willing to approach and interact with an unfamiliar adult than their home-reared, middle-class peers. These findings parallel those of Ricciuti (1974) and of Kagan, Kearsley, and Zelazo (1978).

Finally, Gordon and Feagans (1977) and Gordon and Bernard (1981) have found that the patterns of language skills in these preschool children were altered by enrollment in the daycare program. Children in both high-risk groups and in a General Population Sample (GPS) drawn from local nursery schools (mainly upper-middle-class) were assessed at 3½ and again at 5½ years of age on eight psycholinguistic tasks that measured the domains of basic words, representative sentence structures, and connected discourse. Rank order analyses revealed striking consistencies in performance on the eight subtests, with GPS children's performance exceeding that of the daycare group which, in turn, was significantly greater than that of the control children in all but one instance. The authors concluded that the daycare intervention program facilitated children's abilities on most of the psycholinguistic tasks, especially those concerned with spatial terms, paraphrasing, and sentence comprehension. To the extent that language is used to symbolize action and to mediate interactions with the social and cognitive environment, high-risk children exposed to daycare possess a more refined strategy for dealing with and adapting to the world.

In sum, involvement in the daycare program seems to have affected the stimulus properties of the children. A profile of these children's behavior, as contrasted with that of the control group, would note that they adapt more readily to unfamiliar situations and people, that they respond more appropriately and vigorously to the demands of a task, and that they are more advanced in language development. Succinctly stated, daycare seems to have modified the demand characteristics of these infants so that they are more adept at conducting transactions with the preschool environment.

Cognitive outcomes.

Figure 2 contains a plot of the Bayley Scales of Infant Development administered at 12 months, the Stanford-Binet (Terman and Merrill, 1973) administered at 24, 36, and 48 months, and the WPPSI administered at 60 months. These results have been reported previously by Ramey and Campbell (1981). Analyses of the results indicated a significant difference between the groups at all measurement occasions except the 12-month assessment. Thus, the results suggest that the daycare program has been instrumental in preventing the intellectual decline observed in the control group. Another piece of evidence germane to the intellectual decline issue can be derived from the percentage of individuals in the experimental and control groups who show an educational handicap due to a cognitive deficit. For our purposes we shall define a *cognitive educational handicap* as an IQ score less than or equal to 85. Table 2 is taken from Ramey and Haskins (1981c) and reports the percentage of experimental and control children scoring below IQ 85 at 36, 48, and 60 months for Cohorts 1 and 2 combined. As can be seen, the control group was on the average 3.54 times as likely to have low-scoring children as the experimental group.

That this group of children was truly at high risk for progressive mild mental retardation is also attested to by the performance of older siblings on standard measures of intelligence. Ramey and Campbell (1981) have reported a correlation between the IQs of 41 older siblings of children in the project and their ages (range = 57 to 220 months). Siblings were given the age-appropriate Wechsler Scale. The mean of the IQ distribution was 87.4 with a standard deviation of 10.3 The correlation coefficient was $r = -.45, p < .003$. This finding suggests an apparent progressive IQ decline with age in the absence of an early intervention program.

Because measures of general intelligence do not reveal much about specific psychological processes, we administered the McCarthy Scales of Children's Abilities (1972) at 42 months to determine which components differentiated the treatment and control groups (Ramey and Campbell, 1979a). The educationally treated (daycare) children were superior to the educationally untreated group on the Verbal, Perceptual-Performance, Quantitative, and Memory Scales but not on the Motor Scale. A follow-up administration of the McCarthy Scales at 54 months (Ramey and Campbell, 1979b) revealed that the Verbal, Perceptual-Performance, and Quantitative Scales still differed but the Memory and Motor Scales

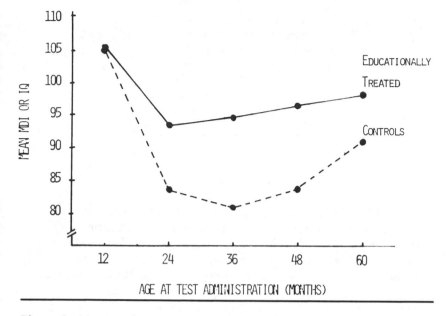

Figure 2. Mean Bayley MDI, Stanford-Binet, and WPPSI scores at five test occasions for the Day care and Control groups.

failed to distinguish between the groups. Thus, early compensatory education appears to improve disadvantaged children's ability to attend to, comprehend, and to carry out abstract and complex tasks. Further, the effect appears broad scale rather than specific, leading us to assume that general intelligence or *g* has been affected.

Effects of infant demand characteristics on outcome.

The principal message of Sameroff's (1975) Transactional Model was that linear relationships between insult to the infant and later cognitive deficits were uncommon in the normal range of environments. Two areas of inquiry from the Abecedarian Project clearly illustrate this process at work. Zeskind and Ramey (1978; 1981) have reported two analyses of the consequences of fetal malnutrition in the two high-risk groups of our project. Using the Ponderal Index (PI) as a measure of fetal growth and nutrition, infants in the daycare and control groups were classified as either malnourished or normal. Bayley mental scale scores at 3 and 18 months and Stanford-Binet scores at 24 months (Zeskind and Ramey, 1978) and 36 months (Zeskind and Ramey, 1981) were analyzed by group (intervention group X PI status). It is clear from Figure 3 that later

Table 2 Experimental and Control Children Performing Below IQ 85 at Three Ages (percentage)

Group	Age (Months)		
	36	48	60
Experimental	26	11	11
Control	61	52	39

NOTE: Averaged across the three ages, Control children are more likely than Experimental children to score below IQ 85 by a factor of 3.54.

IQ cannot be predicted solely from the status of the organism nor from knowing whether or not the infant attended daycare. A supportive environment (daycare) tended to ameliorate the effects of fetal malnutrition. In the unsupplemented home environment of low SES families, fetally malnourished infants showed an even more precipitous decline in IQ than their well-nourished peers.

The synergistic effects of transactions between elements of the system are again illustrated in a recent study by MacPhee and Ramey (1980). As noted earlier, infants in the experimental and control groups were classified as Easy or Difficult in temperament, based on their scores on Bayley's Infant Behavior Record. As in the Zeskind and Ramey studies, four groups representing the two variables (intervention group X temperamental classification) were formed and examined for differences in IQ at each test occasion from 3 to 36 months. The results, shown in Figure 4, again illustrate the transactional nature of development. Although infants classified as Easy fared better through the first 12 months, the effects of the nonsupportive environment began to be asserted in the second year. MacPhee and Ramey concluded that temperament may represent one demand characteristic that makes the infant more or less vulnerable to the stresses of a nonsupportive environment (e.g., Garmezy, 1971).

In sum, we are suggesting that certain demand characteristics of the infant are a product of the individual's biological heritage and learning history. These properties of the infant, however, are not directly related to cognitive and social outcomes. Rather, demand characteristics act upon and modify the environment, resulting in a phenotypic outcome such as IQ or maternal involvement. Some of these characteristics may buffer the child from the full effects of deprivation; characteristics such as task orientation (MacPhee and Ramey, 1980) or activity level (Schaffer, 1966). Other behaviors such as irritability may exacerbate the effects of

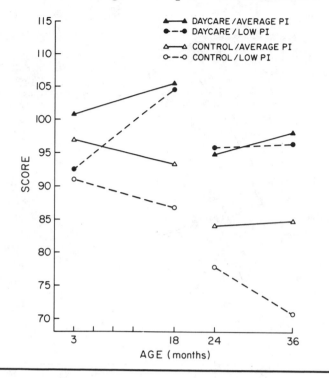

Figure 3. Mental test performance on the Bayley MDI and Stanford-Binet in Day care and Control infants classified as fetally malnourished or average PI.

a stressed home environment, resulting in child abuse (Belsky, 1980). In any event, the demand characteristics of the infant are only one part—albeit an important one—of the story.

Effects at the Level of the Caregiver

History.

In many respects the history of the primary caregivers is the demographic and attitudinal characteristics that they possessed in the year of their children's births. These demographic characteristics have been presented in Table 1 and will not be repeated here except to say that the mothers were from very low income families, had little formal education, were typically black and young, and had IQs which averaged in the low 80s. Almost all the mothers had lived in the local community when they

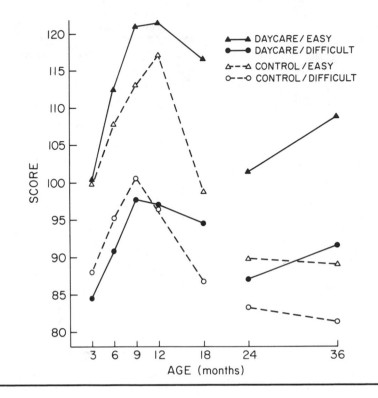

Figure 4. Mental test performance on the Bayley MDI and Stanford-Binet in Day care and Control infants classified as Easy or Difficult on the Bayley Infant Behavior Record.

were children, and they were usually part of a large and extended local kinship network.

Two primary measures of the mothers' attitudes were made about the time their infants were 6 months old. These measures will be conceptualized here as part of their history with respect to their views of life in general and childrearing in particular. Ramey and Mills (1977) reported analyses of the high-risk mothers, responses to Rotter's (1966) locus of control scale and to Emmerich's (1969) version of Schaefer and Bell's (1958) Parental Attitude Research Instrument (PARI). Responses of the high-risk mothers were compared with those of a randomly drawn sample of mothers from the local community with same-aged infants— referred to as the General Population Sample—who tended to be much better educated and financially situated. The experimental and control group mothers did not differ from one another on any of the subscales or total scores from either of these two instruments, but together they differed markedly from the GPS. Specifically, high-risk mothers perceived themselves as much more externally than internally controlled—a perception which to us seems accurate. They also reported themselves to be more authoritarian, less democratic, and less hostile and rejecting of the homemaking role than their more advantaged peers.

Demand characteristics.

The initial demand characteristics of the mothers have been couched in terms of their initial speech characteristics to their 6-month-old infants (Adams and Ramey, 1980; Ramey and Mills, 1977), and by scores on a modified version of Caldwell, Heider, and Kaplan's (1966) Home Observation for Measurement of the Environment (HOME) which we call an Index of Functional Maternal Concern (Ramey and Farran, 1981). This index, unlike the Caldwell, Heider, and Kaplan instrument, restricts itself to overt childcare behaviors that the mother displays during a 45-minute-to-1-hour visit to the family's home. We have found this index to correlate negatively with the mother's authoritarianism and external locus of control and positively with her intelligence and level of education. Further, the index has been shown to be stable during the first 2 years of the child's life. Thus, there is reason to believe that there is substantial congruence between the mother's history as assessed at the level of attitudes and her behaviors, which we construe as demand characteristics.

With respect to speech demand characteristics, Adams and Ramey (1980) have reported a structural analysis of maternal speech to 6-month-old high-risk infants. The results from this sample were compared with those from more advantaged mothers previously reported in the psycholinguistic literature and with other measures we have gathered concerning the risk status of the families in our sample. It was found that the proportion of imperatives, but not the amount of maternal speech, was positively correlated with our High-Risk Index and negatively correlated with maternal education and IQ. Consonant with previous findings on maternal speech to older infants, syntactic complexity was not significantly related to social-risk indexes. Thus, we have some evidence that the risk status of the mothers is translated into a linguistic behavioral style that is likely to affect social interchanges within the dyad.

Outcome characteristics.

Ramey, Farran, and Campbell (1979) have reported repeated assessments using the PARI at 6 and 18 months and found that experimental and control group mothers were not different at either measurement occasion. At 18 months, though, the high-risk groups differed from the GPS sample in the same way that we summarized above for the 6-month assessments. Therefore, at this level of analysis there is not evidence of parental attitudes being affected by daycare intervention, at least during infancy.

Transactions between children and caregivers.

Major alterations in the daily routines of families are likely to have psychological consequences. This topic is particularly controversial with respect to infant daycare. In the United States the sanctity of the intact nuclear family as the premier rearing institution is a particularly strong ethic. Therefore, any proposed supplement or alteration in our traditional ideal is viewed with skepticism and alarm. For example, when former President Richard Nixon vetoed the Mondale-Braddamus Comprehensive Child Care Bill in 1971, one of the main reasons cited for the veto was the potentially devisive influence that expanded availability of daycare would have on families. This public policy decision was based more on an appeal to common sense than on the basis of scientific evidence, which was scant in the early 1970s with respect to daycare in this country. Further, the use of evidence concerning group rearing from other countries such as Sweden, Israel, and Russia was viewed with skepticism because of their pervasive differences in the area of family history and the role of the state in family functioning.

At the time that the Abecedarian Project was begun the controversy over infant daycare was in full force. We had several reasons for wanting to monitor the developing relationship between mothers and children, including the prevailing political zeitgeist basic scientific questions concerning the role of early experience, and a desire to minimize potentially negative consequences to participating families. Three levels of evidence are particularly germane and will be summarized here.

The first type of evidence is derived from observations made in the children's homes using Caldwell, Heider, and Kaplan's (1966) Home Observation for the Measurement of the Environment (HOME), administered when the children were 6, 18, 30, and 42 months of age. The HOME measures the following dimensions of the child's home environment: (1) emotional and verbal responsivity of the mother; (2) absence of punishment; (3) physical and temporal organization of the environment; (4) provision of appropriate toys; (5) maternal involvement; and (6) opportunity for variety in daily stimulation. Neither the scale scores nor the total scores at any test occasion revealed a significant difference between the daycare and control groups, although evidence has been presented to indicate that both groups differ on all assessed dimensions as early as 6 months of age when compared with a representative sample from the local population (Ramey, Mills, Campbell, and O'Brien, 1975). Thus, daycare does not seem to have either a positive or a negative effect on these high-risk homes as they relate directly to childrearing as assessed by the HOME.

The second type of data comes from direct observations of caregiver–child interactions assessed in a 20-minute laboratory session at 6, 18, and 30 months of age. At these ages, a representative sample of same-aged children and their mothers from the local area formed a comparison group. The laboratory sessions were conducted in a room furnished as a small living room and a coding scheme for frequency and durations of discrete behaviors (modified from Lewis and Goldberg's, 1969, procedures) was used.

Ramey, Farran, and Campbell (1979) have presented results that indicate a great deal of similarity among all three groups at 6 months with the only significant difference being the greater amount of talking to their infants by middle-class mothers. At 20 months, however, the middle-class mothers not only talked more to their toddlers but interacted more with them as well. The interaction patterns of the daycare and control groups did not differ significantly from one another on a factor that Farran and Ramey (1980) have labeled *dyadic involvement*. O'Connell and Farran (1980), in a more refined analysis of the videotapes from the 20-month interaction session, found that experimental group infants were communicating to their mothers at a significantly higher level than the control infants. Further, daycare attending infants were communicating at a level equal to middle-class infants on what O'Connell and Farran call "requesting" behaviors. Thus, there appears to be some evidence that the daycare children are presenting different "demand characteristics" when in interaction with their mothers and this, in turn, may affect the quality of the mother–child interactions over time.

Some further evidence for this change in "demand characteristics" is derived from observations of mothers and children conducted in the laboratory when the children were 36 months of age. These interactions have been coded with the Reciprocal Control System developed by Farran and Haskins (1977). Comparisons of the dyadic interactions using conditional probabilities have been made between the experimental and control groups combined and middle-class mother–child dyads (Farran and Haskins, 1980). Preliminary comparisons of the experimental and control groups suggested that daycare may have had the effect of modifying the child's behavior in social interactions with his/her mother. Experimental children were four times as likely to attempt to modify their mothers' behavior (e.g., asking mothers to watch their activity, read them a book, or join them in a tea party) compared with control children. Moreover, the mutual play activities lasted twice as long for experimental dyads, leading one to the speculation that with the child's increasing skills, play becomes more enjoyable to the mother. Thus, the evidence from this level of analysis not only indicates no negative effects on the dyad's behavior but may portend a slightly positive effect mediated by the altered demand characteristics of the child, plausibly attributable to the behaviors encouraged within the daycare center.

The third type of data about caregiver–child interactions derives from direct observations involving the child, the mother, and the child's daycare teachers. The central issue here is whether the mother's saliency for her child, as Kagan, Kearsley and Zelazo (1978) have termed it, has been replaced by that of the child's teachers in the daycare center. Because of our experimental design, this issue is germane only to our experimental group dyads. Farran and Ramey (1977) pursued the issue of saliency of mothers and teachers within a social preference paradigm in which the child, mother, and the child's daycare teacher were simultaneously present in a small playroom. Observations of behaviors were made during a 12-minute free play period and also during a 2-minute period when the infants were given a problem (getting a cookie out of a locked clear plastic container) which they could not solve by themselves. Results indicated a uniform preference for proximity to the mother in this situation. In addition, the children were much more likely to solicit help from the mother in solving the problem. Thus, children overwhelmingly preferred to be near and to interact with their mothers rather than their teachers, indicating that the attachment bond to the mother had indeed been formed. Moreover, they perceived their mothers as providers of help when faced with a mildly difficult, ecologically valid problem. Therefore, our working assumption at this point is that while the concern over daycare and its relation to the disadvantaged family is well intended, the evidence from our own work suggests that it is not necessarily detrimental to mother–child relationships and may, in fact, be mildly positive and mediated by the increased competence of treated children.

Effects of Maternal Demand Characteristics on Infant Outcome.

Fortunately, one of the dividends of the General Systems Model is that new relationships between variables can be spelled out and investigated. In this section, we are interested in the possible relationship between aspects of the parent, such as attitudes, perceptions of the infant, and demand characteristics, and the child's cognitive and social development. While a cause-and-effect linkage between the two has been implicit in some theories of child development (e.g., Schaefer, 1981; Baumrind and

Black, 1967), little research has been done to verify that such a path exists, much less explicate the processes involved. Some findings from the Abecedarian Project are germane at this point, though the connections we are exploring are acknowledged to be tenuous.

Newman and Ramey (1979) investigated the relationship between child self-concept, maternal attitudes, maternal self-esteem, and child outcome as assessed by the Peabody Individual Achievement Test (PIAT) and by the Wechsler Intelligence Scale (WPPSI) administered during kindergarten or first grade. The high-risk group (daycare and control sample combined) did not differ from GPS children on the self-concept scale (Cicirelli, undated). GPS mothers differed from both high-risk groups in their perceptions of their children's temperament using Buss and Plomins' (1975) Inventory. High-risk children were rated as more impulsive and less sociable by their mothers. Furthermore, one of the three PARI factors (democratic attitudes) was correlated with the WPPSI, while maternal self-esteem and perceptions of the child related to both cognitive measures. Although the correlations do not account for more than 25 percent of the variance in any one correlation—suggesting that other processes are mediating or supplementing the effects of parental characteristics—it is important that the processes underlying these findings be examined more closely.

In a study involving only children in the high-risk control group, Ramey and Brownlee (1981) studied variables that might increase the precision of early identification of at-risk children. Predictor variables included maternal attitudes assessed when the infants were 6 months old (the PARI and Rotter's Internal-External locus of control scale), maternal IQ (the WAIS), infant temperament at 6 months (the IBR), measures of the home environment at 6 months (the HOME), and the amount of time the child spent outside the home in the care of others during the first 6 months. Three of the variables showed significant prediction of 24-month infant Stanford-Binet IQ. The three variables included temperament, time outside the home in the care of others in the first 6 months of infancy, and the democratic attitudes factor of the PARI. Ramey and Brownlee concluded that the lack of a well-defined philosophy of childrearing, as exemplified by low scores on the PARI, may translate into inconsistent actions which would leave already stressed mothers ill-equipped to deal with an irritable child or a chaotic setting. If so, this would suggest another transactional process that ultimately may affect the outcome of the infant.

Intervention effects on relationships among variables.
Early intervention may affect development in at least two basic ways. First, it may affect the frequency or type of behaviors that are presumed

or posited to be part of a causal chain, ultimately linked to measures of child outcome. Generally, the form of analysis at this level is a group comparison of the presence or amount of selected variables as a function of differential treatment.

There is a second and perhaps more subtle influence that early intervention may exert. Early intervention may affect the relationships among variables in a causal network. Recall from the General Systems Model that behavior emerges out of the interaction of components of a system so that there are multiple causes of a given outcome. By modifying simultaneously several of these processes, intensive intervention may alter traditionally reported relationships among constellations of parent–child variables. Several pieces of empirical data have given us some tantalizing leads on this topic. Because we do not, as yet, have a unified, detailed, a priori theory of the specific psychological mechanisms likely to be altered as a function of the form and focus of preventive intervention strategies, we will have to make this point by example. We will limit ourselves to two illustrations.

One of psychology's time-honored empirical findings is that the intellectual status of parents is moderately and positively predictive of the intellectual status of their offspring. Generally, the magnitude of parent–child IQ correlations for intelligence averages about .5. Major controversy has existed, and still exists, concerning the meaning of this relationship. Jensen (1981) has argued, for example, that this relationship is best accounted for by genetic inheritance. Others have argued that it represents the shared environments that parents and children typically inhabit. Because experimental tests of either of these positions (or alternative positions) have been virtually impossible to conduct in the past for ethical reasons, the nature–nurture controversy has generated more heat than light.

Because the random assignment to treatment groups in our intervention program is a powerful design feature ensuring, within the limits of sampling theory, initial group equivalence, it has allowed us to pursue this issue without some of the confounding influences characteristic of most earlier studies. We think this is true because our cognitive curriculum is individually prescribed (based on the child's developmental status) and is delivered independently of the child's parents. Thus, there is at least an attenuation of the usual genotype-environment correlation that typically confounds consanguinity studies. Therefore, Ramey and Haskins (1981b; 1981c) have presented parent–child IQ correlations based upon assessments when the children were 3, 4, and 5 years of age. In the control group each of these correlations is statistically significant and not different from the expected coefficient of .5. Thus, our findings for the control group replicate those already in the literature. The correlations in the experimental group are quite different, however. None of the three coefficients are statistically significant and, with one exception of a nonsignificant .34 correlation at 48 months, they are remarkably close to o. At age 3 the correlation coefficient is −.05 and at age 5 the correlation is .14. Thus, the relationship between such a basic psychological construct as parent–child intellectual resemblance has apparently been significantly altered as a byproduct of manipulating other units within the system.

Another example of the alteration among relationships is derived from a paper by Ramey and Campbell (1981). In that report, backwards elimination multiple regression equations were used to predict WPPSI IQ scores at 60 months of age separately for the experimental and control groups. The potential contributors to the prediction equation included maternal age; years of schooling completed by mothers when children were 54 months of age; the family's High-Risk Index Score at the time of the child's birth; family yearly income from the year that the children were 54 months; maternal scores on the PARI authoritarian, hostility, and democratic attitude factors ascertained when the child was 18 months; and the mother's IQ. Of this set of potential predictors of the 60-month WPPSI IQ, four variables remained significant for the control group yielding an R^2 of .57 or 57 percent of the variance in the IQ scores. Significant variables, in order of importance were: (1) maternal IQ; (2) HOME total score at 54 months; (3) PARI Hostility-Rejection from 18 months; and (4) PARI authoritarianism assessed at 18 months.

For the daycare treated group, only the HOME score at 54 months entered significantly into the equation, resulting in an R^2 of .38. Thus, as with the earlier and simpler bivariate correlations concerning parent–child IQ similarity, this more complicated model of developmental forces, as represented by different regression equations, indicates a modification among relationships as a function of preventive intervention. In summary, it appears that the emergent principle from our General Systems Theory model is supported empirically by our data.

Effects at the Level of the Household

The relationship between caregiver characteristics and household characteristics are obviously intertwined and somewhat redundant. The choice of what data to include at the caregiver level of analysis has a direct bearing on what is presented at the family level. Thus, we are aware that initial demographic and psychological attributes such as parental intelligence and the quality of the home as assessed by Caldwell, Heider, and Kaplan's inventory could be justified as measures pertaining to this level. Given that they have already been presented and constitute a "history" section, we will present only two types of data at this level. These can be construed both as demand characteristics of the household and as outcome measures that illustrate the effects of preventive intervention at the family level.

Maternal interviews conducted when the children were 54 months old have revealed what we consider to be some potentially very important changes in the life circumstances of 27 mothers in our experimental group relative to 23 control group mothers. These changes concern the potential availability of intellectual, financial, and role-model resources that may ultimately but indirectly affect the child's progress. With respect to formal education, Ramey, Dorval and Baker-Ward (in press) have reported that mothers of the daycare children have significantly more formal education by the time their children are 54 months old (11.9 years) than the mothers of the control children (10.3 years) although the groups were educationally equivalent in the year of the children's births (10.30 and 10.12 years for the experimental and control groups, respectively). This means that daycare for the children of high-risk mothers has apparently allowed more of them to continue their education. Given that education of the mother again has been validated as a major predictor of children's intellectual and adaptive behavior in first grade in North Carolina (Ramey, Stedman, Borders-Patterson and Mengel, 1978; Finkelstein and Ramey, 1980), this educational differential linked to early daycare intervention may bode well for the experimental group's performance in public school.

When data from the 54 month maternal interview was coded with respect to maternal employment, another striking finding was noted. We classified maternal occupation into: (1) unemployed or unskilled; (2) semiskilled or skilled; or (3) student. Table 3 contains the percentages of both the experimental and control group mothers who fall into each of these categories at 54 months, excluding students. A Chi Square test was completed for the two groups concerning employment. The Chi Square was significant ($X^2 = 4.54$, $p < .05$) indicating that more of the control group mothers were unskilled and/or unemployed and conversely that more of the daycare mothers held semiskilled or skilled jobs. This finding is consistent with the educational advancement just reported and adds optimism to the prediction of the children's subsequent performance in school. We hypothesize that because education and employment represent structural and permanent changes in the families, they may continue to draw the more accomplished high-risk families closer to the resources enjoyed by the mainstream of American society.

Table 3 Employment Status of Experimental and Control Group Mothers when Their Children Were 54 Months Old

Occupational Level	Daycare Group Mothers (N=25)	Control Group Mothers (N=21)
Unemployed or Unskilled	37	65
Semiskilled or Skilled	55	26

$X^2 = 4.54; p < .05$

Effects on the Neighborhood

We have chosen to investigate neighborhood influences on development beginning when children are in their kindergarten year of public school. From each public school classroom in which one or more of our high-risk children are placed, we randomly draw an equal number of same-sexed children. Typically, any given classroom contains only one of our children, although occasionally school district lines and available classrooms result in more than one high-risk child in a given classroom. As part of our school-aged assessments we gather information about neighborhood composition and social functioning through parental interviews and naturalistic observations. Preliminary data from these observations, which are under the direction of Ron Haskins and Neal Finkelstein, have recently been reported by Ramey and Haskins (1981a). The naturalistic observation data were derived from 16 5-year-old experimental and control children and 12 middle-income children from the GPS sample. Children from low-income families were dropped from the GPS sample for the analysis to be reported. On each of 3 days, 4 10-minute blocks of observational data were obtained for each child. Approximately 30 predetermined behavioral categories were scored including talking, playing, attempting to modify or change another person's behavior, crying, striking, and so on.

The results revealed very low levels of aggression both in the neighborhoods of high-risk and middle-income children, more talk by and toward middle-income children and more higher order play (coordinate play) involving explicit rules or games. Thus, these results suggest there may be differences in the neighborhood social experiences of children from low-income and middle-income families. However, not enough data have been gathered to be reported with great confidence because most of the children are not yet old enough. These preliminary data are reported to typify a style of inquiry and a level of analysis rather than for their substance. Results at this level await more complete data collection and analysis.

Effects at the Level of Society

The data germane to this level of analysis are not yet ready for dissemination because the Abecedarian Project is too far from completion. However, two generic types of analyses are anticipated and we will mention them briefly. The first type will involve a more thorough comparison of the fate of the high-risk families relative to that of peers from the local community (society in microcosm). This is similar in form to that reported earlier by Ramey, Farran, and Campbell (1979) but expanded to include larger networks of variables. Thus we have planned a series of analyses based on children's intellectual and adaptive performance through the early elementary school years, with performance at the end of third grade as our criterion. Because most of our children are not yet that old, the analyses cannot be conducted.

A second type of analysis for determining the effects on society must also await the passage of time. However, a brief mention of our general plan may be of interest. We plan an economic cost-benefit analysis of the effects of prevention similar to the one recently and successfully reported by Schweinhart and Weikart (1981). We propose to examine employment histories, special educational placements, health system use-patterns, grade retention, and other relevant variables to determine what, if any, return on the financial investment of preventive services is reaped by the taxpayer. Even preliminary analyses, however, are at least several years in the future.

Summary

Having reviewed the empirical data from the Abecedarian Project in relation to the General Systems Model, we now want to return to a consideration of the Model and its implications for further research. Specifically, we will organize our thinking around the main constructs of the model, namely: the emergent principle, levels of analysis, range of stability, regulatory mechanisms, and the concept of an active organism. We will conclude our summary with a brief discussion of ontogenetic processes.

The Emergent Principle

Development is multiply determined by transactions among many variables. To understand the development of real children, we must go beyond typical laboratory experiments which investigate whether given variables can have an influence on developmental outcome and determine if that variable typically is active in ecologically important ways (McCall, 1977). It is unlikely that an adequate understanding of developmental retardation will emerge from theoretical systems that stress the primacy of single factors. As our data illustrate, the associative paths of active variables are complex and dynamic. For example, the provision of daycare has affected children's cognitive, linguistic, social, and affective development. It also is implicated in changes in parental education and income, which are time-honored predictors of child performance in school. Thus developmental daycare has at least partially restructured the network of influences which impinge upon the child's daily life. The synergistic outcomes of transacting units are not easy to anticipate. Gestalt principles of perception indicate that the whole is greater than the sum of the parts. If true of a psychological process like perception, can it be any less true of the more complicated social mechanisms implicated in developmental retardation? The central issue is whether the system is too complex to permit adequate prediction and ultimate therapeutic control. We find optimism and direction by fixing the criterion performance (developmental retardation) and examining the forces that are related to it.

A corollary of the emergent principle is that unintended consequences, or ripple effects, will result from changes in the system. Several of our findings suggest that such processes have indeed occurred. The most notable example is that the mothers of children in daycare have been able to continue with their education, the implication being that the Abecedarian Project indirectly was able to foster a supportive home environment. We envision additional studies that would focus on such ripple effects as the health of the children, aggressiveness with peers, and changes in the attitudes and socioeconomic status of the family. By ferreting out positive and negative unintended consequences, we will be better able to determine the cost-effectiveness of our own program and forewarn other intervention efforts about the pitfalls of modifying a dynamic system.

Levels of Analysis

Bronfenbrenner's (1977) concept of the ecology of human development argues that effects on development spring from a hierarchy of embedded levels. Our levels of analysis borrow heavily from this concept and so needs little further explication. There are three implications of this idea that merit a parting comment. First, a condition like developmental retardation that is caused by processes occurring within and between levels demands a concerted, multidisciplinary approach. We know from our own work that clear contributions to preventing mild mental retardation can be made by disciplines as diverse as bacteriology and anthropology. The level of analysis and the questions being asked will determine the choice of disciplinary approach. Second, prevention efforts can be targeted at any one level or at a combination of levels. Previous research (Bronfenbrenner, 1975) would suggest that a combination of approaches would be the most effective, although this is an empirical issue. Finally, the design of future programs—and analysis of the data that result—must take the level of analysis into account. As Miller (1978) has pointed out, misleading conclusions about causation can result unless consideration is given to analyses of the data at the appropriate level. Echoing Bronfenbrenner (1977), perhaps the most useful function of this concept is that it makes us aware of the intricacies of developmental processes.

Range of Stability

In a living system, each unit is assumed to operate within a given range of stability. Furthermore, this range of stability is a function of inherent constraints (e.g., the genotype of the child, the income of the family) as well as learned behavior patterns that allow the organism to adapt to changing circumstances. An older child or one reared in an enriched environment should have a range of stability that exceeds that of a young or deprived child. At another level of analysis, a well-to-do family living in a stable, friendly atmosphere should be more able to cope with stress than a poor family living in a fragmented, tough neighborhood. In general, the more isolated the component of the system is from other elements, and the fewer strategies and resources it has at its disposal, the more it is at risk for pathology and dysfunction.

The Abecedarian Project was designed with a range of stability principle in mind, although we did not call it that in 1971. Specifically, a High-Risk Index was used to identify infants at risk for mild mental retardation. This Index (see Ramey and Smith, 1977) contains variables related to sibling status, parental intelligence, and family resources. Implicit in the notion of a threshold score on this scale is that it is a point where the range of stability for the family has been exceeded such that the development of the child is imperiled. Thus risk status can be construed as a measure of the limits of stability.

Intervention programs based on the concept of risk status can also be couched in terms of the range of stability. The Abecedarian Project was designed with two goals in mind: (1) to teach the child those skills that are prerequisite to success in society in general and the schools in particular; and (2) to ensure that the family had at least the minimal resources of nutrition for the child, medical care, and social services. In the first case, our goal was to teach the children how to *adapt* to stress instead of succumbing to a fate of retardation and further poverty or redefining the "range of stability" (e.g., lowered expectations and self-concept). It is too early to tell whether or not we have been completely successful in achieving this aim but the IQ results (Ramey and Haskins, 1981b, 1981c; Ramey and Campbell, 1979a) and the data on self-concept (Newman and Ramey, 1979) are encouraging. As far as stress or the family is concerned, the daycare program seems to have given the family a chance to marshal its resources and to remain within a range of stability (Ramey, Dorval and Baker-Ward, in press). This may be due to the combined effects of support services and the freedom from full-time child care that permitted a return to work or school. Although information on this outcome of daycare is sparse, the Abecedarian Project seems to have been successful in assisting the family as well as the child.

In sum, the range of stability is a concept that was used by the Abecedarian Project to *identify* infants at risk and to *teach* these children how to adapt to stress. Broadly conceived, the goal of the intervention program was to expand the range of stability of the child by fostering adaptive skills and, secondarily, to alleviate some of the stress on the family through social services and time away from caregiving.

Regulatory Mechanisms

The regulation of behavior and development is a concept that is simple to convey yet difficult to study. Perhaps one reason for this is that continuous adaptation to the environment (or to a genotypic "blueprint"—see Tanner, 1963) makes intuitive sense. In order to study cybernetic processes, though, one must examine a system gone awry, as is the case with deprivation or prenatal insult, or study behavior at a molecular level. Two examples from the Abecedarian Project will serve to illustrate regulatory processes in development and behavior.

Effectance motivation is a term that has been used to explain an organism's efforts to affect and master the environment (White, 1959). Research on effectance motivation suggests that exposure to an unresponsive environment can have adverse effects on development while experience with response-controlled stimuli can facilitate social and intellectual growth (Seligman and Maier, 1967; Wachs et al., 1971). Thus effectance motivation is a product of previous experience and, in turn, serves to structure and guide succeeding transactions with the environment. As such, it can be thought of as a mechanism that regulates development through feedback and change.

Finkelstein and Ramey (1977), in a series of three experiments, attempted to tease out the process by which experience with controllable stimulation influences effectance motivation. They concluded that changes in attention to response performance may be the mediating variable. In other words, infants who transferred training to later trials had learned self-monitoring strategies such that "infants who received prior experience learning to control stimulation were subsequently better able to determine the relation between their behaviors and environmental events" (p. 818). In a related vein, two studies of attentional strategies revealed significant differences between the Abecedarian daycare and control groups. MacPhee and Ramey (1981) studied infants through the second year and found significant differences in task orientation by 18 months. Finkelstein, Gallagher and Farran (1980), studying 3 and 4 year olds in both high-risk groups and in the GPS sample, found significant differences between the daycare and control groups in auditory perception and language ability. Both groups, however, fared less well than more advantaged children in attention to complex or demanding stimuli. Thus, there is some evidence for the effects of a responsive environment (daycare) on attention deployment but the results are not conclusive.

At a more molecular level, studies of social interactions have found that behavior is the product of mutual regulation between the actors, whether the dyad consists of peers (Garvey and Hogan, 1973; Mueller, 1972) or caregiver and infant (Fogel, 1977; Bakeman and Brown, 1977). Bell (1968, 1971) has termed this process bidirectionality of effects, stating that an individual's behavior in an interactive setting is co-determined by both partners. A study from the Abecedarian Project illustrates this regulatory mechanism. As mentioned in previous sections, Farran and Haskins (1980) studied mother–child dyads from the high-risk and GPS samples. Important to the present discussion is their finding that, although the quantity of interaction differed between groups, the interactive processes of turn-taking did not. Although the overall duration of mutual play, for example, was longer in the GPS sample, the use of behaviors that modified ongoing activity did not differ.

In summary, we have argued that certain processes regulate development and behavior. Although our list certainly is short and incomplete, this does not imply that regulatory mechanisms are unimportant. On the contrary, it is our fervent hope that more attention will be directed to the study of these processes. For instance, there is a need for more information on how motivation (to control) fuels ability (to adapt). There is a need to find out which regulatory mechanisms do not develop or are interfered with in children reared in poverty. Even though this lament is nothing new, it is worth repeating that effective prevention of psychosocial retardation will occur only when the relevant developmental processes are understood.

The Active Organism

One of the principles of General Systems Theory is that the organism is active rather than reactive. Although this is really nothing more than a philosophical assertion, there is some evidence to support it. The burgeoning literature on early competencies, reviewed by Appleton, Clifton and Goldberg (1975), suggests that neonates come equipped with the means to elicit responses from the environment. Similarly, research on caregiver–infant interactions has found that even young infants actively modify the course of a social exchange (c.f. Bell and Harper, 1977; Lewis and Rosenblum, 1974).

The primary implication of this principle is that an active organism constantly adapts to the environment while modifying it (Sameroff, 1975). In a nonsupportive environment, we might expect the most active infants to be less vulnerable to deprivation (Schaffer, 1966). Even so, as research on learned helplessness (Seligman and Maier, 1967) and effectance motivation (Finkelstein and Ramey, 1977) has shown, an active organism reared in an unresponsive or noncontingent environment may be adversely affected. Evidence for both hypotheses can be found in the MacPhee and Ramey (1981) paper in which it was shown that: (1) daycare caused a change in the infant's demand characteristics; (2) infants classified as easy (more cooperative, task oriented, sociable, and moderately active) fared better in low-income homes than difficult infants; and (3) without the benefit of daycare, the IQ scores of difficult *and* easy infants declined. The moral of this principle seems to be that acting upon the environment may incur some benefits, perhaps through increased stimulation, but it does not ensure adequate development.

Ontogenetic Processes

The Abecedarian Project was specifically designed to alter the course of development in children of low-income families. Several general comments about our success in this endeavor can be made at this point.

Transactional processes.

The General Systems Model views an outcome as the product of interactions among many variables. Coupled with Sameroff's (1975) Transactional Model, this would lead us to conclude that development is not simply the result of a poor environment nor of an inferior or dysfunctional organism. Rather, each can be viewed as multivariate or multilevel components that constantly modify each other. A number of results from the Abecedarian Project demonstrate that there is no such equation as "Child History = Child Outcome" or "Caregiver History = Child

Outcome" or "Family Characteristics = Child Outcome". The results from the fetal malnutrition research (Zeskind and Ramey, 1978; 1981) and the infant temperament research (MacPhee and Ramey, 1981) show that child IQ scores are jointly determined by infant variables and by the presence or absence of a supportive environment. Ramey and Haskins (1981b; 1981c) reached the same conclusion when they found that child–mother IQ correlations in the control group were correctly predicted by a polygenetic model of intelligence but were not significantly different from zero in the daycare group. Clearly, when asking whether organismic or environmental variables determine developmental outcome, one can only reply, "Neither of the above—both do."

Paths versus levels.

One intriguing and important justification for a process approach to development is that a given outcome may be the product of different paths or different levels of functioning. During the 1960s, the prevailing attitude was that low-income children needed *more* education and *more* environmental stimulation to overcome the effects of their "impoverished" surroundings (cf. Zigler and Valentine, 1979). Research on maternal teaching styles (Hess and Shipman, 1966; 1968), dialect, (Baratz and Baratz, 1970) and the characteristics of the home environment (Wachs, Uzgiris and Hunt, 1971) gradually led to the realization that there is a sociocultural *difference* between members of different socioeconomic strata. Therefore, different paths as well as levels of development may be followed.

Some findings from the Abecedarian Project illustrate this concept. Ramey and Campbell (1981) regressed a number of predictor variables onto 60-month WPPSI IQ scores and found that different predictors entered the daycare and control group equations. In addition, recall that there were absolute differences in IQ at this age, suggesting that different paths were taken to different endpoints. The Farran and Haskins (1980) paper suggests that the same processes of dyadic interaction can occur concurrently with differences in the amount of mutual activity. We would hope that more investigators pursue such a course, whether it involves the longitudinal study of developmental processes or the more immediate determinants of behavior.

Plasticity.

Plasticity in development can be defined as the ability to be molded or changed by circumstances. Several processes may act to constrain the plasticity of development, including learning and genetic limitations, such that there is a range of reaction for a given phenotype (cf. Waddington, 1962). The plasticity of development has several crucial implications for intervention programs, most notably for when intervention begins (*timing*) and for the prognosis once intervention ceases (*reversibility*). Results from the Abecedarian Project suggest that intervention should be implemented before 18 months of age if one is to *prevent* (as opposed to ameliorate) developmental retardation. Analyses of our IQ data typically find no differences between groups through 12 months (Figure 2); by 18 months, though, the paths diverge as the control group begins to decline in performance. It could be the case that infant development to this point is so preprogrammed or canalized (Waddington, 1962) that change due to environmental press is not feasible. Rather than "blaming the infant" for not being responsive to daycare, we could ask whether the IQ tests being used are truly sensitive to group differences (Ramey and MacPhee, 1981). In fact, the Bayley Scales are heavily weighted with motor items while the Abecedarian curriculum has focused on linguistic, cognitive, and social development. In reality, some combination of canalization (cf. Gesell and Thompson, 1934) and test limitations may explain our findings more accurately. In any event, further research on the malleability of early development (and ways to accurately measure it) will be needed before a definitive conclusion on the timing of intervention can be reached.

We can only speculate at this point about the prognosis for the Abecedarian children once they have completed the preschool program. Results through 42 months on the McCarthy Scales (Ramey and Campbell, 1979) and through 60 months on the Stanford-Binet (Ramey and Haskings, 1981c) are encouraging but, as of yet, tell us little about their progress in school. Although there is a great deal of plasticity even at this age (e.g., Bronfenbrenner, 1975; Clarke and Clarke, 1976; Kagan, Klein, Finley, Rogoff, and Nolan, 1979), we hope that by providing the children with the cognitive and social skills needed for competing in school, we have been able to give them a chance of success in later life.

Conclusion

The final issues on which we would like to comment have less to do with scientific questions than with ones of ethical responsibility. As scientists, we cannot let ourselves lose sight of the fact that we are dealing with human participants. While we make the assumption that intervention efforts are potentially worthwhile, the fact remains that our knowledge is limited. The range of possible effects of intervention efforts is immense, and some outcomes may fail to be beneficial for those involved. In many ways, intervention programs carry along with them sets of cultural and social values, usually implicit, that may be at odds with the values of program participants. To paraphrase Harriet Rheingold (1976) and Edward Zigler (this volume), we must be careful.

The state of limited knowledge presents several difficulties. The foremost of these is the possible unintended negative consequences of intervention. In preventive efforts children are necessarily selected as being at risk for developmental retardation. The long-term effects that the label *at risk* might have on a child's development are unclear but potentially harmful (Mercer, 1977). While more recent findings have indicated that daycare programs may not be harmful and may even be beneficial (Etaugh, 1980; Belsky and Steinberg, 1978), most of that research has focused on high quality, experimental-type programs. Little is known about the effects of lesser quality programs.

Of course, unintended positive consequences can also occur. Gilmer, Miller, and Gray (1970), for example, found that the addition of parent participation in their preschool program apparently produced benefits for the younger siblings of the participating child, a phenomenon now termed *vertical diffusion*. An unexpected finding of the Abecedarian Project is that mothers of children in the experimental program are more likely to find productive employment and to resume their schooling than mothers of children in the control group. If programs have positive consequences, however, the scientist faces another dilemma. That is, if preventive efforts work, then the continued random assignment of children into experimental and control groups must be questioned. As Hunt (1980) has so cogently noted, the needs of science and the demands of social responsibility can quickly come into conflict. The potential for negative and positive consequences of preventive efforts, then, is a two-edged sword.

An even larger set of ethical questions arises when one examines the social and cultural implications of intervention efforts. Although intervention programs are not forced upon unwilling participants, programs still almost inevitably introduce a strong influence into a child's home and general environment and have implicit sets of values that may conflict with those within the home. While the influence of these conflicts on the results of any given effort is an important question (Stedman et al., 1972) perhaps a larger question surrounds the ethical implications of introducing implicit cultural and social values to relatively unsuspecting families. The influence of large-scale, intense preventive efforts may be an invasion of privacy that is relatively unwarranted given our present state of knowledge (Wallach and Wallach, 1976). As responsible social agents, applied scientists cannot lay claim to the proposition that science is a value-free enterprise. Sensitivity toward and respect for the children and their families is a necessity.

Directions for the Future

It is obvious that the issues involved in preventing developmental retardation are numerous and important. They deserve and must receive thoughtful scrutiny. We think that among the many unresolved issues in preventing developmental retardation, four are particularly important and deserve high places on our research agendas. First, there is a need for more effective and efficient means of identifying high-risk children. Second, there is a need for continuing research into the cost-effectiveness of program variables such as intensity, duration, age of entry, and format. Third, there is a need for more sophisticated measurements of adaptive behaviors. Finally, there is a need for long term follow-up of treated children to determine the full impact of preventive efforts. It is our hope that General Systems Theory will guide our interdisciplinary, longitudinal inquiry along the winding empirical paths to greater knowledge about preventing development gone awry.

References

Adams, J., and Ramey, C. T. Structural aspects of maternal speech to infants reared in poverty. *Child Development*, 1980, *51*, 1280–1284.

Appleton, T., Clifton, R., and Goldberg, S. The development of behavioral competence in infancy. In F. D. Horowitz (Ed.), *Review of child development research* (Vol. 4). Chicago: University of Chicago Press, 1975.

Bakeman, R., and Brown, J. V. Behavioral dialogues: An approach to the assessment of mother–infant interaction. *Child Development*, 1977, *48*, 195–203.

Baratz, S. S., and Baratz, J. C. Early childhood intervention: The social science base of institutional racism. *Harvard Educational Review*, 1970, *40*, 29–50.

Baroff, G. S. *Mental retardation: Nature, cause, and management.* Washington, D.C.: Hemisphere Publishing Corp., 1974.

Bateson, P. How do sensitive periods arise and what are they for? *Animal Behaviour*, 1979, *27*, 470–486.

Baumrind, D., and Black, A. E. Socialization patterns associated with dimensions of competence in preschool boys and girls. *Child Development*, 1967, *38*, 291–327.

Bayley, N. Comparisons of mental and motor tests scores for ages 1–15 months by sex, birth order, race, geographic location, and education of parents. *Child Development*, 1965, *36*, 379–412.

Begab, M. (Ed.). *Psychosocial influences and retarded performance: Strategies for improving social competence* (Vol. 2). Baltimore: University Park Press, 1981.

Begab, M. *Issues in the prevention of psychosocial retardation.* Paper presented at a colloquium at the University of North Carolina Mental Retardation Center on Issues in the Prevention of Psychosocial Retardation, Chapel Hill, North Carolina, December 1978.

Bell, R. Q. A reinterpretation of the direction of effects in studies of socialization. *Psychological Review*, 1968, *75*, 81–95.

Bell, R. Q. Stimulus control of parent or caretaker behavior by offspring. *Developmental Psychology*, 1971, *4*, 63–72.

Bell, R. Q., and Harper, L. V. *Child effects on adults*. Hillsdale, N.J.: Lawrence Erlbaum Assoc., 1977.

Belsky, J. Child maltreatment: An ecological integration. *American Psychologist*, 1980, *35*, 320–335.

Belsky, J., and Steinberg, L. D. The effects of daycare: A critical review. *Child Development*, 1978, *49*, 929–949.

Bernstein, B. B. *Primary socialization, language and education*. London: Routledge and Kegan Paul, 1970.

Bertalanffy, L. V. *Perspectives on general system theory*. New York: George Braziller, 1975.

Birch, H. G., and Gussow, J. D. *Disadvantaged children: Health, nutrition, and school failure*. New York: Grune and Stratton, 1970.

Birch, H. G., Richardson, S. A., Baird, D., Horobin, G., and Illsley, R. *Mental subnormality in the community: A clinical and epidemiologic study*. Baltimore: Williams and Wilkins, 1970.

Blank, M. *Teaching learning in the preschool: A dialogue approach*. Columbus, OH: Charles E. Merrill Publishing, 1973.

Bronfenbrenner, U. Is early intervention effective? In M. Guttentag and E. L. Struening (Eds.), *Handbook of evaluation research* (Vol. 2). Beverly Hills, CA: Sage Publications, 1975.

Bronfenbrenner, U. Toward an experimental ecology of human development. *American Psychologist*, 1977, *32*, 513–531.

Brooks, P.H., and Baumeister, A.A. A plan for consideration of ecological validity in the experimental psychology of mental retardation. *American Journal of Mental Deficiency*, 1977, *81*, 407–416.

Buss, A.H., and Plomin, R. *A temperament theory of personality development*. New York: Wiley, 1975.

Caldwell, B., Heider, J., and Kaplan, B. *The inventory of home stimulation*. Paper presented at the annual meeting of the American Psychological Association, New York, September 1966.

Cicirelli, V.G. *The Purdue self-concept scale for preschool children: Norms-technical manual*. Prepared for the Office of Child Development, pursuant to Contract 50037.

Clarke, A. M. and Clarke, A.D.B. *Early experience. Myth and evidence*. London: Open Books, 1976.

Clarke-Stewart, A.K., VanderStoep, L.P., and Killian, G.A. Analysis and replication of mother-child relations at two years of age. *Child Development*, 1979, *50*, 777–793.

Cronbach, L.J., and Furby, L. How should we measure "change"—or should we? *Psychological Bulletin*, 1970, *74*, 68–80.

Davis, D.E. *My friends and me*. Circle Pines, MN: American Guidance Service, 1977.

Dennenberg, V. (Chapter in this volume.)

Dunn, L.M., Chun, L.T., Crowell, D.C., Dunn, L.G., Avery, L.G., and Yachel, E.R. *Peabody Early Education Kit*. Circle Pines, MN: American Guidance Service, 1976.

Elardo, R., Bradley, R., and Caldwell, B. The relation of infants' home environments to mental test performance from six to thirty-six months: A longitudinal analysis. *Child Development*, 1975, *46*, 71–76.

Elkind, D. Piagetian and psychometric conceptions of intelligence. *Harvard Educational Review*, 1969, *39*, 319–337.

Emmerich, W. The parental role: A functional cognitive approach. *Monographs of the Society for Research in Child Development*, 1969, *34*, (Whole No. 8).

Etaugh, C. Effects of nonmaternal care on children: Research evidence and popular views. *American Psychologist*, 1980, *35*, 309–319.

Farran, D.C., and Haskins, R.T. *Reciprocal control in social interactions of mothers and three-year-old children.* Paper presented at the biennial meeting of the Society for Research in Child Development, New Orleans, March 1977.

Farran, D.C., and Haskins, R.T. Reciprocal influence in the social interactions of mothers and 3-year-old children from different socioeconomic backgrounds. *Child Development*, 1980, *51*, 780–791.

Farran, D.C., and Ramey, C.T. Infant daycare and attachment behaviors towards mothers and teachers. *Child Development*, 1977, *48*, 1112–1116.

Farran, D.C., and Ramey, C.T. Social class differences in dyadic involvement during infancy. *Child Development*, 1980, *51*, 254–257.

Finkelstein, N.W. Enhancing the social development of preschool children: Intervention and evaluation. *Young Children*, in press.

Finkelstein, N.W., Gallagher, J.J., and Farran, D.C. Attentiveness and responsiveness to auditory stimuli of children at risk for mental retardation. *American Journal of Mental Deficiency*, 1980, *85*, 135–144.

Finkelstein, N.W., and Ramey, C.T. Learning to control the environment in infancy. *Child Development*, 1977, *48*, 806–819.

Finkelstein, N.W., and Ramey, C.T. Information from birth certificate data as a risk index for school failure. *American Journal of Mental Deficiency*, 1980, *84*, 546–552.

Finkelstein, N.W., and Wilson, K. *The influence of daycare on social behaviors towards peers and adults.* Symposium paper presented at the biennial meeting of the Society for Research in Child Development, New Orleans, March 1977.

Fogel, A. Temporal organization in mother–infant, face-to-face interaction. In H.R. Schaffer (Ed.), *Studies in mother-infant interaction.* New York: Academic Press, 1977.

Frankenburg, W.K., Coons, C.E., van Doorninck, W.J., Goldstein, E.A., Berrenberg, J. and Moriarty, K.R. *Evaluation of the home environment using a self-administered questionnaire.* Paper presented at the biennial meeting of the Society for Research in Child Development, New Orleans, March 1977.

Gallagher, J.J., Ramey, C.T., Haskins, R., and Finkelstein, N.W. The use of longitudinal research in the study of child development. In T. Tjossem (Ed.), *Intervention strategies for high-risk infants and young children.* Baltimore: University Park Press, 1976.

Garber, H., and Heber, F.R. The Milwaukee Project: Indications of the effectiveness of early intervention in preventing mental retardation. In P. Mittler (Ed.), *Research to practice in mental retardation: Care and intervention* (Vol. 1). Baltimore: University Park Press, 1977.

Garmezy. N. Vulnerability research and the issue of primary prevention. *American Journal of Orthopsychiatry*, 1971, *41*, 101–116.

Garvey, C., and Hogan, R. Social speech and social interaction: Egocentrism revisited. *Child Development*, 1973, *44*, 562–568.

Gesell, A.L., and Thompson, H. *Infant behavior: Its genesis and growth.* New York: McGraw-Hill, 1934.

Gilmer, B., Miller, J.O., and Gray, S. *Intervention with mothers and young children:*

396   CRAIG T. RAMEY ET AL.

A study of intra-family effects. Nashville, TN: DARCEE Papers and Reports, 1970, 4(11).

Gordon, A.M., and Bernard, J.A. *Effect of day-care intervention on the language performance of high-risk children.* Paper presented at the biennial meeting of the Society for Research in Child Development, Boston, April 1981.

Gordon, A.M., and Feagans, L. *Assessing the effects of systematic daycare on the language development of high-risk children.* Paper presented at the biennial meeting of the Society for Research in Child Development, New Orleans, March 1977.

Gottlieb, G. Conceptions of prenatal development. *Psychological Review,* 1976, *83,* 215–234.

Greenberg, P., and Epstein, B. *Bridges to reading.* Morristown, N.J.: General Learning Corp., 1973.

Grossman, H.J. (Ed.) *Manual on terminology and classification in mental retardation,* (1973 Revision). American Association on Mental Deficiency. Special Publication Series No. 2., 1973.

Harms, T., and Cross, L. *Environmental provisions in day care.* Chapel Hill, N.C.: Day Care Training and Technical Assistance System, 1978.

Harper, L.V. The young as a source of stimuli controlling caretaker behavior. *Developmental Psychology,* 1971, *4,* 73–88.

Haskins, R., Walden, T., and Ramey, C.T. *The effects of ability grouping on teacher and student behavior.* Unpublished manuscript, University of North Carolina, 1980.

Heber, F.R., Dever, R.B., and Conry, J. The influence of environmental and genetic variables on intellectual development. In H. Prehm, L.A. Hamerlynck, and J.E. Crosson (Eds.), *Behavioral research in mental retardation.* Eugene, OR: University of Oregon, 1968.

Hess, R.D., and Shipman, V.C. Early experience and the socialization of cognitive modes in children. *Child Development,* 1965, *34,* 869–886.

Hess, R.D., and Shipman, V.C. Maternal influences upon early learning: The cognitive environment or urban preschool children. In R.D. Hess and R.M. Bear (Eds.), *Early education.* Chicago: Aldine, 1966.

Hess, R.D., and Shipman, V.C. Maternal attitudes toward the school and the role of the pupil: Some social class comparisons. In A.H. Passow (Ed.), *Developing programs for the educationally disadvantaged.* New York: Teachers College, Columbia University, 1968.

Hunt, J. McV. *Concepts and factors important for infant education.* Colloquium presentation at the University of North Carolina, Chapel Hill, N.C. April 1980.

Jensen, A.R. How much can we boost IQ and scholastic achievement? *Harvard Educational Review,* 1969, *39,* 1–123.

Jensen, A.R. Raising the IQ: The Ramey and Haskins study. *Intelligence,* 1981, *5.* 29–40.

Kagan, J., Kearsley, R.B., and Zelazo, P.R. *Infancy: Its place in human development.* Cambridge,: Harvard University Press, 1978.

Kagan, J., Klein, R.E., Finley, G.E., Rogoff, B., and Nolan, E. A cross-cultural study of cognitive development. *Monographs of the Society for Research in Child Development,* 1979, *44,* (Whole No. 180).

Kagan, J., and Moss, H.A. *From birth to maturity.* New York: Wiley, 1962.

Karnes, M.B. *GOAL Program: Mathematical concepts.* Springfield, MA: Melton-Bradley, 1973.

Klaus, R., and Gray, S. The early training project for disadvantaged children: A report after five years. *Monographs of the Society for Research in Child Development*, 1968, *33*, (Whole No. 120).

Knobloch, H., and Pasamanick, B. Further observation on the behavioral development of Negro children. *Journal of Genetic Psychology*, 1953, *83*, 137–157.

Kuhn, T.S. *The structure of scientific revolutions.* Chicago: University of Chicago Press, 1962.

Lazar, I., and Darlington, R. (Eds.). *Lasting effects after preschool.* Final report, HEW Grant 90C-1311 to the Education Commission of the States, 1978.

Lewis, M., and Goldberg, S. Perceptual-cognitive development in infancy: A generalized expectancy model as a function of mother-infant interaction. *Merrill-Palmer Quarterly*, 1969, *15*, 81–100.

Lewis, M., and Rosenblum, L.A. (Eds.). *The effect of the infant on its caregiver.* New York: Wiley, 1974.

Lewis, M., and Wilson, C.D. Infant development in lower-class American families. *Human Development*, 1972, *15*, 112–127.

MacPhee, D., and Ramey, C.T. *Infant temperament as a catalyst and consequences of development in two caregiving environments.* Paper presented at the Gatlinburg Conference on Research in Mental Retardation, Gatlinburg, TN: March 1981.

Mann, A., Harrell, A., and Hunt, M., Jr. *A review of Head Start research since 1969.* Washington, D.C.: Social Research Group, George Washington University, 1976.

McCall, R.B. Challenges to a science of developmental psychology. *Child Development*, 1977, *48*, 333–344.

McCarthy, D. *McCarthy Scales of Children's Abilities.* New York: Psychological Corp., 1972.

McClearn, G., and DeFries, J. *Introduction to behavioral genetics.* San Francisco: W.H. Freeman Co., 1973.

McClelland, D.C. Testing for competence rather than for "intelligence". *American Psychologist*, 1973, *28*, 1–14.

Meehl, P.E. Schizotaxia, schizotypy, schizophrenia. *American Psychologist*, 1962, *17*, 827–838.

Mercer, J.R. Cultural diversity, mental retardation and assessment: The case for nonlabeling. In P. Mittler (Ed.), *Research to practice in mental retardation: Care and intervention* (Vol. 1). Baltimore: University Park Press, 1977.

Miller, J.G. *Living systems.* New York: McGraw-Hill, 1978.

Mueller, E. The maintenance of verbal exchanges between young children. *Child Development*, 1972, *43*, 930–938.

Newman, L., and Ramey, C.T. *Maternal attitudes and child development in high risk families.* Paper presented at the annual meeting of the American Psychological Association, New York, August 1979.

O'Connell, J., and Farran, D.C. *The effects of daycare intervention on the use of intentional communicative behaviors in socioeconomically depressed infants.* Paper presented at the Sixth Biennial Southeastern Conference on Human Development, Alexandria, VA, April 1980.

Ogbu, J.V. *Minority education and caste: The American system in cross-cultural perspective.* New York: Academic Press, 1978.

Parmelee, A.H., Kopp, C.B., and Sigman, M. Selection of developmental assessment techniques for infants at risk. *Merrill-Palmer Quarterly*, 1976, *22*, 177–199.

Parmelee, A.H., and Michaelis, R. Neurological examination of the newborn. In

J. Hellmuth (Ed.), *Exceptional infant: Studies in abnormalities* (Vol. 2). New York: Brunner/Mazel, 1971.

Patterson, G.R. A basis for identifying stimuli which control behaviors in natural settings. *Child Development*, 1974, 45, 900–911.

Ramey, C.T., and Brownlee, J.R. Improving the identification of high-risk infants. *American Journal of Mental Deficiency*, 1981, 85, 504–511.

Ramey, C.T., and Campbell, F.A. Compensatory education for disadvantaged children. *School Review*, 1979, 82, 171–189. (a)

Ramey, C.T., and Campbell, F.A. Early childhood education for psychosocially disadvantaged children: The effects of psychological processes. *American Journal of Mental Deficiency*, 1979, 83, 645–648. (b)

Ramey, C.T., and Campbell, F.A. Educational intervention for children at risk for mild retardation: A longitudinal analysis. In P. Mittler (Ed.), *Frontiers of knowledge in mental retardation* (Vol. 1). Baltimore: University Park Press, 1981.

Ramey, C.T., and Dempsey, H. *Social services received by cohorts I and II.* Unpublished document, University of North Carolina, 1979.

Ramey, C.T., Dorval, B., and Baker-Ward, L. Group daycare and socially disadvantaged families: Effects on the child and the family. In S. Kilmer (Ed.), *Advances in early education and daycare.* Greenwich, Conn.: JAI Press, in press. (a)

Ramey, C.T., and Dubinsky, S. *Incidence of illness by cohort.* Unpublished document, University of North Carolina, 1979.

Ramey, C.T., and Farran, D.C. The functional concern of mothers for their infants. *Infant Mental Health Journal*, 1981, 1, 48–55.

Ramey, C.T., Farran, D.C. and Campbell, F.A. Predicting IQ from mother–infant interactions. *Child Development*, 1979, 50, 804–814.

Ramey, C.T., Farran, D.C., Campbell, F.A., and Finkelstein, N.W. Observations of mother-infant interactions: Implications for development. In F.D. Minifie and L.L. Lloyd (Eds.), *Community and cognitive abilities: Early behavioral assessment.* Baltimore: University Park Press, 1978. (a)

Ramey, C.T., and Finkelstein, N.W. Contingent stimulation and infant competence. *Journal of Pediatric Psychology*, 1978, 3, 89–96.

Ramey, C.T., and Finkelstein, N.W. Psychosocial mental retardation: A biological and social coalescence. In M. Begab (Ed.), *Psychosocial influences and retarded performance: Strategies for improving competence* (Vol. 1). Baltimore: University Park Press, 1981.

Ramey, C.T., and Gallagher, J.J. The nature of cultural deprivation: Theoretical issues and suggested research strategies. North Carolina Journal of Mental Health, 1975, 7, 41-47.

Ramey, C.T., and Haskins, R. The causes and treatment of school failure: Insights from the Carolina Abecedarian Project. In M. Begab, H.C. Haywood, and H. Garber (Eds.), *Psychosocial influences and retarded performance: Strategies for improving competence* (Vol. 2). Baltimore: University Park Press, 1981 (a).

Ramey, C.T., and Haskins, R. The modification of intelligence through early experience. *Intelligence*, 1981, 5, 5–19. (b)

Ramey, C.T., and Haskins, R. Early education, intellectual development, and school performance: A reply to Arthur Jensen and J. McV.Hunt. *Intelligence*, 1981, 5, 41–48. (c)

Ramey, C.T., and MacPhee, D. A new paradigm in intellectual assessment? *Contemporary Psychology*, 1981, 26, 507–509.

Ramey, C.T., McGinness, G.D., Cross, L., Collier, A.M., and Barrie-Blackley,

S. The Abecedarian approach to social competence: Cognitive and linguistic. *Socialization of the child in a changing society*. Elmsford, N.Y.: Pergamon Press, in press. (b)

Ramey, C.T., and Mills, P.J. *Mother-infant interaction patterns as a function of rearing conditions*. Paper presented at the biennial meeting of the Society for Research in Child Development, Denver, March 1975.

Ramey, C.T., and Mills, P.J. Social and intellectual consequences of daycare for high-risk infants. In R. Webb (Ed.), *Social development in childhood: Day care programs and research*. Baltimore: Johns Hopkins University Press, 1977.

Ramey, C.T., Mills, P., Campbell, F.A., and O'Brien, C. Infants' home environments: A comparison of high-risk families and families from the general population. *American Journal of Mental Deficiency*, 1975, *80*, 40–42.

Ramey, C.T., and Smith, B. Assessing the intellectual consequences of early intervention with high-risk infants. *American Journal of Mental Deficiency*, 1977, *81*, 318–324.

Ramey, C.T., Stedman, D.S., Borders-Patterson, A., and Mengel, W. Predicting school failure from information available at birth. *American Journal of Mental Deficiency*, 1978, *82*, 524–534. (b)

Rheingold, H.L. Discussant's comments. In T. Tjossem (Ed.), *Intervention strategies for high-risk infants and young children*. Baltimore: University Park Press, 1976.

Ricciuti, H. Fear and development of social attachments in the first year of life. In M. Lewis and L.A. Rosenblum (Eds.), *The origin of human behavior: Fear*. New York: Wiley, 1974.

Richardson, S.A. Reaction to mental subnormality. In M.J. Begab and S.A. Richardson (Eds.), *The mentally retarded and society: A social science perspective*. Baltimore: University Park Press, 1975.

Robinson, H., and Robinson, N. Longitudinal development of very young children in a comprehensive day-care program: The first two years. *Child Development*, 1971, *42*, 1673–1683.

Rothbart, M. K. Laughter in young children. *Psychological Bulletin*, 1973, *80*, 247–256.

Rotter, J. B. Generalized expectancies of internal versus external control of reinforcement. *Psychological Monographs*, 1966, *80*, (Whole No. 609).

Sameroff, A. J. Early influences on development: Fact or fancy? *Merrill-Palmer Quarterly*, 1975, *21*, 267–294.

Sameroff, A. J. The etiology of cognitive competence: A systems perspective. In R. B. Kearsley and I. E. Siegel (Eds.), *Infants at risk: Assessment of cognitive functioning*. Hillsdale, N.J.: Lawrence Erlbaum Assoc., 1979.

Sameroff, A. J., and Chandler, M. J. Reproductive risk and the continuum of caretaking casualty. In F. D. Horowitz (Ed.), *Review of child development research* (Vol. 4). Chicago: University of Chicago Press, 1975.

Schaefer, E. S. Development of adaptive behavior: Conceptual models and family correlates. In M. Begab, H. Garber, and H. C. Haywood (Eds.), *Prevention of retarded development in psychosocially disadvantaged children*. Baltimore: University Park Press, 1981.

Schaefer, E. S., and Bell, R. Q. Development of a parent attitude research instrument. *Child Development*, 1958, *29*, 339–361.

Schaffer, H. R. Activity level as a constitutional determinant of infantile reaction to deprivation. *Child Development*, 1966, *37*, 595–602.

Schaffer, H.R., and Emerson, P.E. Patterns of response to physical contact in early human development. *Journal of Child Psychology and Psychiatry*, 1964, 5, 1–13.

Schneirla, T.C. Behavior development and comparative psychology. *Quarterly Review of Biology*, 1966, 41, 283–302.

Schwarz, J.C., Strickland, R.G., and Krolick, G. Infant day care: Behavioral effects at preschool age. *Developmental Psychology*, 1974, 10, 502–506.

Schweinhart, L.J., and Weikart, D.P. Perry Preschool effects nine years later: What do they mean? In M. Begab, H.C. Haywood, and H.L. Garber (Eds.), *Psychosocial influences and retarded performance: Strategies for improving competence.* (Vol. 2). Baltimore: University Park Press, 1981.

Seligman, M.E.P., and Maier, S.F. Failure to escape traumatic shock. *Journal of Experimental Psychology*, 1967, 74, 1–9.

Sparling, J.J., and Lewis, I.S. *Learningames for the first three years: A guide to parent-child play.* New York: Walker and Co., 1979

Stedman, D.J., Anastasiow, N.J., Dokecki, P.R., Gordon, I.J., and Parker, R.K. *How can effective early intervention programs be delivered to potentially retarded children?* A report for the Office of the Secretary of the Department of Health, Education and Welfare, October 1972.

Stein, Z., and Susser, M. The social distribution of mental retardation. *American Journal of Mental Deficiency*, 1963, 67, 811–821.

Tanner, J.M. The regulation of human growth. *Child Development*, 1963, 34, 817–847.

Terman, L.M., and Merrill, M.A. *The Stanford-Binet Intelligence Scale.* New York: Houghton-Mifflin, 1973.

Thomas, A., Birch, H.G., Chess, S., Hertzig, M.E., and Korn, S. *Behavioral individuality in early childhood.* New York: New York University Press, 1963.

Tough, J. *Listening to children talking.* London: Ward Lock Educational, 1976.

Tulkin, S., and Kagan, J. Mother-child interaction in the first year of life. *Child Development*, 1972, 43, 31.

Wachs, T., Uzgiris, I., and Hunt, J. Cognitive development in infants of different age levels and from different environmental backgrounds: An exploratory investigation. *Merrill-Palmer Quarterly*, 1971, 17, 283–317.

Waddington, C.H. *New patterns in genetics and development.* New York: Columbia University Press, 1962.

Wallach, M.A., and Wallach, L. *Teaching all children to read.* Chicago: University of Chicago Press, 1976.

Watson, J.S., and Ramey, C.T. Reactions to response contingent stimulation early in infancy. *Merrill-Palmer Quarterly*, 1972, 18, 219–227.

Wechsler, D. *Wechsler Adult Intelligence Scale.* New York: The Psychological Corporation, 1955.

Weikart, D.P. (Ed.). *Preschool Intervention: Preliminary report of the Perry Preschool Project.* Ann Arbor, MI: Campus Publishers, 1967.

Werner, H. *Comparative psychology of mental development.* New York: International University Press, 1957.

White, R.W. Motivation reconsidered: The concept of competence. *Psychological Review*, 1959, 66, 297–333.

Wolff, P.H. The causes, controls, and organization of behavior in the neonate. *Psychological Issues*, 1966, 5, (No. 1).

Yarrow, L., Rubenstein, I., and Pedersen, F. *Infant and environment: Early cognitive and motivational development.* New York: Halsted, 1973.

Zeskind, P.S. Adult responses to cries of low-risk and high-risk infants. *Infant Behavior and Development,* 1980, *3,* 167–177.

Zeskind, P.S., and Ramey, C.T. Fetal malnutrition: An experimental study of its consequences on infants in two caregiving environments. *Child Development,* 1978, *49,* 1155–1162.

Zeskind, P.S., and Ramey, C.T. Preventing intellectual and interactional sequelae of fetal malnutrition: A longitudinal, transactional and synergistic approach to development. *Child Development,* 1981, *52,* 213–218.

Zigler, E. (Chapter in this volume.)

Zigler, E., and Trickett, P. K. IQ, social competence, and evaluation of early childhood intervention programs. *American Psychologist,* 1978, *33,* 789–798.

Zigler, E., and Valentine, J. (Eds.). *Project Head Start: A legacy of the War on Poverty.* New York: Free Press, 1979.

PART IV

Social Policy and Service Delivery

Introductory Notes

All efforts to facilitate development require adequate delivery of services and attendant changes in social policy, whether these changes are created by legislation or otherwise. An effective program is one that is not only capable of facilitating development but also of being applied sufficiently widely to ensure that it reaches large numbers of children. Various views are expressed in this section on what is required in the way of social policy for the efficient implementation of programs and, more broadly, for social policy itself to directly or indirectly facilitate development.

The first paper, by J. McVicker Hunt, could have gone in the previous section as an illustration of an intervention program, but we have placed it in Part IV because of its relevance to the shaping of policy, particularly on account of its historical perspective and its description of the shift from the "negative prevention of psychopathology to the positive facilitation of competence." His analysis of the changes in "metatheories" of development and his discussion of the historical changes in approaches to development help provide a major part of the link between theory and research on the one hand and social policy on the other.

As Hunt indicates, conceptions of development influence "not only how data are interpreted but how to change the unwanted aspects of society." This analysis sets the stage for his discussion of the findings of the effects of an educational intervention in the infant-rearing practices in an orphanage in Tehran, as well as for the remaining papers in this section. The beneficial effects of Hunt's intervention on intelligence, language development, and social attractiveness are an illustration of how much can be achieved by teaching caregivers how to provide children with appropriate experiences to promote optimal development. Hunt argues that similar results could be obtained in other populations and that "problems of recruitment for training in parenting and the teaching of mothers are as deserving of research and development as those concerned with how to facilitate early psychological development . . . I believe no culture and very few families have so reared children as to realize half the genetic potential available to them."

The remaining papers deal, in effect, with various aspects of the question of why we, as a society, do not rear children to realize their genetic potential. Zigler and Finn, in their "vision of child care in the 1980s" outline the broad scope of problems our society faces with respect to its children. They start with a review of facts that document the "sorry state" of our nation's children, a listing of information that should disabuse even the most complacent observer of the notion that there are not fundamental and widespread problems. A look at infant mortality, teenage pregnancy, infant and child health, problems with foster care, child abuse, day care, and childhood psychopathology provides an indictment of our efforts—and these data were gathered before the massive recent cutbacks in funding for programs in the areas of health and human services. Although the paper was written before the election of President Reagan, Zigler and Finn were keenly aware of the prevalence of the mentality that would produce the cuts in federal funding for programs to meet the needs of children, and they geared their "agenda for the 1980s" to the premise that benefits will come about "through state and local initiatives and through greater involvement in matters pertaining to family life by the private sector.

Zigler and Finn outline approaches that could be tried in relation to social institutions they consider to be most critical in determining the quality of children's lives, namely the family, the school, and child care outside the home. They suggest that we try out a variety of new programs, almost all of which are of modest cost and of an experimental nature, to modify and improve these institutions. The fiscal restraint and the desire to see a broad range of options attempted and evaluated are a response to economic realities and to their belief that "our nation cannot be transformed into a child-oriented society overnight."

In the paper that follows, Sandra Scarr analyses in greater detail a major point of Zigler and Finn's—evaluating the effectiveness and cost-benefit ratios of interventions—and she reiterates the difficulty of allocating scarce resources in the most beneficial manner. These considerations lead her to pose the important question: "Given some agreed-upon goals for educational or social change, what program will produce the largest intended gain for the least cost?" This, in turn, leads to a detailed consideration of how we should go about quantifying the effects of our interventions, a discussion that is interwoven with consideration of aspects of what we know or theorize about development.

To simplify somewhat, the problems revolve around two parameters of environmental interventions that almost certainly alter their effects (as a function, in part, of the characteristics of the individuals toward whom they are directed). These are the "quantity" of the intervention effort, and its nature. In many cases, if not all, different individuals or groups will benefit to different degrees from the same investment (or, differently stated, some will benefit greatly from small investments, some little from large ones). In addition, the particular intervention may benefit some, leave others unaffected, and even have detrimental effects on others—there is no one perfect intervention or optimal environment. Furthermore, we may be able on theoretical grounds to predict what kinds are not. Scarr suggests that the evolutionary newer behaviors— those "less central to the evolved nature of human kind"—by contrast to behaviors "more central to the evolution of development" are the kinds on which we should concentrate our efforts.

Given developmental considerations of this kind, and in the absence of infinite resources, we have to make decisions about whom we wish to benefit and in what way we wish to benefit them. To make optimal use of the resources we have, we need to be apprised of developmental realities, and Scarr provides an analysis of a way in which a theory of development may constrain our actions, for good or ill.

Richard de Lone, in his paper, gives detailed consideration to the requirements of adequate public policy in the area of child development. De Lone uses the criteria he develops to assess some major choices available in selecting a public policy to facilitate infant and child development. He points out that, in the formulation of social policy, there has been "a persistent tendency to confuse policies which aim at promoting individual development with strategies for changing the social conditions which produce developmental risk." He argues that attempts to remove inequalities and create a just society by facilitating individual development ignore a variety of major determinants of individual success and status, those subsumed under the heading of socioeconomic factors (an analysis reminiscent of Joffe's discussion, in Part II, of the "causes of the causes" of developmental risk).

Two policy options stem from a recognition of a relationship between socioeconomic conditions and development. The first, reflecting what de Lone calls the "micro model" and typifying most efforts at social reform in America, involves identifying individuals at risk and providing them with interventions such as parent education or maternal and infant health care, programs staffed to a large degree by professionals and operated through existing systems of education or health care or welfare. Such programs might be characterized as attempts to obviate the deleterious developmental effects of adverse socioeconomic conditions by modification of the proximal environment of the developing infant or child. The "macro" approach, by contrast, views the proximal environment as a "mediator, a filter" of the effects of the individual's class, race, sex, and cultural group, not as a " 'causal' agent" in itself. Aside from ascribing a much more important role to socioeconomic factors, the macro model differs from the other in adopting relativistic (not normative) criteria of development and in viewing the individual as a more active organism, a "theory builder or map maker."

The implication for social policy of the more active conception of the developing child is dramatic: "It becomes almost meaningless to argue that one child (or group of children) develops less 'well' than another. Rather, the judicious presumption should be made that all develop equally well in response to their circumstances unless proven otherwise. Accordingly, if there are developmental differences which seem socially undesirable in their results, one should look to change the circumstances, rather than attempting to change the individuals." This seems in marked contrast to Hunt's view that no culture and very few families have reared children in such a manner as to realize "half the genetic potential available to them", but opting for the macro choice does not exclude the possibility of interventions deriving from the micro framework having a substantial impact on development (partly because the two choices are not diametric opposites).

Overall, de Lone's analysis echoes a theme of his book, *Small Futures: Children, Inequality and the Limits of Liberal Reform*. Intervening in development to improve society and reduce inequality has had limited success; perhaps it is time to attempt to improve society in the expectation that aside from anything else this will enhance the development of our children.

While de Lone thus focuses primarily on social policy, the final two papers are more concerned with the critical issues of service delivery. Judy Howard describes a service delivery system for handicapped children. Proceeding on the basis of evidence that physical and behavioral systems are linked, she argues that optimal health care for sick neonates requires more than medical intervention. This point is emphasized by the evidence she describes on psychological processes in mothers of at-risk infants and on the possibility of averting physiological crises by altering caregiving procedures (based on observations that behavioral distress signals may occur before physiological crises).

There is, as yet, little evidence available to assess the deduction that infant and child health might be improved by providing support services for parents of sick infants, but initial findings of effects of such programs on mothers' self-concept, feelings of competence, and interactions with their children (see the paper by Minde, Shosenberg, and Marton in the previous section) are promising beginnings, particularly in the light of other findings that improved mother–infant interactions are positively correlated with performance on a variety of developmental tests.

As a number of authors have suggested (see, for example Broussard's and McGillicuddy-deLisi and Sigel's papers), an important mediator of parent–infant transactions and developmental outcome appears to be parental perception of the infant, a point of particular relevance in considering the problems faced by handicapped infants and their parents. Other evidence, including that of Howard and her collaborators, indicates that interventions can improve the quality of interactions of parents and handicapped children, with beneficial effects for both parents and children.

With a need for intervention and its efficacy reasonably established, Howard outlines basic guidelines for developing a service delivery system for handicapped children and their families. Now the primary care physician is not the only source of treatment and support. Since the passing of PL 94-142 in 1975 the education system has also been involved. Howard points out that in designing interventions, professionals, of what ever discipline, need to place the main emphasis on the child while being sensitive to parental responses and attempting to understand parents' reactions, both to the handicapped child and to offers of help. Parents need information as well as understanding, and professionals in different disciplines need to be able to communicate with parents and with each other. Howard's guidelines would improve any program and, as she says, since no perfect program exists, professionals should be prepared to accept advice from parents as well as to provide it.

Earlier in this section Zigler and Finn warned us that an agenda for the 1980s cannot rely on the public purse, and in the last paper Earladeen Badger and Donna Burns tell us how change can be brought about in other ways. They describe in detail how, without federal mandate, individuals strengthened and brought together over 170 parenting programs to create the Ohio United Services for Effective Parenting (USEP). Their account is not merely an outstanding example of how grassroots efforts can create and implement a child and parent advocacy plan but is also a demonstration of the additional power that accrues to people and organizations who create change through their own efforts. The history of the USEP project provides both a model and an inspiration for those who wish to create an effective coalition of programs.

The description of the process can serve as a manual for all who wish to improve services to families and children, and the information on outcomes is an assurance that important goals can be attained through grassroots efforts and with modest funding. Indeed the implications are that this approach increases the likelihood of achieving the ends and that the means themselves become an integral and invaluable part of the process.

Facilitating the Development of Social Competence and Language Skill

J. McVicker Hunt

In 1980, the emphasis of the Vermont Conference shifted from the negative—prevention of psychopathology—to the positive—facilitating the development of competence. In part, this shift may merely have been one of semantic emphasis, for whatever facilitates the early development of competence can probably be said to prevent psychopathology. In part, however, the shift was substantive, for psychopathology has been conceived, ever since Freud's (1920) "general theory of the neuroses" gained wide acceptance, to consist of emotional problems stemming from motivational conflicts. Insofar as facilitating the development of competence concerns the hastening of cognitive and motivational achievements, the shift was substantive, at least at the definitional level. This shift might also involve an implicit theoretical recognition that cognition, emotion, and motivation are essentially unitary in the very young (see, e.g., Ulvund, 1980).[1] At any rate, I wish to applaud this new shift of emphasis. What I have to say is concerned chiefly with intervening in the process of childrearing to facilitate the development of language skill and motivational autonomy in order to prevent school failure, unemployability, and the distressing quality of life associated with such failures. But first a word about emotion-tinged beliefs or metatheories that have strongly influenced the interpretations of observations and even of measurements of human characteristics and attitudes toward infants and children by caretakers, parents, and teachers.

The Major Metatheories

Historically, the major metatheory has consisted of a presumption that whatever exists must be permanent. This presumption may have

The preparation of this paper was supported by a grant from the Waters Foundation of Framingham, Massachusetts, and I wish to acknowledge this support with gratitude.

[1] When used before the author and date in a citation, *see* indicates that the reference is a secondary source which contains references to the relevant original sources.

emerged when, during the history of human epistemology, mankind achieved what Piaget (1947) termed the *concrete operations* shown in the conservation of area, number, quantity, and substance. It was evident at least half a millennium before the Christian era in the preformationistic interpretation of embryonic development (Needham, 1959), and this version of the view persisted for at least 2,300 years, from the writings of the Greek philosopher, Anaxagoras, to the two studies by C. F. Wolff, published in 1759 and 1768, which established the existence of embryonic epigenesis. With the Christian era, this view became theistic, as is manifest in the words of a hymn that was still included in Protestant hymnals of Britain in the early 20th century: "The rich man in his castle/ The poor man at his gate,/ Thank the Lord Almighty,/ He has ordered their estate." According to this theistic metatheory, the divine right of kings included also the divine right to be poor or whatever. It was during the waning years of this long period that Thomas Malthus, a clergyman who had turned to political economy, wrote his *Essay on the Principles of Population: As it Affects Future Improvement of Society* (1798). Even though an agricultural revolution that started about 1700 in the British Isles had increased grain production by 43 percent during the 18th century (Osborne, 1970), Malthus contended, from his mathematical analysis, that the population inevitably increases faster than the food supply. From this theoretical discrepancy, he inferred that poverty is inevitable, and that famine, plagues, and wars were created by God as natural means of sustaining a balance between human and agricultural fecundities. So, despite the Christian teachings on charity, he contended that aid for the poor is a misled effort opposed to the will of God.

This presumption—that whatever is must be permanent and God-given—not only served to justify the inequalities of privilege in society but also permeated epistemology with the concept of innate ideas, the domain of embryology with the doctrine of preformationism, and the domain of behavioral development with the doctrine of "original sin" and the depravity of infants (see Greven, 1973; Smith, 1955). When Martin Luther established schools to teach reading in order to give laymen direct access to the word of God following the Protestant Reformation, it was soon discerned that it was hard to hold the attention of children of 7 years with the Bible as the textbook. John Calvin attributed this inattention to the work of the devil, and this justified physical punishment. Vestiges of his judgment are still embedded in everyday language, for example, "It's the Devil in him," "Beat the Devil out of him," and, of a more secular sort, "Spare the rod and spoil the child." The effects of punishment may have lent some confirmation of this doctrine when anticipating a flogging became more uncomfortable than learning something without inherent interest.

The Controversy: Environmentalism versus Hereditary Predeterminism

Environmentalism appears to have its epistemic beginnings in 1690 when John Locke denied the existence of innate ideas in his famous *Essay on Human Understanding* and asserted that the mind of an infant is analogous to a "white paper" on which experience writes. Following the discovery of differing functions for the dorsal and ventral roots of the spinal nerves and the formulation of the reflex principle, it was but a short step to the idea that original human nature consists of a multiplicity of simple reflexes. These reflexes can come to be elicited by a variety of stimuli and can be combined into an infinite variety of complex chains through something analogous to Pavlovian (1927) conditioning. It was such theorizing that led to Watson's (1928) admittedly exaggerated claim that, given a dozen healthy, well-formed infants, he would guarantee to take any one of them at random and train him to become any type of specialist regardless of his talents. For nearly three centuries, environmentalism has been an alternative to both preformationism and its successor, predeterminism.

With his careful drawings of the epigenesis in the development of the circulatory system and of the gut, C. F. Wolff disposed of the belief in preformationism, at least among the cognoscente. He substituted, for explanatory purposes, Leibnitz's idea of a monad developing into an organism by means of its own inherent force (see Needham, 1959). This notion is a forerunner of the predeterminism that one finds in the 19th century writings of such evolutionists as Herbert Spencer (1860–1862, *First Principles;* 1862–1867, *Principles of Biology*) and in Galton's *Hereditary Genius: An Inquiry into its Laws and Consequences* (1869). According to the predeterministic or hereditarian metatheory, both the rate and the course of anatomical and behavioral development of any individual's characteristics are established once and for all when a sperm enters an egg.

Environmentalism and predeterminism constitute the opposite poles in the metatheories of the causation of organismic development. Although no sensible person would deny a role for both environment and heredity, the existence of this polarity has led to interminable debates over their relative importance. Disciplines have taken sides, with students of sociology following one of the subject's founders, Auguste Comte, in favoring the importance of the environment through the effects of experience controlled by the culture—at least until the advent of sociobiology (Wilson, 1975). Psychology has been divided. Those concerned chiefly with psychometrics and individual differences (with certain exceptions such as Anastasi, 1958a, 1958b) favor the importance of heredity; those concerned with learning, the psychoanalytic theory of psychological development, and social psychology favor the importance of environment or experience (Cronbach, 1957).

Those who devote their attention to the measurement of traits appear to want them to stay put. Thus, even though Binet considered the "verdict that the intelligence of an individual is a fixed quantity [to be] deplorable" (1909, p. 54), he and Simon (1905) introduced the substitutive averaging of test items to obtain the mental age, and Wilhelm Stern (1912) divided it by the chronological age of the tested subject to obtain his or her IQ. Having a metrical measure for an individual's intelligence made it almost inevitable that Galton's hereditarian metatheory would dominate the interpretation and lead to a presumption of its constancy (see Hunt, 1961, pp. 308–315; 1976). There was little change in the resulting climate of opinion until after World War II. Then, according to Steiner (1976), two assemblies of evidence of the effect of experience on development (Bloom, 1964; Hunt, 1961, pp. 308–315), altered opinion. These also had political influence, however, from the accidental fact that President John F. Kennedy was especially sensitive to such problems because he had a mentally deficient sister, and because he and Sargent Shriver, chosen to head the Office of Economic Opportunity, had chosen as their expert consultant, Robert E. Cooke, a professor of pediatrics, who had fathered a mentally deficient child, and was therefore especially cognizant of new knowledge concerning development of intelligence and motivation. The debate still continues even though both of these metatheories interfere with the educational process (Hunt, 1975).

Interactionism: Statistical and Dynamic

Escape from this fruitless debate first came, ironically, from embryology where predeterminism also appears to have originated earlier in C. F. Wolff's evidence of epigenesis. According to Oppenheim (1974, 1981), the experimental embryologists of the 1890s and the 1900s uncovered evidence that even anatomical development is a function of the interaction between the embryo and its changing environmental circumstances in the course of gestation. But it was a botanical geneticist, with the methodological advantage of being able to control heredity by cloning, who first introduced a forerunner of the concept of statistical interaction. Between 1900 and 1910, Johannsen noted that selection for such characteristics as the weight, length, or breadth of beans from a population of these self-fertilizing plants would shift the average measures of these in the direction of the selection. On the other hand, when such selection was applied from a single bean plant, no such shift in the averages of measures of the progeny occurred. Yet, when the seeds from a single bean plant were planted in differing soils and at differing altitudes, definite variations in the measured characteristics of the progeny did occur. Johannsen's investigations were motivated by a fear that acquired characteristics might, despite the then–recent rediscovery of Mendel's findings, be inherited. He discovered that both heredity and environment influence progeny, and this gave him the basis for distinguishing the *phenotype,* the observable and measurable characteristics, from the *genotype,* the hereditary constitution (Dunn, 1965, Ch. 9).

Between 1908 and 1911, Richard Woltereck, a zoologist, conducted a series of quantitative studies of the organic/environmental interaction in a parthenogenetic (i.e., self-fertilizing) species of plankton belonging to the genus *Daphnia.* He discovered that a given genotype can give rise to substantial variations in phenotypic characteristics when developing under differing environmental conditions, and he contended that "the genotype is the inherited norm [or range] of reaction" (Dunn, 1965, p. 96). Had such a concept been available to Darwin, he would probably have been troubled with fewer uncertainties about natural selection in his theory of evolution. On the other hand, if the early intelligence testers had had these concepts, they would have been far less inclined to presume the IQ to be constant.

Within the psychological development of human beings, what one might well term *dynamic interaction* between the achievements of a developing infant or child and the demands of situations encountered is an important factor in determining the rate of development, the structural characteristics of development, and probably also the ultimate level of achievement (Hunt, 1961, pp. 267–288, 1980a; Hunt and Paraskevopoulos, 1980). Such dynamic interaction is implicit in Piaget's accounts of infant and child development in what he terms *accommodation, assimilation,* and *equilibration.* In his discussions of equilibration, Piaget's (1947, 1977) focus was almost entirely concerned with the individual's cognitive appreciation of the demands of a situation encountered. Although cognitive appreciation of the demand appears to be necessary, it fails to take into account the emotional and motivational aspects of the individual's reaction also present in dynamic interaction and their importance for psychological development (Hunt, 1965, 1966, 1980). According to my conception of dynamic interaction, whether an infant's encounter with a situation fosters development or perhaps even hampers it is a function of the discrepancy between the achievements of the child and the demands of the situation combined with the social pressures involved. If the discrepancy is such that the infant has no cognitive appreciation of the demands of the situation, those demands do not exist for the child; the situation is like talk about Sunday to a pig. If the demands of the situation have already been completely mastered by the child, the situation will foster no development and is likely to be boring. If the child can appreciate the demands but cannot make the adaptive modification in her or his existing achievements required to cope with it, then the situation is distressing. If adults make their love and approbation contingent on a child's coping without providing the necessary help to enable the child to cope, real damage can be done (Hunt and Paraskevopoulos, 1980). When the discrepancy between demands and achievements are such that the child can both appreciate them and cope with them, the situation becomes interesting, and development comes with joy. Maximizing the proportion of waking hours during which a child is confronted with situations that excite interest is a problem for caretakers, parents, and teachers. I have called this the "problem of the match" (Hunt, 1961, 1963a, 1965, 1969, 1980, 1981(b), Hunt and Paraskevopoulos, 1980).

The reminders of these metatheories are presented here because they influence not only how data are interpreted but also how to change the unwanted aspects of society and, even more important, perhaps, how an adult interacts with an infant. Moreover, these patterns of interaction during infancy determine in the child what is to be expected of others, and especially those in positions of authority and leadership, throughout life. It is obviously the interactionist's metatheory that I wish to embrace. The empirical work I report illustrates the epigenesis in the structure of this infant–situation interaction, the importance of a solution for the problem of the match in adult–infant interactions designed to facilitate the acquisition of language, and that which we measure in tests of intelligence and admire as social attractiveness.

Social Class Differences in Intelligence and Language Skill

Language skill is an important component of intelligence. Ever since Binet and Simon (1905) published their first scale, vocabulary and understanding of questions posed in verbal language have constituted or been involved in a major portion of the items in tests of intelligence. As already noted, once Binet and Simon (1905) hit upon substitutive averaging as a means of obtaining an "overall index," the mental age, and Stern (1912) divided the mental age by the chronological age to obtain a rate of development, it was easy for the hereditarian metatheorist to shape the interpretation of the IQ into a measure of intellectual potential. Even though Bernstein (1959, 1970), a pioneer in the sociological study of language, described class differences in terms of limitations in the linguistic code, a substantial list of sociolinguists, which includes Baratz and Baratz (1970), Goodman (1969), Labov (1970), Shuy (1969), and Stewart (1969) have contended that children, and especially black children of uneducated parents with low incomes, are in no way deficient in their cognitive, linguistic, and motivational skills; they merely come to school with a dialect that differs from standard English, and they often fail in school merely because they must learn to read in what is, for them, the unfamiliar dialect of standard English. From this diagnosis, they also contend that much, if not all, of the educational handicaps of these black children of poverty could be eliminated by permitting them to begin their learning to read in their own dialect. This is one current version of the traditional professional split between sociologists and psychologists over the nurture-nature issue.

The empirical basis for these contentions of the sociolinguists have come from their studies of the syntax of nonstandard English (Goodman, 1969; Labov, 1970). Kirk and Hunt and their collaborators have put this interpretation to test by comparing not the syntax but the semantic mastery of children of Head Start, both white and black, with that of nursery school children of the same age. Of the parents of the children of Head Start, approximately ⅔rds had less education than high school graduation, while nearly ⅔rds of the parents of children in nursery school had earned a baccalaureate degree from a college. Of the former, about 25 percent were on Aid to Families with Dependent Children; about another 7 percent were unemployed, and less than 10 percent were ever employed at a level above unskilled labor. Of the latter, approximately 70 percent were employed at a level above unskilled labor and none were unemployed or on Aid to Families with Dependent Children. In performance on the Peabody Picture Vocabulary Test, the 3-year sample of children of Head Start had a mean IQ of 72.15, and the mean of the standard deviations for the 3 successive year classes was 21.8. The 3 samples of nursery school children had a mean Peabody IQ of 111.7, and the mean of the three standard deviations was 12.98, or only .6137 that of those of Head Start (Kirk and Hunt, 1975).

The relationship between these groups in mean IQs on the Peabody is highly consonant with the hereditarian metatheory. Moreover, by assuming that the upper ranges of variation in IQ were reduced by the fact that this was a low-cost nursery school, the difference between the standard deviations can also be made consonant with the hereditarian metatheory (see Kirk and Hunt, 1975). One can make the difference of nearly 40 points between the means of the Peabody IQs consonant with the sociolinguistic interpretation only by presuming that the Head Start children, and especially the black children of Head Start, had words other than those of standard English for the objects depicted on the Peabody cards. Such a presumption is clearly contradicted by the findings from the tests of semantic mastery of such elementary abstractions as colors (Kirk, Hunt, and Lieberman, 1975), positions (Hunt, Kirk, and Volkmar, 1975), shapes (Hunt, Kirk, and Lieberman, 1975), and numbers (Kirk, Hunt and Volkmar, 1975). If the black children had alternative words for these elementary abstractions, one would expect their errors on the standard English words to exceed those of the white children, but this is not the case. For none of these elementary abstractions was there significant difference between black and white children of Head Start in semantic mastery of these terms of standard English. Moreover, in a study of child-to-child communication, only one instance occurred in which the black children used a term more commonly than it was used by their white classmates. This was the term *black* as the color for the brown block. Moreover, mothers of the black children knew of no terms for the colors, positions, shapes, and numbers other than those of standard English.

While the children of Head Start were approximately as often correct in matching manually by means of their perceptions colors, positions, shapes, but not numbers, as were the children of nursery school, they showed a substantial semantic deficit. The proportions of Head Start children who either understood correctly (receptive language) or named correctly (expressive language) all six of the colors, or positions, or shapes, or numbers was much smaller than that for those of nursery school. Where, for instance, only about 20 percent of the children of Head Start indicated all six blocks correctly when their colors were named by the examiner, approximately 90 percent of the nursery school children exhibited receptive semantic mastery by indicating correctly all six blocks as the examiner named the colors. On the expressive side, where only approximately 25 percent of the children of Head Start named the colors of all six blocks correctly as the examiner pointed to them, approximately 80 percent of the nursery schoolers did so. The average number of color names understood by those of Head Start was 2.82 as compared with 5.78 by those of nursery school, and the numbers of colors named correctly on the average by children of Head Start was 2.85 versus 5.55 by those of nursery school.

The sociolinguists have contended that black children can communicate with their nonstandard English as well as can white children with standard English, but where colors, positions, shapes, and numbers are concerned, this is not so (Kirk, Hunt, and Volkmar, 1979). In the case of both white and black children of Project Head Start, a demand for communication actually served to reduce the numbers of colors, positions, shapes, and numbers named correctly and also the number of semantic terms for colors, positions, shapes, and numbers that were understood correctly.

We concluded that a genuine deficit in language skill, or in the symbolic processing of information, exists in the children of uneducated parents of poverty.

This deficit need not imply, however, that all, or even a major share, of it is biologically inevitable. Badly educated poor people often fail to have diets for mothers that will foster the development of their progeny in utero during the embryonic and fetal phases (see Cravioto, 1964; Pasamanick, 1962; McDonald, 1966). In consequence, a higher-than-average portion of the children of such parents are vulnerable at birth. Moreover, in families of poorly educated low-income parents, these vulnerable infants typically encounter circumstances which further compound their vulnerability and tendency to defect (Murphy, 1961, 1968). Such children commonly want for the intimate, proximal experiences that foster either cognition or the linguistic and numerical skills in their interactions with both the inanimate and social situations of their homes. For instance, the proneness of mothers to interact vocally with their young has shown positive correlation ranging from .38 to .8 with the level of development on the various branches of the Piaget-inspired scales of Uzgiris and Hunt (1975; Wachs, Uzgiris, and Hunt, 1971), but it is just such vocal interaction that is often scarce in the homes of the poorly educated parents of poverty (Hess and Shipman, 1965; Keller, 1963; Milner, 1951). The number of toys responsive to an infant's manipulation has shown a positive correlation of .731 with IQ at age approximately 2 years (Wachs, 1978), and the positive correlation of the order of .6 with persistence of striving at age 6 months (Yarrow, Rubenstein, and Pedersen, 1975). Conversely, the prevalence of noise that is irrelevant to the infant's actions and from which an infant cannot escape has shown inverse correlations ranging from .371 to nearly .7 with the level of advancement along various items on the Uzgiris and Hunt scales at the age of 22 months (Wachs, Uzgiris, and Hunt, 1971; Wachs, 1978). Such findings help to explain the finding that children of the poor discriminate vocal patterns less well than do children of the middle class (Clark and Richards, 1966), and that the orienting or attentional response to auditory inputs irrelevant to an infant's actions become extinguished or habituated (Deutsch, 1964). Such combinations of lack of the development-fostering experiences and prevalence of experience inimical to development promise to explain a major share of the social class differences in performance on tests of intelligence and in school failure. These differences need not be considered to be biologically inevitable.

Language-Fostering Experience and Intelligence

The findings from an educational daycare program at the Parent and Child Center of Mt. Carmel, Illinois, illustrate the importance of language-fostering experiences for what we later measure in tests of intelligence. The subjects of this study consisted of eight consecutive infants born to the parents served by the Parent and Child Center. These infants were recruited into the educational daycare at various ages during their first 9 months of life. The educational daycare employed the Infant and Toddler Learning Programs of Earladeen Badger (1971a; 1971b). Moreover, it was she who taught some of the mothers how to use her programs. First, she strongly encouraged mothers to believe that how they interacted with the infants in daycare would influence their children's development. Second, she encouraged these mothers-teachers to be quickly responsive to any behavioral indications of distress in order to foster in the infants a learning-set that they could influence their circumstances. Third, to help solve "the problem of the match," she taught these mothers to observe both the behavioral achievements of the infants and the infants' affective reactions in the situations they encountered in order for them to be able, fourth, to maximize the time the infants spent with materials and models that would elicit their behavioral signs of interest. Finally, she showed the mothers in sound cinemas the sequences in which abilities and interests develop along the several branches illustrated in the Piaget-inspired scales of Uzgiris and Hunt.

One surprise came in the highly rapid rate at which object permanence developed. These eight infants, all children of poorly educated parents from the poverty sector of Mt. Carmel, achieved the top step on the Scale of Object Permanence at a mean age of 73.02 weeks. This was 25 weeks ahead of the mean age (98.31 weeks) at which 12 infants from predominantly professional families in Worcester, Massachusetts, achieved this landmark (Hunt, Paraskevopoulos, Schickedanz, and Uzgiris, 1975). This gain, in terms of the IQ-ratio for Object Permanence, is of the order of at least 35 points (98.31 weeks/73.02 weeks = 1.346). I have written "at least 35 points," because one would expect the mean age of attainment for a sample of infants from predominantly professional families to be well above the norm for the population as a whole, so using it as the "mental age" would tend to reduce the IQ-ratio of the Mt. Carmel infants. This is a nice illustration of the great plasticity in early psychological development.

Another surprise, one of a sobering nature, came with the findings for the development of vocal imitation. For reasons to be discussed below, I consider vocal imitation to be an early, epigenetic aspect of language acquisition. The Mt. Carmel infants attained the top step on this scale of Vocal Imitation at a mean age of 114 weeks, and as might be expected from their rearing in the homes of poorly educated parents of poverty, this age of achievement was 20 weeks behind that (94 weeks) at which the Worcester infants from predominantly professional families attained this landmark. This finding that the infants who had been so far ahead of the Worcester children in object construction were so far behind in vocal imitation suggested immediately the need for a supplement in the Badger Learning Programs for Infants and Toddlers to facilitate the development of vocal imitation.

The evidence for the importance of advancement in vocal imitation for the development of intelligence did not come till more than a year later when my colleague, G. E. Kirk, examined these eight children, then in their fourth year, with the Stanford Binet. The results have not been published, but he returned from this experience with a long face. The IQs of all but one of these eight ranged between 75 and 83; that is, they were IQs typical of those of children from poorly educated parents of poverty. The exceptional one was the daughter of a couple both of whom were paraprofessionals on the staff of the center. They participated in the professional planning of the staff and so appreciated what the educational daycare was attempting to do and how it was going about it. Their child had an IQ of 138. Moreover, she had achieved the top step on the scale of Vocal Imitation months ahead of the other seven. Thus, a very substantial advancement in the development of object construction without a corresponding advance in vocal imitation and language acquisition failed to improve intelligence as measured by the Stanford Binet. Such evidence strongly suggests that advances in the early phases of language acquisition must accompany advances in object construction if the latter is to influence the development of intelligence as measured. This finding tends to confirm the importance that Bloom (1964, p. 88) attributed to oportunities for learning verbal behavior for the development of intelligence.

Degree of Plasticity

The means of the IQs from the Peabody Picture Vocabulary Test for the children from poorly educated families of poverty in Head Start and the well-educated families of at least moderate means in the nursery school differ by approximately 40 points (actually 39.4 points) or about 2.5 standard deviations. Although efforts at compensatory education beginning at age 4, or age 3, have demonstrated that the test performance of such children can be improved, such efforts have also shown how difficult it is, following the three or four years of the earliest experience that failed to foster and even hampered development, to make up for all the lost opportunities (Hunt, 1975). Is it feasible to produce differences of such an order of magnitude by means of earlier intervention? This is one of the questions I wish to answer with the results of our educational interventions in the childrearing practices of the Tehran Orphanage.

An Intervention to Foster Language Acquisition in Orphanage-Reared Infants

The interventions at the Tehran Orphanage took place in the decade from 1966 through 1975 (Hunt, Mohandessi, Ghodssi, and Akiyama, 1976). My interest in an orphanage as a setting for research began in the summer of 1958 when I was assembling from the literature the evidences calling for a theoretical reinterpretation of motivation (Hunt, 1960, 1963a, 1963b, 1965, 1971a, 1971b). During that summer, I received a mimeographed prepublication entitled, "Causes of Retardation among Institutional Children: Iran" by Wayne Dennis (1960). If the notions about the role of intrinsic motivation in psychological development that I was gleaning from the literature were anywhere near correct, it seemed to me that it should be possible to prevent a major part of the retardation observed by Dennis in what became the Orphanage of the Queen Farah Pahlavi Charity Society. With encouragement from Dennis, I started a search for an Iranian collaborator and began writing research proposals to obtain the necessary funding. The project was finally launched in 1966, just after the first mimeographed version of the Piaget-inspired Ordinal Scales had been completed (Uzgiris and Hunt, 1966, 1975).

The plan called for "wave design." Thus, the program was to start with a longitudinal study of infants reared from within a month of their births in the orphanage under customary practices. The developmental progress of the infants was to be repeatedly assessed by administering the Uzgiris–Hunt scales every other week during the first year, and every fourth week thereafter so long as the infants remained in this institution for nurslings. The first, control wave, consisted of 15 foundlings without detectable pathology. They were transferred from the municipal orphanage to the Orphanage of the Queen Farah Pahlavi Charity Society when they were no more than an estimated 1 month of age. The average age of transfer of infants to an orphanage for children no longer nurslings was 169 weeks. The second wave, consisting of 10 such foundlings received an abortive attempt at audio-visual enrichment which failed because the person then collaborating as my resident director of the project failed to keep the apparatus in repair. A third wave of 10 such foundlings received what we termed *untutored human enrichment*. The customary infant–caretaker ratio of approximately 30/3 was reduced to 10/3, but the caretakers were given no special instructions and were to do whatever came naturally. This wave was planned, first, as a means of assessing the effect of simply reducing the infant–caretaker ratio and, second, as a control with which to assess the effects of special childrearing practices in what we later called *tutored human enrichment*. Wave IV consisted of 20 foundlings who received the audio-visual enrichment originally planned for Wave II, and this time the apparatus was kept in proper working order. Wave V consisted of 11 foundlings who got the tutored human enrichment.

Although we agreed to welcome any offers of adoption, we chose only foundlings for the subjects of our interventions in order to maximize the likelihood that they would remain in the orphanage for nurslings until the customary time for transfer. We chose the wave design for both ethical and scientific reasons. The ethical reason was to avoid withholding experiences calculated to be advantageous which would be necessary in the case of simultaneous treatment and control groups. The scientific reason was to avoid the tendency of caretakers of control groups to imitate procedures once they discern that these procedures facilitate the development of infants receiving the treatment (see Dennis and Sayegh, 1965).

According to the original plan, the effects of the interventions were to be expressed in terms of the means and standard deviations of the ages at which the infants in each wave attained the successive steps on the ordinal scales of Uzgiris and Hunt (1966, 1975). The original report presents the means and standard deviations of the ages of achieving an intermediate step and the top step on each of the seven scales (Hunt, Mohandessi, Ghodssi, and Akiyama, 1976, pp. 200–201). Here, I need say but little about the effects of untutored human enrichment on Wave III or about the audio-visual enrichment on Wave IV. The relevant comparisons concern the behavioral attainments of the foundlings in the first, control wave combined with those of the foundlings in Wave II, who received the abortive attempt at audio-visual enrichment, with those of Wave V, who received the special experiences designed to facilitate vocal imitation and through it language acquisition. For special issues, we shall also refer to some of the findings from the home-reared infants from predominantly professional families in Worcester, Massachusetts, and the eight children of the poorly educated parents of poverty served by the Parent and Child Center in Mt. Carmel, Illinois. But first, let me present my theory of language acquisition, and describe the experiences provided to facilitate it by the caretakers responsible for the tutored human enrichment for Wave V.

Intervention to Facilitate Language Achievement

As early as 1971, it became evident that the control foundlings of Wave I, even at 3 years of age, lacked both expressive and receptive language. By 1972, the absence of both expressive and receptive language was evident also in the 10 foundlings of Wave II, who received the abortive attempt at audio-visual enrichment. Only two of the 25 foundlings in these two waves ever spontaneously named any object during examinations with the Uzgiris-Hunt scales. Spontaneous naming of objects constitutes the top step on the sensorimotor Scale of the Development of Schemes for Relating to Objects (Uzgiris and Hunt, 1975, p. 204). Additional evidence of lack of expressive language was easy to obtain, for these children used their vocal apparatus only for crying and yelling in anger or exasperation. The essential absence of receptive language derived from improvised tests. One, suggested by memory of the use of instructions at the 3-year-level in the 1916 version of the Stanford Binet Test of Intelligence, consisted of having a caretaker or an examiner request each child to "go to the man," the man being me. At an age of about 30 months, the children of Wave I simply looked blank when they heard this request. Yet, if I were to look at one of these children, smile, and make a gesture inviting approach, I got one of two reactions. One consisted of facial expressions of distress and withdrawal. The other consisted of almost smiling and beginning a tentative approach. Both reactions implied an appreciation of the meaning of my gestures, but there was no sign of such appreciation of the meaning of the verbalized requests even from a familiar caretaker or examiner in Farsi, the language of Iran. Similar results were obtained when a piece of paper was put on the floor and the caretaker or examiner requested the child to: "Put the paper on the table." Not even verbalized questions referring to eating and food elicited any signs of an appreciation of their meaning.

Such a finding led me to make a study of language acquisition. As I examined the recent literature in psycholinguistics, I found most of Lenneberg's (1966, 1967) arguments for a biological basis of language acceptable, but Chomsky's (1959, footnote 48, p. 58) claims that language is analagous to the "complex inate behavior patterns . . . studied in human organisms" and that children must come equipped with an inherent "language acquisition device" (LAD) because children all over the world learn the basic elements of their native tongue during their first 18 months seemed clearly false in the light of the failure of the foundlings in both Wave I and Wave II to achieve either receptive or expressive language by age 3. Moreover, his presumption of an innate LAD showed a lack of appreciation for the epigenetic nature of language acquistion (Hunt, 1980; Hunt et al., 1976). Clearly vocal interaction is crucial, but could one specify those of importance in proper sequence to enable orphanage-reared infants to acquire language?

Students of descriptive linguistics have divided the phenomena of language into three categories or systems: phonology, semantics, and syntactics or grammar (Gleason, 1961). Chomsky's studies and theory have emphasized syntactics, but from Piaget's (1945; 1951) observations of the acquisition of symbolic processes through play and imitation, I theorized that there is an epigenetic, sequential order in the development of both vocal and gestural imitation which was later the basis for two ordinal scales, one vocal and one gestural (Uzgiris and Hunt, 1975, Ch. 13). In this sequence, sounds and gestures highly familiar to the child are imitated before those unfamiliar. This imitation of the highly familiar has been termed *pseudo-imitation,* and its existence illustrates the principle in the development of intrinsic motivation that what is becoming recognitively familiar is motivationally attractive before whatever is unfamiliar (Hunt, 1963a; 1965, pp. 236ff; 1970; Uzgiris and Hunt, 1970; Greenberg, Uzgiris, and Hunt, 1970; Weizmann, Cohen, and Pratt, 1971; Wetherford and Cohen, 1973).

Such notions led me to interact frequently with home-reared infants aged between 2 and 5 months by talking to them briefly in adult fashion, which brought forth eye contact without change of facial expression, and then uttering high-pitched cooings, which brings forth expressions of delight to go with the eye contact. Repetitions of the cooing sounds were often successful in initiating the pseudo-imitation in which the infant would return the cooing sounds. Parenthetically, Kessen's (Kessen, Levine, and Wendriech, 1979) report of infants imitating pitches is probably pseudo-imitation of what is recognitively familiar. From such experiences, came the hypothesis that phonology is acquired through the imitative process. In the early phase, the infant is not genuinely imitating but is responding in kind to the attractiveness of those vocal sounds which have become recognitively familiar. Only considerably later, when most of the home-reared infants of my experience were about 9 months of age, could one elicit genuine imitation of vocal sounds definitely unfamiliar to the infant. Once genuine imitation had emerged, it seemed to me to provide a basis, when combined with association, for at least a beginning of the acquisition of names of objects. Once an infant acquired the names for a number of objects, however, it has been known since the episode of Helen Keller at the pump that a child acquires the generalization that "things have names." This generalization is implicit in repeated asking, in various ways, "What's that?" (see Katz and Schanck, 1938, pp. 371ff).

Early syntactical behavior appeared to me to be a creative act, with an infant employing the phonemic and semantic achievements already acquired for the purpose of imitation. Thereafter, the young child's intuitive syntactical arrangements are gradually shaped toward the standard syntax of the parents' native language through elaborations and corrections which the child imitates, and, from these imitations, gleens the grammatical rules (see Brown, 1965, pp. 286ff; 1973; Brown and Fraser, 1963).

In the meantime, other findings from our own research programs provided useful hints. In one, it became clear that the rate at which a given sensorimotor system develops is a function of the amount that system is used, and this means that there is an unexpected degree of specificity in early development and experience (Hunt, 1977). This was exemplified by Wave III who got the untutored human enrichment. Where the typical age for standing and cruising around the crib had been of the order of 20 months in the foundlings of the first, control wave, and of Wave II, who received the abortive attempt at audio-visual enrichment, for those of Wave III, all but one was standing by the time they were 1 year old. On the other hand, at this time, none of them had shown any evidences of being more advanced than the children of Waves I and II on any of the Piaget-inspired ordinal scales. Moreover, even though pseudo-imitation typically appears among home-reared infants in their third or fourth month of life, it had appeared in none of these throughout the first year. Why? A tentative answer came from asking how the caretakers were using the extra time derived from having reduced the infant–caretaker ratio from approximately 30/3 to 10/3. They had carried the infants around and they put them in strollers. Being carried served to exercise their balancing mechanisms, and being in the strollers prompted them to exercise the stepping scheme and to put weight on their legs. The result was an advance in the posture-locomotion system of between 7 and 8 months in attaining the landmark of standing and cruising while holding onto the edge of the cribs. On the other hand, it did not occur to these caretakers to talk to the infants as they carried them around. They behaved as though they assumed that the task of an infant is to learn to sit and stand and walk but not to talk.

The second hint came from an attempt by Badger to use my suggestion of adults imitating infant cooings to get vocal games going with the adolescent mothers in her classes for parent-education at the Department of Pediatrics at the University of Cincinnati. These maternal imitations of infant cooings served to get vocal games going and to advance the age of attaining vocal pseudo-imitation. But, by roughly 6 months of age, these infants lost interest in such games. Thereafter, they turned out to be considerably delayed in the attainment of genuine imitation of unfamiliar vocal sounds. This clinical finding suggested the need for a transitional experience between pseudo-imitative vocal games and genuine vocal imitation of unfamiliar phonemic combinations. For this purpose, it occurred to me that games of "follow-the-leader" might work. They could capitalize on motivational interest in vocal games with familiar sounds while leading the infant toward caretaker control of her or his vocal patterns. Such a plan would call for caretakers not only to interact vocally with the infants in their care but also to observe carefully the sounds produced by them and to employ the cues from the infants' vocalizing to guide the timing of their sequential changes in their own vocalizing to their infants.

The instructions for the caretakers were introduced into a revision of the Badger Learning Programs for Infants and Toddlers, and these revisions were translated into Farsi. Such instructions would never have worked had not the chief examiner already become familiar with the phenomena of such vocal interaction with infants during an earlier visit in 1972. She had observed my efforts to elicit vocal pseudo-imitation from two infants in Wave III who were most responsive to me. After several weeks of daily trials, these efforts had finally resulted in conversation-like vocal interaction between these infants and me. Such "conversation-like," pseudo-imitative interaction astonished both the college-educated examiners and the almost illiterate caretakers. Nevertheless, these caretakers managed to repeat my efforts with several other infants in Wave III, though only when they were about 14 months old.

In consequence, the chief examiner, Miss Sakhai, was readily able to understand the meaning of these translated instructions and to provide the demonstrational tutelage required for the caretakers in Wave V, who, unlike those in Wave III, had graduated from 3 years of a high school course in nursery training.

In the supplementary instructions added to the Badger Learning Programs for Infants and Toddlers, the caretakers were instructed to imitate the foundlings' cooings in order to get interactive vocal games going as soon as possible after the foundlings were put in their charge. They were to continue these vocal games at every opportunity, but inasmuch as such games are usually fun for both the infant and caretaker, we expected urgings to be unnecessary. The caretakers were also instructed to talk about each of the caretaking operations as they conducted them.

Such instructions prevailed until a foundling had been observed to babble with at least three different vocal patterns. Once three such patterns were manifest, the caretaker was to begin the game of "follow-the-leader." In the instructions for this game, the caretaker was to get an interactive vocal game going with one of these patterns, then shift to another. When the other was established, she was to shift to the third, and then back to the first. This procedure was to transfer the initiation of the vocal pattern in the interactions from the infant to the caretaker in preparation for the establishment of genuine imitation of unfamiliar vocal patterns. In these games of "follow-the-leader," the caretaker was gradually to shorten the number of conversation-like interactions with each vocal pattern until the game became one of the infant following directly the caretaker's lead from one vocal pattern to another. When the infant had become proficient in such following with the familiar patterns, the caretaker was instructed to begin the insertion of phonemic combinations unfamiliar to the child—unfamiliar in the sense that the caretaker had never heard the infant utter them.

As soon as a foundling had begun to produce good imitative copies of several unfamiliar phonemic combinations, the caretaker was to introduce experiences designed to facilitate the semantic mastery, or naming, of parts of the body involved in the caretaking operations. For these experiences, parts of the body were chosen as the referents to be symbolized by the names uttered, because I presumed that nothing could be more discriminable, or more readily identified, than a part of the body being touched. The idea was to have the touching of a part of an infant's body as simultaneous as possible with the caretaker's utterance of the name for the part. This was done to facilitate the infant's associating the part touched with the name heard. For such experiences, the paradigm was tied to earwashing. The caretaker was to say, in Farsi, of course, "Now I am going to wash your ear." As her vocal emphasis hit the word *ear,* her washcloth was to make contact with the infant's ear. This choice may not have been the most fortunate because infants cannot see their own ear; it might have been better to choose a visible part such as a hand, knee or foot. This would have enabled the infant to both see and feel the part named. The caretakers were also instructed to use similar procedures with the materials involved in feeding and in other games. The idea was to provide the infants with names for a large enough number of different objects to establish the generalization or learning set, that "things have names". Once such a generalization was established, it was expected that these infants would take up responsibility for their own vocabulary building by asking, "What's that?" in various ways.

This was as far as the instructions went. They contained nothing about correction of the infant's syntax, nothing about supplying the functors to round out the telegraphic utterances described by Brown and Fraser (1963), and nothing about fostering conversation or using language to ascertain the wishes of children. Apparently such experiences tend to be rare when caretakers are not specially instructed to provide them.

Effects of the Educational Intervention

The effects of this intervention appeared not only in highly improved language achievement by the children of Wave V but also in marked reductions in the means of the ages in weeks at which they attained the intermediate and top step on each of the Uzgiris-Hunt scales. Unexpectedly, there was a marked improvement in social attractiveness, which appeared to derive from greater initiative and trust than was developed in any of the earlier waves and especially in the controls of Wave I and the infants of Wave II, who received the abortive attempt at audio-visual enrichment.

On Language Achievement

The effect on language achievement shows clearly on the Scale of Schemes for Relating to Objects. Of the 25 foundlings in Waves I and II, only two ever spontaneously named an object before they were transferred to another orphanage at about 169 weeks of age. On the other hand, all 11 of these foundlings in Wave V, who received the tutored human enrichment, spontaneously named objects, and they named them at an average age of 90 weeks which is only 4 weeks later, on the average (86 weeks), than this same landmark was attained by the home-reared infants from predominantly professional families in Worcester, Massachusetts.

When infants of Waves I and II used their voices, at 3 years of age, it was only for crying and yelling in anger or exasperation. They showed no appreciation of the meaning of even the simplest of verbalized requests, but many of them manifested an appreciation of the same requests in gesture. Perhaps I can best communicate how markedly these foundlings of Wave V, who received the tutored human enrichment, differed from the language-wanting foundlings of Waves I and II, by describing vignettes of my introduction to them during my last planning visit.

When I arrived at the orphanage, the director detained me in her office for an inordinately long time in the customary tea ceremony. When the chief examiner finally came for me, and I was taken to the door of the playroom for the first time, these now toddlers were standing before their respective caretakers in a semi-circle. Someone gave a signal, and, in unison, they said loudly, "Hello." At that point, I was told that the delay in the tea ceremony had been occasioned by an effort to get these infants, then aged between 17 and 22 months, to say, "Hello, Dr. Hunt." Too many syllables; the caretakers and examiners had to settle for "Hello."

Immediately after this, one of these foundlings in Wave V surprised me by requesting, with both gesture and speech, to be picked up. None of the infants in Wave I and II, and no infant who had been reared from near birth in the orphanage, had ever exhibited such initiative and trust as was manifest in the behavior of this infant. When the chief examiner invited me to see the examining room, I started to put Cambiz, as the child was named, down. He resisted, so I carried him along. Through a window opposite the door of entry to the examining room, was a sprayer.

Cambiz saw it and immediately began shouting, "Ab, ab, ab." *Ab* is the Farsi word for water, a splendid example of spontaneous naming. Impulsively and naively, I decided to teach him the English word, *water*, for *ab*. He was still in my arms when I called his name and modeled the word *water*, yet Cambiz continued his excited shouting of *ab*. When it became evident that I could not get him into the imitation game so long as he could see the sprayer, we went into the hall where the sprayer was out of sight. Then, I called his name and modeled the word *water*, and Cambiz responded with *awter*. After he had responded similarly for two more modelings, I modeled the sounds, *wa, wa*. Cambiz immediately responded in kind. Then, when I modeled the word *water*, Cambiz responded with an utterance of *water* as clear as my own. Later, we had a similiar experience with *glasses*, the English word for the spectacles I was wearing. Cambiz wanted to take them off my face and put them on his own as he repeated the Farsi word for spectacles: *"Enack, enack, enack."* So long as the spectacles were in either view or his knowledge of their whereabouts, I was unable to get him into the imitation game. Once I had given them to one of my collaborators, and we went into the hall, however, Cambiz responded to my modeling the English word *glasses* with *assis*. With further modelings, Cambiz responded with *lasses*. After he had persisted in this response for some three modelings, I tried modeling the *gl* sound: *"Gla, gla, gla."* Cambiz responded in kind. Then, when I again modeled *glasses*, Cambiz responded with as good a pronunciation of the word as my own. This response of Cambiz's surprised Professor Mohandessi, my collaborator and then resident director of the project, who pointed out that there is a phonological rule in Farsi prohibiting the combination of two consonants at the beginning of a word. At age 22 months, the imitative competence of Cambiz was unhampered by the establishment of any such rule in his vocal system.

A few moments after the water incident, I was holding Shabnam, who was then somewhat less than 18 months of age and the youngest of the 11 in Wave V. The chief examiner was demonstrating that this very young girl could imitate the names of all of the infants in her wave. She came finally to Yass. I had no opportunity to see Yass because her adoptive parents had taken her away from the orphanage the week before I had arrived for this final planning visit. As the examiner uttered the name, *Yass*, however, Shabnam removed herself from this imitation game. She twisted in my arm, reached out, looked toward the door, and said, "Yass rafteh." This is a telegraphic Farsi sentence meaning, "Yass gone." No one had deliberately schooled Shabnam in such sentence construction. Yet, she reflected in the symbolism of speech, a state of affairs of which she had full cognitive appreciation. Yass had been her closest friend.

This surprising action of Shabnam led me to ask the examiner how many words she knew. Since no one had asked this question before, the examiner confessed her ignorance. So, after learning how to ask in Farsi, "What is it?" ["Een che aay?"], I gently pulled Shabnam's hair and vocalized my best immitation of, "Een che aay?" Shabnam responded with *muh*, the Farsi word for *hair*. As I touched various parts of her body and repeated the question, she gave correctly the Farsi word for each, except elbow. When I touched her elbow, her face clouded, and I drew the clinical impression that she felt responsible for knowing the names of the parts of her body. So, apparently, did the chief examiner for she quickly supplied the word, and Shabnam repeated it. We continued this procedure with tables, chairs, dishes, and so forth. Before the task of enumeration was done, I was called away. The next morning, I awakened with a Zeigarnik-like recall of this unfinished task. After the experience and writing the English names for the objects about which I had asked Shabnam, they numbered more than 50. Suffice it to say here that later every one of these 4 infants in Wave V, except the one already adopted, named correctly more than 50 objects consisting of parts of their bodies, the garments they wore, and or the various things involved in the caretaking and feeding operation. Furthermore, this procedure failed to measure their full vocabulary, because questions concerned with verbs and adjectives were omitted, even though Shabnam had used the Farsi word for *gone*. Nor was any attempt made to test their receptive vocabularies. In a later attempt to quantify the effects of the intervention involving the tutored human enrichment on language achievement with an improvised test containing 10 categories of items, the performance of these foundlings of Wave V, who had received the tutored human enrichment, was at age 2, equal to that of the four-year-old foundlings remaining in the orphanage from Wave III, who had received the untutored human enrichment, except in understanding terms for position (especially *between, in front of,* and *behind*), and in the length of a sentence that could be repeated after a single modeling. These 2-year-olds were judged to be superior in the distinctiveness of imitative pronunciations of unfamiliar words.

Amount of Effect

When one compares the mean of the ages at which the foundlings in Wave V, who received the tutored human enrichment, attained the top steps on the scales with the mean ages at which those of Waves I and II (combined) attained them, the resulting differences between the means of age range from 34 to 87 weeks. The mean of these seven differences in mean ages for acquiring the top steps of the seven scales is 63 weeks.

This mean transforms to a difference of approximately 47 points in the mean IQ-ratios for the composite of seven Piagetian, sensorimotor achievements in the Uzgiris-Hunt Scales. Since measures of performance on composites of Piagetian tasks show high correlation (.876) with measures of performance on subtests of the Wechsler Scale of Intelligence (Humphreys and Parsons, 1979), this gain of 47 points of the IQ-ratio probably approximates fairly closely what might have been found with the Wechsler Test of Intelligence. Assuming that the samples of foundlings in the successive waves are directly equivalent in genetic potential, the superiority of 47 points of IQ-ratio in those who got the tutored enrichment over those of Waves I and II can be attributed to this educational intervention. This difference is actually about half a standard deviation larger (47 points of IQ-ratio) than that between the children of Head Start and those of nursery school (40 IQ points) on the Peabody Picture Vocabulary Test. Obviously, there are loose points in this chain of reasonings.

Had the revolution in Iran not destroyed the opportunity, we would have repeated this comparison with the use of a Farsi version of the Peabody and the Wechsler in the third year.

One can indicate the amount of effect on the intellectual achievement of these 11 foundlings of Wave V in yet another way by comparing their performances on the Uzgiris-Hunt Scales with those of the 12 home-reared infants from predominantly professional families in Worcester, Massachusetts. The mean (85.7 weeks) of the mean ages at which these foundlings of Wave V attained the top steps of the Piaget-inspired ordinal scales was 7.1 weeks younger than the comparable mean (92.8 weeks) for the children of predominantly professional families in Worcester. This difference favors the foundlings of Wave V in the terms of an estimated IQ by at least 8 points (i.e., 92.8/85.7 = 1.08). I say, "at least," because accepting the mean for the Worcester sample where the children came from predominantly professional families as the mental age norm, even though the children from such families typically have mental ages about 20 percent above the average (i.e., have mean IQs of about 120), would serve to reduce the difference in the IQ-ratio. If no substantial error exists in this reasoning, it means that this educational intervention to foster language achievement has served to bring these 11 foundlings above the norm by nearly 30 IQ points or something approximating two standard deviations of IQ. If these findings are approximately correct, they indicate that one can, by starting early with an educational intervention that makes proper use of the sequential epigenetic changes in early development, produce an effect as great as that commonly found between children from professional families and children from poorly educated families of the unskilled working-class. Moreover, I am confident that this project in Tehran did not achieve the ultimate limits of the average range of reaction for children without pathology.

From this and other evidence, I am inclined to believe that every human infant born without pathology has the genetic potential to acquire all the knowledge, skills, and values required for a productive place in any culture on this spaceship Earth. Even though I find the correlational evidence of heritability quite unconvincing, this statement is not meant to deny inherited individual differences. It should not be taken as a paraphrase of John B. Watson's claim, for I do not claim that one can make an Aristotle, an Einstein, an Isaac Newton, or a Paderewski out of any healthy infant picked at random any more than one can make of that infant a 7-foot basketball star. On the other hand, our evidence does indicate that standardizing the development-fostering quality of the experience of a group of infants serves to reduce the standard deviation in the ages at which they acquire the top steps on our ordinal scales (Hunt, 1980).

Effects on Social Attractiveness: Facial Expression, Initiative, and Trust

The effect on social attractiveness of this educational intervention designed to foster language achievement was quite unexpected. Unfortunately, no scales or metrics exist for assessing such a phenomenon. Even so, the contrast in social attractiveness between the control foundlings of Wave I and Wave II combined and those of Wave V was exceedingly marked. It was most marked in the interactions of the children with adults, as illustrated above in the vignettes of the behavior of Cambiz and Shabnam. I longed for sound cinemas or videotapes to record the interactions between the children in these contrasting groups with adults in standard situations. Nevertheless I can report what I observed.

The children of Waves I and II wore glum expressions. They initiated no interactions with adults and relatively few with other children. They played little with toys, and they tended to be exceedingly wary and withdrawn from anyone but their accustomed caretakers. Several Iranian observers remarked independently that "they behaved like little animals."

The glum or distressed expressions of these children from Waves I and II are obvious in the 8 children pictured in Figure 1. The most attractive expression that I could find among my pictures of the children in Waves I and II is that of the child on the reader's right in the top row of Figure 1. This picture was taken while I was vocalizing my imitation of sounds I had heard this child make. His expression of mild interest, which differed from the glumness shown while I was simply talking to him in adult fashion, accounts for this expression. It is of interest that I cannot recall his

Fig. 1 Children in Waves I and II

name, or the names of any children in Waves I and II. Because they were unresponsive in interaction and lacking in communication skills, they were unattractive little persons, and they seemed to acquire no identity.

The happy, interested expressions of the children from Wave V (see Figure 2) contrast sharply with the glum expressions on the faces of those in Figure 1 from Waves I and II. The one on the extreme left in the top row is Cambiz, who is striking the ball hung from a ring in the ceiling, and his enthusiasm is obvious, even in this snapshot. The second on from the left in the top row is Parvis, and he is obviously interestingly engaged with his stacking toy. The third from the left is Monee. His initiative is evident in his gesture of request for the adult standing by. At the extreme right of the upper row is Shabnam who, although less than 18 months old at the time, was the one who turned in my arms when the examiner modeled the name Yass, and said, in Farsi, "Yass gone." Note her unsollicited wave to me as I took her picture.

It is likely that you will agree that the four infants from Wave V in the upper row of Figure 2 are much more attractive than those in the upper row of Figure 1. You will probably agree, also, that the infants from Wave V in the lower row of Figure 2 are also more attractive than those from Waves I and II in the lower row of Figure 1. These pictures were originally taken only for my personal record, but viewers have been so struck by the contrast that I decided that they must also be accepted as evidence.

I shall not take time here to name and describe the children in the second, contrasting samples of four in the lower rows of Figures 1 and 2, but if you agree that the infants from Wave V are much more attractive than those from Waves I and II, you may be interested to learn that your judgment has been confirmed by several childless couples of Tehran who chose 7 of these 11 foundlings from Wave V for adoption. Again, by way of contrast, of the 57 foundlings who served in the preceding four waves, only two were ever adopted. Moreover, those two were adopted before they were 6 months old because they were pretty babies. These seven from Wave V were adopted because they were attractively responsive 2-year-olds.

As I have already noted, the attractiveness of the children of Wave V derived probably more from their actions implying initiative and trust than from their facial expressions. Although Cambiz was somewhat more forward than others in demanding that I pick him up the first time he saw me, all of the others, at one time or another, endeavored to show me what they were doing or could do. Even at age 2, they had achieved several of the 11 classes of behavior that White and Watts (1973, pp. 41–42) have found to differentiate well-developed from poorly developed

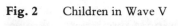

Fig. 2 Children in Wave V

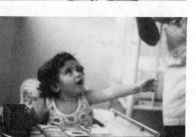

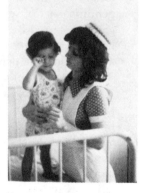

social competence at age 6. These include abilities "(1) to get and maintain the attention of adults when such attention is appropriate, (2) to use adults as resources, (3) to express affection and hostility to adults . . . (8) to resist distractions or to concentrate and persist in effort to achieve a goal . . . and (10) to praise oneself and or show pride in one's accomplishments" as evidenced by showing it to others.

I am inclined to attribute such behavior chiefly to two fairly general traits, trust and iniative. Trust has been emphasized by Erikson (1950) as implying, "not only that one has learned to rely on the sameness and continuity of outer providers, but also that one may trust oneself and the capacity of one's own organs to cope with urges" (p. 220), which Erikson attributed to the nursing experience of infants. The nursing experience of the infants getting the tutored human enrichment differs considerably less from the nursing experience of the foundlings in Waves I and II than do the experiences of vocal interaction. The trust appears to have emerged from the experiences of hearing the caretaker's vocalizations of the child's own vocal productions, at least in the beginning. It is interesting to note, however, that these caretakers claim they could not have loved an infant from their own bodies more than they had come to love these foundlings who had been in their care since early infancy. At first, I was inclined to doubt such claims, but I noted that whenever one of the infants was removed from the orphanage as a consequence of adoption, there were tears in the caretaker's eyes, and her colleagues readily understood her. These tears led me to believe that a genuine bond had been established between these infants and their caretakers which resulted in genuine grief of separation when an infant was adopted. Thus, the vocal games, started by caretakers imitating the cooings of the infants, may have been merely the earliest epigenetic phase of a mutually affectionate interaction that persisted and established the sense of trust, of even a strange American psychologist.

The trait of initiative would appear to be related to that of trust. It corresponds to what Rotter (1966, 1967; see also for bibliography, Thornhill, Thornhill, and Youngman, 1975) has termed the *internal locus of control* and has described as a generalized expectation that the individual can control the reinforcement received. Rotter (1967) also has seen a close relationship between an inner locus of control and interpersonal trust. Initiative may also be seen as the converse of what Seligman (1975) has termed the *learned helplessness* that results, as least in animal studies, from a lack of contingencies between the subjects' actions and the experiences of pain or relief from pain, a state of affairs which resembles "prevalence of irrelevant noise," which has shown inverse correlations of the order of $-.7$ with measures of developmental advance (Wachs, 1978; Wachs, Uzgiris, and Hunt, 1971). Both concepts have excited the interests of many investigators (see Seligman, 1975; Thornhill, Thornhill, and Youngman, 1975). A contrast between the lack of initiative in the control foundlings of Wave I and those of Wave II, who received the abortive attempt at audio-visual enrichment, and the abundant initiative of the foundlings of Wave V who received the tutored human enrichment, tends, in general, to reinforce Rotter's (1966) concept of generalized expectancies.

Nevertheless, I believe I see an epigenetic aspect to the acquisition process. An infant's repeated experiences of hearing the voice of its caretaker uttering sounds with the attractiveness of recognitive familiarity, derived from the infant having just produced them, must lead to a memory of the sequence. Because the central processes that mediate the memory run off more rapidly than events, such a memory gives rise to an expectation that its utterance will produce such an effect. This is little more than a neuropsychological account of Skinner's (1953) operant conditioning, but with the added element of a developmental explanation of the motivational attractiveness of a caretaker's imitations of the cooings of an infant in her care. Moreover, these expectations of pleasurable feedback from vocal productions lead in turn, to an affectionate relationship with the caretaker and help to avoid the complicating effects of control through punishment. As these effects generalize, they produce trust and initiative. Moreover, once a substantial modicum of trust is established, experiences of failure followed by success with efforts and adaptive modification of action can lead to a new realization that adaptive modification of intentional actions improves the likelihood of success in obtaining the desired ends. This is the essence of initiative and adaptiveness.

As I have explained elsewhere (Hunt, 1981a), an infant's experience of being imitated can be the starting point for intentional actions that become modified into the trust and initiative responsible for social attractiveness. Inasmuch as social attractiveness serves to increase the likelihood of a child's obtaining helpful responses from adults other than the caretakers or parents, and initiative serves to render a child more capable of adaptive modifications of the achievements existing at any level of development, the child obtains a persisting developmental advantage. Even though these 2 year-olds of Wave V may encounter conditions that produce learned helplessness in them, it will be more difficult to produce such a trait in them than in those of Waves I and II whose glum lack of initiative and trust already approaches a state of learned helplessness. Moreover, it would be no easy task to rectify the damage already done to the latter by the rearing conditions of the orphanage. Their failure to be adopted is an illustrative confirmation of the damage. The importance of the development-fostering quality of early experience, despite abundant plasticity that is bidirectional, is the inertia of both the facilitative and hampering effects of the early experience.

There may be objections that even though the findings from the Tehran program are interesting, it is unlikely that similar results could be obtained with the progeny of poorly educated parents of poverty. But to a substantial degree, this has been done with the progeny of poorly educated black women of poverty with IQs of 75 or below by Heber (1978). Twenty of these infants given educational treatment from birth on attained a mean IQ of slightly over 120 at age 2 and continued at this level till they entered school at age 6. Another 20 progeny of such mothers who did not receive the educational treatment had at age 2 a mean IQ of about 95, and they continued to one of below 90 by age 6. In Heber's Milwaukee study, the treatment was provided by young women specially selected in a one-to-one relationship 5 days a week. I estimate from the mean of the mean age at which the foundlings of Wave V achieved the top steps on the Piaget-inspired ordinal scales that they attained a mean IQ of at least 128 at age 2, roughly 8 points higher than that attained by the home-reared children from predominantly professional families in Worcester. Moreover, if we could teach the caretakers at an orphanage in Tehran how to foster vocal imitation, language achievement, and social attractiveness well enough to bring them to age 3 in a state of intellectual, linguistic, and social competence to be roughly two standard deviations above the norms for children in the United States, it should be feasible to provide parent training that will teach many, or most, of the poorly educated mothers from the poverty sector to do nearly as well. It may well be necessary to start teaching at the time each mother is giving birth to her first offspring, but such pilot studies are promising (Badger, 1977). These problems of recruitment for training in parenting of mothers are as deserving of research and development as those concerned with how to facilitate early psychological development or any other. Even though genetic individual differences exist, I believe no culture and very few families have so reared children as to realize half of the genetic potential available in them. Parents of the educated middle class achieve more of the potential range of reaction for their children than do uneducated parents of poverty, but parents generally could greatly increase the portion of potential they realize during the preschool years of their young if they could be freed of "what they know," as Mark Twain often said, "that ain't so," and if they had an effective educational technology for infancy and early childhood.

Summary

I have tried to show how the emotionally toned metatheories of psychological development that we are apt to be most confident of knowing, "ain't so." They are fictions. I have noted that it took more than 2,000 years for mankind to give up the metatheory that whatever exists must be permanent. Perhaps it was too easy to blame it on God. I hope it will take less time to give up our debates over the relative importance of heredity and environment because both are all important. Except for genetic counseling to avoid genetic defects and the use of the technology of amniocentesis and therapeutic abortions, I see no hope for the eugenic program Francis Galton envisaged and started. Hope for increasing the portion of the range of reaction achieved in young children through educational intervention is realistic.

I have presented evidence that children from uneducated families of poverty enter school with a genuine deficit in ability to process information with language and numbers, contrary to the claims of some sociological students of language. Yet such differences in the achievements of symbolic skills need not be regarded as biologically inevitable. In support of this claim, I have presented evidence showing that differences in approximate measures of intelligence, language achievement, and social attractiveness can be obtained with an educational intervention in the infant-rearing practices of an orphanage in Tehran as large or larger than those between Head Start children from uneducated parents of poverty and college-educated parents. Moreover, I have contended that what can be achieved with such small samples can be achieved generally if we investigate the development of proper methods of teaching parents how to begin at birth to provide development-fostering experiences of high quality that are modified as the achievements of infants show what modifications are needed.

The effects of the educational intervention in the fifth wave of our Tehran program are the largest of which I know. I believe they were achieved because they were guided by a more accurate theory of the experiences that foster the acquisition of language than is common. The theory recognized the epigenetic nature of language acquisition and provided modifications of caretaker interactions with the infants that solve the "problem of the match" by timing their start to behavioral indicators of infant achievements. This theory attributes the acquisition of phonology to vocal imitation, which has its own epigenesis, the acquisition of semantics to a combination of genuine imitation and association, and the acquisition of syntax to a creative use of phonological and semantic achievements for communication in which creative intuitions get shaped into that of the parental language through elaborations and corrections.

The efforts to foster imitation on the way to fostering language achievement unexpectedly produced dramatic improvements in social attractiveness. This improved attractiveness I attributed to the trust and initiative growing out of the conversation-like vocal games started by having the caretakers begin, as soon as foundlings were put into their care, to imitate the nondistressful vocalizations of the infants. A synoptic theoretical account of the epigenetic sequence in the structure of the infant environment interaction leading to the traits of trust and initiative is also given.

References

Anastasi, A. *Differential psychology: Individual and group differences in behavior.* New York: Macmillan, 1958.(a)
Anastasi, A. Heredity, environment, and the question "How?" *Psychological Review,* 1958, *65,* 197–208.(b)
Badger, E. D. *Teaching guide: Infant learning program.* Paoli, PA: The Instructo Corp., 1971.(b)
Badger, E. D. *Teaching guide: Toddler learning program.* Paoli, PA: The Instructo Corp., 1971.(b)
Badger, E. D. The infant stimulation/mother training project. In B. M. Caldwell and D. J. Steadman (Eds.), *Infant education: A guide for helping handicapped children in the first three years.* New York: Walker and Co., 1977.
Baratz, S. B., and Baratz, J. C. Early childhood intervention: The social science base of institutional racism. *Harvard Educational Review,* 1970, *40,* (1), 29–50.
Bernstein, B. A public language: Some sociological implications of a linguistic form. *British Journal of Sociology,* 1959 *10,* 311–326.
Bernstein, B. A sociolinguistic approach to socialization: With some reference to educability. In F. Williams (Ed.), *Language and poverty: Perspectives on a theme.* Chicago: Markham, 1970.
Binet, A. *Les idees modernes sur les enfants.* Paris: Ernest Flamarion, 1909. (Cited in Stoddard, G. D. The IQ: Its ups and downs. *Educational Record,* 1939, *20,* 44–57.).
Binet, A., and Simon, T. Methodes nouvelles pour le diagnostic du niveau intellectuel des anormaux. *Annee Psychologia,* 1905, *11,* 191–244.
Bloom, B. S. *Stability and change in human characteristics.* New York: Wiley and Sons, 1964.
Brown, R. *Social psychology.* New York: The Free Press, 1965.
Brown, R. *A first language: The early stages.* Cambridge, MA: Harvard University Press, 1973.
Brown, R., and Fraser, C. The acquisition of syntax. In C. N. Cofer and B. Musgrave (Eds.), *Verbal behavior and learning: Problems and processes.* New York: McGraw-Hill, 1963.
Chomsky, N. Review of *Verbal behavior* by B. F. Skinner. *Language,* 1959, *35,* (1), 26–58, footnote 48.
Clark, A. D., and Richards, C. J. Auditory discrimination among economically disadvantaged and non-disadvantaged preschool children. *Exceptional Children,* 1966, *33,* 259–262.
Cravioto, J. *Malnutrition and behavioral development in the preschool child.* Paper presented at the International Conference on Prevention of Malnutrition in the Preschool Child, Washington, D. C., December 1964. Published in *Preschool child malnutrition, primary deterrent to human progress: Papers.* Washington, D. C.: National Research Council Publication No. 1282, 1966.

Cronbach, L. J. The two disciplines of scientific psychology. *American Psychologist*, 1957, *12*, 671–684.

Dennis, W. Causes of retardation among institutional children: Iran. *Journal of Genetic Psychology*, 1960, *96*, 47–59.

Dennis, W., and Sayegh, Y. The effect of supplementary experiences upon the behavioral development of infants in institutions. *Child Development*, 1965, *36*, 81–90.

Deutsch, C. P. Auditory discrimination and learning social factors. *The Merrill-Palmer Quarterly*, 1964, *10*, 277–296.

Dunn, L. C. *A short history of genetics.* New York: McGraw-Hill, 1965.

Erikson, E. H. *Childhood and society.* New York: Norton, 1950.

Freud, S. *A general introduction to psychoanalysis.* New York: Liveright, 1920.

Galton, F. *Hereditary genius: An inquiry into its laws and consequences.* London: Macmillan, 1869.

Gleason, H. A., Jr. *An introduction to descriptive linguistics.* (Rev. ed.) New York: Holt, Rinehart and Winston, 1961.

Goodman, K. S. Dialect barriers to reading comprehension. In J. C. Baratz and R. W. Shuy (Eds.), *Teaching black children to read.* Washington, D.C.: Center for Applied Linguistics, 1969.

Greenberg, D. J., Uzgiris, I. C., and Hunt, J. McV. Attentional preference and experience: III. Visual familiarity and looking time. *Journal of Genetic Psychology*, 1970, *117*, 123–135.

Greven, P. *Child-rearing concepts, 1628–1661: Historical sources.* Itasca, IL: F. E. Peacock, 1973.

Heber, F. R. Sociocultural mental retardation: A longitudinal study. In D.G. Forgays (Ed.), *Primary prevention of psychopathology*, Vol. II: *Environmental influences.* Hanover, N. H.: University Press of New England, 1978.

Hess, R. D., and Shipman, V. Early experience and the socialization of cognitive modes in children. *Child Development*, 1965, *36*, 869–886.

Humphreys, L. G., and Parsons, C. K. Piagetian tasks measure intelligence and intelligence tests assess cognitive development. *Intelligence*, 1979, *3*, 369–382.

Hunt, J. McV. Experience and the development of motivation: Some reinterpretations. *Child Development*, 1960, *31*, 489–504.

Hunt, J. McV. *Intelligence and experience.* New York: Ronald Press, 1961.

Hunt, J. McV. Piaget's observations as a source of hypotheses concerning motivation. *Merrill-Palmer Quarterly*, 1963, *9*, 263–275.(a)

Hunt, J. McV. Motivation inherent in information processing and action. In O. J. Harvey (Ed.), *Motivation and social interaction: The cognitive determinants.* New York: Ronald Press, 1963.(b)

Hunt, J. McV. Intrinsic motivation and its role in psychological development. In D. Levine (Ed.), *Nebraska Symposium on Motivation*, *13*, 189–282. Lincoln: University of Nebraska Press, 1965.

Hunt, J. McV. The epigenesis of intrinsic motivation and early cognitive learning. In R. N. Haber (Ed.), *Current research in motivation.* New York: Holt, Rinehart and Winston, 1966.

Hunt, J. McV. *The challenge of incompetence and poverty: Papers on the role of early education.* Urbana: University of Illinois Press, 1969.

Hunt, J. McV. Attentional preference and experience: I. Introduction. *Journal of Genetic Psychology*, 1970, *117*, 99–107.

Hunt, J. McV. Intrinsic motivation: Information and circumstance. In H. M.

Schroder and P. Suedfeld (Eds.), *Personality theory and information procession.* New York: Ronald Press, 1971.(a)

Hunt, J. McV. Intrinsic motivation and psychological development. In H. M. Schroder and P. Suedfeld (Eds.), *Personality theory and information processing.* New York: Ronald Press, 1971.(b)

Hunt, J. McV. Psychological development and the educational enterprise. *Educational Theory,* 1975, *25* (4), 333–353.

Hunt, J. McV. Utility of ordinal scales derived from Piaget's observations. *Merrill-Palmer Quarterly,* 1976, *22* (1), 31–45.

Hunt, J. McV. *Specificity in early development and experience.* Annual Lecture in Developmental Pediatrics. Omaha, NB: Meyer Children's Rehabilitation Institute, University of Nebraska Medical Center, 1977.

Hunt, J. McV. *Early psychological development and experience.* Heinz Werner Lectures, 1976. Worcester, MA: Clark University Press, 1980.

Hunt, J. McV. The role of situations in early psychological development. In D. Magnusson (Ed.), *Toward a psychology of situations: An interactional perspective.* Hillsdale, N.J.: L. Erlbaum, 1981.(a)

Hunt, J. McV. The experiential roots of intention, initiative, and trust. In H. I. Day (Ed.), *Advances of intrinsic motivation and aesthetics.* New York: Plenum, 1981.(b)

Hunt, J. McV. Language acquisition and experience (Tehran). Unpublished paper, Department of Psychology, University of Illinois, 1981.(c)

Hunt, J. McV., Kirk, G. E., and Lieberman, C. Social class and preschool language skill: IV. Semantic mastery of shapes. *Genetic Psychology Monographs,* 1975, *92*, 115–129.

Hunt, J. McV., Kirk, G. E., and Volkmar, F. Social class and preschool language skill: V. Cognitive and semantic mastery of number. *Genetic Psychology Monographs,* 1975, *92*, 131–153.

Hunt, J. McV., Mohandessi, K., Ghodssi, M., and Akiyama, M. The psychological development of orphanage-reared infants: Interventions with outcomes (Tehran). *Genetic Psychology Monographs,* 1976, *94*, 177–226.

Hunt, J. McV., and Paraskevopoulos, J. Children's psychological development as a function of the inaccuracy of their mothers' knowledge of their abilities. *The Journal of Genetic Psychology,* 1980, *136*, 285–298.

Hunt, J. McV., Paraskevopoulos, J., Schickedanz, D., and Uzgiris, I. C. Variations in the mean ages of achieving object permanence under diverse conditions of rearing. In B. L. Friedlander, G. M. Sterritt, and G. E. Kirk (Eds.), *The exceptional infant,* Vol. 3: *Assessment and intervention.* New York: Brunner/Mazel, 1975.

Katz, D., and Schanck, R. L. *Social psychology.* New York: Wiley, 1938.

Keller, S. The social world of the urban slum child: Some early findings. *American Journal of Orthopsychiatry,* 1963, *33*, 823–831.

Kessen, W., Levine, J., and Wendriech, K. A. Imitation of pitch in infants. *Infant Behavior and Development,* 1979, *2*, 93–99.

Kirk, G. E., and Hunt, J. McV. Social class and preschool language skill: I. Introduction. *Genetic Psychology Monographs,* 1975, *91*, 281–298.

Kirk, G. E., Hunt, J. McV., and Lieberman, C. Social class and preschool language skill: II. Semantic mastery of color information. *Genetic Psychology Monographs,* 1975, *91*, 299–316.

Kirk, G. E., Hunt, J. McV., and Volkmar, F. Social class and preschool language skill: III. Semantic mastery of position information. *Genetic Psychology Monographs*, 1975, *91*, 317–337.

Kirk, G. E., Hunt, J. McV., and Volkmar, F. Social class and preschool language skill: VI. Child-to-child communication and semantic mastery of the information in the message. *Genetic Psychology Monographs*, 1979, *100*, 111–138.

Labov, W. The logic of non-Standard English. In F. Williams (Ed.), *Language and poverty*. Chicago: Markham, 1970.

Lenneberg, E. H. The natural history of language. In F. Smith and G. H. Miller (Eds.), *The genesis of language: A psycholinguistic approach*. Cambridge, MA: MIT Press, 1966.

Lenneberg, E. H. *The biological basis of language*. New York: Wiley, 1967.

McDonald, D. Our invisible poor. In L. A. Ferman, J. L. Kornbluh, and A. Haber (Eds.), *Poverty in America*. Ann Arbor: University of Michigan Press, 1966.

Milner, E. A study of the relationship between reading readiness in grade one school children and patterns of parent–child interactions. *Child Development*, 1951, *22*, 95–122.

Murphy, L. B. Preventative implications of development in the preschool years. In G. Caplan (Ed.), *Prevention of mental disorders in children*. New York: Basic Books, 1961.

Murphy, L. B. Assessment of young children: The concept of a vulnerability index. In L. Dittman, C. C. Chandler, and R. S. Lourie (Eds.), *New Perspectives in early child care*. New York: Atherton, 1968.

Needham, J. *A history of embryology*. New York: Abelard-Schuman, 1959.

Oppenheim, R. W. The ontogeny of behavior in the chick embryo. In D. S. Lehrman, J. S. Rosenblatt, R. A. Hinde, and E. Shaw (Eds.), *Advances in the study of behavior*, Vol. 5. New York: Academic Press, 1974.

Oppenheim, R. W. Preformation and epigenesis in the origins of the nervous system and behavior: Issues, concepts, and their history. In P. Bateson and P. Klopfer (Eds.), *Perspectives in ethology* (Vol. 6). New York: Plenum Press, 1981.

Osborne, J. W. *The silent revolution: The industrial revolution in England as a source of cultural change*. New York: Scribners, 1970.

Pasamanick, G. *Determinants of intelligence*. Paper presented at Symposium on Man and Civilization: Control of the Mind—II, University of California, San Francisco Medical Center, 27 January, 1962.

Pavlov, I. P. *Conditioned reflexes*. (G. V. Anrep, Transl.) London: Oxford University Press, 1927.

Piaget, J. *Play, dreams, and imitation in childhood*. (C. Gattegno and F. M. Hodgson, Transls.). New York: Norton, 1951. (Originally published 1945.)

Piaget, J. *The psychology of intelligence*. (M. Piercy and D. E. Berlyne, Transls.) Paterson, N.J.: Littlefield, Adams and Co., 1960. (Originally published 1947.)

Piaget, J. 1977. Problems of equilibration. In M. H. Appel and L. S. Goldberg (Eds.), *Topics in cognitive development*, Vol. 1: *Equilibration: Theory, research and application*. New York: Plenum Press, 1977.

Rotter, J. B. Generalized expectancies for internal versus external control of reinforcement. *Psychological Monographs*, 1966, *80* (1), Whole No. 609.

Rotter, J. B. A new scale for the measurement of interpersonal trust. *Journal of Personality*, 1967, *35*, 651–655.

Seligman, M.E.P. *Helplessness*. San Francisco: Freeman, 1975.

Shuy, R. W. A linguistic background for developing reading materials for black children. In J. C. Baratz and R. W. Shuy (Eds.), *Teaching black children to read*. Washington, D. C.: Center for Applied Linguistics, 1969.

Skinner, B. F. *Science and human behavior*. New York: Macmillan, 1953.

Smith, H. S. *Changing conceptions of original sin: A study of American theology since 1750*. New York: Scribner, 1955.

Steiner, G. Y. *The children's cause*. Washington, D.C.: Brookings Institute, 1976.

Stern, W. *The psychological methods of testing intelligence*. (G. M. Whipple, Transl.) Baltimore: Warwick and York, 1914. (Originally published 1912.)

Stewart, W. A. On the use of Negro dialect in the teaching of reading. In J. C. Baratz and R. W. Shuy (Eds.), *Teaching black children to read*. Washington, D. C.: Center for Applied Linguistics, 1969.

Thornhill, M. A., Thornhill, G. J., and Youngman, M. B. A computerized and categorized bibliography on locus of control. *Psychological Reports*, 1975, *36*, 505–506.

Ulvund, S. K. Cognition and motivation in early infancy: An interactionistic approach. *Human Development*, 1980, *23* (1), 17–32.

Uzgiris, I. C., and Hunt, J. McV. *An instrument for assessing infant psychological development*. Mimeographed paper, Psychological Development Laboratory, University of Illinois, 1966.

Uzgiris, I. C., and Hunt, J. McV. Attentional preference and experience: II. An exploratory longitudinal study of the effects of visual familiarity and responsiveness. *Journal of Genetic Psychology*, 1970, *117*, 109–121.

Uzgiris, I. C., and Hunt, J. McV. *Assessment in infancy: Ordinal scales of psychological development*. Urbana: University of Illinois Press, 1975.

Wachs, T. D. Relationship of infants physical environment to their Binet performance at 2.5 years. *International Journal of Behavioral Development*, 1978, *1*, 51–65.

Wachs, T. D., Uzgiris, I. C., and Hunt, J. McV. Cognitive development in infants of different age levels and from different environmental backgrounds: An exploratory investigation. *Merrill-Palmer Quarterly*, 1971, *17*, 283–317.

Watson, J. B. *Psychological care of infant and child*. New York: Norton, 1928.

Weizmann, F., Cohen, L. B., and Pratt, R. J. Novelty, familiarity, and the development of infant attention. *Developmental Psychology*, 1971, *4*, 149–154.

Wetherford, M., and Cohen, L. B. Developmental changes in infant visual preferences for novelty and familiarity. *Child Development*, 1973, *44*, 416–424.

White, B. L., and Watts, J. C. *Experience and environment: Major influences on the development of the young child*. Englewood Cliffs, N.J.: Prentice-Hall, 1973.

Wilson, E. O. *Sociobiology: The new synthesis*. Cambridge, MA: Harvard University Press, 1975.

Yarrow, L. J., Rubenstein, J. L., and Pedersen, F. A. *Infant and environment: Early cognitive and motivational development*. Washington, D.C.: Hemisphere, 1975.

A Vision of Child Care in the 1980s

Edward Zigler and Matia Finn

The year 1979, [designated as the International Year of the Child (IYC) worldwide] began with hope. Each nation was charged with the task of examining the unmet needs of its children. In this country, President Carter challenged the United States IYC Commissioners and Honorary Commissioners, the senior author among them, to see what needed to be done to optimize the development of children in America. With the IYC over, the questions have been: Has the year been a success and have we accomplished anything on behalf of children?

Our view is that the IYC was both a success and a failure. The year highlighted some dismal facts regarding our children. Inasmuch as we have not made any clear gains on behalf of children during the year, the IYC may be viewed as a failure. However, if we act on the information we have gathered and use the IYC as a launching pad for greater activity during the 1980s, then the year may yet be considered a success. Before we share with you our agenda for the 1980s, let us review some of the important facts we have learned about the sorry state of our nation's children.

The Unmet Needs of Children

Infant Mortality

Among 42 nations keeping comparable statistics, in 1975 the United States, the richest and technologically most advanced country in the world, ranked 16th in the incidence of infant mortality and death of mothers in child birth (U.S. Department of Health, Education and Welfare, 1976). While significant, these statistics for the nation as a whole mask the disparity in infant mortality and maternal death rates between whites and minority groups as well as between regions of the country. In 1974 the infant mortality rate for nonwhites was 1.5 times greater than for whites and the maternal death rate was 3.5 times greater. There were 14.9 deaths per 1,000 births in the Pacific states in 1973, as compared with 21.6 deaths per 1,000 births in the southeastern United States (Advisory Committee on Child Development, 1976).

Poverty, poor sanitation, malnutrition in pregnant women, and lack of prenatal care are leading contributors to the high infant mortality rate in this country. It is now generally accepted that prenatal care should begin during the first three months of pregnancy in order to have the greatest success in preventing infant mortality and handicapping conditions in children. However, many pregnant women receive no prenatal care during the first trimester. In 1977, 47 percent of black women and 24 percent of white women did not have the minimal level of care suggested by the American College of Obstetrics and Gynecology. This neglect condemns many infants still in the uterus to death at birth or to a variety of physical and psychological handicaps which no amount of intervention can fully remediate.

Teenage Pregnancy

The number of pregnant teenage girls reached epidemic proportions during the last decade. The phenomenon of children having children is associated with complications during pregnancy and delivery. The risk of having infants in poor health and of low birthweight is greater for women below the age of 20. Low birthweight is associated with developmental delays and disabilities later in life. Although some experts believe that this is due to the physical immaturity of the teenage mother, a recent study in Copenhagen suggests that teenage mothers given proper care had the least complications in childbirth (Mednick, Baker, and Sutton-Smith, 1979). The study indicates that the high risk associated with teenage pregnancy may be due to lack of prenatal care rather than young age. No matter what the risks are attributed to, the fact remains that over 550,000 girls age 19 and under are giving birth each year. Of these girls, 10,000 are 10 to 14 years old (U.S. Department of Health and Human Services, 1980). Over 93 percent of girls choose to keep their babies (Zelnick and Kantner, 1978). The effects on the children are devastating. Infants born to teenage mothers often face a life of poverty and neglect because their mothers lack the emotional and financial capability to raise a child.

Health

Good health care for infants and young children is crucial to their chances for healthy and productive lives. Yet over 30 percent of children in the United States receive inadequate medical care and about 25 percent of the children do not receive physical examinations over the course of a year (Advisory Committee on Child Development, 1976). Half the children in this country under age 15 and 90 percent of those under age 5 have never made a single visit to the dentist over their entire childhood (White House Conference on Children, 1970). Despite these statistics and the fact that children constitute one third of our population, only 1 out of 17 federal dollars for health care is spent on children (Keniston, 1977).

Immunization is an easily implemented element of well-child care. Despite our ability to eliminate infectious diseases through immunizations, epidemics continue to occur. The measles epidemics of 1969, 1971, and 1974 resulted from failure of nearly half of the children between the ages of 1 and 4 to get proper inoculations (Knowles, 1977). A recent immunization effort by the Surgeon General resulted in the inoculation of 90 percent of school-age children. However, 2 out of every 5 preschool children are still not immunized against childhood diseases (Edelman, 1980).

Childhood accidents constitute the single major cause of death among children between the ages of 9 and 14 (Furrow, Gruendel, and Zigler, 1979). Of the 22,539 children in this age range who died in 1975, nearly half were killed in accidents. Also in 1975, 28 million accidental injuries occurred among children aged 0 to 16 years. Among Western nations, the United States has the *second* highest rate of childhood deaths due to accidents and is ranked *first* in deaths caused by firearms and poisonings. Motor vehicle accidents are the leading type of accidental death for children of all ages. Yet, with the exception of a still not implemented accident prevention plan (Harmon, Furrow, and Zigler, 1980) approved recently by Dr. Julius Richmond, the Surgeon General, there are few preventive efforts to combat this number one killer and maimer of our young children.

Foster Care

Our complacency as a nation is most evident in the area of foster care. One of the basic tenets of the 1930 Bill of Rights for Children was that every child has a right to a permanent and loving home. Fifty years later we witness some 500,000 children adrift in the U.S. foster care system (Edelman, 1979). The foster care system, supposedly representing temporary care until decisions about permanent placement can be made, subjects children to the impermanency of being placed in one home after another for indefinite periods. In some states, the average time spent in foster care is nearly 5 years (Keniston, 1977). There are reports that 62 percent of children placed in foster care remain out of their own homes for their entire childhood. Only 15 to 25 percent of children placed in foster care return home. The number of children who eventually get adopted is even lower—less than 15 percent (Keniston, 1977).

Removing children from their homes is not necessarily the best solution, nor is it in the best interest of children. In fact, there is growing concern that children placed in foster care suffer permanent emotional damage, or worse. In a recent report in New York City, it was revealed that children in foster care have a death rate twice the national average. Some of the deaths are the result of abuse by foster parents (Lash, Sigal, and Dudzinski, 1980). However, federal dollars are available for a child's room and board away from home, but funds for supportive services such as homemakers or crisis counseling or day care, which could keep the family together and prevent the need for foster care placement, are scarce. With very little money directed at services which might facilitate family reunification or prevent family breakup, many of our children spend a painful journey being shuffled through the maze of our foster care system.

Child Abuse

The facts concerning child abuse and neglect are distressing. It is difficult to quote the exact number of cases of child abuse per year. The available estimates range from a conservative 500,000 (Light, 1973) to 4 million (Gil, 1970). According to the National Center on Child Abuse and Neglect, there are 1 million cases reported per year. Since even the definition of child abuse remains a controversial issue,[1] it comes as no surprise that estimated figures vary greatly. But there is one abusive act that may be measurable objectively—that is, the abusive act which results in the child's death. We can say this with certainty: nearly 2,000 children die each year as a result of abuse and neglect (Martinez, 1977).

Even more distressing are the facts concerning the instances of abuse that occur in America's public institutions—correctional settings, homes for the mentally retarded or otherwise handicapped, and the schools. Documentation of institutional abuse is noted by Blatt and his colleague (Blatt, in press; Blatt and Kaplan, 1966) and by Wooden (1976). Our nation is also supporting child abuse by allowing the barbaric practice of corporal punishment in the schools to continue. The figures of some of our large school systems—for example, Dallas—indicate that tens of thousands of children each year are subjected to physical punishment in the form of paddling (Anderson and Henry, 1976). This form of discipline gives implicit sanction to the use of physical violence within the family. Further, in what amounts to a legal mandate for child abuse, the Supreme Court, in a ruling on a case in which two junior high school

---

1. The research literature on child abuse shows definitions ranging from an emphasis on serious physical abuse (Kempe, C. H., Silverman, F., Steele, B., Droegemueller, W., and Silver, S. The battered child syndrome. *Journal of the American Medical Association,* 1962, *181,* 17–24) to a broader definition which emphasizes maltreatment (Fontana, V. J. *The Maltreated Child: The Maltreated Syndrome in Children* (2nd ed.). Springfield, IL: C. Thomas, 1970). K. T. Alvy, in "Preventing child abuse" (*American Psychologist,* 1975, *30,* 921–928) focuses on the fulfillment of the child's developmental needs.

students received severe beatings, upheld the use of corporal punishment in the schools (Ingraham vs. Wright, 1977). This ruling was made despite our knowledge that over half of child abuse incidents result from overzealous disciplinary actions by parents. If the highest court in the United States condones physical abuse of children, how are we to expect parents to reject this form of discipline?

Day Care

Child care in this nation is a source of a number of problems. The factors in the child care issue are related to both quantity and quality. At the 1970 White House Conference on Children, it was proclaimed that the number one priority for alleviating the problems faced by children and families was quality day care (White House Conference on Children, 1970). Despite this declaration, more than 10 years have passed and there continues to be a need for increased day care services. What is more, we seem unable to impress upon our nation's leaders that we not only need more day care facilities but that we must ensure that those facilities that are in existence provide adequate services.

The need for day care has increased substantially over the past decade as more women have entered the labor force. There are indications that this trend will continue at an even faster pace. The number of children under 6 years whose mothers are working—now 7,166,000—is expected to increase to well over 10 million by the end of this decade (Smith, 1979). In addition, the actual number of young children is expected to increase as the women born during the baby boom era (1946–1964) begin giving birth to their own babies during the next 10 years (Hofferth, 1979). It is estimated that over 50 percent of these mothers will be working by the time their children are 6 years old. A substantial number of them will opt to return to work within the first year after the birth of their infants.

Despite these facts and predictions, representatives of the Carter administration testified in 1979 that there was no need for increased day care services (Martinez, 1979). This statement was made in light of public acknowledgment of the U.S. Bureau of the Census statistic that every school day in this country, nearly 2 million children between the ages of 7 and 13 come home to an empty house (Congressional Record, 1979). These "latchkey" children, so called because they carry their house key on a string around their neck, are left to their own resources to suffer neglect during critical hours of the day. Reports of children encountering burglars or being victimized by molesters are not uncommon. And, in a recent study in Detroit, an investigator discovered that 1/6th of the fires in that city involved an unattended child (Smock, 1977).

While day care facilities are indeed in critically short supply, the quality of group child care in this nation leaves much to be desired. Not much is known about the kind of care children receive in day care since research tends to focus on high quality centers, the least common type of substitute care. However, in a study by the National Council of Jewish Women (Keyserling, 1972), 11 percent of all licensed nonprofit centers were rated as poor in quality; 51 percent were rated fair, 28 percent were rated good, and 9 percent were rated superior. Proprietary centers fared worse: 50 percent were considered poor, 35 percent were fair, 14 percent were good, and 1 percent were superior. In family day care homes, 14 percent were rated poor, 48 percent were rated fair, 31 percent good, and 7 percent were rated superior. These figures may not accurately describe the quality of day care in America since most care is provided in unlicensed homes that are not accountable to public authority. Yet unlicensed settings are not the only such settings that are unmonitored. Even among licensed centers, standards are often lax. Some states, such as New York and Connecticut, have reasonable day care standards that are enforced. But there are other states, for example, Florida and New Mexico, where it is permissible for one adult to take care of up to 10 infants. One has only to think of the difficulties of a mother of twins or triplets to realize that this staff/child ratio is not only not conducive to optimal development, it is downright dangerous. In case of fire, how could one caregiver bring 10 infants to safety?

Efforts to guarantee quality child care in centers across the nation and to enforce uniform standards have been going on for over a decade. After a lengthy moratorium on day care regulation and in the face of considerable opposition, Health and Human Services Secretary Patricia Harris had the courage to approve the Federal Interagency Day Care Requirements (FIDCR) (Federal Register, March 19, 1980). These requirements, representing the absolute minimum standards, imposed nothing on children except protection from fires, nutritious meals, and the right to be cared for by adults who are trained in the principles of child development and recognized as competent caregivers. Yet, several weeks before these requirements were to take effect, their implementation was deferred for yet another year, this time because of so-called budgetary restraints. The decision to defer the requirements was upheld despite a proposal by Senator Cranston that made the budgetary impact of FIDCR negligible (Zigler and Goodman, 1980).

Enforcement of federal day care standards is important in several aspects, especially as these relate to the training of caregivers of infants and young children. The long-term consequences of day care, especially infant day care, are not yet known. Studies conducted over the past decade, however, indicate that the single most important factor in determining children's development is the quality of interaction that they have with the adults in their lives. Children should be reared not only in a safe environment but also in a nurturant environment. We have developed the means to assess caregiver competencies and to credential those caregivers who are competent to take care of children in group situations.[2] But we have yet to implement on a nationwide scale these assessment and credentialing procedures.

Social and Emotional Development

Children today spend less time with their parents or other adults than they did several decades ago. In contrast to children of the 1950s, who encountered a number of adults during the course of a day and who were involved in community activities, many children during the 1970s reported spending most of their time, when not in school, alone or with other children, mainly watching television, eating snacks, and fooling around (Boocock, 1977). Condry and Siman (1974) noted that children today show a greater dependency on their peers than they did a decade ago. They found that attachment to age mates was more influenced by a lack of attention and concern at home than by any positive attraction of the peer group (Condry and Siman, 1976).

What are some of the consequences of these trends? Siman (1973) noted that peer-oriented children have negative views of themselves and their friends, are pessimistic about the future, and are more likely to engage in antisocial behavior. Other investigators relate the rising rate of juvenile crime and the increase in the incidence of childhood depression to the changing way children are growing up. Since 1958, there has been a substantial increase in the number of children with criminal records. What is more, increasingly younger children are involved in serious crimes. In 1975, for example, larceny and burglary accounted for just under 40 percent of all arrests of children under 15; violent crime (aggravated assault, armed robbery, forcible rape, and murder) accounted for 3.3 percent of such arrests (Advisory Committee on Child Development, 1976).

Depression in young children is only now beginning to be recognized so that estimates are difficult to obtain. Kashani and Simonds (1979) estimate that the number of depressed children between the ages of 7 and 12

2. An assessment and credentialing procedure for child care workers has been established by the Child Development Associate Consortium, Inc. (CDAC). CDAC is a nonprofit organization based in Washington, D.C. Since its establishment in 1972, over 7,000 child care workers received the CDA credential, an award signifying competence in child care and knowledge of basic principles of child development.

years in this country is over 400,000, or 1.9 percent of the total number of children in that age range. Albert and Beck (1975) estimate that 33 percent of the population of children between 11 and 15 years experience moderate to severe depression. Suicide may be another indicator of childhood depression. Between 1950 and 1975, the annual suicide rate of white youths between the ages of 15 and 19 increased 171 percent. No other age group had so high a rate of increase. During the same years, the overall white suicide rate increased by only 18 percent (Wynne, 1978).

A Time for Action

Over the course of the International Year of the Child many of the shortfalls outlined above became worse. In large measure, this was due to inflation and inaction, but perhaps our lack of commitment was really the primary cause. Evaluated in these terms, the International Year of the Child can be viewed as a failure.

But let us take another viewpoint. We have come a long way in the process of assessing what we are doing and not doing to optimize the development of our nation's children. In 1979 we were forced to educate each other on the problems facing children and families, and this has resulted in consciousness raising about the unmet needs of children in America. We have garnered vital information. Now is the time for action. The International Year of the Child can serve as our launching pad for greater activity in behalf of children, and, as such, the year may indeed be considered a success. To this end, we want to share with you our vision for child care in the 1980s.

Recommendations

We order our agenda for the 1980s around the social institutions that are most critical in determining the quality of the lives of the children in this country. These institutions, in order of their importance in influencing the lives of children, are, the family, the school, and child care outside the home.

Before we address ourselves to changes that need to be made, we raise a very basic question. That is, will the action be at the federal, state, or local level? While we have come to be dependent on federal initiatives for the many programs begun on behalf of children since the 1960s, it is our belief that the role of the federal government will diminish during this decade. We are in the midst of an era of uncontrollable inflation and Proposition 13 mentality. We cannot afford to wait for federal action. As will become clear in the course of our discussion, any changes to the benefit of children and families will come about through state and local initiatives and through greater involvement in matters pertaining to family life by the private sector.

The Family

The family will remain the first and foremost institution in determining what is going to happen to children. It is imperative, however, that we acknowledge the multiple forms that now constitute a family. Whereas our national policies and rhetoric are directed to the traditional nuclear family where the husband is the breadwinner and the mother the housewife and where there are two or more children living at home, the fact is that fewer the 7 percent of Americans now live in this kind of family arrangement (U.S. Bureau of the Census, 1979). Other arrangements include both parents who are wage earners, with one or more children living at home; married couples with no children, or none living at home; single parent families; unrelated persons living together; and one person living alone.

Families, then, are significantly different today than they were a quarter of a century ago or even a decade ago. There have been deep and far-reaching changes in American society in recent years that have contributed to the changes in family structure. These are significant in that they influence not only the way children are being raised and educated but our attitudes toward young people as well.

These attitudinal changes are reflected in shifting demographics. Because of recent trends, ours has become an aging society, with relatively few children and with mounting numbers of elderly. Twenty-nine percent of today's population is under age 18, in contrast with 34 percent in 1970. Since that year the 25- to 34-year-old group increased by 32 percent, and the number of those over 65 increased by 17 percent. There is an overwhelming trend toward late marriage and childbearing, and an increasing number of couples are choosing to have no children at all (U.S. Bureau of the Census, 1979). During the past decade, the number of children under 15 has decreased by 6.4 million. It is important for us to consider what will be the role of children and youth in an aging society and in an increasingly childless one. Will taxpayers be more caring toward children or will the needs of the young be seen to conflict with adult goals?

The past decade has also been a period of great change in the economic realm. Rampant inflation, sluggish growth, increased energy costs, and balance of payments problems have contributed to pressures on families as well as to people's loss of confidence in the economy. A survey by Yankelovich, Skelly, and White in 1974–1975 found that Americans had less faith in the economy than they previously had and were more fearful of the future. The sluggish economy has also contributed to cutbacks in spending, especially in social services.

Accompanying these changes has been the increase in working mothers. As indicated in an earlier section of this chapter, working mothers now constitute a substantial portion of the labor force and there are indications that the trend will continue, especially in the case of mothers of infants and young children. Women not only constitute a greater proportion of the labor force than ever before, but more and more women have more than one job. Latest statistics reveal that while in 1969 16 percent of the women who worked held more than one job, by 1979 30 percent of the women working held at least two jobs. Eleven percent of these women held two part-time jobs but the remaining 19 percent held two full-time jobs (Brozan, 1980). While changing roles for women contributed to the initial reasons for women joining the labor force, today mothers are working not so much because they want to but because they have to. This has been noted in a recent article by feminist writer Betty Friedan, who contends that women no longer have a choice between staying at home and working, "because it isn't really a free choice when their paycheck is needed to cover the family bills each month; [and] when women must look to their jobs and professions for the security and status their mothers sought in marriage alone" (Friedan, 1979, p. 94).

Another trend reflected in the statistics cited in the beginning of this section is the increase in single parent families. Single parents grew by about 1 million (or 40 percent) between 1960 and 1970 and by nearly 2 million between 1970 and 1978 (Norton, 1979). The majority of single parent families are headed by low-income women, although a small portion is headed by men. One reason cited for the increase in single parent families is the escalating divorce rate. After divorce, the most rapidly growing category of single parenthood, especially since 1970, involves unmarried women (Advisory Committee on Child Development, 1976).

Preceding these recent social changes is the demise of the extended family. With transition from an agrarian to an industrial civilization, the family's role as an economic unit was gradually eroded. Work roles for men and women became more sharply differentiated and children, once an asset in terms of their productivity, came to be regarded as liabilities. At the same time, industry required a mobile labor force. As a result, and in the process of multiple moves, the extended family was lost as a resource in time of trouble and as a natural teaching and socializing agent. Families no longer had immediate access to the experience and wisdom of their elders, nor the support systems for child care and education which they could once count on.

Not only are families separated from their kin but they also face increased isolation and alienation within their own communities. Friendly neighborhood stores have given way to interstate highways, impersonal supermarkets, and shopping malls. With the advent of desegregation and busing, schools no longer serve children from the same community. Having very little in common, families rarely interact with their neighbors. According to a recent survey (Yankelovich et al., 1975), these changes have resulted in serious psychological and emotional problems among people of all socioeconomic levels.

For the family to remain viable during these times of transition and in the face of changing demographic and socioeconomic conditions, we must commit ourselves to supporting and strengthening family life. An important element missing in families today is support, which is perhaps why grass roots help groups proliferated during the 1970s. In numerous communities people joined groups for feminists, single parents, divorced parents, abusive parents, battered spouses, and so on. Some groups depended on their membership for support; others sought the advice of "experts" who ran such programs as reality therapy, sensitivity training, parent effectiveness training, and so on.

With this in mind, every single one of our recommendations for the 1980s is consistent with the notion of family support systems (Zigler and Seitz, in press, a; Caplan, 1978). For the remainder of the chapter, we will focus on several concrete and inexpensive ways to achieve this. It is imperative that we realize, however, that these are but suggestions. Some may work out well, and some may not. It is important that as a nation we begin what Campbell refers to as an "experimental approach to social reform" (Campbell, 1969). With such an approach we try out new programs and learn from the experience whether or not they are effective. If they are, we retain them. If not, we modify or discard them and try new programs.

Referral Centers

One of our suggestions in support of family life involves developing referral information centers in each community. There are several options available—for example, day care centers, food stamps, community legal and health services—which families are often not aware of. Information referral centers would provide the links between families and community services. A network of such services would also provide us with statistics—how many people inquire about day care? What are some of the concerns parents have? With people all over the country showing up at these referral centers inquiring about day care facilities, we doubt that any administration would again proclaim that there is no need for increased day care services in this country.

Home Visitor Programs

Another suggestion is the home visitor program. We are not referring here to a home visitor program for the poor but rather a program for all families regardless of their socioeconomic status. Families today function in isolation. They experience a sense of aloneness, alienation, and helplessness. We know that this isolation and sense of helplessness are contributing factors in many cases of child abuse (Helfer and Kempe, 1972; Maden and Wrench, 1977). With the home visitor program, families who wished to could have someone visit them occasionally to discuss how they were doing, what they might need, and so forth, and could provide them with emotional support and information. For the home visitor program we could utilize an important resource—this nation's senior citizens. Such home visitor programs could prove to be useful not only to families but also to many older retired people who are themselves isolated and lonely. There are several examples of successful home visitor programs. One is Henry Kempe's program in Denver (Kempe and Helfer, 1972); the other is the Home Start program which was started at the instigation of the senior author during his tenure as director of the Office of Child Development (Scott, 1974; Zigler and Valentine, 1979). The Child and Family Resource Program, referred to in greater detail in a later section of this chapter, also includes several home visitors or "family advocates." These individuals work to establish a close, trusting relationship with each family and to serve as resource persons who can advise families of services available in the community (Zigler and Seitz, 1980).[3]

Foster Care

Next to support of the family we recommend that changes be instituted in our present foster care system. Our recommendations are that as many children as possible be kept at home and preventive services to families at risk, as adoption subsidies, be made in order to ensure a permanent home for children. Preventive services and adoption subsidies are cost-effective. Out-of-home care for a child between the ages of 2 and 19 years is $100,000. The alternative we recommend is cheaper. The Children's Bureau, for example, has developed several models for preventive services that have been instituted in several communities (e.g., Burt, 1976). These models show conclusively that minimal financial support to families in times of need as well as other services, coupled with counseling

3. For more information on the early childhood and family education programs in Minnesota, refer to "A Policy Study of Issues Related to Early Childhood and Family Education. A Report to the Minnesota Legislature. January 15, 1979." Available from the Minnesota Council on Quality Education, 722 Capitol Square Building, St. Paul, MN 55101.

and follow-up support, can substantially reduce the number of children placed in foster care. The money now spent on foster care and institutional placement of children should be channeled to these types of family support services.

Subsidizing adoption is also important if we are to achieve permanent homes for children, especially older children, black children, or retarded or otherwise handicapped children. There are many fine families who would adopt such children if only they could afford to. Instead of spending money on foster care or institutionalization of these children, why not subsidize their adoption? Senator Cranston, among others, proposed this idea in legislation to provide for increased adoption assistance (Cranston, 1979).

The School

The second most important socializing institution is the American school. Consistent with the notion of family support systems, we envision that the school of the future will serve children before they are born. Research studies are indicative of the importance of early intervention and our ability to prevent some handicapping conditions. If parents enroll in the school during pregnancy, they could receive support and education relevant to prenatal care that would prevent unnecessary disabilities in children. After birth, parents and children would continue to receive educational services that would further enhance adult–infant interaction and promote optimal development of the child. Should there be anything wrong with a child—speech impediment, or hearing difficulty, for example—these would be identified during the preschool years and help provided before the problem compounded itself to the detriment of both the child and the family. We have available to us screening and other identification devices, as well as programs for handicapped infants and young children. Yet children with disabilities often go undiagnosed until they reach school age simply because their families do not come into contact with an institution such as the school until then.

The types of school services we are referring to are already in existence. The Brookline Early Education Project in Massachusetts is one example (Pearson and Nicol, 1977). Also, many states are cognizant of the school's failure to help preschool and younger children and are developing new programs to combat the problem. The Minnesota Legislature, through the Minnesota Council on Quality Education, has been funding pilot early childhood and family education (ECFE) programs in Minnesota elementary schools. By law, the programs have geographic boundaries to their service area. All families and expectant parents of children o through kindergarten within a program's service area are eligible to participate.

Services offered by the programs include parent/family education, concurrent child development activities, family resource libraries, early health screening and referral, parenting education for adolescents and expectant parents, and coordination of community services for families.

Through these types of services, there occurs a natural situation wherein parents and schools act in partnership. As it stands now, parents do not have to send children to school until the child reaches the age of 5 or 6. By that time, school is viewed as an alien and often hostile environment. Teachers and parents are often at odds or, at best, parents are unaware of what schools are trying to achieve. An important outcome of Headstart and other early childhood education programs of the 1960s has been the realization that the parent is the child's primary teacher. Any help schools try to give children must be in conjunction with the parent if it is to be at all effective (Bronfenbrenner, 1975; Valentine and Stark, 1979).

Education for Parenthood

Besides reaching out to would-be parents and parents of young children, schools should also offer education for parenthood classes to students of all ages. With the demise of the extended family and the increase in two-paycheck families, children no longer benefit from learning about child-rearing and development. To compensate, we should include in school curricula courses relevant to the role and responsibility of parents. Such courses should also offer options of internship in child care. For example, high school students could be sent out to work at Head Start programs and day care centers. There are Education for Parenthood model programs instituted in 2,000 school districts that include internship experiences in child care. These were developed by the U.S. Office of Child Development in 1972.

Corporal Punishment

As we mentioned earlier in the chapter, corporal punishment in schools is not only a barbaric form of discipline, it also serves to further child abuse in the home. We recommend that the practice be abolished. There is absolutely nothing in favor of corporal punishment. Studies are conclusive in indicating that corporal punishment is the least effective way of shaping human behavior (National Education Association Task Force on Corporal Punishment, 1972). Furthermore, it escalates aggression in children and promotes violent tendencies, factors which may contribute to the already rampant crime among our nation's youth. Many states require teachers to report parents suspected of child abuse. Yet very few states have statutes that make schools accountable to the parents by banning corporal punishment and requiring school personnel to use other forms of discipline.

Child Care Outside the Home

The institution which overlaps the school (for the purposes of the discussion we refer to it as a separate institution) is child care outside the home. As we have seen, more and more women are entering the work world and childrearing, once the responsibility of the family, is increasingly delegated to babysitters and other nonrelatives in publicly supported or private child care facilities, day care centers, and family day care homes.

While the need for more day care facilities remains acute, there are other problems associated with child care outside the home. We shall offer suggestions to the solution of some of these problems in two separate, albeit overlapping sections, one dealing with publicly supported programs for low-income families, and the other dealing with the child care needs of all families, regardless of income or structure. The latter section will be discussed under the heading of work and family life.

Publicly Supported Child Care and Early Intervention Programs

Federal spending on child care amounts to more than $2 billion a year. This includes expenditures for Head Start and other related early childhood programs (e.g., Home Start) and subsidizing day care facilities for low-income families through Title XX of the Social Security Act. Intervention programs during the preschool years may prevent unnecessary retardation and/or other complications to development later in the life of children. While some of the programs, Head Start in particular, have been shown to work well (Palmer and Anderson, 1979; Zigler and Seitz, in press, a,b) and are cost-effective, only a small percentage of those families eligible for services actually send their children. One of the problems associated with publicly supported programs is, then, the need for more services to accommodate the numbers of low-income families requiring such services. It may not be realistic to expect that all those eligible receive some sort of preschool experience or day care placement, but priority should be given to those who are most in need, including children of bilingual background, children of single parents, and handicapped children. These children are at a high risk for developmental delays and associated learning and other disabilities, so services should be offered to them regardless of income.

Child and Family Resource Programs

The family support system of the future may be exemplified by the Child and Family Resource Program (CFRP), which has been experimentally

458   EDWARD ZIGLER AND MATIA FINN

implemented in 11 locales across the nation. This model approach to early
intervention has been praised by the Comptroller General in a report
(1979) as comprehensive and cost-effective. Briefly described, CFRPs are
designed to offer a variety of services tailored to the unique developmental
needs of children. The services are provided from the prenatal period
through the child's eighth year and include health, nutrition, and education components. What is unique about CFRPs is that not only do they
offer comprehensive support services for the entire family as well as the
child, but that they utilize existing community services and act as a referral
system and linkage between families and public agencies. According to the
Comptroller General's report (1979), the benefits of CFRPs include better
preventive health care and nutrition for young children; rapid assistance to
families during crises, correction of problems such as inadequate housing,
and general improvement in overall quality of life.

Child Care Professionals
Another important change, already in the offing, is the professionaliza-
tion of child care workers. This applies not only to federally subsidized
centers but to all child care centers. The most important aspect in determining how a child is going to develop rests in the nature of that child's
interaction with adults (Abt Associates, 1979). Providing optimal care to
a group of 15 or 20 children is not as simple as caring for 1 or 2 children
in a home setting. Those who work with children in group situations
should be trained in the principles of child development and should be
cognizant of their impact on the children's growth and socialization. It is
imperative, if we are to have quality child care, that we spend additional
funds on training child care workers.

   In the same vein, parents must be assured that their children are taken
care of by competent adults. To this end, the senior author in 1972 was
supported by several national organizations concerned with child development and welfare who sought the establishment of a consortium
whose sole focus was to upgrade the quality of care children receive.
Known as the Child Development Associate Consortium (CDAC), this
nonprofit organization, with the help of the nation's leading psychologists and early childhood educators, developed an assessment and credentialing system for child care workers (Ward, 1976). Those child care
workers who receive the CDAC credential are regarded as competent
to take care of preschool children in group situations. Since 1972 close
to 7,000 child care workers have received the CDAC credential. While
significant, the number is low given our needs today. We not only need
a greater number of CDACs, but the concept itself should be expanded
to meet the needs of our changing society. We need, for example, to

develop a similar assessment and credentialing system for infant day care workers, school-age day care workers, and family day care "mothers."

The organizational structure of the CDAC should also reflect social changes over the years. In order to mobilize efforts toward professionalizing child care, HEW, as the department was then known, funded the Consortium. Although it is a nonprofit organization and thus able to develop other means of fund raising, the consortium remains operative at the mercy, so to speak, of federal grants (Zigler and Kagan, 1980). The Consortium should be financially independent. We suggest that it reorganize as a mandated corporation, much on the same lines as public television. Although this change would still entail developing an aggressive fund-raising program, the Consortium would nonetheless have a financial security granted to it by Congress and it would operate independently of any government agency.

Regulating Day Care Centers

Regulating responsibility that falls within the realm of the federal government is the regulation of day care centers and the establishment of national day care standards that would be adhered to by all child care facilities. Despite an increase in federal involvement in day care in the last decade and the $2 billion plus price tag that it entails, the principle of federal responsibility for day care has not yet been established. The history of moratoriums and revisions of Federal Interagency Day Care Requirements are explained in other publications (Beck, 1979; Cohen and Zigler, 1977; Zigler and Heller, 1980). Suffice it to add here that child care advocates have been fighting for very basic standards that would do no more than ensure compliance with health and safety codes and a reasonable staff:child ratio. These have not been forthcoming for over 10 years. As mentioned earlier in this chapter, a victory was scored recently with the announcement by Health and Human Services Secretary Patricia Harris that implementation of the revised standards would take effect in October 1980 (Federal Register, March 19, 1980). Several weeks after the Secretary's announcement, a congressional finance committee delayed FIDCR implementation for yet another year, this time due to budgetary reasons. There is considerable dispute as to how much, if anything, will actually be saved by this delay. In the meantime, children and families suffer the consequences. It is imperative that the press and the public impress upon this nation's leaders that day care is not an issue to be treated lightly. Day care should be tailored to the needs of the many children it serves. (Zigler and Goodman, 1980).

Work and Family Life

With the two-paycheck family the norm rather than the exception, and the increase in single parenthood, the impact of the workplace on family life becomes an issue of concern. The relationship between the two institutions has been the subject of several recent studies which emphasize an important point: work and family life are not separate worlds as has been assumed but are, rather, interdependent and overlapping, with functions and behavioral rules within each system influencing processes within the other (Brim and Abeles, 1975; Kanter, 1977).

When there are children present, life for the dual-career family is stressful. Day care arrangements must be made for the infant and preschool child; before and after school facilities have to be found for the older child; school vacations and days when the child is sick bring with them the need for yet other solutions. Since worker satisfaction and productivity have been found to be a function of family stability and other processes within the family system (cf. Kanter, 1977), it behooves industry to offer relevant services and benefits that would facilitate family life.

The role of industry in facilitating family life has been slow to develop. However, some of our suggestions with regard to work and family life have been tried by several of the major corporations. These include changes in the work structure to accommodate flexible working arrangements, part-time work opportunities, and job sharing. Companies are required by law to offer maternity leaves (Bureau of Business Practice, 1979). At best, these constitute 3 months, although school teachers, for example are able to take up to a year's leave of absence without pay in order to stay with their newborn infants. Some school systems offer maternity and paternity leave so as not to exclude the father from childrearing. However, as a nation we lag far behind other countries. According to Kamerman and Kahn (1976), European nations' pronatal policies include 6 to 12 months maternity or paternity leave with pay in order to facilitate childbearing, and provisions for child care are made when both parents work.

Several major corporations have instituted a variety of day care programs in support of their employees. Stride Rite Corporation, in Boston, has a company-based day care center as one of its employee benefits packages. Employees pay at the rate of 10 percent of their salary for the day care to a maximum of $25 a week (McIntyre, 1978). Levi Strauss and Company, in San Francisco, after 7 years of research and experimentation, concluded that day care services should be close to where people live rather than where they work (McIntyre, 1978). As a result of these findings Levi Strauss's policy is to "advocate the concept" of home day care. However, the company, while it is supporting research on the issue, does not have a reimbursement program for employees who use family day care homes.

Since company-based day care centers may not be entirely satisfactory and subsidizing such centers is expensive, several businesses could together support programs central to where their employees work. This would prove convenient to the employees as well as inexpensive because several business would contribute to the cost of one center. Part of the cost for child care might be paid by employees with the rest subsidized either by companies or unions. Children from low-income families who attend the facility could be subsidized by the state or federal government.

Industry could also support other activities that would promote interdependence among families within neighborhoods. For example, a PTA block-mother type arrangement (Mead, 1970) wherein parents take turns looking after children could be instituted. Such an arrangement would only work in conjunction with flexitime or other types of restructuring of the traditional work week. This service would be important not only in alleviating the stresses families currently face but also in promoting neighborhood stability.

Another option might be supporting a referral center or a network of senior citizens who could serve, for pay, as housekeepers or child care workers. This could be done in a center-based location or through referring families in need to those older citizens who wish to work in such capacities. This service might prove especially useful in alleviating the school-age day care problem, since it involves fewer hours per day of care, except at times when children are sick or vacationing. With grandparents usually not in the same locality, the use of senior citizens could also add another important dimension to the lives of children.

Support from Philanthropy

Much of the literature calling for business support of family life is related to industry's involvement through restructuring of working arrangements and including other relevant services as part of employee benefits. Industries could also channel support dollars through their corporate funding program (Zigler and Anderson, 1979). By law, corporations can generally donate as much as 5 percent of their net profits for charitable causes. They choose, however, to contribute less than 1 percent (Cmiel and Levy, 1980), despite the fact that these contributions are tax deductible. Furthermore, money that is donated by industry is channeled to sources that have little to do with family life. According to a recent analysis on corporate philanthropy (Cmiel and Levy, 1980), 49.1 percent of corporations changed their policies to reflect the impact of inflation and the retrenchment of government programs. Of those listing some changes, the most commonly cited changes were increased aid to higher education followed by cultural organizations. This means not so much a change as a reaffirmation of traditional priorities of corporate philanthropy (Finn, 1978). In terms of urban programs and community groups (these include children's programs) that might lose government programs, Cmiel and Levy note that "expressed corporate interest has not yet been translated into action." This is unfortunate considering the investment, in terms of employee satisfaction and productivity, corporations would be making if they provided financial aid in support of family life.

Conclusion

We have outlined in this chapter several ideas that could be tried out in response to problems facing children and families. It would be unrealistic to expect at these times of financial restraints revolutionary changes that involve eliminating societal stresses through the provision of jobs and adequate housing for everyone or the restructuring of our entire economy, as has been suggested by some writers (e.g., Keniston, 1977). We must acknowledge, however, that new patterns of family life that affect all people, but especially our children, are just now beginning to emerge. The social transition we are experiencing is difficult: a simple response is not the solution. Rather, a broad spectrum of options is needed, options that may be tried out without vast organizational expenditures.

Our nation cannot be transformed into a child-oriented society overnight. Progress and changes are gradual processes, and the first steps are undoubtedly the most difficult. The International Year of the Child has brought us to the threshold of our first steps toward becoming a nation that is concerned with and responsible for the optimal development of children. Parents, communities, and industry must now work together to ensure that our most valuable resource, our children, receive the care they deserve.

References

Abt. Associates. *Final report of the national day care study: Children at the center.* Executive Summary. Cambridge, MA: March 1979. (Contract No. HEW 105-74-1100).

Advisory Committee on Child Development. *Toward a national policy for children and families.* Washington, D.C.: National Academy of Sciences, 1976.

Albert, N., and Beck, A. T. Incidence of depression in early adolescence: A preliminary study. *Journal of Youth and Adolescence,* 1975, 4, 301–307.

Anderson, R., and Henry, D. *A literature review and analysis on the use of corporal punishment in the care of children.* Austin, TX: Center for Social Work Research, University of Texas, 1976.

Beck, R. Child care: Story of neglect. *American Federationist,* 1979, *86,* 9–13.

Blatt, B. The pariah industry: A diary from purgatory and other places. In G. Gerbner, C. J. Ross, and E. Zigler (Eds.), *Child abuse: An agenda for action.* New York: Oxford University Press, in press.

Blatt, B., and Kaplan, F. *Christmas in purgatory.* Boston: Allyn and Bacon, 1966.

Boocock, S. S. A cross-cultural analysis of the child care system. In L. G. Katz (Ed.), *Current topics in early childhood.* Vol. 1. New Jersey: Ablex, 1977.

Brimm, O. G., Jr., and Abeles, R. P. Work and personality in the middle years. *Social Science Research Council Items.* 1975, *29,* 29–33.

Bronfenbrenner, U. Is early intervention effective? In H. J. Leichter (Ed.), *The family as educator.* New York: Teacher's College Press, Columbia University, 1975.

Brozan, N. Women now hold 30 percent of 2nd jobs. *New York Times,* June 24, 1980, B6.

Bureau of Business Practice. *Fair employment practice guidelines,* 1979, 170(9).

Burt, M. R. The comprehensive emergency services system: Expanding services to children and families. *Children Today,* 1976, 5(2), 2–5.

Campbell, D. T. Reforms as experiments. *American Psychologist,* 1969, *24,* 409–429.

Caplan, G. Family support systems in a changing world. In E. J. Antony and C. Chiland (Eds.), *The child in his family.* Vol. 5: *Children in a changing world.* New York: Wiley, 1978.

Cmiel, K., and Levy, S. *Corporate giving in Chicago: 1980.* Chicago: Donors Forum Library, 1980.

Cohen, D. J., and Zigler, E. Federal day care standards: Rationale and recommendations. *American Journal of Orthopsychiatry,* 1977, *47,* 456–465.

Comptroller General of the United States. *Report to the Congress: Early childhood and family development programs improve the quality of life for low-income families.* Washington, D.C.: U.S. Government Accounting Office, February 6, 1979. (Document No. (HRD) 79–40).

Condry, J. C., and Siman, M. A. Characteristics of peer and adult-oriented children. *Journal of Marriage and the Family,* 1974, *36,* 543–544.

Condry, J. C., and Siman, M. A. *An experimental study of adult versus peer orientation.* Unpublished manuscript, Cornell University, 1976.

Congressional Record. January 15, 1979, S76–77.

Cranston, A. (Testimony). U.S. Congress. Senate Committee on Finance, Subcommittee on Public Assistance. *Proposals related to social and child welfare services, adoption assistance and foster care,* Ninety-Sixth Congress, September 24, 1979.

Edelman, M. W. Children instead of ships. *New York Times,* May 14, 1979.

Edelman, M. W. Newsletter distributted by Children's Defense Fund. June 1980.

Finn, M. Focus on foundation giving: Education. *The Philanthropy Monthly,* 1978, *11,* 20.

Friedan, B. Feminism takes a new turn. *The New York Times Magazine,* November 18, 1979, pp. 40, 92–106.

Furrow, D., Gruendel, J., and Zigler, E. *Protecting America's children from accidental injury and death. An overview of the problem and an agenda for action.* Unpublished manuscript, Yale University, 1979.

Gil, D. G. *Violence against children: Physical child abuse in the United States.* Cambridge, MA: Harvard University Press, 1970.

Harmon, C., Furrow, D., and Zigler, E. Childhood accidents: An overview of the problem and a call for action, *SRCD Newsletter,* Spring 1980.

Helfer, R. E. and Kempe, C. H. (Eds.). *Helping the battered child and his family.* Philadelphia: Lippincott, 1972.

Hofferth, S. L. Day care in the next decade: 1980–1990. *Journal of Marriage and the Family,* 1979, *41,* 649–657.

Kamerman, S. B., and Kahn, A. J. *European family policy currents: The question of families with very young children.* Unpublished manuscript, Columbia University, School of Social Work, 1976.

Kanter, R. M. *Work and family in the United States: A critical review and agenda for research and policy.* New York: Russell Sage Foundation, 1977.

Kashani, J., and Simonds, J. F. The incidence of depression in children. *Amrican Journal of Psychiatry,* 1979, *136,* 1203–1205.

Kempe, C. H., and Helfer, R. E. Innovative therapeutic approaches. In R. E. Helfer and C.H. Kempe (Eds.), *Helping the battered child and his family.* Philadelphia: Lippincott, 1972.

Keniston, K. *All our children.* New York: Harcourt, Brace, Jovanovich, 1977.

Keyserling, M. D. *Windows on day care.* New York: National Council of Jewish Women, 1972.

Knowles, J. H. (Ed.). *Doing better and feeling worse. Health in the United States.* New York: W. W. Norton, 1977.

Lash, T. W., Sigal, H., and Dudzinski, D. *State of the child: New York City (11).* New York: Foundation for Child Development, 1980.

Light, R. Abused and neglected children in America: A study of alternative policies. *Harvard Educational Review,* 1973, *43,* 556–598.

Maden, M. F., and Wrench, D. F. Significant findings in child abuse research. *Victimology,* 1977, *2,* 196–224.

Martinez, A. (Testimony). U.S. Congress. House Committee on Education and Labor, Subcommittee on Select Education. *Proposed extension of the Child Abuse Prevention and Treatment Act,* Ninety-Fifth Congress, March 11, 1977.

Martinez, A. (Testimony). U.S. Congress. Senate Committee on Labor and Human Resources, Subcommittee on Child and Human Development. *Child Care Act of 1979,* Ninety-Sixty Congress, February 21, 1979.

McIntyre, K. J. Day Care: An employer benefit, too. *Business Insurance,* December 11, 1978, pp. 11–36.

Mead, M. Working mothers and their children. *Childhood Education,* 1970, *47,* 66–71.

Mednick, B. R., Baker, R.L., and Sutton-Smith, B. *Teenage pregnancy and perinatal mortality.* Unpublished manuscript, study supported by the National Institute of Child Health and Human Development, Grant No. 75-7-060, 1979.

National Education Association Task Force on Corporal Punishment. *Report of the task force on corporal punishment.* Washington, D.C.: National Education Association, 1972.

Norton, A. Portrait of the one-parent family. *The National Elementary Principal,* 1979, *59,* 32–35.

Palmer, F.H., and Andersen, L.W. Long-term gains from early intervention: Findings from longitudinal studies. In E. Zigler and J. Valentine (Eds.), *Project Head Start: A legacy of the war on poverty.* New York: The Free Press, 1979.

Pearson, D. E. , and Nicol, E.H. *The fourth year of the Brookline Early Education Project: A report of progress and plans.* Unpublished report, 1977, Brookline Early Education Project, 987 Kent Street, Brookline, MA 02146.

Scott, R. Research and early childhood: The Home Start Project. *Child Welfare,* 1974, *53,* 112–119.

Siman, M. A. *Peer group influence during adolesence: A study of 41 naturally existing friendship groups.* Doctoral Dissertation, Cornell University, 1973.

Smith, R. E. (Ed.). *The subtle revolution: Women at work.* Washington, D.C.: The Urban Institute, 1979.

Smock, S. M. *The children: The shapes of child care in Detroit.* Detroit: Wayne State University Press, 1977.

U.S. Bureau of the Census. *Current Population Reports.* Series P-23, No. 84. Washington, D.C.: U.S. Department of Commerce, 1979.

U.S. Department of Health, Education and Welfare. *Monthly Vital Statistics Report.* Provisional Statistics, June 30, 1976, *24,* 13.

U.S. Department of Health and Human Services. *Monthly Vital Statistics Report.* Advanced Report, Final Natality Statistics 1978, April 28, 1980, *29,* 1 (supp.).

Valentine, J., and Stark, E. The social context of parent involvement in Head Start. In E. Zigler and J. Valentine (Eds.), *Project Head Start: A legacy of the war on poverty.* New York: The Free Press, 1979.

Ward, E. H. CDA: Credentialing for day care. *Voice for Children,* 1976, *9,* 15.

White House Conference on Children. *Report to the President.* Washington, D.C.: U.S. Government Printing Office, 1970.

Wooden, K. *Weeping in the playtime of others.* New York: McGraw-Hill, 1976.

Wynne, E. A. Behind the discipline problem: Youth suicide as a measure of alienation. *Phi Delta Kappan,* 1978, *54,* 307–315.

Yankelovich, Skelly, White, Inc. *The General Mills American family report 1974–1975.* Minneapolis: General Mills, 1975.

Zelnick, M., and Kantner, J. First pregnancies to women aged 15 to 19: 1971 and 1976. *Family Planning Perspectives,* 1978, *10,* 11–20.

Zigler, E., and Anderson, K. Foundation support in the child and family life field. *The Philanthropy Monthly,* 1979, *12,* 12–14.

Zigler, E., and Goodman, J. On day care standards—again. *The Networker: Newsletter of the Bush Programs in Child Development and Social Policy.* New Haven, CT: 1980, *2*(1).

Zigler, E., and Heller, K. A. Day care standards approach critical juncture. *Day Care and Early Education,* 1980, *7,* 7–8; 47.

Zigler, E., and Kagan, S. L. *The Child Development Association: Has the 1970 challenge been met?* Unpublished manuscript, Yale University, 1980.

Zigler, E., and Seitz, V. Social policy implications of research on intelligence. In R. J. Sternberg (Ed.), *Handbook of human intelligence.* New York: Cambridge University Press, in press. (a)

Zigler, E., and Seitz, V. *Early Childhood Intervention Programs: A re-analysis.* Submitted for publication. (b)

Zigler, E., and Valentine, J. (Eds.). *Project Head Start: A legacy of the war on poverty.* New York: The Free Press, 1979.

On Quantifying the Intended Effects of Interventions:

A Proposed Theory of the Environment

Sandra Scarr

Intervention programs are intended to change people's lives in ways that resource managers believe will, in the long run, benefit society and not just those who receive the intervention. Let us be realistic, intervention programs are supposed to have payoffs, not just for the participants but for the larger society, who will not have to pay for these people in the future or at least will pay less for them than if the intervention had not taken place. Occasionally, our moralism gets in the way of our economics, as in the anti-Medicaid abortion forces, but generally intervention programs are supposed to be cost-effective in the long-run. Effective schooling is supposed to create employables and prevent crime; maternal and child health is supposed to reduce birth defects, perinatal trauma, and the welfare load of the lives of the participants, but that is not the major economic consideration. In a capitalist society, the resources of some (you and me) are used to improve the functioning of other individuals or organizations who are perceived to function less well than is acceptable to those who make decisions about resource allocation. Resources are limited by the political allocation process. Poverty is not likely to be abolished in my lifetime, because the "haves" are unlikely to share their affluence and influence in a massive redistribution of resources with the "have-nots." Thus, choices must be made in the allocation of limited resources to those in need. How best to meet their needs?

As Kiesler (1979) pointed out in her article on federal research policy, in the fields of education and welfare the recipients of interventions are generally incompetent to make wise decisions about the allocation of any resources that might be given to them, so that programs for children and the poor most often provide services, not direct allocations of resources. In service programs, of course, the primary beneficiaries of the resources are the salaried professionals who deliver the services, but that is another paper.

Personally, my standard has been to evaluate the effects of a specific intervention program against the benefits of handing the money directly to the people for whom the intervention is designed. Very few interventions pass the test.

Being rational interventionists who work within the system, however, let us accept for the moment social definitions of how and why to intervene. The question then becomes, "Which services will yield the largest *intended* benefits for the fewest resources?"

Intended Change

I must digress a moment to discuss the notion of *intended* changes. The contrast is, of course, to unintended or unanticipated change. In medicine and in cultural anthropology there is appreciation of the perverse nature of interventions: there are intended effects and then there are unintended or side effects. Because both the body and societies are organized systems, one cannot intervene in just one aspect of that organization without changing other aspects that are functionally or structurally related to the site of the intended effect. Drugs that are intended to lower blood pressure in hypertensives, for example, may have effects on alertness or the digestive tract. It is not difficult to think of the effects of psychoactive drugs that make the treatment of anxiety or psychoses problematic.

In cultural anthropology, one memorable example is the introduction of the wagon to the Papago Indians. The roles of men and women and the social organization of the group were profoundly changed by the new technology. Although the intended effect was on economic efficiency, the wagon relieved women of water carrying but they no longer used the well as a place to gather for social support and exchange.

Psychologists most often look to the immediate environment as the source of the "problem" and at intended changes of interventions. Although I cannot here elaborate on this larger context of intervention studies, because I want to elaborate on the system of persons and environments, I think we must always be aware that intended effects are not likely to be the only or even the primary outcomes of interventions. In a current intervention project, we are trying to look for possible negative effects of the intervention on the mother's self-esteem, even though the intervention is intended to teach her to be a more effective teacher of her young child. What effects might there be on the target child's siblings and on the neighbors, whose children are not included in the intervention?

Quantification and the Intervention Fallacy

Given some agreed-upon goals for educational or social change, what program will produce the largest intended gain for the least cost? I suggest that this question is rarely asked because we do not know how to quantify the effects of educational and social interventions. And the reason that we do not is that we have no theory of environmental effects that is more than *naive* environmentalism—a belief that *all* differences among people arise from the cumulative effects of their learning experiences. If we really believe this, then the payoffs for making everyone's environments from the earliest months of life just like those of people who turn out to be what we value will be enormous. All we have to do is spread early stimulation of the middle-class variety, preschool education of the university nursery school kind, and schooling in classrooms like that which occurs in the wealthiest suburbs and private schools. While this program might be expensive, it would be extremely cost-effective, because according to naive environmental theory it would eliminate nearly all reading problems, behavior disorders, mental illness, retardation, criminality, and poverty. After all, the most advantaged environments produce people with very low rates of these undesirable characteristics.

However, as Richard Weinberg and I (1978) have noted:

In its baldest form, naive environmentalism has led us into an intervention fallacy. By assuming that all of the variance in behavior was environmentally determined, we have blithely promised a world of change that we have not delivered, at great cost to the participants, the public, and ourselves. The fallacy runs like this: if people who do X without our intervention have more desirable outcomes than people who do not do X, then we should persuade, or compel, all people to do X. This is unwise, because some of the reasons for the naturally occurring differences between those who do and do not do X are not just environmental differences. Many of these seemingly environmental variations are actually genetic differences or gene-environment correlations. People who are different do things differently.

But here is the most costly part of the intervention fallacy: the erroneous belief that small variations in environments within the "human range" have meaningfully different outcomes for children. If we observe that professional families take their children to the theatre more often than working-class families, or hang mobiles above their cribs more frequently, some social scientists feel justified in recommending to everyone that they take in plays frequently, rather than play baseball in the backyard, or hang mobiles over the crib, rather than carry the baby about wherever they go. Since these are the child-rearing practices of the professional class, whose children excell at IQ tests and in school, all parents are advised to alter their child-rearing practices to follow suit. *It has not been demonstrated that these variations in child rearing are functionally different in their effects on the children,* and we argue that most humane environmental practices, imposed by an "omniscient" professional class.

We can do a better job of designing and implementing effective intervention programs, if we know which variations in the environment make a difference and which ones do not. We can shift our resources to the improvement of those circumstances that have clear, environmentally deleterious effects on people. Many of these we know: we do not have to do research to know that hunger is not good for children, or that child abuse leaves scars. But there are many other marginal and less obvious practices and conditions that we can judge only from sophisticated research on the effects of those environments. So, it is important to know what aspects of the environment have consequences for behavioral differences, and which ones are only apparent variations, based on cultural preferences, genetic differences, or on gene-environment correlations. People deserve respect for self-expression and their own modes of child rearing, unless there is a clear environmental reason to intervene. Behavior genetic methods will help us to gain a far clearer understanding of which environmental variables to worry about. (Scarr and Weinberg, 1978, p. 690)

Theoretical Considerations

There is a problem for intervention studies of separating the effects of environmental differences from those of genetic differences and genotype-environment correlations. Why do we care? Because the amount and kinds of malleability differ depending upon the source of differences. I want, first, to redefine those terms.

Environmental effects.

An example of an environmental effect would be lead poisoning, which damages children's brains. Lead affects all children badly, and the remedy is to remove lead from the environment. This does not mean that all children are affected to the same degree by the same lead concentrations in their brains. There are probably genotype-environment interactions for everything one can think of, but the problem of lead poisoning can be remedied for everyone by removal of lead from paints and auto exhaust, for example. There is no evidence that I know that lead is good for anyone's brain development. If there were, then removing all lead would be less advantageous for some, as in the case of gene-environment interaction in phenylketonuria. Children with the defective enzyme develop better under very low phenylalanine conditions, whereas those with normal enzyme function are harmed by very low phenylalanine diets. On the average, it is important to have phenylalanine in the infant diet as an essential protein, but a very few infants are poisoned by it. One can find many examples of this kind of interaction in allergies and specific responses to environmental agents, such as fava beans, herbs, and medicines. Disordinal interactions as shown in Figure 1 are rare, I think, but *individual responses* to many specific environments do differ sufficiently to constitute gene-environment interaction. There are also "main effects", in the sense that richer, more stimulating, and loving environments are generally better for everyone, even though some genotypes respond a great deal to environmental enrichment and others only a little. A similar case can be made for harmful environments.

For most purposes it is possible to characterize deleterious environments and remedy them. But what about improving environments that are not clearly deleterious, but, rather, different from others that are associated with more desirable outcomes? That is the major conceptual problem, as I see it. Understanding environmental effects is complicated by the fact that different genotypes react in different degrees or different ways to them. Only an evolutionary perspective will help to develop environmental theory, but I will discuss this later.

"Genetic" differences.

Genetic differences are those differences in phenotypes that we do not know how to treat or change environmentally! Once you accept that each genotype responds uniquely to environments and that both genetic and environmental differences are always involved in behavioral development, then it is reasonable to make the distinction between those genetic differences to which we know how to match environments and those that we do not yet. Most complex behaviors remain genetically mysterious, but the fact of genetic differences is there, everywhere. The reaction range concept applies to the application of the same environment to everyone and the differential responsiveness of genotypes to those environments. There are different slopes and intercepts for each genotype. Perhaps this is an exaggeration, but in principle it is true, as shown in Figure 2. There is malleability, but it is tempered and sometimes altered dramatically by the combination of genotypes and environments.

Genotype-Environment Correlations.

These concepts are much misunderstood and understudied in psychology. Basically there are three kinds as described by Plomin, DeFries, and Loehlin (1977).

  ● Passive—Parents' genotypes correlate with their children's genotypes and with the environments they provide for their children.

  ● Evocative—Different genotypes lead to different phenotypes that evoke different responses from the social and physical environments that

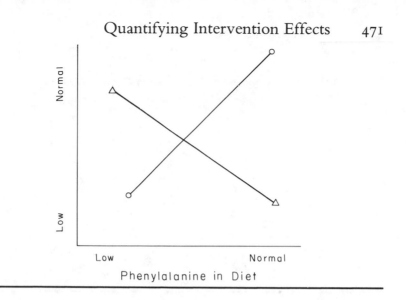

Figure 1. A genotype-environment interaction of the disordinal type. Δ = PKU, o = normal.

further shape the phenotype in ways that correlate with the genotype. Temperament may be like this, leading to personality differences among people. Socially active and engaging infants get more social stimulation than passive, unsmiley babies. In the intellectual arena, bright and cooperative toddlers get more pleasant and instructive interactions from adults around them.

• Active: Niche building; people seek out environments they find compatible and live in them, enlarge and deepen them. We all select from the surrounding environment some aspects to respond to, and our selection is correlated with some aspects of our genotypes.

To the extent that genotype-environment correlations are important in determining differences in development, the mere provision of a different environment will not necessarily change a child's development.

Illustrations of genotype-environment correlations.

The *passive* sort is easy to illustrate with the case of books for children. Parents who like to read, and who think that reading is important will provide their children with more books than less literate parents, regardless of the individual child's preferences. But because the child's genotype is correlated with the parents', the children of parents who are good at reading and who like it are more likely to be receptive to books. The *evocative* sort of genotype-environment correlation is illustrated by the

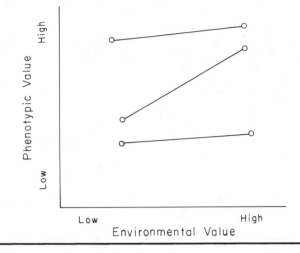

Figure 2. Reaction range model, in which genotypes are differentially responsive to environments across a range of environments, thereby producing a range of phenotypes.

child who reads a lot being allowed go the the library often in school,
being given books for birthday presents by friends, whereas a child who
does not like to read is not given books. The *active* sort of genotype-
environment correlation is represented by the child who spends his/her
own money on books rather than toys, who spends his/her free time in
the library and with other peers who also like to read, who discusses
books rather than baseball, and who selects those people and things in
this environment that are related to reading more than to other things.
He or she builds a book niche.

Genotype-Environment Correlations and Interventions

Keeping in mind that behavioral differences among people are always
due to both genetic and environmental differences, and that often those
differences are correlated in three ways, let us examine interventions.

We observe in the real world that children who learn to read well in the
early school grades come from families with the following characteristics:

- parents read for pleasure.
- parents read to the child.
- the child owns books.
- the child watches less TV.

If we were looking at all of the characteristics that differentiate families
of children who learn to read easily from those that do not, I suspect

our list would include some puzzling "antecedents" of reading facility. My impression, and it is only an impression, is that children who learn to read easily come from families who are more likely to live in single family homes, go to bed at a regular hour, eat fewer refined sugars, and have parents who play bridge rather than poker, work at office jobs, are both in the home, have fewer offspring, and spend less time with their relatives.

The point is that reading facility is associated with a style of life achieved by people whom we can characterize as middle- to upper-middle class. Reading plays a more salient role in the lives of these people than it does in the lives of working- and lower-class parents. On average, middle-class people are better-educated and are better readers, and so are their children, and the differences are not merely in the immediate environment.

In this example I think we can see evidence for environmental differences (if we provided more books for children whose families do not provide them, there ought to be *some* payoff—how much is not determined), for genetic differences (there is evidence for genetic differences in reading facility, as specific kinds of reading problems run in families), and for genotype-environment correlations of all three kinds.

I think that it is important to ask the following question about the behavior to be changed: Do we know that it is malleable and do we know what affects its development? We could all laugh at the impossibility of answering these questions, but we had better venture some predictions of person–environment combinations based on some theory, or we are left with empty words. A global intervention strategy merely distributes goodies willy-nilly.

A Person–Environment View

It seems to me that we need a theory of the environment that takes into account the evolved nature of human development and human differences. There are some behaviors that nearly all normal members of the species will acquire without specific environments: that is, all normal species members will encounter those environments in the course of growing up in any culture, unless by some unlucky circumstance they are deprived of any of the relevant experience. In psychology, we have spent much time and energy detailing the drastic effects of very odd environments on young humans and other animals, to the extent that the sensory deprivation literature threatens to be our only theory of the environment. I think that this is a mistake, because the environments studied in this tradition are completely outside of the range of normal environments in which human behavioral development has evolved. Rather, I propose that most infant and child behaviors develop without specifically provided environments or even conscious tutoring of the young by adults. Walking, talking, and cuddling occur all over the world in young humans whose caretakers received no instruction on the importance of hard surfaces, responsive speech, or physical handling. Oh, you say, but we have analyzed the environments that *cause* the development of those behaviors and we know that infants deprived of experience with hard surfaces are delayed in gross motor skills, those who are deprived of responsive speech to and from their caretakers have poor language development, and those deprived of close physical contact are socially less responsive.

Yes, but we are faced most often with variations in young humans' experiences, not with massive deprivations. Consider the toddler who sits passively on the floor and does not use the hard surface to practice creeping, who prefers to be carried and to be on soft surfaces; the young child who does not use speech to communicate to others, the parents themselves forget to evoke speech from the child; the infant who does not demand cuddling and who arches his or her back to avoid the constriction of hugging. I am not denying that some children experience deprived environments outside of the normal range for the species, but I am saying that most often we are dealing with environments that interact with and are correlated with differences among people.

The three examples I have used so far—walking, talking, and cuddling—are behaviors that seem to be so rooted in the species history that almost any normal environment will serve to promote normal development. Not all behaviors are like that. Reading most often (not always) requires some specific instruction to help the child acquire the component skills. Learning to drive a car and learning specific forms of social contact (with whom, where, when, and why) require conscious adult tutelage for the young to acquire smooth performance.

In addition to the specificity of the environment necessary for normal development, I would guess from evolutionary theory that those behaviors that are less rooted in our species history have more genetic variability than those that are more ancient forms of adaptation. In other words, the selection pressure against reading disorders has not been as strong over the past 100,000 years as the selection against speech disorders that interfere with normal communication among humans. I would suspect that people who cannot communicate through language are not as often chosen as mates and therefore do not reproduce to the same extent as people without communication disorders. I do not think the same can be said for reading disorders until quite recently, even if this is true now. Thus, there ought to be more normal genetic variation in reading facility than in speech.

There are two differences I want to highlight between the more anciently evolved human behaviors such as walking, talking and cuddling, and the more recent ones such as reading: (1) that the ancient behaviors require less specific environments for normal development, and (2) that there is probably less genetic variability in the more ancient genetic programs.

There are several implications for this view. First, it is an inefficient use of resources to intervene in the development of behaviors that will be acquired in the normal course of living in an environment within the range that is normal for the species. One should, of course, provide some exposure to responsive speech for the hearing infants of deaf parents and to physical cuddling for infants in overcrowded institutions. Real environmental deprivation is defined by being outside of the normal cultural variation present in the species. This does not argue for providing infant intervention programs for the promotion of behaviors that develop to the same criterion for all normal members of all groups by an early age. Why is there benefit to be gained from teaching lower-class mothers to provide middle-class rearing for their infants in the first 2 years of life when there are no differences between middle- and lower-class infants on any scales in any studies in the first 18 to 24 months? The rationale that has been provided by the infant interveners is that early skills are the basis for later skills. Unfortunately for this argument, there is not even an empirical basis for the claim that sensorimotor skills or babbling are consistently related to later conceptual intelligence or speech. Even if there were some relationship between earlier and later skills, to justify early rather than later intervention, one would have to believe that there is some critical period for the development of the earlier skills, or else they could be developed more effectively at the later age. I do not know of any evidence for an early critical period for the development of component reading skills, especially since adults acquire literacy at several times the rate of young children. Most of the concepts that are taught to young children are acquired by every adult in the course of living.

Second, for mentally retarded or specifically impaired children, it will be necessary to provide specific environments and instruction for the development of skills that are acquired from the nonspecific environments and experiences of normal children. Something is wrong with their learning apparatus that, in the species, evolved to analyze and synthesize everyday experiences through incidental learning and imitation. By making the learning steps specific and the learning experiences explicit, there is some hope of enhancing the performance of deficient children. They will rarely come to have the same facility or generality of skill that is common to children who learned the central human skills in the evolved way, because the strongly evolved skills require too much incidental learning in too many situations for these situations to be easily simulated.

Third, intervention programs that involve the provision of specific environments are best suited to the development of those skills that usually require specific instruction. If we want 3-year-olds to know esoteric concepts, such as oblique and relative, and to understand arithmetic principles of additivity and commutivity, we shall probably have to teach them. (If we waited until they were 8 or 9 they might need only the label for the concept). And if we want 5-year-olds to know all of the alphabet, letter sounds, blends, left-to-right eye scanning, equivalencies of upper and lower case letters in several scripts, without making equivalent some letter reversals, then we shall have to teach them, intensively. And in order to teach them we will have to make sure that they cooperate with adult wishes and instructions, are susceptible to social approval and disapproval, even from strange adults, and are able to forego what they want to do at the moment for what is defined by adults as legitimate activity. We are no longer talking about early childhood environments that are general to the species. In most societies children under the age of 5 or 6 are not subjected to very specific instruction; rather, at about the age of 6 or 7 children begin their apprenticeships for adult roles through helping in gender-appropriate ways. It has often seemed to me that the small child of 6 climbs down off her sister-caretaker's back one day and is given her younger sibling to carry the next day. There is usually a sharp demarkation between early childhood and childhood.

Let us assume for the sake of this discussion that early literacy and numeracy are important adaptions in Western industrial societies. Then, what are the implications of the theory of person–environment combinations for intervention programs? It means that we shall have to teach people these skills.

Quantitative Prediction

Suppose that we find, as we have in an early intervention project, that some rough and ready measures of mothers' teaching skills are strongly related to children's conceptual development, degree of cooperation with adults in learning tasks, and social competencies. Does this mean that teaching other mothers to be better teachers will enhance their children's intelligence, cooperation, and social competencies? I suppose the answer is yes, but the question of interest is *how much?*

Measured in standard deviation units, the prediction of improvement in a child's scores is a direct function of the unstandardized coefficient from the regression of child scores on mothers' teaching skill scores.

That is, if, as we found for the first 57 families we studied, that the regression of children's cognitive and social competencies on their mothers' teaching skills is about .67, then every standard deviation (SD) improvement in mothers' teaching skills ought to pay off in ⅔ of a standard deviation in children's skills. To use a familiar scale, that of IQ, the regression equation reported predicts that a one SD improvement in mothers' teaching skills yields 10 IQ points in the children, a practically important payoff.

Many studies of family situations in the developmental literature stop right there with the implication hanging and untested. For example, the Caldwell HOME Scale (Caldwell, 1978) is based on such research, which takes naturally occurring correlations of the sort reported and implies that huge gains are to be found in the improvement of mother's interaction or teaching of the child whose family scores below average on such scales.

I suspect that something is wrong with the predicted payoff of 10 IQ points for every SD improvement in mothers' teaching skills. What is wrong, of course, is that a mother's teaching skills are related to many other facts about her, her home, her whole environment, and most likely her genetic background. Her genotype is correlated with the environment she provides for herself and the child, whose genotype is correlated with both her genotype and the rearing environment in the several ways I have described. For example, mother's IQ is correlated .42 with her 24- to 30-month-old's IQ, and her IQ is correlated .62 with her own teaching skills.

Let us model that set of relationships in explicit and plausible ways. I argue that a mother's Wechsler Adult Intelligence Scale (WAIS) vocabulary is not influenced by her 24- to 30-month-old's intellectual or social characteristics. Since the child was born, she has probably not lost vocabulary and certainly has not learned any from the child. The child's IQ, on the other hand, is more likely to be affected directly by the mother's IQ, both genetically and environmentally. Let us also assume that the mother's IQ is not directly affected by her skills in teaching a 2-year-old. Rather, her teaching skills are another manifestation of her developed intellect. These reasonable assumptions give us the following model in Figure 3.

Given the correlation between a mother's teaching skills and her own IQ, and the full impact of the mother's transmission of her IQ to the child by genetic means only (the most conservative assumptions from an intervention point of view), it is still the case that the mothers' teaching skills have a partial coefficient of .35 with children's IQ scores. (In fact, this figure is obtained after removing the variance in child IQ and teach-

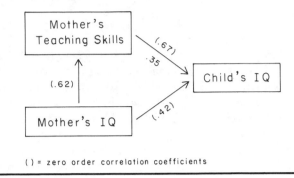

( ) = zero order correlation coefficients

Figure 3. A model of mother–child interaction and child IQ.

ing skills due to the ethnicity and social class of the family.) Thus, an improvement of the mothers' teaching skills by one SD may well improve children's IQ scores by .35 SD or 5 to 6 IQ points, on the average.

Now let us consider another model where the mothers' teaching skills are to some extent a function of the child's attention, responsiveness, and cooperation in learning. We know from our mothers' ratings of their children's personalities and from our own ratings of the children's personalities that young children who are seen by their mothers and us as attentive, cooperative, responsive, and not overly active actually receive better teaching in our experimental situation than children who are seen by their mothers and by us as less attentive, less cooperative, less responsive, and overly active. The child plays a role in how well he or she is taught.

Now we have a mediating variable—child personality—between the mother's teaching skills and the child's IQ. Actually, I think that most of the collaborators[1] on this research would agree that the child's personality affects not just how the mother teaches the child but how able we are to assess the child's IQ. I, for one, take a David Wechsler view of functioning intelligence as part of general personality and not just a set of cognitive skills, because in the real world one has to be able to use effectively what one has cognitively. For 2-year-olds especially, cognition and personality are wedded in performance. Consider Figure 4.

The payoff from improving mothers' teaching skills is complicated by the degree to which the program addresses and "improves" the child's cooperation, attention, responsiveness, and lowers the child's activity in learning situations. If the intervention has no effect on the children's per-

1. J. C. Schwarz, Barbara Caparulo, Kathleen McCartney, David Furrow, Randy Billington.

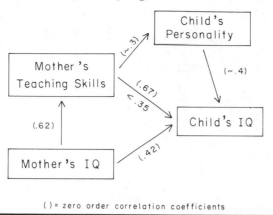

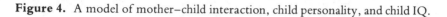

( ) = zero order correlation coefficients

Figure 4. A model of mother–child interaction, child personality, and child IQ.

sonalities then the payoff from raising mothers' teaching skills could be considerably less than the .35 SD cited before. If mothers who teach better have more attentive, cooperative learners, who further reinforce their mothers' teaching skills, then the effect of the children's personalities on the payoff from the intervention may be advantageous.

Now let us consider other possibilities: (1) that a mother's improvement in teaching skills is a function (positive or negative) of her initial intellectual level, (2) that the child's gain in IQ is a function of initial intellectual level (positive or negative correlation), and (3) that both maternal and child interactions of intellectual level with gain from the program occur. These modifications of the prediction models can be fitted on the average results predicted by the former models, but they may be important for policy reasons. If, as rarely happens, those who need the intervention most benefit the most from it, one could rejoice especially at the result illustrated in Figure 5.

Although the best slope might be much the same in the posttest as in the pretest, the R^2 of the child IQ regressed on maternal teaching skills would be greatly reduced by the restriction in variance caused by the negatively correlated gains of both mother and child with their initial scores.

How about the more usual and opposite result? Although everyone benefits from the intervention to some extent, those that got, got more from the program? That result is shown in Figure 6.

Those who had initially high scores gained a lot from the program; those who had low initial scores gained only a little. The only way to

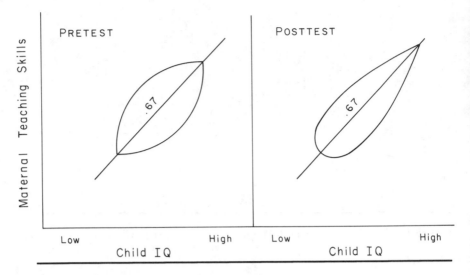

Figure 5. A model of gains in child IQ as a function of gains in maternal teaching skills, where gains are negatively correlated with initial scores.

keep the bright from getting more from absolutely everything is to lock them in closets while you teach the rest. Otherwise they will use their time to learn more and more efficiently than others.

On the other hand, Snow (1981) has shown that certain forms of teaching are actually better geared to slow learners and impede the efficiency of faster learners subjected to the treatment. Making instructional programs highly explicit and redundant enhances the learning of those who do not ordinarily make connections and generalizations and impedes the learning of those who do. If an intervention program is particularly geared to the learning of mothers who do not teach well because they do not know how to make teaching sufficiently explicit for young children, and because they do not spontaneously analyze the tasks that they want to teach, then it may be possible to bore brighter mothers into not gaining and enhance the learning of less bright mothers. Given the social goals of most intervention programs, we ought to gear them to people who need them most, taking into account the functional relationships between the teacher's characteristics and the child's and the functional level of the teacher's intelligence.

General Implications

From my musings about the nature of quantification in the prediction of outcomes from intervention programs, I draw several implications.

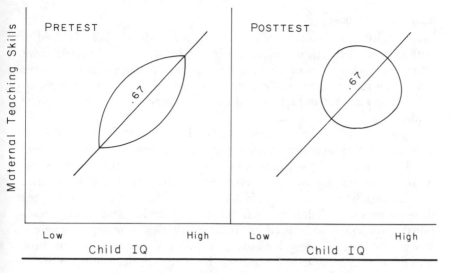

Figure 6. A model of gains in child IQ as a function of gains in maternal teaching skills, where gains are positively correlated with initial scores.

First, we need a theory of the environment that takes into account the evolved natures of human development and of human differences. I propose four characteristics for that theory. One, some human behaviors are more central to the evolution of development and therefore have less genetic variability and less specific requirements for the environments in which they develop. Two, some human behaviors are less central to the evolved nature of humankind, probably have more genetic variability, and require more specific environments for their development—even intentional adult instruction. Third, we ought to concentrate our intervention efforts on those aspects of human development in category two. We often mistake the enhancement of the *rate* of development of behaviors in category one for the necessity of providing instructional intervention for those behaviors in two. Fourth, the prediction of the effectiveness of interventions must take into account the embeddedness of behavioral development in the environmental and genetic contexts in which it develops. In addition, we should see that the genetic differences among people are most often correlated with environments provided for them and in which they choose to live. No version of naive environmental theory can accurately predict the effects of intervention programs designed to emulate the correlations that occur in natural environments. Overprediction and disappointment are the rule, for very good theoretical reasons. *We do not have to continue to self-destruct.*

Resources and Values

The allocation of resources requires us to make choices. I have tried to outline some theoretical reasons for trying some kinds of interventions rather than others. To make further progress in developing quantitative models for intervention studies, we need to know the reaction ranges for different groups for the relevant skills to be taught or adjustments to be made.

Suppose that we have a group of fast learners and a group of slow learners, all of whom must pass a minimal competency exam. Axelrod and I have explored the implications of resource allocation under these conditions in another article (Axelrod and Scarr, 1980). I will summarize our findings briefly here. As Figure 7 shows, the fast learners and the slow learners have different reaction curves to the investment of instructional resources (more teachers' time, textbooks, learning aids, etc.). When resources are very limited, as at point X, investing in the slow learners would be practically useless, because they need much more to make significant progress. When many more resources are available, as at point Y, investing in the fast learners at that level of resources would be wasteful, because they will all reach the criterion with less investment. At what level should resources be available and in whom should we invest them?

This brings us to the really hard choices among values. Shall we invest resources in everyone equally, regardless of payoff? Surely, this is a very inefficient choice, because some will be helped very little by a given level of resources, while others do not need that much to reach a desired criterion. Or shall we invest enough in everyone enough so that each reaches some desired criterion? This means a very unequal input of resources to gain equality of output. This, too, is inefficient (and also impractical), because some will require an infinite amount of resources to make practically insignificant progress toward the criterion. The efficient solution to the problem is to invest at those points in people's reaction curves where the given amount of resources will have the greatest payoff.

Sometimes, the efficient policy is not politically or morally acceptable, because the most needy may receive the least investment, if their reaction curve is relatively flat in the area of resources available, while the "haves" may gain a lot from the same level of investment. I do not pretend to propose solutions to these or other value problems, I can only to try to clarify the choices that are being made every day. By being tough-minded and quantitative about the intended effects of interventions, I hope that we can face the choices and try to serve people's needs better with the resources available.

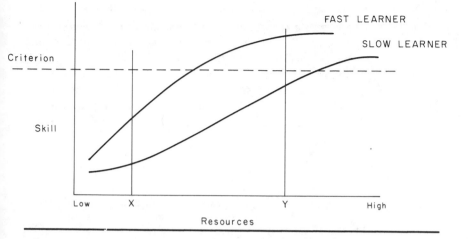

Figure 7. Resource allocation to fast and slow learners under two conditions of resource availability.

My desire for more efficient use of available resources is not an expression of satisfaction with the present investment in social or educational programs. We could certainly make good use of a larger investment. Nor is it an acceptance of inhumane conditions for children and their families. Quite apart from intervention programs that are supposed to have payoffs, there are humanitarian considerations that have precedence in my value system. No one in my society should have to live in squalor, regardless of the causes. Feeding hungry children is justified on humanitarian grounds alone and does not require any long-term payoff, as far as I am concerned. Children should not be hungry, or abused, or deprived of adequate medical care in the United States in the 1980s. We have no excuse for such neglect. I have written, rather, of those educational and social interventions, especially in families, which are designed to improve the long-term functioning of participants in ways that program planners intend. I see many problems in our current lack of theory and inquiry, which could help us to make more informed choices.

The Payoff for Science

Perhaps more important than anything else I have mentioned explicitly is an implication of what I have said. No matter what the outcome of our intervention study is—whether mothers with high or low initial scores gain more, whether children with high or low initial scores gain more, whether the program works, on the average, to a greater or lesser

484   SANDRA SCARR

extent—*the results will teach us about human development.* The best model fit will tell us something important about malleability of development under generalizable conditions. And we will know more the next time about quantitative predictions from this and similar interventions. Explicit quantitative models make hypothesis testing possible for intervention studies. Models that fit well inform us about causal relations in human development. As Urie Bronfenbrenner is fond of saying, quoting his own mentor, "If you want to understand something, try to change it."

References

Axelrod, R., and Scarr, S. Human intelligence and public policy. *Scientific American,* in press.
Caldwell, B. M. Home observation for measurement of the environment. Obtainable from University of Arkansas at Little Rock, Arkansas, 1978.
Jensen, A. R. *Bias in mental testing.* New York: The Free Press, 1980.
Kiesler, S. B. Federal policies for research on children. *American Psychologist,* 1979, *34,* 1009–1016.
Plomin, R., DeFries, J. C., and Loehlin, J. C. Genotype-environment interaction and correlation in the analysis of human behavior. *Psychological Bulletin,* 1977, *82,* 309–322.
Scarr, S. *IQ: Race, social class, and individual differences.* Hillsdale, N.J.: Lawrence Erlbaum Associates, 1981.
Scarr, S., and Schwarz, J. C. Report to the Bermuda Government on the evaluation of the Child Development Project, October 1978 to August 1979. Yale University, 1979.
Scarr, S., and Weinberg, R. A. The influence of "family background" on intellectual attainment. *American Sociological Review,* 1978, *43,* 674–692.
Snow, R. Aptitude-treatment interactions in education. In R. J. Sternberg (Ed.), *Handbook of intelligence.* Cambridge: Cambridge University Press, 1981.

Early Childhood Development as a Policy Goal:

An Overview of Choices

Richard H. de Lone

To speak of facilitating early childhood development is often to imply an agenda for public policy. The implication is that left to their own devices, some or all children do not develop optimally (whatever that means) in our society. Something must be marshalled—information, programs, transfer payments, professionals—through allocation of public resources.

That said, any policy approach to facilitating development must be based on good theory—a sound understanding of what development is and how it occurs—and it must be a theory that can be translated into action: that is, a set of resource allocations and decisions which will reliably lead to the desired outcomes predicted by the theory. In the world of public policy, a theory is no better than its application, and vice versa. So, for instance, Kohlberg's stage theory of moral development may strike one as beautiful and "true," but it has no more relevance for public policy than Keats's "Ode on a Grecian Urn" unless it can be put into operation as programs or strategies that promote moral improvement. Although these comments verge on truism, even a cursory acquaintance with the annals of public policy makes it clear that such policy is often based on interesting theories which cannot be effectively applied, or (more commonly, perhaps) on no theory at all. In the press of politics, any handle may be grabbed, whether it opens the right door or not.

Because developmental theory and public policy concerning family and children have been more closely allied than is true for most other issues in the social and behaviorial sciences, as I have argued elsewhere (de Lone, 1979), it may be worth pursuing this truism in more detail. An understanding of the requirements of public policy may help in deciding which policy alternatives (if any) are most likely to be effective in facilitating infant and child development.

There can, of course, be no public policy worth mentioning unless there is some shared understanding of goals and a consensus that these goals are sufficiently important to merit the allocation of scarce public resources. For present purposes, however, I will assume, perhaps foolishly, that a rough consensus exists that it is in the public interest to allocate resources toward making children smarter, healthier, emotionally better rounded and socially more competent, and that there is a general understanding, as well, of what these things mean. Accepting these givens, adequate public policy—in this or any field—must fulfill four criteria:

- It must be based on sound theory.
- That theory must be translated into an adequate policy framework through the legislative and administrative functions of government.
- There must be a "delivery system" capable of carrying out the policy.
- There must be a practicable and reasonably well-defined set of techniques (applications of theory) at the ultimate point of delivery.

One can be more or less rigorous in deciding what constitutes a sound theory for public policy. In matters of foreign policy, for instance, informed judgment has to serve in lieu of any theory that one might call "scientific," for inaction is not a permissable policy choice. But in matters of human development, as in matters like thalidomide, it is certainly desirable to have a theory that goes beyond mere descriptive plausibility or clinical hunches (valuable as those hunches may be in some settings). A sound theory for public policy aimed at facilitating child development should have predictive value, it should be dynamic, it should facilitate child development, and it should be empirically validated or scientific (in Popper's sense that it is disprovable). I would argue that, in addition, it should have a firm philosophical base, an epistemological self-consciousness. Since most empirical work in social science uses proxies to measure the thing, not the thing itself, it is entirely possible to sustain the illusion of empirical (and even of predictive, dynamic) validity by guileless confusion of epiphenomena with the phenomena. As Kessen (1966) has warned, if we ignore epistemological issues, we face the clear and present danger that "our conclusions about the development of human knowledge may derive in large measure from the preconceptions of the nature of man and the nature of reality that we have stuffed—or, worse, let slip—into our initial conception of the psychological task" (p. 61). Those words could serve as an epitaph for volumes of worthless controversy on the subject of IQ.

A further hazard for the social and behavioral sciences lies in the fact that so much theory is basically taxonomic, not dynamic: we break the phenomenon into pieces; give each piece a label (e.g., IQ; self-concept, demographic characteristic); express the label in quantitative terms; find mathematical relationships between quantities; and—forgetting that the thing itself is something more than, indeed different from, the sum of its labels—yield too often to the temptation to believe that the phenomenon has been explained. Thus, taxonomies masquerade as dynamic theories of causation. This error is particularly likely to occur as one moves from the academic literature to the lay interpretation of that literature for policy-making purposes, and it has a glorious history in the social sciences, too. One can consider, for instance, the history of the so-called Phillip's curve, which led economists to believe that there was an inevitable trade-off between inflation and unemployment (i.e., that high inflation would result from low unemployment and vice versa), a notion that OPEC and "stagflation" recently washed down the drain when it became apparent that the implicit model relating these two factors dynamically was too simple (see, for instance, Lekachman, 1976). Closer to home, the famous assertion of Bloom (1964)—that "in terms of intelligence measured at age 17, about 50 percent of the development takes place between conception and age 4," (p. 88)—was based not only on a questionable definition of intelligence but partly on erroneous reasoning which confused explained variance in test scores (at different times on different tests) with an explanation of development itself.

The second criterion, development of an adequate policy framework, also implies several subcriteria. One is that sound theory will inform legislative and administration policy planning. This, of course, is not always true because of political constraints, or because of the time lag required for research to enter the policy stream, or because of the insouciant ignorance of policy makers. But there is more to an adequate policy framework than good theory. Adequate policy also requires that the goals and objectives of the policy are logically connected to the theory, that resources and timelines are adequate for attainment of those objectives, and that what I will call the "sphere of agency" is properly conceptualized and inherently capable of performing what the theory and objectives of a policy would have it perform.

The well-known story of Head Start provides an illustration of the requirement that goals be logically related to theory. Let us assume for the sake of argument that Head Start was grounded in sound developmental theory about the importance of the early years for cognitive development. Alas, this does not mean that, even if the early cognitive gains experienced by many children in Head Start had been maintained that Head Start would have helped achieve the objectives of the legislation, which were ultimately to improve the economic status of blacks and other low-income children. For in fact, as numerous studies, most of which were thoroughly assessed by Jencks, Bartletts, Corcoran, Crouse, Eaglesfield, Jackson, McLelland, Mueser, Olneck, Schwartz, Ward, and Williams (1979) have shown individual differences in cognitive skills explain at best a minor part of variation in economic achievement.

Examples of policies that are inadequately funded or given impossible time constraints are legion, and the point needs no clarification. The notion of a proper sphere of agency is a bit subtler. At its simplest, it merely means that the delivery system—usually some set of bureaucracies—has the capacity and mandate to implement the policy. This condition is sometimes violated when agencies are asked to take on assignments for which they in fact have little or no experience, capacity, or incentive to perform. There may be subtler problems, however, with the sphere of agency. One major class of problems results from unintended consequences of social programs (consequences which are sometimes serendipitous but more often not). For example, when resources are scarce, policy must generally attempt to define the target population with the "problem" that the policy is supposed to resolve. But the act of definition can easily turn into an act of stigmatization which is counterproductive. Programs for slow learners, the mentally retarded, the emotionally disturbed, the socially maladjusted, and so on are examples. A second major class of problems can occur when the tacit functions of a system are in conflict with the explicit goals of a policy. For example, some have argued that the educational enterprise services the tacit function of social control and perpetuation of the status quo, in direct conflict with the explicit goals of many programs that have tried to use the schools to promote the development and social mobility of disadvantaged groups (e.g., Bowles and Gintis, 1976; Leacock, 1969). A third type of sphere of agency problem results from systemic contradictions. For example, in our cyclic economy, policies and programs intended to alleviate economic hardships are hardest to fund when needed most (i.e., when the economy is in a low). Similarly, many human service programs, because they more nearly resemble an art form than an engineering exercise, depend on the judgment and discretion of local service providers. But a counterforce, the pressure for accountability from remote funding sources (such as the federal government) may generate regulations and stipulations that severely limit the domain of judgement.

The next step in this continuum of policy criteria concerns the adequacy of delivery systems. Assuming the chosen delivery system is the proper sphere of agency, a host of everyday problems results which are no easier to solve because of their familiarity. Here we are largely concerned with intergovernmental relations, effective management, coordination of services, adequate planning, staff training, clinical practice, evaluation, and the like—the entire apparatus of public administration. Suffice it to say that it is always theoretically possible to do things well, but Murphy's law constantly asserts itself. The safest assumption is that large-scale efforts will be implemented with variable quality, and the modal performance will be, by qualitative standards, mediocre. Where excellence is required, public programs will always disappoint. De Lone's law says: if the thing is not worth doing in a mediocre fashion, it is not worth doing at all!

The final criterion is the availability of adequate technique (applied theory) to implement a policy which survives the above tests. To illustrate from another field, economists have a pretty good idea of what makes a small business viable or what makes a good investment. But the ability of economists (or anyone else) to translate that theory into concrete steps which would cut down the rather high failure rate of small businesses, or which would result in an investment portfolio that consistently outperformed the market norm, simply does not exist.[1] Similarly, one may conclude that Piaget has developed a valid model of cognitive growth and be completely unable to tell a teacher what kinds of interventions will hasten the process: perhaps this is just the state of the art, or perhaps it is that growth cannot be nudged; it just happens.

Linked to the criterion of technique is the question of evaluation. How do we know when something has worked? Problems of methodology and instrumentation aside, evaluating programs or policies that aim at fostering *development* is terribly hard to do. Even with adequate controls and pre-post measures, short-term studies are almost invariably subject to the suspicion that they measure learned (and hence forgettable) responses, not development which is, in the absence of extraordinary circumstances, irreversible. But longitudinal studies that are methodologically sufficient are few and far between, slow by definition, time-bound (as are all studies of social phenomena), and rarely capable of providing firm conclusions on more than a few points. Indeed, social science is generally better at telling us what has not worked than what will. But the problems are only in part methodological and logistical. They are also epistemological. Interpreting measurements requires that we reexamine the proxies used in evaluating effectiveness, the assumptions implicit in our theories, and the exogenous factors (for instance, flaws in the delivery system) which may have influenced results. Hence, the question of technique, which requires evaluation, leads to a closing of the loop and a return to the questions and issues posed in the first three criteria.

Table 1 summarizes the criteria listed here. In the balance of this paper,

1. To be sure, the market itself is the mediator of risk.

Table 1: Criteria for Effective Public Policy

Criterion	Tests
Sound theory	Descriptive plausibility
	Predictive value
	Dynamic properties (causal relations)
	Empirical validity
Adequate policy framework	Embodies sound theory
	Goals and objectives congruent with theory
	Resource and logistical adequacy
	Proper sphere of agency not unintended outcomes harmony of tacit and explicit functions absence of systemic contradictions
Effective delivery system	Management
	Planning
	Personnel
	Fiscal systems
	Evaluation systems
Viable technique	"clinical" lore
	"Evaluatability"

these criteria will be used to test some major choices which present themselves to anyone interested in selecting a public policy approach that will in fact facilitate infant and child development.

Traditionally, the children whose development has been of primary concern to public policy are children from low-income families, many of whom are members of minority groups. And while public policy has placed a particular emphasis on cognitive development (through early childhood education programs and other vehicles), the view of development implicit in much policy discussion is a rather broad (perhaps even loose) one. It includes health promotion, emotional growth, and social competence. Its aim is nothing less than facilitating the growth of capable, fully competent, and functional adults who can make their way in society and contribute something to it.

These broad goals are hard to fault. While developmental liabilities know no bounds of class or race, any review of the state of children in the United States leads to the conclusion that the children of low-income families face systematically more severe developmental hazards as a result of their social and economic status (e.g., Keniston, 1977). Yet there has been a persistent tendency to confuse policies that aim at promoting individual development with strategies for changing the social conditions that produce developmental risk. This is an old tendency in our society, as evident in early 19th century school reform (Katz, 1969) as in subsequent waves of social reform up to and through the Great Society (de Lone, 1979). The reasons for this confusion lie deeply rooted in the heritage of classic liberalism which was and is our dominant social, political, and economic heritage. For liberalism, as embodied in American culture, views the individual as the *alpha* and *omega* of society. Not only is the promotion of individual liberty and happiness viewed as the end of society, but the society is viewed as the sum and product of so many individual actors and actions—just as in the classic view of the free market, the economy is the result of myriad individual choices and preferences, guided by the invisible hand of the market.

Our pernicious cultural habit of equating virtue with economic success, and immorality with poverty (evident in 18th century legacies of the British "poor laws" and in 20th century attitudes toward welfare recipients); our Horatio Alger mythology, as alive today as ever; and the reams of regressions run by sociologists studying social mobility with equations in which social status is the dependent variable and a host of individual characteristics serve as the right-hand variables, are but a few examples of the intellectual consequences of "explaining" society by studying individuals. But the apotheosis of this tendency, and a central framework for public policy, has been the doctrine of equal opportunity. This doctrine contains an admirable social goal but, as it becomes confused with a social fact and transmuted into a social theory, is also a dangerous sophistry.

In what I take to be the mainstream version of this cultural ideal/myth/theory, the notion is that once "artificial" constraints such as discrimination, bad diets, and poor schooling are eliminated, individuals can, should, and will make their way in the world more or less as their merits dictate. The result will be a society in equilibrium, with each rewarded in proportion to his or her contribution to the whole (e.g., Bell, 1973; Plattner, 1979). To be sure, individual talents, propensities, and preferences are important and have an important bearing on social outcomes, but it is apparent that this somewhat more sophisticated restatement of the notion that every person is master of his or her fate ignores substantially the effect that social and economic structures may have not only on social outcomes but even on individual development, as will be discussed subsequently. Consider, for instance, the variety of studies which have concluded that social origins (race and class at birth) have more influence than any other factor on the likely status of adults, even when controlling for individual ability (cf. Sewell, 1971, regarding educational attainment; Bowles and Gintis, 1974, 1976; Brittain, 1977; and the comprehensive review and reanalysis of numerous studies by Jencks, 1979).

The relevance of all this to public policy for facilitating child development is simply this: historically, there has been a strange brew of developmental theory and social theory in our public policy. Developmental theory—and programs based on it—have played the role of the alchemical agent dropped in the pot of equal opportunity to turn the lives of the disadvantaged into gold. What the philosopher's stone has yielded is something else: an almost metaphysical confusion of developmental theory and social theory which has served neither policy—nor children—well.

I do not mean to suggest that the problem has been caused by mixing apples and oranges, developmental theory and social theory, or that development should be left to the psychologists and social change to others. Development occurs in society, and no one would seriously argue for long that it makes any sense to think about development out of social context. Conversely, a social theory which does not incorporate an understanding of the ways in which individuals develop will be a pale theory. Public policy based on either will risk failure. The question, in other words, is how to develop a developmental theory in proper relation to social theory (and vice versa) as the basis for policy.

That we need do so is apparent from the abundant literature which suggests the interplay between individual and socioeconomic factors. Virtually all studies which try to identify developmental risk end up listing socioeconomic indicators. For a typical example, there is the paper presented at the Vermont Conference last year by Rutter (1979), who cited the following risk factors associated with child psychiatric disorder: severe marital discord, low social status, overcrowding or large family size, paternal criminality, maternal psychiatric disorder, admission to the care of the local authority (e.g., the child welfare system), and possibly "scope of opportunity." What these have to do with Freud is problematic, but it is striking that almost all are associated, in greater or lesser strength, with parental poverty and its sibling, unemployment. Conversely, a copious literature illustrates the pathogenic effects of unemployment and poverty on adults (and through them, on children in a variety of ways). So Brenner (1976) has found that a rise of 1 percentage point in unemployment is associated with an 8.7 percent increase in narcotics use, a 5.7 percent increase in robberies, a 3.8 percent increase in homicides, and a higher incidence of mental illness; Eisenberg (1979), reviewing a large body of studies, concluded that any major breakthrough in the health status of low-income children in this country is likely to come from employment and income increases; Ross and Sawhill (1975) found that unemployment explains most of the difference between black and white rates of family dissolution. One could go on to cite ad nauseam studies linking poverty and poor nutrition, poverty and low school achievement, poverty and family breakup, and so forth. The ubiquity of these findings pushes us to conclude that there is some relationship between socioeconomic status and development, but the questions remain. Just what is that relationship? How should theory account for it? What are the dynamics of the relationship? What is the proper policy framework for addressing it, and what are the implications for delivery and technique?

To simplify the matter, I would suggest that there are two broad policy options which flow from an effort to accommodate this relationship. Implicitly or explicitly, these options reflect two divergent theories or models, to use a somewhat more apt term, of the relationship between development and socioeconomic conditions.

One approach can be called the micro model, and it has typified most efforts at social reform in the United States. The other I will call the macro model. To so distinguish is somewhat to caricature both, but for purposes of this short discussion, it may also help clarify some basic considerations.

The micro approach is based on essentially normative criteria of development. Although it may draw on a diversity of disciplines for its theories and models of development (biogenetics, epigenetics, behaviorism, neo-Freudianism, etc.), its overarching model of development has three basic parameters: (1) it views the early years as the plastic years, the critical period and even determinative period in human development; (2) it treats development as the result of a series of inputs (genes, nutrients, environmental stimulae) and interactions (between genes and stimulae, parent and child, etc), and (3) it treats environment as the child's immediate surrounding—family, neighborhood, school and, in more studies than not, simply "mom."[2] As a basis for policy, this model of development leads to an emphasis on funding programs which aim at identifying "at risk" individuals—that is, those whose development by normative standards is likely to be deficient—and providing them with targeted interventions which may run the gamut from early childhood education programs, to parent education, to maternal and infant health care, to genetic engineering, and more. These are interventions applied with more

2. Urie Bronfenbrenner and others, using a taxonomy somewhat similar to that used here, have referred to such institutions (family, school, neighborhood) as the mezzo-structure.

or less professional assistance, in a "helper/helpee" clinical framework. Publicly funded programs and hence public bureaucracies, including the education system, the health system, and the welfare system, are assigned the responsibility for implementing these programs, and to a considerable measure, the colleges and universities are involved both in training practitioners in the techniques used in these approaches and in evaluating their effectiveness.

The second broad approach, the macro approach, exists more in literature and argument than it does in fact, for it is by and large the road not taken by public policy. It views the criteria for development as essentially relativistic, not normative. And, while acknowledging the sensitivity and importance of the early childhood years, the macro model (at least in this writer's version) views development as a continuous process of the organism seeking equilibrium with its spatial and temporal environment, not only in early years but into adulthood. It defines the operative developmental environment as including not simply the immediate surround, but also the class, race, sex, and cultural group to which the individual belongs, and the social situation in which that membership finds itself at any moment in historical time (with a past, present, and prospective future). In this perspective, the immediate surround is viewed as a mediator, a filter, not a "causal" agent. The simplest way to make this rather abstract and complex generalization palpable is to consider a cross-cultural example. Michael Cole and his associates have made the point strikingly in their study of the reasoning and performance of American and Kpelle (Liberian) children (and adults). Although Kpelles fail to solve "riddles" which we consider ridiculously simple, Americans perform less well than Kpelles in certain tasks, such as sorting leaves into categories, that are intrinsic to the later group's culture. Yet no one would infer from such evidence that either group is developmentally deficient or incapable of problem solving. Rather, the more plausible conclusion is that "cultural differences in cognition reside more in the situations to which particular cognitive processes are applied than in the existence of a process in one cultural group and its absence in another" (Cole, Gay, Glick, and Sharp, 1971, p. 233). By the same token, children within one society who come from different racial, ethnic, class, and perhaps sex background, insofar as they depart from the norm *as a group* in developmental patterns, may be reflecting differences "in the situations" defined by their group membership.

Finally, this alternative model places an emphasis on the individual as theory builder or "map maker" whose personal contruction of reality, comes from the processing of information derived from his or her "situation", information which, in the early years in particular, is filtered through the immediate surround. The process implied is akin to developing, testing, and refining hypotheses about social reality and the child's likely future in it. These hypotheses guide development (both as internal structure and conscious behavior) of the kinds of skills, behaviors, and attitudes (tacit and conscious) which will be rewarded in it. This map or theory, in turn, structures each new encounter with experience and in some rather obscure sense guides subsequent development. (For a fuller treatment of this concept, and its progenitors, which trace back at least to Kelly, 1955, see Laosa, 1979 and de Lone, 1979.)

With this view of development uppermost, it becomes almost meaningless to argue that one child (or one group of children) develops less "well" than another. Rather, the judicious presumption should be made that all develop equally well in response to their circumstances, unless proven otherwise. Accordingly, if there are developmental differences which seem socially undesirable in their results, one should look to change the circumstances rather than attempt to change the individuals. For instance, if minority youth achieve poorly in school, drop out, cannot find work, and are more frequently convicted of crimes than majority youth, as they do, one should look to changing the circumstantial meaning of being black (or brown, or red) in the United States not only because such changes may be good things in themselves but also because they have developmental implications![3]

From this perspective, a relevant framework for a social policy which facilitates child development must encompass basic structural principles: the skills required by the occupational technostructure; the system of caste and class differentiation; the structure of opportunity (not simply educational pathways but, even more centrally, the distribution and control of capital investments which generate jobs and ration opportunities); and the distribution of income and wealth. The leading programmatic elements of such policy consist of full employment policies, economic development if beneficial to members of low-income groups and communities, affirmative action programs, minimum income supports, and similar efforts aimed at greater equality in the political economy. In current rhetoric, the foundation of a "family policy" is viewed as economic support. Again, one must turn to public bureaucracies to deliver such an approach, but the emphasis goes to the system of taxa-

---

3. This argument, it should be observed, is not equivalent to arguing that subcultural values should be altered, nor is it equivalent to romanticizing cultural differences. As Ogbu (1978) has argued, cultural heritages are not in themselves either an asset or a liability in terms of social outcomes. They may prove to be a strength, a weakness, or entirely neutral only with respect to the way in which they constitute a reactive adaption to the dominant groups' terms or in respect to the way the dominant group reacts to them.

tion and regulatory agencies, as opposed to human service bureaucracies. At the level of "technique," the issue is less one of "helping" or of clinical skill than it is one of creating incentives and opportunities for empowerment of the disenfranchised.

Before applying to these broad alternatives the policy tests suggested in the first part of this paper (which both will flunk in some aspects), it is important to indicate that the choices are not quite as polar as implied. For one thing, the notion of the child as theory builder, constructing reality and a way of processing it through interaction with the environment, has close analogies both in Piagetian and Skinnerian versions of reciprocal action between organism and environment.

For another, there will be individual variance in development even when sociocultural situations are similar, for reasons that are likely to be a problematic mix of genetic, micro environmental, and idiosyncratic "theory building" differences.

For another, to say that the family or other structure in the immediate surround is a mediating, not a primary influence on development does not gainsay the usefulness of studying those micro interactions (although it does alter their interpretation or meaning for policy purposes). Nor does it mean that all developmental liabilities are associated with class or racial status. Nor does the "macro" alternative imply the "micro" interventions can never affect the class- or race-related course of development. What it does suggest, however, is that the intervention, to have impact, must be sharp, major, and sustained. For example, when Kpelle children are placed in Western-type schools for a number of years (a sharp and sustained break with traditional, that is, nonschool, education in the village), they exhibit cognitive processes similar to those of Western children (Cole et al. 1971). By contrast, parent education programs, early childhood education, or other micro interventions are typically marginal and sporadic interventions which do not fundamentally alter the situation of the child. If they have much impact on development, the studies which demonstrate such impact have been carefully hidden.

But what, one may ask, about genes? This paper will not enter the heredity-environment controversy except to make a couple of points: one, there is no doubt a genetic component to intelligence and other aspects of development; two, insofar as genetic endowment places absolute limits on development, this fact is of little use for policy unless one resurrects eugenicism or dreams of a future of clones, for that which can be influenced by policy is the environmental side of the equation; and three, there is no reason to suspect that genes have much to do with determining the class structure or the inequality of social and economic conditions which characterizes this or any other society since individual characteristics explain only a small portion of the variance in social outcomes. Indeed, such specific factors as IQ are only mildly associated with adult success. McLelland (1973), for instance, found correlations of .2 between childhood IQ and adult success as measured by a variety of indicators; this would lead one to conclude that even with a robust claim for the influence of genetic endowment on intelligence, no more than 2 or 3 percent of the variance in social status can be explained by genetic contributions to intelligence!

Let us then consider the claims of these two approaches as the basis for public policy aimed at facilitating infant and early childhood development.

Adequacy as Theory

Current knowledge of the hows and whyfores of child development is, of course, imperfect. Yet, developmentalists can paint a fairly plausible picture of critical events, sequences, and factors (biological and environmental) in human development. However, such plausibility is not in itself sufficient for public policy if one assumes that the goal of policy should be, as suggested above, nothing less than facilitating the growth of capable, fully competent, and functional adults who can make their way in and contribute to society. To support this goal, a theory must not only tell us how children develop, it must include a description of how to intervene in a way that enhances development, and it must include a social theory which is able to identify systemmatically the childhood interventions which will lead with some predictability to adult outcomes. One result of the flurry of interest that occurred in the late 1960s and early 1970s in early childhood development programs was that many leading developmentalists were forced into an agonizing reappraisal of the limits of their knowledge. The effectiveness of interventions—especially in the area of cognitive development—is generally in doubt; the notion that the early years are "critical" to (or determinative of) adult development has been modified to the more modest and supportable claim that the early years are a "sensitive" developmental period, and, indeed, the ability to predict adult characteristics from childhood ones is quite limited (White, Day, Freeman, Hartman, and Messenger, 1973). It is not, in fact, until children reach the age of 8 or 9 (approximately the third grade) that one can begin to construct a plausible future scenario, based on such factors as correlations in year-to-year performance in school achievement, probabilities linking school achievement to school attainment, and the relationship of school attainment to occupational status. But even here, the predictions are very rough and based on crude variables. There remains a tremendous amount of individual variability, and it is by no means clear whether one's scenario is based on developmental stabilities or rigidities in social and institutional process, that is, predictable continuities of socially determined experience, not developmental stabilities (de Lone, 1979).

In short, the theoretical basis for the micro approach to developmental policy is shaky. The more ambitious the goals of that policy, the shakier it becomes. For instance, there is considerable theory and knowledge to support certain targeted services which aim at identifying and correcting individually specific developmental disabilities, from nutritional deficits to learning disabilities, in the sensitive period of childhood. There are important and proper, if modest, goals for public policy. But there is not adequate theory to support the micro approach if the effort is to facilitate the development of that class of children most "at risk" as a class—children of low income and minority groups. As suggested above, it has been the strange conjunction of liberal social theory and developmentalism which have made it easy for policy makers to commit the fundamental error of assuming that microdeterminants of individual development can be manipulated through program interventions to alter social outcomes. Our preconceptions of reality—of social reality, in particular—have been let slip or stuffed into our conception of the psychological task in this regard, and they must be unpacked.

Is the macro approach a theoretically superior alternative? It would be stretching things to attempt a definitive positive answer to this question. But there are reasons to believe it may be superior. It is a perspective which begins by attempting to imbed development in social context. On a priori grounds such an effort appears necessary if one is to take any but a very narrow view of what developmental policy should be. As such, it offers possibilities of yielding a dynamic conceptual framework which systematically relates individual development to social and economic structures and the contexts they produce. Further, it does not negate or disregard the main body of developmental theory so much as it places it in a different perspective and dynamic framework for policy purposes. In particular, its primary policy strategy involves supporting the economic status and security of the family, the agency which, for most of the children most of the time, serves as the source of nurture and the filter of experience. Common sense suggests that publicly funded, professionally delivered interventions are likely to be second-best substitutes for a secure family (however one defines that increasingly nebulous concept), and a body of evidence overwhelming in scale makes it clear that employment, and the economic security which goes with it, is *the* most important *single* determinant of family well-being. Further, such limited evidence as is available suggests that even *without changes in* employment status, simply increasing family income leads to benefits which most of us would conclude enhance the developmental milieu of families. Consider, for instance, this summary of findings from the income maintenance experiments:

The findings on family well-being are not uniformly positive or consistent, and they include some negative as well as numerous beneficial effects. But, taken together, they suggest the potential effects of a more adequate system of income support. These findings indicate that welfare reform that results in the kinds of programs tested in the experiments would contribute to less welfare dependency in the long run, which would (at least partially) offset the disincentive effects on work effort. Many families would use the payments to increase their long-run well-being and their earnings capacity, increase their savings, reduce their debt, obtain additional education and training, and migrate to areas with better opportunities. There would be improvement in nutrition and in the health of children at birth. Drop-out rates among teenagers would diminish, and perhaps there would be improvements in school performance. Finally, there would be less reliance on public housing. (Kehrer, 1979, p. 17)

On the other hand, much of the argument of the developmental payoff of a macro strategy relies on theory that is more intuitive than empirical. Cross-cultural studies are the best empirical source, and they do more to establish the broad fact that developmental patterns differ in distinctly different cultures than they do to illuminate the mechanics of development or the developmental importance of different socioeconomic contexts, social class settings, and subcultures within a society. The notion of the child as an actor in his or her own development through "map making" or the construction of a theory of social reality has a rather mysterious concept at its core, and it gains plausibility more from anecdotal data and analogies to cybernetics than from psychological research. Insofar as one demands a theory that meets all the tests sketched out above, then none is available. Insofar as one is forced to choose among these competing alternatives, however, a modest conclusion on the merits would seem to be that the macro alternative is as worthy of consideration as the prevailing micro choice. A more heroic assumption is that it is preferable. In any event, researchers can rest happy in the knowledge that more research is called for!

Sphere of Agency, Delivery Systems, and Technique

Beyond matters of theory, an effort to test systematically these two broad policy approaches against the criteria suggested above for adequate policy framework, effective delivery systems, and viable technique would require specification of policy strategies and lengthy discussion of implementational issues. It lies well beyond the scope of this paper, and, if theory is wrong, implementational issues are moot. A few overall points are worth making, however, beginning with an examination of micro approaches.

First, if an aim of public policy is to reduce the developmental penalties paid by children guilty of being born to low-income parents, it should be remembered that what is good for the goose is usually good for the gander. Thus, micro approaches which "improve" the development of poor children will also benefit affluent children (and are likely to benefit them more). While this may raise the developmental mean for the society as a whole, it will do nothing to eliminate the relative disadvantage of low-income children, who will remain relatively at risk by standards which are, finally, relative to any given society! Inequality can absorb individual interventions.

Second, when human service programs address the poor, sphere-of-agency problems do arise, as indicated briefly in the examples (stigma, systemic contradictions, etc.) given earlier. It is hard to be sure whether these problems outweigh the benefits, but it is entirely possible that they do, if the kinds of perverse effects frequently found in human service programs for older age groups apply in early childhood. Consider just one example: that recent studies show that vocational education programs not only fail to enhance the earnings and employment records of some (mostly male) recipients, but they also result in lowered aspirations, and in some groups lower rates of school attainment—a fact which probably damages future earnings prospects (Grasso and Shea, 1979).

Third, given the failure of evaluation research to find significant or lasting benefits of early childhood education programs, parent education programs, or similar developmental programs, one must conclude that if clinicians exist whose efforts have consistently positive results for reasons other than chance, they are few and far between. Occasional successes may be the result of exceptionally skilled clinicians, but it seems doubtful that public bureaucracies can replicate this scarce factor.

Again the question arises, do the macro alternatives meet these largely implementational tests any better? Again the answer is equivocal. Little in the past history of welfare programs, employment and training programs, or economic development programs gives one much to cheer about. Full employment, the prerequisite for an effective economic support program, is no easy thing to achieve and has been surprisingly unpopular as a political goal in this country (Nixon, 1973). Bureaucratic as well as technical obstacles exist. Yet, as economist Lester Thurow and others have argued, the basic issues are less those of economic theory, policy framework, or delivery than they are of political will (Thurow,

1973). It is not technically difficult to design or administer a credit income tax that would place a minimum income under every family and that would help to redistribute income (e.g., Keniston, 1977). Despite the bad public relations of the CETA system, evaluations have consistently found that the bureaucratic capacity to create publicly subsidized employment of reasonable (if variable) quality exists. And there is ample theoretical justification for the use of wage and capital subsidy programs which, without fueling inflation, can increase the employment opportunities for the so-called structurally unemployed (Eisner, 1978).

Child developmentalists cannot alone create the political will to drive this country toward an egalitarian family support policy. But in their professional lives, they can raise through research the kinds of macro issues that are important to the development of children, and in their personal lives they can be advocates. Things will not change easily or instantly, but if no one bothers to make the effort, they will not change at all.

References

Bell, D. Equality and merit. *The Public Interest*, 1973, *29*, 20–68.

Bloom, B. *Stability and change in human characteristics*. New York: Wiley, 1964.

Bowles, S., and Gintis, H. I.Q. in the United States class structure. In A. Gartner, C. Greer, and F. Reissman (Eds.), *The new assault on equality*. New York: Social Policy Books, 1964.

Bowles, S., and Gintis, H. *Schooling in capitalist America: Educational reform and the contradictions of economic life*. New York: Basic Books, 1976.

Brenner, H. *Estimating the social costs of national economic policy: Implications for mental and physical health and criminal aggression*. Joint Economic Committee, Congress of the United States. Washington, D.C.: U.S. Government Printing Office, 1976.

Brittain, J.A. *The inheritance of economic status*. Washington, D.C.: The Brookings Institute, 1977.

Cole, M., Gay, J., Glick, J.A., and Sharp, D.W. *The cultural context of learning and thinking*. New York: Basic Books, 1971.

de Lone, R.H. *Small futures: children, inequality and the limits of liberal reform*. New York: Harcourt, Brace, Jovanovich, 1979.

Eisenberg, L. *A research framework for evaluating health promotion and disease prevention*. Paper presented at the First Annual Alcohol, Drug Abuse and Mental Health Administration Conference on Prevention, Silver Springs, MD, 1979.

Eisner, R. A direct attack on unemployment and inflation. *Challenge*, 1978, *21*, 49–51.

Grasso, J., and Shea, J. *Vocational education and training: Impact on youth*. Berkeley, CA.: Carnegie Council on Policy Studies in Higher Education, 1979.

Jencks, C., Bartlett, S., Corcoran, M., Crouse, J., Eaglesfield, D., Jackson, G., McClelland, K., Mueser, P., Olneck, M., Schwartz, J., Ward, S. and Williams, J. *Who gets ahead?* New York: Basic Books, 1979.

Katz, M.B. *The irony of early school reform: Education innovation in mid-nineteenth century Massachusetts.* Cambridge, MA: Harvard University Press, 1969.

Kehrer, K.C. More on the income maintenance and welfare reform debate. *The MPR Policy Newsletter,* Mathematica Policy Research, 1979, *1*, 17.

Kelly, G. *The psychology of personal constructs.* New York: Norton, 1955.

Keniston, K. *All our children: The American family under pressure.* New York: Harcourt, Brace, Jovanovich, 1977.

Kessen, W. Questions for a theory of cognitive development. *Monographs of the Society for Research in Child Development,* 1966, *31* (5, Serial No. 107).

Laosa, L.M. Social competence in childhood: Towards a developmental, socioculturally relativistic paradigm. In M.W. Kent and J.E. Rolf (Eds.), *Social competence in children,* Vol. 3: *Primary prevention of psychopathology.* Hanover, N.H.: University Press of New England, 1979.

Leacock, E. *Teaching and learning in city schools.* New York: Basic Books, 1969.

Lekachman, R. *Economists at bay.* New York: McGraw Hill, 1976.

McLelland, D.C. Testing for competence rather than for "intelligence." *American Psychologist,* 1973, *28,* 1–14.

Nixon, R.A. The historical development of the concept and implementation of full employment as economic policy. In A. Gartner, R.A. Nixon, and F. Reissman (Eds.), *Public service employment: An analysis of the history, problems and prospects.* New York: Praeger, 1973.

Ogbu, J.U. *Minority education and caste: The American system in cross-cultural perspective.* New York: Academic Press, 1978.

Plattner, M. The welfare state vs. the redistributive state. *The Public Interest,* 1979, *55,* 28–48.

Rutter, M. Protective factors in children's response in stress and disadvantage. In M.W. Kent and J.E. Rolf (Eds.), *Social competence in children,* Vol.3: *Primary prevention of psychopathology.* Hanover, N.H.: University Press of New England, 1979.

Ross, H., and Sawhill, I. *Time of transition: The growth of families headed by women.* Washington, DC: The Urban Institute, 1975.

Sewell, W.H. Inequality of opportunity for higher education. *American Sociological Review,* 1971, *36,* 793–809.

Thurow, L. Toward a definition of economic justice. *The Public Interest,* 1973, *31,* 56–80.

White, S., Day, M.C., Freeman, P.K., Hartman, S.A., and Messenger, K.P. *Federal programs for young children: Review and recommendations,* Vol.I. Dept. of Health, Education and Welfare. Washington, DC: U.S. Government Printing Office, 1973.

A Service Delivery System for Handicapped Children, from Birth to Three, and Their Families

Judy Howard

Expanding medical knowledge and improved medical technology are improving the outcome for sick infants and decreasing perinatal complications. Even with improved medical technology, however, there will be handicapped children in the future. This will be due partly to an inevitable delay in providing such techniques to the general population. In addition, new, unanticipated hazards such as drugs, chemicals, and radiation will affect the human fetus. Thus, improvement of intervention methods which will optimize handicapped infants' future and the implementation of these methods into community programs are ongoing concerns.

A service delivery system for handicapped children from birth to 3 and their families requires a theoretical base which is dependent upon current knowledge from medical and behavioral research. The following discussion will focus on medically at-risk infants, the group from which many handicapped children come. We will look at the families' influence on their infants' future development, and the responsibility of the medical and educational disciplines to provide combined services to assist these children and their families.

Medically At-Risk Infants

Evidence is mounting that there may be a linkage system between the physiological and behavioral responses in the neonate and young infant. To ensure optimal care for the sick newborn more than appropriate diagnostic and medical treatment procedures will have to be considered. Professionals will have to take into account their own impact on infants as they care for them medically, as well as how to support the families. Long, Philip, and Lucey (1980) observed that low birthweight infants ex-

This program is sponsored in part by the Office of Education, BEH grant number G007800165.

perienced more hypoxemia when handled by nursery personnel. Furthermore, as the quality of handling improved, the infants demonstrated fewer hypoxemic events.

The ways in which caregiving actions may profoundly influence the course of the infant's progress in the hospital, as well as the success of ultimate recovery, are currently under investigation by Gorski (1980). A complete set of data is not yet available from Gorski's study, yet he believes that he can observe behavioral distress signals before physiologic crises occur. He also believes that the crises may be averted by altering caregiving procedures. He describes how observations of infants' behavior were used to tailor changes in the care. For instance, an infant had had repeated episodes of bradycardia, or slowing of the heart rate, for no discernible reason; careful analysis revealed that most of these episodes were preceded by multiple caregiving interventions, such as the checking of vital signs, physical examination, physical therapy, and laboratory work that followed in close succession. A change in caregiving procedures was instituted. The infant was given a 10-to-15-minute rest period between each caregiving procedure. The result was a decrease in the incidence of the bradycardia from an average of 9 per 8-hour observation period to 3 the following week. This occurred despite any accompanying evidence of change in the infant's medical status.

The importance of promoting opportunities for a healthy parent–child interaction during the neonatal period are also apparent. Interruption of the normal process of mother–infant attachment occurs for parents of medically at-risk neonates. Desmond, Wilson, Alt, and Fisher (1980) describe the experiences of these parents during the early neonatal period. Specifically, the mothers grieve as they withdraw from the relationship established during the pregnancy with the in utero child, acknowledge feelings of failure for delivering an unhealthy baby, prepare to relate to the real baby whose survival is assured, and try to understand the differences and special needs of their medically at-risk infant.

Awareness of these psychological events has led to increased numbers of social support services for parents of infants in neonatal intensive care units affiliated with large medical centers. Presently, longitudinal data are not available that compare the developmental outcome of children whose parents received specific kinds of support services during this early period. However, Minde, Shosenberg, Marton, Thompson, Ripley, and Burns (1980) described the results of their study comparing parental caretaking characteristics of parents who had attended a self-help group for parents of preterm infants with those of an untreated control group. The results indicated that parents who had attended the self-help group demonstrated improved feelings of competence in caretaking procedures and increased interaction with their infants in the nursery and at home, 3 months following their infants' discharge. Experiences such as these assist parents as they plan to care for their infant at home and as they transfer their infant's care to the primary care physician. The importance of the role of this professional cannot be overestimated.

Infants' discharge from the hospital and their return to family care is a stressful period for families. Desmond et al. (1980) describe three events which frequently occur simultaneously: there is withdrawal of the social supportive network to the family, medical care of the infant is transferred to a different physician, and the family receives bills from the hospital and physicians. Parents describe these events as traumatic. Furthermore, once home, parents face the rigors of a 24-hour schedule with an infant who has adapted to extrauterine life in an environment of intensive care with brightly lighted rooms full of music, talking, and motion. The infant may take months to adapt to a predictable sleep-awake cycle which permits a practical family routine.

Even though the parents have support from medical personnel at the time of the infant's discharge from the hospital, many report feeling inadequate to provide proper care for their infant, whom they are likely to perceive as fragile and sick. They continue during the first 4 months to focus mainly on the welfare of their infants and their ability to provide adequate care for survival and normal physical development.

Their concerns are realistic. The medically at-risk infant's vulnerability to illness during the first 2 years is consistently reported in the pediatric literature (Douglas and Mogford, 1953; Littman and Parmelee, 1978). Respiratory tract infections, surgical procedures, and failure to thrive are commonly observed problems (Drillien, 1961; Fitzhardinge, 1978; Harper and Wiener, 1965; Shaheen, Alexander, Truskowsky, and Barbero, 1968).

Multiple medical problems are also observed in handicapped children. As medical director of an early intervention program, I am involved with the pediatric care of young handicapped children. In addition to the program staff and staff from community agencies, the families use a great number of health personnel. During the child's stay in the program, the families, on the average, seek out more than four other health specialists (Howard and Beckwith, 1980). They contact pediatric neurologists, child development specialists, cardiologists, ophthalmologists, gastroenterologists, cardiac surgeons, pediatric surgeons, ear, nose, and throat specialists, audiologists, endocrinologists, geneticists, and orthopedic surgeons. The families' need for medical services are almost overwhelming.

The traditional role of primary care physicians following infants' discharge from the hospital is well-recognized. Health care supervision at frequent intervals and prescribed medical treatments for acute illnesses are routine. The physician's impact on the parent–child relationship is assumed but not often studied. Casey and Whitt (1980) have described the results of a clinical trial with healthy primiparous mother–infant pairs and the effectiveness of physician counseling in nonphysical areas during routine office visits. The children in the control group received thorough physical examinations and their mothers participated in discussions of physical and preventive care such as accident prevention and nutrition. The mothers in the experimental group received, in addition, discussions at all visits designed to enhance the affective interaction between mother and infant and to promote the infant's cognitive development. Specifically, these discussions were about normal infant development, understanding each infant's individuality, the social nature of the infants' behaviors, and encouraging mothers' feelings of confidence and competence to affect their infants' development. The study group, after this early 6 month intervention, demonstrated more appropriate, cooperative, and sensitive interactions and more appropriate play. The infants who had received the intervention demonstrated more advanced vocal imitation, though all infants scored similarly on a developmental test. Thus, it is reasonable to assume that the primary care physicians can influence a family's understanding and enjoyment of their infant.

The significance of healthy parent–infant interaction in the development of medically at-risk infants is furnished by a study conducted by Parmelee and his colleagues at the University of California at Los Angeles. They designed and tested an assessment system for designating infants as potentially at-risk for future disabilities (Parmelee, 1979). The assessments consisted of 14 measures of medical, neurological, neurophysiological, and infant behaviors, and two home observations of caregiver interaction administered between birth and 9 months of age. A medically recognized high-risk group of infants—126 preterms—were selected as the target group. Full-term control infants were also included.

Naturalistic observations were made at the infant's home during everyday routines at 1 and 8 months past expected date of delivery. Approximately 25 caregivers and infant behaviors were noted; these included summary measures of attentiveness, feeding, and physical care, as well as ways of talking to the baby, measures of touching and holding, ways of mediating the environment, social play, behaviors dependent on simultaneous eye-to-eye contact of baby and caregiver, measures of caregiver's contingency to distress, and infant behaviors of fuss-cry, nondistress vocalizations, and social approaches to the observer (Beckwith, Cohen, Kopp, Parmelee, and Marcy, 1976).

The kinds of environmental transactions that occurred between a caregiver and the infant accounted for variance in the child's development beyond that explained by medical events, social class, and other variables. Infants who spent more time in social interaction with their caregivers performed more adequately on a sensorimotor series and a Gesell test in the first year of life. And furthermore, increased social interaction during the first year of life predicted increased competence at age 2 as measured by the Bayley, Gesell, and receptive language tests, whereas obstetrical and postnatal hazards by themselves were not predictive (Beckwith, 1979).

The powerful impact that parents have on the developmental outcome of their children is further strengthened by Broussard's (1976) study of primiparas' perceptions of their full-term neonates and the children's subsequent emotional development. She found that maternal perceptions of the infant during the first month are predictive of the probability of a mental disorder in the child at age 10 to 11, independent of the educational level of either parent, father's occupation, changes in income, maternal age, type of delivery, or family size.

An understanding of the characteristics of a healthy parent–infant interaction can assist medical and educational professionals' identification of the vulnerable family unit. Once this occurs, appropriate intervention methods can be initiated.

Professional recognition of the differences between the response of parents to a normally developing infant as compared with those with a developmentally disabled infant are important when planning intervention strategies. Handicapped infants and their mothers have been studied extensively (Block, 1955; Call, 1958; Marshall, Hegrenes, and Goldstein, 1973; Schlesinger and Meadow, 1972; Shere, 1955). In 1938, Shirley described her observations of mothers relating to their preterm infants following hospital discharge. The mothers were noted to be more anxious than those of term babies, tending to hover over their infants with great solicitude. Protection from the stimulating environment was often followed by over stimulation in the infants' care.

A recent description of an intervention project of parental controlling behavior in responding to the handicapped infant has been reported by Barnard and Kelly (1980). In a study from the University of Washington, 14 handicapped infants between 0 and 18 months of age and their caregivers were observed during a teaching interaction. The treatment group received a home-based intervention program designed to improve the quality of interaction between the infant and the caregiver. The control group received no intervention. Both groups were pretested and posttested using an observation scale which recorded the frequency and duration of initiating and responding behavior of the caregivers and the infants. These behaviors were rated as being either positive or negative. The analysis of the changes between the pre- and posttesting revealed two significant findings: the frequency and duration of positive caregiver behaviors significantly increased as a result of the treatment, and the duration of controlling behaviors significantly decreased as a result of treatment. These changes in the caregivers' behaviors occurred in spite of there being relatively no changes in the frequency of the infants' behaviors.

Their findings are consistent with the study we conducted, evaluating changes in the interaction between the parent and the handicapped child before and after 9 months of intervention (Howard, Laboriel, Burge, and Bromwich, 1980). The observation scale used measured changes in three categories of behavior: affect, language, and play. There were 19 mother–child pairs each in the experimental and control groups. The ages ranged from 8 to 28 months at time of entry into the center-based intervention program. Analysis of the pre- and posttest scores indicated consistently poorer quality in the handicapped children's affective, language, and play behaviors as well as more frequent incidence of nonadaptive behaviors as compared with the control group of children. The impact of intervention was on the mothers of the handicapped children. They improved in their affect and their use of language with their children to a point, approaching the scores of the control group of mothers. The mothers' enjoyment of their handicapped children and their ability to achieve a flow of interaction was significantly improved after intervention. Similarly, their use of language in communication with their children was improved. Thus, with guidance the parents can alter their responses to their handicapped children even without appreciable short-term change in their children's behavior.

However, the importance of tailoring the educational intervention to the needs of the individual mother and child cannot be overemphasized. Because the mother is seen as the key agent of change in the child, the focus of the intervention is to help her gain confidence in observing and responding to her child. The nature of the intervention varies as the needs of the mother and child evolve. In some instances, mothers are entirely focused on the handicap of their children and are unable to perceive those normal aspects of their behavior. In other situations, the interaction is excellent and the mothers need support in times of crisis (e.g., surgery, acute illnesses requiring hospitalization). In still others, the functioning of the child is low enough to be very unrewarding to the mother. The emphasis is on helping the mother to read those cues which the child does give. Over time the inability of the low functioning children to give satisfying feedback to their mothers is a limiting factor in their interaction. Intervention is then directed toward support of the mothers' realistic perception of their children and of their sense of confidence in handling and planning for them.

A Medical-Educational Service System

With our current knowledge from scientific and behavioral research efforts, basic guidelines for developing a service delivery system for young handicapped children and their families can be described. Consideration of the following information is important: Newborn infants who require medical treatment in neonatal intensive care units *can* recover from this insult and develop normally. At this time it is not possible to determine the developmental outcome of medically at-risk infants by their prenatal, perinatal, and/or postnatal complications.

However, medically at-risk infants tend to have more frequent illnesses following their discharge from the hospital through the first 2 years of life. These medical problems beyond the neonatal period seem to have an adverse effect on the developmental progress of the infant. Frequently, the cumulative effect of these illnesses is not apparent on the infant's development until the later half of the first year. Also, time for recovery from neonatal insults is needed before we can determine how much permanent brain damage is present. Thus, it is not possible to identify the mild to moderate developmentally disabled infant until the later part of the first year, using available developmental tests. Those infants with severe disabilities can be recognized earlier.

Developmentally disabled children routinely require multiple medical subspecialty evaluations and treatments during the first few years of life in order to optimally interact with their environment. Common handicapping conditions which require treatment include hydrocephalus, seizures, amblyopia, hearing deficits, orthopedic problems, and congenital cardiac defects. Genetic consultations to determine if a hereditary factor has caused the disability are also commonly needed.

Treatment of the medical needs of the handicapped young child coincide with optimizing the environment in order to provide opportunities for developmental progress. It seems that the medically at-risk infant's development is as influenced by the social enviroment as is the normal infant's. Furthermore, parents of handicapped children tend to be more controlling and intrusive when relating to their children than do parents of normal children. These parental behaviors, no doubt, contribute to the often passive, dependent personalities that many handicapped adults demonstrate (Howard, 1978).

Therefore, we recognized that the medical and environmental needs of developmentally disabled young children require attention. Until recently, the primary care physician constituted the main treatment and support system for these children and their families. Parents continue to expect and need the physician's services. However, as our information about the effects of the environment on young infants has grown, it has become apparent that a more comprehensive service system is required.

With the passage of Public Law 94-142 in 1975, the educational system has become involved. Under this law, all handicapped children within specified age ranges are guaranteed a free, appropriate public education. Many states now have demonstration model programs, funded by the Office of Education, which serve the birth-to-3 population of at-risk children. It is anticipated that the focus of the 1980s will be to mandate educational services for this age group throughout the nation. The flirtation between pediatricians and special educators has been described by the British pediatrician, John Apley (1971). According to him, it was time they were married, if only for the sake of the children! From my perspective, the marriage has now occurred and we are in the midst of sorting out our "family roles."

Our present lack of expertise in designing the perfect intervention program is apparent. However, it is possible to discuss general ways in which the various professional disciplines who have knowledge about normal infant development can work together with these families. The emphasis should be on the child, a person, who happens to have a developmental disability. Sensitivity to parental responses when their fears are confirmed that their infant is not normal is essential. Professionals also need to understand that grief, denial, and anger are normal emotions which will vary in intensity and time according to each parent's personal characteristics and experiences. Knowing when to ask parents if they need assistance from others is crucial. It is also important to recognize that it is not uncommon for parents to refuse help initially. Usually this refusal relates to the parents' disbelief about their infants' disabilities.

Physicians and nurses can assist parents in sorting out the medical and educational needs of their young children. Advising parents in what to expect from different medical specialists and what kinds of questions to ask is an invaluable help. For instance, an orthopedic surgeon who has expertise in evaluating the status of the bones and joints of the physically disabled child may not feel comfortable in answering questions about future cognitive development. Thus, if parents can be helped to ask appropriate questions, increased feelings of competence emerge as they acquire the information they need about their children.

Once infants begin attending an intervention program, the nonmedical staff can better serve the handicapped children and their families if they have information about the clients' medical problems and the behavioral consequences that may be secondary to these problems and/or medications. A further step is necessary before communication can exist between all disciplines. Simplification of professional jargon is mandatory!

The role of the educator with the very young handicapped child is not as clearly understood by the medical disciplines and the parents. During the ensuing years more information will be available. However, an important focus for the educator is helping the parents become more aware of the normal developmental behaviors at their child's developmental age level. Establishment of mutually satisfying interactions—*doing* with the child rather than *to* the child—guarantees a more successful relationship over time. Communicating methods which will enhance the individual child's personal style and tempo is most important as it allows parents an opportunity for success and enjoyment with their children.

A rule of thumb for all professionals working with the young handicapped children and their families, is that the parents, regardless of their past experiences, initially feel unsure about how to plan for the children. The overall goal of all early intervention is to assist the parents as they learn about their handicapped children's strengths and areas of need. Since a perfect program does not exist, parents should be able to question and advise us about our current service methodologies. Many parents have told me, "I must know I did the best I could for my child."

References

Apley, J. Their questions to us. *Clinical Pediatrics,* 1971, *10,* 135–137.

Barnard, K., and Kelly J. *Infant intervention: Parental considerations.* Paper presented at the Conference on Health Issues in Early Intervention Programs, Washington, D.C., May 1980.

Beckwith, L. The influence of caregiver–infant interaction on development. In E. J. Sell (Ed.), *Followup of the high-risk newborn: A practical approach.* Springfield, IL: C.C. Thomas, 1979.

Beckwith, L., Cohen, S. E., Kopp, C. B., Parmelee, A. H., and Marcy, T. G. Caregiver–infant interaction and early cognitive development in preterm infants. *Child Development,* 1976, *47,* 579–587.

Block, W. E. A study of somatapsychological relationships in cerebral palsied children. *Exceptional Children,* 1955, *22,* 53–59.

Broussard, E. R. Neonatal prediction and outcome at 10/11 years. *Child Psychiatry and Human Development,* 1976, *7,* 85–93.

Call, J. Psychological problems of the cerebral palsied child, his parents and siblings as revealed by dynamically oriented small group discussions with parents. *Cerebral Palsy Review,* 1958, *10,* 3–5 & 11–15.

Casey, P. H., and Whitt, J. K. Effect of the pediatrician on the mother–infant relationship. *Pediatrics,* 1980, *65,* 815–820.

Desmond, M. M., Wilson, G. S., Alt, J. E., and Fisher, E. S. The very low birth weight infant after discharge from intensive care: Anticipatory health care and developmental course. *Current problems in pediatrics.* Year Book Medical Publishers: Chicago, 1980.

Douglas, J. W. B., and Mogford, C. Health of premature children from birth to four years. *British Medical Journal,* 1953, *1,* 748–754.

Drillien, C. M. A longitudinal study of the growth and development of prematurely and maturely born children. Part 8. *Archives of Disease in Childhood,* 1961, *36,* 515–525.

Fitzhardinge, P. M. Follow-up studies in infants treated by mechanical ventilation. *Clinics in Perinatology,* 1978, *5,* 451–461.

Gorski, P. A. *Premature infant behavioral and physiological responses to caregiving interventions in the intensive care nursery.* Paper presented at the First World Congress on Infant Psychiatry, Estoril, Portugal, April 1980.

Harper, P. A., and Wiener, G. Sequelae of low birth weight. *Annual Review of Medicine,* 1965, *16,* 405–420.

Howard, J. The influence of children's developmental dysfunctions on marital quality and family interaction. In R. M. Lerner and G. D. Spanier (Eds.), *Child influences on marital and family interaction: A life-span perspective.* New York: Academic Press, 1978.

Howard, J., and Beckwith, L. *Child change in an early intervention program for the developmentally disabled.* Paper presented at the Conference on Health Issues in Early Intervention Programs, Washington, D.C., May 1980.

Howard, J., Laboriel, M., Burge, D., and Bromwich, R. *Assessment of a mother-child interaction measure for handicapped infants.* Manuscript in preparation, 1980.

Littman, B., and Parmelee, A. H. Medical correlates of infant development. *Pediatrics,* 1978, *61,* 470–474.

Long, J. G., Philip, A. G. S., and Lucey, J. F. Excessive handling as a cause of hypoxemia. *Pediatrics,* 1980, *65,* 203–208.

Marshall, N., Hegrenes, J., and Goldstein, S. Verbal interactions: Mothers and their retarded children versus mothers and their non-retarded children. *American Journal of Mental Deficiency,* 1973, *77,* 415–419.

Minde, K., Shosenberg, N., Marton, P., Thompson, J., Ripley, J., and Burns, S. Self-help groups in a premature nursery—a controlled evaluation. *Journal of Pedatrics,* 1980, *96,* 933–940.

Parmelee, A. H. *"Diagnostic and intervention studies of high risk infants."* Final Report NIH. LHD-3-2276. Los Angeles: University of California at Los Angeles, Department of Pediatrics, June 1979.

Schlesinger, H. S., and Meadow, K. P. *Sound and sign.* Berkeley, CA: University of California Press, 1972.

Shaheen, E., Alexander, D., Truskowsky, M., and Barbero, G. J. Failure to thrive: A retrospective profile. *Clinical Pediatrics,* 1968, *7,* 255–261.

Shere, M. Social-emotional factors with families of the twins with cerebral palsy. *Exceptional Children,* 1955, *22,* 197–199.

Shirley, M. Development of immature babies during their first two years. *Child Development,* 1938, *9,* 347–360.

A Model for Coalescing Birth-to-3 Programs

Earladeen Badger and Donna Burns

It is important to recognize that not all or even most of the important events or policies which influence families are the result of governmental action. Ideological changes such as the civil rights movement and individual actions or changes in attitudes can have profound effects on families (Family Impact Seminar, 1978).

"There is no machinery for change. It comes about unexpectedly. It comes about through an individual, through a small group, through prophets. And you can't program prophets, or recruit them. These people just run up and invent their own way. That is the way that change happens" (Wills, 1972, p. 36).

We intend to develop this concept for change by describing how the actions of individuals served to strengthen and bring together over 170 parenting programs in Ohio. The organization which resulted, United Services for Effective Parenting (USEP), helps parents to provide optimal developmental experiences for their children during the first 3 years of life. Its ideology is based on many of the assumptions and values found in *All Our Children* (Keniston, 1977), *Toward a National Policy For Children And Families* (National Research Council, 1976), *Report to the Congress of the United States* (General Accounting Office, 1979), and the *Interim Report of the Family Impact Seminar* (April 1978). Its uniqueness, however, is that USEP came into being without benefit of federal mandate or initiative. USEP, a child and parent advocacy plan executed by program practitioners, succeeds because imagination and adaptability in solving problems are still possible in grass-root efforts.

As public interest mounts in favor of a social policy that will support

Preparation of this manuscript was assisted by funds from Grant #Goo77 00714 (U.S. Office of Education/Bureau of Education for the Handicapped) and the Cincinnati Maternity and Infant Care Project #545. Gratitude is expressed to the many individuals who developed the model for coalescing birth-to-three programs in the State of Ohio (USEP): local pioneers in Cincinnati, members of the original steering committee, and statewide regional leaders who are members of the Ohio Council. Special recognition is due Florence Chamberlin and Joan Mattoz at the state level and Audrey Hodgins and Matia Finn-Stevenson for their reviews and helpful comments in the preparation of the final manuscript.

families in rearing their very young children, we must be wary of how that policy will be institutionalized. Our bias is against federal design or mandate because we have little evidence to suggest that federal programming results in effective translation of policy to service.

The Catalog of Federal Domestic Assistance (1976) considered a total of 1,044 federally funded programs and identified 268, administered by 17 different agencies, with "potential" impact on families. In spite of the number of service programs, concrete effects often seem to be lacking. According to the National Research Council, "fragmentation, discontinuity, lost cases, unsuccessful intervention, and poor service takeup are some of the problems. Despite large federal investments in research and demonstration, specific organizational and professional solutions to these generally acknowledged problems have not been identified" (National Research Council, 1976, p. 93).

The feelings of bewilderment, powerlessness, and alienation that engulf parents, especially low-income parents, when they are forced to deal with bureaucracies, institutions, and professionals in order to receive needed services for their children have been well documented (Berger and Neuhaus, 1977; Keniston, 1977; Steiner, 1976). The inability of parents to perform a mediating role is increasingly cited as an important reason for the ineffectiveness of many well-intentioned public policies.

Most of us would agree that empowering parents to become effective advocates for their children within the maze of agencies is a laudable goal, and how this empowerment might occur has been suggested by many. Three proposals are worth mentioning because of the national attention they have received. The National Research Council (1976) would help parents fulfill their children's basic needs through the creation of Neighborhood Resource Centers which would integrate and coordinate a wide range of existing programs, such as Head Start, Home Start, and the Child Care Associate programs, as well as provide new services as needed. Keniston (1977) would support the primacy of parental authority by enacting extensive reforms in social policy, work practices, and law. And the General Accounting Office (1979) would expand early childhood and family development programs for low-income children during their first 4 years of life.

While all three proposals have long-range merit, a pragmatist would probably opt for the plan of the General Accounting Office because early educational intervention programs for children of the poor have produced demonstrable effects. A 10-year follow-up of the Collaborative Preschool Project, which included 12 federally funded demonstration models with a total of 1,599 children, indicated that developmental programs for low-income children during the first 4 years of life produced lasting, significant gains and helped these youngsters to perform significantly better in school than did control groups of children who had had no early childhood programs (Lazar, Hubbell, Murray, Rosche, and Royce, 1977). And an important discovery related to parent power was reported as part of the results of the collaborative follow-up study. Because the children served were young, parents naturally became co-participants in many programs. Mother love and parental concern often made them apt students in child development and effective imitators of the professional teacher's interactions with children. One of the positive effects of the early education models of the 1960s was that educators began to acknowledge the impact of parents in fostering the development of their children and began to treat the parents as equals. This democratic treatment of low-income parents (Badger, 1971; Gordon, 1969; Klaus and Gray, 1968; Levenstein and Sunley, 1968) not only helped them to become effective teachers of their preschool children but also served to improve their self-concept and feelings of worth. In part, what had been taken away from parents by "helping" institutions during the course of recent social history was restored.

In the senior author's experience as a designer and implementor of early childhood education programs during the past 15 years, most parents respond favorably to support and direction when they are heavily involved in caregiving activities, notably during their child's first 3 years of life. In the original Mother Training Program (Karnes, Teska, Hodgins, and Badger, 1970), children were 12 to 24 months of age; in its replication in Parent-Child Centers (Badger, 1972), children were 6 to 36 months of age; and in an adapted program for teenage mothers (Badger, 1977), the infants were newborns.

According to most of the reviews of parent-focused programs in early childhood, we have not yet developed effective teaching strategies to enhance parenting skills (Bronfenbrenner, 1974; Chilman, 1973; Clark-Stewart, 1977; Horowitz and Paden, 1973; Hunt, 1979; Stevens, 1978). Nevertheless, Clark-Stewart (1977), in a book commissioned by the Carnegie Council on Children, recommends the following proposition: "Parent education programs should be improved and made available to all parents and prospective parents who want them" (p. 105). This is a programmatic rather than a policy recommendation, and while social scientists debate the merits of home-based versus group instruction, the effectiveness of various teaching strategies, or the critical time for entry into parent education programs, there will be designers and implementors who will continue to translate research findings and educated guesses into the programs which ultimately shape social policy.

The Beginnings of USEP

United Services for Effective Parenting began in Cincinnati in 1974. As parenting programs multiplied, largely as a result of a growing interest in early intervention and the training provided through the Infant Stimulation/Mother Training (IS/MT) Program (Badger, 1977), a "buddy" system evolved which transcended the boundaries of agencies and institutions. With token funding and low service priority for birth-to-3 programs in their respective agencies, providers felt the need to get together on a monthly basis for emotional support. They demonstrated that health care, education, and social service agencies could unite at the delivery level to share information, resources, referrals, and staff development programs for the benefit of all. This sharing occurred informally at first, but it soon became apparent that funding needs, program accountability, and a central referral system could be accomplished through USEP's corporate identity. Its constitution and by-laws provided an organizational structure which served to legitimatize programs for high-risk infants and their families in several ways. We subsequently found that we were able to (1) increase the visibility and acceptance of these programs, (2) marshal community and state support for the inclusion of Family Life Programs in Ohio's Title XX service plan, (3) expand promising pilot programs with Title XX monies, (4) involve the University of Cincinnati College of Medicine, the Health Department's Maternity and Infant Care Project, and the State Department of Maternal and Child Health in providing funds and office space for a central referral clearinghouse within the Newborn Division of the Department of Pediatrics, and (5) identify, refer, and track parents with children younger than 3 years of age who were interested in joining programs within the USEP network.

USEP began as an organization of advocacy for birth-to-3 program providers and the families they served. A loose coalition of individuals— teachers, nurses, social workers, psychologists, pediatricians, and experienced mothers—was able to identify problems and solutions related to program development and to follow through on a plan of action.[1] This process has been described by Edelman (1973) who states that "someone or a small group has to stay with the effort throughout, or those whose interest, however genuine, is only a secondary priority will not stay in-

---

[1]An experienced mother is a mature woman who has successfully reared her own children and decides to put her experience and expertise to work as a volunteer or paid employee in a parenting program. She is an independent learner of child development theory and practices and requires only limited training to become highly effective in supporting new parents.

volved long. There is a word for it: leadership" (p. 641). According to Marris and Rein (1967), such an effort is not possible through a strategy of bureaucratic coordination and national planning. Instead, advocacy succeeds when "it demands no prior commitment, and threatens no jurisdiction. It does not predetermine the targets of reform, or theorize its plans, but exploits its chances. The flexibility makes it less vulnerable, more resilient under attack, and surest of its goals" (Joint Commission on the Mental Health of Children, 1969, p. 162).

It became apparent 3 years later (1977) that what 16 agencies were engaged in collectively in Cincinnati was an important translation of interagency coordination and cooperation. We seemed to be ready to spread the USEP concept, if not the organizational model, to other cities in Ohio. And, interest in USEP had been expressed by friends and colleagues who had attended the 4-day short courses (Infant Enrichment Through Mother Training) offered twice a year by the IS/MT Program in Cincinnati.

How to proceed? Our strategy was to try to involve decision makers at the state level since the funding of birth-to-3 programs was, at best, tenuous. Two outside experts, Hunt and Garber, agreed to speak on the significance of early educational intervention in the prevention of mental retardation. A selected audience of 40 state leaders—heads of state departments, therapists, educators, social workers, doctors—attended a 1-day symposium (May 19, 1977) sponsored and supported by Ohio State University Department of Early Childhood Education, to hear Hunt report on the results of his research with experientially deprived infants in Tehran orphanages (Hunt, 1976) and Garber report on the well-known Milwaukee Project (Heber and Garber, 1975). The upshot of this 1-day symposium was that 12 colleagues agreed to form a steering committee to begin to bring together birth-to-3 programs in Ohio. These 12 were, in fact, the only members of the audience who responded enthusiastically to the organizational model embodied in USEP. While others seemed interested in and impressed with the results of early intervention reported by Hunt and Garber, they did not envision how USEP might facilitate the growth and development of primary prevention programs in Ohio. And there was no plan for implementation; that would take time to evolve.

Finding out how the USEP concept might be incorporated across the state occurred during bi-monthly meetings of the 12 members of the steering committee. The first order of business was to find out where the programs were and whom they served. A 21-item program questionnaire (Table 1) was prepared by the committee and circulated by home extension agents in each of the 88 Ohio counties. Completed question-

Table 1. Program Questionnaire
Parenting: Birth to Three

Program Name_____   Sponsoring agency_____

How long operational _____   Address _____

Contact person _____   (street)

Telephone No. _____   _____

                                                     (city)   (zip)

Directions: Check ( ) whatever applies to description of your program. Use *Other* category only if the other options are absolutely *not* applicable and explain.

1. Families served: newborns ( ); firstborns ( ); birth-6 mo. ( ); 0–1 yr. ( ); 0–2 yr. ( ); 0–3 yr. ( ); adolescent mothers ( ); low-income ( ); middle-class ( ); *other:*

2. Number of families served annually (estimate number): _____

3. Families receive program: daily ( ); 2 times weekly ( ); weekly ( ); bi-weekly ( ); monthly ( ); *other:*

4. Duration of program: 1 mo. ( ); 3–6 mo. ( ); 6–12 mo. ( ); 1 yr. ( ); 2 yr. ( ); *other:*

5. Staff includes (specify number); paraprofessional ( ); nurse ( ); volunteer ( ); educator ( ); social worker ( ); P.T. ( ) or O.T. ( ); child development ( ); speech ( ) or hearing ( ) specialist; doctor ( ); *other:*

6. Do you have a plan for staff development: Yes ( ); No ( ).

7. In-service training occurs: weekly ( ); bi-weekly ( ); monthly ( ); and includes: outside experts ( ); out-of-town conferences ( ); *other:*

8. Program facilities: school ( ); church ( ); home ( ); clinic ( ); hospital ( ); agency quarters ( ); *other:*

9. Program model: classes ( ); home visiting ( ); center-based ( ); *other:*

10. Name curriculum model/theoretical base: _____

11. Referral source (estimate percentage): self ( ); central referral system ( ); hospital ( ); clinic ( ); Welfare ( ); mental health ( ); school ( ); doctor ( ); *other:*

12. If you coordinate services with other agencies, name agencies:

13. Educational resources: film library ( ); toy library ( ); books or pamphlets ( ); *other:*

14. Program evaluation: Informal client response ( ); written questionnaire ( ); telephone survey ( ); outside observer/evaluator ( ): infant assessments ( ); parent assessments ( ); *other:*

15. If you use formal assessment instruments, name them: _____

16. Program is funded: tuition or fee ( ); federal ( ); state ( ); county ( ); donations ( ); service organization ( ); *other:*

17. Does your program function with an advisory group? Yes ( ); No ( ).

18. If yes, does this group add to the strength of your program? Yes ( ); No ( ).

19. If no, do you see a need for an advisory group to your program? Yes ( ); No ( ).

20. Would you attend a state conference for infant/family educators? Yes ( ); No ( ).

21. If yes, list three topics you would like to have included in the conference which reflect your greatest program needs. _____

naires were returned to the USEP office in Cincinnati where an item analysis was run and a state directory of birth-to-3 programs compiled. We were especially encouraged by the overwhelmingly positive response to question 20: "Would you attend a state conference for infant/ family educators?" (No attempt was made to locate pre-parenting programs in Ohio, but we expect to do so in a future revision of the current directory.)

What follows is a state of the art in early intervention programs in Ohio. It may be descriptive of what is occurring in other states. We believe the information is sufficiently interesting to share.

Profiles of Birth-to-3 Programs

Approximately 2,200 questionnaires were distributed throughout Ohio between January and June 1978 to both public and private health care, educational, and social service agencies that might be involved in the delivery of early educational intervention programs to children from birth-to-3 years of age. Three-hundred fifty-nine questionnaires (16 percent) were returned. Fifty-one respondents had no such program; 141 indicated that their services were supportive to parents and children (i.e., health care, welfare, mental health) but were not specific educational intervention programs; and 165 positive responses were from infant stimulation/parenting programs across the state.[2] This summary focuses, then, on those 165 programs identified as delivering specific educational intervention services to children birth-to-3.

Infant stimulation/parenting programs for children birth-to-3 and their families are still a relatively new idea and effort. Of the 165 programs, 103 have been operational for 5 years or less. Another 28 programs report that their service delivery systems began less than 10 years ago. Only 16 agencies have been delivering such services for more than 10 years.

Nearly ⅔ of the 165 programs serve children from birth-to-3 years of age; the remaining ⅓ focus on children during the first 2 years of life. Only a few programs limit service to children under 1 year. Of those programs involving birth-to-3 year olds, 28 percent in fact, go beyond 3 to work with children up to 4, 5, and even 6 years of age.

An estimated 15,884 children from birth-to-3 and their families are being served annually in the 165 educational intervention programs across the state. Of the estimated 465,000 children aged birth-to-3 in Ohio,

[2]Of these, over 40 percent sent representatives to the first statewide "Parenting: Birth to Three Conference," held in Columbus, Ohio, on May 19–20, 1980. One-hundred and twenty individuals attended the conference.

therefore, 3 percent are receiving services from the programs included in the directory.

Over ⅓ of the services are delivered on a weekly basis; ⅕ of the services involve families daily. An additional ⅛ of the services are offered on a monthly schedule. The remainder of services are provided according to need and, therefore, the service schedule varies. Program duration varies from agency to agency but is most often dependent upon the needs and service demands of an agency's clients.

The 165 Ohio programs are delivered by 1,563 staff members. Of this number, fully 37 percent are volunteers. An additional 18 percent are paraprofessionals, 13 percent are educators, and 7 percent are nurses. The remaining 25 percent are social workers, child development teachers, speech and hearing specialists, and occupational and physical therapists. Doctors make up just 2 percent of the staff and 5 percent are psychologists and counselors.

A majority of the 165 programs provide for staff development (73 percent). In-service training occurs on a monthly basis in most agencies and typically includes out-of-town conferences as well as visits from outside experts.

Programs operate from a wide variety of facilities, with many agencies using a combination of sites: 39 percent use school facilities to some extent while an almost equal number (37 percent) operate primarily in homes. Churches accommodate a sizable number of programs, as do clinics. Ten percent of the programs are hospital-based.

The programs rely on a variety of formats from classes to home visits to center-based programs with no one format more popular than another.

Diversity among programs is even more apparent in the curriculum models followed by practitioners. The responses of the 68 percent who listed a curriculum model on the survey varied widely—from "Piaget" to "We developed our own model." The most common models mentioned are listed in Table 2.

The initiation of educational intervention as early as possible after birth (or before) hinges on the ability of infant stimulation/parenting agencies to involve community, medical, and social service organizations in the task of early identification and referral. Table 3 illustrates the present breakdown of referral sources:

At present, the single largest source for referrals is the families themselves. An additional 13 percent are recruited for programs by their friends, by program staff, or by door-to-door recruiting campaigns. The medical community, including hospitals, doctors and clinics, comprises the next largest source of identification and referral. Because of its rela-

Table 2 Curriculum Models
Followed by Practitioners

Model	Percentage
Piaget	13
Badger's ITL	11
Portage	8
Nisonger	6
Montessori	4

tively consistent and comprehensive contact with the target population, the medical community has a unique opportunity for early referral and screening.

A sizable number of the 165 programs—⅓—named no other agencies in their communities with whom they had a cooperative working arrangement. It is apparent that cooperation and joint planning among service deliverers in communities throughout Ohio exist on a relatively minimal level.

Educational resources available to practitioners include audio-visual aids; written materials such as books, brochures and pamphlets; and toys for lending, giving, and demonstrating. Nearly all programs have access to books and pamphlets, whereas only 40 percent have film or toy libraries available. Nearby universities function as educational resources and program deliverers avail themselves of relevant seminars and courses.

Evaluation of program effectiveness may focus on changes in the parent as well as in the infant and, therefore, takes many forms. More than ½ of the programs use infant assessments to measure progress, to identify areas of deficit, and to develop an educational plan for the infant. On the other hand, parent assessments are used as an evaluative tool in just 35 percent of the programs. Additionally, ¼ of the agencies bring in outside observers or evaluators to help measure program effectiveness; only 4 percent rely on telephone surveys of clients to provide clues as to the impact of their programs.

A majority of program deliverers (56 percent) provided information about the formal assessment instruments they employ. The Denver Developmental Screening Test, the most frequently mentioned instrument, was listed by 36 percent of the respondents. A combination of instruments is used by many agencies, and 15 percent of the programs assess children with the Learning Accomplishment Profile; 7 percent rely on

Table 3 Referral sources
(percentage)

Self	35
Other (Children's Services, door-to-door, friends, staff)	13
Hospital	12
Doctors	11
Clinics	9
Welfare department	9
School	6
Central referral service	3
Mental health	2

the Bayley Scales of Infant Development; 4 percent on the Vineland; and 3 percent on the REEL.

Several funding sources are often pieced together to support a single program. An overwhelming majority of the 165 programs (130, or 79 percent) receive some public monies. The remaining 21 percent are supported entirely by the private sector, including donations, collection of fees, and support from community service organizations. Public support, on the other hand, encompasses monies derived from federal, state, and county funds.

Fifty-one percent of the programs function with an advisory group. Of those, a clear majority of 88 percent believes that the advisory group adds to the strength of their programs. For those who do not include an advisory group in the operation of their programs, 65 percent are satisfied with that arrangement and do not, in fact, see a need for an advisory group.

Responses to the questionnaire provide some insights into the present scope of early educational intervention throughout Ohio and are useful in planning future service directions and in the organization of programs on the state level.

First Ohio Statewide Parenting: Birth-to-3 Conference

Respondents to the questionnaire indicated an interest in attending a state conference for infant and family educators. The 12 members of the steering committee surmised that enlisting personal support was as important to these practitioners as exchanging program information and strategies. Accordingly, a conference was planned for May 19–20, 1978—the anniversary date of the decision makers symposium a year earlier. The conference, it was hoped, would offer an innovative approach to learning

(Fairfield, 1977). The uniqueness of the conference would be to provide an environment for interaction among the participants based on the recognition that the necessary expertise already existed among the participants themselves. The challenge, then, was for each person to take charge of his or her own learning which would occur in private meetings, in scheduled workshops, and in rap sessions. State department heads were once again invited, and this time they were asked to describe their interest in, commitment to, and funding plans for early intervention programs, on short- and long-term bases.

The 120 persons who attended the conference were a diverse group of practitioners. They came from large institutional delivery systems as well as from small privately funded programs. The latter often included indigenous, paraprofessional, and volunteer staff. They served young children with mental and physical handicaps, poverty populations, young and immature mothers, and inexperienced middle-class parents. In spite of the differences in programs and funding sources, the practitioners were united by their commitment to the fullest development of parent and child.

The steering committee had, in a sense, a private agenda as we planned the conference. We wanted to add to the baseline data gleaned from the program questionnaire and to recognize the expertise of the participants by covering in depth four areas of major concern: Intervention Strategies, Program Logistics, Child Development—Theory into Practice, and Program Evaluation. Topic outlines were prepared for a workshop in each of these areas with members of the steering committee present to facilitate discussion and problem solving. As anticipated, the participants themselves provided a wealth of information.

Each of the workshop summaries which follow is a synopsis of the discussions of two different groups for a total of 8 hours. The summaries merit consideration because they capture the essence of early intervention efforts from the perspective of program deliverers. The development of a sound educational psychology for infancy and the preschool years has begun. The experimental efforts of Ohio's practitioners present evidence of progress. There is some mastery of issues related to program design and delivery and some evidence of effective intervention strategies. And, contrary to accepted belief (Chilman, 1973), program deliverers place a high priority on evaluation of program effectiveness and demonstrate some intuitive skills in measuring the impact of their treatment. Translating child development theory into practice, however, remains an area of major concern. Practitioners seem to reflect the uncertainties of social scientists about how to proceed, but they are nonetheless convinced of the efficacy of their efforts.

Workshop I—Intervention Strategies with Parent and Child

Several general goals common to parenting programs were used to generate and integrate ideas regarding intervention strategies that might accomplish those goals. *Developing parental understanding of child development* was one example of a goal recognized by all participants. Strategies to accomplish this goal were discussed:

●Films and filmstrips in combination with guided discussion have been successful. Advantages included:
 —Motivating parents through visual demonstrations
 —Reaching, without intimidation, parents who have poor reading skills
 —Stimulating parents to think and interact, leading to questions and discussion
 Disadvantages included:
 —Unavailability, inaccessibility, and cost of audio-visual materials
 —Difficulty of determining from advertising information alone which visual materials are applicable and of quality.

●Role playing was another useful strategy in fostering parental understanding of child development. This form of "learning by doing" is successful when the timing is right and when it is initiated by skilled staff.

●Modeling by professionals is a particularly effective strategy when the goal is to teach specific parenting skills or to present activities to be carried out at home.

Identifying the needs of parents before attempting to provide strategies for parent intervention was considered very important by the programmers.

●Some needs of parents relate to their children; others, to underlying personal needs of parents.

●How parents feel toward themselves as parents and adults is critical.

●Strategies might first focus on boosting self-confidence and positive self-concept in parents.

●Intrafamilial influences must be considered.

Identifying the needs, competencies, and performance of children was also discussed:

●Methods of need identification in children seemed to be more straightforward and more clearly delineated than methods used to identify the needs of their parents.

●Informal observations by professionals using general developmental guidelines were common to all agencies.

•Others employed more formal assessment techniques such as standardized tests, developmental profiles, or interdisciplinary evaluations.

Maintaining effective ongoing relationships with parents elicited several suggestions:

•The program deliverer cannot be everything to the parent. After needs are identified, the interventionist can serve as resource person in hooking the family up with other needed services.

•Professionals should not hesitate to tell parents they "don't know" when they don't.

•When a commitment is made to a parent, there should be immediate follow-through. An immediate response will foster trust in the relationship.

•A balance between providing assistance and fostering independence and parent advocacy should be observed.

•Professionals should be aware of issues and problems involved in imposing their own values on parents.

Concluding Remarks:

Conference participants devoted some time to identifying needs of programs for parents and infants in relation to intervention strategies. These needs included (1) additional money and staff for better planning and organization of services; (2) a newsletter sponsored by the network of infant–parent programs for sharing information on a state-wide level; and (3) pooling of resources (i.e., conferences, in-service training, consultants, audio-visuals, and equipment) in the state across programs. Additional needs centered on "how to" access state and community resources, work with parents in a group, and determine the needs of parents. The need for more and better staff training was emphasized; again participants noted that pooling resources in this area may improve the quality of training while keeping costs down. (Scribe: Linda Wnek)

Workshop II—Program Logistics

Participants in this workshop were eager to share their thoughts about recruitment, staffing, transportation, and funding. Their concerns and suggestions are outlined by topic below.

Population to be served encompassed identification of need as well as recruitment of families:

•The importance of early identification of need and the commitment to intervention at or before birth was stressed.

• The problems of how to get infant referrals as early as possible, how to make inroads into hospitals, pediatric offices and clinics, and how to make hook-ups with existing prenatal programs were discussed.

• Participants agreed that the key to early identification and referral lies in developing contacts, interest, and awareness within each community's medical, health, educational, and social service groups—both public and private.

Place was discussed, especially in terms of creative alternatives:

• Use of supplemental space in creative ways has a dual purpose: It may be rent-free and often serves to reinstigate a "sense of community" on the local level.

• Suggestions included use of parks, private homes for group meetings, church basements, rent-free vocational education rooms, clinic waiting rooms, hospitals, and YWCA facilities.

Staff, both salaried and volunteer, was considered:

• Most programs involve volunteers in some capacity.

• Sources for volunteers include the Foster Grandparents Program, the Junior League, graduates of your own program (paraprofessionals), university students (practicums), and mothers from the community.

• The keys to keeping good volunteers were identified as recognition and reinforcement (the importance of saying "thanks").

• Frustration was expressed at being unable to offer enough reward to volunteers. The suggestion was made that our group advocate that legislators consider giving tax breaks (i.e., babysitting, mileage) to volunteers.

• Consider employing mothers part-time—their value in terms of skills, commitment and flexibility is underrated.

Educational materials, audio-visuals, and toys were discussed under the heading, *supplies.* Comments revolved mostly around the use of toys to facilitate interaction as well as the development of the child.

• Half of the group successfully used toy lending libraries (through the County Welfare Department or Jewish Councils).

• Others adapted commercial toys for use with disabled youngsters, bought toys to give away, or relied on donations.

Transportation for clients, most participants agreed, was one of the biggest and most persistent problems.

• A variety of transportation methods had been tried by all: leasing a van, volunteer drivers, parent carpools, owning vehicles, taxi pools, transportation provided by Title XIX.

•Numerous insurance problems arise in relation to transportation, and practitioners reported their frustration in trying to deliver a service program in the face of these worries and concerns.

Community support included coordination of referrals and staff training as well as sharing of equipment, educational materials, staff, and speakers.

•Group concensus was that coordination between agencies is important for all. Without coordination and communication we duplicate services, create rivalries between agencies, divide up the family rather than serve it, and face the possible loss of funding.

•Liaisons within the community and the state will remove these threats and barriers to effective service delivery.

Funding generated the most concern and involvement on the part of workshop participants.

•Funding sources ranged from bake sales to substantial federal grants and included a wide spectrum in between (e.g., Department of Education, Easter Seal Foundation, Women's Clubs, and YWCA).

•Supplemental funding ideas included service organizations (Lion's, Soroptomist, and Kiwanis Club), Justice Department, National Endowment of the Arts (for building innovation/renovation), churches (e.g., Catholic Campaign for Human Development), foundation directories, Titles, V, XIX and XX.

•Help in grant and proposal writing in available through workshops sponsored by the Junior League and through training courses offered through Bill Bell in the Department of Economics and Community Development of Ohio.

•Concern was expressed over the trend for funding to come from the federal and state levels rather than from the private sector. Movement seems to be in the direction of public rather than private (or community) spending; we are missing the rewards of being creative with regard to funding and of involving and strengthening our communities.

•Creative examples of funding were offered:

Organizing fashion shows sponsored by local clothing businesses with the proceeds going to the organization.

Charging middle-class parents for a parenting program and using that money to finance programs for the disadvantaged.

Publizing the organization through the media.

•Importance was placed on looking at long-term program effects in planning and appealing for funding, that is, the cost of prevention versus the costs of remediation.

Concluding Remarks:

Workshop participants were not only eager to share information on program logistics but often served in a joint problem-solving and therapy-giving capacity as well. Overriding concerns among program deliverers seemed to be in the areas of early identification, transportation, and funding. Imaginative solutions to these problems were offered by participants as the workshop fostered a constructive exchange of ideas in the area of program logistics. (Scribe: Donna Burns)

Workshop III—Child Development: Theory into Practice

Understanding the theoretical framework upon which a program is based greatly influences the success and effectiveness of that program. This notion was the primary focus of the Child Development workshop.

Maturational, behavioristic, and psychoanalytic theories of child development were discussed, and participants correlated practical experiences from their programs with the theories. The following are examples:

● A discussion of positive reinforcement and feedback led the facilitator to illustrate the analogous relationship between positive reinforcement and the behavioristic theory.

● The use of behavior modification to help parents learn how to praise desirable behaviors and to ignore undesirable behaviors was also discussed.

● Another topic was the use of a psychoanalytical approach in dealing with parental feelings and emotions. Helping parents come to grips with their own feelings enables them to establish more effective relationships with their children.

● The use of the behavioristic approach in training parents to tune into their babies' cues was another topic shared.

● The most useful method of helping practitioners to understand the theories they are implementing is to share experiences. Then, by analyzing these situations, they can fit them into specific theoretical frameworks.

Professional concerns of translating child development theory into practice were discussed:

● Professionals may need to reprocess their behavior into positive thinking and positive reinforcement. Example: "Try to remember" rather than "Don't forget." The former has a positive connotation, the latter a negative one.

● Most of us are trained to work with children, but, actually, we are training adults, parents.

●Professionals should be cognizant of parental needs and goals. Parents should be involved with the program plan rather than with a program that professionals have planned for them.

●We must not only consider the diagnostic results but the prescriptive measures as well.

Parental concerns of translating child development theory into practice were also considered by the participants:

●Mothers should be familiar with normal child development so that their expectations are realistic.

●Sometimes parents achieve better results using their methods and they should be permitted (encouraged) to give input to their childrens' programs.

Concluding Remarks:

Suggestions from the participants included more structured "how to" methods of implementation and the sharing of workable methods rather than the expression of problems. The recent emphasis on parent and the "whole family" involvement has created a need for training professionals in family dynamics and psychotherapy. Many participants felt that they would benefit from learning more about the various child development theories. (Scribe: Sherry Rosensweig)

Workshop IV—Program Evaluation

The intention of this workshop was to open the door to discussion about the wide spectrum of program activities that evaluation might include. Emphasis was placed on the need to (1) think about how to evaluate the program as program goals are formulated; (2) recognize that evaluation is an ongoing process; and (3) measure how well program goals are accomplished.

General program goals, which seemed to reflect the concerns of the wide range of participants at the conference, included the following:

●to improve the quality of life within families

●to increase parental awareness of alternatives in childrearing methods

●to educate parents regarding the needs of special infants, (i.e., neurologically handicapped or mentally retarded)

●to prevent mental health problems by teaching parents how to have fun with their children

●to promote attachment between parents and infants

●to help parents feel more positive about a special child (i.e., one who is physically disabled)

●to improve referral and tracking systems for high-risk infants (coalition building)

●to measure the community impact of service programs

●to select quality products and resources for use in parenting programs.

Specific program objectives, formulated to measure whether particular goals have been met, included the following:

●to increase the amount of positive attention a mother gives her infant. The interventionist defines what "positive attention" includes and the evaluation quantifies the desirable maternal behaviors.

●to improve infant nutrition. Program input was to inform the mother of the importance of maintaining close emotional contact with her infant during feeding. Measurement included recording whether the mother holds her infant in "cuddly position" during feedings, maintains eye contact, and talks to the infant.

●to increase parental participation in program. Keeping accurate and consistent records permits the interventionist to tally a parent's class attendance, his or her utilization of resource materials, and his or her requests for additional curriculum information.

●to develop survival skills. If the population served is low income and has limited education, has the interventionist been successful in teaching how to read a medicine label, how to child-proof the home, how to plan and budget for nutritious meals?

●to provide an atmosphere where parents can help one another. In a class or group, the interventionist can list the number of ways parents can utilize one another as resources.

●to change a parent's negative feelings toward a disabled child. The mother was asked to keep a written record of her feeding difficulties with her child. Over time, her negative comments became more positive.

●to help parents feel better about their childrearing responsibilities. A pre- and postassessment can provide soft data on how the parents felt when they entered the program and how these feelings might have improved when the program terminated.

Cautions, concerns, and problems in evaluation were expressed as follows:

●Programs cannot be expected to carry out a first rate evaluation unless money is allocated to support it.

●If programs utilize outside evaluators (i.e., university-based researchers) they must be sensitive to an knowledgeable about program goals.

●Maybe we need a position paper on the value of evaluation, in particular, the time and effort it requires. Some funding sources expect us to spend 80 percent of our time on evaluation.

• An infant stimulation program for adolescent mothers tries to promote bonding but is seeing the need to provide counsel on adoption for some of their mothers. Message: Change your program goals to meet the individual needs of parents.

• Do not use other people's evaluative instruments unless goals, staffing, and population are similar.

• A stigma negatively affects participation in certain programs. The Head Start mandate of "serving the poor" and the 169 Board's "mental retardation" programs were examples cited.

• It is important to involve parents in defining the goals of the program. One program leader questioned the funding source's mandate to visit each family 3 times a week. She shared the parents' concern about "why" such frequent visiting is required.

We need to evaluate among ourselves the relevance of widely publicized curricula and training methods insofar as they are or are not able to meet our particular needs.

Concluding Remarks:

It was apparent that documenting the effectiveness of early intervention has a high priority among workshop participants. There seemed to be an appreciation of the difference between the kinds of evaluations carried out in well-controlled studies as contrasted to evaluations of service programs. When evaluation is seen as part of the ongoing process of program delivery, there is a constant review of where you are in relation to your goals and measureable objectives (formative evaluation) which should positively affect later program outcomes (summative evaluation). (Scribe: Earladeen Badger)

Formation of USEP-OHIO

The work of the steering committe from the time of the symposium for decision makers in May 1977 until the Parenting: Birth-to-3 Conference in May 1978 laid the groundwork for a statewide organization. At the wrap-up session of the Birth-to-3 Conference, the leadership of the steering committee was formally recognized. Further, the 120 conference participants delegated the committee to (1) prepare and circulate a state-of-the-art report and directory of programs from the data collected from the program questionnaires and the summaries of the four workshops; (2) to share relevant program information through a periodic newsletter; and (3) continue coalition building among birth-to-3 program providers by planning a second statewide conference.

At a postconference meeting of the steering committee, an organizational format began to evolve which included the following:

●The organization and its membership will be partners in the USEP concept, adopting its name and its goals.

●The USEP staff in Cincinnati will coordinate the meetings and activities of the steering committee, compile and circulate a state directory, and publish and disseminate a periodic newsletter.

●The steering committee of 12 will be increased to 30 members in order to provide representation from all geographic areas and to reflect urban and rural concerns.

●USEP-OHIO will have formal identity when the 30 members of the expanded steering committee meet to participate in a 24-hour "think tank" session (September 24–25, 1978). Individual and group responsibilities of leadership will be determined and defined for the year.

The 12 members of the original steering committee and 18 others who had been identified as potential leaders during the Birth-to-3 Conference came together as planned. In their letter of invitation new members were told that "during this 24-hour period, you will (1) understand the USEP concept, its history, and its development, (2) define the leadership roles you will provide, (3) plan for periodic communications among members through newsletters and a second annual conference, (4) decide on the formation of any working committees, and (5) determine the criteria for USEP-OHIO membership." Additionally, they were promised an "exciting respite from your daily routine, camaraderie, and an opportunity to exercise your leadership qualities."

The incredible energy and enthusiasm of the group were reflected in the outcomes of this extended meeting. Ohio was divided into 12 geographic regions and everyone agreed to work within assigned areas in beginning coalition-building efforts. The Cincinnati experience was shared so that they could replicate the USEP model as it had begun and evolved. Further, they agreed to document their coalition-building efforts by sending progress reports to the Cincinnati office for inclusion in bi-monthly newsletters. And, not surprisingly, they also eagerly agreed to plan and lead workshops for the second annual statewide conference. The spirit of excitement and shared involvement in the agenda of this first meeting set the stage for subsequent meetings. The personal investment that every member promised was a dramatic testimonial to the potency of grass-root efforts as instruments of social action.

USEP-OHIO became a nonprofit corporation with a constitution, by-laws, and IRS tax-exemption status through the assistance of the Cincinnati attorney who had volunteered his services with the Cincinnati chapter. To coordinate the activities carried out by the two authors, and a secretary housed in offices at U.C. College of Medicine, financial support in the amount of $10,000 was secured from the Ohio Department of Health (Maternal and Child Health), the U.S. Office of Education (Bureau of Education for the Handicapped), and the Department of Pediatrics (Newborn Division). This sum included some staff support, all office expenses (telephone, mailings), and the publication of the USEP-OHIO state directory and newsletters. Two of the major corporate officers—the authors—were located in the Cincinnati office; members of the expanded steering committee, later called the Ohio Council, were appointed as the organization's board of trustees. The only monies we expected to generate during the first year of operation were through membership subscriptions ($10) from birth-to-3 program providers and the sale of the state directory ($5). These funds would be used to offset the expenses of the second annual birth-to-3 conference, hereafter known as USEP-OHIO's annual conference.

Progress of USEP-OHIO?

It has been almost 2 years since USEP-OHIO became incorporated and the 30 members of the Ohio Council began to provide leadership and direction in coalition-building efforts within 12 designated regions of the state. Their goals have been to (1) build bridges between programs at the local, regional, and state levels, (2) offer consultation to the membership and community at large, (3) coordinate program services and resources, and (4) establish local central referral sites. These goals have been translated in the following ways:

●through bi-monthly meetings of USEP-OHIO board members (the Ohio Council) who are the planners and doers at the local, regional, and state levels

●through monthly regional meetings of program deliverers which serve to improve in-service training and program coordination and delivery at the local level

●through a bi-monthly newsletter which provides featured articles, book reviews, and items of interest on the technology of early intervention/prevention programs

●through a directory of services which catalogs parenting (birth-to-3) programs in Ohio

●through an annual statewide conference which serves not only to strengthen and coalesce the efforts of program providers but also to address their survival.

It is apparent that the leadership provided by members of the Ohio Council is the strength of the organization. These individuals have worked diligently and creatively to replicate the Cincinnati experience in

their regions. While coordinating programs and services at the local level
is the most difficult and time-consuming part of their job, they have nonetheless persevered. The reinforcement they have received from other
council members as they share their respective successes and failures at
the bi-monthly meetings has served to intensify their efforts in regional
coalition building. We have learned that (1) each city has to develop its
own way; the Cincinnati model can offer only a guideline, (2) a core
group within a limited geographic area needs to be strengthened before
reaching out to far away counties, (3) a change in the monthly meeting
site and an interesting program or speaker are keys to success, and (4) the
strengths of all the members of the regional group must be recognized
and utilized. At this point, none of the 12 regions has established a central
referral site, although three of the cities with the highest density of programs appear ready to do so.

Interestingly, the organization has not grown in numbers over the past
2 years, at least as reflected in the attendance at the last two annual conferences. The announcement of the annual conference has continued to
go to the programs listed in the state directory. The agenda of the last
two conferences has included outside experts who provided the kinds of
program information practitioners requested (i.e., infant attachment,
child development theory, adolescent parenting). We have seen many
programs lose their funding and new ones take their places. Community
colleges, hospitals and health care agencies, and prenatal programs (Red
Cross, Birthline, Birthright) have begun to expand their service commitment to include training in parenting. Thus, USEP-OHIO has func-
tioned to provide sustenance and support to both traditional and nontra-
ditional program providers. It has encouraged a diversity of program
models, recognizing that parents should have choices, based on their
needs and expectations for their children.

Implications for Social Policy

The time and effort spent by members of the Ohio Council on child advocacy activities have increased the visibility of intervention programs
for the birth-to-3 population. It is noteworthy that this has been a new
experience for most of us who have not been involved previously as advocates for our programs.

At the state level, written testimony on the importance of these services was delivered at the Ohio Commission for Children's (OCC) regional meetings. These were followed by council members' attendance
and participation at the state OCC meeting. They were instrumental in
organizing those persons attending the meeting who served preschool

children and preparing a resolution advocating the establishment of a State Department of Child Development. In addition, USEP prepared a statement which was delivered to the State Department of Special Education advocating noncategorical treatment for very young children with handicapping conditions.

On the national level, the Yale University Bush Foundation Program in Child Development and Social Policy is in the process of evaluating the growth and development of USEP-OHIO as a grass-roots model which addresses the survival of birth-to-3 programs. Also, the National Committee for Services to Very Young Handicapped Children and Their Families has identified USEP-OHIO as a viable model for strenghtening and coalescing primary prevention efforts. Finally, based on the leadership qualities of one of the members of the Ohio Council in developing a quality infant day care program, USEP-OHIO wrote a letter of support to the National Day Care Council of America, recommending her appointment to its National Board of Directors.

It is too early to determine the policy impact of any of the above activities, but the members of the organization have begun to evidence their concerns in behalf of their constituents—families with very young children—and they are beginning to be heard and recognized.

Conclusions

Our grass-root efforts hinge on the leadership provided by a small group of program practitioners. What has occurred thus far is largely a "labor of love." Our experience in coalescing birth-to-3 programs in Ohio encourages others to exercise their leadership capabilities on behalf of young children and their parents. Our success thus far, as translated through the leadership of individuals at the regional level, through an annual conference which recognizes the expertise of program deliverers, and through a directory of programs and bi-monthly newsletter which communicates useful information, has resulted in the following outcomes:

• Grass-root efforts to coordinate programs at the service delivery level address the survival of early intervention efforts at a time of tenuous funding.

• Personal development of program practitioners occurs through a support system which provides a forum for sharing, resolving, and directing individual and group concerns.

• Professional development of program practitioners occurs through their collaborative efforts in developing a sound educational psychology for infancy and the preschool years.

●Coordination of programs can be demonstrated at the service delivery level even if it is difficult or impossible at the administrative level.

●Cooperation rather than competition among program deliverers is manifested through the sharing of resources, referrals, staff development, and program information.

●Improved service to families occurs when communication transcends professional disciplines as well as the boundaries of agencies and institutions.

●Program accountability is a natural outcome of a process which promotes self-evaluation and peer approval.

●Child and family advocacy as well as program survival is possible through unified, informed action on social policy issues.

References

Badger, E. *Teaching guides: Infant and toddler learning programs.* Paoli, PA: The Instructo Corp., 1971.

Badger, E. A mothers' training program: A sequel article. *Children Today, 1,* 7–11.

Badger, E. The infant stimulation/mother training project. In B. Caldwell and D. Stedman (Eds.), *Infant education: A guide for helping handicapped children in the first three years.* New York: Walker Publishing, 1977.

Berger, P. and Neuhaus, R. *To empower people: The role of mediating structures in public policy.* Washington, D.C.: American Enterprise Institute, 1977.

Bronfenbrenner, U. *Is early intervention effective? A report on longitudinal evaluations of preschool programs.* Washington, D.C.: Department of Health, Education and Welfare, 1974.

Catalog of Federal Domestic Assistance. Washington, D.C.: Executive Office of the President, Office of Management and Budget, 1976.

Chilman, C. Programs for disadvantaged parents. In B. Caldwell and H. Ricciuti (Eds.), *Review of child development research* (Vol. 3). Chicago: University of Chicago Press, 1973.

Clarke-Stewart, A. *Child care in the family.* New York: Academic Press, 1977.

Edelman, P. The Massachusetts task force reports: Advocacy for children. *Harvard Educational Review, 1973, 43,* 639–652.

Fairfield, R. *Person-centered graduate education.* Buffalo, N.Y.: Prometheus Books, 1977.

Family Impact Seminar. *Interim report.* Washington, D.C.: Institute for Educational Leadership, April 1978.

Family Impact Seminar. *Staff report: Toward an inventory of federal programs with direct impact on families.* Washington, D.C.: Institute for Educational Leadership, February 1978.

General Accounting Office. *Report to the Congress of the United States,* February 6, 1979.

Gordon, I. *Early child stimulation through parent education.* Final report to the Children's Bureau for Development of Human Resources, Gainesville: University of Florida, 1969.

Heber, R., and Garber, H. The Milwaukee project: A study of the use of family intervention to prevent cultural-familial retardation. In B. Friedlander, G. Sterritt, and G. Kirk (Eds.), *Exceptional infants* (Vol. 3). New York: Brunner/Mazel, 1975.

Horowitz, F.D., and Paden, L.Y. The effectiveness of environmental intervention programs. In B. Caldwell and H. Ricciuti (Eds.), *Review of child development research* (Vol. 3). Chicago: University of Chicago Press, 1973.

Hunt, J. McV. Recent concern with early education. In D. Wilkerson (Ed.), *Educating all our children*. Westport, Conn.: Mediax, 1979.

Hunt, J. McV., Mohandessi, J., Ghodssi, M. and Akiyama, M. The psychological development of orphanage-reared infants: Interventions with outcomes (Tehran). *Genetic Psychology Monographs,* 1976, *94,* 177–226.

Joint Commission on the Mental Health of Children. *Crisis in child mental health: Challenge for the 1970's.* New York: Harper and Row, 1969.

Karnes, M., Teska, J., Hodgins, A., and Badger, E. Educational intervention at home by mothers of disadvantaged infants. *Child Development,* 1970,*41,* 925–935.

Keniston, K. and The Carnegie Council on Children. *All our children.* New York: Harcourt, Brace, Jovanovich, 1977.

Klaus, R. and Gray, S. The early training project for disadvantaged children: A report after five years. *Monographs of the Society for Research on Child Development,* 1968,*33,* Serial No. 120.

Lazar, I., Hubbell, R., Murray, H., Rosche, M. and Royce, J. *Summary report: The persistence of preschool effects.* To the Administration on Children, Youth and Families. Washington, D.C.: U.S. Department of Health, Education and Welfare, October, 1977.

Levenstein, P. and Sunley, R. Stimulation of verbal interaction between disadvantaged mothers and children. *Americal Journal of Orthopsychiatry,* 1968, *38,* 116–121.

Marris, P. and Rein, M. *Dilemmas of social reform.* New York: Atherton Press, 1967.

National Research Council. *Toward a national policy for children and families.* Washington, D.C.: National Academy of Sciences, 1976.

Steiner, G. *The children's cause.* Washington, D.C.: Brookings Institution, 1976.

Stevens, J. Parent education programs: What determines effectiveness? *Young Children,* May 1978, 59–64.

Wills, G. Working within the system won't change anything. *The Center Magazine,* July/August 1972, p. 36.

Contributors

Earladeen Badger is associate professor and director of the Infant Stimulation/ Mother Training (IS/MT) Program in the Department of Pediatrics at the University of Cincinnati College of Medicine. She has been actively involved the past 15 years designing (1) mother-training programs for low-income and teenage parents, (2) infant stimulation/parent support programs in neonatal special care nurseries, and (3) training programs for hospital-based maternity and nursery staff. She is president of a grass-roots statewide network of birth-to-3 programs called United Services for Effective Parenting (USEP). The history and development of USEP is described in her chapter.

Jay Belsky is assistant professor of human development in the Division of Individual and Family Studies at the Pennsylvania State University where he currently directs a federally funded research and intervention project. The Infant and Family Development Project seeks to identify factors that facilitate successful adaptation to parenting and the manner in which forces within and beyond the family influence patterns of mothering and fathering and infant development. In addition to this and other empirical work on the ecology of the family system during infancy, his scholarly interests include the effects of day care and the etiology of child maltreatment.

Joanne Benn is a doctoral candidate in human development and family studies at the Pennsylvania State University. Following several years of experience with Head Start, she is dedicated to early efforts to enhance the roles of parents as the primary educators of young children. Her research and teaching interests are focused on the early parent–child relationship, particularly on the effect of expectations on the transition to parenthood. Recently, she has completed a chapter on the ecology of childbearing and childrearing with James Garbarino and initiated a study of factors related to parents' abilities to assess infant development.

Lynne A. Bond is associate professor of psychology at the University of Vermont and previously taught at the College of the Holy Cross. She is active in research on infant interaction with caregivers and siblings, early cognitive development, sex role development, and has done cross-cultural research in Mexico on child cognition. Interested in applications of developmental theory to educational curricula, she has been involved in designing programs to promote the development of social and cognitive competence in young children. She edited, with James Rosen, *Competence and Coping During Adulthood,* the fourth volume of the Vermont Conference on the Primary Prevention of Psychopathology.

Elsie R. Broussard is a psychoanalyst of children and adults. She is professor of public health psychiatry and coordinator of the Health Services Program, Department of Health Services Administration, Graduate School of Public Health and associate professor of child psychiatry, School of Medicine, University of Pittsburgh. Dr. Broussard has been director of the Pittsburgh First-Born Studies since 1963, and in 1973 she received the American Psychiatric Association's Hofheimer Award for outstanding research in mental hygiene in conjunction with these studies. She served as a member of the Task Panel on Prevention for the President's Commission on Mental Health.

Donna Burns is coordinator of special projects in the Infant Stimulation/Mother Training (IS/MT) Program in the Department of Pediatrics at the University of Cincinnati College of Medicine. She is in charge of the central referral system of the Cincinnati Chapter of United Services for Effective Parenting (USEP), matching and tracking referrals of families to one of 32 programs. She also is editor of USEP-OHIO's bi-monthly newsletter, *Parenting Patter,* secretary-treasurer of USEP-OHIO, and a member of the governing council.

Ann M. Clarke is reader in the Department of Educational Studies of the University of Hull, England. She is the author of many research papers and has edited books dealing with mental deficiency and with early experience. In 1977 she received, jointly with her husband, the Research Award of the American Association of Mental Deficiency. She is well known for her challenge to the assumption of the critical role of early experience.

Richard H. de Lone is executive vice president for the Corporation for Public/Private Ventures, a nonprofit social organization concerned with vexing social problems. From 1973 to 1976 he was deputy director of the Carnegie Council on Children. He has published numerous articles and monographs on education, substance abuse, and educational and social policy. He is the author of *Small Futures: Children, Inequality and the Limits of Liberal Reform,* 1979.

Victor H. Denenberg is professor of biobehavioral sciences and psychology at the University of Connecticut. Before coming to Connecticut, he was at Purdue for 15 years. His major research interests include the effects of early experience, maternal behavior, the ontogeny of behavior, and brain laterality. He has been active in the American Association for the Advancement of Science, the Division of Experimental Psychology of the American Psychological Association, and the Division of Physiological and Comparative Psychology. His extensive list of publications deals with exposure to stresses in the early life, maternal behavior, and effects of other experiences such as handling in infancy.

Tiffany Martini Field is associate professor in the Departments of Pediatrics and Psychology at the University of Miami Medical School and the Mailman Center for Child Development. She has been active in research with high-risk infants and has coordinated research activities in neonatal and neonatal intensive care nurseries at the University of Miami Medical Center.

Matia Finn is the editor of *Networker,* a national newsletter of the Bush Programs in Child Development and Social Policy, a faculty member of the Yale Bush Center, and a research associate in the Department of Psychology at Yale University. She was formerly the associate editor for foundation affairs for *The Philanthropy Monthly.* She is the author of several articles dealing with child advocacy issues and the funding of children's services.

Dale Eric Goldhaber is associate professor in the Department of Human Development Studies at the University of Vermont. He is actively concerned with issues in life-span human development, and he has published papers on the changing views of early development and the role of early experience. He also has been involved in the study of changing parental lifestyles and social policy as they affect children and families.

Judy Howard is assistant professor in residence of pediatrics at UCLA and medical director of the UCLA Intervention Program for Developmentally Handicapped Infants and Children. She is also pediatric consultant to the Children's Amputee Project and to other intervention programs at UCLA. She has had extensive training and experience in child development and genetics and in prenursery school work with handicapped infants. Her research has involved work with the play of handicapped children.

David C. Howell is an associate professor of psychology at the University of Vermont. His primary areas of interest are statistics and experimental methodology, and he has collaborated on the design and analysis of research in a number of different areas. At the present time he is actively involved in a prospective study of minimally brain-damaged infants as well as the intervention project with mothers of low birthweight infants. He has published papers in these areas as well as papers and a book on statistical methods.

Joseph McVicker Hunt is professor emeritus of psychology at the University of Illinois. He is widely known as the editor of, and contributor to, *Personality and the Behavior Disorders,* the author of *Intelligence and Experience,* to which Gilbert Y. Steiner, in "The Children's Cause", has attributed a major role in the decision to launch Project Head Start, the editor of *Human Intelligence,* the co-author with Ina C. Uzgiris of *Assessment in Infancy: Ordinal Scales of Psychological Development,* and the author of 180-some papers and chapters. He has received honorary doctorates from Brown University and the University of Nebraska, the Distinguished Scholar Award from Hofstra College (1973), the Distinguished Contributions Award from the Division of Clinical Psychology of the American Psychological Association (1976), and a Citation for Significant Contributions from the American Montessori Society (1975). In

1979, Professor Hunt received the Gold Medal Award of the American Psychological Foundation.

Al Jette was psychological research analyst on the Mother–Infant Transaction Study at the University of Vermont, and he was responsible for the computer program and has researched techniques for examining mother–infant interaction.

Justin M. Joffe is professor of psychology at the University of Vermont. Author of *Prenatal Determinants of Behavior,* he has published numerous papers on developmental effects of early—particularly prenatal—experiences, effects of paternal drug ingestion on progeny, and hormone-behavior relationships. Vice president and treasurer of the Vermont Conference on the Primary Prevention of Psychopathology, he edited, with George Albee, *The Issues: An Overview of Primary Prevention* and *Prevention Through Political Action and Social Change;* he is special features editor of the *Journal of Prevention.*

David MacPhee is a graduate student in developmental psychology at the University of North Carolina at Chapel Hill and has been a participant in the Research Training Program at the Frank Porter Graham Child Development Center. His diverse research interests—including infant termperament, parental knowledge base, and the behavioral sequelae of medical interventions—coalesce around the formation of the mother–infant dyad and the mechanisms of early experience.

Peter Marton received a First Class Honours B.A. in psychology from McGill University and a Ph.D. in clinical psychology from the State University of New York at StonyBrook. The present work was conducted during tenure of a Research Fellowship from the Ontario Mental Health Foundation. Presently he is research coordinator for the Preventive Studies Team at C.M. Hincks Treatment Centre, Toronto, Canada.

Ann V. McGillicuddy-DeLisi is research psychologist at the Educational Testing Service. She has taught at George Mason University, Catholic University, and has done research at Boys Town Center for the Study of Youth Development in Washington. She has been actively involved in research on problem-solving competence of preschoolers, disabled, and atypical children; the effect of atypical children of the family; and birth order. Her publications range across a number of areas of parent–child interaction and family constellation.

Klaus Karl Minde received his medical education in Germany, studied in London, and come to New York on a Fulbright Scholarship to do a residency in pediatrics at Bellevue Hospital and to study developmental psychology at Columbia University. In addition to his medical and psychiatric training he has received a graduate degree in psychology as well as training in psychoanalysis. He is professor of psychiatry and pediatrics at the University of Toronto and senior staff physician at the Hospital for Sick Children as well as director of psychiatric re-search at that hospital. His list of publications is wide-ranging and includes exten-sive work with infants and young children, including parents' relationships with premature infants. He has also studied hyperactive children in Canada and in Uganda and has contributed to cross-cultural studies of children.

Barry Nurcombe is professor and director of child psychiatry, and associate chairman, Department of Psychiatry at the University of Vermont College of Medicine. Before coming to Vermont in 1976, he held several positions in psy-chiatry in Australia. His research and publications span a wide array of issues re-lated to child psychiatry and child and adolescent development including a pre-school intervention and enrichment program for Aboriginal Australians. He is currently involved in the Mother–Infant Transaction Study, with Virginia Rauh and Paul Ruoff.

Craig Thomas Ramey is professor of psychology at the University of North Carolina at Chapel Hill and associate director and director of research at the Frank Porter Graham Child Development Center. He has been involved in an impressive array of studies of infant cognitive development, longitudinal inter-vention with high-risk children, infant vocalization, early education for the handicapped and maternal deprivation. He is currently involved in a number of major projects of intervention with high-risk children and their families and is a consultant to a number of major programs in this country and abroad. He has published extensively reports of his research with high-risk infants and young children and on public policy for children.

Virginia A. Rauh is a clinical instructor at the University of Vermont's College of Medicine, Department of Psychiatry, and a teaching fellow in Maternal–Child Health at the Harvard School of Public Health. She is currently co-investigator (with Drs. Nurcombe and Ruoff) of the Mother–Infant Transaction Study, a longitudinal study involving an educational program for mothers of low birth-weight infants.

Paul Ruoff is the medical director of the Baird Children's Center, Burlington, Vermont, and assistant professor at the University of Vermont College of Medi-cine. His research interests include motor and cognitive functioning in children and the development of behavior rating scales for children. With Virginia Rauh and Barry Nurcombe, Dr. Ruoff is an investigator of the Mother–Infant Trans-action Study, an educational program for mothers of low birthweight infants. His particular interest in this project is in the measurement of mother–infant interactions.

Sandra Wood Scarr is professor of psychology at Yale University. She has been a professor at the Institute of Child Development at the University of Minnesota and a Fellow at the Center for Advanced Studies in the Behavioral Sciences at

Stanford. In addition she has taught at Bryn Mawr, Pennsylvania, and Maryland. She is widely known for her publications in genetics, twin-studies, birthweight, factors affecting IQ, heritability, and infant intelligence. In addition to her research and scholarly activities, she is an active editor and community consultant with emphasis on scientific problems, research design, and program evaluation.

Nancy Shosenberg obtained her B.Sc.N. from Queen's University and following her graduation worked as a Victoria Order of Nursing (V.O.N.) and public health nurse for 5 years. She then took her Diploma in Neonatal Intensive Care Nursing and became an instructor in obstetrics and pediatrics. Since 1975 she has been a research nurse in the Department of Child Psychiatry at The Hospital for Sick Children.

Irving E. Sigel is senior research psychologist at the Educational Testing Service. Prior to coming to ETS, he was area head of developmental psychology at the State University of New York at Buffalo. He was also chairman of research at the Merrill-Palmer Institute for many years. His primary interest is in cognitive development of young children and the social and emotional factors that influence the course of such development. His publications include works on cognitive development, parent–child relations, social factors influencing cognitive development, and methods of assessing the child's cognitive status.

Marian Sigman is associate professor in the Department of Psychiatry and Mental Retardation Research Center at the UCLA School of Medicine. Her research interests are concerned with the development of high-risk infants, and she recently co-edited a book entitled, *Preterm Birth and Psychological Development.* Her current research focuses on cognitive and social development of young autistic and mentally retarded children.

Evelyn Butler Thoman is professor in the Department of Biobehavioral Sciences at the University of Connecticut. Her major research interests involve the interaction of mother-young, the development of communication, and the development of sleep-wake organization. She has published extensively in these fields. She has recently edited *Origins of the Infant's Social Responsiveness,* an important work in the area of infant development.

Keith Owen Yeates is a graduate student in clinical psychology at the University of North Carolina at Chapel Hill and a predoctoral research fellow at the Frank Porter Graham Child Development Center. His research interests include the cognitive and social development of mentally retarded persons and the relationship between the development of interpersonal competence and child/adolescent psychopathology.

Edward Zigler is director of the Bush Center in Child Development and Social Policy at Yale University and Sterling Professor of Psychology at Yale and head of the Psychology Section of Yale's Child Studies Center. Well known as one of the originators of Head Start, he served on Head Start's first National Research Council. He was the first director of the Office of Child Development of the Department of HEW and was also head of the U.S. Children's Bureau. He continues as a special consultant to the secretary of Health, Education and Welfare. He is the author of several books and many scientific and popular articles dealing with children's cognitive development and the impact of social action programs on child and family life and has been widely honored as a major contributor to scholarship and policy formulation affecting children and families.

Name Index

Subject Index

ing developmental dysfunction, 160; identifying for later dysfunction, 159–160; individual differences, 262; interaction with environment, 14; lower-class, 26; of lower SES teenage mothers, 336; malnourished prenatally, 22; motor skills, 9, 18; potential of, 430; preadaptation, 9–10; programmed stimulation of, 5; psychotherapy for, 25–26; requesting behaviors, 377; response to strangers, 16; smiling and cooing, 15; social interaction, 261

Infants, at risk, 5; assessment of, 506; defining, 166; frequent illnesses of, 509; medically, 503, 509; transactions with, 506; vulnerability of, 505

Infants, high-risk, 98, 112, 182, 184, 235, 241, 294; Brazelton demonstration and, 294; mothers of, 182, 184; not included in intervention, 270

Infants, low birthweight, 270; characteristics of, 267; parents of, 267–268. See also Birthweight

Inflation, 451

Instability: as predictor, 169

Instrumental Enrichment program, 74

Intelligence: and birth order, 201; correlation of early/late, 59; defined, 8; and family size, 200–201; longitudinal studies of, 59; sensorimotor, 46

Intelligence measures, 18; compared to Piagetian tasks, 61; inadequate standardization of, 60; invalidity of, 349; as measures of cognitive growth, 348; sensitivity to group differences, 391; unreliability, 349. See also McCarthy Scales, Stanford-Binet, Wechsler

Intelligence Quotient (IQ), 339, 412; Abecedarian project, 387; adult success and, 497; and beyond, 195; as buffer, 372; changes in, 58; Collaborative Perinatal Project, 134; constant, 58; and Consortium for Longitudinal Studies, 70; cut-off points for parent-child correlations, 380–381; and personality, 381; predictive, 70; predictors of children's, 381; and premature infants, 309; and professional classes, 468; and respiratory distress syndrome, 310, 393; sibling comparisons, 67–68; and social class, 545; retardation, 343; early advantage later loss, 70; genetic inheritance of, 380; increased by program, 417; and language intervention, 429–430; maternal, 345, 362; and maternal education,

148; Milwaukee study, 436; mothers' teaching skills, 477–478; origins of, 411; and socioeconomic index, 148; St. Louis Study, 131; studies of cumulative deficit, 67–69; twins, 321; what increases, 348; worthless controversy over, 486

Intelligence tests. See Intelligence measures

Intensive care nursery, 177, 261; improving, 13–14

Intensive Care Unit neonates: cost-effective intervention, 318; sucking stimulation for, 314–318

Interactional Model, 80, 351

Interaction Rating Scales (IRS), 319

International Year of the Child (IYC), 443, 450, 462

Interventions: after age 6, 74; center-based vs. home-based, 336–339; characteristics of early, 41, 112, 359; cost of, 467; cost-effective, 469; cost-free, 326, 329; design of, 359; developmental, 299; disappearing benefits of, 349–350; effects on IQ, 70–71; ethical considerations, 361, 391–392; family-centered, 29; fathers' role, 271; and General Systems Model, 359; global, 473; home-based, 183; low-cost, 335–336; postnatal, 137; "problem of match," 24, 25; prenatal, 137; sleeper effects of, 350; tailoring to individual needs, 508–509

Intrauterine therapy, 140

Iowa Soldiers' Orphan Homes, 63

Iran: institutional retardation in, 419; revolution in, 429. See also Orphanage, Tehran

Isolation studies: in monkeys, 104

Israel, 74, 376

Japanese studies, 92

Junior League, 527

Kauai study: maternal education, 148; standard of living, 148

Kennard Principle, 163

Kiwanis, 527

Knowledge: logico-mathematical, 50–51; social, 50–51

Koluchova twins, 66, 67

Kpelle, 494, 495

Labeling: long term effects of, 391

Language, 40; of black children, 414–415; deficit of poor children, 415–416; development, 19; disorder, 204; -fostering

LIBRARY OF CONGRESS CATALOGING IN PUBLICATION DATA

Main entry under title:
Facilitating infant and early childhood developmnet

    (Primary prevention of psychopathology; 6)
    Papers presented at the sixth Vermont conference,
1980.
Includes bibliographies and index.
1. Child mental health—Congresses.   2. Mental
illness—prevention—Congresses.   I. Bond, Lynne A.,
1949-   II. Joffe, Justin M.   III. Series:
Vermont Conference on the Primary Prevention of
Psychopathology. Primary prevention of psychopathology ;
v. 6. [DNLM: 1. Child development—Congresses
2. Health promotion—Congresses. 3. Mental
disorders—Prevention and control—Congresses.
W3 PR945CK v. 6 1980 / WS 105 V527 19801]
RC454.V46 1977, vol. 6 [RJ499] 616.8'58s 81-69944
ISBN 0-87451-205-0   [618.92'89]AACR2